THE ETHICS AND CONDUCT OF LAWYERS
IN ENGLAND AND WALES

The Ethics and Conduct of Lawyers in England and Wales

ANDREW BOON
University of Westminster
and
JENNIFER LEVIN
University of Wales Swansea

·HART·
PUBLISHING
OXFORD and PORTLAND, OREGON
1999

Hart Publishing
Oxford and Portland, Oregon

Published in North America (US and Canada) by
Hart Publishing c/o
International Specialized Book Services
5804 NE Hassalo Street
Portland, Oregon
97213-3644
USA

Distributed in the Netherlands, Belgium and Luxembourg by
Intersentia, Churchillaan 108
B2900 Schoten
Antwerpen
Belgium

Distributed in Australia and New Zealand by
Federation Press
John St
Leichhardt
NSW 2000

© Andrew Boon and Jennifer Levin 1999

Hart Publishing Ltd is a specialist legal publisher based in Oxford, England.
To order further copies of this book or to request a list of other
publications please write to:

Hart Publishing Ltd, 19 Whitehouse Road, Oxford, OX1 4PA
Telephone: +44 (0)1865 434459 or Fax: +44 (0)1865 794882
e-mail: hartpub@janep.demon.co.uk

British Library Cataloguing in Publication Data
Data Available
ISBN 1 84113–018–4 (cloth)
1 84113–019–2 (paperback)

Typeset by Hope Services (Abingdon) Ltd.
Printed in Great Britain on acid-free paper
by Biddles Ltd, Guildford and Kings Lynn.

Preface

The ethics of the legal profession in England and Wales have, until recently, been largely neglected as an area of study. This is not so true of professional conduct issues, which are described, frequently unanalysed, in a number of texts including the rules published by the Law Society and the General Council of the Bar on behalf of the branches of the profession. The topic has been revitalised for a number of reasons which we explore in this book. Our intention is not merely to describe rules of conduct since, as we acknowledge, this has been done elsewhere. What we attempt here is a critical discussion of the ethics of the legal profession. We locate contemporary rules in a historical, comparative and social context. The main source of comparison is the extensive literature developed by academics and practitioners in the USA. Although there are a number of differences between the two legal systems, the professions and the practice of law, many of the issues facing the profession in the USA and the UK are similar. Because of quite significant differences between the two countries, and their legal professions, we are aware of the substantial risk of treating American discussions of lawyers' ethics as definitive. Nevertheless, we argue that there is much to be gained from comparison in many areas.

Until recently professional ethics were not considered a proper part of legal education. This is changing. Conduct issues now feature strongly in the vocational courses of both solicitors and barristers. The Lord Chancellor's Advisory Committee on Legal Education and Conduct (ACLEC) has consistently urged that ethics should be a part of all stages of legal education, including post-qualification. This reflects an increasing awareness that the work of lawyers, their role in the justice system and the way in which they advise and assist their clients is as much a subject for legal education as are the rules of substantive law. Moreover, the subject is of interest not merely to intending practitioners. It is of vital interest to all who are concerned with the legal system and the delivery of legal services. This book is intended to contribute to the teaching of legal ethics at both undergraduate and professional stages of education and to a growing debate about the relevance of ethics to the practice of law. This, we believe, will increasingly include continuing professional development, where there is much work to be done in exploring the ethical foundations of legal practice.

We are aware that, throughout the book, we do not consistently adopt one analytical approach. Sometimes we explore rules in detail. Sometimes we criticise rules from the perspective of their ambiguity, their relevance or their impact on individuals. Sometimes we look at policy rather than rules. The frame used for particular parts of the study responds to the subject matter of those parts. The book is divided into five parts, each with a unifying theme. In Part I we explore the relationship of ethics to professions using three different perspectives: the source of professional ideals, the relationship between ethics and professional power and the relationship between ethics and the culture of legal professional practice. Part II examines the evolution and current constitution of regulatory frameworks, including legal education and disciplinary mechanisms. In Part III we analyse the core duties of lawyers, particularly towards clients. In Part IV the key duties owed to clients are considered in more detail. Finally, in Part V, we explore the ethics of dispute resolution, the activity which, arguably, provides a defining social role for lawyers. In an epilogue to the book we consider predictions for the future of the legal profession and its ethics.

The approach we have adopted was chosen not just because the subject deserves an academic treatment; we also believe that an approach to ethics which involves the study of rules divorced from a wider contextual understanding distances professionals from responsibility for the ethics of their profession. That is why we begin by examining the role of lawyers in society and the nature of professionalism. This wider context, we hope, will stimulate a deeper understanding of the subject by students and a deeper sense of responsibility for the profession's future. We advocate a need to draw on the best of the legal profession's rich traditions in adapting the ethics of the profession to the challenges which undoubtedly face it. We have tried to avoid being naïve, cynical or judgemental. In order to achieve the purpose we set ourselves, we perceive a need to strike a balance between describing what ethics may have been, what they might have become and what they might be.

ANDY BOON AND JENNY LEVIN

Acknowledgments

In the course of researching and writing this book we have incurred many debts. Many of the foundations of this work were laid in articles appearing in academic journals. Those familiar with the process will know that anonymous referees often contribute much to the development of the piece of writing, and this was certainly the case here. We are particularly grateful to the editors and referees of the *Journal of Law and Society*, the *International Journal of the Sociology of Law*, the *Modern Law Review*, the *International Journal of the Legal Profession* and the *Civil Justice Quarterly* for the opportunities they have given us to develop our initial ideas in print and for the many important comments made on our submitted papers.

Closer to home, colleagues have been influential in developing our ideas, providing references for articles we may have missed and commenting on drafts. We are particularly grateful to Professor John Flood who has taken a keen and lively interest in the development of this project and has been a reliable sounding board for our ideas of how to develop this subject. We are indebted to other colleagues who have read and commented on parts and on individual chapters: Susan Kupfer (Part I); Susan Nash (Advocacy); Sonia Shah-Kazemi and Richard Earle (Alternative Dispute Resolution), Derek O'Brien (Litigation) and Alison Crawley, Head of Policy at the Professional Ethics Division at the Law Society, who provided comments on some of the articles from which the book evolved.

Our book would probably have been considerably longer in gestation had it not been for the research assistance provided by Avis Whyte. Her contribution to the production of the final text spanned virtually every operation apart from the writing. Thanks are also due to our publisher for his enthusiasm and committment.

We would like to thank Leslie Taylor, Helena Twist, Dr Iwan Davies, Ruth Costigan, Leslie Sheinman and John Levin for many useful and helpful discussions and Sean Barr for invaluable library support. Obviously, we take responsibility for any errors.

Contents

PART I
Professional Ethics

Introduction

In this book we consider the ethics of the profession in England and Wales in context. When we speak of the legal profession we adopt the traditional view that "the legal profession" in England and Wales is comprised of two groups, solicitors and barristers. These are usually described as the branches of the legal profession. Others who deliver legal services, such as legal executives and advice bureaux workers, are often treated as ancillary to the branches of the profession. Increasingly, for reasons considered in this book, this established division seems out of date. Nevertheless, we have adopted it in order to mark the main boundaries of this study. The main purpose of this book is to examine the collective ethics of the legal profession, as we have defined it, particularly as they are manifest in rules of conduct. We acknowledge that there are flaws in this approach, which we will deal with in Parts I and II. An ancillary aim is to increase awareness, not just of the rules of conduct, but of the origins and potential of professional ethics. We take seriously the argument that ethical actions are actions based on knowledge *and* understanding, particularly an understanding of the rationale for rules. Where possible we explore *the reasons* for professional action.

By examining reasons for professional action we acknowledge that individual behaviour is shaped by a number of influences. Indeed, many have argued that ethical orientation is determined well before a person enters law school. Whether or not this is true, the personal history of individuals and their moral convictions are important. Selznick argues that what the individual brings to the subject of ethics, whether a personal morality or "parochial experience", is an important, but not sufficient component of developing ethical awareness:

> "From the standpoint of critical morality . . . parochial experience may not be taken as final or treated as an unqualified end in itself. There must be a corollary commitment to press the particular into the service of the general, that is, to draw from one's special history a universal message. To do so is, inevitably, to create a basis for criticising one's own heritage, not only from within but also from the standpoint of others" experiences and more comprehensive interests. This is a two step process. The first is inward looking. It consists of examining the received culture to identify its moral premises. The latter serve as principles of criticism by means of which particular rules or practices can be assessed, revised or rejected . . . In a living political community these starting points for moral and legal reasoning are not static; they require continuous review and clarification."[1]

---

[1] P. Selznick, "The Idea of a Communitarian Morality" (1987) 75 *California Law Review* 445 at 461.

Consistently with this approach, Part I touches upon some important questions. What are the sources of ethics of legal professions and how can they be analysed and evaluated? Other, more problematic, questions are raised. Must a profession have ethics and, if it must, can it be left to define them? Can the profession misconstrue its ethical obligations or is it the sole arbiter of them? This leads to the consideration of central issues about professional responsibility, the formulation of ethical commitments and changes in those commitments. If professionals disagree with the conventional ethics of their profession must they try to change them, evade them or is their only conscientious action to leave the profession? If the answer is that they must try to change the profession's ethics, what mechanisms are there for achieving this? Such questions raise issues about personal and collective responsibility. Some of these questions may be unanswerable, given the current state of thinking about the ethics of the legal profession. By raising them and, on occasions, offering some preliminary thoughts we hope to contribute to a growing debate about the ethics of the legal profession.

Another starting point in preparing this text is the view that the ethics of legal professions cannot be considered out of context. Bordieu argues that the juridical field, a "structured socially patterned activity or 'practice', . . . disciplinarily and professionally defined", is "strongly patterned by tradition, education, and the daily experience of legal custom and professional usage".[2] Therefore, he argues, we are liable to misconstrue the internal protocols and assumptions of a legal culture unless we see it in its totality. The field of professional ethics shares this aspect of the field of law. Lawyers in Anglo-American society have developed positions of considerable power and prestige within society founded on private practice, the right to represent parties in court and a recognised role in the mediation of the exercise of state power.[3] The historical traditions of law and of legal professionalism are a source of considerable status for lawyers.[4] They contribute to an ideology of the legal profession based on independence from the state. Just as professional jurisdiction and power have a historical context, professional ethics are shaped by historical tradition which is rooted in, and still reflects, this context.

Understanding these connections is essential to understanding contemporary frameworks of ethics, conduct and regulation. Therefore, in Part I, we explore the impact of ideals, legal jurisdiction (broadly, the control a profession exercises over an area of work) and culture on the ethics of the legal profession. In this task we must acknowledge "both the tensions within professions and their ambivalent relations with the state, holding in uneasy juxtaposition the two faces of professionalism—the one monopolistic, even narcissistic, and the other

[2] R. Terdiman, "Translator's Introduction to Bordieu, P. 'The Force of Law: Toward a Sociology of the Juridical Field' " (1987) 38 *The Hastings Law Journal* 805.

[3] R. L. Abel, "Lawyers in the Civil Law World" in R. L. Abel and P. S. C. Lewis (eds.), *Lawyers in Society: The Civil Law World* (Berkeley, Calif., University of California Press, 1988).

[4] E. Friedson, "The Theory of Professions: State of the Art" in R. Dingwall and P. Lewis (eds.), *The Sociology of the Professions* (London, The Macmillan Press Ltd, 1983).

benign, even altruistic".[5] Each of the chapters in Part I, Professional Ideals, Professional Power and Professional Culture, explore the legal profession's commitment to ethics from a different perspective. In Chapter 1, "Professional Ideals", we explore the philosophical foundations of legal ethics and search for an organising theme which harmonises and explains the rules which govern the legal profession in England and Wales. Both codes of conduct and other sources, including some comparative material, are used for this purpose. In that Chapter we ask whether institutionalised ethics, of the kind favoured by legal professions, still have place in a society in which the idea of a collective morality has been overtaken by individualism and materialism.

In Chapter 2 we consider the relationship between professional ethics and professional power. Changes external to the profession have, over the past 25 years, undermined professional jurisdiction over defined areas of work. Change has been partly brought about by public expectations of the service that should be given by professionals. This leads us to explore two main themes in Chapters 2 and 3. In Chapter 2 we focus on the tensions between the professional commitment to ethics and the pressure to conduct legal practice as a business. In Chapter 3, we look at the impact on lawyers" ethics of the internal and external pressures generated by commercialism, competition and the demands of the state and consumers. In Chapter 3 the emphasis is on the implications of changes in the "legal culture" for the ethics of the legal profession. Each of these areas are fundamental to understanding the context which gives professional ethics life. They are also central to understanding the argument for change in the ethics of the profession.

---

[5] T. C. Halliday, *Beyond Monopoly: Lawyers, State Crises, and Professional Empowerment* (Chicago, Ill., London, University of Chicago Press, 1987), at 3.

1

The Nature of Professional Ethics

". . . whilst civic morals change according to the State, everyone is nevertheless the subject of a State and for that reason has duties, which everywhere have a similarity in their basic features- (duties of loyalty, service). No man exists who is not a citizen of a State. But there are rules of one kind where diversity is far more marked; they are those which taken together constitute professional ethics."[1]

A. INTRODUCTION

A conventional view of professional ethics is that they represent the highest ideals of an occupational group providing important services to society in a spirit of public service. For various reasons this view has been challenged. One reason is that the claims of professions have been subject to closer scrutiny in recent years. This is certainly true in relation to the ethics of the legal profession. In this chapter we consider some of the reasons for this. Our main focus, however, is the source of the values which comprise the ethics of lawyers. As our opening sentence implies, the ethics of the legal profession are intimately linked to wider social values but are adapted to recognise the special role that lawyers play in society. This chapter starts by considering the differences between ethics and the legal profession's codes of conduct, the nature of professional norms and the need to establish the legitimacy of these norms in order to build public trust in the professional group. It then examines the relationship between wider social norms, sometimes called morality, and professional virtues, some of the problems presented by contemporary thinking on the nature of morality, the sources of legal professional values and ways of evaluating ethics.

B. PROFESSIONAL ETHICS: NORMS, TRUST AND LEGITIMACY

"Professional ethics" is a phrase with a multitude of possible meanings. These meanings tend to change according to the disciplinary background of the person viewing the problems of ethics, whether lawyer, philosopher or sociologist. One issue is, however, fundamental. "Professional ethics" is a term frequently used interchangeably with the rules governing professionals. Those who equate

---

[1] E. Durkheim, *Professional Ethics and Civic Morals* (Translated by C. Brookfield, London, Routledge and Kegan Paul, 1957).

ethics with rules may define "rules" narrowly, as those appearing in a code of conduct, or broadly so as to embrace wider frameworks, such as rules governing entry to the profession. Those who argue that rules and ethics are the same usually argue the first of these positions. But, even those central to the regulatory process distinguish between regulatory issues and ethics[2]; ". . . ethics and professional responsibility are more than a set of rules, they are also a commitment to honesty, integrity and service in the practice of law".[3] Thus, there is an expectation that lawyers understand that conduct is wrong even where it is not expressly covered by rules of conduct.[4] From the early days of self-regulation by professions it was recognised that, in order to be guilty of misconduct, a lawyer must do "something which was dishonourable to him as a man and dishonourable in his profession".[5]

We share this broader perspective. We argue that *professional ethics* are principally concerned with the moral dimensions of professional work and that these dimensions cannot be covered comprehensively by rules alone. While, therefore, it might be argued that ethics described expectations of professional conduct at a time in history when ethics were lived, rather than written down, but, we argue, professional ethics embrace a broader framework of values, in education, in local communities and in new thinking about old problems.[6] We treat the distinction between ethics and rules as one which continues to be important.

It may be useful here to consider "ethics" as a discipline with a contribution to make to the subject of professional ethics. As branches of philosophy, ethics are concerned with individual conduct and social philosophy with the conduct of groups. Both are implicitly concerned with norms of behaviour,[7] the "characteristic spirit and beliefs of community, people, system . . . or person".[8] Both the ethicist and the social philosopher go beyond describing what norms of behaviour are, or what rules govern them. Their mutual concern is with the questions, "how the world should be, what will make it better, how one ought to live".[9] Both are concerned with "what people should do and how they ought to behave".[10] The method of both disciplines involves the analysis of the value judgements used to justify behaviour. Their tools are the evaluation of logical

---

[2] A. Crawley and C. Bramall, "Professional Rules, Codes, and Principles Affecting Solicitors (Or What Has Professional Regulation to do With Ethics?)" in R. Cranston (ed.), *Legal Ethics and Professional Responsibility* (Oxford, Clarendon Press, 1995) at 100.

[3] R. Cranston, "Legal Ethics and Professional Responsibility" in *ibid.*, 1, and see D. Nicolson, "Mapping Professional Legal Ethics: The Form and Focus of Codes," (1998) 1 *Legal Ethics* 51.

[4] *Ibid.*, at 5.

[5] *In re G. Mayor Cooke* (1889) 5 Times Law Reports 407.

[6] R. Cranston (ed.), n. 2 above.

[7] In the social sciences the term "norm" is often used to refer to "behaviour accepted within a group or to the statistical average of characteristics". Note that the term "norm" can also be used in an evaluative sense, that is in describing what behaviour should be: M. D. Bayles, *Professional Ethics* (Belmont, Calif., Wadsworth Publishing, 1981), at 16.

[8] *Ibid.*, at 356.

[9] For fuller discussion see P. A. Facione, D. Scherer and T. Attig, *Values and Society: An Introduction to Ethics and Social Philosophy* (Englewood Cliffs, NJ, Prentice Hall Inc., 1978), at 11.

[10] *Ibid.*

arguments. At the end of this chapter we return to the issue of evaluating ethics and ethical systems. For the present we argue that the broad perspective offered by the questions typically posed by the ethicist and the social philosopher are as important in the field of professional ethics as they are important in their own fields of enquiry. As we shall see, the rules governing professional behaviour seldom present a vision of how to conduct legal work that is self-evidently correct. This moves the focus of professional ethics away from rules of conduct. It raises issues about the boundaries between individual and collective responsibility, about how to reinforce individual responsibility and about how to formulate the policy behind collective responsibility. A study of professional ethics, therefore, is not merely a study of what has been enacted as the rules of professional conduct, as legal rules. It raises questions about the sources, coherence and enactment of the rules. It is concerned with why and how rules of conduct have been adopted by the profession, and in what social and political context.

It may be useful to consider the limitations inherent in treating professional ethics and the rules of professional conduct as the same thing. On a purely practical level, an exclusive emphasis on rules denies the relevance of what actually happens in practice, of how the rules, or the gaps in them, are, or should be, interpreted by practitioners. At a more profound level, to argue that professional rules of conduct are the same as professional ethics means that conduct sanctioned by the professional body cannot be questioned on moral or other grounds.[11] Such an argument would deny that professionals have any social responsibility which transcends their professional rules. Rules might, for example, permit the professional to enforce immoral laws or participate in sharp practices, whereas, it could be argued, this is not be what the professional "ought" to do. Although we suggest that professional codes of conduct cannot be definitive ethical statements, we do not deny that professional associations are crucial to the idea of professional ethics. Professional bodies do not merely enforce rules. They are responsible for developing the normative systems which are designed to anticipate and mediate the conflicting expectations of professionals. They provide social support to professionals when the performance of their professional role exposes them to attack. Professional rules minimise the need for professionals to improvise responses to situations in which there may be conflicting expectations of how the professional should behave.[12]

Formerly it was often assumed that ethics were a manifestation of a profession's high ideals. Although in recent years more complex explanations have been suggested for professional action, we do not discount the idea that altruism underlies professional ethics. For the present, however, we make some fairly

[11] T. W. Giegerich, "The Lawyer's Moral Paradox" (1979) 6 *Duke Law Journal* 1335. For reasons which are discussed below, some argue that the use of the word "moral" is inappropriately applied to norms. This is because the definition of morality involves making judgements about the value of norms which are, in fact, context dependent for their meaning. The word "moral" is useful to distinguish norms which are legal from those which are not.

[12] R. K. Merton, "The Role-Set: Problems in Sociological Theory" (1957) 8 *British Journal of Sociology* 106 at 117.

neutral assumptions based on the discussion thus far. The first is that professional ethics concern the moral dimensions of work practices. In that sense, ethics, for lawyers, are inevitable. Secondly, professions are often distinguished from other occupations because they try to make the ethic of their work universal and binding. They may also engraft onto the ethic of their work obligations which reflect the collective aspirations of the profession as a group. The focus of professional ethics is, however, work. Thirdly, rules of conduct are an attempt to capture the ethic of the profession's work and to prescribe standards of performance. They may be wholly successful in this, but it is more likely that they only partially or imperfectly describe the conduct of practitioners in the field. Codes of conduct may also refer to the aspirational aims of the profession, its ideals, or they may help to shape the profession's view of the ethics of work. Based on these assumptions we make an initial proposition which is neutral regarding the motives and means of professional ethics but recognises the importance of relationships within the professional group and the relationship of that group to the wider society. We propose that professional ethics claim *legitimacy* for those *norms of behaviour* which promote *trust* in the professional group. We now explore the relationship between norms, trust and legitimacy.

Professional Norms

The norms of behaviour of professions emerge from, and are organised around, the way in which the group conducts its work. The norms of a professional group are likely to be different from the norms of other groups. Indeed, one of the founding fathers of sociology, Emile Durkheim, observed that, within every society "there is a plurality of morals that operate on parallel lines".[13] He argued that parallel systems were produced by different groups and, in order to survive, they had to be protected by the authority of a group. Durkheim saw that:

> ". . . the greater the strength of the group structure, the more numerous are the moral rules appropriate to it and the greater the authority they have over their members. For the more closely the group coheres, the closer and more frequent the contact of the individuals, and, the more frequent and intimate these contacts and the more exchange there is of ideas and sentiments, the more does a public opinion spread to cover a great number of things . . . Accordingly, it can be said that professional ethics will be the more developed, and the more advanced in their operation, the greater stability and the better the organization of the professional groups themselves."[14]

But it would be naïve to ignore the probability that this apparent consensus conceals a diversity of views within the profession. Likewise, it would be naïve to assume that Durkheim's parallel systems do not influence each other. If a professional ethic arises out of work, it is never a novel invention. It is linked to

[13] Durkheim, n. 1 above, at 5.
[14] *Ibid.*, at 9.

wider social structures and norms, derived from society generally or from particular classes or groups, including other professions. Professional norms and professional rules may change at a different, usually slower, rate than wider social norms, thus creating conflict between professionals' behaviour and the expectations of the groups they serve.

In its infancy, a profession may be drawn from a homogeneous social group performing work of a similar kind. As professions grow, the membership may become more differentiated. A professional community typically comprises members from diverse backgrounds. It is geographically spread. The nature of work may change and become more diverse. As the profession becomes more heterogeneous in these ways, the individuals comprising the professional community may be in infrequent contact with each other if, indeed, they have any contact at all. The production of rules, enforcing group norms through disciplinary procedures, may help to address the problem of increasing differentation within the professional group. This presents practical and theoretical problems. The fact that professional ethics no longer emerge from the frequent contacts of the group changes their character. Professional ethics acquire the flavour of law. Professional bodies then have many of the same problems as governments have in creating and enforcing law. They may also have problems in binding together "parallel systems" of norms emerging within a disparate community, of identifying a common purpose manifest in shared goals and common values. Building trust and claiming legitimacy are central to these tasks.

Trust

At its most basic, trust is the foundation of co-operation between people and it is essential to the functioning of society. The need to trade is perhaps one of the earliest reasons why humans trusted those outside their immediate families. Today, even legally sanctioned relationships, such as those based on contract, depend on a degree of trust. Trust, in all its diverse meanings, is crucial to professional ethics.[15] Social co-operation is itself the precondition of virtue, a notion examined in more detail below, and virtue is the foundation of morality and ethics.[16] Encouraging trust is therefore a fundamental part of "trade" in the professional relationship because clients are dependent on the professional's superior knowledge. Indeed, the mutual advantages gained by different interest groups from trade are one of the main countervailing forces against naked self-interest.[17] This is a particularly important consideration in professional practice. In basic matters such as the price of professional services clients may fear that their ignorance could be exploited. But beyond this, trust between a lawyer

---

[15] M. Little and M. Fearnside, "On Trust" (1998) 2 *The Online Journal of Ethics* http://www.depaul.edu/ethics/ontrust.html.

[16] M. Ridley, *The Origin of Virtue* (Harmondsworth, Penguin, 1996), chap. 13.

[17] *Ibid.*, at chap. 10.

and her client is important if the lawyer is to obtain the full facts relevant to the client's concerns. A client's trust, therefore, expresses faith or confidence in the expectation of honesty, of competent performance and diligent service. The betrayal of the trust of individual clients undermines faith in the professional group. How to engender trust in a suspicious world is a central question for professions. Without trust in the legal profession, for example, people will be loath to engage lawyers.

Professionals are fortunate because the mere fact that someone is a professional engenders trust. Traditionally, professionals tend to be invested with power, and authority, the culturally legitimised organisation of power.[18] They were generally assumed to be trustworthy. But traditional authority has been undermined by "globalisation", the dominance of economic and material forms of life, and the rapid circulation of information.[19] Capitalism and industrialisation have created systems and institutions which have undermined reliance on traditional habits, customs and authorities. Thus, argues Giddens, trust now tends to be vested in expert systems, not in individuals. People are attuned to interacting with expert systems *reflexively,* taking information selectively. Given that individuals have such a highly developed facility in processing information it is not surprising that trust is no longer the automatic right of individual professionals;[20] to some extent it must be continually earned. Ethics, the underwriting of individual professional performance by the collective, is one way in which professions seek to elicit the trust of the public in relation to matters which are usually of fundamental concern to individuals or where they may be particularly vulnerable through ignorance, anxiety or grief; for example in the purchase of a home, the breakdown of family life or dealing with the consequences of the death of a loved one.

Although gaining public trust is central to the ethical project of professions, professionals must also have trust in their fellow professionals. Otherwise they will not make the sacrifices necessary to sustain an ethical community. As with law, the central problem is one of securing widespread and willing compliance by practitioners without constant recourse to sanctions. One answer is to institutionalise suspicion, to provide mechanisms of surveillance of professional work[21] which can be both internal and external to the organsations in which

---

[18]   Merton, n. 12 above, at 113.

[19]   D. Harvey, *The Condition of Post Modernity* (Oxford, Blackwell, 1989), A. Giddens, *Modernity and Self-Identity: Self and Society in the Late Modern Age* (Cambridge, Polity Press, 1991).

[20]   "The idea of holding an *office* . . . confers trust on the office-holder, presumptively, from clients and outsiders just as does professional certification; but it also embodies expectations by the principal, or body conferring the office, of certain standards of behaviour on the part of the agent, or office-holder, which are contingent": A. Dunsire, "The Concept of Trust" in R. M. Thomas (ed.), *Teaching Ethics: Government Ethics* (London, HMSO, 1996), at 335.

[21]   A good example of this is the requirement for auditing of the annual accounts of voluntary organisations. Everybody knows that relatively few Treasurers are crooked but, by making auditing a universal requirement, honest auditors are unlikely to be offended: R. Dore, *Trust and the Workings of Market Capitalism* (Edinburgh, International Social Sciences Institute, 1997).

lawyers work. Such surveillance is expensive and leads to a considerable loss of professional autonomy. Less intrusive, and more effective, is to ensure that practitioners police themselves and their colleagues. For this to be a realistic proposition lawyers must see their professional ethic as good, or right. Otherwise they will evade regulation and assist colleagues to avoid surveillance. Not only is it necessary to engender the trust of clients in the law, and in the lawyer's role in that system, it is also necessary to secure the trust of lawyers in the system. Thus, Parsons asks, "why do people follow rules?":

> "The first problem concerns the basis of legitimation of the system of rules. The question is why, in the value or meaning sense, should I conform to the rules, should I conform to the expectations of the others with whom I interact? What in other words is the *basis* of right? Is it simply that some authority says so without further justification? Is it some religious value, or is it that I and the others have some natural rights it is wrong to violate? What is the basis of *legitimation*?"[22]

A profession must seek a legitimate basis for its ethic, both to convince the public that its confidence and trust are justified and also to convince its own members to subscribe to its ethics and, thereby, to justify public trust.

Legitimacy

In order to assert the validity of its ethical system a profession asserts the *legitimacy* of its goals. One way of achieving legitimacy is to show that the profession supports and reinforces the structures, values and politics of a wider society. Is it possible to identify structures, values and politics to which most people would subscribe? Giddens argues that the liberal state has, as a central political purpose, the pursuit of human emancipation from exploitation, inequality and oppression. Emancipatory politics attach primary importance to justice, equality and participation[23] with the end goal of organising collective life in such a way that people are autonomous i.e. capable of independent action and responsibility. This has led to the emergence of "life politics", the goal of which is the creation of "morally justifiable forms of life that will promote self-actualisation in the context of global interdependence".[24] Legitimacy for professions, therefore, might be secured by an ethical foundation which promotes, or is consistent with, these central goals of the liberal state.

There are, however, reasons to be cautious about the direction in which "globalising" forces are driving society. Silbey detects several narratives of globalisation, each with relevance to professional ethics.[25] One of these envisages

---

[22] T. Parsons, "The Law and Social Control" in W. M. Evan (ed.), *The Sociology of Law: A Social-Structural Perspective* (New York, London, The Free Press 1980), at 60.

[23] Giddens n. 19 above, at 212.

[24] *Ibid.*, at 215.

[25] S. S. Silbey, "Let Them Eat Cake: Globalisation, Postmodern Colonialism, and the Possibilities of Justice" [1997] *Law and Society Review* 207.

the increasing domination of the social and the political by economics, whereby governments will be increasingly impatient of the attempts of law to mediate the operation of markets. Indeed, the state itself is forced to shrink as private property is recognised as paramount: "[b]y subordinating reason and law to desire, the market narrative is a parable about lowering expectations about what collectives can or should do".[26] Another is the story of the enlightenment, wherein science and technology facilitate increasingly rational forms of social organisation, "in the end overcoming ignorance, superstition, myth, religion, and scarcity to create relative abundance, human freedom and worldwide mobility".[27] Even this vision of globalising forces, Silbey predicts, has its casualties; those who cannot keep up, who do not embrace globalisation, fall by the wayside. Professions, as organisations within the liberal state which traditionally resisted the domination of market forces, must be conscious of where the logic of globalisation might lead.

Another implication of the transformations in the liberal state for professional ethics is recognition that the reasons professionals observe ethical standards might change. One of the more important changes is that people may be less likely to regard moral imperatives as "given".[28] Therefore, one way of coopting people to behave in a particular way is to foster belief in, and ownership of, ethical rules. The implication of this is that the ethical project of professions should be participatory, should promote the ethical autonomy of their members and their members' clients. In order for professionals to subscribe to ethics they must have convincing reasons for ethical behaviour. It follows that, as with law, professional ethics cannot merely operate through a system of coercive sanctions. They must also operate to shape emotions and attitudes by giving reasons for behavioural norms. An obvious rationale for professional action, and another way to claim legitimacy, is to demonstrate that the profession pursues a "common good" which is beneficial to society, whether or not the norms of behaviour which the pursuit of this good promotes are praiseworthy.

It will be obvious that the legal profession in England and Wales, possibly more than any other, is steeped in tradition. But tradition is closely linked to ideology and, therefore, can be viewed either as a device for encouraging trust or as a way of misleading outsiders. Whatever the roots of ideology, contrasted with scientific knowledge, it is often presented as a "full and true understanding within its sphere of concern", and appears as a mode of thought which is self evidently correct and which therefore, is resistant to modification through experience.[29] As we shall see in the remainder of this chapter, and in Part I generally, the traditions of the legal profession, the ideology which supports them and hence the way in which the profession has traditionally staked its claim to

---

[26] *Ibid.*, at 217.

[27] *Ibid.*, at 212.

[28] *Ibid.*, at 207.

[29] See further R. Cotterrell, *Law's Community: Legal Theory in Sociological Perspective* (Oxford, Clarendon Press, 1995), particularly at 11.

legitimacy, are under considerable strain. The ethics of the profession are intimately connected with these traditions and ideologies. It follows that a serious study of professional ethics must seek to investigate the ends of the profession, to examine the validity of these ends and investigate the extent to which the profession's rules support "the good" the profession pursues.

C. SOCIAL AND PROFESSIONAL NORMS

The issue of the legitimacy of professional norms arises in an environment of considerable political and academic scepticism which crosses international boundaries. The reasons offered for this crisis of confidence are as varied as the proposed responses to it. Some take the view that there is no moral basis to professional ethics, others that professional ethics are not particularly idealistic; that they are no more than is expected of other occupational groups or, indeed, groups in society in general.[30] Yet another view is that ethics are merely a reflection of professional ideology which attempts to justify the profession and confuse or mislead those who may wish to undermine its privileges. In the United States the legal profession has responded vigorously to allegations that the ethics of business are overtaking the traditional ethics of lawyers.[31] In the United Kingdom the response of the profession to similar concerns has been more ambivalent reflecting, perhaps, a loss of confidence in the ethical project.[32]

Sceptics have argued that professional groups are not interested in acting genuinely as moral agents. Rather, it is said, they use the language of ethics and morality in a self-serving manner in order to legitimise their status, privileges and power. This view is examined in more detail in Chapter 2. Here we are concerned to examine certain charges brought against the ethics of lawyers; that they are neither idealistic nor distinctive or that they reflect the norms of a society which is itself amoral or, at least, accomodates many different visions of morality. In order to do this we must examine the relationship between social and professional norms and the problems raised by any such relationship. We

---

[30] Bayles identifies four senses in which professional norms may relate to ordinary or social norms: (1) they may be the same as ordinary norms, thus undermining a need for the study of professional ethics; (2) they may specify how professionals relate ordinary norms to the situations in which they find themselves, e.g., holding other people's money for long periods of time; (3) they may take into account the role of the professional in applying ordinary norms; and (4) they may be completely independent of ordinary norms so that, e.g., absolute loyalty to clients could justify professionals acting in ways which broader society might call immoral: Bayles, n. 7 above, at 16–17).

[31] In 1984 the American Bar Association established a commission, the Stanley Commission, to investigate the decline of professionalism in lawyers: R. L. Nelson and D. M. Trubeck, "New Problems and New Paradigms in Studies of the Legal Profession" in R. L. Nelson, D. M. Trubeck and R. L. Solomon (eds.), *Lawyers' Ideals/Lawyers' Practices* (Ithaca NY, and London, Cornell University Press, 1992).

[32] A former president of the Law Society recently doubted the viability of self-regulation, arguing that the practice rules have no ethical basis but are a hotchpot evolved to respond to various crises arising since the 1930s: T. Holland, "Taking the Self out of Regulation", *The Lawyer*, 7 July 1998, at 9).

then explore the distinctive virtues required of professions in general and lawyers in particular. What is attempted here is merely a sketch of legal professionalism. It seeks to show how lawyers subscribe to a standard of conduct which exceeds that expected of non-professionals and different from that of other professionals. It is suggested that such a standard of behaviour reflects *virtues prized in society in general, adapted to reflect the specific social role assigned to the legal profession.* The two separate parts of this proposition are examined in the following section.

Values in Legal Practice

The Decline of Morality

In asserting that lawyers share and observe common norms, and that these norms draw on wider social norms, a further problem must be addressed. Many scholars, including philosophers and lawyers, maintain that the notion that society shares a common morality cannot be sustained, that there is no accepted understanding of how people should behave.[33] In other words, there is no rational basis for professional ethics because there is no common understanding of "morality" in society.[34] To the extent that there is agreement about "right" or "wrong" there is little consensus beyond fundamental injunctions such as "thou shalt not kill". Even with such basic propositions there are exceptions which reveal fundamental differences between the interest groups which constitute society. The relationship between accepted facts and the conclusions based on those facts is almost always contentious; it is not possible to derive from some statement of fact, i.e. that something "is", the conclusion that something "ought" to happen, in the sense that it should rationally be accepted as flowing from the statement of fact. From this it is often concluded that "there is nothing to judgements of virtue and vice except the expressions of feelings of approval and disapproval".[35] All is relative and we lack any yardstick against which to measure competing claims.[36] Since ethics are generally held to be linked to

[33] This situation arises in societies with "pluralistic" values (A. D. Macintyre, *After Virtue: A Study in Moral Theory* (London, Duckworth, 1985) at 32), from doubt about the existence of "an unchallengeable creator of the right and good" and from our inability to devine a creator's concept of the right and the good: see further A. A. Leff, "Unspeakable Ethics, Unnatural Law" (1979) 6 *Duke Law Journal* 1229.

[34] "Ethic . . . 1. *a.* relating to morals, treating of moral questions; morally correct, honourable . . . 2. *n.* Set of principles of morals . . . science of morals, moral principles, rules of conduct, whole field of moral science . . .": *The Concise Oxford Dictionary of Current English* (Oxford, Oxford University Press, 1976), at 355.

[35] i.e., it reflects the philosophical school of emotivism (Macintyre, n. 33 above, at 11–22 and 230 summarising the view of David Hume).

[36] The generation of evaluative concepts, e.g. utility, rights, produces viewpoints which are "incommensurable", i.e. they radically diverge from each other and are resistant to tests of truth (see J. G. Merquoir, *Foucault* (London, Fontana Press, 1991)). An example is provided by the use of competing views of rights and universalism. If we take the notion of rights, for example, we could argue

morality, and philosophers have abandoned the attempt to establish the idea of a universal morality,[37] is there any basis for professional ethics?

This situation does not merely derive from a philosophical premise that there is no schema behind human existence. It flows also from the reality of economic existence in the modern liberal state where emancipation is linked with the dominant values of individualism and the consumerism; the predominant values are those of the market-place.[38] This leaves little scope for notions of shared values, except the values of commercialism and choice. For adherents to this view, society has no universal ends or goals which can provide a framework of values to structure behaviour. Here we must distinguish between the ideas of pluralism, recognition that there are many normative systems which may claim to represent "the good", and relativism, the idea that they are all equally valid. Some will assert that some systems of values are preferable, socially, philosophically or morally, to others.[39] But one of the features of modern society is tolerance of difference. People are assumed to be *moral agents,* capable of making choices and responsible for their own acts and values. They are able to monitor their behaviour and are able to give rational explanations for the way they act.

Although one of the features of modernity is almost perpetual surveillance of individuals, a strong mechanism of social conformity,[40] mastery of the self has become a substitute for what was once understood as "morality".[41] It is not only the concept of morality that has been thus undermined, it is all grand theories, those all-embracing explanations of social phenomena, which are now unfashionable.[42] All evaluative judgements, the social, the æsthetic as well as the ethical, have been categorised as little more than expressions of individual feeling or personal choice, incapable of being established or objectively verified. In an

---

that people have the right to enter contracts freely. However, a competing argument is that everybody has an equal right to education and health. In order to achieve this, no education or health can be provided privately. Both original propositions are based on different premises, they are incommensurable; the invocation of one basic premise against the other becomes a matter of assertion and counter assertion: Macintyre, n. 33 above, at 8.

[37] The last serious attempt was in the middle ages. Kant and Kierkegaard tried to establish a foundation for a universal morality, respectively by reference to reason or to acts of choice between models e.g. ethical or æsthetic: Macintyre, n. 33 above, at 47.

[38] The rise of this view is coextensive with Max Weber's theory of bureaucratic rationality, i.e., matching means to ends economically and efficiently: Macintyre, n. 33 above, at 26. It is also consistent with one interpretation of the globalisation process (see Silbey, n. 25 above).

[39] A number of different positions can be identified. Ethical nihilists believe that any claim that something is desirable is meaningless. Ethical sceptics believe that normative claims make sense but cannot be justified. Ethical relativists believe that normative claims can be justified but the justification does not extend beyond a particular community: Facione, Scherer and Attig, n. 9 above, at 22, and see B. H. Smith, "Judgment After the Fall" (1990) 11 *Cardozo Law Review* 1291, particularly at 1302.

[40] This is consistent with Foucault's view that discipline, the enforcement of normalising judgements, in society, just as in closed communities, such as armies or prisons, discipline is fostered by hierarchical, continuous and functional, surveillance: M. Foucault, *The Foucault Reader* (P. Rabinow (ed.), Harmondsworth, Penguin, 1986), at 192.

[41] Giddens, n. 19 above, at 202.

[42] Merton , n. 12 above.

individualistic world, it is suggested, all expressions of feeling are of equal value, one person's preference for classical music being the equivalent of another's for popular music. Further, it is suggested that, by presenting as moral imperatives what are essentially the feelings or preferences of a particular group or class,[43] it is arguable that those in power have controlled and fettered the individuality of less dominant groups by demanding social conformity.[44] In other words, society has no universally accepted or objectively verifiable goals which can provide a framework for evaluating behaviour. In such a society how can a profession be expected both to identify common values and ensure that its members live up to them?

This account of the decline of faith in a universal morality cannot do justice to a complex field of legal philosophical and political inquiry.[45] It is important to note, however, that there are objections to the rather nihilistic implications of this kind of philosophical analysis. If society, or groups within society, abandons all resort to and development of ideas about "the good" or the moral, society will descend into a Hobbesian view of life as "solitary, poor, nasty, brutish, and short".[46] If we accept the limitations of conventional conceptions of "morality", the impossibility of proving moral laws, we need not forego all pursuit of any higher goal.[47] As Ridley argues:

> "Human beings have some instincts that foster the greater good and some instincts that foster self-interested and anti-social behaviour. We must design a society which encourages the former and discourages the latter."[48]

Moreover, it might be argued, the absence of moral consensus in society is irrelevant to professional ethics because, for all practical purposes, the professional body fulfils the role of defining the principles of "professional morality". As with Parliament, in its own sphere, the professional body is sovereign. Its rules of conduct provide guidance that has a moral quality and its mechanisms of enforcement, in theory at least, ensure compliance.

Although, because of the coercive powers of the professional body, it might be argued that professional ethics share many of the features of law,[49] there are

---

[43] This is Nietzsche's view of morality as "a creation of individual will in search of power": Macintyre, n. 33 above, at 258.

[44] Theorists as diverse as J. S. Mill and Foucault perceived this tendency of society: Merquoir, n. 36 above. "The web of discipline aims at generalising the *homo docilis* required by 'rational', 'efficient', 'technical society', an obedient, hard working conscience ridden useful creature pliable to all modern tactics of production and warfare . . . discipline thrives on 'normalizing judgement' "(at 94). See also J. Simons, *Foucault and the Political* (London and New York, Routledge, 1995), at 22 and 116–18.

[45] See further D. Lloyd, *The Idea of Law* (Harmondsworth, Penguin Books, 1991).

[46] T. Hobbes, *Leviathan*, (ed. M. Oakeshott) (Oxford: Blackwell, 1946) chap. 13.

[47] Difficulties of proof are not unique to moral inquiry. The inherent difficulty in proving facts beyond all doubt has never deterred man from successfully pursuing scientific inquiry.

[48] Ridley discusses this by reference to research which showed that economics students who were told that self-interest is natural became markedly more selfish: n. 16 above, at 260.

[49] It is indeed true that disciplinary control can be seen either as a subordinate form of state law or as a system of law quite distinct from the state (see further Cotterrell, n. 29 above, at 28–40).

problems with the view that professions can, through rules alone, establish independent moral empires within society. Many ethical obligations are not mandatory, legally enforceable or even enforced by the profession. We must examine, therefore, why people conform to social norms. Some scholars have observed that there is a high degree of conformity in human behaviour, a tendency which operates for both good and ill.[50] The impulses which ensure conformity are not clear, but it is arguable that they have changed over time. Modernity, Giddens argues, has changed the nature of social being and the motivation for human action. The primary motivation for human action, anxiety, may have once been induced by guilt, which is associated with breaking traditional norms. The breakdown of fixed moral codes renders guilt less important as a mechanism for controlling behaviour. Shame has, Giddens argues, superseded guilt as the primary motivating force. This is because shame represents anxiety about the adequacy of self-identity and self-identity, shaped by the reflexive process, is highly individualised and freed from local contexts. Shame, therefore, reflects the individual's sense that their biographical narrative "cannot withstand engulfing pressures on its coherence or social acceptability".[51]

The importance that modern society attaches to self mastery has profound implications for ethics. The more self-identity becomes internally self-referential, rather than dependent on traditional values or customs, the less likely are codes of behaviour to be accepted as definitive statements of how they should act.[52] People respond reflexively to *reasons for action*, because reasons for action are more likely to be absorbed as part of the individual's self-identity. This suggests that, rather than being unconcerned about their behaviour, individuals are acutely attuned to expectations of how they should behave. But the conclusions that each individual draws from the reflexive process are likely to reflect a multitude of different engagements with that process; they are idiosyncratic. We must therefore ask whether there are core values which could be accepted by individuals as characteristic of professionals and lawyers in particular.

Professional Virtues

MacIntyre links the notion of "the good" with *virtue*,[53] a normative concept which reflects the ends that particular societies value and strive for. This approach derives from Aristotle's proposition that all living things have a specific nature which determines their end state or *telos*.[54] Aristotle's *polis*, or city

---

[50] Ridley, n. 16 above, at 183.

[51] Giddens, n. 19 above, at 65.

[52] *Ibid.*, at 153.

[53] Aristotle conceived of virtue as the point on a scale of actions which represented the mean between extremes of behaviour. Of the qualities important in Greek society a prime virtue was courage, the median point between cowardice and rashness.

[54] Macintyre, n. 33 above, at 148.

state, pursued "friendship" between citizens and the common pursuit of the good society. The human *telos*, therefore, comprised "intellectual virtue", which was developed by teaching, experience and time, and practical virtues, for example honesty, which sprung from habit.[55] In such a state a higher value was placed on certain civic virtues than would be in other types of society. The societies of the Northern European Dark Ages, for example, of necessity placed greater value on the obligations of kinship, fidelity and courage.

Morality, MacIntyre argues, is tied to social structure, and we can understand and "possess" it only as part of the tradition which we inherit.[56] While MacIntyre sees virtue as the product of a particular society, it should also be noted that the idea of virtue is also connected to the social role an individual performs and to *practices* which are central to the performance of that role. MacIntyre defines a role as "any coherent and complex form of socially established cooperative human activity".[57] There are many forms of practice within a particular society. MacIntyre gives as examples farming, scientific inquiry, artistic activity—and we could add legal practice.

As with many philosophers, including legal philosophers, MacIntyre illustrates his thesis by using the game of chess as an example of what he means by a practice and of the way virtue is inherent in practice. In playing the game of chess there are two kinds of goods that the players may achieve. Certain goods are external to the game, such as fame, fortune and prestige, and these goods flow to those who play well. But such goods are only contingently attached to the activities which constitute practice; they are not obtainable through the game of chess alone. The internal goods of playing chess *can only* be acquired by playing the game of chess well, according to the rules and the judgement of those who have experience of the game. A cheat may acquire the external goods of fame or fortune, but he will not acquire internal goods, for these flow only to those who play the game honestly, according to the rules, *and* with knowledge and skill.

From this analysis MacIntyre derives two basic propositions, First, "a virtue is an acquired human quality the possession and exercise of which tends to enable us to achieve those goods which are internal to practices and the lack of which effectively prevents us from achieving any such goods" and secondly, "goods can only be achieved by subordinating ourselves within the practice in our relationship to other practitioners".[58] On this view, the ethical practice of law is conducted for internal rather than external goods and reflects those

---

[55] "What constitutes the good for man is a complete human life lived at its best, and the exercise of the virtues is a necessary and central part of such a life, not a mere preparatory exercise to secure such a life . . . to act virtuously is not . . . to act against one's inclination; it is to act from inclination formed by the cultivation of the virtues": *ibid.*, at 149.

[56] *Ibid.*, at 127.

[57] *Ibid.*, at 187.

[58] *Ibid.*, at 191. It follows that a book on legal ethics has nothing to say to a lawyer whose *sole* aim in practising the law is to achieve an external good such as money.

virtues which are accepted as the core virtues of lawyers.[59] The notion of virtue remains central to professional ethics. An indication of core "virtues" is explicitly stated in Practice Rule 1 which the Law Society's *Guide to the Professional Conduct of Solicitors* acknowledges as the source of the principles governing solicitor's professional practice.[60] It provides that:

> "A solicitor shall not do anything in the course of practising as a solicitor, or permit another person to do anything on his or her behalf, which compromises or impairs or is likely to compromise or impair any of the following:
> (a) the solicitor's independence or integrity;
> (b) a person's freedom to instruct a solicitor of his or her choice;
> (c) the solicitor's duty to act in the best interests of the client;
> (d) the good repute of the solicitor or of the solicitor's profession;
> (e) the solicitor's proper standard of work;
> (f) The solicitor's duty to the Court".[61]

The virtues of duty, competence, independence, integrity and freedom of choice are thereby explicitly made an intrinsic part of the ethical obligations of solicitors. Therefore, although it is the detailed interpretation of principles of conduct which delineate the performance of the professional role, the exercise of the relevant virtues are a source of these principles and yardstick against which that performance is judged.

---

[59] The relationship between morality and law has been a popular theme in jurisprudence. One debate explores the relationship between law and morality, but it is generally argued that the two are not coextensive. While law may be seen to embody social norms standards of conduct are not subject to immediate change in the way that laws, or rules of professional conduct, are (see H. L. A. Hart, *The Concept of Law* (Oxford, Oxford University Press, 1961); H. Kelsen abstracts in M. D. A. Freeman (ed.), *Lloyd's Introduction to Jurisprudence* (London, Sweet and Maxwell, 1994), at 271–326). There is an excellent summary of these and other relevant writers' views on the relationship of law, morality and norms in Freeman, *ibid.*, chap. 5 (and see also P. Harris, *An Introduction to Law* (London Edinburgh and Dublin, Butterworths, 1998), chaps. 1 and 2). Lawyers may compare MacIntyre's ideas with those of Lon Fuller and his search for the inner morality of law. Fuller considered the law was a purposive enterprise, that of subjecting human conduct to the guidance and control of general rules. This is not dissimilar to MacIntyre's notion of a practice. In subjecting human conduct to rules, certain minimal "virtues" or standards must be acknowledged or the enterprise must fail. To be fully successful in the enterprise requires the observance of a greater quantity of those virtues or standards. The legal system will completely fail if, for example, the lawmaker does not acknowledge that, in general, laws must be prospective and not retrospective in effect, and that it must be possible for persons to understand and obey them. There is therefore an internal morality of law without which the legal system cannot exist as an undertaking. Similarly, it might be argued, there is an internal morality to the practice of the law without which a person cannot be said to be practising as a lawyer (for a more detailed exposition of Fuller's arguments see L. L. Fuller, *The Morality of Law* (Yale, NJ, Yale University Press, 1964), chap. 2.

[60] "The Guide comprises, in addition to the practice rules and other statutory material, the Council's interpretation of the basic principles summarised in rule 1, as applied to the various circumstances arising in the course of a solicitor's practice": R. Taylor (ed.), *The Guide to the Professional Conduct of Solicitors* (London, The Law Society, 1996), rule 1.02, para. 5 at 2, hereafter referred to as *The Guide*.

[61] Solicitors' Practice Rules 1990, rule 1, *ibid.*, at 1.

The virtues of "good professionals", are often explicitly related to wider social norms[62] such as integrity, justice, wisdom and truth.[63] But professions are also associated with the notion of service to others which, culturally and religiously, has been assumed to be a public good since antiquity.[64] Therefore, the manifestation of virtue in relational terms finds its strongest expression in the duties owed by a lawyer to his or her client. Indeed, the most obvious concern of professional ethics, to protect the interests of clients when their interests conflict with the lawyer's own interests, reflects the virtue of altruism. Honesty, candour, competence, diligence, loyalty and discretion are often assumed to be general requirements of all professionals in their dealings with clients.[65] They are reflected in rules governing the protection of confidences (Chapter 10) and the handling of money, whether the money of clients (Chapter 12) or of third parties (Chapter 8). Professions are, however, distinguished from other occupations not only by their obligation to serve clients, but by an obligation to embrace wider considerations. The broader scope of professional vision includes consideration of interests such as those of third parties directly affected by the lawyer's actions and of the interests of wider society.

There are, however, some areas of professional conduct that are less conspicuously related to virtues. Some rules appear to be designed simply to delineate the limits of the professional's role and set out the etiquette for dealing with other professionals at the margins of professional jurisdiction. These rules prevent legal professionals encroaching on areas of work typically conducted by other professions and vice versa.[66] These kinds of rules are often characterised as restrictive practices. Historically, they served the purpose of encouraging specialisation, thereby promoting distinctive communities. Their value in creating the conditions for professional expertise may be less relevant today. The acid test of the legitimacy of such rules is the extent to which each professional community performs a necessary social role and is seen to operate in the public

---

[62] An example of this is found in the 1936 ABA Canons of Professional Ethics which provided that "[a lawyer] advances the honour of his profession and the best interests of his client when he renders services or gives advice tending to impress upon the client . . . exact compliance with the strictest principles of moral law" Canon 32 (G. C. Hazard, "The Future of Legal Ethics" (1991) 100 *Yale Law Journal* 1239 at 1263).

[63] Bayles, n. 7 above.

[64] A similar doctrine of vocation was prescribed several thousands of years ago by Lord Krishna in Bhagavad Gita: "[o]ne must perform his prescribed duties as a vocation, keeping in sight the public good": see O. P. Dwivedi, "Ethics for Public Sector Administrators: Education and Training" in R. M. Thomas (ed.), *Teaching Ethics: Government Ethics* (London, HMSO, 1996), 339 at 345.

[65] This can be illustrated by a number of examples, e.g. honesty—handling clients' money; candour—being truthful with client, but lying for client's benefit; competence—only to handle work able to do; diligence—timeliness in dealing with work; loyalty—avoid conflicts of interest; discretion—beyond confidentiality covering facts disclosed from clients: see M. D. Bayles, "Trust and the Profession–Client Relationship" in A. Flores (ed.), *Professional Ideals* (Belmont, Calif., Wadsworth Publishing, 1988), at 67.

[66] Examples are legion, e.g. "securing appointments, conducting referrals, handling consultations, acquiring and receiving clients, recompensing a sponsor and relating to peers, supervisors and subordinates": T. J. Johnson, *Professional Power* (London and Basingstoke, Macmillan, 1972), at 56.

interest. Similarly, the exercise of virtue depends on the nature of the professional role. If I am asked by a client to deceive someone on their behalf, and the rules of conduct do not provide any guidance, which virtue prevails? Should I be loyal to my client or should I be honest? The answer depends on my vision of *how* lawyers serve the social good.

Lawyers and the Social Good

The exercise of virtue is not enough, of itself, to legitimate the activity of a profession. The ethics of a profession are a manifestation, in specific rules and ideal actions, not merely of virtues but of virtues set in the context of a defining "good".[67] The evolution of the role to serve that good may have been a historical necessity or accident. But the continuing legitimacy of a profession's social role derives from the nature of the good which it secures for citizens and on its effectiveness in securing that good. Health is the good pursued by the medical profession and, it is usually asserted, justice is the good pursued by the legal profession. Professional conceptions of this good are manifest in professional ideology, and professional ethics, as ancient traditions. The key to these traditions lies in the legal system and the roots from which it sprang. They are bound up with the development of Europe in the medieval era.

In order to consolidate the nation state and educate and civilise populations with diverse roots and traditions, medieval monarchs centralised their power, creating codes of law to replace blood feuds, trial by combat and appeals to divine judgement.[68] Pagan virtues, such as loyalty to family and friends, melded with Christian virtues but medieval society was still close to a kin organised society. To the virtues derived from kinship-based society, justice, prudence, temperance and courage, were added theological virtues—faith, hope and charity.[69] Many of the core values associated with professional life were assimilated in these times. Not surprisingly, they often had a quasi-religious character. As the clergy, the original "learned occupation" gradually surrendered responsibility for medicine and the law, these emergent professions continued clerical traditions such as confidentiality and altruism towards "clients" and the public in general.[70] The virtues of

[67] T. L. Beauchamp and J. F. Childress, "Virtues and Conscientious Actions" in Flores, n. 65 above, at 27.

[68] See Merquoir, n. 36 above, at 89, Macintyre, n. 33 above and D. Thurbin, *Crime and Punishment: A Critical Survey of the Origins and Evolution of the Common Law*, (Long Ditton, Surrey: Idle Press, 1998).

[69] Macintyre, *ibid.*, at 167–8.

[70] Prior to the development of the legal profession, the clergy was involved in early methods of proof, e.g. performance of oaths. This was because God was presumed to be the judge of guilt or innocence. This continued until the Lateran Council of 1215: E. E. Sward, "Values Ideology and the Evolution of the Adversary System" [1989] *Indiana Law Journal* 301 at 321. Altruism towards those who cannot afford the professional's services has been associated with professions from the earliest times: see J. A. Brundage, "Legal Aid for the Poor and the Professionalisation of Law in the Middle Ages" (1988) 9 *The Journal of Legal History* 169. The continued relevance of professional virtues rooted in medieval Christianity in an increasingly secular and materialistic society is considered in Chap. 9.

the time are reflected in legal structures and ethical traditions. The adversarial trial stood as proxy for trial by battle, for as Prest observes "going to law in early modern England was often rather a means of of expanding and continuing conflicts than bringing them to an end".[71] This was a task which emphasised the legal virtues of commitment and courage. Similarly, existing social structures influenced the emergent professions. The bar organised along family lines, living as an extended kin group. They ate and worked together in houses, Inns, and developed strong communal norms supported by educational and disciplinary procedures.[72] This supported the growth of familial responsibilities owed one to another.

Although the legal professions of the different European countries may have shared similar antecedents, in each legal profession different virtues are pre-eminent. This reflects different traditions. We can see this even in relation to areas as fundamental as the core duties owed to clients. In France, for example, an *avocat* was bound to keep secret from his own client communications with another *avocat*. This rule reflects the ideal of independence, in this case from clients, and the desire to foster collegial relations between lawyers.[73] The Anglo-American tradition is, in contrast, that control over information is the client's not the lawyer's.[74] In order to discover the rationale for the prioritisation of interests it is necessary to look at the way the profession interprets its social role.[75] There is often much ambiguity in this, even in societies sharing common traditions and values. In Anglo-American society, for example, a popular view is "that the central function of the lawyer—a function that is he alone is capable of fulfilling in our complex democracy—is to stand beside his client and protect him as an individual" in his dealings with others, and particularly in

---

[71] W. R. Prest, *The Rise of the Barristers: A Social History of the Bar 1590–1640* (Oxford, Clarendon Press, 1986), at 300.

[72] Pound notes that the Serjeants, the senior advocates, addressed each other as "brother": R. Pound, *The Lawyer from Antiquity to Modern Times: With Particular reference to the Development of Bar Associations in the United States* (St. Paul, Minn., West Publishing, 1953), at13.

[73] This may be thought to represent the different place which clients have in lawyer loyalties in common law and inquisitorial systems, but it will be noted that lawyers can have a duty of partisanship (see below) in an inquisitorial system: M. Taruffo, "The Lawyer's Role and the Models of Civil Process" (1981) 16 *Israel Law Review* 5; J. Leubsdorf, *The Independence of the Bar in France: Learning from Comparative Legal Ethics* (Draft paper, 1997). In the Eastern European communist states the lawyer was not bound solely by client loyalty but by loyalty to the state. Therefore lawyers were under a duty to persuade clients to avoid proceedings which conflicted with the interests of the community or society. Lawyers in the former soviet block are now redefining their basic affiliations: see M. Bohlander, M. Blacksell and K. M. Born, "The Legal Profession in East Germany—Past, Present and Future" (1996) 3:3 *International Journal of the Legal Profession* 255.

[74] Privilege may, therefore, only be waived by a client, expressly or by implication: *Lillicrap* v. *Nadel & Co.* [1993] 1 All ER 724, although it should be noted that barristers, in common with *avocats*, have a notion of confidence between themselves: J. Flood, A. Boon, A. Whyte, E. Skordaki, R. Abbey and A. Ash, *Reconfiguring the Market for Advocacy Services: London and Four Fields of Practice* (London, Report for the Lord Chancellor's Advisory Committee on Legal Education and Conduct, 1996), hereafter ACLEC report.

[75] See also Flores, n. 65 above.

resisting the oppressive power of the state.[76] Another view is that the "ultimate function of the lawyer is to administer and to facilitate the operation of law".[77] The differences in these conceptions of the lawyer's role have profound implications for the exercise of virtue by lawyers and the way in which they seek to realise the social good of justice.

Conceptions of Justice

Most discussions of the lawyer's role take the commitment to the pursuit of justice as a starting point.[78] The promise of justice to citizens legitimates the state and the central role of lawyers in delivering justice legitimates the lawyer's role in the liberal democracies. Justice is, however, conceived in different ways.[79] Compared with the social good of health, there is considerable ambiguity and lack of consensus regarding what constitutes the good of justice.[80] The lawyer's role in securing the good of justice is, therefore, equally ambiguous. Indeed, it has been said that the lawyer's "primary loyalty is to an overarching system of value orientations that represents, beyond a clear-cut core, an ambiguous compromise among several influential conceptions of justice".[81] Because of the ambiguity inherent in the concept of justice, it has been suggested that the way in which legal professions conceive of it is intrinsically tied to the role of law in society. In common law countries, lawyers tend to conceive of their role in securing justice as achieving three main objectives. These are striving to achieve an efficient and effective legal system, supporting the legitimacy of law as an institution and promoting the merits of procedural justice and legalism.[82] These objectives tie the professional ethics of lawyers in a common law country to the adversarial system and to a position that equates justice with the defence of rights.[83]

---

[76] J. Weinstein, "On the Teaching of Legal Ethics" (1972) 72 *Columbia Law Review* 452; and J. F. Sutton and J. S. Dzienkowski, *Cases and Materials on the Professional Responsibility of Lawyers* (St. Paul, Minn., West Publishing, 1989), at 3.

[77] Giegerich, n. 11 above.

[78] Flores, n. 65 above.

[79] Generally, for the Ancient Greeks, justice tended to be equated with "what is in the interests of the stronger". In Aristotle's account of the virtues, i.e. the mean between the more and less; justice is the mean between doing injustice and suffering injustice: Macintyre, n. 33 above at 154. But, even in the city states of Ancient Greece there were different understandings of what doing justice might mean. In the modern world the concept of justice is again plagued by the incommensurability of values. Macintyre gives the example of A's belief in the justice of his right not to be taxed; B's belief in the justice of redistributive taxation. Pluralist culture has no means of weighing these competing claims. Theories which might suggest answers are also incommensurable, e.g. Robert Nozick's account of justice is a rational articulation of A's position, John Rawl's of B's. Nozick prioritises entitlement, Rawls needs: Macintyre, n. 33 above, at 249.

[80] D. Rueschemeyer, "Doctors and Lawyers: A Comment on the Theory of the Professions" [1964–5] *Canadian Review of Sociology and Anthropology* 17.

[81] *Ibid.*, at 20.

[82] T. C. Halliday, *Beyond Monopoly: Lawyers, State Crises, and Professional Empowerment* (Chicago, Ill., and London, University of Chicago Press, 1987), at 369.

[83] C. Douzinas and R. Warrington, *Justice Miscarried: Ethics, Aesthetics and the Law* (Hemel Hempstead, Harvester Wheatsheaf, 1995).

The adversarial system has many distinctive procedural characteristics. Particularly significant in relation to the role of lawyers is party control of the investigation and presentation of evidence and argument. The decision-maker, for example a judge, adopts a passive role. He or she listens to both sides and renders a decision based on the evidence and argument presented. In contrast, under the inquisitorial system adopted by civil law countries, the judge controls the development of the case.[84] The adversarial system gave lawyers considerable control over the processes of litigation. If lawyers did their job well, it was assumed, a court was able to reach a wise decision. But, in fact, as explained in Part V, the litigation process often transforms the idea of *control by the parties* over the conduct of the dispute into *control by lawyers* of the conduct of the dispute. Nevertheless, the idea of party control legitimated both the system and the role of lawyers within it. This gave the legal profession a strong incentive for adherence to the adversarial system and the ethic which evolved to support the lawyer's role in that system.[85]

The way in which lawyers can reinforce a view of justice which is most consistent with the goals of the liberal state is to seek the fair treatment of social groups and individuals. It follows that they should also support social values consistent with these goals. Although the lawyer's defence of the adversarial system is often viewed as self-interested, Cotterrell argues that "in many legal systems, the appeal to democratic will and the insistence on procedural propriety are genuine contributions to the safeguarding of legal values".[86] In all systems, he suggests, the ideological significance of these goals is not to be underestimated. Given this orientation to justice, the task for those involved in the administration of justice is to ensure that there is sufficient order—certainty and consistency—in the system, and to ensure that officials, including lawyers, maintain predictable patterns of behaviour.[87] As we have already suggested, these patterns of behaviour, behavioural norms, are a source of professional ethics and a professional ideology. The emphasis on procedural justice is a defence against a clash of different conceptions of justice. It gives rise to and is reflected in a positivist tradition which espouses faith in formal rules and procedures and separates these from moral considerations such as the social impact of the rules.[88] On the other hand, there is the experience of law in action, whereby unequal access to law and the service of lawyers is offered to different groups and classes. This is a potential source of alienation between the values of the legal profession and the various sections of society it serves.

---

[84] Sward, n. 70 above.

[85] *Ibid.*, at 354.

[86] See further Cotterrell, n. 29 above, at 156.

[87] *Ibid.*, at 154.

[88] Positivism undoubtedly has its virtues in a pluralistic society because it provides "mandatory rules of such clarity, precision and scope that they can be routinely understood and and applied without recourse to contentious moral and political judgements": T. Campbell, "The Point of Legal Positivism" (1998–9) 9 *The King's College Law Journal* 63 at 66.

But more, proceduralism undermines the notion of individual responsibility in the practice of law.[89]

D. THE ADVERSARIAL ETHIC

Philosophical Foundations of the Adversary System

The ethic associated with adversarialism both reflects and reinforces wider social values. Sward argues that human societies balance an individualistic ethic which reinforces the values of creativity, autonomy and reward for effort with a communitarian ethic which promotes social co-operation. Both the communitarian and the individualistic ethic have weaknesses.[90] Communitarianism suppresses the individual and can create disincentives to effort. Individualism can lead to a lack of concern for the consequences of one's actions. Most societies lean more towards one than the other of these ethics. Adversary adjudication, which gives parties substantial control over the process of dispute resolution, reflects an individualistic ethic which is consistent with the individualistic and materialistic society produced by unrestrained capitalism.

The weakness of the individual ethic, its lack of concern for consequences, is strongly expressed in the adversarial ethic of lawyers. This places it at odds with the social values which have emerged as dominant since the Middle Ages. As Ridley observes, many of the "conspicuously virtuous things we all praise— cooperation, altruism, generosity, sympathy, kindness, selflessness—are concerned with the welfare of others" and arise out of a co-operative and reciprocal society.[91] The emphasis on the individual in society, reflected in the adversarial system, means that there are circumstances in which lawyers may do things for clients which they may well have moral qualms about doing for themselves; particularly misleading others or bullying weaker parties. Legal professionals may be required to exercise virtue in the context of the relationship with clients, yet, in pursuing the selfish objectives of their client, be less than fair, wise or beneficent in their dealings with others. Not only are they are expected to be selfish for their client, they are required to be unco-operative for their client, not to reciprocate in their client's interests.

---

[89] It has been argued that a serious risk arising from a lack of consensus on the meaning of justice is that members of the profession will see the professional norms simply as conventions with little moral force: *ibid.*, at 21.

[90] See D. Kennedy, "Form and Substance in Private Law Adjudication" (1976) 89 *Harvard Law Review* and Sward, n. 70 above.

[91] Ridley, n. 16 above.

The Ethic of Lawyers in an Adversary System

The commitment of lawyers to notions of adversarialism may be reflected in their codes of conduct. But this is not the only source of the lawyer's ethic. As already discussed, a "professional ethic" can be seen as an ideology through which a professional group claims legitimacy and status. An ideology can be seen as a narrative, or story, constructed by a group, such as a profession[92] through which it seeks to justify its social role.[93] Hazard maintains, for example, that the narrative of the American legal profession "conveys a . . . clear ideal: that of the fearless advocate who champions a client threatened with loss of life and liberty by government oppression".[94] It is clear that the particular concept of justice pursued by lawyers is the defence of the rights of individual citizens against a powerful enemy, the state.[95] On this view, the lawyer's role in society, the good the profession promotes, is access by citizens to vigorous representation within closely circumscribed rules provided by a court which is independent of the state. This supports the key ethical obligations, loyalty, confidentiality and candour to the court, and balances the legal profession's two basic affiliations—to clients and to the judiciary.[96] It also justifies the structural independence of lawyers, including judges, from the machinery of the state. But, Luban argues, this view of the adversarial ethic also demands a compensating loss of autonomy by lawyers. This sacrifice is manifest in the "standard conception" of the lawyer's role; the expectation that lawyers subscribe to two overarching principles which are central to the legitimacy of the adversary system. These principles are partisanship and neutrality.

Neutrality is manifest in the obligation to represent any cause, irrespective of personal feelings and regardless of the moral merit of that cause.[97] It is embodied in the English bar's "cab rank" rule; the requirement that barristers accept

---

[92] Macintyre, n. 33 above, argues (at 216) that there is no way of understanding societies except through the stock of stories, the myths, which are their dramatic resources. Such narratives have a "key character" whose moral dilemmas reflect the dominant conflicts of the time, e.g. the knight on his quest or the Athenian gentleman. Heroic sagas present a view of the world, a narrative, for which they claim truth; the writers claim an objectivity for their own standpoint. In the medieval quest, for example, everything previously wrong with a person's life could be remedied, thus reflecting the Christian belief in redemption (at 175). Although Macintyre argues that bureaucratic managers are the "key characters" of the modern age, lawyers also have a claim to such a role. Lawyers control the law. The "blindness" of law to social position legitimises centralised state control of a society with pluralistic values: D. Phillips, "Some General Thoughts on the State of the Republic and the Obligation of the Legal Profession to it" (from an address to a conference of the fourth judicial Court of the United States at Hot Springs, Virginia, 27 June 1969 (cited in Sutton and Dzienowski, n. 76 above, at 12)).

[93] Halliday, n. 82 above, at 33.

[94] Hazard, n. 62 above, at 1243.

[95] Bayles *Professional Ethics*, n. 7 above, at 18–19.

[96] Hazard, n. 62 above, at 1246.

[97] D. Luban, "The Adversary System Excuse" in D. Luban (ed.), *The Good Lawyer: Lawyers' Roles and Lawyers' Ethics* (Totowa, NJ, Rowman and Allanheld, 1984), although it can also be taken to mean the maintenance of distance from clients (see below and S. Scheingold and A. Bloom, "Transgressive cause lawyering: practice and sites from the politicization of the professional," (1998) 5 *International Journal of the Legal Profession* 209 at 213).

instructions irrespective of their personal feelings about their client or the case.[98] Partisanship is reflected in a duty to put the client's interests before those of any other party, a duty which flows from the assumption that justice results from the vigorous presentation of conflicting views. Brougham's much quoted statement justifying his partisan defence of Queen Caroline against the King's charge of adultery in the early nineteenth century perfectly encapsulates the essence and the implications of the partisan ideology[99]:

> "An advocate, in the discharge of his duty, knows but one person in all the world, and that person is his client. To save that client by all means, and expedients, and at all hazards and costs to other persons, and among them, to himself, is his first and only duty; and in performing this duty he must not regard the alarm, the torments, the destruction which he may bring upon others. Separating the duty of a patriot from that of an advocate, he must go on reckless of consequences, though it should be his unhappy fate to involve his country in confusion."[100]

Both partisanship and neutrality remain important parts of the structure of ethical obligation. The extent of each obligation is, however, uncertain because the profession itself is ambivalent about them. Although many query the applicability of Brougham's description of the advocate's duty, we see examples of it every day; the trial of O.J. Simpson and Kenneth Starr's dogged pursuit of President Clinton are classic examples of Brougham's philosophy in action.[101]

Cases illustrating problems surrounding partisanship and neutrality need not involve celebrities in order to stir controversy. A case in 1990 relating to neutrality illustrates this. Two firms of London solicitors, both well known in the field of criminal defence, refused to accept as a client a man accused of raping his girlfriend. Although there is no explicit obligation on solicitors to accept clients, an editorial in a popular legal magazine attacked the firms on the ground that there is a *moral* obligation to represent unpopular causes.[102] Individuals in both firms defended their decision robustly.[103] Both accepted the argument that a profession should provide comprehensive service and, in general, the principle of neutrality. Both argued that they did not handle the particular kind of case, one on the ground that it did not specialise in rape cases and the other that it

[98] So, e.g., a female barrister must, in theory, defend an accused rapist if asked to do so, even if she has moral objections to promoting the type of defence he wishes to put forward.

[99] Brougham had threatened to expose the King's own adultery and other moral shortcomings. It has been suggested that few lawyers now adopt this as a definitive statement of the adversarial obligation: L. R. Patterson, "On Analyzing the Law of Legal Ethics: An American Perspective" (1981) 16:1 *Israel Law Review* 28.

[100] 2 Trial of Queen Caroline 8 (J. Nightingale (ed.) 1821) quoted in Frankel, "The Search for Truth: An Umpireal View" (1975) 123 *University of Pennsylvania LR* 1031 at 1036, and Hazard, n. 62 above, at 1239.

[101] Many explanations of why Starr was so determined to "get" Clinton were offered. Some commentators thought his motive was personal, others that it was political. Lawyers would find it less surprising than other people that Starr thought that he was just doing his job as a lawyer.

[102] *New Law Journal*, 9 Feb. 1990.

[103] A. Hall, "We Say No and we Mean No!", *New Law Journal* 2 March 1990 at 284, B. Raymond, "The Profession's Duty to Provide; A Solicitor's Right to Choose", *New Law Journal* 2 March 1990 at 285.

chose not to appear where the defence was consent.[104] A senior barrister commented that solicitors had not been subject to the cab rank rule because clients have a greater choice of solicitors than barristers and because, being paid by solicitors, barristers do not have to check the creditworthiness of clients.[105] But, he argued, the rule might have to be considered since, in the circumstances of the particular case, the public might well reach the damaging conclusion that lawyers were allowed to make moral judgements about potential clients.

Neutrality, therefore, remains an important principle because it underwrites access by citizens to partisan representation. Partisanship itself is, arguably, the principle that underpins the way in which lawyers actually approach their work. Partisanship is intrinsic to the adversarial system and will be considered in the next section. In general, however, it has been argued that neutrality and partisanship, as a "standard conception" of the lawyer's role, are incomplete explanations of the lawyer's professional ethics, at least as represented in the American Bar Association's code.[106] This is also true in England and Wales where solicitors, unlike barristers, are under no obligation to accept particular clients. It is better, therefore, to regard both principles as essential pillars of legal ethics, but they do not represent a complete framework for them.

The Lawyer's Adversarial Role

The lawyer within an adversary system has a distinctive role; he or she represents or advocates the position of one of the parties. This requires a stance in relation to the client, and the client's opponent, which is quite different from that taken by other professions. Even in those professions which habitually deal with conflicting interests, the professional role is usually to arbitrate rather than represent. In adversarial situations there is a temptation to be forceful and insistent. This can become, or be seen as, aggressive behaviour on the part of representative lawyers. This aggressive partisanship is perplexing to non-lawyers. Lawyers often have little opportunity to foster the genuine concern for their client's interests that grows out of interpersonal relationships. So their aggressive presentation of client wishes or client interests appears shallow. Other representatives, other lawyers, may be the focus of this aggression. Thus, while "normal civility and fairness can minimise the tension, . . . the lawyer's role as advocate of his client's best interests requires that a certain untrodden area of

[104] This was on the ground that "consent" defences generally involved attacking the reputation and character of the alleged victim (see Chap. 14) and because the firm may, as a result of links with women's organisations, have been exposed to accusations of a conflict of interest (see Chap. 11), A. Hall n. 103 above.

[105] D. Latham Q.C., "Solicitors and the Cab Rank Rule", *New Law Journal* 2 March 1990 at 286.

[106] It is notable that the Kutak Commission's (see generally ch. 4 section E below) model rules permitted lawyers to reject clients whose aims they found "repugnant or imprudent" or to withdraw from a case when clients wished to pursue such objectives: T. Schneyer, "Professionalism as Politics: The Making of a Modern Legal Ethics Code" in Nelson, Trubeck and Solomon (eds.), n. 31 above, 95 at 142.

potential interaction be left on lawyers on the opposing side of a controversy".[107] In short, the adversary system creates concern for winning and losing
which stirs up enmity between professional colleagues and between the parties
who are their clients.

The ideology and ethic of lawyers associated with adversarial justice confuse
non-lawyers because the behaviour of lawyers often seems to conflict with what
is regarded as fair or just in wider society. Various attempts have been made to
justify such behaviour in a professional context. The priority which lawyers char-
acteristically attach to the virtues of loyalty, courage and valour has been called
"role morality" and the acts of lawyers themselves "role-differentiated behaviour".[108] In theory, the lawyer tempers this aggressive partisanship by adopting a
purely technical orientation to the client's problem, a "professional approach".
They are "affectively neutral" which means that they resist becoming emotionally
involved with the client but focus on the legal merits of the cause.[109] It has been
argued that this is demanded by the rule of law and reinforced by the positivist
tradition in legal education. The lawyer's role in maintaining the rule of law leads
to an obsession with formal rationality.[110] The emphasis on the consistent application of rules known in advance blocks an empathetic response by lawyers,
including judges,[111] to the human issues raised by legal problems.[112] At its
extremes, legal socialisation can develop these tendencies to an extreme degree so
that, to ordinary people, affective neutrality can seem cold and uncaring. Feminist
and critical legal scholars have argued that the law curriculum achieves this by
equating logic with reason and understanding, while denying the value of feeling
and imagination.[113] Given the rapidly changing ethnic and gender balance in the
profession[114] and the increased attention the profession is seeking to give to the
lawyer and client relationship,[115] these values are increasingly questioned.

The distinctive position of lawyers in adversarial dispute resolution presents
another problem to those subscribing to classical professional virtues. This
problem is that, while professionals may be expected not to harm others, the
good of opponents in a legal action is generally low on the list of the lawyer's
considerations. Unlike most other professionals, the lawyer's specialist know-

---

[107] Giegerich, n. 11 above.

[108] R. Wasserstrom, "Lawyers as Professionals: Some Moral Issues" (1975) 5 *Human Rights* 1.

[109] Johnson, n. 66 above, at 36, and see also V. Denti, "Public Lawyers, Political Trials and the
Neutrality of the Legal Profession" (1981) 1 *Israel Law Review* 20 (proposing four different ways in
which lawyers are "neutral" including, first, the lawyer's interest only in "the fact", divested of all
passional elements and all that does not fall within the legal rule and, secondly, the lawyer's indif-
ference with regard to the final outcome of litigation).

[110] C. Sampford, "What's a Lawyer Doing in a Nice Place Like This? Lawyers and Ethical Life"
(1998) 1 *Legal Ethics* 35. But see Campbell, n. 88 above.

[111] L. H. Henderson, "Legality and Empathy" (1986/87) 85 *Michigan Law Review* 1574.

[112] T. M. Massaro, "Empathy, Legal Storytelling, and the Rule of Law: New Words, Old
Wounds?" (1988/89) 87 *Michigan Law Review* 2099.

[113] *Ibid.*, at 100.

[114] See Chaps. 2 and 6 below and D. B. Wilkins 'Fragmenting Professionalism: racial identity and
the ideology of bleached out lawyering' (1998) 5 *International Journal of the Legal Profession* 141.

[115] See Chap. 7 below.

ledge and skill are deployed to bring another down; the inevitable consequence of a system in which there is usually a winner and a loser. From this position it is a small step to a situation where lawyers justify acts through the need to put their own client first. They may find that they do not even consider the impact of their actions on third parties.[116] But the exact limits have always been unclear. This position is reflected in a decision in a key case at the end of the last century. In it, the Master of the Rolls said that:

> "A professional man, whether he were a solicitor or a barrister, was bound to act with the utmost honour and fairness with regard to his client. He was bound to use the utmost skill for his client, but neither a solicitor nor a barrister was bound to degrade himself for the purpose of winning his client's case. Neither of them ought to fight unfairly, though both were bound to use every effort to bring their client's case to a successful issue. Neither had any right to set himself up as the judge of his client's case. They had no right to forsake their client on any mere suspicion of their own or on any view they might take as to the client's chance of ultimate success. The duty of a solicitor to his client arose from the relationship of solicitor and client. A solicitor had no relation with his client's adversary which gave rise to any duty between them. His duty was, however, not to fight unfairly, and that arose from his duty to himself not to do anything which was degrading to himself as a gentleman and a man of honour."[117]

It has, over time, been convenient for lawyers to assume that their fidelity to the pursuit of justice is limited to an obligation to use their technical expertise at the expense of their own interests but with limited regard for any other consequences.[118] Some scholars have argued that lawyers must put aside moral considerations when their professional role requires it.[119] Others have sought to align the role morality of lawyers with wider social norms by arguing that what lawyers may have to do for clients is no more than society would expect friends to do for each other.[120] Such explanations are seldom wholly satisfying[121] and

---

[116] This perspective is strongest in the American literature. See e.g. Schneyer, who suggests that the primary purpose of professional ethics is to guard against lawyers' co-operation with, or co-optation by, third parties whose interests conflict with those of clients: T. Schneyer, "Moral Philosophy's Standard Misconception of Legal Ethics" [1984] *Wisconsin Law Review* 1529, and Freedman, n. 59 above, chap. 11); J. Leubsdorf, "Three Models of Professional Reform" (1982) 67 *Cornell Law Review* 1021.

[117] *In re G. Mayor Cooke* (1889) 5 Times Law Reports 407 at 408.

[118] Koehn cites the example of the campaign waged by dentists for the fluoridisation of water, even though this would decrease their work: D. Koehn, *The Ground of Professional Ethics* (London and New York, Routledge, 1994) at 178.

[119] See, e.g., S. Pepper, "The Lawyers Amoral Ethical Role: A Defense, A Problem, and Some Possibilities" [1986] *American Bar Foundation Research Journal* 613 and C. P. Curtis, "The Ethics of Advocacy" (1951) 4 *Stanford Law Review* 3.

[120] This is illustrated by attempts to liken the lawyer–client relationship to a friendship. Friends typically do, and are forgiven for doing, things for friends which they would not do for others: C. Fried, "The Lawyer as Friend: The Moral Foundations of the Lawyer–Client Relation" (1976) 85 *Yale Law Journal* 1060. Fried asks whether a lawyer—a decent and morally sensitive person—can conduct himself according to the traditional conception of professional loyalty and still believe that what he is doing is professionally worthwhile? He argues that the best way of favouring the abstract collectivity is to concentrate on those to whom one has a special relation.

[121] For a highly critical comment on Fried's argument see E. A. Dauer and A. A. Leff, "Comment on Fried's Lawyer as Friend" (1976) 85 *Yale Law Journal* 573.

the relationship between the professional ethics of lawyers and ordinary morality is strained by a lack of concern for the impact of the lawyer's efforts on third parties. A popular view of lawyers is that they are amoral technicians; skilful manipulators of legal rules in their clients' legal interests,[122] who, by definition, suppress their own moral convictions. This vision of the lawyer has been described as "pure legal advocacy", a model which discourages behaviour conducive to the attainment of virtues such as truth, honesty and justice. Clearly, when the lawyer remains silent when a client lies under oath he compromises the professional commitment to truth and "justice".[123] He contradicts the idea of professionalism "as an ideal defining a standard of good conduct, virtuous character, and a commitment, therefore, to excellence going beyond the norm of morality ordinarily governing relations among persons".[124] Although such behaviour is rarely condoned it may still happen. It is assumed that, when it happens, the lawyer concerned suffers anxiety about what it is right and proper to do for clients.

In Chapter 7 these issues are considered in the context of the obligations owed to clients. In Chapter 14 it will be seen that professional rules of advocacy, which incorporate a "duty to the court", strain against the more extreme examples of adversarial behaviour. But the economic interests of the advocate, the expectations of the advocate's clients and peers and, indeed, the logic of the adversarial system may encourage an aggressive amoral stance. This creates for the individual a struggle between ethos, in the sense of habit, and ethic[125] which can lead to a lawyers suffering from a "debilitating psychic tension".[126] The question arises, can a lawyer be a "morally good person" in an adversary system? Some argue that it is possible. It requires that lawyers treat others justly, are truthful, benevolent, trustworthy and morally autonomous and have moral courage and morally respectable financial habits.[127] The problem is that the adversary system produces strains and temptations which other systems do not. One example will serve to illustrate this. The adversary system relies on lawyers to interview witnesses before the trial and decide which witnesses to produce. It has been argued that this encourages lawyers to exercise influence over wit-

---

[122] E. D. Cohen, "Pure Legal Advocates and Moral Agents: Two Concepts of a Lawyer in an Adversarial System" in Flores, n. 65 above, at 87.

[123] As we have noted, there may be many notions of what constitutes justice. In these circumstances it may well be argued that a lawyer does not treat people justly in these circumstances because he does not treat them equally.

[124] A. Flores, "What Kind of Person Should a Professional be?" in Flores, n. 65 above, at 1.

[125] See Chap. 12.

[126] L. E. Fisher, "Truth as a Double-Edged Sword: Deception, Moral Paradox, and the Ethics of Advocacy" (1989) 14 *The Journal of the Legal Profession* 89.

[127] Doing what is morally right, even though by doing so one suffers substantial hardship, following Aristotle, spending the right amounts on the right objects and taking the money from the right sources, being disposed to do good for others when reasonably situated to do so and doing no harm, keeping confidences even when it does a greater injustice to do so and performing ones own moral thinking: Cohen, n. 122 above, at 82.

nesses which can lead to the distortion of evidence.[128] In an inquisitorial system, in contrast, lawyers generally have no prior access to witnesses but can suggest those to be interviewed. The responsibility for presenting evidence, and therefore the temptation to distort evidence, is removed.

The Decline of Adversarial Values?

In many common law systems the value of adversarialism is increasingly being questioned. Advocates of the system who have sought a justification for its individualistic values have offered two main theories. The first is that the presentation of conflicting views is the best way to test the facts and to arrive at the truth. The second, and later theory is that the adversary system offers the best way of protecting individual dignity and autonomy. Despite this defence, in many common law countries, adversarial processes are tempered by procedural devices, such as discovery, which equalise the power of the parties.[129] Increasingly, adversarial dispute resolution has been supplemented by alternative methods which reflect less individualistic and more communitarian values.

The profession in the UK has already gone further than the American Bar Association in modifying the adversarial ethic both in its rules and in its narrative. Yet the narrative of the legal profession in the UK is remarkably similar to that described by Hazard. This is not surprising, since the founding principles of the legal profession of England and Wales are similar to those in the professional code of the American Bar Association.[130] Like the legal profession in the United States, lawyers in England and Wales see the profession as a bulwark against state oppression.[131] In the 1980s, when the legal profession's privileges were under sustained attack, the Marre Committee, which included representatives of both branches of the profession, asserted that[132]:

[128] See G. L. Wells and E. F. Loftus (eds.), *Eyewitness Testimony: Psychological Perspectives* (Cambridge, Cambridge University Press, 1984), and Sward, n. 70 above, at 312.

[129] Sward, n. 70 above.

[130] A classic example is the duty not to discuss a client's confidences. Noonan cites the English case *Annesley* v. *Anglesey*, 17 How. St. Tr. 1140, 1223–6, 1241 (Ex., 1743) as an example of the root of the privilege of confidentiality, *viz.* "(1) A 'gentleman of character' does not disclose his client's secrets. (2) An attorney identifies with his client, and it would be 'contrary to the rules of natural justice and equity' for an individual to betray himself. (3) Attorneys are necessary for the conduct of business, and business would be destroyed if attorneys were to disclose their communications with their clients": J. T. Noonan, "The Purposes of Advocacy and the Limits of Confidentiality" (1966) 64 *Michigan Law Review* 1485.

[131] This position was clearly expressed in the 1880s, when the Law Society advanced solicitors as a counterweight to state authoritarianism, "officialism" or the growth of the bureaucratic machinery of the modern state, and "state socialism": D. Sugarman, "Bourgeois Collectivism, Professional Power and the Boundaries of the State. The Private and Public Life of the Law Society, 1825 to 1914" (1996) 3:1/2 *International Journal of the Legal Profession* 81 at 111.

[132] The Committee was established by both branches of the profession to review the extent to which the services offered by the legal profession met the needs of the public for legal services, how such services could be made readily available to meet such needs and demands, where changes in structure practice and education might be in the public interest, to make recommendations to the professional bodies on such changes and to consult both inside and outside the profession as thought fit.

"the rights which can give rise to the strongest feelings usually concern a principle or cause, or involve a real or perceived oppression or abuse of power, either by the state or by a person or corporation which is more powerful and influential than the injured citizen. It is in these circumstances that the public needs an independent lawyer to ensure that justice is achieved . . .[133] [and] [L]awyers are frequently asked to advise clients who wish to assert or uphold their rights against the government or other public authorities, whether in the field of criminal or public law. A lawyer should therefore be entirely independent both of outside pressures which might interfere with his independence and of conflicts of interest . . . The public interest which requires that citizens are free to have access to, and protection for, their legal rights may transcend the interests even of government where those rights conflict with the wishes and interests of government."[134]

This particular claim to legitimacy has been increasingly challenged. The binding of professional ideology and its ethics to litigation, and particularly with criminal proceedings,[135] ignores the fact that both branches of the legal profession conduct a large amount of non-contentious work.[136] Moreover, it is precisely in the area of contentious work used to launch ideological claims, criminal representation, that the failure of the adversarial ethic is most sharply exposed. Lawyers have been deeply implicated in this failure, both for their neglect of adversarial values in magistrates' court proceedings[137] and for their emphasis on formalism in more serious cases. As the Australian judge, Mr. Justice Kirby, noted in connection with miscarriages of justice:

"the greatest injustice arises from the way in which operators of the present system at every level allow it to be manipulated, pre-trial, at trial and on appeal, with too much attention to rules and procedures and insufficient concern about the risk of injustice. It is lawyers' faults that we are accused of: attention to the familiar, comparatively simple rules and procedural requirements. Unconcern about the substantive issues of injustice and innocence that lie behind."[138]

The concern reflected in critiques of the operation of the adversarial ethic was matched by concerns about the expense of civil proceedings and the way in which cost denied access to justice. By the 1980s, change was omnipresent. As successive governments struggled to control public expenditure, state sponsorship of the adversary system was deemed less important than health or education. Moreover, the professional monopoly was increasingly perceived to be an

---

[133] Lady Marre CBE, *A Time for Change: Report of the Committee on the Future of the Legal Profession* (London, General Council of the Bar and Council of the Law Society, 1988), para. 6.8, hereafter the Marre Report.

[134] *Ibid.*, para. 6.7.

[135] Patterson, n. 99 above.

[136] Indeed, until fairly recently, domestic conveyancing was the bedrock work of a significant number of solicitors' firms.

[137] M. McConville, J. Hodgson, L. Bridges and A. Pavlovic, *Standing Accused: The Organisation and Practices of Criminal Defence Lawyers in Britain* (Oxford, Clarendon Press, 1994).

[138] M. Kirby, *Miscarriages of Justice: Our Lamentable Failure?* (a public lecture delivered by Michael Kirby on 4 June 1991 (London, Inns of Court School of Law 1991)) at 6.

impediment to *access* to justice. Access had become as pressing a concern as procedural propriety because access to justice was increasingly seen as fundamental to the legitimacy of liberal democracy. With state support in the form of legal aid, the profession in the UK had acted for a wider range of social interests than its counterpart in the United States. But adversarial justice is notoriously costly and, as the main expense of the increasingly unacceptable legal aid bill, lawyers were set on a collision course with the state. In defending the adversarial system, lawyers fostered the suspicion that they did so, at least partly, in their own interests. The legal profession, struggling to justify its position and in danger of losing the argument, had to adapt its narrative. This is strikingly illustrated by the General Council of the Bar's response to the government's proposed changes in the legal profession in the late 1980s. The Bar accepted the validity of the government's aim, to enhance competition and standards, but asserted the importance of its own "first principles". These were:

> "Access to justice for all at fair and reasonable cost; independence of barristers and acceptance of the 'cab-rank rule'; choice between barristers in strong competition; the same high quality of service for rich and poor alike; fair and reasonable remuneration; efficient administration of justice in the interests of all; the high quality of judges."[139]

The implications of the shift in the rhetoric of proceduralism to one of access are further considered in Chapter 9 and Part V.

The Anglo-American legal professions' commitment to defending adversarial justice was under considerable pressure. The public interest now required that justice was seen to be done; that disputes were resolved expeditiously at the lowest practical cost; that client's interests had to be buttressed at the expense of lawyers' interests.[140] A lesser concern for policy-makers, but one which should concern the profession, was that the adversarial system placed such demands on lawyers that their own personal wellbeing was threatened. The adversary system was being run at a lower cost. Lawyers were under increasing work pressures. It was more difficult to prepare cases adequately and there was an increasing temptation to cut corners. Lawyers were concerned on the one hand that their capacity for partisanship was undermined and on the other that unrestrained partisanship was not morally justifiable in many situations.

As legal aid declines, lawyers in the UK may be forced to adapt the narrative that legitimises their special position in society. It has been argued, for example, that the role of lawyers is to provide access to *law*,[141] not specifically access to

---

[139] General Council of the Bar, *Quality of Justice: The Bar's Responce* (London, Butterworths, 1989) para. 1.3.

[140] T. D. Morgan, "The Evolving Concept of Professional Responsibility" (1977) 90 *Harvard Law Review* 702 (see also Rawl's reference to two principles defining justice, i.e. maximum liberty consistent with the liberty of others and equality of opportunity subject to priority given to need: J. Rawls, *A Theory of Justice* (Cambridge, Mass., Harvard University Press, 1975) at 60–7).

[141] See S. L. Pepper, "Counselling at the Limits of the Law: An Exercise in the Jurisprudence of and Ethics of Lawyering" (1995) 104 *The Yale Law Journal* 1545, and for more detailed analysis see I. M. Ramsay, "What Do Lawyers Do? Reflections on the Market for Lawyers" (1993) 21 *International Journal of the Sociology of Law* 355.

justice through the courts. In deal-making or advising on drafting documents, lawyers anticipate and pre-empt disputes. This is an important social role, one which is at least as important as adversarial representation. To change the narrative of legal professions to reflect this has implications for ethics, not least because adversarial principles cease to be their *raison d'être*. The changes in professional ideology which such a shift implies are always difficult, but Hazard argues that it was forced in the United States as it became clear that most lawyers defended the interests of powerful corporations in civil actions. American lawyers were employed in resisting government regulation, or were dealing with disputes involving other business entities, their employees or consumers.[142] The profession was forced to reinvent an image of lawyers as protectors of individual rights and as protectors of property.[143] The problems presented by changing or adapting ancient traditions force us briefly to consider the relationship between tradition and change.

Tradition and Change

Professions serve the public good but perceptions of the public interest can be quick to change. In contrast, the norms of stable communities are relatively slow to change. Longstanding traditions can become ritualised whereas, in the wider community, they may seem to be anachronistic.[144] This supports the view that "law is a profession and an intellectual discipline which is profoundly engaged with the here and now, and which often seeks for authority and legitimacy in a real or imagined past".[145] There may, of course, be good reasons for retaining traditions precisely because changing them creates confusion or conflict within the profession. Following the conventions of a society is a relative good because convention reflects a consensus, past or present, and minimises the risk of conflict. Therefore, before any tradition is rejected, it is important to understand its

---

[142] The role of the American legal profession had been to develop and protect business property within a political system committed to both popular government and constitutional restraints on government. Therefore, the narrative of the profession in the USA has changed; it remade itself as a counterbalancing force against "the vagaries of popular government with the pressures of the market": Hazard, n. 62 above, at 1241.

[143] This produced a justification and legitimisation of the profession as defender of due process or "resistance to government intervention in the lives, liberty or property of private parties" *ibid.*, at 1245, but even this narrative was threatened when American courts, in the 1960s and 1980s, did not accept the primacy "under the rubric of due process, of the parity between property on the one hand and life and liberty on the other": *ibid.*, at 1266. The fact that the narrative proved not to be sufficiently robust suggests that this particular attempt to legitimise the role of lawyers, as mediators between property and democracy, is justified only by two circumstances. First, if the protection of property is essential to a stable and prosperous society and, secondly, if property is "continually threatened by majoritarian democratic politics": *ibid.*, at 1267.

[144] Macintyre cites the example of anthropological studies where certain kinds of social behaviour were "taboo". The rules themselves were often rooted in a specific context which gave them intelligibility but the context had changed, leaving taboo rules as arbitrary prohibitions (n. 33 above, at 112).

[145] H. W. Arthurs, "Lawyering in Canada in the 21st Century" (1996) 15 *Windsor Yearbook of Access to Justice* 202.

role in sustaining contemporary values. But, far from suggesting an ethical decline, change can give it renewed life, particularly when new conventions are sustained by the exercise of the relevant virtues. Only through understanding tradition can we grasp the possibilities which the past has made available to the present.[146] Understanding change also offers the best prospect of adapting successfully to new environments.[147] It could be argued that the decline of adversariality offers an opportunity for lawyers to review ethical commitments. It is therefore necessary to evaluate traditions as new social conditions arise.

E. EVALUATION

Methodologies

The study of ethics is linked to a range of specific methodologies. Two are discussed here because they are broad enough to encompass other approaches. These two are deontology and teleology. The word deontology is derived from the Greek *deon* meaning binding duty. Deontology is defined as the study of duty partly or wholly independently of consequences.[148] Deontology looks to the internal logic of value systems and rules and the moral content of these are seen as "given". Deontological approaches assume that it is possible to identify principles that make behaviour right or wrong. A good example is the study of divine law. Applied to professional ethics such approaches tend to explore and criticise the logic of rules, or the prioritisation of some interests over others, but do not look at the relevance or utility of the rules within a wider framework of values.

A deontological approach tends to accept the proposition that professionals are entitled to do whatever is permitted by the regulations promulgated by their profession.[149] This is attractive to practitioner lawyers because it provides a framework of regulation, like the law, within which they can comfortably operate. It might be attractive to academic lawyers because it is consistent with the positivist tradition in study of the discipline of law.[150] However, it is self-evidently a narrow approach which closes down a number of avenues of enquiry. Deontology is an inadequate framework for identifying the content of

---

[146] MacIntyre, n. 33 above.

[147] Arthurs, n. 145 above.

[148] J. Pearsall and B. Trumble (eds.), *The Oxford English Reference Dictionary* (Oxford, New York, Oxford University Press, 1995) (and see Luban, n. 97 above, at 424–8).

[149] Bayles, n. 7 above, at 13.

[150] Bordieu notes that the law tends to formalise and codify everything which comes into its sphere. This, he argues, is part of the law's ability to obtain and sustain social consent. Formalisation is seen as a sign of the law's impartiality and neutrality. It is also important in the "maintenance and universalisation of the tacit grant of faith in the juridical order, and thus to the stability of the juridical field itself": R. Terdiman, "Translator's Introduction to Bordieu, P. 'The Force of Law: Toward a Sociology of the Juridical Field' " (1987) 38 *The Hastings Law Journal* 805 at 810.

professional obligations because codes, however comprehensive they are, represent "a single piece of a larger mosaic of considerations that are morally relevant to a lawyer's conduct".[151] Some of the highest ideals of legal professionals, like acting for the poor free of charge, or *pro bono publico*, are not required by professional codes. Therefore, it is proposed, deontology must be supplemented by other frameworks of analysis which seeks an explanation of phenomena with reference to the purpose they serve. Teleology serves this purpose.

Teleology looks to criteria outside the value system being studied and uses these values as a yardstick for judging rules or conduct.[152] For Aristotle, for example, the *telos*, or end-state, of human beings is a "good life", based on both moral actions for their own sake and the ability to think and reason.[153] Similarly, in evaluating professional ethics we might ask, "what social good does the legal profession promote and how do its rules promote this 'good'?" or "should the profession try to help its members to be 'better' people and, if so, how do its rules achieve this?". In assessing social goods, well established concepts such as utilitarianism, which seek policies which will achieve the greatest good for the greatest number,[154] may be of value. This requires that justifications of professional action consider the consequences of that action for a wide group of people.[155] But utilitarianism is not sufficient on its own, for its assumptions do not recognise that certain relationships may give rise to specific obligations which are valid without any wider benefit to those outside the relationship. The relationship between lawyers and their individual clients is a classic example of this.

In this book, therefore, our focus moves between these methodologies. In Parts I and II the approach is mainly teleological. A number of explanations of professional action and motivation are explored which have a direct significance for an understanding of why professional ethics take the form they do and the pressures and potential for change. In Part III some of the fundamental duties of lawyers are explored in the context of trends in the demands on the profession. The approach here is both deontological and teleological, because specific rules and cases are examined as examples of wider theories relevant to each area. In

---

[151] Giegerich, n. 11 above.

[152] Bayles, n. 7 above, at 11.

[153] Flores, n. 65 above citing Aristotle, *Nicomachean Ethics*, Book II, section 6 (Oxford, Oxford University Press, 1925).

[154] Utilitarianism involves (a) ranking the outcome of actions solely according to how much welfare (i.e. pleasure or pain or satisfaction of human preferences) they produce and (b) determines total welfare by summing the welfares of all affected individuals by reference to intensity, duration, propinquity and extent: D. Luban, "Freedom and Constraint in Legal Ethics: Some Mid-Course Corrections to Lawyers and Justice" (1990) 49 *Maryland Law Review* 424 at n. 11 and Facione, Scherer, and Attig, n. 9 above. This can be further refined; act-consequentialism evaluates the rightness of each act by appraising its consequences while rule-consequentialism evaluates the rightness of each act by appraising the consequences of general rules requiring or permitting such acts (a distinction made by J. Rawls, "Two Concepts of Rules" (1955) 64 *Philosophical Review* 3. See also D. Luban, "Freedom and Constraint in Legal Ethics: Some mid-course corrections to *Lawyers and Justice*", (1990) 49 *Maryland Law Review* 424; R. Posner, "Utilitarianism, Economics and Legal Theory" (1979) 8 *Journal of Legal Studies* 103.

[155] Facione, Scherer and Attig, n. 9 above.

Parts IV and V, which explore specific obligations, for example in relation to confidentiality or advocacy, the approach tends to be more deontological in nature.

Applications: Ideology and Ethics

In this chapter we have attempted to dispel the notion that professional ethics are found only in codes of conduct. Useful as they are as a source of guidance or as indications of ethical principles, the ethical project of professions has changed and will continue to change. If professional ethics are to develop, new ways have to be found to ensure that professionals interact with the subject of ethics. This is not important only because practitioners are unlikely to follow rules for their own sake but because the development of the field of professional ethics demands participation. Participation in the consideration of questions relevant to professional ethics is, however, likely to be impaired without some understanding of tradition and context. The impact of social and political change on the profession could have profound implications for professional ethics. The transitions which may be necessary will be less painful if they are implemented before the need for change becomes a crisis.

We have seen that a deontological approach is consistent with the positivist tradition which dominates the law and law teaching and is consistent with "legal" ways of thinking. The problem with deontology as the sole foundation for the study of professional ethics is that the obligations accepted by a profession may go beyond the rules of professional regulation promulgated by Parliament and by the legal profession.[156] A deontological approach accepts the limitations of the framework of rules found in codes of conduct. Yet, in order to understand the relationship between ends and means it is often necessary to look beyond the forms of writing and rules with the "intention to unsettle apparently closed systems and empires of meaning".[157] A purely deontological approach to ethics tends to deny the need and inhibit the capacity for change in response to changing conditions.

It is argued that, since professions aspire to serve society, they have an obligation to pursue social values. It follows that a legitimate standpoint for evaluating "the good" a profession serves is the standpoint of average members of society, both as consumers and as third parties affected by the delivery of professional services.[158] Average members of society are probably self-interested, and have limited benevolence, but would support the notion that the values of

---

[156] "Practice rule 1 [discussed below] sums up, in the form of a statutory rule, the basic principles of conduct derived from the common law": n. 60 above, at 1.03, para. 3(c).

[157] C. Douzinas, R. Warrington and S. McVeigh, *Postmodern Jurisprudence: The Law of Text in the Texts of Law* (London, Routledge, 1991), at 4.

[158] Bayles, n. 7 above, at 3. See also Rawls, n. 140 above, discussed by S. G. Kupfer, "Authentic Legal Practices" (1996) 10 *Georgetown Journal of Legal Ethics* 33, at 77–81.

a liberal society are available to all. They therefore support governance by law.[159] For various reasons they may accept that a legal profession must play a role in delivering governance by law. But precisely what that role is, and how they would wish it to be manifest as a commitment to professional ethics and conduct, is more debatable. In what circumstances can individuals expect unswerving loyalty from lawyers? Would they, for example be happy that a wealthy party in litigation should make that litigation so expensive that justice is less achievable for the other party? Would they accept that loyalty to clients should take precedence over the protection of society? In short, does the legitimation of liberal society require that lawyers have an amoral role? These are issues which will be considered in Parts III, IV and V. But it must be remembered that the study of professional ethics demands the exercise of a critical faculty. The social values promoted by a profession must be balanced against the social harm that might result from professional monopoly and self-regulation. This is an issue considered in the next chapter.

CONCLUSION

Both the deontological and teleological approaches to the analysis of professional ethics are reflected in the mainstream of philosophical enquiry. The deontological character of moral judgements is a remnant of belief in divine law which underpins the philosophical tradition represented by Kant. Teleology represents the ghost of the moral philosophy of Aristotle, which examined human nature and human activity as the foundation of morality. Both assume the legitimacy of certain ends. If we are to establish a platform for a teleological analysis of professional norms, practices and ethics it is necessary to identify the social good promoted by the legal profession and the implications for legal professionals of the pursuit of that social good.

Professional ethics encourage behaviour which promotes the intrinsic goods of the practice of law and the virtues of legal professionals. The social role of lawyers is reflected in an ethic of dedicated service to individual clients and commitment to public service. The interpretation of these broad aims has been shaped by the adversary system which, for centuries, has provided the framework within which lawyers pursue justice, the defining goal of legal professionals. Recently, there have been doubts whether the adversarial ethic, and the focus on process which it engenders, is consistent with or can be reconciled with personal virtues such as honesty and integrity. As demands for wider access to justice have increased, the commitment of lawyers to defending the integrity of

---

[159] They can act so as to avoid penalties, to rely on the conduct of others and act as they wish so long as this does not infringe upon other values. In a liberal society individuals are entitled to protection from injury, equality of opportunity, privacy in terms of the control over the personal information which others have access to and welfare, as manifest in a minimum standard of living: Bayles, n. 7 above, at 11.

the adversarial legal process seems increasingly self-interested and out of step with the times. The crisis of adversarialism is, however, only one of the ideological problems facing legal professionals. As we shall see in the remainder of Part I, ethics are a matter of context and the context in which the profession operates is changing fundamentally.

2

Professional Autonomy and Power

". . . it is not possible, when considering the legal profession and the need for change, to be guided solely by considerations of price, cost and convenience. Considerations which may be appropriate to the sale of goods, or to the supply of other services, are not always relevant to the supply of legal services . . . the raison d"être of an independent legal profession is, and should remain, its ability to fulfil [its duties as traditionally conceived] and any change which would derogate from those duties should not be encouraged."[1]

A. INTRODUCTION

This chapter is concerned with the relationship between professional power and professional ethics. Professional power is a gift of the state. Its most obvious manifestation is in the professional monopoly of the market in which the profession offers its services. It is, however, also manifest in the ability of a profession to influence government policy and to control its own affairs. Ethical commitments place limitations on what practitioners can do. They can work against the commercial interests of professionals and their natural desire to be autonomous individuals. If professions are willing to accept the constraints of ethical commitments, they will expect some advantage in return. Some argue that ethics are used to justify privilege and that if privilege is withdrawn ethical commitments will fail.

The key to the privileges of market control and self-regulation is the monopoly of professional knowledge. Knowledge also gives professionals control over relationships with clients. This underlies the need for the exercise of virtue, particularly altruism, by professionals. In order to explore the ethics of contemporary professionalism it is important to consider changes in the perception of professional knowledge. This may help to explain how and why professional power has declined, and why the professions' relations with the state have changed. If professional power and autonomy are reduced, as has recently happened in the case of the legal profession in the UK, why should ethical commitments be maintained? In tackling this question we look briefly at the historical development of the legal profession, at the theories used to explain the

---

[1] Lady Marre, CBE, *A Time for Change: Report of the Committee on the Future of the Legal Profession* (London, General Council of the Bar and Council of the Law Society, 1988), para. 6.9, hereafter the Marre Report.

phenomenon of professional power and at the economic, social and political position of the legal profession.

B. THE RISE OF LEGAL PROFESSIONALISM

A range of theories has been advanced about what motivates collective professional action. Some recent analyses suggest that the driving motivation is the domination of markets and that the height of this aspiration is securing a monopoly over work. This and other theories are considered below. First, however, it is necessary to put the debate in its historical context. What follows is merely a sketch of some of key stages in the development of legal professionalism.

Legal professions can be seen as the product of two developments in western society; the rise of capitalism and the evolution of the modern state system.[2] The emergence of groups identified as "lawyers" seems only to occur when there is a high level of occupational differentiation in society. A point is reached when it is convenient to have practitioners knowledgeable about rules and regulations, where to find them and what to do about them.[3] Johnson observes that this advanced division of labour creates a social and economic dependence on lawyers and increases the social distance between lawyers and their clients. Legal services comprise both technical knowledge and also an element of "indeterminacy" in the relationship. This, in turn, creates a demand from professionals for autonomy in defining the content of practice and the exercise of judgement.[4]

The kind of work performed by lawyers is, neither fixed or stable.[5] Therefore Johnson's argument, that professionalism merely describes the way in which an occupation uses its social resources to impose a vision of its services on a large and fragmented demand, is particularly true of the legal profession. Professions find it easier to make a claim for autonomy when their work involves more indeterminacy than technique so that the mystery of their work is maintained. The balance between technicality and indeterminacy in the construction of knowledge was also changing. Traditional professional knowledge was in the nature of a craft involving a large measure of practical judgement in diagnosis and response.[6] This was superceded in the modern world by more transparent forms

---

[2] D. Rueschemeyer, "Professions Cross-Nationally: From a Profession Centred to a State-Centred Approach" [1986] *American Bar Foundation Research Journal* 415.

[3] Friedman notes that some societies do not have a legal profession. There must also be a sufficient volume of distinctive work to support the work of the professional group; the emergence of professions may also, therefore, be a sign of a society with a dominant middle class majority: L. M. Friedman, "Lawyers in Cross Cultural Perspective" in R. Abel and P. Lewis (eds.), *Lawyers in Society* (Berkeley, Calid., University of California Press, 1995).

[4] T. J. Johnson, *Professional Power* (London and Basingstoke, Macmillan, 1972), at 43.

[5] Friedman, n. 3 above, at 131.

[6] M. J. Osiel, "Lawyers as Monopolists, Aristocrats and Entrepreneurs" (1990) 103 *Harvard Law Review* 2009 at 2023.

based on reason, whereby the material of professional practice was discoverable in the library.

We saw in Chapter 1 that, as one of the original "learned professions" of the medieval European states, lawyers assumed some of the functions of the clergy. As a part of that process they acquired some of the mystique associated with theology.[7] The legal profession, together with medicine, became a prototype for professions in Western, industrialised societies.[8] As Western states moved to rational systems for resolving disputes, based on evidence and rules of logic,[9] lawyers acquired an important social role.[10] By the thirteenth century a group of professional pleaders known as narrators emerged in England. Some evolved into sergeants-at-law and, from their ranks, barristers emerged. During the reign of Edward I (1272–1307) attorneys, the forerunners of solicitors, emerged. Their appearance in court was equivalent to that of the client, a great benefit to landowners and ecclesiastical bodies who did not then have to appear person-ally.[11] The status of the legal professions of the UK and the USA derives from their emergence at a time of these major social transitions. Social control began to move from a feudal system, based on social stratification, to control exercised by means of formal rules or law. Professional autonomy grew from collective action to consolidate and enhance this advantage.

The Consolidation of Professional Power

The acquisition and use of power by different legal professions did not follow a uniform pattern. The lawyer in American society, for example, fulfilled a dif-

---

[7] The legal profession began appearing in the reign of Edward I (see generally R. Pound, *The Lawyer from Antiquity to Modern Times: With Particular Reference to the Development of Bar Associations in the United States* (St. Paul, Monn., West Publishing, 1953), particularly at 78).

[8] There are, however, differences between the Anglo-American and continental models. Friedson suggests that Anglo-American society is distinguished in particular by training for corpo-rately organised occupations to which specialised knowledge, ethicality and importance to society are imputed, and for which privilege is claimed: E. Friedson, "The Theory of Professions: State of the Art" in R. Dingwall and P. Lewis, *The Sociology of the Professions* (London, The Macmillan Press, 1983). On mainland Europe, in contrast, the state prescribes education and status is derived from membership of the educated class. In civil law countries graduates in law tend to enter a range of occupations, each with additional qualifications. The private practitioner is not "the core of any notional legal profession" because members of civil law legal occupations, do not see themselves as part of a wider "profession": see Abel and Lewis (eds.), n. 3 above, Vol. 2: *The Civil Law World*.

[9] M. J. Saks and R. Van Duizend, *The Use of Scientific Evidence in Litigation* (National Centre for State Courts, 1983), at 5.

[10] The democratisation of Western society led to "softening social mores and manners of per-sonal deportment which a class based society contributes along with the less beneficial aspects of its paternalism" but "also opened the door for unseemly scrambling, for divisive jealousies and resent-ments resulting from massive social displacement": D. Phillips, "Some General Thoughts on the State of the Republic and the Obligation of the Legal Profession to it", from an address to a confer-ence of the Fourth Judicial Court of the United States at Hot Springs, Virginia, 1969 (J. F. Sutton and J. S. Dzienowski, *Cases and Materials on the Professional Responsibility of Lawyers* (St. Paul,. Minn., West Publishing, 1989), at 12).

[11] T. F. T. Plucknett, *A Concise History of Common Law* (London, Butterworth, 1956).

ferent social role from his British counterpart. It has been suggested that lawyers in the USA fulfilled an "aristocratic" role; mingling with democratic elements of society and serving as intermediaries between property and poverty.[12] England was a more class based society and lawyers had to fight hard to achieve social status. But the English profession arguably enjoyed a greater degree of independence from the state than the legal profession of any other country. From the sixteenth century a number of organisations, guilds, cities and universities were given significant powers by central government. As a result professional groups could both assert their independence from the state and control their area of expertise. Following a period of threat from the Stewart monarchs, the position of the legal profession was further enhanced by the "unwritten constitution" resulting from the "Glorious Revolution" of 1688 and the accession of William and Mary. This not only established the pre-eminence of law but protected various kinds of groups including municipal corporations and livery companies, from the powers of the state. Professions benefited from these constitutional guarantees, and the lack of definition of their power and status provided scope for the consolidation of professional autonomy.[13]

The Bar, which was well established by this time, was the senior branch of the profession. It controlled the defining task of lawyers in a common law system, advocacy, and from its ranks the judiciary was drawn. By the seventeenth century the attorneys were excluded from being members of an Inn and the institutional foundations of the divided profession were laid.[14] Barristers had a long tradition and effective discipline but the attorneys at law and solicitors in chancery had none, having no organisation or tradition of their own. By the second half of the seventeenth century, however, barristers had withdrawn from direct contact with clients, being retained directly by attorneys who provided instructions. Subsequently, solicitors and attorneys merged.[15] The rise of the solicitors' branch since then illustrates three points which are relevant to the

---

[12] A "natural aristocracy" as opposed to one endowed by inheritance: G. C. Hazard, "The Future of Legal Ethics" (1991) 100 *Yale Law Journal* 1239 at 1272; see Hazard's discussion of A De Tocqueville's *Democracy in America, ibid.*, at 1267.

[13] M. Burrage, "From a Gentleman's to a Public Profession: Status and Politics in the History of English Solicitors" [1996] *International Journal of the Legal Profession* 45 at 60–4. Thus, in 1610, the judiciary, in the person of Coke CJ, asserted that the King had no extra-legal or personal prerogative and, subsequently, that the King should not judge cases personally because he was not versed in the "artificial reason and judgement of the law": *The case of Proclamations* (1610) (see D. Sugarman, "Bourgeois Collectivism, Professional Power and the Boundaries of the State: The Private and Public Life of the Law Society 1825 to 1914" (1996) *International Journal of the Legal Profession* 81 at 83–4). Under the "balanced constitution" (1) English law was based on customs which were slow to change and, therefore, not amenable to change by legislation; (2) "freedom" was guaranteed by law; (3) the judiciary must be independent (Sugarman, *ibid.*, at 84, and see M. Burrage, "Mrs. Thatcher Against the "Little Republics": Ideology, Precedents, and Reaction" in T. C. Halliday and L. Karpik (eds.), *Lawyers and the Rise of Western Political Liberalism* (Oxford, Clarendon Press, 1997), 124 at 148).

[14] W. R. Prest, *The Rise of the Barristers: A Social History of the Bar* 1590–1640 (Oxford: Clarendon Press, 1986), at 9.

[15] Solicitors were originally people who "conducted business on behalf of someone else without being an attorney or a barrister" (Pound, n. 7 above, at 107).

discussion of professional power. First, the development of professional power and influence was possible even as late as the nineteenth century.[16] Secondly, the accumulation of power can be incidental to other aims and, in a sense, accidental. Thirdly, profit is not necessarily the driving force behind the professionalisation of occupational groups.

Burrage argues that the primary concern of the emergent solicitors' branch was to elevate the status of the professional group rather than to make business for itself. The Society of Gentlemen Practisers, formed in 1739, sought to persuade its members to give up low status tasks as a means of enhancing social status. The Society probably never numbered more than 200, and disappeared after the creation of the Law Society in 1825.[17] Before it did so, however, it achieved, almost by chance, a very significant coup; it secured a monopoly over conveyancing.[18] The character of developing professions was also influenced by the institutions of the time. The eighteenth century was an age of learned societies; public bodies linking learning, science and the public interest. This culture, and the example of the Bar, was very influential in developing the role of the Law Society as the professional body of solicitors.[19]

The power of the solicitors' branch developed exponentially with the creation of the Law Society, first mooted in 1823, incorporated in 1831 and granted its Royal Charter in 1833. This was an exclusive body. The cost of membership of the Law Society was initially pitched at a price beyond the reach of ordinary practitioners. The funds were used to build an impressive, club-like building, the Law Society Hall in Chancery Lane.[20] From the 1830s the Law Society set up a committee to lobby on proposed legislation, often using the influence of solicitor MPs. It was generally anxious, however, to ensure that its comments were limited to technical legal issues or to lobbying which was seen to be in the interests of the public. In 1838 the Master of the Rolls encouraged the Law Society to draft a bill consolidating existing legislation relating to solicitors. The draft was accepted and the government collaborated with the Law Society in the passage of the bill through Parliament. The resultant Solicitors' Act 1844 created the office of Registrar of Attorneys and delegated it to the Law Society. The success of the collaboration subsequently led to the Law Society being consulted by the Attorney General on other legislative measures.[21]

---

[16] Burrage argues that the story of the rise of the solicitors' branch gives grounds to consider solicitors the most successful profession. It has the largest voluntary membership of the professional body of any profession ("From a Gentleman's to a Public Profession", n. 13 above).

[17] Sugarman, n. 13 above, at 88; Pound, n. 7 above, at 105.

[18] In the late 1700s Pitt the Younger sought to establish a tax on the annual practising certificates of solicitors and attorneys in order to finance the Napoleonic Wars. The Gentleman Practisers sent him a draft clause for bill, which was adopted, which limited the right to conduct conveyancing to those holding practising certificates: Sugarman, n. 13 above, at 89.

[19] *Ibid.*, at 89–90.

[20] *Ibid.*, at 91.

[21] It also played a significant part in establishing the new Royal Court of Justice on the Strand (Sugarman, n. 13 above, at 93–4, 96). The process was aided because the responsibility for initiating legislation had moved from private individuals to the state and because the civil service was relatively small. The Law Society subsequently prepared the Acts of 1860 and 1870 (*ibid.*, at 97 and 101).

In the second half of the nineteenth century the rise of the urban middle class produced an increased demand for technical services. The profession was in a powerful position. It had historic associations with aristocratic members and patrons[22] and a wide client base. Whereas by the 1800s, the solicitors' branch had achieved its aim of being regarded as "respectable", by the end of the nineteenth century, the Law Society had achieved unparalleled influence in law reform.[23] This strong position was not just the product of its expanding social role. It was made possible by a mode of government which built upon "elite consensus seeking and co-optation", by the blurring of the public and private spheres and by the widespread assumption that technical issues were best left to experts.[24] The Bar and the Law Society co-existed in mutual respect and harmony. Marking the meteoric rise of the solicitors' branch, the Bar and the Law Society issued a statement in 1973 acknowledging their equality of status.[25] The Bar, however, continued to maintain distance from the solicitors' branch by rules of etiquette governing relations between solicitors and barristers. Solicitors, though keen to close the status gap, were resistant to the idea of fusion of the branches of the profession. Their reluctance, perhaps, arose from the reliance of most solicitors' firms on the specialist advocacy services of the Bar.[26]

This history, albeit brief, is a useful basis for comparison with contemporary theories of professional collective action. The extent to which lawyers, through their professional bodies, continue to exercise political influence and, in particular, how they continue to shape legislation, particularly in areas that affect them is not clear. It is clear however, that the legal profession no longer enjoys exclusive access in the preparation of legislation directly affecting its organisation. Consultation on proposed legislation now encompasses contributions from any interested party and the profession is increasingly forced to publicly justify it position.[27] Encroachments into powers of self-regulation, considered in more detail in Part II, suggest that many of the gains of the last 100 years are being lost. Nevertheless, lawyers, and their professional associations, have arguably had a considerable influence on the building of modern liberal states around the world.[28] While the profession in the UK appears to be more conservative than some of its continental counterparts, it has been a fundamental supporter of the "moderate state" and institutions such as the rule of law and the institutional separation of powers within the state.[29] It seems unlikely that opportunities to perform such a role are at an end.

[22] Johnson, n. 4 above.

[23] Sugarman, n. 13 above, at 105.

[24] *Ibid.*, at 119–20.

[25] Burrage, "From a Gentleman's to a Public Profession", n. 13 above, at 59.

[26] *Ibid.*, at 58.

[27] See, e.g., General Council of the Bar, *The Quality of Justice: The Bar's Response* (London, Butterworths, 1989).

[28] See generally T. C. Halliday and L. Karpik, (eds.) *Lawyers and the Rise of Western Political Liberalism* (Oxford, Clarendon Press, 1997).

[29] T. C. Halliday and L. Karpik, "Politics Matter: A Comparative Theory of Lawyers in the Making of Political Liberalism", in Halliday and Karpik, *ibid.*, 15 at 21 and 30.

C. PROFESSIONAL PRIVILEGE, JURISDICTION AND AUTHORITY

Professional Privilege

What have been and are the social and political aspirations of the legal profession as their power has grown over the last 200 years? The declared aim of the Society of Gentleman Practisers was ethical in character: "supporting the honour and independence of the profession [and the] moral elevation of its members, [who] being placed under the constant observation of the whole body, the least tendency to ungentlemanly conduct or dishonourable or illiberal practice will be immediately noticed and checked".[30] In seeking to establish its credentials the SGP, and the Law Society, pursued three major policies identified with the success of the Bar; control over entry to training, jurisdiction and self-government,[31] so that it could guarantee the conduct of its members.[32] While the Gentleman Practisers had been largely ineffective in controlling misconduct, by 1834 the Law Society had initiated its first disciplinary proceedings and had begun to collect and publish "best practice" on issues of etiquette and costs.[33] A proposal by the Gentlemen Practisers that, with the support of Parliament, they would guarantee the behaviour of their members was not expressly taken up. The lawyers, however, acted as if there was an agreement, and by 1941 structures of self-regulation were completed when powers were vested in the Law Society to inspect the accounts of practitioners and with the creation of the compensation fund.[34]

This tacit agreement between lawyers and the state continued until the 1970s when it began to be perceived that the lawyers' view of the public interest was at best misconceived or, at worst, partial and self-interested. This change was reflected in theories of professional power and privilege. In the early 1970s Johnson identified two sociological approaches to defining professional status.[35] First, "trait" models attempted to list the attributes identified as the common core of professionalism.[36] Subsequently, "functionalist" models

[30] Burrage, "From a Gentleman's to a Public Profession", n. 13 above, at 49.

[31] Unlike the Bar, which operated from the Inns of court, the Law Society, organised nationally, needed statutory support in order to implement these policies: *ibid.*, at 51.

[32] Johnson sees the regularisation of recruitment and practice as the key feature of the professionalising process: Johnson, n. 4 above, chap. 2). Others have seen professionalisation as the acquisition of other features and one therefore able to assimilate a wider diversity of professional models: see C. O. Houle, *Continuing Learning in the Professions* (California and London, Jossey-Bass, 1980); C. W. Wolfram, "Modern Legal Ethics" (St. Paul, Minn., West Publishing Co., 1986); E. Schein, *Professional Education* (New York, McGraw-Hill, 1972); and M. D. Bayles, *Professional Ethics* (Belmont, Calif., Wadsworth Publishing, 1981) and see Chap. 6.

[33] Burrage, n. 13 above, at 94.

[34] *Ibid.*, at 50.

[35] Johnson, n. 4 above, at 23–35.

[36] E.g. the professional practitioner was seen to possess high status knowledge, often taught in universities and usually acquired during a long process of education and training. The connection with universities also fulfilled the need for research into their own distinctive field of knowledge. The work of the profession was perceived to have a high value to many people and involved

attempted to isolate those traits which had functional relevance to society or to clients. Functionalists considered that professions had certain essential features. These varied in detail but centred on a few key factors: a high degree of generalised and systematic knowledge; a primary orientation to the community interest rather than the individual self-interest[37]; a high degree of self control of behaviour through codes of ethics internalised in the process of work socialisation and through voluntary associations organised and operated by the work specialists themselves; a system of rewards, both monetary and honorary, that operated as symbols of work achievement.[38]

Specialist knowledge was seen as a prerequisite to professional power because neither bureaucratic control nor judgement by customers was likely to be an effective way to counteract the natural inclination of all individuals, including professionals, to act in their own economic interest.[39] Self-control, institutionalised in the structure and culture of the profession and socialised into new entrants, was the solution.[40] Ethics, manifest as the self-disciplined pursuit of the public interest, was the natural corollary of professional power and central to the professional ideal. But ethical professions were also perceived to offer widespread social benefits. The functionalist model produced a view of professions as cohesive, altruistic communities in a socially stratified, pluralistic society driven by materialism.[41] They were seen to provide cohesion to society as a whole and a counterweight to the increasing power of the state.[42] Accordingly they were accepted as worthy trustees of the apolitical and specialised disciplines which they controlled.[43] Professionals were honoured servants of public need, distinguished by their orientation to public service. The establishment of professions as *moral* occupational communities was an important counter-

processes which were surrounded by mystique, limitation on entry, social prestige, wealth from specialised knowledge and autonomy (See Houle, n. 32 above; Wolfram, n. 32 above; Schein, n. 32 above; and Bayles, n. 13 above, at 7). Greenwood claimed to have identified five features of all professions: (1) systematic theory, (2) authority, (3) community sanction, (4) ethical codes, and (5) a culture: E. Greenwood, "Attributes of a Profession", *Social Work*, July 1957 at 45.

[37] See also Pound, n. 7 above, at 95.

[38] Johnson, n. 4 above, at 38.

[39] "It is not possible for a social function to exist without moral discipline. Otherwise, nothing remains but individual appetites, and since they are by nature boundless and insatiable, if there is nothing to control them they will not be able to control themselves": E. Durkheim, *Professional Ethics and Civic Morals* (translated by C. Brookfield, London, Routledge and Kegan Paul, 1957), at 11.

[40] D. Rueschemeyer, "Doctors and Lawyers: A Comment on the Theory of the Professions" [1964–5] *Canadian Review of Sociology and Anthropology* 17.

[41] R. M. Rich, "Sociological Paradigms and the Sociology of Law: An Overview" in C. E. Reasons and R. Rich (eds.), *The Sociology of Law: A Conflict Perspective* (London, Butterworth & Co., 1978), 147 at 148.

[42] This approach, rooted in the work of the French sociologist Emile Durkheim, argues that structures and institutions can contribute to maintenance of social order: see A. M. Carr-Saunders and P. H. Wilson, *The Professions* (Oxford, OUP, 1933); Johnson, n. 4 above, at 12–14 and R. L. Abel, *The Legal Profession in England and Wales* (Oxford, Basil Blackwell, 1988), at 5–6, 26–30.

[43] W. H. Simon, "The Ideology of Advocacy" (1978) 29 *Wisconsin Law Review* 38, quoting A. M. Carr-Saunders (1934) 12 *Encyclopaedia of the Social Sciences* 476.

weight to the fragmentation of the traditional moral order brought about by the division of labour. Ethics, the regulation of members of the profession by a professional body, and the development of codes of conduct, was seen as the final stage of professionalism.[44]

The central rationale for professional privilege was that professions were committed to higher ideals than commercial interests. The conferment by the state of autonomy and independence was therefore conceived of as a "bargain with society", the terms of which were that professions had the exclusive right to conduct particular kinds of work provided they also served the public interest. Professions justified this relative autonomy by guaranteeing, through their disciplinary procedures, the performance of their members, and by indemnifying those who had been unjustifiably harmed by them.

Gradually this perception of professions as ethical communities operating in the public interest was undermined. It was said that the analysis ignored the significance of ideology in the presentation, by professions, of professions. Far from being stable and cohesive communities, professions were seen to be involved in perpetual conflict with other occupations and professions in the defence of their privileges.[45] For the critics of the conservative analysis of professional power, the ideology of professionalism and the institutional structures which supported professionalism were little more than propaganda.[46] Professions presented a caring and acceptable veneer which concealed the worst consequences of the powerful and destructive forces of the capitalist system which created them and which they served.[47] They pursued collective status and economic reward by forging relations with the state and with the universities so as to dominate markets. Sociologists, therefore, adopted the view of economists, who focused on the closed and monopolistic nature of professionalised labour, that professionalism was a means of concentrating and exercising power.

Policy-makers also came to doubt the commitment of professions to the public good and the benefits offered by professions to wider society.[48] By seeking to control markets, professions created systems of control over their work so as to exclude potential competitors.[49] This is the view adopted in one of the most

[44] Johnson, n. 4 above, at 28; M. S. Larson, *The Rise of Professionalism: A Sociological Analysis* (Berkeley, Cal., University of California Press, 1972), and Abel, n. 42 above, at 29.

[45] This also marked a shift in sociological thought. Theorists increasingly saw society as based on conflict and focused on the role of power in the arrangement of social roles and social organisation: Rich, n. 41 above, at 148–9).

[46] H. Jamois and B. Peloille, "Changes in the French University-Hospital System" in J. Jackson (ed.), *Professions and Professionalisation* (Cambridge, Cambridge University Press, 1970), at 117 and Johnson, n. 4 above, at 57. This calls into question the whole notion of "profession": P. Bordieu and L. Wacquant, *An Invitation to Reflexive Sociology* (Chicago, Ill., University of Chicago Press, 1992), at 242.

[47] Larson, n. 44 above.

[48] Friedson, n. 8 above.

[49] Larson, n. ,44 above, C. Harrington, "Outlining a Theory of Practice" in M. Cain and C. Harrington (eds), *Lawyers in a Postmodern World: Translation and Transgression* (Buckingham, OUP, 1994); A. Abbott, "The System of Professions: An Essay on the Expert Division of Labour"

recent and comprehensive analyses of the legal profession in England and Wales[50] in which Abel proposes that professionalism is "a specific historical formation in which the members of an occupation exercise a substantial degree of control over the market for their services, usually through an occupational association".[51] The pursuit of competitive economic advantage came to be seen as the motivational force behind professional organisation.[52] For Abel the professional project therefore has both a political and economic dimension.[53] But, he suggests, while the strategies of market closure and social closure are not only the keys to the historic success of the legal profession, the failure of these mechanisms in controlling the market for legal services will cause the continuing decline of professionalism so defined.[54] The extent to which the legal profession has both failed to sustain a monopoly over its work and failed to control the numbers of producers of legal services by controlling entry to the profession[55] are examined below. For the present we return to the notion of professional knowledge since this is generally recognised as the foundation of professional power.

Knowledge and Power

A theory which bridged the gap between the functionalist and market analyses of professions proposed that the monopoly of important knowledge was the source of the institutional power of the professions.[56] Professional knowledge has been seen as mysterious, unique and highly individualised. "Professional knowledge" came to be seen as a "commodity". But, while both the "product" and the "producer" were presented as standard, there remained sufficient imprecision in the

(Chicago, Ill., University of Chicago Press, 1988), hereafter, "The System"; and A. Abbott, "Jurisdictional Conflicts: A New Approach to the Development of the Legal Professions" (1986) 2 *American Bar Foundation Research Journal* 187, hereafter "Jurisdictional Conflicts".

[50] Abel, "n. 42 above, at 4.

[51] R. L. Abel, "The Decline of Professionalism?" (1986) 49 *Modern Law Review* 1 at 1.

[52] This view derives from Weber who noted that English barristers were a strong and organised guild which protected its corporate economic interests and "had a measure of power which neither King nor Parliament could have easily brushed aside": M. Weber, "Economy and Law (Sociology of Law)" in G. Roth and C. Wittich (eds.), *Economy and Society* (Berkeley, Cal., University of California Press, 1978), at 794.

[53] See further R. L. Abel, "Towards a Political Economy of Lawyers" [1981] *Wisconsin Law Review* 112.

[54] See generally Johnson, n. 4 above.

[55] Abel, n. 42 above, at 11.

[56] E. Freidson, *Professional Powers: A Study of the Institutionalization of Formal Knowledge* (Chicago, Ill., University of Chicago Press, 1986). The corollary is that among the factors that contribute to low status, recent origins for example, the lack of a distinctive field of knowledge or a disciplinary base in universities contributes to an occupation's relatively low status despite its undoubted public service orientation: R. A. Barnett, R. A. Becher and N. M. Cork, "Models of Professional Preparation: Pharmacy, Nursing and Teacher Education (1987) 12:1 *Studies in Higher Education* 51 at 61.

[57] Larson, n. 44 above, at 30–1.

nature of that product that "non-standard producers" could be excluded from the market.[57] This conception of legal knowledge was undermined by the contribution of legal realism. Socio-legal scholarship also revealed the limitations of legal positivism, the assumption that legal action is rule bound.[58] A host of studies and theories demonstrated that legal action is "situationally responsive, it involves extralegal decisions and actions".[59] At the heart of the work of lawyers is the inevitable exercise of discretion, "how it is invoked, confined, and yet ever elastic".[60] Discretion, therefore, came to be seen as an intrinsic part of professional knowledge. The practice of law came to be seen as the management of uncertainty through the exercise of discretion, technicality, art and science[61] rather than the application of rules. Professional knowledge was conceived as a construct designed to convince consumers that they could not produce the professional services themselves.[62]

While all professions suffered from the changing perception of professional knowledge, none was more vulnerable than the legal profession. For, as Rueschmeyer argued, unlike medicine, lawyers' knowledge is not scientific. Medical science assists the physician in diagnosis and prediction. The practice of law, in contrast, involves facility with a system of social norms, formed in part by lawyers themselves, and involving the use of a good deal of non-specialist "worldly knowledge" and skills. Indeed, Rueschmeyer suggests that legal practice depends on "generalised interpersonal skills" rather than complex technical knowledge.[63]

In addition to the above developments the legal profession has experienced pressure to improve the technical skills of its members, including through specialisation. Professional knowledge has been analysed and reconstructed as packages of technical skills. Professional judgement itself came to be seen as more technical, and therefore routine. The value of professional services was undermined. This created the possibility that non-professional competitors could claim to enter the market. The professional monopoly in law came under constant threat and the demand for professional autonomy, which hinged on the indeterminacy of the tasks performed, was weakened.[64] The importance of these developments for lawyers, and for the theory of professions, was recog-

---

[58] Socio-legal scholarship backed the claim of the legal realist movement that there is a gap between the law in books and the law in action; this is generally perceived as a gap between the equality of law in theory and the inequality of law in operation.

[59] S. S. Silbey, "Let Them Eat Cake": Globalisation, Postmodern Colonialism, and the Possibilities of Justice" [1997] *Law and Society Review* 207 at 231.

[60] *Ibid.*

[61] Jamois and Pelloille, n. 46 above; Abel "The Legal Profession in England and Wales", n. 42 above, at 8; and Rueschemeyer, n. 40 above.

[62] Abel, "The Legal Profession in England and Wales", n. 42 above.

[63] Surveys of lawyers tend to show that client communication, fact gathering, presentation etc. are the most highly rated skills: see A. Boon, "Skills in the Initial Stage of Legal Education: Theory and Practice for Transformation" in J. Webb and C. Maughan (eds.), *Teaching Lawyers' Skills* (London, Dublin, Edinburgh, Butterworths, 1996), 99 at 107 and see discussion by Johnson, n. 4 above, at 35).

[64] Johnson, n. 4 above, at 47; Abel, *supra* n. 42 at 10.

nised by Abbott, who noted both the importance and vulnerability of legal knowledge in the construction and control of markets. Abbott observed that the nature of professional work is not given; professionals construct it as they deal with clients. Having established expertise they seek to establish "jurisdiction" over the area of work. Their ability to do so depends on the impermeability of the work, i.e. the extent to which it is comprehensible or can be performed by outsiders, and this in turn depends on the way the profession has constructed it. When the work is highly impermeable professions are more likely to be given an exclusive right to conduct the work, a monopoly, which Abbott calls legal jurisdiction. Other privileges, such as self-regulation, inevitably follow. But, Abbott argues, jurisdiction is not just legal. It has a public and workplace dimension. The public face of jurisdiction is the use of ideology, codes of conduct, reports and advertising as a way of defending legal jurisdiction.[65] Professional work, therefore, ceases to be solely technical; it has a considerable ideological component.

Legal jurisdiction is slow to change. When professions design their educational curriculum and set standards, they defend their workplace and legal jurisdiction. They provide a foundation from which they can attack interlopers on the grounds that they do not have the expertise and they cannot meet the standards of the established professionals in the field. But, try as they may, the control of workplace jurisdiction is always vulnerable. Just as the Bar and the solicitors did in the last century, professional groups reach "settlements", agreements on a division of labour.[66] Competing jurisdictional claims are, however, often generated by social, technological and organisational change.[67]

In summary, both trait theorists and functionalists saw exclusive control of an area of knowledge, an area of knowledge with central importance to society, as the foundation of professional power. They saw the need for self-regulation, and hence ethics, as a manifestation of responsibility arising from the control of exclusive knowledge, and a key indicator that an advanced level of professionalism had been achieved by an occupation. Trait theorists saw the mere existence of codes of ethics as indicative of a profession, while functionalists tended to assume that an ethical commitment meant that professions acted in the public interest. They assumed that, because a profession claimed to have ethics, its members had ethics. Later theorists shifted the focus of analysis to the control of work. They tended to see professional ethics as an ideological weapon in an armoury used to defend professional power. This explains why professional etiquette, the demarcation of boundaries and the governance of work relationships

[65] Abbott, n. 49 above, at 196. See also Johnson, "legends, symbols and stereotypes operate in the public sphere to formulate public attitudes to the profession"(n. 4 above, at 55). Bordieu argues that this must be seen further as the attempt of sub-groups within the professional hierarchy to impose their internal norms on the wider field; to establish the legitimacy of their own self-conceptions and interpretations of that field: R. Terdiman, "Translator's introduction to Bordieu, P. 'The Force of Law: Toward a Sociology of the Juridical Field' " (1987) 38 *The Hastings Law Journal* 805.
[66] Abbott, n. 49 above, at 191.
[67] E.g. the growth of business and administrative bureaucracy in the nineteenth century: *ibid.*

between different groups, has a central role in ethical codes. In Abel's analysis, ethical commitments depend on the ability of an occupational group to defend the market for its services. If market control fails, ethics, as a secondary feature of professionalism, must follow. In order to consider the implications of these theories for legal professionalism it is necessary to examine changes in the market for legal services.

Jurisdiction over the Law

To some extent these theories of professional power have been both tested and enriched by the events of recent decades. In the nineteenth century, the drive to dominate the whole field of law was not a principal concern of the solicitors.[68] Sugarman argues that, rather, strong central self-governance of professions tended to depress the provision of services. It led the solicitors to seek a protected market where they could conduct a narrow range of work and enhance their status. In the eighteenth and nineteenth centuries both the Bar and solicitors surrendered jurisdiction over work deemed less honourable so as to secure control over work deemed more honourable. Eventually solicitors gained the exclusive right to conduct conveyancing, probate and primary legal advice and referral while barristers provided advocacy and specialist advice. Thus, when provincial solicitors sought county court rights of audience in the nineteenth century, the Council of the Law Society rejected the proposal on the grounds that gentlemen did not frequent the county court.[69]

Although the jurisdictional settlement between barristers and solicitors was remarkably stable for over 100 years, more recently it has begun to break down. The two obvious reasons for this are that it has become more difficult to confine work to traditional disciplinary boundaries and because monopoly is seen to be an inefficient way of providing goods or services.[70] The undermining of the solicitors' conveyancing monopoly in the early 1980s is an illustration of the termination of monopoly with the aim of increasing the efficiency of markets. Most fundamentally, in terms of the established jurisdiction of the legal profession, it upset the historic settlement between solicitors and barristers governing rights of advocacy in higher courts.

[68] This leads Burrage to challenge Abbott's thesis that professions collide and compete to enlarge jurisdiction: see Abbott, "The System", n. 49 above, and Burrage "From a Gentleman's to a Public Profession", n. 13 above, at 55.

[69] Sugarman, n. 13 above, at 98 and 109.

[70] Both these factors are illustrated in the case of insolvency practice, an area where, traditionally, different professional groups have collaborated. The Insolvency Act 1986 recognised this by creating "insolvency practitioners", a new occupational group. Solicitors and accountants both entered the area and, across the field in general, reached a new settlement in relation to aspects of the work: see J. Flood and E. Skordaki, *Insolvency Practitioners and Big Corporate Insolvencies* (London, Certified Accountants' Educational Trust, 1995). In the area of arbitration in construction disputes, jurisdictional battles, between lawyers, engineers and architects, tended to be more fractious: see J. Flood and A. Caiger, "Lawyers and Arbitration: The Juridification of Construction Disputes" (1993) 56 *Modern Law Review* 412.

In 1983 legislation allowed licensed conveyancers to compete with solicitors. This stimulated unprecedented competition within the profession, far greater than was necessary to respond to the commercial threat from licensed conveyancers. Between 1983 and 1986 solicitors reduced their conveyancing fees by an average of 30 per cent.[71] The solicitors' branch, which in the 1960s had derived 60 per cent of its income from conveyancing,[72] was galvanised. Almost immediately the Law Society sought the right to conduct advocacy in higher courts. The Bar's response was to assert that:

> "the public will be best served by continuance of the independent barristers and solicitors' professions with their separate and specialised functions . . . The cornerstones of the Bar as a specialist profession are cost effectiveness and strong competition in 'the most competitive business going', as the Lord Chancellor has described the Bar."[73]

The solicitors' claim to increased advocacy rights, a claim which was swiftly followed by the creation of enabling legislation,[74] was also a response to other factors. The higher court advocacy settlement had preserved the Bar's monopoly of the bench, which was symbolic of its claim to superior status. Entrants to both branches of the legal profession in terms of background, education and qualification were similar and this undermined this claim.[75] In some areas of work, solicitor specialisation had undermined barristers' claims to offer unique expertise. The government, encouraged by its success in driving down the cost of conveyancing, was also already poised to tackle the professional monopolies over litigation and advocacy.

The Courts and Legal Services Act 1990 not only created the mechanism whereby bodies other than the Bar would be able to accredit their members in the exercise of advocacy rights, it created a similar mechanism to threaten the solicitors' control of litigation. In fact, while solicitors benefited from the abolition of Bar's only formal monopoly, there was no real inroad into their jurisdiction. Although they lost the exclusive right to brief barristers when some other professional groups were granted this right (known as "direct professional access"),[76] the Law Society remained the only body authorised under the Courts and Legal Services Act to conduct litigation. This jurisdiction is now threatened by the government's latest proposal that the Bar and legal executives also be given this right.[77] Advice agencies are now entitled to claim legal aid for clients

---

[71] S. Domberger and A. Sherr, "Competition in Conveyancing: An Analysis of Solicitors' Charges" (1987) 8:3 *Fiscal Studies* 17.

[72] Conveyancing provided less than 30% of solicitors' gross income. Despite this, most high street firms still derive more than half of their income from that source: C. Glasser, "The Legal Profession in the 1990's: Images of Change" (1990) 10:1 *Legal Studies* 1.

[73] N. 27 above, para. 2.2; the Bar's response to the 1989 Green Paper proposing the widening of groups allowed to offer litigation and advocacy services.

[74] The Courts and Legal Services Act 1990.

[75] Glasser, n. 72 above.

[76] E.g. patent agents, parliamentary agents, Local Authority employed lawyers, etc.

[77] The Lord Chancellor's Department, *Rights of Audience and Rights to Conduct Litigation in England and Wales: The Way Ahead* (London, Lord Chancellor's Department, June 1998).

and may be given an even greater role in the proposed National Legal Service. These developments threaten further to undermine the traditional monopoly of expertise by both solicitors and barristers. Thus, Abel argues, legal professionalism in England and Wales now depends not on expertise but on independence.[78] But how independence by itself can serve as a new form of legitimation is far from clear.

D. CHANGES IN THE MARKET FOR LEGAL SERVICES

We now examine the changes in the market for legal services and the threats they pose to the ethics of the legal profession.

Supply and Demand

The massive expansion in demand for legal services since the second world war is attributable to changing patterns of ownership (including personal ownership of real property or national ownership of industry), the increased regulation of social life and the development of technology.[79] Most important, however, the growth in the personal resources of the employed, and the advent of legal aid,[80] brought the services of lawyers within the scope of more people. The profession expanded in response to this demand. During and after the 1960s the tight controls traditionally exercised over the supply of lawyers were gradually relaxed.[81] Between 1961 and 1986 the numbers of lawyers in England and Wales increased by 147 per cent.[82] Recent figures suggest that there are currently around 68,000

[78] R. Abel, "Ten Years on: Changes in the Regulatory Framework", paper delivered at the Law Society Research and Policy Planning Unit, Annual Research Conference (London, Law Society, 3 July 1998).

[79] Ramsay identifies a range of factors which influence demand. These include the increasing need to legislate over the relations of individuals and corporations, demand created by the way in which lawyers organise their business, e.g., by creating or reinforcing monopolies, the internationalisation of legal work with the potential of bringing together geographically remote parties, greater population diversity increasing the need for normative ordering, changing demographics, wealth levels, levels of complexity in life, increasing bureaucratisation of society and a growth in the range and use of administrative remedies, changes in the methods of production of goods and services, transactions affecting the allocation of resources, complexity in business transactions and financial innovation, changing technologies: I. M. Ramsay, "What Do Lawyers Do? Reflections on the Market for Lawyers" (1993) 21 *International Journal of the Sociology of Law* 355 and see Abel, n. 42 above, at 20.

[80] Funding work which arises particularly from increases in the levels of crime, family breakdown and debt (Marre Report, n. 1 above, paras. 3.14–3.31).

[81] During the past 100 years the solicitors' branch was always more numerous and therefore less exclusive. The Law Society was the first to move to meritocratic selection by examinations but, in more recent times, both branches have relaxed control of "production" at the undergraduate stage: Glasser, n. 72 above.

[82] In the USA and Canada the number of lawyers increased by 129% and 253% respectively: M. Galanter, "Law Abounding: Legalisation Around the North Atlantic" (1992) 55 *The Modern Law Review* 1 at 4, hereafter "Law Abounding".

solicitors holding practising certificates, over 55,000 of whom work in private practice, and 9,369 practising barristers.[83] The pattern of growth in the size of the solicitors' branch since 1966 is demonstrated in Table 1.

Table 1: Solicitors holding practice certificates 1966 to 1996.[84]

Year	Practising Solicitors	% Change	Solicitors in Private Practice	% Change
1966	21,672	19.3	18,823	N/A
1976	31,250	44.2	26,992	43.4
1986	47,830	53.1	41,483	53.7
1996	68,037	42.2	55,673	34.2

One of the features of this growth in the size of the practising profession is the growth in numbers of solicitors who are not in private practice, an increase from around 3,000 in 1966 to 15,000 in 1996. The implications of this are considered in more detail in Chapters 3 and 6. Similarly , the growth in the number of barristers and the number of barristers' chambers since 1979 is set out in Table 2.

Table 2: Barristers and their chambers in London and the provinces 1979–97[85]

Year	London		Provinces	
	Barristers	Chambers	Barristers	Chambers
1979	2,894	197	1,182	109
1987	3,977	227	1,665	114
1997	6,171	302	3,198	274

What is the impact on the market for legal services of these changes? Social closure restricts the numbers of professionals, so that the status and work of the existing profession are maintained. The price of open and meritocratic entry policies is the loss of control over the character of the profession. But the

---

[83] The figures for solicitors are as at 31 July 1996 (*Trends in the Solicitors' Profession: Annual Statistical Report* (London, The Law Society, 1996) at 10) and for barristers as at 1 Oct. 1997.

[84] *Ibid.*, Table 2.2. at 10 (The Law Society has confirmed that 71,637 hold practising certificates as at July 1997).

[85] The figures for 1979 were reported by the Benson Commission (1979) for 1987 the Marre Report, n. 1 above, para. 5.16 (representing an increase of 11.4% between 1979 and 1987) and for 1997 The General Council of the Bar. The increase between 1979 and 1987 (38.4%) was, in fact, less than in preceding years. So, e.g., the increase in the size of the Bar between 1975 and 1985 was 47% (Marre Report, *ibid.*, para. 5.17).

implications of this are debatable.[86] One dilemma is clear. If the profession fails to respond to demand, it creates a vacuum which sucks in professional competitors. These new groups acquire skills and experience and may eventually threaten core areas of the profession's work.[87]

One issue is whether the profession uses the opportunity presented by the increased supply of lawyers to make the services it provides to society more comprehensive. Legal aid has assisted the profession in expanding the services it offered and the groups it served. One consequence of competition is that, as existing areas of work become saturated, lawyers are encouraged to find and enter new areas of work. Legal services are spread through society. The oversupply of lawyers, therefore, ensures that the legal profession offers a comprehensive service to society, and is more responsive to legal need.[88] As Table 3 shows, solicitors have developed new areas of work. The main area of additional income, the miscellaneous category, suggests that the small firms included in this survey actively developed new areas of work in response to the decline of residential conveyancing income.[89] But, although the legal profession has increased in size, this expansion was not born of a desire simply to meet need. In the case of the legal needs of the poor, for example, it has been suggested that the Law Society sought control of the legal aid scheme to prevent others gaining a foothold in the market. Thus, Goriely concludes, there is a four-stage process of expansion in relation to low status work. First, the profession denies that there is a need for legal services in the particular area; secondly, having been forced to accept that there is such a need, the profession devises a plan but does nothing about it; thirdly, the advice sector develops the area of work and involves local solicitors; finally, the profession defends the market which has been established.[90] But, for whatever reasons it expanded, as it did so the legal profession faced increasing problems in controlling the market for legal services. This issue is dealt with in more detail in Chapter 9.

The effect of limited supply in relation to demand is to create a monopoly for the professional class and this then attracts additional entrants. The twofold effect of this is to devalue the credentials by which access is gained and to drive down the price of the service.[91] It is not surprising, therefore, that enquiries into professions suggest that the over-supply of lawyers is the cause of the declining income of lawyers, the quality of legal services and increases in unethical behav-

---

[86] One example of the different interpretations of the same phenomena will illustrate this. Trait theorists perceive long training as a guarantee of quality services. Abel, in contrast, argues that the weak correlation between high levels of education and training and the low level of skill or knowledge actually required in practice, is evidence of the operation of social closure: see Abel, n. 42 above, at 13.

[87] Abbott, "Jurisdictional Conflicts", n. 49 above.

[88] Therefore, the expansion of producers is often a means by which the state attempts to expand access to professional services (Johnson, n. 4 above, at 79).

[89] M. Hope, *Expenditure on Legal Services* (London, Lord Chancellor's Department, 1997), at 7.

[90] T. Goriely, "Law for the Poor: The Relationship Between Advice Agencies and Solicitors in the Development of Poverty Law" (1996) 3:1/2 *International Journal of the Legal Profession* 215 at 216.

[91] Abel, n. 42 above, at 16.

iour.[92] While there is a connection between over-supply and falling income,[93] Ramsay suggests that there is no proven connection between over-supply and standards of behaviour or competence.[94] In fact, he argues, increased competition should lead to the provision of *better* services by lawyers.

Table 3: Sources of the income of solicitors (for firm with fewer than 25 partners and gross fee income of more than £15,000) in 1989 and 1994 by area of work[95]

Category of Matter	Year	
	1989	1994
Commercial property	20%	11%
Business affairs	22%	19%
Residential conveyancing	22%	16%
Housing law	3%	2%
Probate, Wills etc.	8%	10%
Personal bankruptcy	1%	2%
Personal finance	1%	1%
Family law	7%	10%
Personal injury	7%	9%
Crime	4%	7%
Welfare benefits	0%	0%
Consumer problems	1%	1%
Employment law	1%	2%
Other	3%	9%

If the legal profession correctly predicted expanded demand for legal services,[96] the assumption that the state would support that demand proved incorrect. Moreover, as both branches of the profession expanded in response to demand, the value, exclusivity and mystery of legal services declined. The profession became more willing to embrace new areas of work; alternative dispute resolution, transnational practice, financial services and, for solicitors,

[92] See also C. E. Reason and C. Chappell, "Crooked Lawyers: Towards a Political Economy of Deviance in the Profession" in T. Fleming (ed.), *The New Criminologies in Canada: Status, Crime and Control* (Toronto, Oxford University Press, 1985), 206 at 212.

[93] Abel, *supra* n. 42 at 21.

[94] But see Reason and Chappell, n. 92 above, at 206.

[95] J. Sidaway and B. Cole, *The Panel: A Study of Private Practice 1994/5* (London, The Law Society, 1996).

[96] In 1988 the Law Society predicted growth in both the private-client and commercial sphere of legal activity as a result of changing social conditions. It identified 14 areas of work and the factors which would increase the demand for private-client services including divorce, unmarried parenthood, unemployment, home ownership, inheritance, consumer credit and debt, environment, law and order, personal mobility, equal opportunities and product liability: The Report of the Training Committee of the Law Society, *The Recruitment Crisis* (London, The Law Society, 1988), at 11–17.

advocacy in higher courts all offer new opportunities which mop up surplus supply. But, as lawyers seek work outside their traditional sphere, their claim to exclusive jurisdiction in their traditional sphere may be undermined. This is particularly the case where the work has a limited "legal" component, as with the provision of financial services. Although lawyers define their own expertise widely[97] they find it increasingly difficult to argue that they should have exclusive jurisdiction over core areas of their existing work.[98]

Consumerism

The mechanisms of supply and demand are not the only causes of the decline in the power of the legal profession. The growth of consumerism has also been blamed for the diminishing power of lawyers. There are three ways in which this has happened: first, the extent to which lawyers have been called upon to act in the service of large corporations; secondly, the growth of the consumer movement; and thirdly, through increasing demand for dispute resolution services which creates pressures for cheaper access to justice. The impact of the service offered to large corporations is dealt with in the next chapter. The growth of the consumer movement has had a number of implications for legal practice. It seems clear that consumer demand for change in the delivery of legal services strengthened the government's resolve to undermine the professional monopoly. Consumers, as clients, demanded more accountability from lawyers.[99] Additionally the decline was fuelled by more effective research into the activities of professions in general,[100] falling confidence in the legal profession and inept public relations by the legal profession.[101]

Consumers have also brought about change by becoming more litigious. Although lawyers are sometimes held partly to blame for this development, it

[97] Legal services have been defined as "any service which might be available to help people to deal with legal problems regardless of whether payment is made from public or private funds . . . including criminal and civil legal services . . . legal advice, legal assistance (for example in conveyancing and the making of wills) and legal representation" (Marre Report, n. 1 above, para. 7.3).

[98] E.g., although lawyers have established a monopoly as counsellors and advocates, they have failed to gain a stranglehold on the adjudication of construction disputes: Flood and Caiger, n. 70 above.

[99] Consumers complain about goods and services generally worth about £2.5 billion per annum which complaints are dealt with by local authorities. Over the past 5 years there has been a 21% increase in such complaints (C. Taylor "Cause for Complaint" (1998) 21 *Fair Trading* 10. The phenomenon has not been limited to the UK. Galanter suggests that in the UK, USA and Canada have, since the 1960s, the populations became more educated and enjoyed higher incomes. The economies of these countries greatly expanded, becoming more service driven and more internationalised: Galanter, n. 82 above, at 3.

[100] Legal academics, media and consumer groups began a critical examination of the profession through research and, as a result of what was discovered, undermined its claim to act in the public interest. Civil servants attached to state agencies used academic and other research to create the climate in which corrective measures became inevitable: Burrage, n. 13 above, at 68.

[101] Burrage suggests that the Law Society's inept handling of accusations of chronic overcharging by one of its own leading members (the Glanville Davies affair) helped to create the climate for the political onslaught in the 1980s: Burrage, *ibid.*, at 69.

can also be seen as reflecting decreasing tolerance of harm caused by others.[102] Increasing demand for access to courts places pressure on the system and on funding, and calls into question the cost of professional interventions. A survey of consumer attitudes in the UK suggested that people saw the legal system as "out of date, slow, too complicated and easy to twist".[103] Only a quarter of respondents supported the proposition, usually promoted by the profession, that the legal system was something to be proud of. Middle-income groups, ineligible for legal aid but not rich enough to fund litigation, were the most likely to be dissatisfied with the legal help available to them.

It is not surprising that there has been considerable pressure to expand access to legal services and to increase the quality of services offered. The Marre Report observed that:

> "More members of the public are now inclined to complain about poor quality or costly services (or what they perceive as poor quality or costly services) and to demand that the traditional ways of doing things should be justified. Moreover, members of the public are no longer deferential to those who provide professional services and will no longer tolerate secretiveness. This is not to say members of the public are better informed about legal matters (although they may be) but simply that consumers are less willing to accept uncritically the authority which used to be attached to professional people."[104]

A powerful consumer movement, headed by the National Consumer Council and the Consumers Association, has consistently criticised the legal profession.[105] The NCC assesses goods and services against criteria such as access, choice, information, quality and value for money, safety and representation[106] and has argued that consumers should have a voice in the process of professional regulation.[107] It has been an influential advocate of the expansion of the advice sector through legal aid funding.[108]

The power of the consumer movement can be gauged from the fact that the government's success in ending the conveyancing monopoly was due, in part, to consumer pressure. This arose from the growth of owner occupation[109] and the

---

[102] W. F. Felstiner, R. L. Abel and A. Sarat, "The Emergence and Transformation of Disputes: Naming, Blaming, Claiming" (1980–1) 15 *Law and Society* 631.

[103] National Consumer Council, *Seeking Civil Justice* (London, NCC, 1995), at 8.

[104] Marre Report, n. 1 above, at para. 3.52.

[105] See, e.g., the following National Consumer Council (NCC) publications, *Making Good Solicitors: The Place of Communication Skills in their Training*" (London, NCC, 1989); *Professional Competence in Legal Services: What is It and how do you Measure it?*" (London, NCC, 1990); *Eligibility for Civil Legal Aid: Response to the Lord Chancellor's Department* (London, NCC, 1991); *Out of Court: A Consumer View of Three Low-Cost Arbitration Schemes* (London, NCC, 1991); *Court Without Advice: Duty Court-Based Advice and Representation Schemes* (London, NCC, 1992); *Seeking Civil Justice: A Survey of People's Needs and Experiences* (London, NCC, 1995).

[106] C. Ervine, *Settling Consumer Disputes: A Review of Alternative Dispute Resolution* (London, NCC, 1993).

[107] NCC, *Ordinary Justice* (London, HMSO, 1989), at 3.

[108] NCC, *Civil Justice and Legal Aid* (London, NCC (1995).

[109] Glasser, n. 72 above.

barrier to the government's policy of selling council houses presented by solicitors' scale charges for conveyancing.[110] It will be observed that this was a case where the middle class was demanding quality service and reasonable prices from the lawyer, its social peer.[111] The legislative attack on the profession began with the attempt to deal with a single monopoly and was broadened to encompass other areas where the profession charged high fees for essentially routine work. The profession was put to the proof of the proposition that restrictions on competition were in the public interest.[112]

E. PROFESSIONALIZATION AND DEPROFESSIONALISATION

Osiel argues that different conceptions of the lawyer are competing for ascendancy in Western society. Lawyers are cast as aristocrats, entrepreneurs or, latterly, as monopolists.[113] Most legal professions demonstrate, in some degree, aspects of all these conceptions simultaneously. No one of these conceptions is "superior" in terms of representing the position of a legal profession in society. Indeed, Osiel argues, the different degrees of prominence that the lawyers of different nations have achieved are "attributable not to the relative success of their projects of monopolisation, but to the different opportunities presented to them by industrialisation during the nineteenth and early twentieth centuries and the differing propensity of national bars to seize such opportunities".[114] Abel, Osiel argues, seeks to demolish faith in existing professional institutions and the possibility of ethics in the workplace in order to create a blank page on which a more satisfactory ethic can be devised.[115] In doing so Abel "denies a complex possibility: that the public service ideal of the independent professional functions simultaneously as an ideology, masking unpleasant institutional realities, and as a noble aspiration, prompting successful attempts at piecemeal improvement".[116] The fact that lawyers regularly choose status rather than wealth, Osiel argues, suggests that there is a future for the public service ideal.

Does the decline of legal professionalism charted by Abel in England and Wales leave opportunites for the pursuit of this ideal? The profession's inability to control the supply of lawyers and the demand for cheaper legal services have

---

[110] Owner-occupied dwellings increased from around 7 million in 1961 to over 14 million in 1986: The Marre Report, n. 1 above, at paras. 3.16–3.17.

[111] A Sherr, "Coming of Age" (1994) 1:1 *International Journal of the Legal Profession* 3.

[112] N. 27 above, at 3.19. In a response to the chairman of the Bar in 1989, the permanent secretary of the Lord Chancellor's Department affirmed that the twin themes of the Green Paper on the work and organisation of the legal profession was competition and the maintenance of standards; "it is against this background that the existing practices and structure of the legal profession should be judged". The same para. indicates that the government believed that the onus should be on those who support restrictions as a way of achieving standards to justify them.

[113] Osiel, n. 6 above.

[114] *Ibid.*, at 2013.

[115] Ibid., at 2021.

[116] *Ibid.*

led to serious questions concerning the nature of professionalism and the role of the legal profession in society. Are there alternative ways of providing services, of ensuring comprehensiveness and quality? Can changes in regulation make professions more responsive to new social demands, or is competition with non-professional groups the only solution? Johnson observes that there are a number of ways in which an occupation can be controlled. Professionalism offers a means of control whereby the occupation defines consumer needs and the way in which those needs are met. Johnson suggests three main alternatives to professionalism. First there is patronage whereby, in the modern world, major clients such as corporations define the kind of service they require; secondly, communal control, whereby consumer organisations attempt to define consumer needs and affect the way in which occupations organise themselves in order to satisfy need; thirdly, control may be exercised by state mediation of the relationship between producers and consumers.[117]

Each of the alternatives to classical professionalism have gained ground in recent years, but none offers a total replacement. What we see is the emergence of a much more complex relationship between professionalism and other means of occupational control. What is emerging is a multiple regulation environment. This has fundamental implications for professional ethics. Whereas professionalism relies on the mechanism of collective peer review, with each of the alternatives to professionalism, the producer of legal services looks beyond his occupational peers for the evaluation of those services. Some believe that ethics are redundant or are, at least, compromised by these fundamental changes in the nature of professional regulation.

An example of this kind of scepticism is provided, as we have seen, by Abel's analysis. He suggests that their commitment of professions to ethics declines with the loss of market and political control. Manifestations of professionalism, altruism, self-governance, self-regulation, ethicality and competence are, he argues, secondary to the need to dominate the market.[118] Therefore, legal professionalism in the UK has been fatally undermined, partly as a result of the loss of control over the supply of lawyers but, more importantly, as the result of the increasing intervention of the State.[119] The growth in external regulation undermines the notion that ethical commitments are voluntarily accepted in the public interest.

There are a number of examples of how control is being wrested away from the profession. The transfer of the administration of the Legal Aid Scheme from the Law Society to the Legal Aid Board, the quality controls imposed before firms are granted a legal aid franchise[120] and the statutory remit of the Lord Chancellor's Advisory Committee on Education and Conduct (ACLEC) are

[117] Johnson, n. 4 above, at 46, 65 and 86.
[118] Abel, n. 42 above, at 7.
[119] Ibid., Abel, n. 51 above and R. Abel, "Between Market and State: The Legal Profession in Turmoil" (1989) 3 *Modern Law Review* 285.
[120] T. Goriely, "Debating the Quality of Legal Services: Differing Models of the Good Lawyer" (1994) 1 *International Journal of the Legal Profession* 159.

significant. It is worth looking at franchising in particular. The 1995 Green Paper and the 1996 White Paper proposed a system whereby solicitors and advice agencies would bid for, and be contracted to conduct, a fixed number of cases at set prices.[121] In the contracting process, price would not be the only consideration; the quality offered was to be significant also. The quality of providers was to be measured by a range of indicators, such as the result of the case, length of time taken, client satisfaction and the accuracy of predictions of success. This has led to concentrations of specialization in relatively few firms.[122] Such controls upon the profession are, arguably, more likely to determine lawyer behaviour than those imposed by the profession's own self regulatory processes.[123]

The powers given to ACLEC under the Court and Legal Services Act 1990[124] could be a significant threat to the capacity of the profession to control its jurisdiction over litigation and advocacy. ACLEC was also given another important responsibility which has traditionally resided with the profession; education and training. Under the Courts and Legal Services Act ACLEC was given: "the general duty of assisting in the maintenance and development of standards in the education, training and conduct of those offering legal services".[125] It is not yet clear whether any of ACLECs reports will have any long-term impact on legal education, but the increasing incidence of external control of the legal profession undermines important symbols of legal professionalism. It is symptomatic of declining confidence in the effectiveness of self-regulation and, therefore, of the power of professional ethical commitments to work in the public interest.

Could these developments, therefore, signal the end of legal ethics? Paterson challenges Abel's historical construction of legal professionalism by suggesting that, in relation to both market and social control, the profession has always exercised limited control over both the supply of lawyers and its markets.[126] He suggests that, although the changes of the past 15 years have been far-reaching for the

[121] *Legal Aid: Targeting Need,* Cmnd. 2854 (London, HMSO, 1995), and see E. Gilvarry, "Mackay Taken by Fundholding" [1994] *Law Society Gazette,* 7 Sept. at 3 and *Solicitors Journal,* "550 firms Offered Franchises" [1994] *Solicitors Journal,* 29 July, at 755, T. Watkin, "Govt. to ration legal aid cases" *The Lawyer* 8 December 1993 at 1.

[122] By 1995 over 100 offices were approved for welfare work: Goriely, n. 90 above. Latterly, the Legal Aid Board has proposed giving criminal law franchises twice the space on dity solicitor quotas, effectively reducing the work of non-franchised firms by half (E. Davidson, "LAB to slash firms' duty solicitor work" *The Lawyer* 15 Dec. 1998 at 1.

[123] P. Abrams, A. Boon and D. O'Brien, "Access to Justice: The Collision of Funding and Ethics" (1998) 3:1 *Contemporary Issues in Law* 59.

[124] See s. 19(1) and, for composition of the committee, see s. 19(2) and (3).

[125] S. 20(1). However, note that the Legal Services Act also preserves areas of independence. E.g. the Legal Services Ombudsman established by s.21 does not have powers to investigate a matter "which is being or has been determined by . . . (ii) the Solicitors' Disciplinary Tribunal; (iii) the Disciplinary Tribunal of the Council of the Inns of Court . . .". A clearer indication of the scope and impact of the ACLES's role can be gained from its 1997–8 Annual Report (London: The Stationery Office, 1998).

[126] A. A. Paterson, "Professionalism and the Legal Services Market" (1996) 3:1/2 *International Journal of the Legal Profession* 139.

legal profession, Abel's analysis overestimates their significance. In Paterson's view there has been an adjustment of the "bargain with society" which reflects a re-evaluation of the market for legal services.[127] Current changes in the UK address the specific problem; namely that the profession did not deliver its side of the bargain, particularly in relation to conveyancing and criminal legal aid.[128] This does not, he believes, signify a massive change in the relationship with the state or portend a further decline in professional power. It is consistent with Paterson's analysis to suggest that the legal profession may prevent further encroachment on its jurisdiction by improving its performance in key areas of its social responsibility. Ethical commitments would then be strengthened.

We therefore have two views of contemporary legal professionalism. The pessimistic view is that the legal profession is one of those occupational groups going through the process of losing the characteristics of a profession,[129] or "deprofessionalising". An alternative view is that the model of legal professionalism now undergoing change is itself of fairly recent vintage, and that it is merely adapting to a new environment. [130] Within either interpretation it is plausible, but not inevitable, that ethics will become less important. In our view there could be an even more significant role for ethics in the future but, in order to make that case, we have to make sense of the past. It is conceivable that the attacks of the Thatcher years were partly motivated by the desire to strengthen the state and to weaken institutional counterbalances to the power of the state. Professions in general were one of the most significant institutions to be challenged during this period for, not unlike trade unions, they controlled "human, symbolic and material resources' and exercised "the capacity of acting even against the state".[131] While the kinds of changes instigated in the 1980s are still occurring, there does not appear to be the same ideological commitment to curbing professions.

[127] Oligiatti suggests that the professional project in Italy is also undermined by internal (market) forces: V. Olgiati, "Self-Regulation of Legal Professions in Contemporary Italy" (1997) 4 *International Journal of the Legal Profession* 89.

[128] Paterson, n. 126 above, at 140–3.

[129] See also Johnson, n. 4 above, at 18, and Houle, n. 32 above, at 29.

[130] See R. Dingwall and P. Fenn, "A Respectable Profession? Sociological and Economic Perspectives on the Regulation of Professional Services", (1987) 7 *International Review of Law and Economics* 51 who argue that adherence to a strict code of conduct is the *quid pro quo* for the rights and privileges of a legally sanctioned cartel. The withdrawal of privilege when that position is abused is, they argue, 'ultimately the only workable real and effectual discipline' (at p. 62) Paterson argues that the loss of the conveyancing monopoly was sponsored by the Consumers' Association with the support of the Office of Fair Trading but was not desired by the government as a whole; that many of the features of professional privilege are of fairly recent origin and are not therefore fundamental to the notion of professionalism. As regards public protection, e.g., Paterson points out that the compensation fund, separate client accounts and consistent disciplinary enforcement did not mature until this century. As regards restricted competition, despite acrimonious debate for much of the 19th century, bans on advertising and touting, fee-cutting and fee-sharing with non-qualified persons were either not prohibited or not enforced until the 1930s. Finally, the deregulation of legal professions was a worldwide phenomenon in the 1980s and was caused by international initiatives towards free trade, consumer and commercial pressures and pressures from within professions for greater competition: above, n. 128, at 146–8.

[131] Halliday and Karpik, n. 13 above, at 34.

The state has become more pragmatic about lawyers: it does not appear to desire any more control over the profession than is necessary to ensure that it adapts its public role. This suggests the possibility of a new *rapprochement* between the legal profession and the state. Indeed, recent analyses predict that modern states will be increasingly "confronted with a surfeit of expectations and an incapacity to resolve them internally", which will create the necessity for the delegation of some of the functions of the state to professions.[132] What is noticeable is that, in most of its planning, for example the implementation of conditional fees, the state assumes that lawyers will retain high ethical standards. As they stand at present, incursions into professional autonomy are relatively minor.

We now have a plural system of professional regulation which combines self-regulation and external regulation. This may become far more effective than self-regulation alone. In the meantime, the legal profession retains significant control over its own affairs and still has considerable influence in society. Indeed, it could be argued that legal professions are more successful and therefore, perhaps, more inclined to be ethical when forced out of their monopolist mode into more overt entrepreneurial activity.[133] One way of securing the future of legal professionalism is by ensuring that the new entrepreneurial spirit of the profession reflects professional virtues, and by ensuring that judgement and social responsibility are seen as an intrinsic part of legal knowledge.[134] Far from being redundant, ethics could hold the key to the future of legal professionalism.

CONCLUSION

The ability to control work has come to be seen as a defining feature of professions. In the case of the legal profession a number of circumstances have combined to undermine this aspect of the professional project. This may be a result of conditions which have particularly affected the UK or a symptom of deeper problems, such as a crisis of confidence in professional knowledge or an undermining of the moral standing and authority of professionals. For, as Bordieu writes:

"In The Conflict of Faculties, Kant noted that the 'higher disciplines'—theology, law and medicine—are clearly entrusted with a social function. In each of these disciplines, a serious crisis must generally occur in the contract by which this function has

[132] T. C. Halliday, *Beyond Monopoly: Lawyers, State Crises, and Professional Empowerment* (Chicago , Ill., and London, University of Chicago Press, 1987), at 28.

[133] See further Osiel, n. 6 above.

[134] This could include requiring lawyers to hold a wider range of obligations to third parties in particular and the community in general and by changing the emphasis of legal education (See Part III, below, and R. W. Gordon and W. H. Simon, "The Redemption of Professionalism" in R. L. Nelson, D. M. Trubeck and R. L. Solomon (eds.), *Lawyers' Ideals/Lawyers' Practices* (Ithaca NY, and London, Cornell University Press, 1992), 230 at 236.

been delegated before the question of its basis comes to seem a real problem of social practice. This appears to be happening today."[135]

Despite the optimistic conclusion that lawyers are well adapted to survive in a competitive environment, the traditional trappings of legal professionalism are being undermined. The fact that legal professions in many parts of the world are experiencing these pressures differently cannot conceal worldwide concerns about the future of ethical commitments.[136] In the Netherlands, for example, lawyers have adjusted their aspirations for status and prestige while using other dimensions of professional ideology for competitive advantage.[137] Out of a situation of considerable uncertainty ethics may acquire a new role—to keep the forces of commercialism and professionalism in balance.[138]

Faced with a considerable reduction in privilege and public trust professionals can either retreat to the view that their practice is purely a business or they can renew their professional commitments and seek new ways of realising the professional ideal. The central issue is, therefore, whether, in the light of the scale of change, the providers of legal services continue their commitment to a common culture and to professional ideals and *how these are supported*. The success of strategies of support depend on a number of factors. One of these is the impact of organisational change, precipitated by the changes outlined in this chapter, on professional culture. This will be considered in the next chapter, as will the implications of cultural change for existing approaches to professional ethics.

[135] P. Bordieu, "The Force of Law: Toward a Sociology of the Juridical Field" (1987) 38 *The Hastings Law Journal* 805 at 819.

[136] In the US concern that law was becoming "big business' has been prevalent since the 1920's, whereas in the Netherlands it has never been an issue: L. E. De Groot-van Leeuwen, "Polishing the Bar: The Legal Ethics Code and Disciplinary System of the Netherlands, and a Comparison with the United States" (1997) 4 *International Journal of the Legal Profession* 14.

[137] In the Netherlands 1986 legislation shifted the focus at the core of regulations from the "honour of the order of lawyers" to "the interests of the client". Meanwhile, confidentiality was reinforced in the 1992 Dutch code—possibly because it confers a competitive advantage.

[138] A. Paterson, "Legal Ethics in Scotland" (1997) 4 *International Journal of the Legal Profession* 25.

3

Professional Organisation and Culture

"Psychologists, organization theorists, and economists all know that the ethics of ethical decision-making change dramatically when the individual works in an organisational setting. Loyalties become tangled and personal responsibility gets diffused. Bucks are passed and guilty knowledge bypassed. Chains of command not only tie people's hands, they fetter their minds and consciences as well. Reinhold Niebuhr called one of his books *Moral Man, Immoral Society*, and I suggest for students of ethics no topic is more important than understanding whatever truth the title contains."[1]

A. INTRODUCTION

In the first two chapters we dealt with the relationships of the legal profession to society at large and to the state. Although in Chapter 2 we considered the considerable threat to the legal profession posed by the state, internal threats, arising from the nature of legal practice, are often significant. Thus, writing in the 1950s Pound noted the dangers, in the USA, of the "increasing bigness of things in which individual responsibility as a member of a profession is diminished or even lost", the exploitation of young lawyers producing pressures to organise in trade unions and the desire of the service state to replace professional services with administrative bureaux.[2] Similar pressures continue to threaten professional culture and professional norms. This chapter therefore examines the way in which the norms of the professional community might vary because of differences in fields of practice and the way in which different firms are organised. A particular concern is the ability of the profession to sustain a community with common norms and culture as the tendency towards differences within the profession, the fragmentation of interests and identity, increases.

B. Culture and Ethics

Professional organisation in its widest sense consists of the professional bodies and interest groups within them, educational institutions, the basic units of pro-

---

[1] D. J. Luban, "Milgram Revisited" (1998) 9:2 *Researching Law: An ABF. Update* 1 at 4.
[2] R. Pound, *The Lawyer from Antiquity to Modern Times: With Particular Reference to the Development of Bar Associations in the United States* (St. Paul, Minn., West Publishing, 1953), at 354.

duction in the practising profession, firms and chambers, other cliques and clusters of colleagues such as employed lawyers in public bodies. Even those in marginal positions have a role, although at first sight this may appear to be negative from the point of view of the profession. Lawyers in universities provide a critique of professional action, for example, and lawyers employed outside practice present a challenge to the homogeneity of professional practice. All of these contribute, albeit in varying degrees, to the culture of the profession. Culture can be defined in a number of ways, but we will adopt a simple working definition. We suggest that culture consists of values, norms and symbols.[3]

Professional organisation, and the culture it sustains, is important to an understanding of professional ethics because it is only through the symbolism associated with culture that social events, behaviours and institutions can be understood.[4] The notion of culture conveys the sense that those involved in an activity have, and perceive that they have, a common sense of the character and potential of the activity.[5] Nowhere is the notion of legal culture stronger than at the English Bar. Arthurs, a Canadian academic, observes:

> "For the Canadian legal profession, the real (or imagined) culture of the English bar is the point of reference (not to say reverence). We all recognise the power of the bar's ability to secure a high degree of cultural conformity as manifest in its professional customs and conventions, ideology, geographic concentration in chambers in or adjacent to the Inns of Court, dress and formal speech, shared understanding of law and legal knowledge, concentration on advocacy and legal opinions, relations with clients and so on. Indeed, if there is any legal profession whose culture can be identified with some precision, it is surely this one. Accordingly, in the case of the English bar, culture can be seen as an important vehicle for the transmission of values and the regulation of behaviour."[6]

Although in this chapter we focus mainly on the solicitors' branch, the culture of the Bar had not been immune from pressure for change. Changes in the culture of legal practice are, arguably, at least as important to professional ethics as are changes in the market for legal services; occupational culture is central to the legitimation of professional work because it integrates principles and procedures with the actual conduct of work.[7] Whether we see ethical norms as the idealised behaviour promoted by professional bodies or the actual behaviour of professionals in the field, both of these are the product of the environment in

---

[3] E. Greenwood, "Attributes of a Profession" (1957) *Social Work*, July, 45 at 52.

[4] C. Geertz, "Thick Description: Toward and Interpretive Theory of Culture" in C. Geertz (ed.), *The Interpretation of Cultures* (New York, Basic Books, 1973). Culture can therefore be seen as "conventional understandings made manifest as act and artefact": R. Redfield, *The Folk Culture of Yucatan* (Chicago, Ill., University of Chicago Press, 1941), at 132).

[5] H. Becker, *Doing Things Together: Selected Papers* (Evanston, Ill., Northwestern University Press, 1986).

[6] H. W. Arthurs, "Lawyering in Canada in the 21st Century" [1996] *Windsor Yearbook of Access to Justice* 202 at 223.

[7] R. Cotterrell, *Law's Community: Legal Theory in Sociological Perspective* (Oxford, Clarendon Press, 1995), at 36.

which professions operate.[8] Given that the legal profession brought into each era the symbols and organisational characteristics of preceding ages,[9] we must ask "what do changes in the external environment signify for legal professional culture?"

The environment in which ethical norms are developed is extremely complex. Despite the impression that the legal profession is subject to one set of ethical standards, firms and chambers develop their own organisational culture and respond in different ways to regulation. It is the environment provided by institutions and organisations which shapes the way that the people within it behave. Suchman and Edelman argue that organisations respond, much like individuals, to factors which are part of their everyday life; rituals, norms, shame and the desire for legitimacy. They are less responsive to rules and sanctions which are not part of the particular organisational culture. This is not to say that the imposition of legal sanctions or ethical rules does not have the capacity to transform organisational ideas, but this may take time. In the meantime, firms are part of the wider professional culture and, through multiple interactions external to the organisation, the individuals within them affect the wider culture. Therefore, the relationship between normative rules and institutions and organisations is reciprocal.[10]

How can we characterise the culture in which legal practitioners operate? The answer is difficult because of the wide diversity of practice settings and the difficulty of conducting research.[11] Ethicality is strongly associated with sole practice in professional and legal culture.[12] This is because professionalism is an individualistic notion; the individual is the unit of service and individual qualities, judgement and responsibility are the essence of professionalism.[13] Yet, paradoxically, Canadian research shows that it is busy sole practitioners, acting for individuals in conveyancing, estates and litigation, who are the most likely to be the subject of complaints.[14]

---

[8]   G. C. Hazard, "The Future of Legal Ethics" (1991) 100 *Yale Law Journal* 1239 at 1241.

[9]   T. J. Johnson, *Professional Power* (London and Basingstoke, Macmillan, 1972), at 47.

[10]   M. C. Suchman and L. B. Edelman, "Legal Rational Myths: The New Institutionalism and the Law and Society Tradition" (1996) 21 *Law and Social Inquiry* 903.

[11]   See B. Danet, K. B. Hoffman and N. C. Kermish, "Obstacles to the Study of Lawyer Client Interaction: The Biography of a Failure" (1980) 14 *Law and Society Review* 905 and A. Sherr, *Solicitors and Their Skills: A Study of the Viability of Different Research Methods for Collating and Categorising the Skills Solicitors Use in Their Professional Work* (London, The Law Society, 1991).

[12]   The Bar is a good example of this. Note the argument that the most ethically powerful lawyer is the sole practitioner because only s/he can make an autonomous decision on how to represent— most other lawyers are constrained by the policy and bureaucracy of larger organisations: L. Sheinman, "Looking for Legal Ethics" (1997) 4 *International Journal of the Legal Profession* 139 at 151. Negligence actions are typically against 3–5 partner firms rather than sole practitioners. Sole practitioners are more likely to be guilty of fraud, but the largest claim against the Compensation Fund was in respect of fraud, £13 million, which was committed by the senior partner of a 35 partner practice: A. Sherr and L. Webley, "Legal Ethics in England and Wales" (1997) 4 *International Journal of the Legal Profession* 109 at 130.

[13]   Johnson, n. 9 above, at 13 and 53.

[14]   In this research those sole practitioners subsequently disbarred had a similar profile; typically they were 10-year qualified with an average law school performance and the predictable life

Most solicitors practise in partnership with other solicitors. Compared with other organisational forms, such as the company, partnership is synonymous with professionalism precisely because it implies individual independence, autonomy and responsible conduct.[15] The traditional image of professional practice is that of "the solitary, disciplined, highly educated, and deeply ethical practitioner dealing with clients one by one". As Houle observes, this was always both over-idealised and over-generalised, and, nowadays, is an image which is increasingly atypical. He suggests that the modern professional is more likely to be part of a collective group enterprise, consisting of many people representing layers of specialism. One of the problems arising from this is that, today, professional practice is "flawed by a lack of concern for comprehensive and dedicated service, by a marked self-interest, and by incompetent performance".[16] In examining the shift in perception marked by this change, we consider the traditional structures in which professional norms were embedded, the changes in the nature of legal work and impact of such change on professional culture and the ethics of the legal profession.

C. PROFESSIONAL ORGANISATION AND STRUCTURES

Traditionally, professional work is structured around and supports collegial relations between members of a profession. The character of collegiality was defined in ancient times when craftsmen's organisations, *collegia*, provided a focus of loyalty for members which rivalled the loyalty owed their own family groups.[17] The *collegia* collected dues from members and distributed them as benefits, but their character was defined by the rituals peculiar to each group. Key among these rituals was frequent feasting that linked the associates in familial ties of brotherhood.[18] Durkheim saw this as an entirely benign process whereby:

---

problems of family debt, children and business commitments. Usually they had been the subject of previous disciplinary proceedings: C. E. Reason and C. Chappell, "Crooked Lawyers: Towards a Political Economy of Deviance in the Profession" in T. Fleming (ed.), *The New Criminologies in Canada: Status, Crime and Control* (Toronto, Oxford University Press, 1985), at 206; and see Arthurs, n. 6 above).

[15] R. Greenwood and C. R.Hinings, "Understanding Radical Organisational Change: Bringing Together the Old and the New Institutionalism" (1996) 21 *Academy of Management Review* 1022 at 1027.

[16] Houle based his observations on the professions of the USA, but his description is also a true and accurate image of the traditional solicitor or barrister: C. O. Houle, *Continuing Learning in the Professions* (London, Jossey Bass, 1980).

[17] Durkheim notes that the Roman Empire enforced a division of labour built on crafts formed into *collegia* all of which had duties and privileges. They re-emerged in Europe as guilds in medieval times: E. Durkheim, *Professional Ethics and Civic Morals* (translated by C. Brookfield, London, Routledge and Kegan Paul, 1957), at 19.

[18] *Ibid.*, at 21.

"when individuals who share the same interest come together, their purpose is not simply to safeguard those interests or to secure their development in face of rival associations. It is, rather, just to associate, for the sole pleasure of mixing with their fellows and of no longer feeling lost in the midst of adversaries, as well as for the pleasure of communing together, that is, in short, of being able to lead their lives with the same moral aim."[19]

In recent usage, "collegiality" describes both a model of occupational control, of which professionalism is an example,[20] and the relations between members of the producer class.[21] Here, we are concerned with the second meaning of collegiality, the sense in which Durkheim used the term, the relationship between professionals. Collegiality, in this sense, characterises the relations between people "belonging to a body or society of people, invested with special powers or rights, performing certain duties, engaged in some common employment or pursuit".[22] Traditional forms of professional organisation, like the model of the classical solicitors' firm or the barrister's chambers, are said to support collegiality. By working closely or in parallel with colleagues, professionals are supported in foregoing their short-term interests for the common good. In informal discussion, professionals are reminded that short-term self-sacrifice is in the interests of the profession as a whole and, therefore, their own long term interests as professionals.[23]

Barristers, despite their sole practitioner status, are organised in small units, chambers, administered by a clerk. Historically, the Bar was an archetypal collegial structure whereby barristers associated not only with members of chambers but with all of those in their Inn of Court. Collegiality, "this good spirit, a part of the professional tradition, enables them to contest with their professional brethren all day in the forum, and meet outside on the friendliest terms and with respect for those with whom they have been engaged in the strife of litigation".[24] It is notable that, prior to the expulsion of the attorneys from the Inns, discipline had deteriorated there as a consequence of the pressure on space which forced students to live outside the Inns, in particular because many gentlemen wished to join an Inn for social, rather than professional, reasons. Hence the introduction of the requirement of "dining" at the Inn as a symbol of residence.[25] But collegial structures existed outside the Inns. Through the early Circuit Mess and its Grand Council a strong surveillance was exercised over the

---

[19] *Professional Ethics and Civic Morals*, at 25.
[20] Johnson, n. 9 above, at 45.
[21] Ihara defines collegiality as involving support and co-operation between colleagues, a reciprocal respect for colleagues' ability to further professional ends through their knowledge and skills, a commitment to common professional values and goals, a willingness to have confidence in colleagues as responsible autonomous agents, a sense of "connectedness", or sharing with others the bond of being part of a longer independent whole: C. K. Ihara, "Collegiality as a Professional Virtue" in A. Flores (ed.), *Professional Ideals* (Belmont, Calif., Wadsworth Publishing, 1988), at 56).
[22] *Ibid*.
[23] P. F. Camenisch, "On Being a Professional: Morally Speaking" in Flores, *ibid*., at ???
[24] Pound, n. 2 above, at 127.
[25] *Ibid*., at 109.

Bar in England.[26] But, beyond this, most early professional constitutions had the aim of cultivating "a spirit of friendship and good will toward each other".[27]

Professionals have traditionally practised alone or in partnership, generally supported by non-qualified personnel, such as secretaries and para-legals. But the main focus of activity is the professional around whose practice the unit is organised. Solicitors' partnerships were, until about 30 years ago, relatively small. Joint and several liability for the firm's debts was a powerful incentive to maintain a controllable and well organised practice. The relatively small scale of operations meant that personal relationships were not only possible but necessary. Today, however, this type of practice is only one of a number of models. In order to understand the changes in professional culture of the last two decades or so it is necessary to identify other models of professional practice. We concentrate on solicitors' practices because, although there is no doubt that barristers' practices have also changed, they have to a large extent been maintained at a similar size and retained traditional forms of organisation.

A Typology of Solicitors' Practices

There is a wide variety of solicitors' firms, and any attempt to classify will almost certainly oversimplify. McConville *et al.* describe four main kinds of firm engaged in criminal defence work; classical, managerial, political and routine.[28] These descriptions apply to the organisation of criminal defence within larger units, but they are also useful in describing many firms operating in other fields. Firms often represent a combination of the features of one or more of these ideal types. We briefly outline the essential features of these types before considering two more "ideal types", large firms, often operating in the corporate/ commercial field, and boutique firms.

Classical

The classical model is broadly coextensive with the traditional image noted above and that promoted by professional bodies. The firm is organised around solicitors who handle a relatively low volume of cases. The solicitors are therefore able to be centrally engaged in all the legal tasks: research, interviewing clients and advocacy. In addition the solicitor inducts trainees and non-qualified staff and allocates and supervises their work. The staff are loyal, there is rarely a high turnover, and the firm is therefore cohesive and stable.

[26] *Ibid.*, at 12.
[27] *Ibid.*, at 15.
[28] M. McConville, J. Hodgson, L. Bridges and A. Pavlovic, *Standing Accused: The Organisation and Practices of Criminal Defence Lawyers in Britain* (Oxford, Clarendon Press, 1994), chap. 2.

Political

The political firm is organised around personal commitment to particular types of clients. This kind of work has recently been characterised as "cause lawyering". The law is used politically in order to highlight injustice or bring about political change. The firm's members empathise with poor and disadvantaged clients in their disputes with the state, corporations or employers.[29] These firms attract highly motivated staff who are committed to providing quality services. Such firms are often keen to change the law in the interests of their client group by pursuing test cases.

Managerial

Firms with a strong managerial structure have responded to competition and reduced funding by introducing systems and procedures aimed at reducing administration and delay. This has the effect of routinising procedures, for example for time recording and billing, training and the delegation of work.

Routine

Routine firms comprise the majority in McConville *et al.*'s study and, to some extent, their work describes some of the work in other firms; it is routine, physically demanding, repetitive and unending. Because of this there is likely to be frequent "poaching" of qualified and non-qualified staff either for advocacy or for their local connections, leading to instability in firms and variable service to clients.

In all of the firms described in McConville *et al.*'s research, staff perceived themselves to be providing a public service in poor working conditions and for relatively low pay. Despite this they felt they lacked the respect of the public. The same story would probably be heard from lawyers working primarily in civil legal aid or doing other small civil work. The pressures which result in the clients of some of these firms receiving perfunctory or discontinuous service contrasts markedly with those instructing large corporate commercial firms. Large firms will rarely deal with a criminal case unless it is corporate crime. Such firms are, by virtue of their size alone, subject to different but powerful forces which have also led them to depart from the classical model.

Large Firms

The increasing number of large firms, and the concentration of legal resources within them, is one of the most significant developments in the legal professions

---

[29] See S. Sheingold and A. Sarat (eds.), *Cause Lawyering: Political Commitments and Professional Responsibilities* (New York, OUP, 1998).

of the United States, Canada and Britain. They have grown faster than the profession as a whole and receive a larger proportion of the money spent on legal services, mainly from their business clients.[30] While in the United States large firms have been a feature of the landscape since before the turn of the century, in the UK partnerships of solicitors were not permitted to exceed 20 until the passing of the Companies Act 1967.[31] This opportunity for expansion was fuelled by the "Thatcher revolution" in the 1980s leading to the "big bang" in the City of London and the deregulation and reregulation of financial services.[32] This created substantial work for solicitors' firms and the opportunity to play a part in a growing international market for corporate and commercial legal services.[33] The firms organised around four broad categories of work: corporate and commercial, property, litigation and tax, but their principal focus was on corporate/commercial work.[34] Within a short time large firms transformed the way legal work was conducted and the way in which the legal profession was perceived. Table 4 lists the largest firms, their location and their personnel and financial profile.

The resources of large firms stand in stark contrast to those of most other solicitors[36] reinforcing a dichotomy, already established in the USA,[37] between wealthy firms serving corporate/commercial clients and smaller "general

---

[30] M. Galanter, "Law Abounding: Legalisation Around the North Atlantic" (1992) 55 *Modern Law Review* 5; Lady Marre CBE, *A Time for Change: Report of the Committee on the Future of the Legal Profession* (London, General Council of the Bar and Council of the Law Society, 1988), hereafter The Marre Report, noted that, between 1984 and 1986 the number of firms with more than 11 partners increased by 8% and the number of principals in those firms by 12% (para. 5.22).

[31] S. 120(1)(a). Corporation law practice had emerged in the USA by the turn of the 20th century. It became "a business" in its own right stressing high quality service and demanding large staff, a high degree of organisation, a high overhead and more intense specialisation. The "law factory" emerged with the mass of work performed by the ablest product of the best law schools. The partners lent their name to this work but were principally business getters and the repository of the goodwill of the corporate clientele: see K. Llewelyn, "The Bar Specialises: With What Results?" [1933] *The Annals of the American Academy* 176 and M. Galanter and T. Palay, *Tournament of Lawyers: Transformation of the Big Law Firm* (Chicago, Ill., University of Chicago Press, 1991).

[32] See J. Flood, "Megalaw in the UK: Professionalism or Corporatism?: A Preliminary Report" (1989) 64 *Indiana Law Journal* 569. Other factors encouraging expansion may have included the abandonment of fee regulation in England and Wales: see E. Skordaki and D. Walker, *Regulating and Charging for Legal Services: An International Comparison*, Research Study No.12 (London, Research and Policy Planning Unit, The Law Society, 1996), at para. 3.6).

[33] This prospect led to the merger of Coward Chance and Clifford Turner creating Clifford Chance which in 1988 had 168 partners, 386 assistants and 123 articled clerks, which by 1998 had doubled the numbers of partners and trainees, and quadrupled the numbers of fee earners (see Table 4).

[34] Flood, n. 32 above.

[35] *Legal Business*, Student Special, Feb. 1998 at 44. Note: turnover figures do not include VAT, disbursements, interest or anything other than worldwide fees generated by fee-earners for their work.

[36] It became accepted that 100 firms, having more than 20 partners, could earn one fifth of the income of the whole solicitors' branch of the profession: C. Glasser, "The Legal Profession in the 1990s—Images of Change" (1990) 10 *Legal Studies* 1.

[37] Galanter and Palay, n. 31 above.

Table 4: Large law firm finances[35]

No	Firm	Location	Gross fee (£m)	Profits per partner (£000)	Fees per fee-earner (£000)	No. of fee-earners	No. of equity partners
1	Clifford Chance	London	310	347	212	1,459	248
2	Linklaters & Pains	London	213	418	231	922	176
3	Freshfields	London	182	445	222	819	163
4	Allen & Overy	London	167	540	237	704	121
5	Slaughter & May	London	140	566	243	577	107
6	Lovell White Durrant	London	130	284	176	739	137
7	Eversheds	National	125	176	122	1,028	199
8	Herbert Smith	London	104	350	188	553	93
9	Dibb Lupton Alsop	National	100.6	271	132	763	88
10	Simmons & Simmons	London	92	174	150	615	110
11	Norton Rose	London	81	252	171	475	80
12	Nabarro Nathanson	London	70	169	139	502	102
13	Ashurst Morris Crisp	London	66	332	198	334	73
14	Denton Hall	London	61.3	201	163	377	72
15	Hammond Suddards	Leeds	53	278	131	404	42
16	Richards Butler	London	52.8	329	187	283	48
17	McKenna & Co.	London	52	253	161	323	53
18	Clyde & Co.	London	50.5	221	184	275	66
19	Wilde Sapte	London	50	240	156	320	77
20	Cameron Markby Hewitt	London	45.9	185	152	302	74

practice" firms handling lower value work on behalf of individual clients.[38] Most of the firms are located in the City of London and provide legal expertise in solving complex problems on a massive scale.[39] Like their American forerunners, large firms in the UK are adept at "custom work",[40] solving the multitude of problems raised by complex commercial transactions.[41] In order to do this they organise large teams of lawyers, accountants, economists and architects; they provide a multi-disciplinary approach to legal practice.

[38] J. Heinz and E. Laumann, *Chicago Lawyers: The Social Structure of the Bar* (New York, Russell Sage Foundation, 1982).

[39] The de-nationalisation of publicly owned companies also created new areas of work for lawyers which continued as ambiguous drafting and the discretionary decisions of new regulators for these industries created fresh legal problems to solve: C. Stanley, "Enterprising Lawyers: Changes in the Market for Legal Services" (1991) 25:1 *Law Teacher* 44.

[40] See Skordaki and Walker, n. 32 above, at paras. 2.5.4, 2.9.1 and 2.10.1.

[41] See generally M. Galanter, "Mega-Law and Mega-Lawyering in the Contemporary United States' in R. Dingwall and P. Lewis (eds.), *The Sociology of the Professions: Doctors, Lawyers and Others* (New York, The Macmillan Press, 1983), at 166.

Large firms were considerably more commercially orientated and entrepreneurial than solicitors' firms had been in the past. Emerging in response to the enterprise culture fostered by government policy in the 1980s and having close contact with business and financial institutions, the large firms absorbed the ethic of that period.[42] The firms, and the individuals working within them, were "becoming more corporate, more specialist, more competitively aware, and more orientated to economic productivity".[43] As a response to these changes, large firm lawyers were more concerned with technique to the exclusion of the traditional professional virtues.[44] Indeed, Stanley has argued that such firms had begun to place industry, initiative, responsibility and success over the traditional virtues of benevolence and altruism and even concerns about justice.[45] Manifestations of this changing professional ethos were said to be found in the commodification of legal services, in overcharging and in subservience to client demands.[46]

It would be surprising if such firms did not exercise powerful effects on the profession. Some of these are negative. They attract corporate commercial work away from smaller firms which, therefore, become less viable. They present a powerful image of legal practice which influences the perception of the public and policy makers. They attract the most able entrants to the profession.[47] They can change professional relationships and influence the policies of professional bodies.[48] Examples have occurred in relation to legal education and the regulation of legal services.[49] The influence of large firms can be positive. Large firms offer a democratic and meritocratic environment for employees, providing

[42] Firms located in the City of London, e.g., were major beneficiaries of the work produced by the policy of denationalisation and became identified with enterprise economics.

[43] E. H. Greenebaum, "Development of Law Firm Training Programs: Coping with a Turbulent Environment" (1996) 3:3 *International Journal of the Legal Profession* 315 at 322.

[44] So, e.g., Galanter and Palay, n. 31 above, observe that by the 1950s in the USA "efficiency, accuracy and intelligence" were the only values sought in large firm lawyers.

[45] Stanley, n. 39 above, relates this to the conditions in which the UK firms developed, but others have suggested that the structure of the work of large firms places them on "a collision course with humanistic values such as truthfulness and altruism": see H. T. Edwards, "A Lawyers Duty to Serve the Public Good" (1990) 65 *New York University Law Review* 1148.

[46] Stanley, n. 39 above.

[47] See M. J. Powell, *From Patrician to Professional Elite: The Transformation of the New York City Bar Association* (New York, Russell Sage, 1988), and note that the American television programme "LA Law", a glamorous representation of life in a corporate commercial law firm, is credited with increased demand to enter the legal profession in both the UK and USA.

[48] As long ago as 1933 Karl Llewellyn observed that large law firms in the USA had attracted the profession's "best brains [and] most of its inevitable leaders": Llewellyn, n. 31 above. An example of large firm domination of professional relationships in the UK is the way they have redefined the traditional relationship between solicitors and barristers: see Flood, n. 32 above, at 574, and 578; A. Boon, "The Skills of Litigation Solicitors' in *Skills for Legal Functions II: Representation and Advice* (London, IALS, 1992); and M. Humphries, "An Artificial Divide That's Had Its Day" [1995] *The Lawyer*, 21 Nov. at 12. The Law Society itself grew out of "intimate links with elite City firms": see D. Sugarman, "Bourgeois Collectivism, Professional Power and the Boundaries of the State: The Private and Public Life of the Law Society 1825–1914" (1996) 3 *International Journal of the Legal Profession* 95.

[49] A. Sherr, "Of Super Heroes and Slaves: Images and Work of the Legal Profession" (1995) 48 *Current Legal Problems*, part II, 327.

better opportunities for the advancement of women and ethnic minorities. This is because, as large organisations, they are more likely to absorb the current norms and standards of public life.[50] They are more likely to have dedicated personnel functions and to be proximate to the public sector where norms such as those relating to equal opportunities are most strongly expressed.

From the wider professional perspective, however, large firms present three further problems. First, their growth has made the solicitors' organisational and ethical model, originally based on that of the bar, increasingly irrelevant. This is not purely a question of scale; it arises from the bureaucracy necessary to run such firms and the attendant changes brought about in their cultures.[51] Further, the cultures of large commercial firms were seen to be as diverse as their management structures, making it difficult to find a model of education or regulation equally acceptable to all.[52] Finally, despite the relatively small number of large firms, they offer a large proportion of solicitor traineeships.[53] To the extent that large firms offer a commercial alternative to traditional professionalism, their influence is bound to grow. The evidence concerning whether large firm lawyers are more ethical than their counterparts in general practice is inconclusive. It is not clear, for example, whether professional disciplinary procedures treat the transgressions of large firm lawyers with the same rigour with which they treat those from small and sole practices.[54]

Boutique Firms

Boutique firms also represent a high degree of organisational specialisation. They are generally smaller than typical large firms, with a narrow area of highly specialist work, albeit work crossing different areas of legal practice. They may specialise in one aspect of a larger field, for example, childcare work or immigration cases. Boutique firms, however, often have a strong overlap with the work of large firms or do work which is ancillary to large firm work, for example intellectual property or entertainment law. Such firms could be organised on the lines of the classical, managerial or political models.

C. THE FORCES SHAPING ORGANISATION AND CULTURE

Competition

The aim of the government in the 1980s was to stimulate competition in the legal services market. The policy reduced the cost of some legal services, particularly

---

[50] W. W. Powell, "Fields of Practice" (1996) 21 *Law and Social Inquiry* 956.

[51] M. Burrage, "From a Gentleman's to a Public Profession: Status and Politics in the History of English Solicitors" (1996) 3:1/2 *International Journal of the Legal Profession* 45 at 69.

[52] Greenebaum, n. 43 above.

[53] The largest 5% of firms employ 40% of solicitors and offer the majority of training contracts: Sherr and Webley, n. 12 above, at 113 and see R. Abbey, "The Crisis in Solicitor Training" (1993) *New Law Journal*, 17 Dec.

[54] Reason and Chappell, n. 14 above, at 221.

conveyancing, but had a detrimental effect on other aspects of legal practice. Conveyancing services had been the bedrock of the majority of small practices and had subsidised less profitable areas of work. The decline in conveyancing income undermined the economic stability of many small firms. In response to the new environment, the profession generally became more business orientated. A sense of this can be gained from firms' response to the recession in the market for legal services which occurred in the years 1991 to 1994. A survey conducted by *Commercial Lawyer* found that a number of themes were dominant in the strategies of large and medium sized firms for coping with the recession:

> "the switch to litigation, pressures on fees, the strong and intensifying competition, and the need to invest in marketing. But there are also clear differences in strategy between firms of different sizes. The largest shifted their targets for expansion to overseas markets. The second tier, the worst affected by redundancies, fought hard on fees to maintain workloads. Firms with a large national presence, but not in the 'full-service' category, created new departments and redeployed staff from those areas that declined. Medium-sized firms recruited specialists from the larger firms and moved rapidly into growth areas created by the recession."[55]

There are a number of consequences of this shift to more entrepreneurial activity. Increased movement in the employment market reflected a more overt concern with fees. The Bar even wanted to abrogate the cab-rank rule on the grounds that legal aid fees were not "adequate in all cases".[56] Two examples considered below, advertising and competition, however, go to the heart of the professional ethic.

One immediate impact was the relaxation of the rules relating to advertising. Anticipating the need to respond to competition from licensed conveyancers, the Law Society changed its rules prohibiting advertising in 1984.[57] In the early 1960s all professions restricted or prohibited advertising, thereby symbolising the distinction between professions and business. The rule did not merely signify a disdain for the business ethic. It was consistent with the position of professions that their clients were, unlike customers of businesses, unable to assess the technical standards achieved. Competitive pressures, including advertising, were thought to lead to unprofessional conduct. A critical argument against advertising was that the inability of professionals to claim individual distinction reinforced the need for them to identify with the professional community and collective control.[58] Permitting advertising conceded one of the dearest

---

[55] M. Chambers and P. Wilkins, "Recession in Retrospect" [1995] *The Commercial Lawyer*, July/Aug. 34.

[56] J. Malpas, "Bar Council to Confront Cab Rank Rule", *The Lawyer*, 16 July 1996.

[57] Restrictions on advertising were also lifted in the Netherlands in 1990: L. E. De Groot-van Leeuwen, "Polishing the Bar: The legal Ethics Code and Disciplinary System of the Netherlands, and a Comparison with the United States" (1997) 4 *International Journal of the Legal Profession* 14.

[58] D. Rueschemeyer, "Doctors and Lawyers: A Comment on the Theory of the Professions" [1964–5] *Canadian Review of Sociology and Anthropology* 17.

principles of professional elites and changed the image of lawyers.[59] Soon, advertisements appeared in local papers, alongside advertisements for plumbers, builders and estate agents: "[h]ave you suffered an accident? We are specialists in personal injury. Free initial consultation".[60]

Secondly, competition stimulated the need to locate and develop new markets, that is to become more entrepreneurial. This has a wide range of effects. It undermines a tenet of professionalism that it is the client who seeks the expert's services and not the professional who seeks out the client. Lawyers who in the past might have turned down an invitation to broker shady deals for clients might be relieved just to have the business.[61] It also risks unseemly "turf wars" with other professions and sub professions. Lawyers were forced to redefine and compromise their distinctive claim to jurisdiction and to try and reconcile their ethic with the demands of the market.[62] Competition puts loyalty to clients at a premium. Duties to the courts or to third parties are inevitably marginalised in a highly competitive market.[63] Competition forces professionals either to be market leaders, so that they can obtain a good proportion of high paying work, or to perform more work cheaply. Whichever choice is made it creates a pressure for specialisation and hence the routinisation of work.

Specialisation

The model of the classic firm, noted above, is based on general practice in an age when competition was not intense. In the UK, classic firms were often built on conveyancing, and typically offered criminal or civil litigation, family law and perhaps one or two other specialist areas. Litigation was generally a relatively minor area of specialisation. Where it was offered, solicitors relied heavily on barristers who were seen as specialists, not just specialist advocates but also experts in the law. As a result the bar was the senior branch, the legal consul-

---

[59] Even as late as 1979 Orojo stated "[i]mproper attraction of business will include all those acts which tend to give an unfair advantage in obtaining legal business. Such acts lower the prestige of the profession and, therefore, constitute unprofessional conduct": J. O. Orojo, *Conduct and Etiquette for Legal Practitioners* (London, Sweet & Maxwell, 1979). In the USA advertising was said to have "changed the image of lawyers from professionals who deplored self-laudation into that of aggressive self-promoters": Hazard, n. 8 above, at 1256. Since lawyers were permitted to produce promotional brochures in 1984 virtually all have done so: J. Flood, "Megalawyering in the Global Order: The Cultural, Social and Economic Transformation of Global Legal Practice" (1996) 3:1/2 *Intenational Journal of the Legal Profession* 169.

[60] Barristers were allowed to advertise in 1990 but, because of the nature of their practices, usually resort to more subtle forms: see *Practice Management for the Bar—Standards and Guidelines for Barristers and Chambers* (London, General Council of the Bar, 1998).

[61] Reason and Chappell, n. 114 above, at 212.

[62] Stanley, n. 39 above.

[63] This trend was marked in the USA as early as 1870, at the end of the civil war: L. R.Patterson, "On Analyzing the Law of Legal Ethics: An American Perspective" (1981) 16:1 *Israel Law Review* 28 at 31 *et seq.*

tants of the profession. This had a profound effect on the way work was conducted, with solicitors seeking advice on the drafting of pleadings from barristers even in relatively straightforward litigation matters. When a barrister advised in conference the solicitor took the client to the barrister's chambers. Barristers were consulted frequently, on issues of liability, quantum and evidence, and took strategic decisions in cases on which they were instructed.[64]

This division of labour reinforced the idea that barristers were socially and intellectually superior to solicitors. It also made the ethical issues of representation clear, as responsibilities for areas of work were separated. The expertise of solicitors in the process of settlement was seen as complimentary to the advocacy expertise of barristers, thus supporting different roles and ethical structures. As one solicitor comments:

"when you come to settlement discussions most advocates, and that means, at the moment, barristers, will tell you that they would rather not get involved in settlement discussions for the very good reason that if you are an advocate you want to see things slightly black and white. Your case is white and his case black. To be a successful negotiator, settler, you have got to see the shades of grey in the situation. I have no experiences as an advocate but I have spoken to people who have, including my father who was a chancery silk, and he says that it is very, very difficult in the late stages of preparing and during a big trial you can severely damage your effectiveness as an advocate by getting sucked into the averaging process, if you like, which is negotiation. If you spent a day trying to see the common ground between the two parties and see the strengths of the other chap's case it is obviously much more difficult to get up and argue in the black and white terms that one wants an advocate to argue that the other chap's case is hopeless and your case is very strong."[65]

But specialisation has undermined this traditional demarcation of work between the branches of the legal profession and with it the ethical clarity the traditional division of labour produced. As competition in new areas of work intensified solicitors in large firms or "boutique practices' became more specialised[66] leading to concentrations of expertise in these firms. Consequently, smaller numbers of lawyers were regarded as competent to do work in certain fields.[67]

---

[64] "Even in litigious matters, the solicitor instructs the barrister, makes all preliminary enquiries and prepares "all the preliminary papers needed for a brief. It is he who is constantly in touch with the client": Orojo, n. 59 above, at 5). This reliance until recently was so great, it is reflected in law. So, e.g., solicitors are still entitled to plead reliance on counsel as a defence to negligence actions in areas where they might not have experience: see *Manor Electronics* v. *Dickson* (1990) 140 New Law Journal 590.

[65] J. Flood, A. Boon, A Whyte, E. Skordaki, R. Abbey and A. Ash, "Reconfiguring the Market for Advocacy Services: A Case Study of London and Four Fields of Practice", a report for the Lord Chancellor's Advisory Committee on Legal Education and Conduct, 1996, at 99, hereafter the ACLEC. Report.

[66] R. G. Lee, "From Profession to Business: The Rise and Rise of the City Law Firm" in P. Thomas (ed.) *Tomorrow's Lawyers* (Oxford, Blackwell, 1992), at 31.

[67] In the early 1990s there were around 12 solicitors' firms and two barristers' chambers specialising in construction law: J. Flood and A. Caiger, "Lawyers and Arbitration: The Jurisdiction of Construction Disputes" (1993) 56 *Modern Law Review* 412 at 426.

In large solicitors' firms high levels of specialisation undermined respect for the generalised skills of barristers, particularly as advisors. This is particularly marked in the corporate field. A barrister specialising in corporate work has observed:

"When I started at the bar, those who were my seniors were plainly regarded by solicitors as being great lawyers and great men whose advice was required and whose advice was taken in relation to the conduct of litigation, invariably. That reflected, in commercial litigation, the fact that the litigation departments of the big City firms were run by unqualified though often very talented people. Two things have changed since then. Firstly, litigation has become much more important financially to City firms, therefore the quality of the man has got much greater . . . [W]e are equal in terms of legal expertise as a mass to the City firms of solicitors. We no longer offer great expertise in the law that they cannot get themselves . . . That means that the role of the bar in taking critical decisions, I suspect, has gone down."[68]

Thus the role of the barrister as *primus inter pares* in the litigation team was undermined. If counsel was instructed he or she was expected to be "part of the team" and was chosen with compatibility, even compliance, in mind.[69] This paved the way for a concerted attack by leading large firms on the advocacy monopoly of the Bar. When solicitors were granted rights of audience in higher courts, large firms in the provinces took referral work from solicitors in the same area. The commercial Bar faced real competition in its most lucrative areas of work.[70] Specialisation by solicitors' firms is, then, a major threat to the jurisdiction of the Bar.[71]

But specialisation was not just a feature of large and boutique practices. Specialisation affected the work of small firms of solicitors also. While the large firms had nothing to do with the staple diet of smaller practices, like legal aid work or domestic conveyancing, other firms increasingly specialised in these areas. Working on lower profit margins they depended on familiarity with an area of work to ensure efficient processing of files. Not all firms dealing with personal work fitted this pattern. Some personal injury firms, for example, obtained considerable volumes of personal injury work by acting under trade union personal injury schemes. They also grew to be both large and highly specialised.[72] Other firms specialised in legally aided "disaster litigation" or medical negligence cases, making a boutique practice out of work which was often unglamorous and legally aided. The result of these developments was that, by 1990, 70 per cent of the solicitors' branch claimed to be moderate or extreme

---

[68] ACLEC Report, n. 65 above, at 115.

[69] Greenebaum, n. 43 above, at 321.

[70] Marre Report, n. 30 above, at para. 5.22

[71] A. Abbott, *The System of Professions: An Essay on the Expert Division of Labor* (Chicago, Ill., University of Chicago Press, 1988).

[72] Approximately one third of claims are handled by solicitors' firms which have stable arrangements with trade unions for bringing claims in relation to accidents suffered by trade union members: A. Boon, "Client Decision-making in Personal Injury Schemes" (1995) 23 *International Journal of the Sociology of Law* 253.

specialists.[73] Solicitors used counsel more selectively for tasks such as drafting pleadings, appearing in interlocutory hearings in chambers and advising.[74] A solicitor specialising in personal injury work observed:

> "We still use counsel to draft a lot of the pleadings and I think that that is likely to change fairly soon. In the smaller cases we are doing more and more of our pleadings; we should be doing them in all road accident cases. But otherwise we use counsel. I, personally, never go to counsel at all in a smallish case if I am dealing with one. I would only go to counsel when I genuinely think I need them."[75]

Similarly, in relation to advocacy, counsel are used more selectively by solicitors. As one barrister has said:

> "The big firms who instruct me, who do virtually nothing but personal injury, will do the vast majority of the interlocutory applications themselves. They will do them unless they perceive there to be some kind of a problem, it seems to me. They will instruct counsel if they think that there is an awkward point that they may not succeed on, which I think is probably a sensible approach. I occasionally find myself in the position, as I did the other day, where I'm instructed on three matters and there is a fourth one for the same solicitor in the same court on which for one reason or another they haven't instructed me and so I watch the woman who's sitting behind me on the other three do the fourth one."[76]

The Law Society has itself encouraged specialisation. Stung by criticisms of the handling of personal injury work by non-specialists, the Law Society established a Personal Injury Panel, dominated by market leaders, to vet and accredit individual applicants according to their experience and expertise.[77] The panel often adopted rather restrictive definitions of specialisation which tended to favour extreme specialists and also conferred competitive advantages on them.[78] The selection criteria included norms which reflected and reinforced the norms of this elite practitioner group.[79] The trend towards specialisation among legal aid providers was also encouraged by the government's proposal for franchising legal aid firms on the basis of expertise and efficiency (see Chapter 2 and 9).

---

[73] G. Chambers and S. Harwood, *Solicitors in England and Wales: Practice Organisation and Perceptions, First Report* (London, Research and Policy Planning Group, The Law Society, 1990), at 150.

[74] R. Hill, "Higher Aspirations" [1995] *Solicitors Journal*, 14 Apr. 34.

[75] ACLEC. Report, n. 65 above, at 49.

[76] *Ibid.*, at 63.

[77] The Law Society has developed a number of specialist panels since 1983. Five areas were within the Panel Scheme as at 31 July 1996. Medical Negligence had 100 panel members, Children 1,597, Personal Injury 2,233, Planning 197, and Mental Health Review Tribunals 367. Other specialist panels include Local Government Diploma, Licensed Insolvency Practitioners, Rights of Audience in Higher Courts and Qualified to Conduct Discrete Investment Business: see further Sherr and Webley, n. 12 above.

[78] *Ibid.* Note that the Family Law Committee of the Law Society follows a more inclusive definition of specialisation which depends on competence in the field (Report by the Family Law Committee of the Law Society, 1995).

[79] A. Boon, "Ethics and Strategy in Personal Injury Litigation" (1995) 22:3 *Journal of Law and Society* 353.

Specialisation by solicitors has a number of implications. These include the possibility that specialist solicitors will come to dominate certain areas of higher court advocacy. Another possibility concerns the development of multi-disciplinary practices (MDPs) which will bring together the human resources necessary to conduct the custom work required by corporate clients. We have noted that, in order to deal with the complexity of work, large firms often formed teams representing different kinds of legal expertise and professionals from other disciplines. The success of this kind of co-operation between professionals raises the possibility of collective multiple professions in one firm. Solicitors, accountants and merchant (investment) bankers, chartered surveyors and stockbrokers may well form practices together.[80]

Hitherto, public policy, and the policy of the professions, has opposed MDPs. In 1979 the Benson Report concluded that MDPs were not in the public interest.[81] The 1990 Courts and Legal Services Act permitted the Law Society to retain restrictions on solicitors entering unincorporated associations with other professionals.[82] This is not the policy of governments on the continent. In a number of European countries, MDPs are allowed and accountants are the dominant partners. The possibility that this may be the pattern established in the UK was enhanced when, in 1993, Arthur Anderson, a multi-national accounting firm, established a law practice. This rapidly spread to separate offices, operating alongside its accounting business, employing 100 lawyers and with projected income of £22 million.[83] Such arrangements avoid the Law Society's ban on fee splitting by the maintenance of separate accounts.[84] Recognising the inevitability of MDPs the Law Society has formally ended its opposition and their arrival in the mainstream of corporate/commercial work now seems inevitable.[85]

The Law Society originally resisted MDPs on the ground that it was "not satisfied that the public's need for independent legal advice can be properly achieved in a multi-disciplinary practice". It argued that, "if the Government does decide to permit multi-disciplinary practices, further safeguards would be needed in primary legislation".[86] The Bar weighed in with objections of its own to the proposals contained in the government's Green Papers of 1989. They

[80] MDPs have received wide support from some European governments and the World Trade Organisation. Because of protectionist provisions in the ABA code there are fears that MDPs would not be possible in the USA without major revisions. This may place American lawyers at a global competitive disadvantage: C. W. Wolfram, "Multi-Disciplinary Partnerships in Global and Domestic Law Practice of European and American Lawyers" (conference paper, 1997).

[81] Report of the Royal Commission on Legal Services (1979) Cmnd. 7648, at 401.

[82] S. 66(2).

[83] Wolfram, *The Lawyer*, 27 May 1997, at 18.

[84] Solicitors' Practice Rules 1990, r.7.

[85] "Medium Sized City Partners Accept Need for MDPs", *The Lawyer*, 11 Feb. 1997 at 48; S. Parker "Introduction to Legal Ethics and Legal Practice" in S. Parker and C. Sampford (eds.), *Legal Ethics and Legal Practice* (Oxford, Clarendon Press, 1995), at 1. A Law Society Consultation Paper on MDPs is currently out for discussion.

[86] The Law Society, "Striking the Balance: The Provisional Views of the Council of the Law Society on the Green Paper" (London, Law Society, 1989), at 4 and 17.

feared the loss of independent barristers to MDPs. They were also concerned with the loss of the benefit of cross-monitoring of the work of solicitors and barristers by each, reduced entry to the independent Bar as a result of the ability to enter a career in advocacy in large firms or MDPs, "without the uncertainties of the bar", and the loss of small local solicitors' practices through unfair competition with larger units.[87] Finally, as ever, the Bar was concerned at the loss of the public benefit of the "cab rank" rule.[88]

The main difficulty in relation to MDPs is the level of financial and management integration permitted between the different professional groups comprising the MDP. It was particularly difficult to imagine how MDPs could function as partnerships with members of different professional frameworks being subject to different regulatory and, therefore, ethical requirements. When different professions function together in the workplace, do they pursue their own occupational ethics, are the different ethics integrated into one code or, if neither of these, which professional ethic governs the work performed? The obvious solution is that MDPs adopt a business framework subject to external regulation. This raises the possibility that such practices would be incorporated and subject to limited liability.[89] If "[t]he ideals of professionalism may be harder to preserve when a majority of lawyers are employees",[90] imagine the tensions that will be created when MDPs are permitted to operate combined management and profit sharing arrangements. The suggestion that MDPs may need to incorporate would raise further questions about the compatibility of the commercial and professional ethics.

Advocacy, perhaps the last of the three areas of the bar's jurisdiction to be threatened by solicitor specialisation, is itself undergoing a process of demystification. It is now said that there is "no magic to advocacy"[91] and advice is even given to litigants that they should consider bringing their own cases.[92] The Bar will increasingly depend on its own degree of specialisation, its capacity to offer specialised advocacy services and its ability to offer new kinds of services.[93] It is widely predicted that the Bar will lose its grip on general criminal and common law advisory work and advocacy. Its future, therefore, could depend on its being able to offer areas of expertise which firms of solicitors will be unable to offer in-house.[94] The specialisation which this necessitates is already under way. According to one barrister:

---

[87] The General Council of the Bar, *The Quality of Justice: The Bar's Response* (London, Butterworth (1989), at para. 2.35.

[88] *Ibid.*, at para. 2.57.

[89] Flood, n. 32 above.

[90] R. L. Abel, *The Legal Profession in England and Wales* (Oxford, Basil Blackwell, 1988), at 306.

[91] J. Edwards, "Revolution: Solicitors March on Bar's Territory" [1995] *Legal Business*, Mar. at 46.

[92] M. Randle, "The DIY Defence", *The Guardian*, 26 Sept. 1995.

[93] S. Hall-Jones, "Is Fusion An Illusion?" [1992] *Law Society's Gazette*, 23 Sept. 20.

[94] *Ibid.*

"The reason why, and I have always had a broad band of work, the chambers itself in the last ten years has increasingly specialised in family work. We used to do right across the board—family, crime, civil. The criminal part of chambers in effect evaporated, much to everyone's distress, including those who left, about five years ago. One of the senior civil practitioners went off into a specialist practice because he decided that he wanted to specialise even more in environmental law and the rest of it and for that you need a degree of back up and there were not enough of us who wanted to go down that particular line which inevitably would mean giving up other areas of work."[95]

Routinisation

Much of the work conducted by lawyers is essentially routine,[96] and this is certainly not new.[97] But the increasing rationalisation and formalisation of procedures, in courts, Land Registries etc., increases routinisation. As we have seen, competition encourages specialisation and tends to concentrate work in the hands of a few providers as they attempt to dominate a sub-market. Issues which can be difficult when encountered for the first time, and which require a high level of professional judgement, become routine the thirtieth time and require little in the way of professional problem-solving. Systems can be devised whereby less qualified staff can carry out routine tasks, reserving the professionals for the role of overseer and dealing with the rare difficult problems. This, however, increases the risk that problems which would be detected by a professional, totally familiar with the file, will be missed by a less qualified worker. This may be one explanation of why cost cutting in conveyancing work has caused a massive increase in claims for negligence.[98]

The pressure towards routinisation has not been generated entirely by competition and specialisation. Since the 1960s a technological revolution, including photo-reproduction, computerisation, on-line data services, overnight delivery services, electronic mail and fax machines, has transformed legal practice.[99] Some of these developments, such as word-processing and IT generally, increase the potential for certain aspects of work to be made routine and, therefore, in theory, the professional is freed for less routine tasks. In practice this tends not

[95] ACLEC Report n. 65 above.
[96] This is not to minimise the importance of substantive knowledge, but the matters dealt with often involve repetitive procedures which do not call for original analysis of legal issues.
[97] T. Goriely, "Debating the Quality of Legal Services: Differing Models of the Good Lawyer" (1994) 1 *International Journal of the Legal Profession* 159 at 163, citing L. Bridges, B. Sufrin, J. Whetton and R. White, *Legal Services in Birmingham* (Birmingham, Birmingham University, 1975), suggesting that some legal aid firms handled high volumes of work in a routinised way.
[98] Glasser, n. 36 above. See also S. Domberger and A. Sherr, "The Impact of Competition on Pricing and Quality of Legal Services" (1989) 9 *International Review of Law and Economics* 41. Note that it was the collapse of the conveyancing market in 1988 that most affected the profession, not the cuts in costs which occurred between 1983–6.
[99] Galanter, n. 30 above, at 6.

to happen. The capacity to carry out work more quickly reduces the economic return from work; more has to be done for the same return. Additionally, information technology has the potential further to unbalance the relationship between the technical dimension of legal practice and the element of indeterminacy or discretion in professional judgement.

D. CHANGES IN CULTURE

Bureaucracy and Collegiality

There are three main threats to collegiality in the current environment. First, professional stratification threatens both colleague relationships and professional control.[100] Secondly, collegiality is threatened by institutional pressures towards bureaucratisation and profit.[101] Thirdly, collegiality may be undermined in an environment where rapid changes in staff are necessary because of the need to respond to the rapid changes which occur in a highly competitive market.

The dominance of the profit motive not only undermines the central ethical commitments of professions,[102] it marginalises the structures which support these ideals.[103] The commercial pressures unleashed in the 1980s certainly threatened collegial structures, particularly in so far as these structures opposed "the tidal pull of the profit motive".[104] We now examine the mechanisms through which collegial structures are undermined by focusing, first, on large firms. Large firms became more managerial in their structures, not just because of the need to compete with each other but also because of their increasing size. Large firms were under pressure to centralise their management structures and, therefore, to become more bureaucratic.[105] They became more like "businesses"

[100] Johnson, n. 9 above, at 80.

[101] R. Gordon, "The Independence of Lawyers" (1983) 68 *Boston University Law Review* 63 [in no 121], and Ihara n. 21 above.

[102] It is useful to recall and expand Macintyre's argument (see Chap. 1) that practices are sustained by institutions but that institutions, paradoxically, prioritise external goods. Without the virtues, practices cannot withstand the corrupting power of institutions: A. Macintyre, *After Virtue: A Study of Moral Theory* (London, Duckworth, 1985), at 194. If, in a particular community, the pursuit of external goods become dominant the virtues might first suffer attrition and then extinction. The conflict between internal goods, such as the development of virtues, and external goods, such as fame, fortune and power, are exacerbated by a disjunction between the values of professional practitioners and the institutions through which they practise (e.g. the firm or the courts). The rich rewards at one end of the profession and the poor living to be had at the other provide little incentive for young lawyers to prioritise the public nature of their calling rather than their personal self-interest: "[w]hy be a virtuous person in one's professional role if the goods that are regarded as most important are the external goods the institution emphasises?"

[103] Ihara, n. 21 above.

[104] W. M. Sullivan, "Calling or Career: The Tensions of Modern Professional Life" in Flores, n. 21 above, at 41.

[105] This position is to be contrasted with that in France, where the risk that the independence of lawyers is threatened by their place in a larger bureaucracy has been specifically addressed. Following the *avocats* and *conseils juridiques* (lawyers specialising in non-contentious commercial

and less like the "gentlemen's clubs" of old.[106] They appointed partners or officers to deal with functions which might formerly have been shared by practitioners within the firm. Increasingly, they also needed specialist expertise in service departments as diverse as finance, marketing, personnel, library, information technology and training.[107] This contrasts with the classical model because the solicitor is not the centre of all activity.[108] The partnership structure of the classical model presents an image of equals, which is in stark contrast with the massive hierarchy and bureaucracy of the large firm. Finally, the large firm is under extreme competitive pressures which affect all aspects of its systems including its methods of promotion and reward.

There are two main criteria for making decisions regarding promotion and reward; "lockstep" policies reward seniority while "eat what you kill" rewards client getting and retention. "Lockstep" is consistent with the classical firm model because it fosters stability and collegiality. "Eat what you kill" encourages hard work, the cultivation of a client base and the pursuit of profit. However, it can lead to competition between firm members and is therefore a threat to partnership harmony. In the UK, "lockstep" is still common, even in large firms, whereas, in the USA, "eat what you kill" is popular. English large firm lawyers are said to be resistant to the idea of introducing "eat what you kill" promotion policies.[109] Competition and the fight to retain the services of bright young "stars" may, however, change this. The pressure towards a managerial culture is not experienced only in large firms. The Law Society itself promoted the managerial ethos through the introduction of its compulsory course for solicitors in their third year following admission. The "Best Practice Course" was intended to ensure that all firms were helped to prosper by providing "solicitors with a reference manual of basic management techniques suitable for application to private practice".[110]

---

work) salaried *avocats* must have a written contract guaranteeing, *inter alia*, autonomy in the organisation of working time: see J. L. Leubsdorf, "The Independence of the Bar in France: Learning from Comparative Legal Ethics" (conference paper, 1997).

[106] Stanley, n. 39 above. See also Galanter and Palay, n. 31 above, chap. 4, describing the transformation of the big firm in the USA in the 1980s and M. Galanter and T. Palay, "Public Service Implications of Evolving Law Firm Size and Structure" (in R. A. Katzmann, (ed.) *The Law Firm and the Public Good* (Washington, The Brookings Institute, 1995) at 41) where they suggest that the increased size of firms is coextensive with increased rationalisation, specialisation, hierarchy, meritocracy and market orientation. See also K. I. Eisler, *Shark Tank: Greed, Politics and the Collapse of Finley Kumble, One of America's Largest Law Firms* (New York, Plume, 1990 and Powell, n. 50 above.

[107] Greenebaum, n. 43 above, at 322.

[108] This contrasts with "ordinary lawyering" in a number of ways including the detail of organisation, span of operation, relation to clients and operating style: Flood, n. 32 above, citing Galanter, "n. 41 above, and also L. Bishop, "Regulating the Market for Legal Services in England: Enforced Separation of Function and Restrictions on Forms of Enterprise" (1989) 53 *Modern Law Review* 326.

[109] Flood, n. 59 above, at 178.

[110] R. Steele, "The Best Practice of Management" (1991) 20 *The Law Society's Gazette*, 29 May at 21.

The loss of collegial structures and relationships obviously undermines the notion of peer evaluation associated with traditional ethical structures. This can be seen in the case of the Bar, the collegial structures of which were also affected, both positively and negatively, by the pressures of competition. The close physical proximity of barristers in Chambers and Inns is an explanation of why the Bar is seen to be able to acculturate entrants and exercise effective "informal discipline". Because of expansion and the pressure on accommodation an increasing number of chambers have moved outside the Inns of Court, including to chambers in regional centres. The Bar, therefore, has become more able to serve "local need" but its culture may have become more diffuse. Competition has also affected the nature of barristers' work in a way that affects collegiality. Chambers have become more specialised, concentrating on particular areas of work and dropping others. This could be seen to strengthen collegiality because of the support practitioners working in similar fields are able to offer each other. Indeed, it has been stated that many barristers' chambers became more supportive environments, as specialisation increased. They also became more client-centred and commercially orientated, with barristers offering conferences out of chambers and seminars to which solicitors and lay clients were often invited.[111]

This example shows that it is not competition itself which undermines collegiality; it can survive a competitive environment.[112] What is more important is the way in which organisations adapt to competition. Where a collegial form of organisation remains possible, a competitive environment reinforces the need for support. It should be noted, however, that the changes that have occurred at the Bar are relatively minor when compared with those occurring in the solicitors' branch.

Fragmentation of the Professional Community

The increasing specialisation, and hence diversity, of professional practice presents significant problems of professional coherence. For, as Durkheim saw, the larger size of the profession, of itself, undermines the possibility of common understandings. Hence,

> "when the group is small, the individual and the society are not far apart; the whole is barely distinguishable from the part, and each individual can therefore discern the interests of the whole at first hand, along with the links that bind the interests of the whole to those of each one."[113]

---

[111] ACLEC Report, n. 65 above.

[112] The adversary system, with the co-operation between lawyers on different sides of a case, may be a good example of this: see Chaps. 9–11.

[113] Durkheim, n. 170 above, at 15.

Although the situation is complex and nuanced we have seen that, in general terms, the sharpening of the rich/poor divide between law firms has created sharper distinctions between the main areas of private practice; corporate client and personal client. It is clear that the differences between legal practice within each of these "hemispheres", typified by large firms and "high street" practice, is enormous. In the USA it has been said that "only in the most formal senses do the two types of lawyer constitute one profession".[114] An example of the fundamental differences in approach is the professional relationships of lawyers with clients. Lawyers in the corporate sphere are dominated by their commercial clients because these clients have the power to offer high-paying repeat business.[115] Lawyers acting for private clients are more willing to act contrary to their clients' wishes, even when these clients have socio-economic power, because private clients tend not to have a regular need for lawyers.[116] There are also regional differences in the structure of the profession. The Marre Report noted what it called the "increasing dominance of London and the south east of England" in terms of the increase in numbers of partners,[117] of trainees[118] and in gross fees.[119] This may exacerbate fragmentation brought about by differences in types of practice.

The work of different kinds of lawyer, and the organisational cultures in which they operate, have never been homogeneous The differences have, however, been recently magnified at the ends of the spectrum. This is illustrated in attitudes to recruitment. Large firms recruit trainees with a view to the long-term development of the recruit and the firm. Small firms, especially legal aid firms, have short-term goals in recruiting trainees, who are often used as cheap labour for conducting routine tasks.[120] In such different cultures, ethical obligations are bound to be interpreted in different ways. The different attitude of lawyers to clients within each hemisphere illustrates this. The public service dimension of a lawyer's work represented by the handling of the "poor man's

---

[114] Heinz and Laumann, n. 38 above, at 905; J. P. Heinz, "The Power of Lawyers" (1983) 17 *Georgia Law Review* 891.

[115] *Ibid.*, at 899 (lawyers in general, "serve those clients they are likely to see and who occasionally bring them the cases they prize" (*ibid.*, at 900).

[116] Whereas, in relation to clients, corporate sector lawyers are said to be timid and weak, personal service sector lawyers are arrogant and imperialistic: A. Sarat, "Lawyers and Clients: Putting Professional Services on the Agenda of Legal Education" (1992) 41 *Journal of Legal Education* 43 at 44. So, e.g., according to Sarat, there is mutual suspicion between lawyers handling divorce cases and their clients. Divorce lawyers, in this study, emphasised the lack of reliability in the process and in the rules for resolving matrimonial disputes so as to increase client dependence on them (at 50).

[117] Between Mar. 1985 and Mar. 1986 there was a 3.5% growth in the number of principals in London compared with 1.2% in the North and 0.8% in the south: Marre Report n. 30 above, para. 5.22.

[118] The articles registered from the Greater London area represented 47% of the total for England and Wales in 1986/7: *ibid.*, para. 5.22.

[119] Gross fees (before deduction of expenses) earned by solicitors in London were £73,000, in the south £53,000 and in the north £48,000: *ibid.*, at para. 5.22).

[120] T. Goriely and T. Williams, *The Impact of the New Training Scheme: Report on a Qualitative Study* (London, The Law Society, 1996).

case" is absent in large firm practice.[121] Moreover, the vision of professionalism that regards professionals as capable of excluding external and non-technical questions, i.e. affective neutrality, is undermined. A form of practice where corporate clients define their needs, and the way they are met, has become a common, rather than a variant, theme. Ways in which these differences might be accomodated within the framework of professional ethics are considered in Part 3.

In law, as happened in accountancy in the 1920s,[122] large firms have an influence on professional policy which is disproportionate to their number.[123] This is potentially problematic, particularly when large firm lawyers develop an idealised view of the ethical standards their less advantaged professional peers should be able to achieve. They do not recognise that their perspective of the needs of the profession, or of the needs of wider society, is shaped by their day-to-day experience. Llewellyn captured this when he observed that:

> "any man's interests, any man's outlook, are shaped in greatest part by what he does. His perspective is in terms of what he knows. His sympathies and ethical judgements are determined essentially by the things and people he works for and on and with. Hence the practice of corporation law not only works for business men towards business ends, but develops within itself a business point of view toward the work to be done, toward the value of the work to the community."[124]

Another concern is that large firm practice may produce practitioners who are experts and technocrats with narrow vision. As such they may have a "trained incapacity for social responsibility".[125]

The tendency towards diversity is not, however, confined to types of firm. Driven by specialisation, it affects areas of work also and drives those within these areas to claim representation for their area as well as increasing control over the competence of practitioners. An example of this arises from the efforts of the specialist plaintiff personal injury solicitors and barristers who established the Association of Personal Injury Lawyers (APIL) in 1990. APIL operates as a pressure group "dedicated to the improvement of services provided for victims of accidents and disease". Members of the Association subscribe to objectives which include the promotion and development of expertise in the practice of personal injury law, campaigning for improvements in the law and wider

---

[121] See also Gordon who argues that commercial firms had become tainted by commercialism, to the detriment of "their lofty professionalism": Gordon, n. 101, above, and H. F. Stone, "The Public Influence of the Bar" (1934) 48 *Harvard Law Review* 1.

[122] Johnson, n. 9 above, 67–8.

[123] H. W. Arthurs, "Lawyering in Canada in the 21st Century" 15 *Windsor Yearbook of Access to Justice* 202 at 213. But see T. Schneyer, "Professionalism as Politics: The Making of a Modern Legal Ethics Code" in R. L. Nelson, D. M. Trubeck and R. L. Solomon (eds.), *Lawyers' Ideals/Lawyers' Practices* (Ithaca NY, and London, Cornell University Press, 1992), at 95 and discussion in Chap. 4, below.

[124] K. Llewellyn, n. 31 above. See also Johnson, n. 9 above, at 90: "practitioners subject to corporate patronage . . . will exhibit beliefs, attitudes ideologies which diverge from and sometimes conflict with those exhibited by practitioners subjected to meditative or collegiate forms of control". See also Eisler, n. 106 above.

[125] Johnson, n. 9 above, at 16–17.

redress for personal injury and promoting safety and alerting the public to hazards wherever they arise.[126] Recently the organisation proposed its own code of conduct comprising 11 brief paragraphs, some of which overlap directly or by implication with those in the Law Society Guide.[127] A clause which went beyond the Law Society's own regulations, designed to prevent "ambulance chasing" by prohibiting members from charging referral fees, was amended after complaints by members.[128] This illustrated the point that even in small professional subgroups, it is difficult to achieve consensus on ethical issues. The larger point is that specialist groups of lawyers are setting up their own codes of ethics. In the longer term, they may threaten the professional consensus as to the good the profession pursues and how it pursues that good.[129]

Finally, there is the fragmentation created by the gulf between private practitioners and employed lawyers. In the last chapter it was noted that the growth of the employed sector is one of the significant trends of recent years. Many young lawyers, who are unable to enter private practice, seek employment in the civil service, local government, Crown Prosecution Service, in commerce and in law centres. The employed sector, both private and public, expanded significantly between the 1970s and 1980s.[130] Employed lawyers can find it difficult to conform to ethical rules. Thus, a leading employed lawyer said recently:

"On the one hand the in-house legal counsel is supposed to be the corporate conscience, and on the other hand they're supposed to assist the company in achieving its commercial objectives. Sometimes these requirements clash."[131]

This presents a conundrum to professional bodies. How far are their ethical ideals likely to be sustained in employed practice? But, beyond this, an ancillary problem is that the Law Society, and to a lesser extent the Bar, has the problem of trying to speak effectively for a variety of groups within the profession which may have fundamental interests in conflict.[132]

---

[126] APIL code of conduct (1996).

[127] Para. 1, e.g., APIL members will act in the best interests of clients' replicates Practice Rule 1(c): R. Taylor (ed.), *The Guide to the Professional Conduct of Solicitors* (London, The Law Society, 1996), at 1, hereafter referred to as *The Guide*. The prohibition on contacting potential clients does not apply to "permitted advertising" which is defined as "advertising which complies with the Code of Practice of the Advertising Standards Authority and with the rules of the member's relevant legal professional body": para. 9.

[128] C. Fogarty and A. Laferla, "Protests Force Apil to Relax Ambulance-Chasing Clause" [1997] *The Lawyer* 21 Jan.

[129] See Schneyer, n. 123 above. It will be noted that medical negligence defence lawyers set up a group (the Healthcare Lawyers' Association) to give them a "balancing voice" in legal debates traditionally dominated by plaintiffs' groups: N. Hilborne, "New Voice for Defendants' Solicitors" [1996] *Law Society Gazette* 13 Nov. at 1.

[130] By 1985/6 there were 3,241 solicitors employed in local or national government and 3,106 in commerce and industry, a growth of 10% and 100% respectively since 1975/6. In 1988, approximately 500 employed barristers subscribed to the General Council of the Bar but the total number of employed barristers was not known: Marre Report, n. 30 above, paras. 5.24–5.

[131] "Ethics on Agenda at in-house Conference" [1995] *The Lawyer*, 14 Nov.

[132] Note that, in 1995, the Bar Council removed the rule which prevented employed barristers from being elected Chairman or Vice Chairman of the Bar so as to address the perception that

These various developments underline a fact which is independent of any of them. The swelling of the numbers of qualified lawyers, and the diversity of their backgrounds, undermines the notion that the professional group initially can or will, without more, share or develop common values. It is difficult to see how, without some considerable effort, multitudes of local understandings can be harnessed in a collective enterprise, let alone a collective ethic. This threatens collective action and collective status for both ends of the professional spectrum. For, as one large firm lawyer recently said, "[f]irms of our size would not rely on the Law Society to represent our interests . . . we recognise that we've got to look after ourselves".[133]

How can the profession resist pressure from large firms for regulatory changes which suit their interests?[134] Where does the professional body stand when in-house lawyers seek rights of audience and the rest of the profession opposes this? How can the profession justify a common education and training when students have such widely different career options?[135] How does the professional body set ethical standards for professional sub groups which are so different?[136] The attempt to develop high standards of competence or ethical standards of practice may be thwarted by the economic and other realities in which the vast majority operate.[137] One way of coping with this diversity is to make rules of conduct either basic or aspirational. They are likely to be vague in

---

employed barristers were inferior and to enable the Bar Council to claim that it represented all barristers equally: "Employed Barristers Eligible for Office" (1995) *New Law Journal* 3 February at 134.

[133] "Law Soc Damned by Members" [1997] 11:22 *The Lawyer*, 3 June.

[134] E.g., under threat from large law firms who wanted to offer their own LPC training, the Law Society has fundamentally changed the patterns of study in the LPC, dropping Wills and Probate as a subject assessed as part of the core and increasing the component of Business Law and Practice so that it contributes a maximum of 40% to the overall assessment. Litigation and Advocacy (up to 30%) and Conveyancing (up to 30%) represent the other components: *Legal Practice Course: Guidelines on Assessment Regulations* (May 1977), para. 2.1(a).

[135] Attempts to include a universalistic approach to management issues for solicitors three years into qualification (via "The Best Practice Course") failed, in part, because of the divergence of experience of young lawyers in different parts of the profession: A. Sherr, "Professional Legal Training", (1992) 19:1 *Journal of Law and Society* 163 at 171.

[136] While the "non-elite" sector of the profession struggles for existence, corporate lawyers, with secure goodwill, can demand the highest ethical standards and lead the attack on "the ambulance chasing evil". Abel argues that elite firms promote high standards in order to preserve the image of the profession as broad-minded and unselfish but that, in fact, their position conceals self interest. He cites attitudes towards advertising as an example. Although advertising tends to be resisted by professional elites, who already have an established client base, firms wishing to grow larger and new firms building a clientele need to advertise. See also Galanter and Palay, n. 31 above, and extracts from the speech of Senator John V. Tunney, Chairman, Senate Judiciary Committee's Subcommittee on Constitutional Rights, 5 *Juris Doctor* (July/Aug. 1975) (cited in J. F. Sutton and J. S. Dzienkowski, *Cases and Materials on the Professional Responsibility of Lawyers* (St. Paul, Minn., West Publishing, 1989) at 11—"[t]he economically marginal lawyer should rightly fear these changes. They are precisely the ones who do not have certifiable specialities, who cannot meet rigid trial practice criteria, and who can be most easily replaced by paraprofessionals . . . [and while] [t]echnological advances and their application to legal practice are generally considered to be good . . . [f]or the small practitioner, they are vaguely threatening".

[137] Goriely argues that the franchising standards tacitly recognise that legal aid solicitors will have a lower standard than large city solicitors: Goriely, n. 97 above, at 161.

order to be widely accepted and will therefore be open to a number of interpretations. It will then be argued that are useless as guides to action.[138] But, as the Kutak Commission discovered, the development of rules which govern the different roles which lawyers fulfil might be too unwieldy.[139]

Finally, it is necessary to consider the extent to which fragmentation threatens the acceptance of professional norms. Larson states that professionalism contains within itself a powerful ideological force which enables a professional elite to dictate standards. Larson thought that these standards were accepted by professionals lower down the internal hierarchy of the profession, and internalised as a part of themselves,[140] because they were content with the esteem bestowed by professional status, and association with the elite as a reference group, as compensation for a lack of more material rewards. It has been argued that this is probably an oversimplification of the operation of professional socialisation and culture.[141] Therefore, the extent to which the ethics of lawyers are dictated by elites may be a moot point. Nevertheless, the increasing differentation in the market for legal services creates the strong possibility that the interests of different groups will become more strongly defined and, perhaps, opposed. The content of ethics, the need for ethics, may become increasingly contested issues. Meanwhile, it became even more apparent that "the appeal of bar leaders to a common, if vaguely defined, set of values tends to serve a legitimating function".[142]

Loss of Independence

In the last chapter we identified various encroachments on the autonomy of the legal profession. These examples undermine the image of independence, from both the state and from clients, which is a powerful part of the ideology of the legal profession. The increase in external regulation suggests that independence is realised only when it is buttressed by financial independence from the state. The significance of conveyancing to the profession was that it provided a core area of work based on private paying clients. As conveyancing income declined, solicitors were forced to explore new areas of work; legal aid from the state often filled the gap. In 1975 the solicitors' branch still derived a relatively small part of its income from legal aid work,[143] but this has steadily risen and now constitutes approximately 15 per cent of the income of the solicitors' branch.

---

[138] R. Abel, "Why Does the ABA Promulgate Ethical Rules?" [1981] *Texas Law Review* 639.

[139] Schneyer, n. 123 above, at 138.

[140] M. S. Larson, *The Rise of Professionalism: A Sociological Analysis* (Berkeley Cal., University of California Press, 1977), at 227.

[141] R. L. Nelson and D. M. Trubeck, "New Problems and New Paradigms in Studies of the Legal Profession" in *Lawyers' Ideals/Lawyers' Practices*, n. 123 above, at 17.

[142] R. L. Nelson and D. M. Trubeck, "Arenas of Professionalism: The Professional Ideologies of Lawyers in Context" in *ibid.*, 177 at 196.

[143] In 1975/6 this was 6% (Glasser, n. 36 above).

The Bar is much more dependent on legal aid. At the time Glasser commented on the decline of the financial independence of lawyers, barristers were receiving half of their income from the state in the form of legal aid especially in criminal cases.

Whereas a profession supported by a variety of privately paying clients has considerable freedom in the way it organises itself, a profession dependent on the public purse is open to criticism of its most deeply embedded structures,[144] and the way in which it provides services. The involvement of the Treasury in supporting the finances of the profession has been used to justify government intrusion into professional affairs. The independence of the solicitors' profession from the state, and its claim to autonomy and self-regulation, is thereby undermined. Heavy reliance on public funds raises the issue of whether legal services, particularly in the field of welfare law, should be provided by state funded agencies. This, in turn, generates new ethical issues. One question, for example is whether "public" lawyers remain within the established profession as members of one professional body. Another is, to whom do they owe their primary loyalty; to clients or the state?[145]

CONCLUSION

Changes in the market for legal services created or, more accurately, stimulated competition and a competitive ethos. Competition has brought about change in the organisation and culture of solicitors' firms and barristers' chambers. One change has been the decline of the "classical" model of the solicitor's firm and the rise of the managerial model. At the elite end of the professional spectrum, the arrival of large firms of solicitors working for an exclusively corporate clientele marked clearer distinctions in the practice of law in the UK. Competition, specialisation and diversity threaten professional culture and particularly collegiality, the mutual respect and support of professionals for each other. These pressures undermine the structures that support professional values. The vision of the British lawyer as an isolated and committed general practitioner, working alone or in a small partnership or chambers, has been overtaken by changes in the organisation of practice.

---

[144] A good example is the way in which the Marre Committee deliberated over the role of barristers' clerks. The Committee asked whether an arrangement which left so much of the organisation of a professional practice to a clerk was desirable (Marre Report, n. 30 above, paras. 19.34–19.45). It recommended that, if chambers were to continue to employ clerks, they should be salaried "with an incentive to reward effort and efficiency" rather than on a commission basis (*ibid.*, at para. 19.42). See generally J. Flood, *Barristers' Clerks: The Law's Middlemen* (Manchester, Manchester University Press, 1983).

[145] This is a debate already well established in the USA and Israel. It is often argued, e.g., that the obvious role of public service lawyers should be to assist the judge reach a wise decision rather than to be partisan: M. Taruffo, "The Lawyer's Role and the Models of Civil Process" (1981) 16 *Israel Law Review* 5.

At one end of the spectrum, large firm lawyers are increasingly seen as wealthy business people who challenge the traditional expertise of barristers. Junior barristers and small firm or legal aid lawyers are increasingly poor relations, more subject to the pressures of the market and, therefore, having a different professional perspective, status and range of concerns. These and other developments raise vital questions. Can a universal ethical commitment survive the tensions produced by such diversity? Should the legal profession forsake its ethical commitments and become a pressure group for business people providing legal services? Can professional standards be left to the markets to define and the civil and criminal law to enforce? In considering these matters it is important to bear in mind that the pressures and tensions identified in this chapter may be neither novel nor insurmountable. Indeed, the alleged "crisis of professionalism" can be seen as the attempt of professional leaders to invoke the spirit of bygone ages.[146] While there may be something novel, or more threatening, about recent changes in the profession there is a sense in which we have been here before. In the 1950s, for example, Pound wrote of the profession in the United States:

> "Integration of the Bar has [become], therefore, a mission of the first importance. By keeping the followers of the different specialities of practice, the different groups into which the lawyers in the large cities of today tend to regroup themselves, conscious of a higher organization of which they are members and to which, as the profession itself, they are responsible, it can stand fast against the disintegrating tendencies which, threatening professions, threaten ultimately the law."[147]

But there is a substantial issue, not only whether the various sub-cultures of the legal profession can continue to perform their traditional roles of "instructing, mentoring, censuring, defending, nurturing and regulating, their members",[148] but whether they can do so while maintaining a common core of interests, norms and aspirations. Clearly, such is the mission of the professional bodies. The failure to perform this mission will bring agencies external to the profession to the fore in professional education and regulation. The issues of governance, representation, regulation and education are therefore considered in more detail in Part II.

---

[146] R. L. Solomon, "Five Crises or One: The Concept of Legal Professionalism, 1925–1960" in *Lawyers' Ideals/Lawyers' Practices* n. 123 above, at 114.

[147] Pound, n. 2 above, at 362.

[148] Arthurs, n. 6 above.

PART II
Professional Commitments

Introduction

In Part I we saw that ethics relate to individual behaviour and that clients rely on the competence, dedication and commitment of professionals. Although professionals are expected to place the interests of their clients above their own interests, there are everyday pressures to ignore that responsibility. Collective action, through the professional group as a whole provides a counterbalance to such pressures. It is also a means of protecting the interests of the occupational group as a collective. The ethical commitment of individuals is supported by disciplinary, educational and other mechanisms controlled by the profession; this collection of powers is known as self-regulation. It is frequently argued that self-regulation serves the interests of clients best, because only professionals can effectively review professional performance. Self-regulation was necessary historically because the art of the professional practitioner was made impermeable; external regulation was therefore seen as impracticable. In Part I we considered why that view has been challenged. We outlined alternative means of occupational control which have encroached on legal professionalism.

In Part I we also saw some of the pressures which make the development and maintenance of a professional ethic among lawyers a complex and difficult task. Lawyers operate in a market for their services which is more overtly commercial than that in which most other professions operate. It is increasingly more fluid, competitive and differentiated. While there is a need for enforceable standards of regulation, this diversity makes detailed regulation difficult. Moreover, disciplinary mechanisms are not the only mechanism of control. There are arguably expectations of standards of conduct from legal professionals which transcend enforceable standards. Such expectations might only be realised through the process of education and training.[1]

In Part II we deal with these issues by examining the practical ways in which the profession discharges its commitment to achieving ethical standards. Chapter 4 examines the establishment and evolution of disciplinary procedures and the publication of codes of conduct, the tension between the central role of the professional body in regulation and representation and some possibilities for alternative ways of promoting or adapting self-regulation. Chapter 5 explains the operation of the current disciplinary framework in some detail. Chapter 6 looks at legal education, and the role of ethics in the preparation of law students, and considers some possibilities for change.

---

[1] J. F. Sutton and J. S. Dzienkowski, *Cases and Materials on the Professional Responsibility of Lawyers* (St. Paul, Minn., West Publishing Co., 1989), at 2.

4

Governance and Representation

"Governing bodies are formally responsible for the regulation of professional practise: within the scope of their statutory authority they admit and disbar, they educate and exhort; they legislate and speak as the official voice of the profession. But it would be foolish to pretend that no sparrow falls without the knowledge of the governing body, that no norms of conduct exist save for those they proclaim, that no system of sanctions or rewards influences lawyers' conduct except those which bear an official imprimatur. To the contrary: it is the governing body which occupies a marginal role in directing professional behaviour, albeit a role which does become more central at the defining moments of entry to and exit from practise."[1]

A. INTRODUCTION

In this chapter we are concerned with the systems used to promote ethical practice. It deals with the way in which the legal profession acquired and exercised its powers of self-regulation, the dual role of the professional bodies as both representatives of members and the disciplinary authorities of the profession. The details of the current framework of regulation is described in Chapter 5. The background in the current chapter is important in understanding the ways in which changing social, economic and political conditions, bring about changes in jurisdiction and the need for new kinds of rules.[2] We also consider changes in the codes of legal professions outside the UK, particularly those influenced by the common law tradition. At present we have little idea of the extent to which professional bodies in different countries influence each other. Professional bodies often attempt to expand the influence of their ethical codes. The attempts of the American Bar Association (ABA) to establish a common code for State Bar Associations is one example.[3] One of the results of "globalisation", described in more detail in Chapter 1, may be to increase the harmonisation of

---

[1] H. W. Arthurs, "Lawyering in Canada in the 21st Century" (1996) 15 *Windsor Yearbook of Access to Justice* 202 at 223.

[2] This can be illustrated by the Law Society's relaxation of rules relating to advertising and in the differences in approach by the American Bar Association and the Law Society of England and Wales to the provision by lawyers of legal services *pro bono publico*: R. Abbey and A. Boon, "The Provision of Free Legal Services by Solicitors: A Review of The Report of the Law Society's Pro-Bono Working Party" (1995) 2 *International Journal of the Legal Profession* 261.

[3] R. Pound, *The Lawyer from Antiquity to Modern Times: With Particular Reference to the Development of Bar Associations in the United States* (St. Paul, Minn., West Publishing, 1953) at 270–349.

the ethics of legal professions in different countries.[4] This prospect is considered in more detail in the Epilogue.

The Development of Disciplinary Machinery

As already noted, professions are distinguishable from other occupations because the regulations governing their conduct are self-imposed, i.e. they are not imposed by governments or employers. In practice, powers of self-regulation are exercised by professional bodies in a representative capacity. The Law Society provides the regulatory framework and professional representation for solicitors, and the General Council of the Bar of England and Wales for barristers. The evolution of self-regulation, towards the present framework of regulation, has a long history. Prior to the sixteenth century discipline was maintained by the judiciary for the whole profession which comprised a number of different categories; barristers, attorneys (advisers in law suits) and solicitors (who specialised in real property). From the sixteenth century barristers became more differentiated from the others. Barristers were sufficiently established and well organised to offer formal education in the Inns of Court[5] and to exercise disciplinary authority over their own members. It appears that discipline did not operate at a formal level and was often used to emphasise etiquette and to reinforce the status and reputation of the bar. Discipline employed shame more than formal sanctions.[6]

In contrast to Bar self-regulation, for solicitors the power was hard won. As we saw in Chapter 2, professionalisation of the solicitors' branch occurred much later and only really gathered speed with the creation of the Law Society. The desire for self-regulation was the manifestation of concern by elite practitioners for their personal and professional reputations, status and honour. In 1836 the Law Society was made responsible for maintaining the roll of solicitors and in 1839 it was allowed to appear when solicitors were accused in court of

---

[4] The growth of international trade and political co-operation increases the prospect that both the laws of different countries and the ethics of lawyers will move towards closer harmonisation.

[5] Education at the Inns can be traced to the Middle Ages: D. Sugarman, "Bourgeois Collectivism, Professional Power and the Boundaries of the State. The Private and Public Life of the Law Society 1825 to 1914" (1996) 3:1/2 *International Journal of the Legal Profession* 81 at 85.

[6] A good example of this is provided by Pound (n. 3 above, at 127). In early times barristers who had progressed to the point that they could not conveniently carry their briefs were permitted to carry a purple brief bag. This had to be presented by King's Council. Thus, the Circuit Grand Court preferred an indictment against one barrister who received a purple bag from a King's Council to whom he was related by marriage; the terms of the indictment were that he carried "one purple bag wholly collapsing by reason of emptiness". It will be noted that the unfortunate holder of the purple bag had not broken a specific rule but that he, and the donor of the bag, had ignored norms of behaviour. The indictment was a rebuke to them both for engaging in nepotism and a warning to others that similar conduct risked exposure.

disciplinary offences for which they might be struck off the roll. A solicitors' disciplinary committee was established under the Solicitors' Act 1888, but it had no power of sanction.[7] In 1874 the Law Society was permitted to conduct preliminary investigation before disciplinary proceedings[8] and in 1907 it was given power to investigate solicitors' accounts and to issue annual practising certificates.[9] Not all of the Law Society's battles were easily won. The Law Society began to run disciplinary tribunals with power to impose sanctions only in 1919. Prior to that it was often in conflict with the political and legal establishment on many issues. Advertising, for example, was regarded as unprofessional conduct by the Law Society but, during the nineteenth and early twentieth centuries, judges were not supportive of the Society's attempts to suppress either advertising or touting by solicitors.[10]

Currently the Law Society's grip on self-regulation is being considerably weakened. The increasing separation of the complaints system from the Law Society's control and the existence of ACLEC may suggest that self regulation is in decline.[11] This has already been mentioned in Chapter 2 and will be dealt with in detail in Chapter 5. It is too early to judge whether there is a long-term trend towards external regulation, although this is a pattern which has emerged elsewhere.[12] The Bar, although now subject to some external regulation, has been less affected in this respect than the solicitors' branch. Clearly there are circumstances in which self-regulation is still seen as appropriate[13] presumably where the promotion of professional norms within a professional group is still thought to be viable. Is this just a question of the size and organisation of the group or is it more to do with the mechanisms used for promoting and enforcing norms?

The Promulgation and Enforcement of Ethical Norms

The most obvious way in which self-regulating professions reflect and disseminate professional norms is through codes of conduct. Codes of conduct are a normal, though not necessary, incident of complex disciplinary machinery.

---

[7] See further R. Cranston, "Legal Ethics and Professional Responsibility" in R. Cranston (ed.), *Legal Ethics and Professional Responsibility* Oxford: Clarendon Press), at 3.

[8] M. Burrage, "From a Gentleman's to a Public Profession" [1996] *International Journal of the Legal Profession* 45 at 56.

[9] Sugarman, n. 5 above, at 106.

[10] *Ibid.*

[11] Burrage, n. 8 above, at 74. It is via membership of ACLEC that for the first time lay persons have been given a role in defining the responsibility of lawyers: A. A. Paterson, "Professionalism and the Legal Services Market" (1996) 3:1/2 *International Journal of the Legal Profession* 137 at 153.

[12] A number of Australian Law Societies are no longer self-regulating: A. Evans, "Professional Ethics North and South: Interest on Clients' Funds and Lawyer Fraud. An Opportunity to Redeem Professionalism" (1996) 3:3 *International Journal of the Legal Profession* 281 at 283.

[13] Burrage observes, that many critics have acknowledged the high standards of the bar but the solicitors' profession receives little praise for its disciplinary efforts: Burrage, n. 8 above, at 57.

They are not necessary because discipline is usually reserved for actions or neglect which are illegal in any event or are clear breaches of professional standards. Codes of Conduct, while they will deal with such instances, also contain exhortations to high standards which are not intended to have disciplinary force. The ambiguous role of codes gives rise to two views of their significance. As we saw in Chapter 2 they are seen as indications of professionalisation and symbolic of the evolution of the role of the profession.[14] Alternatively, they are also seen as a part of a profession's attempts to justify a monopoly position and to control its market. What evidence is there to support these views? There are four areas that can be considered: first, the commitment to codes as a manifestation of the commitment to effective self-regulation; secondly, the substance of the codes and other regulations governing the profession; thirdly, the use of disciplinary mechanisms; fourthly, the actual observance of ethical norms which do not necessarily carry sanctions.

The Commitment to Self-regulation

The adoption of formal codes by the professions in the United Kingdom was a fairly late development and the formal enforcement of ethical principles even later. The first account of etiquette for the Bar was published in 1875[15] but it did not prescribe standards and so could not be seen as a disciplinary code.[16] The first Royal Commission on Legal Services, in 1979, recommended that the Bar adopt written standards. This recommendation resulted in the publication of the Code of Conduct for the Bar of England and Wales in 1981.[17] The Law Society unenthusiastically accepted powers to make regulations for governance of the profession given to them under the Solicitors Act 1933. Two reasons overcame the Law Society's unwillingness. The first was the need to pre-empt government regulation in the wake of a growing scandal surrounding the embezzlement of client funds by solicitors.[18] The second was the desire to increase the Law Society's credibility in the eyes of the government.[19]

[14] See also L. H. Newton, "Lawgiving for Professional Life: Reflections on the Place of the Professional Code" in A. Flores (ed.), *Professional Ideals* (Belmont, Calif., Wadsworth Publishing, 1988), at 47.

[15] R. Abel, *The Legal Profession in England and Wales* (Oxford, Basil Blackwell, 1988), at 133.

[16] The first formal code of ethics in the USA was adopted by the Alabama State Bar Association in 1887. This served as a model for the ABA's Canons of Professional Ethics in 1908: L. R.Patterson, "On Analyzing the Law of Legal Ethics: An American Perspective" (1981) 16:1 *Israel Law Review* 28.

[17] (1979 vol.1 310) and see Abel, n. 15 above, at 133.

[18] L. Sheinman, "Looking for Legal Ethics" (1997) 4 *International Journal of the Legal Profession* 139. See C. Maughan and J. Webb, *Lawyering Skills and the Legal Process* (London, Butterwoths, 1995), at 92 n. 4. The problem remains significant and is not limited to the UK. Evans recounts that one firm in Wellington, New Zealand, defrauded clients of NZ$60 million, bankrupting the New Zealand fidelity fund. Thefts of A$10 million are "not uncommon" in Australia: Evans, n. 12 above.

[19] Hence, the Law Society improved its prospect of taking control of the infant Legal Aid scheme in 1949: C. Glasser, "The Legal Profession in the 1990s: Images of Change" (1990) 10 *Legal Studies* 1.

Since the legal profession began to issue codes, its rulemaking has increased apace, particularly in the solicitors' branch. Yet it remains the case that neither branch of the legal profession in the UK has highly developed codes of conduct.[20] The Bar Council's code remains relatively brief. The Law Society's collection of rules[21] and principles of conduct, *The Guide to the Professional Conduct of Solicitors* (the *Guide*), is more comprehensive and has grown rapidly in the last few years. It does not currently aspire to be a "code". On this evidence, therefore, the legal profession has not, historically, sought to develop codes of conduct with effective sanctions. The fact that it may now be attempting to do so could be seen as a reaction to the pressures outlined in Chapters 2 and 3.

The Substance of the Rules of Conduct

What does the actual substance of the codes reveal? In general terms the kinds of professional obligations found in codes of conduct can be classified into three distinct types[22]: first, "standards" set by the professional body which usually describe character traits such as honesty and competence; secondly, "rules" which prescribe duties in particular terms and leave little room for interpretation; thirdly, "principles" which prescribe general responsibilities and allow a degree of discretion in interpretation and implementation. Disciplinary sanctions are normally imposed for breaches of rules rather than for breaches of principles. Therefore, in creating a rule, as opposed to creating principles, it must be quite clear that the conduct involved is recognisably wrong. There is certainly a large amount of material, particularly in the solicitors' *Guide*, which is not intended to lead to disciplinary action. Where codes are most detailed, in the area of professional etiquette, they operate so as to reinforce legal jurisdiction. It is therefore arguable that such rules support restrictive practices rather than the ethical conduct of practice.

What of rules which do concern ethical practice? It has been argued that such rules of conduct rarely place legal professionals at a commercial disadvantage and are so vague that they do not set clear boundaries for professional behaviour.[23] To these accusations there are two defences. The first defence is that the

[20] J. Levin, *An Ethical Profession?* (Swansea, University of Wales, 1994), at 8.

[21] The rules are made by the Council of the Law Society, with the concurrence of the Master of the Rolls, under the Solicitors Act 1974, s.31.

[22] M. D. Bayles, *Professional Ethics* (Belmont, Calif., Wadsworth Publishing, 1981), at 22. See further Chap. 5 for a more detailed analysis of the nature of the rules contained in the Law Society's *Guide*.

[23] See the following works by R. Abel, *The Legal Profession*, n. 15 above, at 30, "Why Does the ABA Bother to Promulgate Ethical Rules?" [1981] *Texas Law Review* 639 and "The Decline of Professionalism?" (1986) 49 *MLR* 1, which cites the report of the KUTAK Commission in support of the proposition that it is impossible to come to grips with the intrinsic problem of enforcing professional rules. KUTAK argued that compliance with rules depended "primarily upon understanding and voluntary compliance—the rules of conduct are frequently forgotten". It favoured "reinforcement by peer and public opinion" rather than coercion, although, "finally, when necessary, by enforcement through disciplinary proceedings". Nicholson suggests that the vast majority of the practice rules summarising the basic principles of solicitors' practice "deal with matters of internal bureacracy or the protection of the interests and self-image of the profession"

inadequacy of professional codes is not deliberate; the second that it is inevitable. As regards the coincidence between professional self-interest and professional codes, it is often said that the main failing of professionals is that, in the ethical sphere, they do not perceive interests at odds with their own.[24] It does not follow that professional self-regulation is a charade and professional ideology self-serving. It may follow that professionals need to be alerted to this tendency when drafting their rules. As regards the allegation of vagueness, it can be argued that principles of conduct are intended to be inspirational, aspirational or for guidance. As such they are an unsuitable basis for imposing sanctions. If this argument is accepted, it may be thought that the acid test of the importance of ethical aspirations to the profession is how they are used in education and training. Unfortunately, as we shall see in Chapter 6, the profession's record in that respect is patchy at best.

The Nature and Use of Disciplinary Machinery

The third area for consideration, disciplinary mechanisms, is often a focus of criticism. Critics of self-regulation argue that complaints and disciplinary procedures are, typically, slow and offer inadequate redress. Abel's analysis of complaints against barristers suggests that, since 1957, the majority of complaints have been dismissed before reaching the Senate. The Senate rejected a recommendation of the Royal Commission that it should interview all complainants, a measure that might have improved the success rate.[25] This suggests that there was a lack of commitment to dealing with unethical behaviour. This impression is reinforced by the fact that, of the complaints reaching the Disciplinary Tribunal, fewer than 3 per cent led to disbarment and only 1 per cent in suspension.[26] Is there any explanation of this phenomenon apart from the fact that the legal profession is not serious about enforcing discipline? It must be acknowledged that professions have a conflict of interest in pursuing disciplinary sanctions against members. One aim is to maintain public confidence; ensuring that complaints are properly handled is a key part of this aim. But, by dealing with dishonesty and incompetence openly and publicly, professions highlight their inadequacies. This threatens, rather than enhances, the future, not only of their powers of self-regulation, but of other professional privileges.[27] From this point of view it is sensible for professional bodies to use disciplinary sanctioning only in the clearest cases. There is a strong argument that a profession should rely on informal measures whenever possible.[28] It follows that

(D. Nicholson, "Mapping Professional Legal Ethics: The Form and Focus of the Codes" (1998) 1 *Legal Ethics* 51 at 56.

[24] D. L. Rhode, "Why the ABA Bothers: A Functional Perspective on Professional Codes" [1981] *Texas Law Review* 689.

[25] Abel, n. 15 above, at 135–6.

[26] *Ibid.*, at 136.

[27] *Ibid.*, at 30.

[28] This is evident from the reports of the Bar's new Complaints Commissioner whose appointment was followed by a 30% increase in complaints and a first report form Scott which suggested

formal disciplinary procedures are likely to be used only in cases where offences will become public anyway.[29] Unfortunately, recent analysis of the last two hundred cases brought before the Solicitors' Disciplinary Tribunal suggests that, even in cases involving alleged misappropriation of client funds, the tribunal has not used its full powers.[29a]

The Voluntary Observance of Norms

An effective commitment to ethics requires practitioners and the professional bodies to take both observance and enforcement seriously. Our final area, therefore is observance of norms and standards in areas in which sanctions do not operate. We have already noted that where rules are ambiguous or do not relate to specific practice contexts, there is scope for interpretation. If the rules do not recognise the economic and practical realities of practice, there is also an incentive for non-observance. There is very limited evidence available in this area. Carlin's study of the New York City Bar in the 1970s suggested that ethical standards were differently accepted by lawyers, depending on the status of the field in which they operate.[30] Carlin analysed the acceptance of ethical norms by status of firm and found that a large majority of lawyers in all firms accepted certain basic standards, usually pertaining to lawyer client relations.[31]

Only high status (large firms) lawyers accepted norms which went beyond wider social norms. Carlin also found that the lower the status of the lawyer's clientele, and the lower the status of courts in which s/he worked, the higher was the rate of violation of ethical standards.[32] Lower status lawyers also reported more frequent pressure from clients to violate professional norms. In the absence of consensus on ethical norms Carlin suggests three possible models: random disagreement, where it was not possible to predict adherence to particular norms; plural standards, where different groups uphold different or opposing norms; and a norm hierarchy where certain norms are universally upheld, but in relation to which some groups adhere to additional, more demanding norms. Recent qualitative work in the UK confirms differences in norms accepted in different

that "a very small percentage of barristers are disciplined as a result of criminal conviction. A slightly larger percentage make mistakes through incompetence or cutting corners. Overwork or laziness leads to mishaps. Arrogance and self-importance result in rudery and bombast. Sometimes these can cause real disadvantage and distress ("Barristers Accused of Arrogance and Self Importance", *The Lawyer*, 19 May 1998). See further Chap. 5 below.

[29] Burrage, n. 8 above, at 57.
[29a] Of the 200 solicitors 64 were accused of misappropriating client funds. Thirty (47%) were struck off, twelve (19%) were suspended and twenty-two (34%) were fined. Thus, 53% of those found guilty of misusing client funds were not struck off, usually on the grounds that dishonesty was not found (M. Zander, "Only the talk is tough", *Gazette* 95/46 December 2nd 1998.
[30] J. Carlin, "Lawyer's Ethics" in *The Sociology of Law: A Socio-Structural Perspective* (London, The Free Press, Collier Macmillan, 1980), at 257.
[31] Carlin distinguished Bar norms proscribing behaviour which is generally socially unacceptable, e.g., cheating and bribery. Elite or paper norms proscribe behaviour acceptable in the wider community (he cites the case of advertising or accepting commissions for referring business).
[32] Carlin attributed this to the instability of clientele and the temptation offered by personal gain: n. 30 above, at 264.

areas of practice, but not that large firm lawyers are intrinsically more ethical in the way they handle cases than solicitors in smaller firms.[33] They may, however, be more committed to activities such as *pro bono* work.[34]

The Future of Self-regulation

The last 20 years have seen a large increase in activity around the issues of ethics and conduct. The extent to which regulation became external rather than internal to the profession is considered in the next chapter. Here, we are concerned with the philosophy of regulation. The amount of regulation by the profession has increased at the same time as external regulation is increasing. How can this be explained? It probably reflects a number of influences described in Part I. These include the increasing complexity of practice, the increasing incidence, or at least appearance, of professional malfeasance, the demand for professional accountability from government and other bodies outside the profession and the desire of the profession to combat the argument for external regulation. So, in some vital areas, obligations to clients have been reinforced and in other areas rules and principles have been clarified. There is increasing attention to criticism. Assuming that the volume of regulatory material is increasing, what are the implications for professional ethics?

Simon argues that there are two contrasting ethical philosophies which typically underly a profession's approach to the regulation.[35] The first is the libertarian stance under which the lawyers' freedom of conduct is constrained only by duties to clients. A libertarian approach places procedure over substance. Typically, if a particular course of action is permitted by a code of conduct the lawyer can pursue that course of action. This orientation is often reflected in codes which are loosely drawn and ambiguous, the guiding spirit for the classification of ambiguity is the lawyer's perception of the client's interests. The doubt whether or not particular conduct is ethical is resolved by asking whether the conduct is in the client's interest. One consequence of the libertarian philosophy is that professional norms are placed above ordinary social norms. It is the fact that lawyers are acting for another which is taken to justify the action. The libertarian conception of lawyer responsibility is therefore consistent with the image of the adversarial advocate who places his or her client's cause above every other consideration.[36]

Contrasted with libertarianism is a more regulatory philosophy that places the substance of rules over procedure. It is reflected in principles of conduct

---

[33] A. Boon, "Client Decision-making in Personal Injury Schemes" (1995) 23 *International Journal of the Sociology of Law* 253; A. Boon, "Ethics and Strategy in Personal Injury Litigation" (1995) 22:3 *Journal of Law and Society* 353.

[34] See further Chap. 9.

[35] W. H. Simon "Ethical Discretion in Lawyering" (1988) 101 *Harvard Law Review* 1083.

[36] This is discussed further in Chaps. 1 and 12.

which are more detailed and allow practitioners less scope for interpretation or discretion. Where this model applies the professional body may, for example, reinforce its rules of conduct with guidance from its officers in individual cases. The emphasis of the regulatory philosophy is on the public responsibility of the lawyer as a facilitator of informed dispute resolution, an officer of the court and the distiller and transmitter of information. This tempers the idea of the lawyer as a partisan advocate and increases the scope of obligation. As the codes of conduct in the legal profession become more explicit we might anticipate that the partisanship of lawyers will be tempered by more explicit obligations to others and to the system of justice. Whatever the reasons for the accumulation of rules in recent years, therefore, the change has deeper implications. We argue that we are witnessing a movement from a libertarian system to a system which is more regulatory in nature.[37] This may indicate that the profession, and the solicitors branch in particular, wishes to enhance the ethical content of legal practice.

C. REPRESENTATION

In Chapter 2 we noted that the profession of law lacked a scientific knowledge base, a fact which made the professional monopoly of law fragile. This, arguably, has advantages in terms of the profession's ability to influence social institutions and public policy. It is worth examining this claim in more detail since it is a point which is material to the influence a profession can wield in fulfilling its representative function. Halliday draws a distinction between professions whose knowledge base is primarily scientific, e.g. the natural and biological sciences, and those in which it is primarily normative e.g. the clerical and legal professions.[38] Halliday postulates that the normative professions "lose the authority of science but thereby obtain a broad mandate to range extensively over moral terrain"[39] because moral and ethical questions are relevant to public policy and to everyday issues of practice. Thus, the normative professions may be seen to have a legitimate view on issues relating to the governance of society which exceeds the narrow area of their technical competence. Further, the very weakness of lawyers, that they can move across employment boundaries, is also a strength in that it allows them to permeate secondary institutional spheres i.e. areas of social activity in which the profession's technical skill is of marginal relevance. Halliday, therefore, considers that professions have degrees of expert

[37] Since the 1930s the solicitors code of conduct has grown in complexity. Its current manifestation, *The Guide to the Professional Conduct of Solicitors*, was published in 1993 and 1996, on each occasion substantially revised, and is updated by supplements on a regular basis. The growth of a regulatory philosophy is also evidenced by the fact that the Law Society encourages solicitors to telephone its Division of Professional Ethics with ethical queries.
[38] T. C. Halliday, *Beyond Monopoly: Lawyers, State Crises, and Professional Empowerment* (Chicago, Ill., and London, University of Chicago Press, 1987), at 32. It should be noted that Halliday identifies a third group of professions who straddle this divide e.g. the academic and the military, but detailed consideration of this group is not relevant here (at 34).
[39] *Ibid.*, at 36.

and moral authority and spheres of primary and secondary influence. The degree of legitimacy, and therefore influence, which can be exercised by a profession varies according to the conjunction of the type of authority it can exercise on an issue and the spheres of influence in which it operates.

In their primary institutional sphere, in the case of lawyers the operation of the legal system, and on technical issues professions can expect to have a high degree of legitimacy. Even in its primary sphere, however, its moral authority is contingent as, for example, where it attempts to influence public policy. In secondary institutional spheres its authority is likely to be contested by experts from other disciplines who will approach problems with a different perspective. Likewise, in secondary spheres a profession's moral authority will have marginal influence.[40] Although individuals from the normative professions may have considerable influence in secondary spheres of activity, professional bodies are the main means by which professions seek to influence public policy. Here, professions have a choice in terms of how they claim legitimacy for their views. Large and inclusive professional groups confer a degree of legitimacy on the professional body and, therefore, allow it to speak with authority. The more inclusive professional membership, however, the wider the range of views which are represented. This increases the possibility that the profession will not be able to come to a common view on any issue. Small exclusive bodies can more effectively mobilise their membership. Their problem is that they may lack legitimacy and, therefore, influence.[41] In order for an organisation with a large membership to move beyond legitimacy to effective collective action it must involve its members in a collective project and control the tendency to pursue sectional advantage at the expense of the higher goals the profession may set itself.

Professional bodies have had, historically, a key role in defining, sustaining and promoting the professional ethic. At times when the membership shows common values and assumptions this may be achieved without any participation by the membership. At times in the history of the legal profession this has, perhaps, been seen as quiescent. The role of members is often seen to be to obey the rules, not to make them. But this expectation is built on very fragile foundations:

> "For the effective enforcement of a professional ethic, it is not necessary that all members of the profession adhere to it with total commitment . . . But . . . there must be excellent leadership and good morale. The leadership is necessary to provide definition and application of the professional ethic in constantly changing circumstances; and morale is necessary if this leadership is to be effective. The ordinary members of the profession must respect the leaders according to their criteria of skill and success, and be prepared to accept their guidance and control. Also, they must have some degree of commitment to doing good work, so that a consensus can operate against those who betray the good name of the profession. Otherwise the enforcement of a professional ethic is impossible."[42]

[40] *Ibid.*, at 41–7.
[41] *Ibid.*, at 47–51.
[42] J. R. Ravetz, "Ethics in Scientific Activity" in Flores (ed.), *Professional Ideals* (Belmont, Calif., Wadsworth Publishing Co., 1988) 147.

Effective leadership and consultation are important because the observance of rules depends on the support of members. This support, being easier to achieve when the members of the profession are cohesive, sharing a common purpose and common values[43] is more difficult when the membership has only an occasional interest in governance. Democratic governance, therefore, may foster a sense of "ownership" of the profession's ethic and encourage observance of ethical rules and other norms.[44] As the poor turnout in Law Society elections tends to show, conventional democracy does not guarantee even the limited degree of participation which it notionally permits. Moreover, the difficulty of providing effective leadership is exacerbated by the declining influence of the professional body on government. This is perhaps the reason why, after 40 years of uncontested elections for senior positions in the Law Society, there have been four contested and acrimonious elections in the past four years. As the professional bodies are forced more openly into the role of negotiator and lobbyist, it is more difficult for them to maintain a lofty detachment from the concerns of both the state and its membership.

As a result of the need to combine its representative and regulatory roles the profession faces three problems which hamper its effort to develop its commitment to professional ethics. First, there is the problem of maintaining the image of disinterestedness in investigating and pursuing disciplinary issues. Secondly, there is the problem of providing protection to consumers while promoting individual responsibility among members.[45] Thirdly, there is the problem of representing a diverse constituency and various factions within it. It is to the last of these problems that we now turn. The task of the professional bodies in dealing with these problems is complicated by the fact that one of their key tasks is to articulate the membership's demands for autonomy in the way that they conduct their work.[46]

In Chapter 1 we considered the legitimacy of professional norms of behaviour in terms of wider social norms. We noted that the acceptance of the legitimacy of rules depends on acceptance by practitioners of the legitimacy of the authority propounding the rules. There are different reasons why people accept this kind of domination; because the rules are consistent with the actor's own purposes, because the rules are believed to be worthy in their own right, because they accord with the actor's feelings or emotions or because, by virtue of tradi-

---

[43] Although professional bodies assume responsibility for the ethics of a profession, professionals must also accept responsibility, not only for their own performance, but for the performance of fellow professionals. Membership of professional bodies and local associations is perhaps indicative. In a recent survey of solicitors it was found that over 50% of respondents were not involved with the Law Society or their local law societies: "Law Soc Damned by Members" (1997) 11:22 *The Lawyer*, 3 June at 1.

[44] For a discussion of governance and constitution of the Bar see J. M. Gibson, "The Bar—What Price Democracy?" (1995) *New Law Journal* 16 June.

[45] This is often problematic because financial consequences are spread through insurance. The weakness of compensation funds is that the whole professional group takes responsibility for individual misbehaviour.

[46] Bayles, n. 22 above, at 8. Many critics suggest that this is all that professional bodies achieve and that "what is done is largely trivial or irrelevant, what needs to be done is left unaccomplished": J. C. Payne, "The Weakness of Bar Associations" [1977] *The Journal of the Legal Profession* 55.

tion, observance is habitual.[47] One means of securing legitimacy for regulatory regimes is through participation of the objects of regulation, in this case members of the profession, in the creation of regulation. But the problem here is of securing mutual interpersonal trust between the members of the professional community. Here, the embodiment of the professional project, the professional body must be an appropriate repository of *trust*[48] between the various groups in the professional community. As we saw in Chapter 3, the increasing differentiation of the legal profession creates tensions between the so-called professional elite, whose interests tends to dominate professional bodies and shape the rules of conduct, and the bulk of the membership. There are increasing pressures for professional leaders to be made more accountable to the rank and file.[49] This is an issue we return to at the end of the chapter. For the moment, however, we note that inter-professional conflict is by no means new. Examples of these tensions have occurred throughout the history of the solicitors' branch.

During the periods 1840–50 and 1880–1914 tensions between the London-dominated Law Society and provincial solicitors became severe, particularly when the Law Society was thought not to be defending the conveyancing monopoly or other work sufficiently strongly. Various alliances of provincial law societies threatened the control of the Law Society but failed to gain a significant foothold.[50] As the Law Society struggled to maintain the idea that it advanced the public interest, it became increasingly diffident in defending the profession's interests against the government. The ultimate humiliation occurred when country solicitors' opposition to a land transfer bill forced the government to back down after the Law Society had agreed its terms. Thereafter the Law Society was forced to become more vocal in protecting its members' interests.[51] In the debates regarding the legalisation of trade unions in the late nineteenth century the Law Society increasingly saw its representative role as both legitimate and necessary.

The strains of articulating the views of an increasingly diverse membership have recently become quite severe. In 1995 the election of a President of the Society was contested for the first time since 1954. In an acrimonious election campaign, Martin Mears was elected on a populist ticket to represent the interests of the "ordinary" practitioner. His themes were the damage done to standards of conveyancing by the ending of the solicitors' monopoly, the oversupply of lawyers and the bureaucracy of the Law Society. His period in office highlighted the tension between the elite and the remainder of the profession and his challenge to the liberal establishment both within and outside the Law Society

---

[47] R. Cotterrell, *Law's Community: Legal Theory in Sociological Perspective* (Oxford, Clarendon Press, 1995), particularly at 140, discussing Weber's theory of legitimate domination.
[48] See Chap. 1 and Cotterrell, *ibid.*, particularly at 330 and references to Giddens in Chap. 1.
[49] R. Owen, "The Governance of the Bar: Constitutional Reform" [1997] *Counsel*, May/June at 3.
[50] Sugarman, n. 5 above, at 103.
[51] *Ibid.*, at 115.

excited much disagreement about its role.[52] Thus a lawyer in a large personal injury firm commented:

> "The Law Society under Mears regards itself as a Trade Union to make sure that lawyers earn enough. It isn"t actually looking at how we serve the public. If someone doesn"t start looking at that someone is going to take it away from us."[53]

These tensions are exacerbated where a professional body acts both as regulator and as "trade union"; roles that are increasingly difficult to harmonise. This is particularly so when the threat of external competition has forced the Law Society to become a "central marketing agency for the profession".[54] Moreover, the fact that the leadership of the Law Society has become a political issue reflects deeper problems. As practitioners experience a fall in public esteem, their professional bodies receive more criticism from members. An independent survey conducted for the Law Society in 1997 established that that only 8 per cent of solicitors in private practice felt that the Law Society was doing a good job of promoting the profession to the public and only 21 per cent that it was doing a good job of representing the views of the profession to decision-makers and Parliament.[55] The Law Society, for its part, has emphasised that it cannot accept full responsibility for the fortunes of the profession. A spokesperson for the Law Society said "I fully accept that the Law Society must bat more strongly. Individual solicitors must do so too. The Law Society cannot single-handedly guard and promote the reputation of the profession". One cause for concern in terms of participation and legitimacy therefore is that so few solicitors vote on issues of fundamental importance to the profession.[56] On the issue of whether the Law Society should divide its representative and regulatory role, for example, less than 30 per cent of the membership voted.[57]

The nature of the representative task has, however, fundamentally changed. It is no longer assumed that professions are servants of public need. The Law Society has to counter a flood of research and opinion which undermines the image of ethicality. In an attempt to do so it has developed its own research

---

[52] Henry Hodge, the official Council candidate, was defeated by over 3,000 votes (*The Guardian*, 11 Apr. 1995). On 21 Sept. 1995 Mears proposed a reduction in powers of the Secretary General at a Council Meeting (*The Independent*, 11 Sept. 1995). In Oct. 1995 Mears excited adverse press reaction with attacks on the Equal Opportunities Commission and the Commission for Racial Equality (Lawtel doc. z51024 10 Oct. 1995).

[53] J. Flood, A. Boon, A. Whyte, E. Skordaki, R. Abbey and A. Ash, *Reconfiguring the Market for Advocacy Services: A Case Study of London and Four Fields of Practice* (Research Report for the Lord Chancellor's Advisory Committee on Legal Education and Conduct, 1996), at 55.

[54] Burrage, n. 8 above, at 73.

[55] *The Lawyer*, n. 43 above. A similar survey in 1989 had found that 32% of solicitors thought that the Law Society was good at promoting the profession and 53% that it was good at representing the profession.

[56] Only 23,000, of over 65,000 solicitors eligible to vote voted in the election in the 1995 presidential elections (*The Times*, 11 July 1995), 8,881 (29.8%) voted on the proposal to separate the Law Society's disciplinary and representative function: see N. Hilborne, "Voters Reject Split Society" (*The Gazette*, 16 Oct. 1996 at 1 et seq.).

[57] The vote was rejected and was therefore seen as a desire to retain self-regulation although 40% voted for the division of functions: *ibid*.

capability and has become more "conscious of the need to justify its policies publicly, and to demonstrate how the public and professional interest may be reconciled".[58] Therefore, the multiple tensions in its role are exposed for all to see:

> "the strength and weakness of the Law Society (and the profession) has stemmed from its propensity to express several contradictory tendencies side by side: its claim to act in the general interests of society; its much asserted independence and relative autonomy from external influence, notably that of the state; its "gentlemanly" character, in part sustained by the image of the barrister, its "national" character; its claims to act as an effective pressure group and trade union on behalf of its membership; and its inherent dependence upon and imbrication within the state."[59]

In 1996 the membership of the Law Society rejected a motion which could have led to a formal separation of the regulatory and representative functions.[60] The then President of the Law Society said; "[t]he profession has sent a clear message that solicitors do value self-regulation. It is time to draw a line under this divisive and costly argument".[61] Nevertheless, the separation of the traditional roles of professional governance and professional representation will be increasingly difficult to sustain.

D. ALTERNATIVE MODELS

A number of alternatives to traditional modes of self governance have been suggested. Two will be considered here—individual professional autonomy and legalisation—because they are polar opposites of the present system. The philosophical foundations of the first, professional autonomy, were discussed in Chapter 1 and the implications for legal education are considered in Chapter 6. This model recognises the futility of trying to enforce universal norms and seeks to provide a framework whereby lawyers take greater responsibility for developing their own professional conduct. The second model, legalisation, is the focus of attention in this chapter. Legalisation involves strengthening key principles of conduct by methods of enforcement other than self-regulation. The rules become, in effect, rules of law and give rise to individual rights of action in ordinary courts rather than in disciplinary tribunals. This is quite different from the stated position of the professional bodies, which is that principles of conduct generally *follow* the common law. Legalisation means that the power and publicity of public adjudication is used to ensure professional compliance.

---

[58] Burrage, n. 8 above, at 75.
[59] Sugarman, n. 5 above, at 121.
[60] See the discussion of the proposal in a paper published by Anthony Bogan, leader of the Solicitors' Association (*The Times*, 30 Apr. 1996).
[61] Hilborne, n. 56 above.

Legalisation

Developments in the USA offer a classic example of the incremental legalisation of professional ethics. In 1964 a committee was established by the ABA to draft a new professional code of conduct. This resulted in the Code of Professional Responsibility (CPR) which replaced the 1908 Canons in 1970.[62] The code comprised a three-tier system: Canons, Ethical Considerations and Disciplinary Rules, the last of which were rapidly adopted by 40 states and recognised by federal courts in dealing with lawyers appearing in federal litigation.[63] The authority of age-old rules,[64] "the shared understandings of a substantially cohesive group" were replaced by "rules of public law regulating a widely pursued technical vocation whose constitutional position is now in doubt".[65] The Disciplinary Rules were intended to be adopted by State Bars as an enforceable code. The Ethical Considerations were intended as both a statement and aid to the interpretation of the Disciplinary Rules and as guidance to lawyers in "grey areas". This model was not entirely successful because courts began to interpret the "considerations", as well as the Disciplinary Rules, as binding and enforceable.[66]

In 1980, the Kutak Commission was therefore established to revise the 1970 CPR. It circulated Model Rules of Professional Conduct. These replaced the Code of Professional Responsibility in 1983. The Model Rules retained the idea that they should be enforceable but substituted commentary as a replacement of the ethical considerations. It has been suggested that the Kutak Commission's proposals, by searching for general unifying principles, settled for lowest common denominators.[67] In any event, many states either adopted only parts of the Model Rules or retained the old Code of Professional Responsibility.[68] Moreover, the attempt by the ABA to universalise standards exacerbated problems, exposed differences and encouraged separate bars to go their own ways.[69]

While these political ramifications of legalisation are less likely to arise in the more centralised system of England and Wales, other problems experienced in

---

[62]   The early ethics of the professions were found in "canons of ethics" which took the form of guidance to new members on the behaviour expected by their fellow professionals: Hazard chap. 1 n. 62 at 1250).

[63]   *Ibid.*, at 1251 and n. 63.

[64]   *Ibid.*, at 1255.

[65]   *Ibid.*, at 1279.

[66]   Moreover, the schema concentrated on the adversarial process at the expense of office-based work and the rules on advertising and solicitation were outdated: J. F. Sutton and J. S. Dzienkowski, *Cases and Materials on the Professional Responsibility of Lawyers* (St Paul, Minn., West Publishing Co., 1989) at 20; and see L. R.Patterson, "The Limits of the Lawyer's Discretion and the Law of Legal Ethics: National Student Marketing Revisited" (1979) 6 *Duke Law Journal* 1251.

[67]   T. Schneyer, "Professionalism as Politics: The Making of a Modern Legal Ethics Code" in D. Nelson, R. Trubeck and R. Solomon (eds.), *Lawyers' Ideals/Lawyers' Practices: Transformations in the American Legal Profession* (New York, NY, Cornell University Press, 1992), chap. 3.

[68]   Sutton and Dzienkowski, n. 66 above, McCrate Report, *Legal Education and Professional Development—An Educational Continuum, Report of the Task Force on Law Schools and the Profession: Narrowing the Gap* (Chicago, American Bar Association, 1992).

[69]   Burrage, n. 8 above, at 73.

the USA are likely to be similar. One is that the legalisation of ethical norms (giving them the status of rules of law), actually diminishes their ethical status.[70] They become the same as any other legal rule and their moral quality is thereby diminished. This detracts from the personal responsibility of the practitioner.[71] The profession must therefore exercise care before going down the route of legalising ethical norms. Not only does legalisation of ethics diminish the lawyer's personal responsibility but, once begun, it is unlikely that there can ever be a return to self-regulation. Legalisation can, by reducing ethical responsibility, also legitimise the use of ethically based rules as unethical tactics in litigation. An example of this arises in relation to rules on conflicts of interest which can be used to harass the other side.[72]

Individual Moral Autonomy

Moral autonomy, the principal advocate of which is William Simon,[73] is the reverse of legalisation. Rather than operating within a system of formalised ethical rules, lawyers are asked to exercise their own judgement and discretion in deciding what clients to represent and how to represent them. Lawyers exercising moral autonomy would seek to do justice and would be required to consider the merits of a client's claim relative to those of opposing parties and other potential clients.[74] For example, the lawyer might need to consider the resources available to each side in deciding what behaviour may be justified. Further, "the lawyer must be granted discretion in the representation of a client, sometimes to go beyond the letter of the law, sometimes not to utilise the law to its full extent".[75] This requires lawyers to analyse the substantive merits of a client's claim and the reliability of standard legal procedures for resolving the particular problem. Under this, the "discretionary" approach, rules of conduct are framed as rebuttable presumptions; instructions to behave in a certain way unless the circumstances suggest that the values relevant to the rule would not be served by doing so.

---

[70] Hazard concludes that the bar in the USA is too large, diverse and balkanised in its practice specialities for the old system of governance and will be increasingly subject to regulation, common law, public statutes and external disciplinary agencies: Hazard, chap. 1 n. 62 above, at 1279. It will be noted that these are precisely the forces at work in the UK. And see T. W. Giegerich, "The Lawyer's Moral Paradox" (1979) 6 *Duke Law Journal* 1335.

[71] A simple example has been used to illustrate this. When the judge admonishes the parties in court for some unethical conduct it is often "the plaintiff" or "the defendant" who is criticised rather than their lawyer: L. R.Patterson, "On Analyzing the Law of Legal Ethics: An American Perspective" (1981) 16:1 *Israel Law Review* 28 at 32.

[72] J. Flood, "The Cultures of Globalisation: Professional Restructuring for the International Market" in Y. Dezalay and D. Sugarman (eds.), *Professional Competition and Professional Power: Lawyers Accountants and the Social Construction of Markets* (London, Routledge, 1995),at 139.

[73] Simon, n. 32 above.

[74] Ibid., at 1090.

[75] Patterson, n. 71 above, at 35.

The value of the discretionary approach is that it addresses the central weakness of the regulatory approach, namely that ethical responsibility is simply a question of following rules,[76] and also the central weakness of the libertarian approach, the tendency to limit lawyers' responsibilities to clients only. There are, however, risks. These include the potential harm to the client which may result from any failure by the lawyer to prioritise his or her interests and the potential subversion of the client's role in exercising judgement. There is a risk that lawyer-power is increased and that the client has no clear idea of how the lawyer may choose to interpret her ethical obligations. The relationship of trust between lawyer and client could break down if lawyers were perceived to abuse ethical autonomy. Acting ethically would become more complex, more a question of individual judgement and, less susceptible to external criticism. Therefore, while the adoption of a philosophy of ethical discretion would strengthen the lawyer's own "ethical autonomy", there is a substantial risk that this kind of ethical regime would cause confusion. It is therefore unlikely to be acceptable to the profession as a whole or to the public. Nevertheless, an adaptation of the notion of moral autonomy is perhaps necessary if ethics, as opposed to regulation, is to survive. We consider this idea in more detail at the end of Chapter 6.

E. THE REVIEW AND REFORM OF PROFESSIONAL ETHICS

In general, the development of professional ethics in England and Wales has proceeded in a piecemeal way with little debate or consultation with the profession as a whole or with outsiders. The advantages, and perils, of a more public review of the ethics of a legal profession were demonstrated by the process adopted by the Kutak Commission for its review of the ABA's ethics code in 1977.[77] The process encouraged an association mainly comprised of personal injury lawyers to propose the adoption of a code that they had developed and, in effect, to challenge the authority of the ABA to make ethical rules for the whole profession. In the result, compromise was reached. On one view the process was intensely political and divisive, presenting an image to the public of a profession at odds with itself, unable to agree on the most fundamental principles. On the other hand the process by which the Kutak Commission produced the Model Rules of Professional Conduct has been described as the "most sustained and democratic debate about professional ethics in the history of the American bar".[78] It could therefore be justified on the grounds that it engendered participation, exposed, and helped to reconcile, differences and claimed increased legitimacy for the rules produced. It is worth considering the process adopted by Kutak in more detail.

---

[76] J. Ladd, "Legalism and Medical Ethics" in Flores (ed.), n. 14 above, at 96.
[77] Schneyer, supra n. 67 above, at 95.
[78] *Ibid*.

The first stage of the Kutak review, beginning in 1977 and ending with the publication of a discussion draft in 1980, operated under conditions of secrecy. This was partially to ensure that the shape of the new model rules could emerge before interest groups within the profession began to shape them. At this stage the Commission sought to address academic criticism of existing rules, particularly that they went too far in prioritising client interests over those of third parties. It also garnered lay comment and fostered relations with the press.[79] Early drafts included some radical provisions. These increased accountability to third parties in non-contentious proceedings,[80] including imposing an obligation to warn of the threat of serious bodily injury by clients. They extended the duty to the court by imposing a duty to draw the judge's attention to adverse evidence which would have a substantial impact on a material issue of fact.[81] They imposed a mandatory *pro bono* obligation.[82]

The leaking of the first draft of the Kutak proposals before the end of the first stage caused uproar and almost persuaded the ABA to abandon the project. A compromise was struck when a nine-month adjournment was agreed so that Bar interest groups could consider the proposals. Between the end of the first stage and final stage Kutak's radical proposals were considerably diluted following fierce debate and political struggle within the profession.[83] The criticism which apparently caused the most damage was made by the small but influential American College of Trial Lawyers. It charged that Kutak's proposals, particularly in so far as they undermined the obligation of confidentiality, were contrary to both the adversary system and effective legal representation. But neither the process of revision nor the concerns of the Kutak Commission, as might have been expected, were monopolised by elite firms.[84] While this may be taken to challenge the theory that such firms in fact dominate ethical rule formation, it perhaps illustrates something more limited. Given an extensive and overtly democratic process of rule revision, organisations and interest groups representing the views of small firm lawyers could bring considerable pressure to bear. It is not clear how far they can do so within the more secretive and incremental processes of rule revision favoured by the legal profession in England and Wales.

The passage of the Kutak proposals suggests that any legal profession should be very cautious before embarking on a root and branch reformation of its professional ethics. Such a move may be welcomed on the grounds that it would stimulate debate and thought and force the profession to articulate what it really thought about ethics; it would be a sign that ethics are at least taken seriously by the legal profession. Alternatively, the process could be divisive and counterproductive in terms of public relations. It would almost certainly stir up and

---

[79] *Ibid.*, at 97.
[80] See Chap. 8.
[81] See Chap. 14.
[82] See Chap. 9.
[83] The second stage ended with the presentation of a proposed final draft in 1981. The final stage ended with the adoption by the ABA of the model rules in 1983.
[84] *Ibid.*, at 141.

exacerbate internal divisions in the profession and invite press criticism and public controvery. For these reasons a compromise process may be preferred whereby the views of practitioners and others are sought before any drafts are produced. Such a public consultation would enable the rules to be revised and given the coherence and rationale which many critics claim they currently lack. The process could also have an educative function. This dimension of a possible review process is considered in Chapter 6.

CONCLUSION

Burrage predicts that, as the work of the profession becomes more diverse, and the status and circumstances of solicitors becomes more differentiated, the problems of governance will become more extreme.[85] One change, brought about by the pressure on the profession to account for itself as a public body, is a perceptible shift from a prevailing libertarian philosophy to one which is increasingly regulatory in matters of conduct. There have been considerable efforts, in the solicitors' branch in particular, to revise and enlarge the rules and principles of conduct. But there has been no obvious or open debate with practitioners, or with the lay recipients of legal services, about the guiding principles of the profession's ethics. This could make a significant contribution to the development of the professional ethics of lawyers because participation potentially increases the legitimacy of the profession's efforts to regulate itself in the eyes of both its members and the public. In the meantime, there continue to be demands from outside the legal profession that it should be stripped of all powers of self-regulation,[86] that the profession share the burden of self-regulation with other professions[87] or that there should be other adjustments to the existing system.[88] To assess these claims we must examine the existing system in more detail.

[85] Burrage, n. 8 above, at 73.
[86] R. Lindsay, "Fabian Society Calls for End to OSS", *The Lawyer*, 2 June 1998 and "OSS backlog leak fuels new row", *The Lawyer* 9 December 1998 at 1.
[87] "Law Society to Hear Super Watchdog Plan", *The Lawyer*, 24 Mar. 1998.
[88] S. Pye, "OSS Admits to Substandard Service as Complaints Surge", *The Lawyer*, 24 Mar. 1998 at 1.

5

The Regulatory Structure in England and Wales

"Bar Associations are notoriously reluctant to disbar or even suspend a member unless he has murdered a judge down town at high noon, in the presence of the entire Committee on Ethical Practices."[1]

A. INTRODUCTION

The historical and philosophical context of professional self-regulation, and the role of the professional body in this process, was discussed in the last chapter. This chapter is intended to be largely descriptive of the current regulatory structure for barristers and solicitors in England and Wales. Each branch has its own professional body. The General Council of the Bar regulates barristers, both practising and employed. Its current structure dates from 1985. It has 98 members and three officers. The Law Society, which is a statutory body, governs solicitors. It works through a Council consisting of 70 members, 56 elected by the profession and 14 by the Council for their specialist knowledge.

As has been seen in the previous chapters, the claim of the profession to regulate its own affairs, promulgate its own rules and discipline its members free from outside interference can create many problems and tensions. There is little agreement on whether this element of professional autonomy is in itself desirable. If it is desirable it is not clear what combination of self-regulation and external regulation and review is optimum. Nor is it clear what, if anything, should be required from the profession in return for regulatory autonomy. Presumably a minimum requirement is that the system of self-regulation should work effectively and efficiently in the interests of the profession, its members and the public at large. Reconciling these potential conflicts presents a number of problems.

One example relates to the profession's claim that, in the public interest, it subjects its members to internal disciplinary processes which are additional to the normal legal processes that bind everyone else. The public therefore enjoys double protection and the profession endures double jeopardy. The implication is that standards are thereby effectively upheld. But, in almost the same breath, the profession also claims immunity from suit in relation to negligence

[1] S. J. Harris, quoted in M. Teigh Bloom, *The Trouble with Lawyers* (New York: Simon and Schuster, 1968). 157.

connected to advocacy. This immunity, upheld in *Rondel* v. *Worsley* in 1967,[2] has not been seriously challenged in any of the reviews of the legal profession that have taken place since 1969.[3] The Bar also claims immunity from contractual liability.[4] Ironically, these immunities have been used by the profession to limit (rather than expand) the scope of its own internal complaints procedures so as to exclude complaints about advocacy, as is explained later in this chapter. Double jeopardy gives way to no jeopardy at all.

In other contexts it is true that the legal profession often faces more controls than the lay public, but these are imposed by the courts rather than the professional body. Court control via taxation of costs and the wasted costs jurisdiction are examples. Moreover, the court exercises a general summary jurisdiction controlling the conduct of solicitors who fail to fulfil their duty to the court. The remedy is discretionary and can include an order that the solicitor compensate the applicant in some way. This jurisdiction provides an alternative to suing the lawyer in contract or tort and has procedural advantages for the applicant.[5]

In relation to the professions' rule-making powers, it has already been noted that their autonomy in this context has been limited by the provisions of the Courts and Legal Services Act 1990 (CLSA) and the setting up of the Lord Chancellor's Advisory Committee on Legal Education and Conduct (ACLEC). Changes in the rules relating to rights of audience and the conduct of litigation must now be approved by the Lord Chancellor and the four designated judges. They act after receiving advice from ACLEC, which consists of both lawyers and non-lawyers.[6] Although the Committee's functions are advisory only, its existence means that, for the first time, the professional bodies must submit changes in their rules to outside scrutiny and comment. This system represents a compromise; the government originally wanted all professional rules to be made by the Lord Chancellor.[7]

The role of ACLEC is now under attack from the Government itself. In the Access to Justice Bill 1998 the Lord Chancellor proposes that ACLEC be abolished. He considers that it had not furthered the objectives of the 1990 Courts

---

[2] [1967] 1 AC 191. See also *Saif Ali* v. *Mitchell* [1978] 3 All ER 1033; *Kelley* v. *Corsten* [1997] 4 All ER 466; and *Atwell* v. *Perry & Co.* [1998] 4 All ER 65.

[3] On the contrary, the Courts and Legal Services Act 1990 extends this immunity to anyone acquiring advocacy rights under the Act: see s.62. For recent cases on immunity in relation to solicitors see *Smith* v. *Linshalls*, 1996, *New Law Journal* 16 February; *Acton* v. *Pearce* [1997] 3 All ER 909; and *Atwell* v. *Perry & Co.*, n. 2 above.

[4] The power conferred by the CLSA 1990, s.61, to allow barristers to make contracts has been overridden by the *Bar Code of Conduct*, under a power also conferred by the CLSA. See *Code of Conduct of the Bar of England and Wales* (London, The General Council of the Bar of England and Wales, 1997), Annex D, paras. 25 and 26, hereafter *The Bar Code*.

[5] See *Myers* v. *Elman* [1939] 4 All ER 484; *Udall* v. *Capri Lighting Ltd.* [1987] 3 All ER 262. See also Hon. A. D. Ipp, "Lawyers' Duties to the Court" (1998) 114 *Law Quarterly Review* 63.

[6] See CLSA 1990, Sched. 4, for the complex procedure which it is not proposed to detail in this book.

[7] See A. Crawley and C. Bramall, "Professional Rules, Codes and Principles Affecting Solicitors (or What has Professional Regulation to do with Ethics?)" in R. Cranson (ed.), *Legal Ethics and Professional Responsibility* (Oxford, Clarendon Press, 1995), 99 at 101.

and Legal Services Act to develop new means of providing legal services but had upheld the *status quo*. This, of course, was what the profession had hoped for. The Lord Chancellor is also concerned by the amount of time it took to obtain approval for any change. Accordingly he proposes just what the profession managed to avoid in 1990—namely that changes in rules on rights of audience should require the consent of the Lord Chancellor only. He will take advice from the designated judges and also from a newly formed Legal Services Consultative Panel. The final decision, however, will be his alone.[8]

There are also other challenges on the horizon. For example, it is proposed to remove the Law Society's recently acquired powers to regulate solicitors who act as financial advisors. The Home Secretary also threatened to set up a statutory body to regulate immigration lawyers and advisers because of the unsatisfactory and sometimes unscrupulous service provided by some organisations in this field.[9] This threat has receded a little but has not been abandoned.[10]

B. SOLICITORS

The Rules and Regulations

The formal position in England and Wales on the ethical rules governing solicitors is somewhat confusing. Solicitors claim to be subject to special rules of ethics and conduct imposed upon them by their professional body. In fact the majority of these rules of professional conduct are to be found either in the ordinary law, such as that on contract, agency or trusts, or in statutes or statutory instruments specifically concerned with solicitors. The main statute directly affecting solicitors is the Solicitors' Act 1974. Other rules are to be found in delegated legislation made, not by a government department, but by the Council of the Law Society under the 1974 or similar Acts.[11] Examples are the Solicitors' Practice Rules 1990 and the Accounts Rules. The profession's claim to autonomy in relation to professional conduct therefore rests substantially on this rule-making power. These Rules are proposed by the Law Society and must be approved by the Master of the Rolls (or, in the case of rules relating to investment business, the Securities and Investment Board). In the case of rules relating to solicitors' advocacy rights and litigation generally, advice must be sought from ACLEC, as noted above, and also from the Director General of Fair Trading. Such rules must be approved by the four designated judges and the

---

[8] Consultation Paper, *Rights of Audience and Rights to Conduct Litigation: The Way Ahead* (London, Lord Chancellor's Department, June 1998), chap. 4. The Access to Justice Bill received its first reading in December 1998.

[9] Consultation Paper from the Home Office, Jan. 1998. See *The Lawyer*, 27 Jan. 1998.

[10] See *The Lawyer*, 4 July 1998, and *Improving the Quality of Immigration Advice and Representation A Report* (London, The Lord Chancellor's Advisory Committee on Legal Education and Conduct, July 1998), especially para. 7.3.

[11] See the Solicitors' Act 1974 ss.32–34.

Lord Chancellor under Schedule 4 of the CLSA 1990. The Law Society has the power to waive many of the rules in individual circumstances, which is a significant self-regulatory power.

Apart from this power of waiver, it might be thought that these rules would be binding in the same way as any other delegated legislation provided they are *intra vires*. However, the courts do not seem to follow this line. First, it has been held that the fact that the Solicitors' Practice Rules prohibit a practice does not, by itself, mean that the practice is illegal.[12] In *Giles* v. *Thompson*, Lord Mustill stated that the rules (or at least those banning contingency fees) were simply rules of professional conduct. Secondly, Lord Justice Millett in *Thai Trading Co.* v. *Taylor* stated that the rules "are based on a perception of public policy derived from judicial decisions". In that case he overturned those judicial decisions on public policy grounds and so he also, in effect, declared the relevant Solicitors' Practice Rule to be inapplicable.[13] It is not clear whether the Disciplinary Tribunal (or any other adjudicatory body) has the power to take the same view as the courts.

Other professional guidance is to be found in codes issued under the rules, such as the Solicitors' Publicity Code. Their legal status is even more debatable, as is the case with many other codes of guidance issued under statutory authority. Conventionally they are regarded as not being binding.[14] However, in common with many other varieties of guidance that now proliferate, adverse legal consequences may well follow for those who disregard it. As the Law Societys *Guide* firmly notes, Law Society guidance "is treated as authoritative by the Adjudication and Appeals Committee [now the Compliance and Supervision Committee], the Solicitors' Disciplinary Tribunal and the Court". "Authoritative" does not necessarily mean binding, and these bodies could conclude that such guidance was either contrary to law or inappropriate in some other way if the issue came before them. Breach of the guidance could clearly be the basis of, or evidence of, a complaint or disciplinary allegation, but is not conclusive of the issue.[15]

The Law Society also issues less formal guidance, ranging from the notes added to the discussion of the "principles" laid down in the *Guide to Professional Conduct*, to the more formal guidance laid down from time to time. An example is the guidance contained in the Written Standards on Costs. Such guidance is not regarded as authoritative in the sense that to disregard it would be a disciplinary offence (although in fact such guidance sometimes encapsulates a legal rule and as such is binding). Disregard of informal guidance

---

[12]   See *Picton Jones & Co.* v. *Arcadia Developments Ltd*. [1989] 1 EGLR 43 and *Thai Trading Co.* v. *Taylor* [1998] 3 All ER 65 at 69.

[13]   [1998] 3 All ER 65. In this case the relevant rule was r. 8 of the 1990 Rules relating to contingency fees. A contrary view has subsequently been expressed by the Divisional Court in *Hughes v. Kingston upon Hull City Council*, 9 November 1998, LAWTEL. For further details see Chap. 12 on Fees and Costs.

[14]   See H. W. R.Wade, *Administrative Law* (Oxford, Clarendon, 1994), at 857; also R. Baldwin and D. Houghton [1986] *Public Law* 239.

[15]   See below on the definition of "conduct unbecoming" in the context of disciplinary proceedings.

might well be evidence of a good cause for a complaint. It would be evidence which might be considered in proving a disciplinary offence or evidence of actionable negligence. Finally, guidance on conduct may be sought from the actual decisions made by the Disciplinary Tribunal and related bodies, who tend to follow precedent.

The Law Society's published *Guide to the Professional Conduct of Solicitors* dates from 1960 and contains all these varieties of laws, rules and guidance. The Society also issues regular *Professional Standards Bulletins* and additional guidance from time to time to keep all its rules and guidance up to date.[16] The problem for the novice is to find a way through this morass of material. This is not easy, as the Legal Services Ombudsman has pointed out.[17] The *Guide* itself speaks of the rules being sometimes "based on a common law ethical requirement".[18] The latter is an odd phrase implying that the common law creates ethical rules as opposed to some other form of rule. In fact, of course, ethical considerations, broadly conceived, may form the basis of common law rules, but their binding force derives from their accepted legality as the common law and not from any assumed ethical basis. Some of the non-statutory guidance issued by the Law Society is stated to be based on "an interpretation of statutory rules".[19] On normal principles such interpretation could be challenged in the courts, but the *Guide* nevertheless claims that all the "requirements of professional conduct", statutory and non-statutory, will be treated as authoritative by the courts and the disciplinary tribunal.

Finally the *Guide* also states that the rules of professional conduct should not be "confused with the requirements of the general law of contract or tort or . . . criminal law". But a large number of the rules as stated in the *Guide* are in fact part of that general law as applied in the particular context of solicitor and client. This law is, of course, constantly changing and growing so that rules, which may well have been regarded originally as being in some way based on ethical principles rather than legal requirements, have become incorporated into the law. An example of this can be seen in the developing law on confidentiality and legal privilege. Crawley and Bramall, who work in the Professional Ethics Division of the Law Society, plead for a broad approach: "[t]he codes of conduct . . . should not be treated as if they were tax statutes to be scrutinised for loopholes. They establish rights and responsibilities that must be viewed broadly and in the spirit".[20] This approach is essential if the codes are to be properly regarded as embodying *ethical* obligations, as was noted in the last chapter.

[16] In addition there is a regular column in the *Law Society Gazette* answering professional ethics queries from solicitors.
[17] See both the 1995 and 1996 *Annual Reports*.
[18] Para. 1.03, n. 3.
[19] N. Taylor (ed.), *The Guide to the Professional Conduct of Solicitors* (London, The Law Society, 1996), at para. 1.03 n.3, hereafter *The Law Society Guide*.
[20] In Cranston, n. 7 above, at 103.

The *Law Society Guide* adopts the following organisation. Each chapter contains a number of basic principles printed in bold type. These are followed by explanatory notes. A number of appendices to each chapter expand the material. It is not always clear where the legal or other authority for these basic principles comes from. Some of them are clearly to be found in the Statutory Rules, such as rule 1 which "sums up the basic principles of practice" governing solicitors.[21] Other principles are clearly solely advisory, e.g. "an employed solicitor in putting forward a claim for costs against a third party, must have regard to the proper indemnity basis for costs",[22] or just provide information, for example, the statement that "[s]olicitors may offer ADR services as part of their practice". Others represent clear statutory obligations, for example, Principle 5.03 which states that a solicitor is under a duty to report certain information about his client's circumstances to the Legal Aid Board. This is contained in the relevant Legal Aid regulations. Others are based on common law but provide very little help to solicitors seeking to work out their legal or ethical obligations, for example, Principle 16.02, which states that confidentiality can be overridden in "certain exceptional circumstances". A particular problem is ascertaining what are really the *basic* principles that the Law Society considers underlie the rules of ethical professional practice as often these are not stated, and certainly not elaborated or debated in the *Guide*. It is hoped that Parts III, IV and V of this book will provide some assistance with this in relation to key ethical obligations and areas of practice.

Authority to Practise

Solicitors, once they have satisfied all the educational and other requirements and been admitted by the Law Society, cannot lawfully practise without holding a current practising certificate.[23] Practising means holding oneself out to be a solicitor in private practice or otherwise, or undertaking for a fee certain activities which are the monopoly of solicitors, such as executing certain conveyancing documents (a function now shared with licensed conveyancers), probate documents and the administration of oaths. Under sections 20 and 21 of the 1974 Act no unqualified person shall "act as a solicitor" or pretend to be a solicitor. Both are criminal offences.

Solicitors can practise in partnership with other solicitors or as sole practitioners. They cannot practise as limited companies or as partners with other professionals.[24] Neither can they practise on their own for the first three years after admission. Practising certificates are issued by the Law Society annually on payment of the appropriate fee (currently £430) and a contribution to the

---

[21] *Law Society Guide*, n. 19 above, at 2. See Chap. 1, p. 20.
[22] *Ibid.*, para. 4.07.
[23] Solicitors' Act 1974 s.1, see Chap. 6 below, on educational requirements.
[24] On multidisciplinary partnerships, see Chap. 3 above.

Solicitors' Compensation Fund. It must also be shown, where appropriate, that the solicitor has complied with the Indemnity Rules. In general the issue of a certificate is automatic if the conditions are fulfilled. However the Law Society can issue conditional certificates where:

- there has been lapse of over 12 months in taking out a practising certificate;
- there is a failure to satisfy the Office for the Supervision of Solicitors;
- the solicitor has entered into a composition with creditors; or
- there has been late delivery of an accountant's report.[25]

There is a requirement, under the Training Regulations 1990, that all newly qualified solicitors undertake continuing education for the first three years. This was extended to all solicitors from November 1998. A practising certificate will be refused if the Society is not satisfied that the Training Regulations 1990, *inter alia*, have been complied with.[26] This sanction has never been applied in this context, however, and it is suggested by ACLEC that some lesser penalties might be devised for non-compliance, such as financial sanctions or taking non-compliance into account where there are other disciplinary proceedings against the solicitor.[27]

Accounts rules visits can be made to a solicitor by the monitoring unit of the Law Society, and there were 1,144 such visits in 1996.[28] Where a breach of the accounts rules is discovered a reference can be made to the OSS (see below) or it can result in a refusal of or restriction on the practising certificate.

Dealing with Client Complaints

Apart from the processes that accompany the yearly issue of practising certificates, the main way by which the profession enforces its ethical and regulatory rules is by receiving, investigating and acting on complaints received from clients or, sometimes, from other solicitors. The Law Society can also act on its own initiative and sometimes does so where there is a risk of public scandal. A recent example is the case of multi-murderer Frederick West's solicitor. He proposed to write a book on his client's case and was subject to disciplinary proceedings for breach of confidentiality. Another example occured in relation to the proposed take-over of the Co-operative Wholesale Society where it was alleged that the solicitors for a predator investor acted on the basis of documents they knew were confidential and stolen.[29]

---

[25] Solicitors' Act 1974 ss.10 and 12 and *Law Society Guide*, n. 19 above, para. 2.05.
[26] See Solicitors' Act 1974 s.10.
[27] *Continuing Professional Development for Solicitors and Barristers* (London, The Lord Chancellor's Advisory Committee on Legal Education and Conduct, 1997), at para. 2.25.
[28] Law Society, *Annual Report* 1996–7 at 11.
[29] See *The Lawyer*, 6 May 1997.

The way the Law Society has dealt with complaints against solicitors has been a source of conflict and criticism for many years.[30] The Government recognised this criticism in the 1989 Green Papers. The Solicitors' Complaints Bureau (SCB) was seen to be slow and insufficiently independent of the Law Society. It would not deal with complaints of negligence as the Law Society considered that these should be dealt with by the courts. It would, however, deal with shoddy work, but this concept was not defined in written professional standards and clients found it difficult to establish that work was shoddy to the satisfaction of the SCB. Clients also found it difficult to perceive the difference between negligence and shoddy work. Indeed it is difficult even for lawyers to draw a clear line between them. In any case the layperson considers negligence to be just the kind of serious conduct that should be dealt with by a profession claiming to be self-regulating. It seemed odd that when an allegation is made about a solicitor which directly affects the client, the profession suddenly abandons its insistence on self-regulation and tells the client to take his chance in the courts, a course of action that will be costly, lengthy and wearing to the complainant who will also have to rely for help on a member of the profession about whom he is complaining. Criticisms of the SCB, however, were not limited to the scope of its jurisdiction.

Communications to complainants from the Bureau were legalistic and often perceived to be evasive and protective of solicitors. Such criticisms showed, according to both the Lord Chancellor's Department and the National Consumer Council, that self-regulation in the profession was not working.[31] In his last report, covering the work of the SCB for 1996, the Legal Services Ombudsman, Michael Barnes, repeated many of these criticisms and gave the following example of the way the Bureau could approach a complaint. A woman had complained about the way her solicitors had handled her divorce:

> "She had clearly listed her complaints as 'lack of information about costs, incorrect advice and failure to comply with instructions'. The SCB told her that they could not become involved until 'the possibility of negligence had been canvassed' ".

The Ombudsman took the view that there were here clear allegations of failure to adhere to the now written professional standards which should have been investigated by the SCB.[32] In his conclusions to his 1996 Report he noted, "[i]n . . . 1995 . . . I expressed the view that, unless the professional bodies were able to deliver a higher level of consumer satisfaction with the way that complaints were dealt with, it was unlikely that self regulatory complaints handling would

---

[30] For the most recent see the reports of the Legal Services Ombudsman for 1996 and 1997. Even the Benson Commission on Legal Services in 1979, which was notoriously gentle with the legal profession, made criticisms: see chap. 22 of the Report. See also the National Consumer Council Report, *Ordinary Justice* (London, HMSO, 1989).

[31] See p. 105 above, the NCC report, *ibid.*, and the 1995 Annual Report of the Legal Services Ombudsman and the complaint of Conrad Burnham described in the *New Law Journal*, March 1997.

[32] *1996 Annual Report*, at para. 3.9.

survive into the next century". In the 1997 Annual Report the newly appointed Ombudsman, Ann Abraham, warned that poor communication in dealing with complaints "pervades the dealing of both practitioners and the professional bodies with clients and complainants [which] suggests a . . . significant and deep-rooted introspection which fails to engage with the legitimate expectations of the contemporary consumer of legal services".[33]

Solicitors also were not happy with the SCB which they saw as an expensive public relations disaster which did not protect them but leaned in favour of clients. The SCB cost £13,213 million in 1994–5, a rise of 23.4 per cent on the previous year.[34] The creation of the Office for the Supervision of Solicitors (OSS) in 1996, was a response to this widespread dissatisfaction. It represents a last chance to retain a measure of self-regulation for solicitors in the field of complaints.[35]

Complaints are now dealt with under Practice Rule 15, which came into force in May 1991, and by the Office for the Supervision of Solicitors (OSS), which replaced the SCB in September 1996. Practice Rule 15 requires every solicitors' firm to set up a complaints procedure for clients. The nature of the procedure is not prescribed by the rules. Clients must be informed about the system unless they are established clients who will already know of it. Clients must be given details of which member of the firm is handling their affairs. Solicitors are encouraged to deal with complaints themselves in order to minimise the number that reach the OSS, which, in its old persona as the SCB, was becoming overwhelmed with work, receiving some 20,000 complaints a year. The Law Society advises that the complaints system should be set out in writing. It should specify to whom the complaint should be made, which may be a senior partner, a supervisor of the solicitor handling the issue or even someone outside the practice. The investigation should be prompt, 14 days is recommended, and an explanation should be given to the client. Staff should all be made aware of the procedures and records kept. It is, however, clear that many solicitors are not complying with these requirements. In 1997 86 per cent of all firms stated that they had a formal complaints procedure, but in the case of single partner firms, only 66 per cent had complied with this requirement. Only 29 per cent of solicitors had received any training in handling complaints.[36] One study of solicitors' complaints handling has shown that very few complaints enter the formal system operating in solicitors' offices. The formal system was felt to be over-elaborate and unworkable in small firms. The researchers concluded that it is "probably a mistake to press solicitors to adopt systems which do not accord

[33] See article in *Legal Action*, Aug. 1998, at 8. Nevertheless in the 1997 Report the Ombudsman considered that complaints handling had improved but there was still "a long way to go".

[34] Solicitors' Complaint Bureau, *Annual Report 1995*, at 17.

[35] Complaints rose sharply at the end of 1997 and the delays in dealing with them have, again, become unacceptable: *The Lawyer*, 24 Mar. 1998.

[36] Client Care Survey reported in the *Law Society Gazette*, 25 June 1997, at 26.

with their sense of professional obligation, and which, in the context of their particular practice, do not make economic sense".[37]

The Office for the Supervision of Solicitors (OSS)

The OSS was set up by the Law Society using its powers under the Solicitors' Act 1974 and the Law Society Charter. Whilst it is funded by the Law Society, the OSS claims independence from it, a situation which was approved by the Law Society Council. It reports to the Compliance and Supervision Committee of the Law Society which consists of 23 members appointed by the Master of the Rolls, ten of whom must be laypersons. By including laypersons it is hoped that the independence of the OSS will be guaranteed. The Compliance Committee can refer a complaint to the Disciplinary Tribunal.

The OSS has 200 staff. They are divided into the Office for Client Relations and the Office for Professional Regulation. They operate through two sub-committees; the Client Relations sub-committee (chaired by a layperson) and the Professional Regulation Sub-Committee with a solicitor chair. The Client Relations sub-committee receives complaints relating to standards of service and also deals with reviews of solicitors' bills.[38] The Professional Regulation sub-committee deals with complaints and other work relating to professional regulation and conduct, such as practising certificates and the accounting rules. It deals with the serious cases and cases brought before the Solicitors' Disciplinary Tribunal. Complaints about service can generally be received from clients only about their own solicitors, not from third parties affected by the conduct of another's solicitors. However where the complaint is about a breach of the rules of professional conduct, non-clients may complain. Other solicitors have a duty to report their fellow solicitors under principle 19.03 where there is any "serious misconduct". The OSS is very wary of complaints from lay non-clients, however, and warns that "most complaints we receive about someone else's solicitor cannot be investigated further".[39]

In relation to complaints about standards of service, the aim is that a single member of staff sees the complaint through from start to finish, in order to resolve the issue fairly, preferably with agreement and without the need for a formal investigation. The OSS is most anxious to cut down on the need for investigations. It has set up a "hotline" to help solicitors who are complained about to resolve the issue speedily with their clients. Conciliation is therefore the key but, if this is not possible, then a more formal investigation will be launched.

[37] See G. Davis, C. Christensen, S. Day and J. Worthington, "The Client as Consumer" (1998) *New Law Journal* 832. They recognise that political pressure forced the complaints system on the Law Society. The Law Society view is that the failure of in-house complaints systems creates the impossible workload for the OSS: see *The Lawyer*, 7 July 1998 and A. Darling "Firms 'Failing' on Client Complaints" (1998) *Gazette* 95/21 28 May, 1.
[38] On which see Chap. 10 on fees and costs.
[39] *This is the Office for the Supervision of Solicitors* (OSS Leaflet, 1996).

The OSS aims to be both consumer-friendly and to "serve solicitors fairly, acting as a guardian of their professional standards".[40] Complaints have risen recently, and delays in dealing with them are still a problem.[41] In yet another attempt to improve the system the Law Society is now considering proposals to introduce a "fast track" system. A period of only two weeks will be allowed for conciliation of the complaint, and if this does not succeed the solicitor will have a period of 21 days to respond to the substance of the complaint. A decision by the OSS will then be made. The penalty for failure to comply with complaints provisions will increase to £1,000. A case-handling fee is also being considered, to be paid by the solicitor complained of.

Powers of the OSS

The Office can require a solicitor to produce files. Failure to do so can amount to professional misconduct, as can failure to deal adequately with a complaint. Having investigated a complaint and upheld it in whole or in part, the main powers of the OSS are:

1. To issue a rebuke to the solicitor;
2. In the case of inadequate professional services, to disallow costs, require any error to be rectified or order the solicitor to undertake any other action in the client's interests, and order compensation of up to £1,000;
3. To refuse a practising certificate or impose conditions on it;
4. To intervene in the practice under the Solicitors' Act 1974, Schedule 1 (which confers extensive powers, sometimes requiring the leave of the court, to control money, documents and other matters);
5. To institute disciplinary proceedings against the solicitor.[42]

An appeal can be made to the Appeals Adjudications Committee. In 1996 the OSS made 1,568 original decisions of which 287 were appealed, 67 successfully.[43]

The Solicitors' Disciplinary Tribunal (SDT)

Further details of the jurisdiction and procedure of this tribunal can be found in a guide by Barrie Swift, a former President of the SDT.[44] This Tribunal is constituted under the Solicitors' Act 1974 section 46.[45] It is independent of the Law Society though funded by it. The 24 members of the SDT are appointed by the Master of the Rolls and eight of them are lay members. Three members,

---

[40] *Ibid.*
[41] There are now 30,000 per year. *New Law Journal*, December 4 1998.
[42] The full powers are listed in the *Law Society Guide,* n. 19 above, at 684.
[43] *Law Society Gazette*, 8 Oct. 1997.
[44] B. Swift, *Proceedings Before the Solicitors' Disciplinary Tribunal* (London, The Law Society, 1996).
[45] As amended by the Administration of Justice Act 1985 and the CLSA 1990.

including one lay person, sit for each hearing. It sits in public, and evidence is given on oath. The tribunal has powers to compel attendance.[46] Anyone may apply to the tribunal in relation to an allegation of conduct unbefitting a solicitor. The usual applicant is the Law Society itself or the OSS. The latter may make the application only where the issue relates to breaches of the rules such as the accounts rules or those relating to practising certificates.

Unbefitting Conduct

The tribunal adopts the criteria for unbefitting conduct which was laid down in *Re A Solicitor*.[47] This includes reprehensible conduct "such as to be regarded as deplorable by his fellows in the profession". In the words of Barrie Swift, it must be "[a] serious and reprehensible departure from the proper standards of a solicitor as a professional".[48] Mere negligence is not enough. The primary issue whether there has been a violation of one of the principles laid down in the *Law Society Guide* though this test is neither exhaustive nor conclusive. The *Guide* is "a Highway Code" for solicitors.[49] Swift also warns that what was considered unbefitting conduct 20 years ago might not be so today. Normally an element of culpability is required but "impecuniosity will not excuse failure to discharge a professional liability".[50] Conduct prior to admission can be used to establish unbefitting conduct.[51]

Procedure

The tribunal makes its own procedural rules, which are currently the Solicitors' (Disciplinary Proceedings) Rules 1994, with the consent of the Master of the Rolls. It is not proposed to go through these here. The proceedings are public, formal and court-like.

Powers

These can be found in full in the Solicitors Act 1974 section 47 and include:

- striking a solicitor off the roll;
- suspension from practice indefinitely or for a fixed period;
- a fine of up to £5,000 for each established allegation;
- exclusion from legal aid work permanently or for a fixed period;
- the issue of a reprimand;
- an order for payment of costs.

[46] See the Solicitors' (Disciplinary Proceedings) Rules 1994 and Solicitors' Act 1974 s.46(11).
[47] [1972] 2 All ER 811.
[48] Swift, n. 44 above, at 12.
[49] *Ibid.*, at 13.
[50] *Ibid.*, at 17.
[51] *Re A Solicitor* (Co/2860196), May 1997, *Current Law* 421.

The tribunal has no authority to act in relation to the issue of practising certificates, but it may make recommendations to the Law Society to impose conditions on the issue of a certificate.

Guidance on actual penalties imposed can be gained from Swift's account, noted above. He advises that cases of dishonesty will lead to striking off. Breaches of the accounting rules involving substantial sums will normally result in striking off or a suspension. In *Bolton* v. *The Law Society*,[52] the Court of Appeal noted that the most serious charges against solicitors involved dishonesty and "in such cases the tribunal almost invariably, no matter how strong the mitigation, ordered that the solicitor be struck off". Where no dishonesty was found "it remained a matter of very great seriousness in a member of a profession whose reputation depended on trust. A striking off order might, but would not necessarily, follow." The tribunal should be concerned fundamentally to maintain the reputation of the profession "as one in which every member . . . might be trusted to the ends of the earth". In fact, however a number of dishonest solicitors, even some with criminal convictions have not been struck off or suspended by the Disciplinary Tribunal.[52a]

In 1996, from a total of 249 applications made to the Tribunal, the following actions were taken against solicitors:

Struck off	76
Suspended	26
Fined	80
Reprimanded	11
Censured	1
No order made (though allegation substantiated)	2
Order for costs only	1
Allegation not substantiated	1
Application for restoration to the roll	2

In addition the tribunal dealt with the following matters:

Cases involving s.43 orders[53]	55
Prohibition Orders[54]	6
Application to determine period of indefinite suspension	2
Solicitors Complaints Bureau Referral[55]	9
Application withdrawn	1

[52] *The Times*, 8 Dec. 1996.

[52a] See *ante* p. 106. Research showing this was presented by the Channel 4 programme *Dispatches*. See *New Law Journal*, December 4 1998, 1797 and *Law Society Gazette* December 2 1998.

[53] These relate to solicitors' clerks; they may only act as clerks with the permission of the Law Society.

[54] These are made with regard to former solicitors who have not been struck off but who cannot practise as solicitors, i.e. they do not have practising certificates and cannot obtain one unless the tribunal orders it.

[55] The Bureau (now the Office for the Supervision of Solicitors) may make an order/direction against a solicitor. If this is not complied with the Bureau may refer the matter to the tribunal for enforcement. The order then made by the tribunal is equivalent to an order made by the High Court.

Appeals

Appeals from decisions of the SDT go to the Divisional Court of the Queen's Bench Division or, in the case of applications for restoration to the Roll, to the Master of the Rolls.

Compensation for the Client

Compensation for clients for losses connected with the work done by their solicitors comes from two main sources, the solicitors' indemnity insurance organised by the Law Society and the Solicitors' Compensation Fund which is run by the Law Society. These are now considered in turn.

Indemnity Insurance (SIF)

All practising solicitors must contribute to and be covered by the Solicitors' Indemnity Fund (SIF) run by the Law Society under the Solicitors' Indemnity Rules 1995. The claims limit is £1 million for each claim (up to August 1996). Premiums for a sole practitioner for 1997–8 were £12,500. For large firms of 50 or more partners, the premium could be £1 million. Currently the fund is in severe financial trouble with a shortfall in the region of £454 million. Cover is given for losses arising from any civil liability, except where it arises from the fraud or dishonesty of a *sole* practitioner or where *all* the partners in the firm are party to the fraud. The client in such a case will have to seek compensation from the Solicitors' Compensation Fund described below.

The cost to practising solicitors of this insurance has escalated in recent years, to the distress of smaller firms which carry a low risk of being liable for high rates of compensation. The high cost has also encouraged proposals that higher premiums should be charged to those who offer cut-rate conveyancing services, and thereby are regarded as running greater risks. Premiums are substantially higher than for other professional group insurance and the cover is more comprehensive. The cost to the profession is considerable and the SIF has become a highly political issue. There are currently moves to scale down the system, and recurring calls to abolish it altogether.[56]

Solicitors' Compensation Fund (SCF)

This fund is run by the OSS and contributions of about £1,000 per year are made to it by all practising solicitors holding client monies under the Solicitors' Act

---

[56] E. Davidson, "Fury as SIF Fees Hike Hits Home", *The Lawyer*, 19 Aug. 1997 at 1; S. Pye, "City Sounds SIF Death Knell", *The Lawyer*, 28 July 1998, at 1; E. Davidson, "SIF Fudge Infuriates City Firms", *The Lawyer*, 29 Sept. 1998, at 1.

1974 section 36. It is a "discretionary fund of last resort"[57] set up in 1942 and makes grants to those who have suffered loss as a result of a solicitor's dishonesty or failure to account for money that is due. The dishonesty will have to be proved by the applicant either by establishing that there has been a conviction for, or a civil finding of, fraud or by presenting evidence leading to the "inevitable presumption" of theft.[58] The Fund does not compensate for personal negligence. The claimant does not necessarily have to be a client of the defaulting solicitor. Certain losses will *not* normally be compensated. These are listed in paragraph 3 of the Schedule to the Compensation Fund Rules 1995 and include:

• Losses which are not part of the fraud even though caused by it;
• Losses "tainted with the applicant's" own dishonesty;
• Losses contributed to by the applicant's own acts or omissions including the applicant's own professional negligence;
• Losses caused by a solicitor's failure to honour an undertaking. However if the solicitor gave the undertaking dishonestly in order to obtain funds and the applicant reasonably relied on this undertaking, their right to compensation will be "considered."

Applications to the SCF will be entertained where there is no other source of compensation from the SIF, other insurance or elsewhere. It will not normally pay sums in excess of £1 million, inclusive of the legal costs of the application. The claim must be made normally within six months of the date of the loss or the applicants' knowledge of it.

Major claims have been made on the fund in recent years in connection with mortgage fraud and the collapse of the property market in the late 1980s. The discretionary powers of the Law Society in compensating for such frauds were the subject of litigation in *R.* v. *Law Society, ex parte Mortgage Express Ltd.*[59] This was a test case and behind it lay claims by lenders of up to £25 million. The case concerned inflated valuations made of properties about which the solicitor failed to warn the mortgage lender (the solicitor represented both borrower and lender, on which see Chapter 7). As a result, when the borrowers defaulted, the lenders lost a considerable amount of money. The Law Society's policy that compensation from the fund would be refused where the dishonest solicitor did not commit the fraud for his own benefit was upheld by the Court of Appeal. Lord Bingham considered that the profession was not called upon to make good any loss caused by a solicitor's dishonesty. "The Law Society have always . . . made clear that they regard the fund as, first and foremost, a source from which to replace money which has been taken by dishonest solicitors for their own benefit."[60] This case

---

[57] See E. Skordaki *et al.*, *Default by Solicitors* (London, The Law Society, 1991).
[58] See the Solicitors' Compensation Fund Rules 1995, Sched., para. 4; *Law Society Guide*, n. 19 above, at 685.
[59] [1997] 2 All ER 348.
[60] *Ibid.*, at 360.

was subsequently applied in R. v. *Law Society, ex parte Ingram Foods*[61] where the Law Society was held to be entitled to reduce the compensation that would otherwise have been ordered by 100 per cent because of the applicant's own reckless conduct in accepting an undertaking in relation to a $5 million deposit from a sole practitioner without any documentation or other checks.

The majority of the defaulters whose clients are compensated from this fund are sole practitioners.[62] However this is not unexpected in view of the fact that the indemnity fund will not provide compensation for fraud in multi-partner firms unless *all* the partners are involved in the fraud. Although defaulters do not appear to be a homogenous group, common factors include a history of submitting late accounts to the Law Society and personal problems at the time of the default.

C. BARRISTERS

The Code of Practice

The Bar Code of Conduct is much shorter than that for solicitors, and much more recent, having been first published by the Incorporated Council of the Bar in 1981. Neither the Code nor the powers of the Bar Council are derived from statute.[63] The Bar Council's existence is now recognised by statute, in the Courts and Legal Services Act 1990 section 31. The Act gives the Bar Council the power to confer rights of audience on barristers subject to any changes in the rules of conduct being approved under section 27 of the Act. Changes to the Code generally are currently subject to the same procedures and consultation with ACLEC under the 1990 Act as in the case of solicitors outlined above. The Bar undoubtedly resents the fact that it has lost the power unilaterally to change its rules of conduct and there have been at least two occasions on which it has come into conflict with ACLEC about its powers and procedures.[64] In addition to the Code, Consolidated Regulations govern the Bar's training requirements and Chambers Administrative Guidelines govern practice organisation issues. Both are published by the Bar Council.

---

[61] [1997] 2 All ER 666.

[62] 46 of the 49 defaulters were sole practitioners in 1988 according to the Report: Skordaki *et al*, n. 58 above.

[63] Like the Law Society, the Bar Council has the power to waive any duty imposed on a barrister by the code: see *The Bar Code,* n. 4 above, at para. 104.

[64] The conflicts related to barristers' contact with witnesses and a proposed ban on barristers giving advice at police stations: see *The Lawyer,* 11 June 1996.

Authority to Practise

A barrister must be called to the Bar by one of the four Inns of Court (Gray's Inn, Lincoln's Inn, Inner Temple or Middle Temple) after having satisfied the educational requirements of the Bar.[65] The powers of the Inns are now recognised by statute in the Courts and Legal Services Act 1990 section 41(3). Having once been called to the Bar and served the necessary period of pupillage there is no further process of renewal of practising certificates similar to that of the solicitors' annual practising certificate. In this respect the Bar is remarkably unregulated, whether by itself or anyone else. This is unlikely to continue. A small foretaste of the future is the creation of a scheme for mandatory continuing education for barristers qualifying after October 1997 in the first three years of qualification which came into operation in October 1997. Failure to comply will lead to a suspension of the right to practice. There is no further requirement for continuing education but one was recommended by ACLEC in 1997.[66]

Practising Arrangements

Barristers are sole practitioners who practise in chambers in groups of an average size of 22 members and must normally employ the services of a clerk.[67] It is no longer mandatory to employ a clerk but most chambers do so. The traditional clerk acts as a chambers' manager and, most importantly, allocates work to the barristers and negotiates their fees with the solicitors.[68] Barristers' chambers are situated in both London and provincial centres and, since 1987, those in London no longer need to be within any Inn of Court. Barristers who have practised in chambers for three years may practise at home without a clerk, though very few do this.[69] Barristers may not "have a seat in the office" of any person entitled to instruct them, such as a solicitor.[70] Members of chambers share the costs of rent, clerks, secretarial services and other overheads.

Barristers must belong to an Inn of Court (which calls them to the Bar). The Inn provides a library and other collegiate benefits. Barristers are encouraged to join one of the six circuits throughout England and Wales, but this is not compulsory. Circuits have their own committees and rules but no disciplinary powers.

[65] On which see Chap. 6 below.

[66] *Continuing Professional Development for Solicitors and Barristers,* n. 27 above.

[67] Barristers share the cost of accommodation and clerking, with senior members paying more: Lady Marre CBE, *A Time for Change: Report of the Committee on the Future of the Legal Profession* (London, General Council of the Bar and Council of the Law Society, 1988), hereafter The Marre Report, at para. 5.7.

[68] For a study, now somewhat out of date, of the clerking system, see J. Flood, *Barristers' Clerks: The Law's Middlemen* (Manchester, Manchester University Press, 1983).

[69] Less than 1% according to M. Zander, *Cases and Materials on the English Legal System* (London, Butterworths, 1997) at 545.

[70] *Bar Code,* n. 4 above, para. 207 (c).

Barristers may not form partnerships or companies, nor, in general, may they share their fees with any other person including other barristers.[71] Some fee pooling within chambers is now permitted subject to certain conditions.[72] Barristers must practise as independent persons and cannot delegate their work to anyone else. Traditionally barristers could not make binding contracts for their services and neither could they sue for their fees. This rule has been formally abolished by the Courts and Legal Services Act 1990, section 61. However, that section also allows the Bar Council to make a rule continuing the prohibition from entering into contracts, and this the Council has done.[73]

In general, barristers may be briefed only by solicitors, not by clients directly. There are now, however, many exceptions to this rule. Parliamentary and patent agents have been able to brief barristers directly for some time. Since 1989 the Bar has allowed direct access to barristers by members of recognised professional bodies such as accountants, surveyors and members of the Institute of Taxation, the Association of Average Adjusters, the Institute of Chartered Engineers, the Incorporated Society of Valuers and Adjusters and Chartered Secretaries and Administrators. When briefed by these professionals, barristers cannot appear in the higher courts, county courts or the Employment Appeal Tribunal. Barristers can also be directly briefed by foreign clients, an exception which is becoming increasingly important. Most recently it has been decided to allow non-solicitor employees of advice agencies to brief barristers directly.[74]

Whilst barristers are normally briefed by solicitor, whom they refer to as their "professional client", their primary duty is to their lay client. They must not allow their professional client to limit their "discretion as to how the interests of [the] lay client can best be served". Where a conflict arises between the lay and professional client, the barrister must "advise that it would be in the lay clients' interest to instruct another professional adviser".[75]

About 10 per cent of the practising Bar are appointed, after application to the Lord Chancellor, as Queen's Counsel.[76] The appointment is honorary but most senior judicial appointments are made from the ranks of QCs. QCs are normally more highly remunerated than junior counsel and do not normally undertake paperwork. For this reason they are generally, although not necessarily, instructed with junior counsel in difficult cases. Junior counsel handle their own cases and, when instructed with Queen's Counsel, deal with drafting and less difficult procedural matters.[77]

---

[71] *Bar Code*, n. 4 above, para. 207.

[72] See *Law Society Gazette*, 27 May 1987, at 1566.

[73] *Bar Code*, n. 4 above, Annexe D, paras. 25, 26.

[74] *Ibid.*, paras. 210, 305, 306 and Annexes E and F. See also *The Lawyer*, 4 Nov. 1997. A consultation paper has been issued by the Bar (Oct. 1998) proposing widening direct access to barristers.

[75] *Ibid.*, paras. 203(b) and 605.

[76] For the origins of this office in Tudor and Stuart times see R. Pound, *The Lawyer from Antiquity to Modern Times: With Particular Reference to the Development of Bar Associations in the United States* (St. Paul, Minn., West Publishing, 1953), at 114.

[77] Marre Report, n. 68 above, at para. 5.9.

Complaints

Until April 1997 there was no effective complaints system for barristers' clients. In so far as a system did exist, its function was to alert "the Professional Conduct Committee to possible breaches of the Bar's code of conduct".[78] There was no indication in the Bar Code of Conduct of what should be done if a client or solicitor wished to complain, although it did set out, in an appendix, details of the workings of the Professional Conduct Committee. About 400 complaints were received by this committee each year. After lengthy and often acrimonious negotiations[79] the Bar Council agreed to and launched a new complaints system in April 1997. This deals with matters of discipline and also with complaints about inadequate service. Full details of it are to be found in Annexe M to the Bar Code which, incidentally, is drafted so poorly and legalistically that it might have been deliberately designed to confuse the most intelligent layperson. What follows is a summary of the main provisions.

There are now four levels at which complaints may be dealt with. The first level is to make the complaint to a new officer, the Complaints Commissioner (currently Major General Michael Scott), who is appointed by the Bar Council.[80] The second level is the renamed Bar Professional Conduct and Complaints Committee (PCCC). This body consists of 40 barristers and a panel of laypersons appointed by the Commissioner. The third level is for the PCCC to refer the case to an Adjudication Panel which consists of the Commissioner, a lay member and two barrister members (one being a QC) appointed by the PCCC. The forth stage is the Disciplinary Tribunal dealt with in the next section.

Complaints (other than those laid by the Bar Council) go first to the Commissioner. His function is to consider whether there is a *prima facie* case of either professional misconduct or inadequate professional service which should be put before the Committee. He can:

- refer the matter to the Inn or circuit if appropriate;
- dismiss the complaint if there is no *prima facie* case, it is trivial or "obviously lacks validity";
- where there is no evidence of misconduct, attempt to conciliate the complaint of inadequate service with the complainant and the barrister;
- adjourn consideration of the complaint for conciliation, or during the currency of legal proceedings or other reason;
- following investigation by the Commission secretary, if a *prima facie* case is made out, refer the case to the PCCC.

---

[78] See *1996 Report of the Legal Services Ombudsman* (London, HMSO, 1997), at para. 3.23.

[79] For a summary, see M. Zander, *Cases and Materials on the English Legal System* (7th ed. London, Butterworths, 1997) at 578–9.

[80] V. Cowan, "Great Scott? Not Quite but Showing Promise", *The Lawyer*, 9 June 1998, at 7.

The PCCC must consider any complaint referred to it by the Commissioner and may:

- dismiss the complaint "provided that each of the lay members present at the meeting consents to the dismissal";
- take no further action on the complaint;
- postpone consideration of it for any reason it thinks fit;
- where no misconduct is found but the "barrister's conduct is nevertheless such as to give cause for concern, draw it to his attention in writing". He may then be required to attend on the chair of the committee to receive advice on future conduct;
- refer to the Adjudication Panel any complaint from a lay client where there is a *prima facie* case of inadequate service (not misconduct), provided that it is not covered by the barrister's immunity from suit in respect of the conduct of litigation;
- deal with a *prima facie* case of professional misconduct which is not serious by holding an informal hearing;
- deal with other *prima facie* cases of misconduct summarily where such a procedure can deal with any remaining disputes of fact and which is unlikely to lead to disbarment;
- refer other *prima facie* cases of misconduct to the Disciplinary Tribunal.

Where an informal hearing is held under the above powers and the case is made out, the Panel may admonish the barrister and give him advice on future conduct. If, whether or not misconduct is found, the informal panel makes a finding of inadequate service then it may, *inter alia*, order the barrister to apologise to the complainant, repay or remit any fee and pay compensation of up to £2,000. The latter will be ordered only if the panel consider that the complainant has suffered a "loss recoverable at law" in respect of the inadequate service. Finally, further to protect the barrister, "no finding by a panel under this procedure shall be publishable" except in certain circumstances to the barrister's Inn.

Adjudication Panels, which deal with cases of inadequate service referred to them by the PCCC under the powers listed above, are governed by rules laid out in Annexe R of the *Bar Code*. The standard of proof required is now the civil standard (it used to be the criminal standard). In the event of a tie the barristers prevail. As with the informal panels noted above, Adjudication Panels also have the power to order the barrister to apologise, to pay up to £2,000 compensation for such service and remit or repay fees. Again, the determinations of this body are not publishable except as above or anonymously reported in the Annual Report of the Commissioner.

As has been noted, the complaints machinery (including the disciplinary machinery) cannot deal with allegations of negligence in court, a rule justified by the Bar on the ground that barristers are immune from suit in respect of such negligence. The Review Body which recommended the new complaints system, considered that it should cover negligence in court, pointing out that "complaints of poor service in and at court make up a significant part of the complaints received". The Bar would not accept this recommendation. The Ombudsman in his 1996 Report added his voice to that of the Review Body, [81] and at least one member of the judiciary is unhappy with this limitation on the complaints procedure. In *Kelly* v. *Corston* Lord Justice Judge commented, "the immunity of the advocate is not founded on some special protection granted by the court to the legal profession to enable lawyers to avoid justified complaints by dissatisfied clients . . . The immunity arises in very limited circumstances when the general public interest prevails against even a meritorious claim."[82]

The new system is obviously still very barrister dominated. The Ombudsman in 1996 considered it to be an improvement but feared that it would be operated in an over-legalistic fashion by the Bar.[83] His successor found this could be the case and has written that "[o]ne complainant who had rashly exposed himself to the Bar's complaints procedure recently described the experience as being like that of Alice at the Mad Hatter's tea party. I could well see what he meant."[84] Complaints against barristers have risen by 25 per cent since the introduction of the new system. Of the 551 complaints in 1997, 140 were referred to the Professional Conduct and Compliance Committee.[85]

Discipline

The Bar Disciplinary Tribunal consists of five persons, a judge, three barristers and one lay representative nominated by the President. The charges are laid before the Tribunal by the Professional Conduct and Compliance Committee. The hearing is normally in private. The standard of proof is criminal for professional misconduct and civil for inadequate professional services. If the charge is found to be proved the main powers of the Tribunal are:

- disbarment;
- suspension for a prescribed period;
- a fine of up to £5,000;
- an order to forgo fees;
- a reprimand by the treasurer of the barrister's Inn;
- admonishment by the Tribunal;
- advice from the Tribunal on future conduct;
- an order for the reduction or cancellation of legal aid fees;
- exclusion from legal aid work.

---

[81] *1996 Report of the Legal Services Ombudsman*, n. 79 above, paras. 3.29 and 4.28.
[82] [1997] 4 All ER 466 at 471.
[83] *1996 Report*, n. 79 above, para. 1.4.
[84] See A. Abrahams, "Ethical Lawyering: Public Expectation", *Legal Action*, Aug. 1998, at 8.
[85] See *Law Society Gazette*, 20 May 1998.

The Tribunal can make such order for costs as it thinks fit, and may also order compensation to the complainant of up to £2,000.[86] An appeal may be made to the Visitors who are the High Court judges. One or three will hear the appeal, depending on the issue involved.

Barristers' Insurance

Barristers must be insured against claims for professional negligence with BMIF in accordance with the terms approved by the Bar Council from time to time.[87]

D. LEGAL SERVICES OMBUDSMAN

Before 1991 solicitors were subject to the jurisdiction of an official called the Lay Observer. He was established under the Administration of Justice Act 1985 section 3, and dealt with complaints from the public where complainants did not receive satisfaction from the Solicitors' Complaints Bureau. This office was replaced under the CLSA 1990 sections 21–26 by that of the Legal Services Ombudsman who has jurisdiction over both solicitors and barristers. The Ombudsman can consider complaints which have first been considered by the relevant professional body (which includes the Council for Licensed Conveyancers and ILEX as well as those for barristers and solicitors). The Ombudsman's main task is to investigate the way in which the professional body has dealt with the complaint. He can also investigate the complaint itself. In the case of barristers, he cannot investigate complaints of negligence which are covered by their immunity from liability for negligence or contract, a restriction which severely limits his ability to supervise the Bar.

On completing the investigation, the ombudsman must send a written report to the complainant, the lawyer against whom the complaint was made and the relevant professional body. The ombudsman can recommend that:

- the professional body reconsider the complaint;
- the professional body initiate disciplinary proceedings;
- compensation be paid to the complainant by the lawyer for loss, inconvenience or distress caused;
- compensation be paid by the professional body for the loss, distress or inconvenience caused by the way it dealt with the complaint;
- the costs of making the complaint be paid by the professional body or the lawyer complained of.[88]

---

[86] For full details of the procedure see the Disciplinary Tribunal Regulations 1993, *Bar Code*, n. 4 above, Appendix N.

[87] *Ibid.*, para. 302.

[88] See CLSA 1990 s.23(2).

The report is a public document and absolutely privileged. A failure by the lawyer complained of, or the professional body, to do what the Ombudsman orders within three months may result in that failure being publicised. The costs of that exercise may be borne by the defaulter. The Ombudsman's reports are not directly enforceable in any other way.

The number of new cases reviewed by the Ombudsman in 1996 was 1855, a 11 per cent drop on the year before. That number represents just under 10 per cent of the total of complaints dealt with by the professional bodies. In 1996, 81 reports recommended the payment of compensation ranging from £100 to £6,000.

CONCLUSION

The framework of regulation for the legal profession is complex and is open to accusations that it is slow, cumbersome and offers inadequate redress. There has been a gradual response to criticism with the creation of independent watch-dogs, the separation of complaints-handling procedures from professional bodies and small increases in lay participation. It is not yet clear whether or not these measures will eventually diminish demands that powers of self-regulation should be removed from the professional bodies. This is unfortunate since it would appear to replicate mistakes made during the process of deprofessional-ising legal professions in the past. For, as Pound noted in relation to the USA:

> "It must not be supposed . . . that an organized profession of lawyers or of physicians is the same sort of thing as a retail grocers' association or that there is no essential difference between an organised bar and plumbers' or lumber dealers associations. The conditions of an organised body of lawyers, with no differentiation between advocates and agents for litigation, which obtained in the United States in the last century, gave to bar associations in the decadence of professional organizations something of the look of trade associations or else of dinner clubs. But this condition, as it existed in the last third of the century, was the lingering effect of a general movement to deprofessionalize the traditionally professional callings and put all callings in one category of money making activities, which was characteristic of frontier modes of thought in the formative era of American institutions."[89]

---

[89] Pound, n. 77 above, at 7.

6

Ethics and Legal Education

"I always was of opinion that the placing a youth to study with an attorney was rather a prejudice than a help. We are all too apt by shifting on them our business, to incroach on that time which should be devoted to their studies. The only help a youth wants is to be directed what books to read, and in what order to read them."[1]

A. INTRODUCTION

In preceding chapters we have seen how the professional ethics of lawyers are, in part, manifested in norms of behaviour found in codes of conduct, in public and private documents published by the profession, in fields of work and in units of organisation within those fields. We have also argued that individuals bring to the practice of law their own individualised ethical commitment. This reduces the scope for common understanding of ethical commitments. It follows that it is not plausible to expect entrants to the legal profession to know intuitively what is "professional conduct", much less that they will accept automatically the need for professional ethics. It might therefore be expected that, at degree level and beyond, some attempt would be made to explore this core of legal professionalism. This has not happened.

As we have described in Chapters 2 and 3, the numbers entering the legal profession have increased, as has their diversity of background. This gives strength to the profession. It is more representative in terms of gender, class and ethnicity. It is consistent with the rhetoric of the meritocracy and it makes it more likely that the profession is equipped to deal with the problems of the whole society. There are still problems which inhibit this diversification, for example, the high cost of qualifying, and the fact that many more graduates are produced than can be absorbed by the profession. Diversification, along with the other pressures which have made the profession more heterogeneous, which have been described in Chapters 1 and 2, undermines the idea that the profession consists of a single community with a common goal or purpose holding it together.

This is a problem which, arguably, should to be addressed by legal education. But the inculcation of an explicit common ethic has not been required of legal education nor voluntarily assumed by it. In this chapter we explore the reasons for this and look at some of the ways in which the deficit could be met. The

---

[1] T. Jefferson, Letter to Thomas Turpin, 5 Feb. 1769, in *Papers of Thomas Jefferson* 1:24 (J. P. Boyd (ed.) 1950).

chapter starts with a brief historical overview of legal education. It then moves to look at the reasons for, and some of the educational issues raised by, the increasing heterogeneity of the profession. Finally, developing some of the themes of previous chapters, the possibilities and implications of adopting a more radical approach to promoting professional ethics through education are explored.

B. HISTORICAL CONTEXT

Education and training are essential to the process of professionalisation[2] because the claim to exclusive knowledge is the foundation of professional autonomy. The length of education and training is often taken as a sign of the intrinsic difficulty of the knowledge required by the professional in order to carry out her role in society. The form and content of education are therefore highly indicative of those things which the profession not only requires but prizes in its entrants. But the evolution of any education system builds on existing structures and assumptions. Like professions, intellectual disciplines make claims for legitimacy. These claims become entrenched in the ideology and tradition not just of the producers of education but of the agencies with which they interact, the profession and organs of the state.[3] It is often difficult to change such systems. In Chapter 1 we considered the importance of traditional structures and ethical assumptions in shaping the contemporary ethics of the legal profession. In legal education, as in these other areas, the legacy of the past is a powerful influence on the present. It is therefore necessary to examine the inheritance of legal education in more detail.

In medieval England the Bar provided the blueprint for a communal and oral tradition of education based on lectures, moots and taking notes in court. A senior barrister was chosen to lecture, raising questions for debate which were taken up by an audience of practitioners. Established lawyers were required to engage in debates which often lasted for two hours and were followed by further debate after a communal dinner. Moots were also judged by senior barristers. Attendance at these events was a condition of call to the Bar.[4] Formal training did not begin until much later. The Inns of Court attempted to standardise their training in 1852 by creating the Council of Legal Education. Passing an examination became compulsory in 1872 but the educational process

---

[2] It is indicative that, after its Royal Charter was granted in 1831, one of the first things the Law Society did was to institute a programme of public lectures (in 1833): see D. Sugarman, "Bourgeois Collectivism, Professional Power and the Boundaries of the State: The Private and Public Life of the Law Society, 1825 to 1914" (1996) 3:1/2 *International Journal of the Legal Profession* 81.

[3] See generally M. Young (ed.), *Knowledge and Control: New Directions for the Sociology of Education* (London, Collier-Macmillan Publishers, 1971).

[4] R. Pound, *The Lawyer from Antiquity to Modern Times: With Particular Reference to the Development of Bar Associations in the United States* (St. Paul, Minn., West Publishing, 1953), at 90.

remained haphazard. The Inns of Court School of Law was, by 1925, responsible for vocational preparation for the Bar, a monopoly it enjoyed until 1996. A
small number of additional providers were then accredited to offer the Bar
Vocational Course, which had been devised by the Inns of Court School of Law
in 1988.[5]

Legal education could have acquired status by the connection with universities, but in fact the central role of university education in the professional preparation of lawyers is a recent phenomenon. Both branches of the profession, in
the initial development of their education, relied heavily on the apprenticeship
model.[6] The five year apprenticeship was the Law Society's preferred route. So
strong was this commitment to apprenticeship that university education became
a route to qualification almost by accident. The Bar, with the intention of
attracting higher status entrants, granted two years' exemption from the qualification process for entrants with a university degree in 1756. The Law Society
did so in 1821. During the formative years of the profession both branches
regarded university lectures as merely supplementary to their own apprenticeships.

Burrage argues that apprenticeship was not primarily intended as a cognitive
training but a moral training in the widest sense. Of the solicitors' branch he
says:

> "By forcing clerks and pupils to submit to a period of hardship, drudgery and semi-
> servitude, it necessarily conveyed a due appreciation of the value of membership of the
> profession. It also necessarily instilled respect for one's elders, for their experience, for
> their manners, conventions and ethics and for their sense of corporate honour. Articles
> and pupillage could, therefore, provide cast-iron guarantees about the attitudes,
> demeanour and commitment of those who were to enter the profession. A university
> degree, by contrast, guaranteed only the acquisition of a certain amount of knowledge
> of uncertain relevance to the actual practice of law."[7]

In both branches therefore, apprenticeship served a wider purpose than the
development of technical competence.[8] It inducted entrants into the ethos of the
profession.

Student preference for the university route to qualification dates from the
1960s. Although articles had been an exploitative way of recruiting entrants,
they ensured that they were highly committed and motivated. Articles provided
an opportunity to induct entrants into the prevailing norms, including the ethical norms, of a stable community[9] and therefore fostered that stability. The

---

[5] "The Providers", *Counsel*, May/June 1997, at 12.

[6] I.e., barristers served pupillage and solicitors articles of clerkship.

[7] M. Burrage, "From a Gentleman's to a Public Profession: Status and Politics in the History of
English Solicitors" (1996) 3:1/2 *International Journal of the Legal Profession* 45 at 54.

[8] The Bar, it could be argued, did not need such an extensive induction because of the smaller
numbers and greater concentration of barristers in the Inns. Pupillage gave the Inns a coherent role,
identity and means of recreating their culture. Burrage argues that pupillage created the Inns rather
than the reverse: at 52–4.

[9] *Ibid.*, at 68.

reduction of the period of articles undermined this pervasive ethical training. For, as Burrage notes, law schools achieved none of the wider outcomes of articles; respect for rules of etiquette, of practice or of ethics. The primary interest of university law schools was cognitive. This may be one cause of the perceived decline in feelings of responsibility for the "collective honour of the profession"[10] which has led to recent calls to increase the attention paid to ethics in legal education. The deficits produced by the decline of articles suggest a number of key aims for legal education; the cultivation of an ethos of public service, the fostering of an awareness of ethics and professional responsibility and the link between practical skills and ethics. Before these are considered in more detail however, it is necessary to look at some of the issues which came to the fore when the university became the main route into practice in the 1960s.

C. ENTRY INTO LEGAL EDUCATION AND TRAINING

Historically, professions derived much of their status from the class background of their members and of their clients.[11] This was particularly true of the legal profession in England and Wales, in relation to which Glasser, for example, refers to the image of a pyramid with barristers representing a higher level, particularly elite social characteristics, than the lower branch of solicitors.[12] Selection according to such criteria, i.e. ascriptive characteristics such as class background, rather than more objective assessments of merit maintains the homogeneity and status of the professional group. The elevation of one group above another in this way through the role of character, emphasises tradition and continuity and builds trust. The assumptions of such a community are often unspoken. Close social ties increase the pressure to conform to common expectations of a social role.

As professions become more publicly accountable they find it more difficult to justify the perpetuation of professional elites in this way. After all, in a democratic society the legal profession claims to represent the whole of society. The profession became sensitive to criticism that its entry procedures were not meritocratic. The Law Society, and subsequently the Bar, operated a system of public examination as a prerequisite of entry. When a law degree became the basic entry requirement for taking these public examinations, the profession could not control the supply of intending lawyers.[13] The move to meritocratic entry

---

[10] *Ibid.*, at 72.

[11] The numbers qualifying for practice at the Bar were contained by an "invisible" process of selection which prioritised "ascribed" characteristics such as social class. The expense of training and the requirement that non-graduates were required to sit examinations in Latin and Greek were effective controls on the numbers of barristers: C. Glasser, "The Legal Profession in the 1990s: Images of Change" (1990) 10 *Legal Studies* 1 and R. Abel, *The Legal Profession in England and Wales*, (Oxford, Basil Blackwell, 1988) at 17–18, hereafter *The Legal Profession*.

[12] *Ibid.*

[13] In times of crisis the profession is now reduced to bemoaning the underproduction or overproduction of law graduates. Both professional bodies have considered, or have achieved,

and the absence of control over the numbers of law graduates meant that, with the explosion in higher education opportunities at the end of the 1960s, the supply of graduates was likely to expand at least as rapidly as demand for lawyers.[14] Entry to the profession was restricted only by the availability of vocational stage places, by finance and by the numbers of available pupillages and traineeships.[15] Both of these means of controlling supply have created qualification bottlenecks but, for intending solicitors, the problem has receded lately (see Tables 1 and 4).

Table 4: Traineeships available to those completing solicitors' vocational stage.[16]

Year	No. completing Voc. Course	Year/s	Traineeships Available
1987	2,059	1987–8	2,918
1988	2,379	1988–9	3,058
1989	2,583	1989–90	3,254
1990	3,170	1990–1	3,841
1991	3,828	1991–2	3,941
1992	4,201	1992–3	3,681
1993	4,319	1993–4	3,874
1994	No figures noted	1994–5	4,170
1995	4,755	1995–6	4,063
1996	4,775	1996–7	4,739
1997	4,338	1997–8	4,826
1998	4,460		

restrictions on the numbers qualifying by excluding students with particular classes of law degree from vocational courses. The Law Society briefly considered reducing the number of Legal Practice Course places so as to control the numbers of solicitors. Despite this only a few years before, in 1988, the Law Society was reporting a recruitment crisis, particularly in local government, the CPS, and in private practice in the North East, parts of the North West, the Midlands—"even firms in the City of London report difficulties": *The Recruitment Crisis: A Report by the Training Commission of the Law Society* (London, The Law Society, 1988). Recently, the Law Society briefly attempted to turn back the clock; to reduce the number of entrants to the solicitors' branch by further restricting entry to the Legal Practice Course. It was advised that such a move would be illegal and the attempt was abandoned. Numbers are in any case already restricted because LPC providers are permitted by the Law Society to offer only a limited number of places.

[14] In 1995 the total number of law graduates was over 8,000, an increase of 32% over the previous year. It is not known how many of these hold a qualifying law degree, i.e. a degree which permits entry to the vocational stage. The Law Society's Legal Education Department, estimates that a further 2–3,000 students with joint honours degrees may hold a qualifying degree: (*Trends in the Solicitors' Profession: Annual Statistical Report* (London, Law Society, 1996).

[15] In 1995 there were 9,849 applications to study the LPC and a total of 6,921 full-time and 954 part-time places. 7,800 students studied the LPC but only 4,063 training contracts were registered with the Law Society that year: A. Sherr and L. Webley, "Legal Ethics in England and Wales" (1997) 4 *International Journal of the Legal Profession* 109 at 112.

[16] Training places available taken from *Trends in the Solicitors' Profession: Annual Statistical Report*, n. 14 above, Chart 12 at 73. Number of students passing, and traineeships available 1996–7 and 1997–8, provided by the Law Society.

Table 5: Number called to Bar and admitted to the Roll[17]

Year	No. called to Bar	New solicitors admitted to Roll
1991–2	1,340	
1992–3	1,584	4,417
1993–4	1,445	4,801
1994–5	1,593	4,695
1995–6	1,685	4,620
1996–7	1,608	5,417

Nevertheless, as shown in Table 5, there has been an expansion of people entering the profession.

The expansion of the profession in this way tends to lead to a younger, less experienced and better educated professional group which includes more women and members of ethnic minorities.[18] Indeed, in the UK, by the second half of the 1980s, more women than men were qualifying as solicitors and with better qualifications.[19] Further, approximately 20 per cent of students accepted for a first degree in law are from ethnic minorities.[20] Table 6 shows ethnic minority participation in the solicitors' branch, as a proportion of the total number of solicitors with practising certificates, compared with ethnic minorities as a proportion of the total population

Women and ethnic minorities are not necessarily represented in the same proportions in private practice as in education. One reason for this is the selection policies of many firms, which tend to offer training contracts to those from "elite" universities, where women, ethnic minorities and working class entrants tend to be underrepresented.[21] In the case of solicitors, Goriely and Williams identify two other factors; the gaining of prior work experience, especially with the firm in question, and interview performance, as being decisive in

[17] The figures for the Bar were provided by the General Council of the Bar and for solicitors by the Law Society.

[18] Galanter notes that, by the late 1980s, 20% of lawyers in the USA and Canada were women: M. Galanter, "Law Abounding: Legislation Around the North Atlantic" (1992) 55 *Modern Law Review* 1 at 4.

[19] A. Sherr, "Coming of Age" (1994) 1:1 *International Journal of the Legal Profession* 3 at 4. Between 1977 and 1987 the number of women practising at the Bar increased from 336 to 572, an increase from 8% to 14% of the practising Bar in each year: Lady Marre CBE, *A Time for Change: Report of the Committee on the Future of the Legal Profession* (London, General Council of the Bar and Council of the Law Society, 1988), para. 5.18, hereafter The Marre Report.

[20] *Trends in the Solicitors Profession*, n. 14 above, Table 9.4. There are no figures on ethnic minority graduation.

[21] The RPPU. Cohort Study (3rd Report, London 1997) showed that academic achievement, attending elite universities and having relatives in the profession were positive factors in obtaining a training contract, whereas ethnicity and social class were negative factors. There have been various claims that ethnic minorities in particular are discriminated against: see T. Growney, "Bar to Equal Opportunity", *The Guardian*, 27 May 1997 (allegation that clerks systematically deprived black pupils of work and that senior barristers did not remove such clerks because they operated in their interests).

Table 6: Ethnic minority solicitors as a proportion of total solicitors with prac-tising certificates compared with people from ethnic minorities as a proportion of the total population[22]

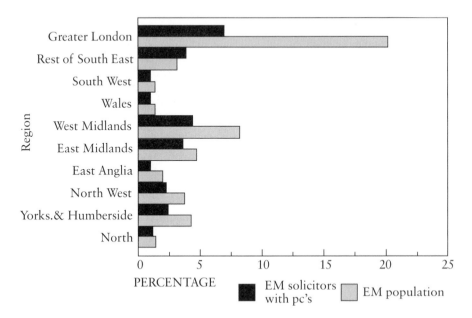

employment decisions.[23] It has been suggested that over-reliance on such factors tends to increase the possibility of discriminatory practices, not as a conscious decision but because appointment decisions are still influenced by personal rela-tionships. Solicitors, therefore, appoint people they think they will get on with; the key question is "are they one of us?".[24] It is to be hoped that the arrival of the first woman senior partner in a top 100 law firm signals a more widespread change.[25]

A number of implications arise from the increasing diversity of entrants to the profession. We have already noted that, from the profession's point of view, the risk of stratification of private practitioners according to type of work intensi-fies[26] and that the expansion of the employed sector creates additional problems

[22] *Trends in the Solicitors Profession*, n. 14 above, at 7 (taken from the Law Society database and the Office for National Statistics).

[23] T. Goriely and T. Williams, *The Impact of the New Training Scheme: Report on a Qualitative Study* (London, The Law Society, 1996).

[24] *Ibid.* In order to improve the efficiency of the process of applying for pupillage the Bar intro-duced the Pupillage Applications Clearing House Scheme (PACH) but around seventy per cent of chambers are not in the scheme and it is not clear whether it has addressed the problem of equal opportunities (see General Council of the Bar, *PACH (The Pupillage Applications Clearing House Scheme*: Report of the Review Working Party (1998)).

[25] *The Lawyer* (1998) 20 Oct. 3.

[26] A. Abbott, "Jurisdictional Conflicts: A New Approach to the Development of the Legal Professions" (1986) 2 *American Bar Foundation Research Journal* 187 at 197.

of achieving professional coherence. For the moment, however, let us consider the employment prospects of women and ethnic minorities coming into the profession. If the profession fails to accommodate minority groups, its commitment to the values of the liberal state, i.e. to equal opportunities and a commitment to serve wider society, is undermined.[27] This has had a number of interesting consequences. Increasingly it is not unusual to find equal opportunities in entry to the profession canvassed as an ethical issue for the profession.[28]

Partly as a result of efforts by the professional body, the number of solicitors from ethnic minorities appears to be increasing. The greatest concentration is in Central and South Middlesex, where 20 per cent of solicitors are from ethnic minorities. As will be seen from Table 6, this participation rate approaches the proportion of ethnic minorities in the population of Greater London as a whole.[29] The number of ethnic minority solicitors is currently 4.1 per cent of solicitors with practicing certificates compared with 3.8 per cent in 1995.[30] Fifty-five per cent of ethnic minority solicitors on the Roll hold practising certificates and 78 per cent of those with practising certificates are in private practice. In contrast, 83 per cent of white or European solicitors on the Roll in 1996 held practising certificates and approximately 82 per cent of solicitors holding practising certificates are in private practice. It is less clear how far ethnic minority students have penetrated the large commercial corporate firms and boutique practices where the rewards, status and prestige are the highest. At the Bar, it is estimated that 10 per cent are from ethnic minorities.

Just as there are suspicions that subtle forms of discrimination may pervade employment practices, so legal education has come under scrutiny for the same reason. Allegations of discrimination arising from differential pass rates for white and ethnic minority students at the Inns of Court School of Law led to the establishment of a Committee of Enquiry in March 1994. The Committee concluded that, while direct discrimination did not explain why fewer ethnic minority students passed the course than white students:

> "the school and the course were designed to reproduce the model English barrister, who is white, male and upper class. Anyone who does not conform and has no wish to, or is unable to, may feel uncomfortable. This is equally so of pupillage, tenancy

---

[27] See, e.g., H. W. Arthurs, "Lawyering in Canada in the 21st Century" (1996) 15 *Windsor Yearbook of Access to Justice* 202.

[28] C. Thomson, "Fairness for all", *The Lawyer*, 20 May 1997 (student supplement p. vi). And see The General Council of the Bar Education and Training Committee, *Report of the Working Party on Financing Entry to the Bar: Investing in the Future* (The Goldsmith Report) 1998, which noted that the cost of the BVC had increased by 174% from October 1989 to October 1997 compared to inflation of only 31% partly as a result of the end of the Inn's subsidy of the BVC (para 3.6). Goldsmith argued that, in order to attract the best and brightest students from the complete cross-section of social, cultural and racial backgrounds the degree of financial hardship needed to be reduced for disadvantaged groups, if necessary by getting chambers to sponsor 500 students per annum.

[29] The majority of those holding practising certificates and in private practice are from the Asian community: Thomson *ibid.*

[30] *Ibid.*, para. 2.12.

Table 7: Gender balance of solicitors holding practising certificates 1986–96.[32]

Year	Total	Men		Women	
1986	47,830	40,420	84.5%	7,410	15.5%
1991	57,167	42,986	75.2%	14,179	24.8%
1996	68,037	46,681	69%	21,356	31.4%

and further eminence at the Bar but it is less noticeable then because those who have reached the later stages will already have successfully conformed."[31]

The increasing number of women entering the profession (see Table 7) appears to contradict the view that the legal profession is unresponsive to wider social changes.[33] In recent years one quarter of solicitors holding practising certificates have been women, but many were working part-time, were unemployed[34] or were unlikely to reach partnership level.[35] Indeed, it seems that women must typically come from higher social groups than men to make a success of practice,[36] which suggests that informal barriers remain significant.[37] There are other problems which women are reported to face. A disturbing 40 per cent of women who enter the Bar, for example, report sexual harassment at work.[38]

The entry of substantial numbers of women might have profound implications for lawyers' ethics. Some scholars have argued that the adversarial ethic reflects a masculine preference for confrontation over a female preference for negotiation.[39] Therefore, the increasing numbers of women in the profession

[31] *Equal Opportunities at the Inns of Court School of Law: Final Report of the Committee of Inquiry into Equal Opportunities on the Bar Vocational Course* (The Barrow Report, 1994), at 99, para. 8.10. The report in general offered a compelling criticism of the ethos of the Bar as mirrored in the Inns of Court School of Law and offered a summary of 25 conclusions which read like recommendations (at 85–7).

[32] *Trends in the Solicitors' Profession*, n. 14 above, Table 2.3 at 11.

[33] This may seem unremarkable but for the fact that women were refused access to the Bar and solicitors' branch before the first world war. The proportion of women entering practice as solicitors rose by 43% from 1983/4 to 1985/6 reflecting the expansion of higher education. By 1993/4 women admitted as solicitors rose to 52.5%: E. Skordaki, "Glass Slippers and Glass Ceilings: Women in the Legal Profession" (1996) 3:1/2 *International Journal of the Legal Profession* 7 at 10 and 11.

[34] H. Sommerlad, "The Myth of Feminisation: Women and Cultural Change in the Legal Profession" (1994) 1:1 *International Journal of the Legal Profession* 31.

[35] Marre Report, at para. 5.22. and see Somerlad, n. 33 above, at 34.

[36] Abel above n. 11.

[37] D. Rhode, "Perspectives on Professional Women" (1988) 40 *Stanford Law Review* 1163.

[38] J. Shapland and A. Sorsby, *Starting Practice: Work and Training at the Junior Bar* (Sheffield, Institute for the Study of the legal Profession, 1995), table 5.3 at 71, based on a survey of 822 students entering practice: B. Hewson, "A Recent Problem", *New Law Journal* 5 May 1995 at 626.

[39] The cultural norms of legal professionalism, "instrumental rationality, ambition, competitiveness, aggression" are often contrasted with arguably more important but less significant norms of "empathy care or compassion": see further R. Collier, " 'Nutty Professors', 'Men in Suits' and 'New Entrepreneurs': Corporeality, Subjectivity and Change in the Law School and Legal Practice" (1998) 7 *Social and Legal Studies* 27. Maughan and Webb base an outline of an "ethics of care" on the work

might produce a pressure for more collaborative ways of working. The assumptions behind this are not necessarily valid, for example that men are competitive and women co-operative or that the adversarial ethic is sustained by men's preferences rather than the nature of the legal system. Moreover, a competitive environment imposes pressures to conform on all. The idea that an increasingly equal gender balance will change the way work is performed is, therefore, probably misplaced. Entrants to well-established structures are more likely to have to adapt to those structures. A more realistic view therefore is that, despite large numbers of women entering the profession, the professional identity of lawyers remains a masculine construct in which masculine expectations, for example full-time commitment, is seen as a prerequisite of progression.[40] Indeed, Sommerlad argues that "behind the facade of the professional code, the professions are gendered and patriarchal structures which are predominately anti-female".[41] The content of work, and the normative assumptions surrounding the way it is conducted, is likely to be resistant to revision by groups of new practitioners, however great their numbers.[42]

These factors governing the make-up of the solicitors' branch are significant. Burrage observes that:

> "The solicitors' branch is becoming a more public profession than its predecessors . . . more educated and heterogeneous, less concerned with its corporate honour, more market-oriented and competitive, with others and amongst themselves, and therefore less secure . . . all these things make it more unruly and fractious, more unethical and disloyal."[43]

This paragraph of itself tends to conflate the issues, linking the growth of the profession and its education with certain kinds of decline. As we saw in Chapter 2 the relationship between wider access to the profession and declining ethicality is unproven and, we suspect, unprovable. If there is an increase in dishonesty it might be simply because the profession itself has become larger, thus increasing the numbers of infractions. There may be more opportunities than previously for serious misconduct and more conduct requirements on which the

of Carol Gilligan, *In a Different Voice* (Cambridge, Mass. and London, Harvard University Press, 1982). This suggests that men are predisposed to a rights *v.* justice approach to resolving problems whereas women approach problems with empathy and a concern to minimise the violence involved in different solutions. They argue that the key elements are making connections (membership of a network of lawyers and others in which there is open and empathetic communication), obtaining consent (i.e. participatory lawyering) and seeking resolution (a greater emphasis on alternatives to trial based on methods of resolving disputes): see C. Maughan and J. Webb, *Lawyering Skills and the Legal Process* (London, Butterworths, 1995), at 116–20.

[40] Sommerlad, n. 33 above, at 36–9.

[41] Women who took a career break to raise families were unlikely to make partnership and, when firms laid off solicitors, those affected were disproportionately women: *ibid.*, citing J. Ames, "Late Bloomer" (1993) 90:12 *Law Society Gazette*, 24 Mar., at 10.

[42] It has been argued that the addition of women to male environments does not necessarily bring about a demand for changes to the violent ways of doing things which characterise male domains: A. Giddens, *Modernity and Self-Identity: Self and Society in the Late Modern Age* (Cambridge, Polity Press, 1991), at 229–30.

[43] Burrage, n. 7 above, at 75.

professional bodies are likely to act. Because such matters are more frequently detected, treated more seriously and dealt with more openly it does not follow that the profession as a whole is less honest. For unethicality which is not dishonest we must look to explanations such as Carlin's; that ethics are imposed by elites and are differentially accepted by sub-groups within the profession. This may be because of the different economic pressures experienced by elite and other groups and because the norms of elite groups within the profession do not correspond with those of the wider profession. Education offers one way of dealing with this problem. Education has a role in a two-stage process; professional norms must reflect a wide professional consensus, a consensus which can only evolve through knowledge and understanding, and this consensus must be vigorously promoted at all stages of legal education, including post-qualification. We now consider the extent to which legal education has this potential or has demonstrated this potential in the past.

D. THE STRUCTURE OF EDUCATION AND TRAINING AND THE PLACE OF ETHICS IN IT

The education and training requirements for lawyers in the United Kingdom consist of a first degree in law[44] (the "initial stage") followed by a one-year vocational course, currently the Bar Vocational Course for barristers and the Legal Practice Course for solicitors. There then follows an "apprenticeship", a one-year pupillage for barristers and a two-year traineeship for solicitors. Therefore, the quickest route to qualification as a solicitor is six years and as a barrister five years.

There have been three major reports in the past 30 years which have grappled with some of the issues, Ormrod,[45] Benson[46] and Marre.[47] Ethics have usually had a neglible role in the recomendations of such reports. This may be because they have usually been an implicit rather than an explicit part of brief of these committees. The Benson Report, for example, suggested that:

> "It is essential that throughout their training students should be impressed with the importance of maintaining ethical standards, rendering a high quality of personal service, maintaining a good relationship with clients, providing information about work in hand for clients, avoiding unnecessary delays, maintaining a high standard in briefs and preparation for trial, promptly rendering accounts with clear explanations and attending to other matters mentioned elsewhere in this report."[48]

---

[44] Graduates in a non-law discipline can enter the vocational stage by passing a one year "Common Professional Entrance Examination".

[45] *Report of the Committee on Legal Education*, Cmnd.4594 (London, HMSO, 1971).

[46] *Report of the Royal Commission on Legal Services*, Cmnd.7648 (London, HMSO, 1979).

[47] *Report of the Committee on the Future of the Legal Profession "A Time for Change"* (London, The General Council of the Bar and the Law Society, 1988).

[48] Benson, *Final Report: Volume 1*, para. 39.47.

Many of the positive ideas to emerge from the reports were not implemented or, as with the introduction of legal skills in the vocational stage, implemented late.[49] Some were not implemented at all.[50] Why was this? One reason was that the reports take the needs of the legal practice, and particularly the demand for technical competence, as their starting point, ignoring the considerable complication that law was also an academic discipline in the universities. Ormrod, for example, described the fundamental problem as one of finding alternative ways of allowing entrants to the profession to "develop wings" following the decline of the apprenticeship system. This was seen as a problem of combining an education which is necessary to enable someone to follow a learned profession, "with the skills and techniques which are essential to its actual practice".[51] These were a perspective and an agenda that were always resisted by the university law schools, particularly the elite schools.

Ormrod has been, and continues to be, the most influential of the reports, because it espoused a liberal agenda which, at the time, was broadly acceptable to all the interest groups, including the professional and the academic. Some of its more far-reaching proposals, unfortunately those which may have had direct benefits for ethics, including a closer integration of the stages of legal education and the setting up of a Institute of Professional Legal Studies, have not been realised.[52] Much of the difficulty encountered in the reports, which also affects introducing ethics into legal education, stems from the fact that there has been a rigid separation of the three modes of learning in professional preparation; inquiry, instruction and performance.[53] Traditionally, the notion of inquiry has pervaded the initial stage, instruction the vocational stage and performance the apprenticeship stage. This structure is based on the partnership model of professional preparation and it assumes that professional education:

1. should enable students to analyse and reflect on practice so as to encourage them to assume responsibility for their continuing professional development;
2. undertake the development of students' professional skills as a partnership between practitioners and academics, with academics offering the theoretical framework and practitioners the introduction to skills;
3. provide a body of knowledge which directly underpins practice.[54]

[49] W. Twining, *Blackstone's Tower: The English Law School* (London, Stevens & Sons/Sweet & Maxwell, 1994), chap. 2.

[50] Both Ormrod and Benson recommended common training for the vocational stage. The profession's own Marre Committee felt it did not have enough evidence to form a conclusion: Marre Report, n. 47 above, at para. 14.20. The Lord Chancellor's Advisory Committee on Legal Education and Conduct has recently repeated Ormrod's call and proposed a six-month common stage followed by six months' training for each branch of the profession.

[51] Ormrod, n. 45 above, at para. 82.

[52] W. Twining, "The Benson Report and Legal Education: A Personal View" in P. A. Thomas (ed.), *Law in the Balance: Legal Services in the 1980s* (Oxford, Robertson, 1982) at 186.

[53] C. O. Houle, *Continuing Learning in the Professions* (London, Jossey-Bass Publishers, 1980).

[54] R. A. Barnett, R. A. Becher and N. M. Cork, "Models of Professional Preparation: Pharmacy, Nursing and Teacher Education" (1987) 12:1 *Studies in Higher Education* 51 at 61.

The model separates the theoretical and practical dimensions of professional education so that university teachers and the profession each retain responsibility for the different elements. In legal education, as in other professional preparation, this rigid separation has broken down to the extent that practical work, i.e. performance, has become an assessed element of all three stages. Practical work has not been uniformly introduced into the academic stage, however, and the problem with this is that practical work is often seen as a way of imbuing ethical issues with relevance and, thereby, developing ethical awareness. Yet neither practical work nor the teaching of ethics has been central to traditional legal education. Nor have ethics been central to clinical or legal skills work.[55] This was because of both the assumption that ethical preparation was unnecessary, and also to the way in which legal education developed.

The Undergraduate Stage

Law degrees are available at both universities and private colleges. Law school curricula are often a compromise between the needs of the legal profession, which most law students aspire to join, and the academy, where law has a fragile foothold as a discipline. Twining observes that:

> "In all Western societies law schools are typically in a tug of war between three aspirations: to be accepted a full members of the community of higher learning; to be relatively detached, but nonetheless engaged, critics and censors of law in society; and to be service-institutions for a profession which is itself caught between noble ideals, lucrative service of powerful interests and unromantic cleaning up of society's messes."[56]

As a result of these multiple demands, undergraduate legal education has a number of conflicting aims.

Moreover, unlike many other professional disciplines, law has generally received inadequate support[57] in the universities and is currently funded on the least generous formula available to the Higher Education Funding Council. This provides resources for classroom teaching, or "chalk and talk" as it is often called, but little for the more labour-intensive, and many would say vital, "clinical" education, such as working with real clients, found in university medical schools. A more direct practical emphasis would, it has been argued for some time, maintain "an environment in which every aspect of legal work can be the object of the most painstaking planning, reflection and review".[58] This is not to

---

[55] See, e.g., K. Economides and J. Smallcombe, *Preparatory Skills Training of Trainee Solicitors* (London, The Law Society, 1991).

[56] Twining, n. 52 above, at 2.

[57] See, e.g., J. F. Wilson, *The Resources of Law Schools* (Society of Public Teachers of Law and the Committee of Heads of University Law Schools, 1991).

[58] M. Meltsner and G. Shrag, "Scenes From a Clinic" (1978) 127:1 *University of Pennsylvania Law Review* 1. See also R. Barnhizer, "The Clinical Method of Legal Education: Its Theory and Implementation" (1979) 30 *Journal of Legal Education* 67.

suggest that there has been no pressure for change. From the mid 1960s there was criticism of the "expository orthodoxy" of academic law teaching and a range of changes were proposed.[59] One of these was the introduction of "clinical" legal education and "legal skills", both of which have made some inroads into the curriculum since that time but have not become universal.

One of the reasons for the relative lack of innovation is the fact that law schools are constrained on several fronts. The profession prescribes approximately half of the curriculum for qualifying undergraduate law degrees. The core curriculum for the undergraduate stage, the minimum requirement for a qualifying degree, is found in the "Seven Foundations of Legal Knowledge". This curriculum, prescribed by both the Bar and the Law Society,[60] focuses exclusively on substantive areas of law.[61] None of the subjects, nor the professional bodies' stated objectives for this stage, makes reference to ethics. Nor would this be easy because pressure to expand this core is usually resisted by the university law schools.[62] The curriculum is seen as overcrowded and there is great variation in the content taught at different institutions. In view of this it is not surprising that ethics are not a compulsory component in law degrees.

A consultation paper on the revision of the joint announcement was published by the professional bodies in September 1998.[63] This cited the view of the ACLEC that the law degree should stand as an independent liberal education not tied to any specific vocation. Two innovations proposed in the joint announcement are relevant here. The first proposal is the introduction of a requirement that general transferable skills be assessed. The form of assessment could, however, be formative rather than summative, which means that it need not contribute to the award of a degree. Secondly, the joint announcement proposed that students should acquire, *inter alia*, knowledge, "where relevant of the social economic political, historical, philosophical, moral, ethical, cultural and comparative contexts in which law operates."[64] These proposals, while obviously well intentioned, continue to deny ethics, and the learning activities which hold most potential for developing ethical awareness, a central role in the initial stage of legal education.

Academic resistance to the expansion of the core is often based on arguments that the addition of compulsory ethics is not necessary. It is argued, for example, that the qualities required of the ethical practitioner, "vision, range, depth, balance and rich humanity", are, in any case, fostered by the study of law as a

[59] H. T. Edwards, "The Growing Disjunction Between Legal Education and the Legal Profession" (1992) 91 *Michigan Law Revue* 34; Twining, n. 52 above, at 141–2.

[60] This forms the core of most undergraduate degrees and comprises the Common Profession Entrance Examination (or Graduate Diploma in Law) which provides exempting legal study for graduates of other disciplines.

[61] "Announcement on Qualifying Law Degrees", issued Jointly by the Law Society and the Council of Legal Education, Jan. 1995, at 6.

[62] Twining, n. 49 above, chap. 2, nn. 47 and 53, chap. 3 and 162–6.

[63] The Law Society and the General Council of the Bar, *A Consultation Paper on the Revision of the Joint Announcement on Qualifying Law Degrees* (Sept. 1998)

[64] It is not clear what the "moral and ethical" context includes.

liberal art.[65] The study of law itself has the study of morality at its core.[66] But, more fundamentally and probably inconsistently, it is not thought to be a part of mission of a liberal legal education to "indoctrinate" students.[67] This argument may seem naïve. The absence of an explicit ethical core to legal studies creates a vacuum which is filled by the, often unarticulated, values, not of the liberal university, but of a narrow, traditional legal education.[68] Despite its "liberal education" label, traditional legal education often stresses the ethic of individualism, competitiveness, legalism and authoritarianism.[69] Such values conflict with the notion of personal ethical commitment and the idea that the role of the lawyer is promoting justice or public service.[70] These problems are exacerbated by the social composition of the undergraduate body which tends to be dominated the by middle classes[71] for whom law school provides access to a lucrative career. University legal education is often a rite of passage.[72]

Research tends to confirm this view. The most popular objectives of law students are acquiring the legal knowledge and intellectual skills which it is assumed are appropriate preparation for practice. Personal development, understanding of the social context of law, law reform and preparation as

---

[65] K. Llewellyn, "The Study of Law as a Liberal Art" (1960) reprinted in *Jurisprudence: Realism in Theory and Practice* (Chicago, Ill., University of Chicago Press, 1962), at 376 (and see discussion by Twining, n. 49 above, chap. 4, n. 42).

[66] Twining, n. 49 above, at 159–62.

[67] *Ibid.*, chap. 7 and n. 54.

[68] "students are absorbing, from the day they enter law school, a sense of what the functions of the profession are and what their individual role is to be in that profession": J. Weinstein, "On the Teaching of Legal Ethics" (1972) 72 *Columbia Law Review* 452 and J. F. Sutton, and J. S. Dzienkowski, *Cases and Materials on the Professional Responsibility of Lawyers* (St. Paul, Minn., West Publishing Co., 1989), at 3.

[69] J. Webb, "Ethics for Lawyers or Ethics for Citizens? New Directions for Legal Education" (1998) 25 *Journal of Law and Society* 134.

[70] C. Stanley, "Training for the Hierarchy? Reflections on the British Experience of Legal Education" (1988) 22:2/3 *The Law Teacher* 78, argues that the narrow pursuit of rule-handling techniques and the retention of largely irrelevant amounts of knowledge is a form of educational socialisation which provides a foundation for the generation of hierarchical power relationships. The core curriculum prioritises private law (70%) over public law (30%) and marginalises theoretical analysis of law and skills courses. The result is that "responsible" jurists are produced who do not question. Having served their apprenticeships "the power is theirs": they become "zealous partisans and promoters [of hierarchy], anxious to secure their moral empire".

[71] A study conducted for The Law Society by the Policy Studies Institute found that the A level grades typically required to study law were matched only by the requirements for studying veterinary science or medicine. While ethnic minorities were generally well represented at degree level, those from a working class background were less well represented than those from professional and managerial backgrounds: D. Halpern, "Tomorrow's Lawyers", *The Gazette*, 16 Dec. 1992, at 23.

[72] A more comprehensive analysis will be possible on the conclusion of an extensive longitudinal study which is following the careers of lawyers from the undergraduate stage into practice. The data already produced are already too complex to do justice here: see further D. Halpern, *Entry into the Legal Professions: The Law Student Cohort Study* (London, The Law Society, 1994); M. Shiner and T. Newburn, *Entry into the Legal Profession: The Law Student Cohort Study Year 3* (London, The Law Society, 1995); M. Shiner, *Entry into the Legal Profession: The Law Student Cohort Study Year 4* (London, The Law Society, 1997).

policy-makers appear at the bottom of their list of objectives.[73] The Lord Chancellor's Advisory Committee on Education and Conduct, concerned with this trend, has recently proposed that "students must be made aware of the values that legal solutions carry and of the ethical and humanitarian dimensions of law as an instrument which affects the quality of life".[74] It is not clear whether ACLEC is recommending teaching professional ethics, as opposed to a jurisprudence curriculum. It is unlikely that universities will voluntarily embrace the teaching of ethics or that most will be able to link ethics to practical work. For, as Twining observes:

> "one reason for the seeming fragmentation and pluralism of modern legal studies is a reluctance to confront some of the problems of broadening academic law in a coherent way that combines appropriate theory (generally middle order) with explicit concern for method."[75]

New proposals for developing and monitoring the achievement of threshold standards by all undergraduate degrees have again focused on skills. Those for law include autonomy and the ability to learn, communication and literacy and problem solving. The Knowledge component includes understanding the ethical and cultural context in which law operates.[75a]

The Vocational Stage

In general, education for professional life balances "scientific knowledge" ("knowing that") with skills of interaction, needed to deal with clients ("knowing how").[76] Until quite recently the emphasis of vocational legal education was on "knowing that". The Law Society Finals Course was remodeled in 1980 but remained a "bastion of old-style legal education", heavily favouring the instruction mode. This curriculum was ripe for change. There was a crisis of confidence in the traditional forms of "professional knowledge",[77] mounting criticism of lawyers' level of competence and, for some in the professional bodies, a desire not to lag behind developments in the training regimes of other common law countries.[78] Increasing change in work led to an emphasis on

---

[73] Halpern, n. 71 above, but contrast Glasser who argues that, because of the commitment to professionalism, entrants to Anglo-American professions are therefore more likely to have a high sense of "calling": Glasser, n. 11 above.

[74] Lord Chancellor's Advisory Committee on Legal Education and Conduct, *First Report on Legal Education and Training* (London, the Committee, 1996), at para. 1.19.

[75] Twining, n. 52 above, at 173.

[75a] J. Bell, *Benchmark Standards for Law: Preliminary Draft and Commentary* (1998) and 'General Transferable Skills and the Law Curriculum' (1996) 2 *Contemporary Issues in Law* 1.

[76] Barnett, Becher and Cork, n. 54 above.

[77] D. A. Schon, *The Reflective Practitioner: How Professionals Think in Action* (New York, Basic Books, 1983).

[78] The USA, Canada and Australia had already incorporated clinical or skills components in the education and training of lawyers.

adaptability, flexibility and the capacity for action.[79] It was recognised that, to avoid being sporadic and opportunistic, continuing development must be self-directed. Learning therefore had to become the responsibility of the learner and the focus of education had to become to "learn how to learn". This presented a considerable challenge to legal education which required law graduates to absorb a large volume of legal material and relied heavily on a pedagogy of instruction. As both academic and practising lawyers had been educated in this way, they were suspicious of alternative methods. Nevertheless the new training regime introduced by the Law Society for solicitors in the early 1990s purported to revise assumptions about the technical knowledge needed by intending practitioners and the kind of legal practice they would enter.[80]

The Law Society changes followed those already made by the Bar. The introduction of the Bar Vocational Course in 1989 and the Legal Practice Course in 1993 brought a shift in the content of vocational stage from instruction to inquiry and performance, i.e. to knowing how. These changes were, generally, positively received.[81] One reason was that they promised increased attention to practical issues like how to deal with solicitors and clients. The old course had not dealt with some of the most basic ethical issues.[82]

In May 1990 the Training Committee of the Law Society identified two principal reasons for the change to a more practically orientated curriculum: "the continuing needs to improve the quality of entrants to the profession and to increase the system's ability to respond flexibly to changes in demand for solicitors' services".[83] The original proposals made by the Law Society's Training Committee did not emphasise technical competence or skills and were criticised on the ground that they had taken insufficient account, *inter alia*, of "the extent to which the final course is dominated by the requirements of the written examination at the expense of training in practical skills". It was said that:

"the primary purpose of the vocational stage of training should not be to add to the body of factual knowledge but to develop the analytical skills and to add to them the practical skills that will be needed in practice. The emphasis of the course and of the methods of assessment associated with it should not be on knowledge but on skill.

---

[79] "The fixed person for the fixed duties, who in older societies was such a godsend, in the future will be a public danger": Whitehead (1926), quoted in C. O. Houle, *Continuing Learning in the Professions* (London, Jossey-Bass Publishers, 1980).

[80] It was also modelled on an assumption that students were being prepared for practice in a typical high street firm or a "four partner firm in Oldham" but, by 1992, 70% of trainees worked in large firms dealing with commercial law: A. Sherr, "Professional Legal Training" (1992) 19: 1 *Journal of Law and Society* 163.

[81] V. Johnston and J. Shapland, *Developing Vocational Legal Training for the Bar* (Sheffield, Faculty of Law, 1990).

[82] *Ibid.*, at 42–7.

[83] Law Society Training Committee, *Training Tomorrow's Solicitors: Proposals for Changes to the Education and Training of Solicitors* (The Law Society, London, 1990), at para. 1.2. The conclusions of the review may have been influenced by the fact that the review took place at the time of a recruitment crisis: *The Recruitment Crisis: A Report by the Training Committee of the Law Society* (London, Law Society, May 1988);

What should be tested is . . . the development of competencies that are needed to be an effective member of the profession."[84]

The Report recommended that skills teaching on the Legal Practice Course should be increased compared with the Law Society Final Course and that the amount of skills teaching should increase still further "as institutions develop their expertise in this field".[85] Integral to the methodology of the LPC was the idea that students would work with "transactions", the processes of legal practice, in the context of each subject. The LPC also prescribed standards for the performance and assessment of skills such as drafting, research, advocacy, interviewing and negotiation in the context of transactions. These skills were apparently selected for two reasons:[86] first, because they had been adopted in other common law countries which had skills at the vocational stage; secondly, these skills were undeveloped in solicitors' practices and their inclusion would serve to increase the competence of practitioners.

The move towards a skills orientated curriculum in vocational training had implications for undergraduate law degrees, most of which had also been dominated by instruction rather than performance. This was regarded as poor preparation for a more practical vocational stage in which existing skills had to be employed in context. The Training Committee therefore recommended that the Law Society should "encourage law schools to improve their students' oral and written powers of communication and their skills of initiative, leadership and teamwork, particularly where this can be done in a legal context",[87] develop their students' understanding of the practical application of law[88] and "ensure that their students proceed to the Final Course with an adequate knowledge of . . . the skills of legal research and problem solving".[89] Reactions to the LPC were mixed, with complaints that it still emphasised "black letter" law and allegations that the standards required to pass were not demanding enough.[90]

The new vocational courses made some progress in addressing issues of competence but the attempt to place ethics in the curriculum was less successful. Ethics is not included among the four aims of the BVC issued by the Bar Council. A fair summary of the first three aims is that students are expected to acquire such knowledge, skills and *attitudes* as will prepare them for pupillage and future

---

[84]   J. Randall, *Review of Legal Education: An Alternative Approach* (Sept. 1989) at 5. There were also to be significant changes in delivery and assessment. More universities were encouraged to offer the finals course than had offered the LSFC. The need to assess the skills of students would have made assessment by Law Society appointed markers expensive and impracticable.

[85]   *Training Tomorrow's Solicitors*, n. 83, above, at para. 5.10.

[86]   It was hoped that skills training, both on the LPC and in mandatory CPD, would be informed by two research reports: A. Sherr, *Solicitors and their Skills* (London, The Law Society; 1991), and Economides and Smallcombe, n. 55 above, but neither report was substantially reflected in the scheme ultimately implemented: see A. A. Paterson, "Professionalism and the Legal Services Market (1996) 3:1/2 *International Journal of the Legal Profession* 137 at 149.

[87]   Para. 4.1.

[88]   *Ibid.*

[89]   Para. 5.1.

[90]   Goriely and Williams, n. 23 above

practice. The final aim clearly has ethical bias, which goes beyond issues of competence and relates more explicitly to attitudes; thus it is intended that the BVC should "emphasise the importance of being able to practise in a culturally diverse society, communicate effectively with everyone involved in the legal process, and of recognising the role of other professionals and their expertise".[91] In a section describing the "ethos" of the BVC, it is said that the course will "seek to inculcate a professional approach to work and to develop in students a respect for the principles of professional conduct".[92] Providers were left to decide how to include issues of professional ethics. Both the Legal Practice Course and the Bar Vocational Course treated ethics as a "pervasive" topic rather than dealing with it as a discrete subject.[93] This was not a bad thing in itself but, a few introductory lectures notwithstanding, students hardly had a thorough grounding in ethics. As with other pervasive subjects, the way in which they are dealt with depends on the subject staff who deliver each course and the time made available for consideration of ethical issues. Lawyers will be quick to note that "developing respect" is a rather vague goal. Unfortunately, the continuing domination of substantive law on the LPC was felt to marginalise both skills and the consideration of ethics.[94]

The Apprenticeship Stage

Trainee solicitors continue their formal education during their apprenticeship. In theory they develop by observing and assisting more experienced lawyers and become attuned to the ethics of the profession. This was noted by a practitioner in one study who said:

> "It is essential for Articled Clerks to sit in with a partner or someone who is doing litigation all the time so they learn the law and how to look for it and they can see these skills being exercised daily on the telephone and in letters. Putting them in a room and giving them instructions is not the same. You must show and explain why . . . if you have bad habits it tends to be exposed fairly early on in this type of work."(Litigation solicitor).[95]

There is, however, a temptation for experienced lawyers not to take the training task seriously; to use the trainee for running errands or performing minor clerical tasks and to downgrade the expectation of training.

[91] General Council of the Bar Validation Steering Committee, *Application Procedure to be Validated to Offer the Bar Vocational Course: Course Specialisation Guidelines* (London, General Council of the Bar, 1995), at 3, para. 1.1.

[92] *Application Procedure to be Validated to Offer the Bar Vocational Course: Course Specialisation Guidelines* (London, General Council of the Bar, 1995), at para. 1.1.(2)(6).

[93] Some formal and discrete ethics classes are a feature of some schemes. The Inns of Court School of Law, has three lectures and three tutorials on ethics in its BVC (The Inns of Court School of Law, *Bar Vocational Course Handbook, Full Time Studies 1997–98*, para. 4.7).

[94] H. Brayne, "LPC. Skills Assessments—A Year's Experience" (1994) 28 *Law Teacher* 227.

[95] A. Boon, "Assessing Competence to Conduct Civil Litigation: Key Tasks and Skills" in P. Hassett and M. Fitzgerald (eds.), *Skills for Legal Functions II: Representation and Advice* (London, Institute of Advanced Legal Studies, 1992).

For some years there had been concerns at the quality of articles. At the same time as the LPC was introduced, the Law Society also introduced a more comprehensive regime to improve the quality of training at the apprenticeship stage. The Professional Skills Course (PSC), comprising four weeks of continuing professional development for trainees, was intended to accommodate "professional conduct, ethics, interviewing skills and accounts rules".[96] The rationale was that trainees generally knew little of these subjects before entering the office; nor could they be sensibly taught it until they had an understanding of how legal offices operate. The Law Society also introduced measures to monitor training by authorising firms to take trainee solicitors only if they agreed to observe a code of conduct incorporating monitoring and appraisal of trainees.[97] These requirements led many large firms to appoint directors of education and training to organise the "in-house" delivery of courses. By 1987 four London law firms had appointed full-time directors of education and training. By 1990 it had increased to 96.[98] In many cases this diminished the time devoted to training by partners, often to the detriment of the programmes.[99] Directors of Training, in many cases, took over the role of mentor to trainees.

Some smaller firms, concerned at this advantage gained by the large firms, grouped together to provide joint courses for their trainees and also extended this training to more senior staff. Research commissioned by the Law Society and published in 1996 concluded that "on the job" training was still regarded as the most important element of a solicitor's education.[100] But the research noted that supervision often amounted to no more than sharing a room with a more senior person, or more accurately the four supervisors in each of the departments attended by trainees in larger firms. The "supervisor" often found it difficult to articulate what the process of training actually involved and the rotation of supervisors undermined the continuity of pastoral care. Both trainers and trainees were dismissive of the PSC, except the advocacy component, and regarded the day spent on professional conduct as a "token gesture". Few supervisors had actually read the *Guide to the Professional Conduct of Solicitors*, regarding it more as a reference work than an integral part of working life.

Measures were also taken to improve the quality of barristers' pupillages. Many different studies have confirmed that the most useful "training" barristers

[96] A. Sherr, "Professional Legal Training", n. 80 above, at 167.
[97] *Ibid*.
[98] Although this was partly a response to the recruitment crisis of that time there were a number of reasons why this development continued when the recruitment crisis receded. Firms aimed to attract the ablest recruits by showing that they took training seriously. They wished to develop economic in-house PSC and CPD programmes. They also aimed to develop more participatory formats of education, i.e. to depart from the pervasive "talking heads format", and to develop new subjects of particular relevance to the firm, e.g. marketing (E. H. Greenebaum, "Development of Law Firm Training Programs: Coping with a Turbulent Environment" (1996) 3:3 *International Journal of the Legal Profession* 315 at 318–19, 331 and 345).
[99] The Law Society *The Recruitment Crisis*, n. 83 above, at para. 11(c).
[100] Goriely and Williams, n. 23 above.

receive is in the second six months of pupillage. Here, being in court several times a day provides the neophyte with valuable experiences of advocacy. However, this opportunity to appear in court in a multitude of minor matters is now declining through competition with solicitors, cutbacks in legal aid or decisions not to prosecute in criminal cases.[101] Apart from this experience there is little intrinsic to the barrister's background or training which can be assumed to confer superiority in advocacy.[102] Since the Bar is built on specialist advocacy, its education should perhaps develop relevant skills and, thereby, protect young barristers from competition or the impact of market change. Perhaps this is why there are ambitious proposals for the continuing professional development of barristers which aims to recreate the system of involving senior barristers and judges in the clinical training of "young tenants".[103] The same paper proposed seminars on ethical and other practical issues including such matters as costs and legal aid. A working party established by the Bar under the chairmanship of James Goldsmith QC has recommended that students intending to enter the Bar should receive a subsidy from the profession.[104]

Continuing Professional Development (CPD)

The professional bodies' educational requirements do not end with qualification. The Law Society has now realised its long-term project to subject all solicitors to CPD requirements.[105] There is no ethical component in this CPD scheme after the PSC. The General Council of the Bar introduced, in 1997, "The New Practitioners' Programme", a compulsory CPD requirement, under which 42 hours of continuing education must be completed in the first three years following qualification. At least three of the hours must be devoted to ethics, with the objective of enabling the new practitioner to identify those situations which raise ethical problems, understand the principles that govern professional conduct and apply these principles to given situations. Chambers are "authorised providers" under the scheme and are "specifically encouraged to offer the ethics component of the programme. The chambers environment is regarded as particularly suited to the small group discussions that are essential to effective

---

[101] J. Morison and P. Leith, *The Barrister's World and the Nature of Law* (Buckingham, Open University Press, 1992). See also the Goldsmith Report, *The Work of the Young Bar: Report of the Joint Working Party of the Young Barristers' Committee and Legal Service Committee of the Bar Council* (London, General Council of the Bar, 1993).

[102] Indeed there is a strong suspicion that the standards of qualification for advocacy are higher for solicitors than for barristers, e.g. a Scottish member of the Faculty of Advocates retrained as a solicitor and failed the qualification tests ([1995] *Legal Business*, 50).

[103] *Second Report of the Bar Council's Working Party on Continuing Education and Training* (Chaired jointly by the Honourable Justice Potter and Richard Southwell QC) Bar Council (1991) at 5.

[104] Supra, n. 28 and see S. Pye, "Cash Crisis and Poor Prospects for Young Bar" (1998) *The Lawyer*, 20 Oct.

[105] For further details see Chap. 5.

ethics teaching."[106] The rhetoric of the profession is that CPD represents a commitment to "lifelong learning". The requirement that continuing professional development is mandatory, the tendency of much of it to be dull and unimaginative lectures requiring no involvement by practitioners, undermines this objective.[107] This is particularly unsatisfactory in relation to the development of ethical awareness as a part of CPD.

E. FUTURE DIRECTIONS FOR LEGAL EDUCATION AND TRAINING

Building on the Present System

A significant feature of the increasing number of research reports on entry to the legal profession is the virtual absence of any discussion of ethics. Ethics are a vital but invisible part of legal education. How to fill the gap is not obvious. It has been said that "[e]thical theory alone does not create morality. It can only cast light on morality by analysing and appraising moral justification. Ethics require thought, while morality must be lived."[108] What, among other things, this tells us is that there is no necessary correlation between understanding what it is right and doing what is right. What can and should legal education contribute to the making of an ethical profession has been a hotly contested issue precisely because of the factors considered thus far. If self-regulation is doomed, commercialisation is rampant and the profession is increasingly fragmented and fractious, is not ethical education a bit like putting a finger in the breach in the dam?

Since, as we argued in Chapter 1, ethics are inevitable, they may as well be as soundly grounded as possible. Legal education is the key because, while understanding ethics may not guarantee ethical behaviour, understanding ethics is surely an essential prerequisite of ethical conduct. This makes some discussion of ethics in legal education important. The Lord Chancellor's Committee on Education and Conduct (ACLEC) has, in a number of its reports, drawn attention to this, but it has not dwelt on the detail of how ethics programmes would be delivered at the undergraduate stage. The result of the ACLEC's initiative could be the addition of yet another substantive subject to an already overcrowded undergraduate curriculum.[109] ACLEC's proposal for a lengthy

---

[106] *The New Practitioners' Programme* (London, Continuing Education Unit, General Council of the Bar, 1997), at 3 and 4. This initiative was presumably a response to the ACLEC proposals in *Continuing Professional Development for Solicitors and Barristers: A Second Report on Legal Education and Training* (1997) para. 2.33.

[107] K. Rockhill, "Mandatory Continuing Education for Professionals: Trends and Issues" (1983) 33 *Adult Education* 106.

[108] F. Beauchamp and J. F. Childress, "Virtues and Conscious Actions", in A. Flores (ed.), *Professional Ideals* (Belmont Cal., Wadsworth, 1988).

[109] J. Webb, "Inventing the Good: Prospective for Clinical Education and the Teaching of Legal Ethics in England" (1996) 30:3 *The Law Teacher* 270 at 271 and nn. 4 and 6.

Master's programme built around "a more rigorous basic education in common professional values" to replace the vocational stage seems unlikely to succeed.[109a] How then can ethics be incorporated into the education of lawyers? This depends on defining the goals of such a curriculum.[110] Before considering this issue, it is useful to look at the position in the United States, where some of the problems have already been encountered.

Since 1974 the American Bar Association has required that accredited law schools instruct all students in applied ethics and professional responsibility.[111] While the catalyst for this was the fact that large numbers of government lawyers were involved in the Watergate scandal, it also reflected "a growing sense of moral malaise, a declining faith in professional leaders and a perceived erosion of traditional forms of social control through families, churches and communities".[112] Even early advocates of ethics teaching recognised that it would not raise the standards of morality amongst students.[113] Rather it was argued that by raising and discussing the problems of legal practice during the formative educational stages, entrants to the profession might be more able to analyse, and even resist, induction into the "discrepant moral reasoning" of some practice cultures.[114] In 1992 a major report by the American Bar Association task force argued that the acquisition of lawyering skills and values must be part of an educational continuum from the initial stage to continuing professional development. This was to be built around four key objectives: the provision of competent representation; the responsibility to promote justice, fairness and morality; the responsibility to maintain and improve the profession; the personal responsibility for one's own professional development.[115]

One continuing debate in the USA has been whether ethics should be taught as a discrete subject, i.e. allocated its own place in the curriculum, or whether it should be pervasive, i.e. taught as an element of other courses throughout the curriculum.[116] There are attractions, and problems, in both approaches. One of

[109a] Private practitioners and professional bodies objected on the grounds that it would raise the cost of access to the profession and be confused with other postgraduate master courses, ACLEC, *First Report on Legal Education and Training* (1996).

[110] Paterson suggests goals which avoid the objective-led approach of the LPC i.e. to sensitise students to ethical issues, to encourage moral development, to work against ethical relativism, to encourage reflection: P. Paterson, "Legal Ethics in Scotland" (1997) 4 *International Journal of the Legal Profession* 25.

[111] D. L. Rhode, "Ethics by the Pervasive Method" (1992) 42 *Journal of Legal Education* 31. Such instruction was to include the "duties and responsibilities of the legal profession including the history, goals and responsibility of the bar and its Code of Professional Responsibility".

[112] *Ibid*.

[113] J. Weinstein, "On the Teaching of Legal Ethics" (1972) 72 *Columbia Law Review* 452 at n.2. But see Webb, n. 109 above, at 281.

[114] E.g., the range of factors, pressures and tensions which undermine ethical practice of law including the pressures arising from billing practices, law firm promotion pressures and the problems of underfinanced disciplinary systems and overburdened judiciaries: Rhode, n. 111 above at 42–43).

[115] R. MacCrate, "Preparing Lawyers to Participate Effectively in the Legal System" (1994) 44 *Journal of Legal Education* 89.

[116] The "pervasive" approach favoured for the Legal Practice Course in England and Wales is frequently criticised by academics in the USA. For an account of an attempt to establish a non-perva

the problems when ethics are pervasive is the risk is that no one teaches them; "there is no place in which students and institutions confront in any probing and systematic way, the central ethical concepts, institutional and political under-standings and regulatory alternatives that underline all areas of professional ethics and regulation".[117] When taught as a discrete subject ethics can easily mirror traditional law teaching. Students often receive ineffective instruction or training in "unethics", indicating how far lawyers can go without disbarment, with suggestions for circumventing the rules.[118] Nevertheless, there are power-ful reasons why many ethics courses in the USA are taught in this way. The approach is less likely to expose anomalies, contradictions and conflicts because learning "ethics" becomes a case of learning rules.[119] Further, this is a method with which teachers and students are already very familiar.

England and Wales have advantages over the United States. First, the perfor-mance-oriented curriculum of the BVC and LPC presents opportunities for the development of ethical awareness through performance and reflection on the problems of the real world.[120] The inhibiting factor is the lack of time because of the continuing dominance of substantive material which competes for time with skills teaching. It is arguable, however, that ethics already forms a signifi-cant part the vocational stage because the LPC standards incorporate ethical norms. In the standards for litigation and advocacy, for example, LPC students are required to "advise the client on the legal consequences of his or her pro-posals . . . to agree a [case preparation] strategy with the client" and "under-stand the ethics of advocacy and be able to apply them". If taken seriously this requirement would mean that students understand much about the ethics of participative decision making (see Chapter 7) and advocacy (see Chapter 14).

Despite their potential for ethical development, there are a number of prob-lems with the LPC standards. One is the risk that due to the pressure of time,

sive approach see S. M. Bundy, "Ethics Education in the First Year: An Experiment" (1995) 58 *Law and Contemporary Issues* 19. This article notes "strong student resistance to required legal ethics education" (at 29).

[117] Bundy, n. 116 above, at 32. Note also that research referred to suggests that short courses have no impact on ethical judgements. See also J. R. Rest, *Moral Development: Advances in Research and Theory* (Praeger, Westport, Conn., 1986), and Rhode, n. 111, above.

[118] Rhode, n. 111 above at 38–42.

[119] See Bundy, n. 117 above, noting that theory and empirical evidence courses are less well estab-lished than "materials which stress law rather than ethics, and the external rather than the internal regulation of lawyers" (at 31).

[120] Schon adopts the proposition that professional students cannot be taught what they need to know about professional practice but can be coached. They must see on their own behalf and in their own way the relations between means and methods employed and results achieved proposes the development of a "reflective practice" aimed at helping students acquire of essential to compe-tence in the indeterminate zones of practice: D. A. Schon, *Educating the Reflective Practitioner: Toward a New Design for Teaching and Learning in the Professions* (London, Jossey-Bass Publishers, 1987), at 17. See also Schon, n. 77 above. In relation to the initial stage see A. Boon, "Skills in the Initial Stage of Legal Education: Theory and Practice for Transformation" in J. Webb and C. Maughan (eds.), *Teaching Lawyers' Skills* and A. Boon and P. Hodgkinson, "Life and Death in the Lawyer's Office: The Internship in Capital Punishment Studies" (1996) 30:3 *The Law Teacher* 253 and Webb, n. 109 above.

deeper issues of ethics, for example the quality of the lawyer–client relationship, are squeezed out by technical performance issues, for example, is the advice given credible?.[121] Another problem is that the standards do not in fact reflect the principles of conduct required by the profession. Solicitors are not required by any rule to "agree a case preparation strategy with their clients"; indeed as advocates they enjoy the same immunity as barristers in relation to strategic decisions which they alone make. Further, while client involvement in decision-making may be "good practice" for lawyers,[122] it may be unrealistic in certain practice settings.[123] The standard, therefore, reflects the aspirations of the course designers rather than ethical standards grounded on any empirical reality. The meaning of other LPC standards is obscure. As we shall see in Chapter 14, while there are certain rules of conduct which govern advocacy, there is considerable doubt about what constitutes the "ethics of advocacy". Relying on performance standards to develop ethical awareness or ethical practice is therefore problematic. It risks sowing seeds of confusion rather than furthering the cause of ethics.[124] In addition, students are not encouraged to explore the ethical rationale for their actions.[125] If they do not understand *why* it is ethically sound to act in one way rather than another they are less likely to adopt it but will follow the culture of practice uncritically.

The integration of skills and ethics on the LPC therefore remains underdeveloped. The majority of teachers on LPCs are recruited from practice to ensure the relevance of the course. Now that many of these practitioners work in academic institutions the possibility exists for fusing skills work with more ambitious ethics programmes. Different insights can be brought to ethics by academics and practitioners. But, despite the existence of a partnership committee to explore such issues, the dialogue between practitioners and academics remains muted. LPC teachers rarely teach on academic programmes, and academic research marginalises practical work as opposed to theory. The insights, research and materials which might bridge the divide between the academic and practice in the field of ethics have been slow to arrive.

There are no easy answers to the problem of introducing ethics to the legal curriculum. If we accept the limitations of the present system we must try to har-

[121] E. H. Greenebaum, "How Professionals (Including Legal Educators) 'Treat' Their Clients" (1987) 37 *Journal of Legal Education* 554.

[122] A. Sherr, "Lawyers and Clients: The First Meeting" (1986) 49 *Modern Law Review* 323 at 324. Sherr suggests that the first interview with a client is a "crucial period of mutual assessment. Mutual confidence must be built up, the lawyer must be given basic information on the client's case and the client must be given some basic understanding of how the law operates in relation to his/her problem."

[123] A. Boon, "Client Decision-making in Personal Injury Schemes" (1995) 23 *International Journal of the Sociology of Law* 253.

[124] Similar points can be made about the interviewing standards which can be seen to promote participative decision-making and the negotiation standards which promote interest based and problem-solving methods.

[125] It has been suggested that even real life "legal clinics" are not the solution to the problem of how to teach ethics because the nature of the obligation implied is not understood and is undesired: but see D. Rhode, 'Institutionalizing Ethics' (1994) 44 *Case Western Reserve Law Review* 665 at 734–5.

ness the strengths of each stage of legal education; to recognise their distinctive orientation which provides both opportunities and constraints. The academic stage could take primary responsibility for the inquiry element essential to the teaching of ethics. It could cover ethical concepts, the fundamentals of ethical reasoning and an introduction to the traditions and ethos of the legal profession. The material could be covered in courses such as English legal system, legal theory or philosophy and legal skills; possibly in all three. This is a fairly unambitious route which might find acceptability because it would not disrupt the curriculum too much. It may be possible, however, to radicalise it somewhat by incorporating ideas from the alternative agendas considered in the next section.

The vocational stage could then build on this foundation by refocusing the skills components so as to explore ethical issues explicitly and in greater detail. Finally, and perhaps most important, is the post qualification stage. CPD programmes provide opportunities for ethics seminars in which practitioners share and discuss the problems they encounter in their work. These seminars could form a two-way dialogue between participating practitioners and the wider profession.[126] Examples of the ethical issues discussed with tentative solutions could be published, with suitable commentary, by the ethics committees of the professional bodies and used in the deliberations of the relevant professional rule making bodies. The emphasis of this shift in legal education would be to encourage reflective judgement rather than conformity.[127]

In summary, there is an argument that ethics should be taught at every stage of legal education. There is also an argument that, in order for ethical instruction to have any impact, it should involve more than learning rules. Possible alternatives include simulated tasks and clinical activity which can provide graphic illustrations of real life ethical issues.[128] But teachers must be skilled in dealing with questions and able to stimulate thought on ethical issues.[129] Some legal educators have argued for ambitious programmes; courses which would encourage students to "subject ethical norms to critical scrutiny, to argue the merits of prioritising practice norms or regulatory structures and to make self determined, responsible, self reflective and critical judgements about themselves

---

[126] At present the rationale for "collecting" CPD points is often professional updating which therefore relates to the professional obligation of competence. This tends to have a "ballooning effect", resulting in an experience of dubious value which is the antithesis of "self-directed learning": Houle, n. 53 above at 266. ACLEC's proposal for a sustained postgraduate course incorporating professional responsibility issues suggests one way forward. It is consistent with Schon's advocacy of a significant intellectual component in developing high levels of professional skill: Schon, "Educating the Reflective Practitioner", n. 120 above at 312, and his proposal that the best place for this is in the professional's "mid-career" phase (at 342).

[127] See further R. W. Gordon and W. H. Simon, "The Redemption of Professionalism" in R. L. Nelson, D. M. Trubeck and R. L. Solomon (eds.), *Lawyer's Ideals/Lawyer's Practices* (Ithaca NY, and London, Cornell University Press, 1992), 230 at 236–40.

[128] Winfield argues that clinical studies might lure more graduates into the welfare field of practice and increase the appeal of law to the young and idealistic: M. Winfield, "The Legal Profession Must not be Allowed to Lose its Way", *The Lawyer*, 28 July 1998, at 19.

[129] See P. Brest, "The Responsibility of Law Schools: Educating Lawyers as Counsellors and Problem Solving" (1995) 58 *Law and Contemporary Problems*.

and their work".[130] Others stress that students must understand how moral conduct might be affected by stress, competition, authority, peer and time pressures.[131] As was well recognised by the Benson Commission in 1979:

> "As students join the profession year by year in the future it should be emphasised to them, in the course of their formal training and education and during service under articles or in pupillage, that the responsibility for bringing about and maintaining this change [a transformation in the image of the profession] rests in their hands."[132]

Changes in the profession increase the need for rethinking the role of ethics in legal education. As has already occurred in the USA, the curriculum of law schools is theoretical and may become more so. Meanwhile, law firms are becoming more commercial. This leaves a potentially significant gap in the preparation of lawyers in terms of both technical competence and ethical responsibility.[133] The need for a fully integrated curriculum, one which deals with both issues of competence and values, becomes more pressing as the tensions within legal professionalism become more acute.[134] The need to coordinate the effort to create a more ethical profession calls for an overarching body. Both of these proposals were made by the Ormrod Report in 1971.[135] The fact that they have not been acted upon does not bode well for their future. Unfortunately, the capacity of education to bolster professional distinctiveness, and therefore professional monopoly, ensures that it is often a part of the profession's repertoire for resisting wider change.[136]

Alternative Agendas

We have already noted the problems of the legal profession in embracing the pluralistic and relativistic values of the liberal state and of maintaining a "common morality" when the profession has fractured and fragmented and of absorbing entrants from diverse backgrounds. It has been argued that mature professions can embrace and harmonise a wide range of interests and moral positions. But, in order to do this, traditional assumptions about the transmission of ethical norms may have to be revised. One of the more radical suggestions on how this might be achieved is by providing a legal education which promotes moral agency. It will be recalled that in Chapter 1 we explained that

---

[130] S. G. Kupfer, "Authentic Legal Practices" (1996) 10: *Georgetown Journal of Legal Ethics* 33.

[131] Rhode n. 111 above at nn. 67 and 71.

[132] The Royal Commission on Legal Services (1979) Vol.1 para. 3.40 (Cmnd. 7648).

[133] H. T. Edwards, "The Growing Disjunction Between Legal Education and the Legal Profession" (1992) 91 *Michigan Law Revue* 34, discussed in Twining, n. 52 above, at 140.

[134] For further discussion of this issue see A. Boon, "History is Past Politics: A Critique of the Legal Skills Movement in England and Wales" (1998) 25 *Journal of Law and Society* 151.

[135] Twining, n. 52 above. This proposal was recently repeated by ACLEC with a call for a new Institute of Professional Legal Studies the primary function of which would be to research and develop CPD (ACLEC, n. 106 above at paras. 3.7 to 3.9).

[136] "Earthworks against ACLEC", *SPTL Reporter*, Spring 1996.

moral agents are able to stand back from situations, ignoring personal and social characteristics, and judge from a universal and abstract point of view. The idea of moral agency is coextensive with Simon's notion of moral autonomy discussed in Chapter 4 and with the idea that practitioners are not, and cannot have their behaviour, bound by codes.

What kind of legal education promotes moral agency? Goldsmith argues that education might help professionals to decide whether or not to accept or reject the practices into which they are settled. He argues that, for preparation for practice to be reflexive and consciously moral, rather than simply mecahnical, legal education would need to develop wider goals. These would include redefining the orientation of the law school and the introduction of a more complex understanding of community obligations and social responsibilities. Students would theorise "about the conditions of legal practice in ways informed largely or partly by empirical studies of different practice fields and interdisciplinary scholarship".[137] But there must be serious doubts about the success of such an attempt through the initial and vocational stages of legal education education alone. So, how could the idea of promoting moral agency be taken beyond the stages of formal education?

A number of fundamental changes would be required in the ethic of the profession, in its rules and in methods of education. Osiel, for example, argues that Simon's notion of moral autonomy is not feasible unless all lawyers in competition with each other are subject to a similar obligation to refuse unethical representation.[138] Otherwise those who refused to be unethical would be at a competitive disadvantage and might not succeed in practice. Similarly, in order to counteract the lawyer's self-interested pursuit of client objectives, a strong sense of commitment to a common obligation to protect third party interests would need to evolve. This would require active participation by members of the professional community in ethical deliberation which might include the formulation of rules of conduct.

We might argue therefore that what is needed for the idea of moral agency to take root is to supplement the traditional, hierarchical structures of professional discipline with mechanisms which enable professional bodies to interact with small communities of practitioners. These communities are the most effective way of developing and transmitting professional norms because it is they who work with new entrants and ensure social reproduction, the continuity of the professional order. We envisage communities of lawyers in diverse practice settings, both feeding ethical insights to the professional body and receiving ethical guidance from that body. Both the rules of conduct and professional education would be informed by this process. Both would become more relevant to professional practice. This is another example of reflexivity. Despite some doubt that "communities of virtue" such as these are credible in the

---

[137] *Ibid.*, at 416.
[138] M. J. Osiel, "Lawyers as Monopolists, Aristocrats and Entrepreneurs" (1990) 103 *Harvard Law Review* 2009 at 2016.

contemporary environment[139] there have been a number of attempts to establish such a "communitarian" model for the regeneration of ethics. These models offer the possibility of reconciling professional ethics with the changed position of the self in modern society; of combining notions of rationality, autonomy and self-interest within the pursuit of a greater social good.[140] These ideas are in fact not as radical as they may seem at first sight. Durkheim, for example, went to the heart of the problem when he observed that:

> "the discipline laid down by an individual and imposed by him in military fashion on other individuals who in point of fact are not concerned in wanting them, is confused by us with a collective discipline to which the members of the group are committed. Such discipline can only be maintained if it rests on a state of public opinion and has its root in morals; it is these morals that count . . . As to the rules, although necessary and inevitable, they are but the outward expression of these fundamental principles. It is not a case of co-ordinating any changes outwardly and mechanically, but of bringing men's minds into mutual understanding."[141]

The starting point would be to produce ethical rules and guidance, based on a general foundation, appropriate to the various specialities and sub-groups that the profession now consists of. This cannot be done in a purely haphazard or incremental fashion, as has been the case so far. It can no longer be assumed that ethics will flow from a consensus developing within a small group of homogenous professionals. There must be a conscious effort within the various groups within the legal profession to develop an ethic appropriate to each field of work. These ethical norms may well differ, but they must be based on the reality of actual practice within each speciality.[142] In some specialities responsibility to the client may have priority (as in possible in relation to the accused client), in others responsibility to others may have a greater claim. But it may no longer be credible to expect that practitioners will identify with or follow a single code.[143] Practitioners must take responsibility for their own behaviour. They will obviously be assisted by the professional organisations devoted to their own specialities. Such moral autonomy is, in fact, vital to the very idea of moral agency and it is relevant to both professionals *and* clients.

The role of legal education would be to lay the foundations of "moral agency" by developing the capacity for independent reasoning using moral

---

[139] Many commentators reject attempts, such as Macintyre's, "to retreat from the public vices to the private virtues of small communities of like-minded citizens in search of virtue . . . the advent of the megapolis of post-modernity further undermines the possibility of even small scale communities of virtue. The corruption of moral agreement narrated by Macintyre finds no answer in the nostalgia for Aristotelian virtue": C. Douzinas, R. Warrington and S. McVeigh, *Postmodern Jurisprudence: The Law of Text of Law* (London, Routledge, 1991), at 6.

[140] "Community" is not a special purpose organisation but a framework for life; "community implies integration, shared symbolic experience and self regulating activities groups and institutions": see P. Selznick, "The Idea of a Communitarian Morality" (1987) 75 *California Law Review* 445 at 449.

[141] E. Durkheim, *Professional Ethics and Civic Morals* (translated by C. Brookfield, London, Routledge and Kegan Paul Ltd., 1957), at 28 and 29.

[142] M. Davis and F. Elliston (eds.), *Ethics and the Legal Profession: An Educational Text* (New York, Prometheus Books, 1986).

premises. This would be most valuable if the material for such processes arose out of the ethics of practice. An ethic emerges from a willingness to discuss, understand and, on occasions, assume the perspectives of others.[144] This is a reflexive process in which personal intuitions are shaped in discussion with the professional group including opposing lawyers. The scope of such an exercise is not limited by geography or even areas of work. Just as academics often maintain an international community of ideas, it is possible to conceive of communities of legal professionals. Networks of practitioners interested in *pro bono publico* would provide opportunities for practitioners from different areas of practice, including elite firms, to communicate ethical ideas. The idea of communitarian ethics could, therefore, be based on mutually supportive communities, participating in developing collective understandings. This could be united to public altruism which infuses morality into social relations and provides a way of stabilising the professional community.[145] The aim of this process is authentic legal practice; a congruence between personally held values and the actions of the practitioner in her work.[146] Some advocates of this view see codes of conduct ceasing to become regulatory, but operating as an influence in moral choice. We argue that this does not necessarily follow since, as we have argued, codes of conduct could be informed by these processes as part of the reflexive process. While many will see visions of practitioners debating ethical issues in communities of their peers as impracticable,[147] if professional ethics is to survive the diffusion of a common culture, it may need to become a reality.

CONCLUSION

It may seem an obvious proposition that legal education has a significant contribution to make in identifying and sustaining the profession's ethics. Despite this, ethics have never featured prominently in the core curriculum of either the undergraduate or vocational stages. This lack is troubling because it tends to perpetuate the *status quo*. While an education in common ethical values might be "the cement" which can bind the legal profession together,[148] education cannot provide an answer to all the tensions within modern legal professions. If

[143] P. Bordieu, *The Logic of Practice* (1980) at 52; Kupfer, n. 130 above.

[144] The attempt to map a postmodern ethic is therefore built on the notions of reflexivity (see Chap. 1), and the recognition and accommodation of difference (i.e., reciprocity). In this way it attempts to deal with the main problems presented by postmodern analysis; the revival of pragmatism and the failure of foundational beliefs, the incommensurability of values and the fragmentation of self: see *ibid.*, at 62–7.

[145] R. Cotterrell, *Law's Community: Legal Theory in Sociological Perspective* (Oxford, Clarendon Press, 1995), particularly at 246 and 332–7.

[146] *Ibid.* and see Kupfer, n. 130 above and A. C. Hutchinson, "Legal Ethics for a fragmented society: between professional and personal" (1998) *International Journal of the Legal Profession* 175.

[147] L. Sheinman, "Looking for Legal Ethics" (1997) 4 *International Journal of the Legal Profession* 139.

[148] Glasser, n. 11 above.

ethics are to be "taught" should lawyers be required merely to be thoroughly familiar with their professional code or should they be encouraged to develop "moral autonomy"? Should they question the code, even be permitted to disobey it on occasions? The answers to these questions depend on which of the philosophies or approaches to ethics the profession adopts. Each philosophy suggests a different approach to education. The ethical regimes which have emerged are often a kind of hybrid. Professionals are relied on to understand ethics intuitively. But this is unrealistic. The alternative—moral autonomy and ethical awareness—is difficult both to teach and verify.[149] What will emerge from the current interest in the idea of using legal education to promote professional ethics? It is to be hoped that it is something ambitious, a scheme which does justice to the importance of ethics to the future development of the legal profession.

[149] Kupfer, n. 130 above, at 112.

PART III

The Focus of Professional Duties

Introduction

In the next three chapters we consider the basic ethical principles and rules of conduct governing a lawyer's duties to clients and the consequences which flow from that obligation in relation to duties to others such as third parties, the profession and the state.[1] We are concerned with the balance the lawyer is expected to achieve between the needs and rights of clients, third parties, the profession and society in general. In Part IV we deal in more detail with the conflicts that may arise between the client's interests and those of the lawyer (for example in relation to fees), and conflicts between the client's interests and those of other relevant persons or bodies, such as the other side, the court, opposing lawyers or other third parties.

All professions share a commitment to the service of clients. Four virtues attempt to reconcile the notion of service to clients with wider obligations. These are beneficence, doing good to others when it is possible to do so without harming ourselves; non-malificence, avoiding needless harm to others, including the profession; justice, seeking equality between interests, often manifest in the provision of professional services on the basis of need rather than ability to pay; autonomy, an obligation to recognise the right of individuals to make their own decisions.[2] Although each profession may represent these virtues in different ways in their ethical codes, Koehn argues that the fundamental virtues can be reconciled: professionals have authority and justify trust, (a) because of a public pledge, (b) to promote the good of both individual clients and those in need,[3] (c) while being committed to consider the good of other members of the community affected by service to clients.[4] In Chapter 7 we explore the nature of the lawyer–client relationship and in Chapter 8 the duty to third parties. The position of those in need is considered in Chapter 9.

In addition to an examination of the rules and guidance, we also consider in greater detail a fundamental question raised in Part I. Given the longstanding

---

[1] We have not considered here the duties owed by lawyers as employers or as employees. This is not to underestimate the significance of such duties or their relevance either to the nature of duties owed to clients or to the quality of relationships with clients. These may well be affected by how an employer deals with an employee; how she is trained, instructed or treated. This issue is dealt with indirectly in several places and detailed treatment is not within the scope of this book, but see further M. D. Bayles, *Professional Ethics* (Belmont Calif., Wadsworth Publishing, 1981).

[2] S. C. Childs, "Ethics and the Professional Family Mediator" (1992) 10 *Mediation Quarterly* 155.

[3] D. Koehn, *The Ground of Professional Ethics* (London and New York, Routledge, 1994), chap. 4. (Note that, in reaching this conclusion, Koehn dismisses both expertise and contract as the "ground"—the source of professional authority, i.e. which distinguishes professional authority from authority as such at 7–9—as insufficient explanation of the trust placed in professionals.)

[4] *Ibid.*, at 174.

obligations of secrecy, diligence and fidelity owed by advocates to clients,[5] how far can, or should, a lawyer depart from his or her own personal ethics in advancing the interests of the client? This issue also clearly arises in the context of the lawyer's advocacy role, which is discussed in more detail in Chapter 14.

[5] This was asserted to be the central triumvirate of duties as long ago as the 17th century (see futher R. Cranston "Legal Ethics and Professional Responsibility" in R. Cranston (ed.), *Legal Ethics and Professional Responsibility* (Oxford: Clarendon Press, 1995).

7

Lawyers and their Clients

"In certain respects the legal profession occupies a position which differs from that occupied by other professions. Lawyers must always act in their clients' best interests and must refuse to act if a conflict of interest occurs; lawyers have a duty to the court; they are sometimes required to represent clients in unpopular causes; they have a duty to uphold the rule of law; for all these reasons the ordinary commercial considerations cannot be decisive if the traditional character and functions of an independent legal profession are to be preserved."[1]

A.INTRODUCTION

This chapter is concerned with the general principles that currently govern the relationship of the lawyer with the client. These duties may conflict with obligations owed to other parties or with wider public duties, such as the lawyer's duty to the court. This is dealt with in Chapter 14 on advocacy.

A useful starting point for the consideration of the ethics of the lawyer and client relationship is Luban's identification of two principles which are fundamental to the role of lawyers in a democratic society; neutrality (or non-accountability) and partisanship.[2] These principles are central to the issue of who lawyers should accept as clients and what they are entitled to do on behalf of those clients. The principle of neutrality suggests that lawyers adopt a neutral stance in relation to their client and their client's cause. An unrestrained requirement of neutrality, therefore, requires that lawyers defend causes that they find morally repugnant. "In representing a client, a lawyer is neither legally, professionally, nor morally accountable for the means or the ends achieved." The principle of partisanship requires that lawyers "maximise the likelihood that the client's objectives will be attained". Both principles require that the lawyer puts aside questions of his or her personal morality in deciding whether to represent a client and, once that decision is taken, how to represent that client. This enables lawyers to avoid responsibility for having to assist a client to achieve a purpose about which the lawyer would otherwise have moral qualms. The justification for this is that neutrality and partisanship reinforce the notion of

[1] Lady Marre CBE, *A Time for Change: Report of the Committee on the Future of the Legal Profession* (London, General Council of the Bar and Council of The Law Society, 1998), hereafter the Marre Report, at para. 6.1.

[2] See D. Luban, "Partnership, Betrayal and Autonomy in the Lawyer/Client Relationship" (1990) 90 *Columbia Law Review* 1004 and *Lawyers and Justice* (Princeton, NJ, Princetown UP, 1998). See also the discussion in Chap. 1 of this book, at 27–9.

equality before the law which is itself a social good, particularly in a society of pluralistic values. Nevertheless, it also means that, instead of striving to do justice, lawyers must follow rules which may, *or may not*, lead to justice being done.[3]

B. GAINING AND REFUSING CLIENTS

The process of gaining clients may have a profound effect on the nature of particular lawyer and client relationships. The basis on which the lawyer provides services as well as the expectations of the client may be influenced by the process by which each client has been acquired and what the client is told during the process of acquisition. Advertising, previously banned as being unethical, is one way of attracting and informing clients. Personal contact and word of mouth were the methods traditionally used, methods which favoured lawyers with established clienteles. Paying for client referrals is still unacceptable according to the codes of conduct. Given that the principle of neutrality prioritises access to representation, the question of when clients can be refused or existing retainers terminated, and on what basis, is also relevant in this context.

Advertising

Advertising legal services is now permitted but is regulated by both the Bar and the Law Society. Advertising can be a valuable source of information for consumers, enabling them to make an informed choice of advisor. Alternatively it can be a way of concealing problems or inflating virtues. Since 1989 the Bar has permitted barristers to advertise in accordance with the British Code of Advertising Practice. Fees and methods of charging can be advertised but certain other claims are banned. In particular barristers may not "make comparisons with or criticisms of other barristers or members of any other profession". Nor may they make claims about the quality of their work or their success rates. Their advertising must not "diminish public confidence in the legal profession or the administration of justice or otherwise bring the legal professional into disrepute". Nor must it indicate that the barrister will restrict the clients who will be represented other than in compliance with the *Bar Code*.[4]

Solicitors' advertising must, of course, comply with any legal requirements, for example in relation to investment advice and services. Apart from such provisions, the Solicitors' Practice Rules 1990 rule 2 permits advertising in compliance with the Solicitors' Publicity Code promulgated by the Council of the Law

---

[3] L. J. Tapp and F. J. Levine, "Legal Socialisation" in W. M. Evan (ed.), *The Sociology of Law* (London and New York, The Free Press, 1980) at 121.

[4] *Code of Conduct of the Bar of England and Wales* (London, The General Council of the Bar of England and Wales, 1990), at paras. 307.1 and 307.2, hereafter the *Bar Code*.

Society.[5] Publicity must not be "in bad taste" and must not be misleading or inaccurate. Examples of misleading advertisements in relation to conveyancing are given in the Advertising Code. If the advertisement states a fixed fee for conveyancing and then the solicitor charges as disbursements "expenses which are in the nature of overheads such as normal postage and telephone calls", this is misleading.[6] Solicitors can now claim to be experts in a particular field provided they can justify such a claim. As with barristers, they may not advertise success rates or compare their charges or quality with that or other solicitors.

Fees can be advertised but with restrictions. To advertise that fees "start from £X" is not allowed. It must be clear what is being offered for the fee or the basis on which a fee is charged. The position in relation to VAT and disbursements must be stated. Solicitors can advertise a free service but such a service must not be conditional on the client retaining the solicitor subsequently or on the solicitor receiving any commission in relation to the matter. There are a number of other rules relating to the description of staff, multi-national practices, etc. which need not be detailed here. Breaches of the Code should be reported to the Office for the Supervision of Solicitors

Personal Contact and Referrals

Many clients are obtained through personal contacts. There is, according to the *Law Society Guide*, nothing unethical in seeking clients by contacting other solicitors *or potential professional* connections. Seeking clients through professional contacts with estate agents or insurance agents on the golf course or in a club therefore is acceptable. Cold-calling in old people's homes to make their wills is not. The solicitors' Introduction and Referral Code[7] stresses that in accepting such business the solicitor must not compromise the duty to the client or any of the other obligations listed in Practice Rule 1. The "introducer" should be told the basis upon which the solicitor accepts instruction and also the fees charged. Solicitors are also warned that they should not "become so reliant on a limited number of sources of referrals that the interests of an introducer affect the advice given by the solicitor to clients".[8] How this advice is policed is not clear. However, the danger is clear. If a solicitor becomes over-reliant on introductions from a particular firm of estate agents, for example, he or she may be hesitant in giving any advice to the client which might cause conflict with that estate agent and risk the source of business drying up. The solicitor has a duty to warn the client of any potential problem in relation to a house purchase but

---

[5] See N. Taylor (ed.), *The Guide to the Professional Conduct of Solicitors* (London, The Law Society, 1996), at 196, hereafter the *Law Society Guide*.

[6] Which illustrates the general problem of the definition of disbursements mentioned further in Chap. 12 on Fees and Costs.

[7] *Law Society Guide,* n. 5 above, at 205.

[8] *Ibid.*, s.2(4) and (5).

in so doing the client might withdraw from the purchase. This could compromise the solicitors' relationship with the estate agent who introduced the client.

The introduction to the Referral Code suggests that firms should keep a record of agreements for the introduction of work, that they should review the situation every six months to ascertain whether or not the provisions of the Code have been complied with, that such referred clients have indeed been given "impartial advice" and the amount of income that had been earned from such introductions. In general, if more than 20 per cent of a firm's income has been derived from a "single source of introduction", then the firm should "consider whether steps should be taken to reduce that proportion".[9]

Whether this advice is in fact adhered to is doubtful. This Code does not require that the *client* is given any information about the relationship of the introducer and the solicitor or the amount of work that the solicitor obtains from that introducer. If there is an agreement between the solicitor and the introducer for the provision of services (e.g. where an insurance company uses the services of a particular solicitor in relation to the work of its customers) then the *introducer* (not the client) must be reminded that the solicitor is subject to the instructions of the client and that there is a privileged relationship between them.[10] It appears, therefore, that the code is more concerned to protect the referral relationship than to protect the interests of clients where information is concerned.

A major rule governing referrals of business concerns payment. The code states clearly that "solicitors must not reward introducers by the payment of commission or otherwise. However this does not prevent normal hospitality."[11] This rule must be read with Rule 7 of the Solicitors' Practice Rules which prohibits fee sharing with anyone other than another solicitor or *bona fide* employee of the practice. As Mr Justice Lightman commented in a recent case, "clients are not merchantable commodities to be bought and sold".[12] The reason for the rule is obvious. The acceptance of introduction fees would create a clear conflict of interest between the solicitor and the client. Despite Rule 7, it appears that paying for lists of possible clients, such as lists of accident victims, is ethically acceptable at present. This issue, as well as the general issue of professional referrals, is being reviewed currently by the Law Society.[13]

Refusing to Represent

A lawyer may be asked to take on a client who might be regarded as an immoral person or who wishes to implicate the lawyer in a scheme that the lawyer con-

---

[9] *Introduction and Referral Code*, sect. 2, paras. 10–12.

[10] *Ibid.*, sect. 3, para. 4.

[11] *Ibid.*, sect. 2, para. 3.

[12] In *Mohamed* v. *Alaga & Co.*[1998] 2 All ER 720 at 724.

[13] See *Law Society Gazette*, 21 October 1998 at 40 for the draft new referral code which is now subject to consultation with the profession.

siders immoral or improper. Equally, an existing unobjectionable client may want the lawyer to undertake an immoral or improper action in the course of his or her retainer. Can and should a lawyer refuse to represent a person who is regarded as immoral or undesirable in some way, such as a member of an extreme political party, a serial rapist or a major polluter of the environment? Many lawyers strongly adhere to the view that, however unpleasant, every person is entitled to representation. This is akin to the idea that however much one may disagree with another's views, the right to express those views will be resolutely defended. Alternatively, lawyers may appeal to the idea that in representing the objectionable client they are defending a wider principle. Lawyers for the American Civil Liberties Union defended Nazis on the basis that "our real client is the Bill of Rights". As David Luban comments, this justification is unlikely to be relevant to the vast majority of cases; a business lawyer does not accept an unpleasant corporate client on the basis that the real client is the Uniform Commercial Code.[14]

The barrister is subject to the cab-rank rule, a rule which embodies the above idea. This rule, which applies to all the work of barristers but which is linked mainly with their role as advocates, obliges a barrister to take on a client irrespective of the nature of the client's case or any views the barrister may have of the client's character or reputation.[15] It is a rule which expresses the fundamental nature of the lawyer–client relationship in England and Wales, namely that the lawyer is not to be identified personally with the client's aims or objectives but will provide access to his or her legal skills, in the interests of justice, to all who need them. The cab-rank rule is subject, however, to many exceptions. For example the barrister can refuse the brief if already fully employed, the fee offered is not what the barrister normally charges, the case is not within the barrister's competence or there is a conflict of interest. The cab-rank rule can be manipulated by both clients and barristers. Clients may seek to enforce it on a barrister so as to confuse the opposing party or the jury, as where a person accused of a racial attack briefs a black barrister. Barristers may avoid its operation by resorting to the many exceptions.

A recent example related to Lady Porter's appeal against a surcharge of £27 million imposed on her in connection with alleged gerrymandering activities carried out when she was leader of Westminster Council in London. She wished to brief Lord Neill QC, who, in addition to being a practising barrister, was Chair of the Committee on Standards in Public Life, the "Government watchdog on public ethics".[16] The brief was seen as a propaganda coup for Lady Porter—she would be represented by a barrister identified with the promotion of high ethical standards. The acceptance of the brief was defended by Lord Neill by reference to the cab-rank rule, saying "[b]y long tradition, members of

---

[14] Luban, n. 2 above, at 1009.
[15] *Bar Code*, n. 4 above, paras. 209, 501–503. See further on the cab-rank rule, Chap. 14 on advocacy.
[16] *The Guardian*, 20 June 1998.

the Bar accept instructions on . . . the cab-rank principle. They do not pick and choose their cases on the basis of the popularity or unpopularity of the case or the client." This explanation was treated with some disbelief. Lord Neill could clearly have avoided the brief by claiming to be too busy or that there was a conflict of interest with his public office. In the event he withdrew from the case on the ground that to continue would damage the interests of the client and because of the "perceived" conflict of interest.[17]

The solicitor, unlike the barrister, is not subject to the cab-rank rule and can in general refuse clients. Subject to the provisions of the Advocacy Code,[18] a solicitor is "free to decide whether to accept instructions from any particular client".[19] In practice many solicitors adopt the principle behind the cab-rank rule, namely that no person should fail to obtain representation because of the unpopularity of his views or unpleasantness of his character. The right of solicitors to refuse clients is limited by a general obligation not to discriminate unlawfully, that is on the basis of sex, race, colour, national or ethnic origins, marital status or, now, disability. The Law Society Anti-discrimination Rules also require solicitors not to discriminate on the ground of creed or sexual orientation.[20] A solicitor should not accept a client if he or she believes that the client wishes solely to gratify his or her "malice or vindictiveness".[21] On this basis, presumably, the solicitor must refuse to accept, for example, a anti-Semitic client who wishes to pursue a trivial case solely to harass a Jewish opponent. On the other hand, there is no obligation to take on that client even if the client wishes both to enforce an undoubted legal right and to harass the defendant. Equally there is no obligation to represent the anti-Semitic client in a case where his or her civil rights are threatened by the police. Many solicitors would, however, take the view that such a person is entitled to representation if only to ensure that a wider interest—that of justice—is served.

Some commentators state that there is an exception to these rules in legal aid cases. Under the provisions of the Legal Aid Act 1988, section 32(1), "[s]ubject to the provisions of this section, a person entitled to receive advice or assistance or representation may select the legal representative . . . from among the legal representatives willing to provide [it] under this Act". In *Cordery* it is concluded from this that a solicitor cannot refuse a client who is eligible for legal aid.[22] This seems to be a misunderstanding of the section. Not only does section 32(1) not impose any obligation on the solicitor (being selected by a prospective client does not imply an obligation to accept selection), but section 32(6) specifically provides that "the selection or assignment to a person of solicitor or counsel shall not prejudice the law and practice relating to the conduct of proceedings

---

[17] *The Guardian*, 24 June 1998.
[18] See further Chap. 12 on solicitors' advocacy code.
[19] *Law Society Guide*, n. 5 above rule 7.02, para. 3 and rule 12.01.
[20] *Ibid.*, and see Chap. 12 below.
[21] *Law Society Guide*, n. 5 above, rule 12.01, para. 5.
[22] See J. A. Holland (ed.), *Cordery on Solicitors* (London, Butterworths, 1995), Sect. E, para. 253 (4).

by a solicitor or counsel or the circumstances in which a solicitor or counsel *may refuse or give up a case* or entrust it to another".[23]

Terminating the Retainer

Having accepted the client, can a lawyer later withdraw from the representation? Despite the fact that solicitors are under no formal cab-rank obligations to accept clients, once the client has been accepted the solicitor must not terminate the relationship except for "good reason and upon reasonable notice".[24] Examples of good reasons provided in the *Guide* are breaches of the rules of conduct (e.g. where there is a conflict of interest), inability to obtain clear instructions from the client or "where there is a serious breakdown of confidence" between solicitor and client. Such a breakdown could, possibly, be created where the client was determined on a course of conduct to which the solicitor had grave moral objections. Such an idea is not canvassed in the *Guide*. There are other grounds for termination, including failure to make agreed payments on account, bankruptcy of either solicitor or client and mental incapacity.

Barristers must cease to act if continuation would cause them professional embarrassment.[25] This phrase embodies all the reasons, such as lack of skill or time, which justify refusing the brief in the first place.[26] They can also cease to act where legal aid has been wrongly obtained and the client refuses to remedy the situation and also in circumstances where to continue to act would involve a breach of the law or professional conduct rules.

C. THE NATURE OF THE LAWYER AND CLIENT RELATIONSHIP

The most basic premise of professional ethics is that the client's interests should take precedence over those of the lawyer.[27] Can this vision of professional commitments as essentially altruistic be reconciled with suggestions that human beings are motivated purely by self-interest? Here we must distinguish unrestrained self-interest, the pursuit of present impulses and feelings, and enlightened self-interest which is more subtle and long term.[28] Enlightened self-interest might predispose professionals to act with integrity. In this way they may achieve both the intrinsic good of self-respect and the extrinsic good of status

---

[23] Emphasis added.
[24] *Law Society Guide*, n. 5 above, rule 12.10.
[25] *Bar Code*, n. 4 above, rule 504.
[26] *Ibid.*, rule 501.
[27] *Ibid.*, rule 203, and see *The Law Society Guide*, n. 5 above, rule 1.01c.
[28] P. A. Facione, D. Scherer and T. Attig, *Values and Society: An Introduction to Ethics and Social Philosophy* (Englewood Cliffs, NJ, Prentice Hall Inc., 1978), at 39–40.

and power. So, by behaving ethically, practitioners serve their own long term commercial interests, for:

"The client is dependent for his welfare on the accomplishment of the task; but he is not competent to assess the adequacy of the work done; recognised competence in the set of tasks is legally restricted to those certified to have completed a training of a scientific character; and in exchange for the monopoly of practice the group accepts responsibility for the achievement of the purposes of clients. The situation of the professional thus involves an essential fiduciary element; incompetence or malfeasance constitutes a betrayal of the clients' trust. Should this occur, there is a risk of scandal, and the erosion of or loss of the legally enforced monopoly enjoyed by the professional group . . . It is thus in the long term collective interests of the profession to maintain standards of work and to protect the interests of clients."[29]

Giving priority to the interests of the client may be the basic principle, but how should that principle be translated into everyday practice? The relationship of all professional persons with their clients, or patients, has been the subject of considerable debate in the last 25 years or so. The modern view is that the relationship with clients should be one that, like many other professional relationships, has the capacity to empower them by treating them as an individual and allowing them to reach their own decisions. Indeed, the feature which unites professional skills and virtues is precisely the professional commitment to treating clients as individuals. Therefore, the professional must hear a client's individual story before deciding what can be done. This sensitivity to human individuality ensures that professionals do not subvert clients' personal values or take over and manage their lives.[30]

This participatory approach implies a continual dialogue between lawyer and client. At each stage the progress of work should evaluated in the light of the client's aims and interests. New agreements are reached on the steps to be taken. The relationship between lawyers and clients should be client-centred because:

"Client-centred relationships entail shared decision-making responsibility and mutual participation by lawyer and client. By avoiding the trap of either lawyer or client-dominance, these relationships provide greater opportunities for facilitating wise client decisions in a supportive atmosphere."[31]

In effect, the client has control over decision-making and the lawyer is a technical advisor and counsellor. This conception of the lawyer–client relationship

---

[29] J. R. Ravetz, "Ethics in Scientific Activity" in A. Flores (ed.), *Professional Ideals* (Belmont Calif., Wadsworth Publishing, 1988), 147 at 152. It may be of concern that professionals might place the interests of others before their own interests for selfish, rather than altruistic, reason. Philosophers have long debated the issue of whether altruism must have a generous motive as well as a generous act. As more is discovered about human motivation, however, the less relevant this objection seems. For a scientific discussion of this issue see M. Ridley, *The Origin of Virtue* (Harmondsworth, Penguin, 1997), particularly chap. 1.

[30] Koehn, n. 3 above, at 176.

[31] R. D. Dinerstein, "Client-Centered Counselling: Reappraisal and Refinement" (1990) 32 *Arizona Law Review* 501 at 556.

can be contrasted with the traditional or paternalistic view. This is that, once the lawyer has been engaged by the client and been broadly instructed on what the client wants to achieve, the lawyer should be left to take the decisions in the best interests of the client. The lawyer, argues the paternalist, has superior knowledge, skills and experience of the matter in hand and therefore knows what is best. The issues involved are far too complicated for clients to understand: this is why they need lawyers. This view, writes the American commentator, Deborah Rhode, is now "seldom preached but often practised".[32]

In England, however, the paternalistic view of the lawyer and client relationship *is* preached by the profession, as is clearly reflected in Practice Rule 1. This requires the solicitor to "act in the best interests of the client" but says nothing about how much information should be given to the client or about the lawyer's responsibility for following the client's instructions. In view of the fact that Practice Rule 1 is meant to express the basic principles of professional conduct,[33] this omission is surprising. In an experiment reported in 1986 one of the most significant "failures" of newly qualified solicitors conducting an initial interview was that they recorded what they had to do for the client in their notes but did not share this information with the client.[34]

The Bar Code says virtually nothing about relationships with clients; presumably this is considered to be the solicitor's concern. Barristers are required by their Code simply to promote the client's best interests fearlessly.[35] Indeed the barrister is told not to "compromise his professional standards in order to please his client".[36] One concession to the client mentioned in the Bar Code is the injunction to write clear comprehensible advice.[37]

This presents a considerable contrast to the Code of the American Bar Association which does not mention the client's best interest. It stresses that the role of the lawyer is to do what the client requires even if this is unwise. The lawyer should "abide by a client's decisions concerning the objectives of the representation".[38] David Luban concludes, "the American model is loyalty to the client's wishes and not his interests".[39] However, in reality, the paternalistic, and even domineering, lawyer is to be found as much in the United States as in the United Kingdom. In research conducted in the USA it was found that higher levels of participation by clients in their personal injury claims tended to

---

[32] D. Rhode, *Professional Responsibility: Ethics by the Pervasive Method* (Boston, Mass., Little Brown, 1994), at 411.

[33] *Law Society Guide*, n. 5 above, at 2, para. 4.

[34] A. Sherr, "Lawyers and Clients: The First Meeting" (1986) 49 *Modern Law Review* 323 at 330. It will be noted that this experiment was conducted before the introduction of interviewing on the Legal Practice Course. This may have remedied some of the problems identified in this research.

[35] *Bar Code*, n. 4 above, para. 203 and Annex H, para. 5.1.

[36] *Ibid.*, para. 205. Nor must the barrister compromise those standards in order to please the court or a third party.

[37] *Ibid.*, Annex H, para. 5.7.

[38] Model Rule 1.2.

[39] D. Luban, "The Sources of Legal Ethics" (1984) 48 *Rabels Zeitschift* 262.

increase the sums that they recovered in damages.[40] This suggests that paternalistic professional relationships are not in the best interests of clients.

Some paternalism is unavoidable in many lawyer–client relationships, and the more vulnerable the client the more paternalistic that relationship is likely to be. However many would prefer to develop a model of the relationship which accords a high level of respect for client autonomy and collaborative working practices. This view is also prevalent in relation to other professional relationships such as doctor, or nurse, and patient. The reasons for attacking the paternalistic model are generally based on the notion of personal autonomy. People should be allowed and enabled to make as many decisions as possible for themselves; to exercise free will. They should be seen not as passive recipients of advice or assistance, but as consumers. As such they have a right to obtain what they want in a form which is appropriate to their circumstances.[41] Professional help may be needed, and in some cases may be essential, to achieve this but sufficient information should be given to allow clients to make their own informed decisions on their own interests.

Many solicitors argue that they should not be passive in the relationship either, that promoting client autonomy is not simply a question of doing what clients say. It may include a responsibility to ensure that *clients* make ethically defensible decisions. Further in many cases the slavish pursuit of the client's wishes may produce an unsatisfactory result. In one study, for example, a litigation solicitor said:

> "Many solicitors come unstuck because, at the end of the day, it is very difficult to deceive the court . . . if a case is properly investigated, prepared and looked after there is little chance of you being taken by surprise. In that connection, over the years I have . . . listened to what the client has said but will also taken steps to investigate what the other side has said and investigate this with my own client. I am not blinded by what they [clients] tell me. By asking questions I test the truth or otherwise of what they say and discuss it with them . . . if the client tries to trick me they usually come unstuck . . ."[42]

The value of patient autonomy has, in the medical field, led to much discussion of the need to ensure that the patient makes an informed consent to treatment. In many jurisdictions this has led to the abandonment of the *Bolam* test[43] which states that it is for the doctor's professional judgement to decide what to tell the patient. Instead the "prudent patient" test is preferred—what would the prudent patient in his or her particular circumstances need to know about his

---

[40] See D. E. Rosenthal, *Lawyer and Client: Who's in Charge?*, which dates from 1974 and therefore might not reflect current practice (New York, Russel Sage Foundation, 1974). See also A. Gutmann, "Can Lawyers be Taught Virtue" (1993) 45 *Standford Law Review* 1759.

[41] See Chap. 2 on consumerism.

[42] A. Boon, "Assessing Competence to Conduct Civil Litigation: Key Tasks and Skills" in P. Hassett and M. Fitzgerald (eds.), *Skills for Legal Functions II: Representation and Advice* (London, Institute of Advanced Legal Studies, 1992), hereafter *Assessing Competence*.

[43] *Bolam* v. *Friern Hospital Management Committee* [1957] 1 WLR 582.

medical condition in order to decide what treatment to follow? Little of this discussion has arisen in the context of lawyer and client, which is ironic as one of the lawyer's main functions is to facilitate client autonomy.[44] No cases on the issue have come before the English courts, probably because of the immunity from suit enjoyed by litigation lawyers.

D. MODELS OF LAWYER–CLIENT RELATIONSHIPS

One approach to examining the nature of the lawyer and client relationship is by analogy with existing legal relationships. The relationship and its obligations have been compared with agency, contract and trust relationships. These concepts are illuminating in terms of defining the legal nature of the relationship. The ethical approach adopted in relation to key issues such as confidentiality, conflict of interest, the financial relationship between lawyer and client and the nature of the bargaining and advocacy role will be influenced by the model of the lawyer–client relationship which is adopted by the profession. But to some extent they have been overtaken by other concerns. Over the years the issue of control of decision-making has become an important issue. Whether or not the lawyer or the client has primary responsibility in this area is somewhat obscured by focusing on legal obligations.

Agency

One model is that of the professional as agent for the client. In this model the client directs the professional as to the broad remit of the task, but the professional, as an agent, has considerable latitude as to how the task is achieved. There are constraints on the agent but the constraints are often fixed by the general law or by custom and practice. Such constraints are mainly concerned with the duty the agent owes to the principal. Therefore, they largely operate so as to reinforce the fidelity of the agent to the principal's prime objective. In the context of legal practice this model is consistent with visions of the lawyer as a "hired gun" or the client's mouthpiece.[45] There are two problems with this model. First, it seems to require the lawyer to abandon any moral evaluation of the client's objectives or methods of achieving them. The lawyer is unconcerned with the moral or other worth of the client or with his or her objectives, since lawyers cannot presume to question the task given to them. Secondly, the lawyer may lose his or her own personal autonomy and his or her capacity to act in a

---

[44] For a good discussion of this idea see S. L. Pepper, "The Lawyer's Amoral Ethical Role" [1986] *American Bar Foundation Research Journal* 613 and reply by Luban [1987] *American Bar Foundation Research Journal* 637. See also S. Spiegel, "Lawyering and Client Decision Making: Informed Consent and the Legal Profession" (1978) 128 *University of Pennsylvania Law Review* 41.

[45] See Chap. 14, on the implications of this in relation to advocacy.

professional manner may be compromised. The model cannot easily be reconciled with the requirements of both the law and professional conduct codes. It is not consistent with the lawyer's obligation to take into account the public interest, the interests of justice and the duty to the court.

Contractual Relationships

Another model is that of contract: this conception of the relationship sees lawyers and clients as parties to a bargain where they have agreed their respective rights and duties on both sides. Some of these duties are assumed, i.e. they are imposed by the law or professional codes. This model presumes an equal relationship which may not exist. The client may be ignorant or poor and at a disadvantage in agreeing terms. Alternatively, a rich and powerful corporate client is capable of dominating the lawyer. The contractual model may incorporate a high degree of lawyer paternalism or alternatively a high degree of client autonomy. What determines this is the respective bargaining power of the client and the lawyer and, where the client has power, the degree to which he or she wishes to be involved in decision-making.

The Fiduciary Model

Under the fiduciary model the superior knowledge and skills of the professional are acknowledged, in that he or she is required to take special care to ensure that no advantage is taken of the client, and that there will be no undue influence.[46] This is based on the concept in the law of trusts whereby a trustee is subject to a high degree of responsibility for protecting the interests of the beneficiaries of the trust. There is a presumption that any profit made from dealings arising from the relationship by the trustee is a breach of trust. The fiduciary model often involves a higher level of participation than is necessary in the other models. If the lawyer is expected to act in the client's best interests, clearly the client has to be consulted and counselled so as to establish exactly what his or her best interests may be. But consultation is only necessary thereafter when vital interests are affected, possibly only at the end of the transaction. So, the fiduciary model does not always conform to the participatory model of decision-making. True, the lawyer must make every reasonable effort to inform the client and then to obtain his or her authority to act. But, the day-to-day conduct of a transaction is a matter purely for the lawyer and all kinds of decisions which may or may not affect the client, including ethical decisions, may be taken on his or her behalf by the professional. The client is expected to trust the lawyer and the lawyer to justify that trust.

---

[46] This is the model favoured but not discussed in detail in Holland, n. 22 above, at sect. F, para. 87. For a full discussion of this model in the American context, see Dinerstein, n. 31 above.

E. APPLICATION OF THE MODELS TO PRACTICE

As with all models, the three alternatives outlined have limitations in describing what the profession is trying to achieve, what is happening "on the ground" and in terms of conceptualising the lawyer–client relationship.[47] In different fields of practice or in any particular client–lawyer relationship any one of the models or all three may be in operation. A few examples may serve to illustrate this point. One fundamental difference is in the dimensions of problems presented by different kinds of clients. So, for example:

> "In company/commercial work the client is aware through their own experience and so the solicitor is helped by the client. Also the possible permutations of problems have been explored before. In a High St. firm it can be anything; emotional, legal and quasi-legal problems all need to be unravelled . . ."[48]

The relationship between lawyer and corporate client can be very different from that of lawyer and individual client. The role of the lawyer in the "mega lawyering" context of big corporate or class action litigation as described by Galanter may well be more akin to a cog in a machine rather than that of autonomous independent professional person. The corporate client involved in heavy strategic litigation may be served by teams of lawyers who provide a customised service for years.[49] This is very different work from the high street lawyer making a living from a series of individual criminal or matrimonial clients. Representing a child, a confused elderly person or a mental patient may justify a more paternalistic approach than representing a healthy adult. It is nevertheless important not to ignore the shift towards participatory decision-making because it is often expected by clients and, indeed, by the courts. In *Griffiths* v. *Dawson*,[50] for example, a solicitor failed to oppose a divorce petition based on five years' separation on the ground of financial hardship because he considered such opposition to be "unsporting". The wife lost pension rights as a result. The solicitor was held to be negligent—he should have filed the defence, unless specifically instructed not to do so, and not have decided himself on the basis of his own personal views.

The fiduciary model, which we consider is closest to what the profession is presently trying to achieve, demands more of some weaker clients than they are either capable of or desire. Equally, the powerful clients may wish to insist on an arrangement which is closer to the contractual or agency model. Some

---

[47] For a fuller discussion of these models see M. Bayles, *Professional Ethics* (Belmont, Calif., Wadsworth Publishing, 1981).

[48] Boon, n. 42 above.

[49] This was the case in the USA, e.g., where litigation involving Braniff Airlines went on for 12 years to try to eliminate competition from lucrative routes. Lloyd's of London have produced a code regulating the relationship of Lloyd's Underwriters and their lawyers. The lawyers must justify their fees, provide advance notice of bills, standardise their advice and make greater use of ADR. See *Law Society Gazette*, 1 July 1998, at 9.

[50] [1993] FL 315.

clients, those with comparatively simple or routine legal needs, will just want the lawyer to get on with the work efficiently and not bother them with information or alternatives to choose from. Moreover, funding constraints may impose limitations on what the lawyer would wish to do if he or she had no concerns about who was paying for his or her time. Thus, in one study, a personal injury lawyer said:

> "In PI you are getting to the sort of Tesco stage: pile it high and sell it cheap, get turnover moving as quickly as you can. The service that we are going to deliver to our clients in the future will be much less than it is at the moment, you will be saying to clients, "Don't phone me up, if you do I will charge you. Don't write me letters unless I want something from you . . ."[51]

The model in use must, therefore, respond to the needs and abilities of the client in question, the nature of the work involved and the economic circumstances in which it is done.

There is, however, one issue which is raised by the shift to participative decision-making which perhaps arises less where a lawyer fulfils a more paternalistic role; what is the lawyer to do when the client seeks advice in such a way as to suggest that he intends to break the law? Pepper gives two hypothetical examples.[52] In the first example, a lawyer advising on the drafting of a contract is asked by the client what the consequences would be if he broke the contract three years hence. In the circumstances, the lawyer knows that the client will break the contract if the consequences are not financially unfavourable. In the second example, a client asks the lawyer about the legal consequences for someone who participates in consensual euthanasia where his or her own parent is terminally ill and in immense pain. Pepper speculates that full legal advice would include reference to extra-legal factors, which are not strictly legal knowledge but which could be relevant to the client's query. The advice could, therefore, include reference to court backlogs which might encourage the other contracting party to accept a lesser sum in damages than the claim is worth, or the practice of local prosecutors not to bring charges in cases of consensual euthanasia. By giving such information to the client, the lawyer could be seen to be counselling the commission of breaches of contract or crimes.

Pepper argues that in cases of contract or tort breaches are not prohibited; they merely invoke financial sanctions (a view that would be contested by many contract lawyers). Therefore, advice on financial consequences is ethical. Where criminal conduct has consequences for third parties however, he argues that lawyers should not provide advice which may assist in the commission of an offence. Beyond this, the multitude of situations which can arise make it diffi-

---

[51]   J. Flood, A. Boon, A. Whyte, E. Skordaki, R. Abbey and A. Ash, *Reconfiguring the Market for Advocacy Services: A Case Study of London and Four Fields of Practice* (a report for the Lord Chancellor's Committee on Legal Education and Conduct, 1996), hereinafter "ACLEC Report", at 36.

[52]   S. L. Pepper, "Counselling at the Limit of the Law: An Exercise in the Jurisprudence and Ethics of Lawyering" (1995) 104 *The Yale Law Journal* 1545.

cult to formulate clear rules or even guidelines. He suggests four relevant principles. The first principle is that the client is presumed to have a right to know
the law. The second is that the lawyer has an obligation to counsel the client if
the client is likely to use the advice in order to violate a significant legal or moral
norm. The third is that the lawyer is bound to consider a number of factors
regarding the impact of the conduct to which the advice may give rise.[53] Finally,
he argues, in addition to using these technical aids to decision-making, lawyers
must self-consciously balance the good of providing access to law with their
own obligation to their role as a lawyer.

F. THE POLICY OF THE LAW SOCIETY

The Bar continues to maintain a distance between barristers and lay clients. The
Law Society has, however, developed its rules and guidance recently to encourage a greater flow of information between solicitor and client. On the surface, it
appears that the Law Society favours the fiduciary model with a reasonably high
level of client participation. However, as we shall see, whether this is in fact
achieved in the current "client care" regime is open to doubt.

Central to any regime of participatory decision-making in the professional
context is the concept of informed consent, which, as has been noted, has been
developed primarily in relation to the doctor–patient relationship rather than
that of lawyer–client. In a participatory client care regime it would be expected
that this concept would take a central place. Unfortunately this does not appear
to be the case. The current client care regime is concerned more with standards
of work and with processing client complaints, rather than with promoting a
particular model of client–lawyer relationships.

The Client Care Guidance

> "Many [solicitors] are far too verbose, others insist on using legal jargon . . . there is
> nothing to be gained from keeping some mystique about the profession and coming
> out with phrases and procedures which the client does not understand and telling them
> its something they needn't be concerned with . . . they want to be able to conceptualise
> what's going on . . . It's when they don't quite understand what you have said and they
> ring you with the same question and you give them the same answer . . ."[54]

[53] Pepper acknowledges that the kinds of distinctions he draws are highly complex, but the kinds
of factors he indicates might be relevant include the distinction between criminal and civil law; conduct wrong in itself and conduct "merely" prohibited; the exent to which the particular law is
enforced; whether the query relates to procedural rules, substantive law or the enforcement of law
(e.g. where a criminal client seeks information relating to police procedures which might be known
to lawyer); whether the information is in the public or private sphere; whether the lawyer or client
initiated the discussion of the particular issue; the likelihood that the information will assist unlawful conduct: *ibid.*, at 1586.
[54] Boon, n. 42 above.

As this quotation by a solicitor suggests, client participation supported by good client care is usually in the professional's interest because, in the long run, it can save time. The fact that the Law Society came rather late to the notion of regulating client care suggests that it probably attempted to hang on to the paternalistic model for too long. The relevant rule[55] came into force in 1991 as a result of a number of scandals relating, in particular, to solicitors' charges. It was also linked to the failure of the old Solicitors' Complaints Bureau to convince the public that it could deal fairly with the resultant complaints.[56] Despite public dissatisfaction with the complaints system, it cost the profession a considerable sum to run. In 1991 it cost £7 million and this rose to £13 million by 1994–5. Solicitors felt they were paying a high price for what was often a public relations disaster, and the best way to manage the issue was to try to minimise the numbers of complaints by introducing new rules on client care.

Another pressure which led the Law Society to do something about client care was the need to protect solicitors' Legal Aid work. The government wanted value for money and made this very clear both in the context of the Legal Aid Efficiency Scrutiny[57] and in its plans for the development of Legal Aid franchising. Government concern was also expressed in the context of the general reform of the legal profession embodied in the Green Paper, *Legal Services: A Framework for the Future*, published in 1989. If the Law Society was going to retain its regulatory powers and protect the economic base of its members who depended on legal aid, it had to do something about standards of work and the treatment of complaints about bad service. In addition to the new rules and issuing guidance, the Law Society has promoted research into the issue. It is also possible for firms to acquire a Kite Mark (BS 5750) for effective practice management.

Practice Rule 15 was the result of this pressure, along with the Written Professional Standards and the Transaction Criteria. The Rule forms "the basis of a 'client care' regime which has gained a high profile in the general climate of accountability and consumerism to which legal services are being subjected".[58] Rule 15 is an odd compromise which aims to meet the consumer's desire for information, the demand for an effective response to complaints and the profession's desire to minimise regulation. Instead of beginning with some clear general rules on client information, it begins with the rule which requires every practice to set up a procedure for handling complaints.[59] Similarly, the Law Society publication, *Client Care, A Guide for Solicitors*,[60] stresses the need to

---

[55] Solicitors' Practice Rules 1990, r.15. Proposed new client care rules will be published by the Law Society in early 1999 and will be accompanied by new Terms of Business letter intended to assist solicitors in complying with the professional standards for costs information to clients (1998) and, in due course, with the changes to practice rule 15 *Gazette* 95/36 23 September 1998, 36.

[56] See the cases of Glanville Davies and Peggy Wood. See O. Hansen, *Legal Action,* Oct. 1993, at 9.

[57] *Legal Aid Efficiency Report* (London, Lord Chancellor's Department, 1986).

[58] N. Harris, "Do Solicitors Care for their Clients?" (1994) 13 *Civil Justice Quarterly* 359.

[59] On which see Chap. 5.

[60] (London, the Law Society, 1991).

improve communication between solicitor and client in order to prevent complaints.

Rule 15(2) is concerned with client information. *Unless it is inappropriate in the circumstances*[61] solicitors in private practice must inform their clients:

- of the name and status of the person dealing with their case and any principal responsible for supervision;
- who to approach with any problem;
- of appropriate information at relevant times on the issues raised and progress of the matter.

Rule 15 provides no further help. The rest of the chapter on client care in the *Guide to Professional Conduct* is guidance only, not rule, and the written professional standards concern only fees and costs.[62]

The Law Society guidance on client information in chapter 13 is vague. The principle is "to help clients who are unfamiliar with the law to understand what is happening".[63] Clients must be told the issues in the case and how they "will" be dealt with "in appropriate language".[64] Note the use of the word "will"; "may" would have been more appropriate if informed consent were the guiding principle and the client's instructions were really being sought. Other recommendations are discretionary and tentative. Solicitors "should consider" whether to confirm instructions in writing, for example. Nowhere is it clearly stated that clients are entitled to be properly consulted and informed before confirming the instructions or authorising a further step in the progress of the matter. The rules on costs are similarly discretionary.[65]

There are other provisions, apart from the written professional standards and rule 15, which encourage some solicitors to adopt a more informative and client-friendly approach. Firms which have, or wish to obtain, a Legal Aid franchise must reach certain standards in relation to client care. For example, it is mandatory for franchised firms to record the instructions and requirements of the client, to record the advice given and to comply with the written standards on costs, all of which must be confirmed with the client "ordinarily in writing".[66] The need for written communications with clients and the use of plain English is stressed. In complex cases (e.g. a High Court case or one with costs over £25,000), clients should agree a case plan which is periodically reviewed and updated.[67] In all cases information about the client's costs liability (e.g. relating to the statutory charge) must be given at least every six months. Many of the other franchise requirements on training staff, office management and main-

---

[61] Emphasis added.
[62] These, which also came into force in 1991, are dealt with in detail in Chap. 12 on fees and costs.
[63] *Law Society Guide*, n. 5 above, r. 13.04, para. 1.
[64] *Ibid.*, r. 13.04, para. 2.
[65] See Chap. 12.
[66] Franchise Specification 1993, paras. 3.70 and 3.71.
[67] *Ibid.*, para. 3.76.

taining records should have a beneficial influence on the quality of client care. Firms which fail to reach these standards may lose their Legal Aid franchise.

Finally, and very oddly, there is guidance in the chapter on confidentiality in the *Law Society Guide* on informing clients.[68] "Usually" a solicitor must give the client "all information which is material to the client's business".[69] Failure to do this would probably be negligence and also give rise to disciplinary proceedings. This means also that a solicitor should not agree to receive information that will not be disclosed to the client. There are some exceptions to this principle. For example solicitors, like doctors, claim a "therapeutic privilege" and need not disclose information that might harm the client, such as a report that the client suffers from a terminal illness.[70] No legal authority for this is provided in the *Law Society Guide*. However, it may be related to the discovery provisions in the Supreme Court Act 1981, section 33(2). This section permits the court in personal injury cases to order the production of certain records to the applicant's legal advisers or medical advisers, but not directly to the client-applicant.

Thin though they are, the client care practice standards are not adhered to by all firms, and these failures are the most common cause of client complaints, especially in relation to fees. The first Report of the Solicitors Complaints Bureau noted that "[a]bout 90% of complaints are resolved immediately once the client understands what has been going on".[71] Pressure for change is also found in Lord Woolf's proposals on civil litigation. Lord Woolf recommends that it should be mandatory for solicitors to inform clients how fees are calculated and what the overall costs are likely to be. Clients should be present at case management conferences so that they can understand what is happening and the likely cost. Woolf also suggests that clients should impose eight requirements on their solicitors, including eliminating unnecessary research, controlling the use of experts, preventing meetings when the phone will do and emphasising "that the case belongs to the client".[72] The Law Society has accepted the need for change and the Council agreed, in March 1997, to a new client care and costs code, details of which are not yet available.

The fact that the Law Society is promoting a model of practice which gives freer rein to clients' wishes and preferences addresses the central problem of the lawyer–client relationship; the paternalistic and disempowering effect of expert authority. It does however, create another problem. If the lawyer is more closely tied to the client's preferences and prejudices, what limits, ethical constraints, are there on the lawyer's actions? For, if the fiduciary model strengthens the

---

[68] Does the Law Society consider confidentiality a right of the solicitor, disclosure to the client being an exception to the right? This is what is implied by placing disclosure to the client in this chap. rather than in that on client care.

[69] *Law Society Guide*, n. 5 above, at 16.06.

[70] *Ibid.*, r. 16.06, para. 4. For other exceptions see r. 16.01, paras. 5 and 7.

[71] See also the study done for the National Consumer Council in 1993, and Harris, n. 58 above.

[72] Lord Woolf, *Access to Justice: Final Report to the Lord Chancellor on the Civil Justice System in England and Wales* (London, HMSO, 1996), hereafter *Final Report*, at 84 ff. Some of these ideas appear in the civil procedure rules due to come into force in April 1999.

hand of clients, what of the interests of third parties, opponents in a suit or participants in a transaction, who may be damaged, financially, socially or psychologically, by what a client requires the lawyer to do in the interests of the client? As we have seen, in the United States the pursuit of client preferences has been seen as the dominating principle of professional ethics. This leads lawyers to do things for clients which they would feel ashamed to do for themselves. How can this be justified? The justification provided is that the unique role of the lawyer requires a quite distinctive set of norms which are amoral in character; in effect that the practice of law has its own role morality, a proposition discussed in Chapter 1 and in the next section.

G. ROLE MORALITY

A professional, as noted above, may sometimes be required to do something for a client that he or she would not feel morally justified in doing for themselves, something which conflicts with the moral rules prevailing in the wider society. This conduct may be justified by the lawyer by appealing to the particular demands of the professional role. As we saw in Chapter 1, the distinctive and unique role of lawyers has, in the UK and the USA at any rate, been firmly linked with the concept of adversarialism. Adversary adjudication gives the parties substantial control over the conduct of their cases. The role of the lawyer is to act as the neutral and partisan advocate of the client in conducting that case. Lawyers are seen, stereotypically, as technicians, as skilful manipulators of legal rules for the benefit of their clients. Such pure legal advocates must suppress their own moral convictions concerning both the worth and the objectives of the client.[73] Paradoxically, whilst lawyers are expected to act co-operatively, altruistically and ethically when dealing *with* their clients, they are expected to be unco-operative, selfish and possibly unethical in pursuing the objectives *of* their clients, assuming that this is what the client wishes. This creates considerable moral strain.

Adversarialism is a concept which reflects a highly individualistic ethic. It is based on the idea that the best way to get at the truth is to allow each side to present its case in the way it thinks best. This approach has, however, been increasingly modified in the context of civil practice to encourage greater fairness and reciprocity, as greater pre-action discovery of evidence exemplifies. The other main justification of the adversarial ethic is that it protects individual autonomy and dignity. Each of the parties may decide for itself what it wishes to claim and how it wishes to support its claims. The role of the lawyer is to facilitate that exercise of autonomy. It is this idea that lies behind the cab-rank rule, previously discussed, and which leads lawyers to claim that their role morality enables them to do for their clients what they would not do for themselves. Indeed if

---

[73] E. D. Cohen, "Pure Legal Advocates and Moral Agents: Two Concepts of a Lawyer in an Adversary System" in Flores, n. 29 above, at 82.

lawyers were to exercise moral censorship on their clients they could be accused of adopting an unacceptably paternalistic attitude towards them.

Attempts to resolve this dilemma have so far not been successful. In a seminal article on the issue, Wassertrom discusses a number of examples.[74] Should a lawyer draft a will for a client who wishes to disinherit a child because he opposed the war in Vietnam? Should the lawyer represent a corporation which manufactures harmful substances like tobacco? He assumes that both of these actions would be immoral (which can be disputed), but comes to no conclusion about what the lawyers should do, recognising the force, in many contexts, of the "role differentiated way of approaching matters". At the same time he is concerned that lawyers will fail to confront the moral dilemmas that these two examples raise by taking refuge in the requirements of the role.

A slightly different approach is adopted by Simon.[75] He considers that lawyers have a "professional duty of reflective judgement" and should evaluate the instructions of the client to see if they are "likely to promote justice". It may be, for example, that a lawyer acting on behalf of a large corporation should not plead the limitation rules if, by so doing, a poor person is unable to enforce a debt which undoubtedly is owing. The lawyer should not, in other words, lend assistance to the client who wants to use procedural rules or technical devices to defeat, rather than promote, the interests of justice. Even when working in a adversary context, the interests of justice should take priority for the lawyer. It is clear that Simon is thinking primarily of the powerful corporate client in putting forward this view. It begs the question why clients, corporate or otherwise, should engage the services of a lawyer who seeks to limit their autonomy, impose values upon them and deny "them the opportunity . . . to seek vindication of hypothetically legal interests".[76]

Another attempt to reconcile the role morality of lawyers with ordinary morality comes from Charles Fried[77] who argues that the lawyer–client relationship is like that of friendship. Friends will typically do things for each other that they would not do for a stranger, and this is regarded as acceptable in the wider society. The basis of this justification is however very doubtful, and the idea has been subjected to considerable criticism.[78] The conception of the lawyer as a pure legal advocate in an adversarial system, therefore, could discourage behaviour which is conducive to promoting such virtues as truth, justice and also honesty. For example, when the pure legal advocate remains silent when a client lies under oath he compromises a commitment to truth and also justice. In interviewing witnesses before trial, which is required in the adversarial but not the inquisitorial system, the lawyers will be tempted to influence their

---

[74] R. Wasserstrom, "Lawyers as Professionals: Some Moral Issues" (1975–6) 5 *Human Rights* 1.

[75] See "Ethical Discretion in Lawyering" (1988) 101 *Harvard LR* 1083.

[76] Dinerstein, n. 31 above, at 558.

[77] C. Fried, "The Lawyer as Friend: The Moral Foundation of the Lawyer–Client Relation" (1976) 85 *Yale Law Journal* 1060.

[78] E. A. Dauer and A. A. Leff, "Comment on Fried's 'Lawyer as Friend' " (1977) 86 *Yale Law Journal* 573.

evidence and distort the truth. Add to these pressures the economic interests of the lawyer and the expectations of both clients and peers, and it can be seen that this creates for the individual lawyer a struggle between ethos (in the sense of habit) and ethics.

Professional rules of advocacy can, however, attempt to restrain the more extreme examples of the behaviour apparently allowed to the pure legal advocate. How far does the guidance contained in the current professional codes do this? It can be argued that in both the USA and the UK the adversarial ethic and its consequent role morality has been modified, arguably more so in the UK than in the USA.

In the USA the obligation of partisanship, historically, flows from a commitment in the ABA's code to the notion of "zealous advocacy" on behalf of the client.[79] As this concept has now been replaced by a duty of diligence, much of the writing on the professional obligation to clients, based on the concept of zealous advocacy, must be treated with caution. There is no corresponding obligation in the UK in either the *Law Society Guide* or the *Bar Code of Conduct*[80] although it is sometimes said that the duty of "diligence", which is found in the solicitors' *Guide*,[81] is closely related to zeal.[82] Whereas "zealous advocacy" implies that lawyers are bound to pursue their clients' every desire, the *Guide* specifically states that a solicitor "must refuse to take action which he or she believes is solely intended to gratify a client's malice or vindictiveness".[83] The Marre report also reflected this when it observed that:

> "the client is frequently acting under physical, emotional or financial difficulties and may well wish to take every step he can, whether legal or extra-legal, to gain advantage over the other party. In this situation the a lawyer has a special duty and responsibility to advise his client as to the legal and ethical standards which should be observed and not to participate in any deception or sharp practice."[84]

The balance between duties to clients and the wider system varies considerably between countries as a result of complex interactions; between conceptions of the judicial process and its purpose, between theories and ideologies about procedure and substantive justice and between different ideologies relating to the role of the judge and the legal profession.[85] Based on the ABA's code, on the writings of American scholars interpreting that code and the guidance in the codes of both branches of the domestic profession, we deduce that the balance

---

[79] American Bar Association Code, Canon 7. See R. J. Condlin, "Bargining in the Dark: The Normative Incoherence of Lawyer Dispute Bargaining Role" (1992) 51:1 *Maryland Law Review* 1 at 72.

[80] J. Levin, *An Ethical Professional* (Swansea, Swansea University, 1994), at 23.

[81] R. 12.11 of the *Law Society Guide*, n. 5 above, states a solicitor is bound to exercise diligence in carrying out a client's instructions.

[82] Bayles, n. 47 above, at 86.

[83] The *Law Society Guide*, n. 5 above, r. 12.01, para. 6.

[84] The Marre Report, n. 1 above, at 6.1.

[85] M. Taruffo, "The Lawyer's Role and the Models of Civil Process" (1981) 16 *Israel Law Review* 5.

here is tipped more towards the legal system than it is in the USA.[86] This is the clear implication of the *Law Society Guide*, which states that "where two or more of the principles in practice rule 1 come into conflict, the determining factor in deciding which principle should take precedence must be the public interest and especially the public interest in the administration of justice".[87]

H. PUBLIC PRESENTATION: LAWYERS AND THE PRESS

The dealings which a lawyer is entitled to have with the press are an interesting reflection of the lawyer's wider role. If it was seen as acceptable for lawyers to be aggressively partisan, lawyers could be forgiven for using the press to pursue their clients' ends and, incidentally, to promote their own services. As we shall see, however, there are constraints on the way lawyers are expected to deal with the press. This may be a remnant of the conservatism reflected in rules against advertising and a quite sensible attempt to prevent some lawyers from bringing the profession and legal system into disrepute. It could also recognise that there is a substantial difference between what must be done for clients under the cloak of professionalism and the image of professionalism that should be presented to the public.

A lawyer's primary role, in relation to litigation, is to provide the client with legal advice and representation in a court or similar tribunal and to negotiate with the other side. Non-contentious work is often confined to advice and assistance with the legal work involved in, say, making a will or contract or setting up a company. However, many lawyers adopt a wider role as "men of affairs", assisting generally in promoting the business or other interests of their clients, This may include lobbying, presentational and educational work. How far should a lawyer seek to use the press and other media in promoting their clients' interests and, even incidentally, their own? What may lawyers tell the press about their cases or the behaviour of their opponents?

It is not unusual for lawyers to give their clients' statements to the press, to comment on their clients' position or the adequacy of the law in dealing with the clients' particular problem. This is common in high profile criminal cases and also in test cases or other public interest litigation. The lawyer hopes, thereby, to mobilise public opinion in the client's favour or correct adverse publicity generated by the press, often with considerable help from the police. What ethical or other principles govern this activity? First, and most obviously, press state-

---

[86] Although the idea that obligations of candour to the court and fairness to others significantly qualified loyalty to clients has also gained ground in the USA. See L. R.Patterson, "The Limits of the Lawyer's Discretion and the Law of Legal Ethics: National Student Marketing Revisited" (1979) 6 *Duke Law Journal* 1251.

[87] The *Law Society Guide*, n. 5 above, r. 1.02.6. Basic principles—additional guidance at 2 (note the examples given in the *Law Society Guide* under para. 7 of situations where a solicitor may find a conflict between r. 1(c) (client's best interests) and 1(b) choice of solicitor where "the public interest demands that the latter takes precedence . . .").

ments should be made only with the consent of the client. Without that they will probably involve a breach of confidence and may bring the lawyer into conflict with the client. Secondly, statements to the press must not involve a contempt of court. The Law Society's general guidance on press statements amounts to no more than this: "[a] solicitor who on the client's instructions gives a statement to the press must not become in contempt of court by publishing a statement which is calculated to interfere with the fair trial of a case which has not been concluded".[88] Thirdly, solicitor-advocates are advised in the Solicitors' Advocacy Code that they must not, in relation to any "current matter" on which they are or have been briefed, offer *personal* views to the "news or current affairs media". Personal views can therefore be given where the solicitor is not acting as an advocate, and any comment (subject to the contempt laws) may be made in publications not regarded as being "news or current affairs". Learned articles in legal journals, and possibly in the popular legal press, would presumably not come within the latter description.

Barristers are advised that they must not comment *at all* to the news or current affairs media on any issue arising from a *current* matter on which they are or have been briefed.[89] The underlying reason for this rule is that barristers must retain their professional independence and must not appear to be personally committed to their client's cause. These rules are vague and inconsistent. What is a "current matter"? How long is a matter current? Does it include non-contentious matters? How is the phrase "news media" to be defined? Is a statement of fact a "personal view"? Finally, is the distinction between solicitors and advocates valid?

The issue of press comment by lawyers in criminal cases was the subject of a report by ACLEC in 1997.[90] The Committee considered that it was not adequate for the Law Society to rely solely on the law of contempt as a guide, with its requirement of proof of intention and the criminal standard of proof. In criminal cases the Committee considered that a solicitor should not say anything that might prejudice the outcome of the proceedings. He or she should be able to say anything on behalf of the client that the client can lawfully say, i.e. "[m]y client denies any involvement with this charge and considers the evidence against him flimsy and unreliable". The Committee would, however, retain a rule that prohibits an advocate from expressing a personal opinion about the merits of the case whilst it is current and would extend it to solicitors generally. The prohibition should cover the period from charge to acquittal or the disposal of any appeal. It would not prevent a solicitor from commenting on issues which did not go to the merits of the case, such as any delay in prosecuting. The same rules should also apply to barristers. The reasoning behind these proposals is the

---

[88] *Law Society Guide*, n. 5 above, r. 21.18 at 341, which restates the Solicitors' Practice Rules 1990, r. 22.13.

[89] *Bar Code*, n. 4 above, para. 604.

[90] *Lawyers' Comments to the Media* (London, Lord Chancellor's Advisory Committee on Legal Education and Conduct, May 1997).

elimination of any risk that personal comments from lawyers on the merits may prejudice the outcome of the proceedings and "detract from public recognition of the principle that these are matters to be decided by the courts and the courts alone". They were also concerned that "lawyers may come under pressure to express views [to the press] that they do not genuinely hold on the merits of their clients' cases". The Committee did not look in detail at civil cases but recommended to the profession that it consider adopting the same rules in relation to such cases.

CONCLUSION

In public life in general, adversarial traditions are under attack. The adversarial ethic of legal professionals is not only out of step with the times, it creates a potential problem for non-practitioner lawyers and for all lawyers in their personal lives. This statement deserves some explanation because it is contentious. The problem arises when professionals cease to perceive the difference between their professional and personal selves, and they allow their professional role to determine their self-identity and to shape their thinking and their behaviour. The tendency of lawyers to adopt a partisan perspective in situations where it is inappropriate, in political life for example, can lead to very damaging results.[91] In public life, the "discrepant moral reasoning"[92] which characterises the professional ethics of lawyers is seen to undermine the integrity of individuals and public trust in lawyers as public figures.

The process of socialisation is considered in Chapter 6 in the section on legal education. Goffman touched on a troubling aspect of the adoption of professional roles as the dominant influence on personality. He noted that the self is capable of adapting to different settings but that certain kinds of personality cannot cope with the "fragmentation" of the self which is required in order to achieve this. Such individuals tend to adopt a "false self" in order to fit in. Not surprisingly, they experience themselves as empty and "inauthentic".[93] It is of concern that professional ethics should have this potential, both for the individuals concerned and for their professional relationships with clients. The "reflective project of the self", described by Giddens, prizes authenticity, the capacity of people to know themselves and to reveal self-knowledge discursively and in the behavioural sphere.[94] Professionals are precisely the kind of people who

[91] One explanation for the involvement of so many government officials, trained as lawyers, being involved in the Watergate scandal is that they brought the discrepant moral reasoning of their profession both to the political problem and to their attempts to defend the Nixon administration: Wasserstrom, n. 74 above.

[92] *Ibid.*, at 15.

[93] A. Giddens, *Modernity and Self-Identity: Self and Society in the Late Modern Age* (Cambridge, Polity Press, 1991).

[94] *Ibid.*, at 187 (the demand that professionals are able to cope with this dynamic of client relationships is increasing and is considered in more detail at the end of Chap. 3).

clients should experience as being capable of participating in "authentic dialogue". This is the key to the client being able to articulate his or her true wishes and to the lawyer being able to offer constructive counsel.

This kind of approach requires courage and honesty. It is encapsulated in the view of one solicitor who argued:

"You must be able to communicate with the client. It is no good if you treat the client like dirt as some do . . . solicitors should advise the client, discussing the case with the client, telling them what they think; it avoids misunderstanding. Even if you tell the client he is wrong and put your position to him, even though he may feel bitter or aggrieved, you have acted within the law and are giving them you best advice. This, I think, touches on the question of personal honesty: I think if you are straight with everyone its a good start; it's the proper thing to do and does not leave the client with false hopes. Also it helps the solicitor in that, if the case fails and the client has been told this is possible, he cannot then turn round and criticise the solicitor . . ."[95]

Honesty or loyalty; which comes first? While a client is entitled to a full measure of both of these virtues from professionals, the prioritisation of one over the other has significant implications for the lawyer's role. In particular it may well affect how the lawyer must deal with non-clients. This is now considered.

[95] Boon, n. 42 above.

8

Obligations to Third Parties

A. INTRODUCTION

This chapter examines the rules governing the way in which lawyers should deal with others when acting on behalf of their clients, for example, the solicitors and barristers on the other side, the unrepresented opponent, other third parties who are affected by the transaction in question, such as beneficiaries under wills or trusts, or third parties paying for the legal work done for clients. Duties in relation to third parties do not figure large in the ethics of legal professions. As we saw in Chapters 1 and 7, it is sometimes asserted that the sole responsibility of the lawyer is to advance the interests of the client.[1] Even if this is accepted it does not follow that the lawyer owes no duties to third parties. There are many such duties imposed on lawyers in order to *advance* the interests of the client. Examples are the duties owed by solicitors to the barristers they brief and vice versa. The personal responsibility imposed on solicitors to honour undertakings given to third parties is intended to advance the efficiency and speed of legal business in the interests of clients.

However, other duties owed to third parties do raise a conflict between the interests of the client and the interests of the third party. Examples dealt with in this chapter include the duty not to take unfair advantage of the other side, duties to the Legal Aid Board in respect of legally aided clients and the wasted costs jurisdiction which, in effect, requires lawyers to consider the effect of their behaviour on the other side. The general duty of the advocate towards the court, in the interests of justice, also can present a conflict with the interests of the client.[2] It is therefore necessary to construct an ethic of the profession which encompasses three basic duties—loyalty to clients, candour towards the court and fairness towards third parties.[3]

B. GENERAL PRINCIPLES

The general principles governing solicitors are set out in paragraph 17.01 of the *Law Society Guide*. Solicitors must not be deceitful, fraudulent or act in a way

---

[1] See, e.g., T. Schneyer, "Moral Philosophy's Standard Misconception of Legal Ethics" [1984] *Wisconsin Law Review* 1529 and J. Leubsdorf, "Three Models of Professional Reform" (1982) 67 *Cornell Law Review* 1021.

[2] This is dealt with further in Chapter 14 on advocacy.

[3] See further L. R.Patterson, "On Analysing the Law of Legal Ethics: An American Perspective", (1981) 16:1 *Israel Law Review* 28 at 33.

that is "contrary to their position as solicitors". Nor should they take unfair advantage "either for themselves or another person". This principle therefore modifies the "zeal" with which a solicitor may promote the interests of the client. The solicitor should not, at the behest of the client, take unfair advantage of another, even if it is lawful to do so. However, solicitors are not under an obligation to protect the other side by refusing to represent their clients in hopeless cases; they need not impose a screen on the client's case before litigating. It is obviously difficult to draw a line between indulging in vexatious conduct and simply taking on a client's case even where it has a slim chance of success, as is exemplified in the cases concerning wasted costs. The main constraint on the conduct of cases which are not vexatious or frivolous is the rules of court. These allow considerable latitude. This area is considered in more detail in Part V.

Of course everyone, including solicitors, has an obligation not to deceive or defraud as such acts are contrary to the law. If solicitors are subject to additional constraints, imposed by their professional ethics, these must be contained in the phrases referring to action "contrary to their position as solicitors" and taking "unfair advantage". It is difficult to establish from the *Law Society Guide* what conduct is covered here. However there are three other important guidelines that solicitors are bound by and which would seem to be within this basic principle. First, they must not write "offensive letters" to third parties, or behave offensively.[4] Good manners are required, however appalling the solicitor or his client considers the other side to be.

Secondly, solicitors should not send letters making claims that they know have no foundation in law. This is stated in Principle 17.05 which, somewhat inconsistently, is confined to letters before action. In fact, this principle must extend to all letters or claims if it is to be consistent with the general principle set out in Principle 17.01. It is unprofessional to use the authority of the solicitor's role to bolster a claim which the solicitor knows, or should know, is not within the law and which therefore must be intended to frighten or pressurise the other side illegitimately. An example would be for a husband's solicitor to write to a wife demanding that she immediately vacate the matrimonial home owned by the husband. The law protects wives from summary eviction in such circumstances and all solicitors know or should know this. The example given in the *Law Society Guide* is that "a solicitor must not seek to enforce a gaming debt except in cases permitted by the gaming acts".[5] Thirdly, they must abide by their undertakings whether or not they are enforceable under the law of contract, on which see further below.

A recent case provides an example of the operation of principle 17.01. In *Ernst & Young* v. *Butte Mining Co.*[6] the court had approved a consent order setting aside a judgment by default and the defendants were permitted to serve a

[4] See N. Taylor (ed.), *The Guide to the Professional Conduct of Solicitors* (London, The Law Society, 1996), hereafter the *Law Society Guide*, r. 17.01, para. 5 and r. 19.01.
[5] *Ibid.*, r. 17.05, para. 3.
[6] [1997] 2 All ER 471.

defence and counterclaim within a set time. The plaintiff's solicitor had the carriage (i.e. drafting and issuing) of the order and, immediately after obtaining it, filed a notice to discontinue the action. This was intended to, and did, prevent the defendants from filing their counterclaim. It was held to be an abuse of process. The plaintiff's solicitors had misled the defendants as to their intentions and sought an unfair advantage by obtaining the defendants' agreement to the plaintiff having carriage of the order. Delivering judgment, Mr Justice Robert Walker said, "[h]eavy, hostile commercial litigation is a serious business. It is not a form of indoor sport and litigation solicitors do not owe each other duties to be friendly (so far as that goes beyond politeness) or to be chivalrous or sportsmanlike (so far as that goes beyond being fair). Nevertheless even in the most hostile litigation . . . solicitors must be scrupulously fair and not take unfair advantage of obvious mistakes." This duty "is intensified if the solicitor in question has been a major contributing cause of the mistake".[7]

Undertakings

In, addition to Principle 17.01, which applies to a solicitor's relations with "anyone", Principle 19.01 requires solicitors to deal with other solicitors with "frankness and good faith consistent with his or her overriding duty to the client". This principle is most important in relation to solicitors' undertakings. Solicitors frequently give undertakings to the other side—to discharge mortgages, produce or return documents, hold monies to order, exchange contracts for the sale of land, etc. Much business could not be speedily or efficiently carried out without reliance on undertaking, and the guidance governing such promises form an important part of a solicitor's professional ethics. An undertaking is defined as "any unequivocal declaration of intention" made to a person who reasonably relies on it by a solicitor or a member of a solicitor's staff either in the course of business or as a solicitor.[8] This covers undertakings made to both solicitors and non-solicitors. Undertakings may be oral or in writing. Indeed an undertaking can in some circumstances be implied, as where a solicitor receives documents or money subject to a condition. He or she must return them if unwilling to abide by the condition.

A solicitor is personally bound by an undertaking and breach will *prima facie* be professional misconduct. The Law Society is rigorous about undertakings.

[7] See also *Haiselden* v. *P & O. Properties, Law Society Gazette*, 3 June 1998, where the defendant realised that a case had been mistakenly set down for trial in the county court when it should have been dealt with as a small claim. The defendant did not alert either the court or the unrepresented plaintiff to this mistake. It was held that he was under an obligation not to take advantage of the mistake. See also *Vernon* v. *Bosley* [1997] 1 All ER 614 (CA) on the duty to inform the court of changed circumstances arising after the conclusion of the hearing. See further *post* p. 358.
[8] *Law Society Guide*, n. 4 above, para. 18.01.

They endure for as long as the solicitor remains on the roll, they cannot be unilaterally withdrawn, nor can the Council release a solicitor from an undertaking, even where there has been a delay in notifying the Law Society of the breach.[9] All partners are liable on the undertakings of each of them. The Law Society cannot specifically enforce the undertaking itself, though the court may be able to. From the Law Society's point of view the remedy for the recipient of the undertaking is disciplinary proceedings against the solicitor. Compensation may be available from the SIF. It will not be available from the Solicitors' Compensation Fund unless the solicitor gave the undertaking dishonestly in order to obtain funds, when compensation will be considered.

Unsurprisingly the Law Society is concerned that undertakings may be too easily given by solicitors, and be too vague in scope. Compensation for broken undertakings is a considerable drain on the SIF. Solicitors can also find themselves personally liable for them; for example, the SIF does not cover undertakings that amount to a bare guarantee of a client's financial obligations. The Society points out that there is no obligation either to give or receive undertakings even where it might be in the client's interest to do so. If given, they should be specific, confirmed in writing and realistic, in the sense that a solicitor should not promise to do something that is not in his or her control. An undertaking is regarded as binding even if its discharge proves to be outside the control of the solicitor.[10]

The Court, in the exercise of its inherent supervisory jurisdiction over solicitors in relation to litigation, can order the performance of the undertaking, or can award compensation if this is not possible. An illustrative case is *Udall* v. *Capri Lighting Ltd*.[11] In this case the solicitor undertook orally to secure charges over the property of the directors of a company in favour of the plaintiff if the latter would adjourn judgment summonses he had obtained. The charges were not executed. Judgment was entered against the company, which then went into liquidation so that it could not be enforced. It was also impossible for the charges to be executed. The Court of Appeal held that failure to implement an undertaking was, *prima facie*, misconduct even where the solicitor had not acted dishonourably or could not implement it. The court could, in the exercise of its inherent jurisdiction, either order the implementation of the undertaking, where possible, or order compensation from the solicitor where it was not.[12]

Contacting an Opposing Party

Once a party is represented by a solicitor, the opposing solicitor should not contact that party directly, except with the consent of that solicitor. This principle

[9] However the Council does have a discretion in the latter case, see *Law Society Guide*, n. 4 above, 18.05 note 7.
[10] For further detail of Law Society guidance on undertakings see *ibid.*, chap. 18.
[11] [1987] 3 All ER 262.
[12] See also *Fox* v. *Bannister* [1987] 1 All ER 737.

does not however prohibit client to client communication. Contacting witnesses is allowed.

Reporting Other Solicitors to the Law Society

Luban relates an incident in 1977 in which a senior lawyer in the United States, "an upright and courtly man", lied to an opponent to conceal discoverable documents, perjured himself to conceal the lie and, upon confessing the truth, resigned his job and spent a month in prison.[13] What is particularly interesting is the reaction of the associate who worked for the partner concerned who "saw [the partner] lie and really couldn't believe it. And he just had no idea of what to do. I mean, he . . . kept thinking there must be a reason. Besides what do you do? The guy was his boss and a great guy." The complicity of the associate was partly due to the ambiguity of the ABA's model rule which permitted a subordinate lawyer to defer to a senior lawyer's reasonable resolution of an arguable question of professional duty. Luban argues that it is also the product of working in a large organisation where lines of responsibility are confused and ambiguous, and result in a gradual desensitisation to these issues.

In England and Wales disciplinary whistle-blowing is not only allowed, it is formally encouraged. A solicitor has a duty to report suspicions of *serious* misconduct to the OSS. The report can be anonymous. The OSS operates a "red alert" line for solicitors concerned about the activities (or, often, the lack of activity) of another solicitor, guaranteeing that the informant's confidentiality will be preserved. The *Guide* states that "where necessary" the client's consent to such a report must be obtained, but gives no indication of when it is necessary. A client may well be loath to get involved in the unprofessional conduct of the other side's solicitor unless it impinges directly on his or her case. Indeed such a report may delay matters or cause other problems to the client. This raises further questions. Does the client's consent have to be sought in such circumstances? Does the seriousness of the misconduct have any effect on this?

D. RELATIONSHIPS WITH BARRISTERS

The primary relationship with the client is that of the solicitor but, of course, the solicitor will often brief a barrister on behalf of the client. How does this affect the relationship with the client? The basic principle is that solicitors have a duty to brief appropriate counsel and "may not abrogate their responsibility to clients by instructing counsel".[14] In particular, solicitors should not follow counsel's advice blindly; they must continue to exercise their own judgement,

---

[13] D. J. Luban, "Milgram Revisited" (1998) 9 *Researching Law: An ABF. Update* 1 at 4.
[14] *Law Society Guide*, n. 4 above, chap. 20.

especially where counsel is obviously or seriously wrong.[15] This raises the interesting possibility of solicitor and counsel presenting differing advice to the client, a position that only the client can resolve by deciding whose advice to accept.[16]

The solicitor has a personal responsibility to pay the barrister's fees (but not a formal legal liability as there is no legal contract between solicitor and barrister or between barrister and client), whether or not the client has put the solicitor "in funds". Solicitors must provide adequate instructions in good time. The solicitor or "a responsible representative" must attend the barrister in court, with certain exceptions.[17] In the magistrates' court and in the Crown Court on guilty pleas, appeals against committal and committal for sentence, attendance may be dispensed with. But this must be reasonable, in the interests of the client and not prejudicial to the interests of justice. The Law Society states that "careful judgement" is required on dispensing with attendance and suggests various situations where attendance is desirable even where a case falls within the exceptions. For example where a client is a juvenile, handicapped in some way, is a "difficult character" or where a substantial sentence of imprisonment is likely.[18]

In criminal cases it is not uncommon for the barrister to return the brief at a late stage and a substitute to take over at the last minute. This can also happen in civil cases, though it appears to be less common. Where this happens the *Guide* states that, even if the case falls within the exceptions noted above, solicitors should nevertheless attend court "unless the solicitor is satisfied that the change of counsel is unlikely to be prejudicial to the interests of the client". It is also noted that, in the event of a complaint, where the rules on attendance at court have not been complied with by a solicitor faced with a last-minute substitution of counsel, the Law Society Council, in considering the complaint "will take into account all the practical difficulties".[19]

The client may well wonder why two lawyers must be employed and paid for where one would do, in the situation where a last-minute return of the brief means that the barrister is not familiar with the case and has probably never met the client before the day of the hearing. Solicitors also find this a problem as the following quotation shows:

"You get called to a case conference by the court at which the client is also required to attend, are you going to have to instruct a barrister to turn up and speak to the judge

---

[15] See *Locke* v. *Camberwell Health Authority* [1991] 2 Med. LR 249; *Davy-Chiesman* v. *Davy-Chiesman* [1984] 1 All ER 321; and *Matrix Securities Ltd.* v. *Theodore Goddard* (1997) 147 NLJ 1847. See also, on wasted costs, *Tolstoy* v. *Aldington* [1996] 2 All ER 556.

[16] Barristers have a professional obligation to advise their lay clients of any conflict of interest between them and their solicitors and advise the lay client "to instruct another professional adviser". This must be done in writing or at a conference at which both client and solicitor are present. See *Code of Conduct of the Bar of England and Wales* (London, The General Council of the Bar of England and Wales, 1990), hereafter the *Bar Code*, rule 605.

[17] *Law Society Guide*, n. 4 above, para. 20.04.

[18] *Ibid.*, 20.04, para. 2.

[19] *Ibid.*, 20.04, para. 4.

when you are the one who knows the case because the client says, well, you know my documents, and you know my witnesses, you have spoken to them, why do I need another person to come along and tell the judge what this case is about? Don't you know what the case is about? Clearly the answer has got to be we have got to do it ourselves."[20]

This leads to the more general issue of the division between solicitors and barristers. Is it in the interests of clients? There are often good practical reasons for a solicitor to employ a separate advocate. A partner in a big city firm is expected, mainly, to be a client getter and pleaser and cannot be out of the office for days or weeks at a time undertaking advocacy. Advocacy is a special skill and needs constant practice which few solicitors can undertake in combination with running an office and attending to the demands of all their clients, In addition to these practical reasons, two other justifications are put forward in favour of the current rules. First, the existence of an independent bar enables even the smallest firm of solicitors to retain an expert advocate for their clients. As one solicitor has expressed it:

"The great thing for small firms like us is what I have always said: we have on tap the best advocates without having to pay them a retainer or employ them and if we have the right case or the right fee, we can get the right person to do it."[21]

Even larger firms also appreciate the range of expertise available to them:

"A department . . . cannot have the pools of specialist expertise that may be available in a larger firm. What it does have of course is access to an independent bar, barristers numbering two thousand six hundred within half a mile of this office who are all, more or less, experts in particular fields and are all, more or less, trained advocates who do little else but."[22]

Secondly, the barrister is supposed to maintain a greater distance from the client than the solicitor and can provide more objective and independent advice.

Whether, in order to achieve these benefits, it is necessary to maintain an entirely separate Bar with its accompanying restrictive practice rules is doubtful. The government intends, under the Access to Justice Bill 1998, to give full advocacy rights to all solicitors and barristers, including employed solicitors and barristers such as those employed by the CPS.[23] This will be subject to the provision of adequate advocacy training before or after qualification. The government is not convinced that independence will thereby be impaired: "independence is a matter of ethos, professional discipline and frame of mind, rather than a matter

---

[20] J. Flood, A. Boon, A. Whyte, E. Skordaki, R. Abbey and A. Ash, *Reconfiguring the Market for Advocacy Services: A Case Study of London and Four Fields of Practice* (a report for the Lord Chancellor's Committee on Legal Education and Conduct, 1996), hereinafter "ACLEC Report", at 101.

[21] *Ibid.*, at 186.

[22] *Ibid.*, at 129.

[23] See the White Paper, *Modernising Justice*, Cm 4155, 1998 and Access to Justice Bill 1998 clauses 30–37.

of how a lawyer is engaged or paid".[24] Nor is it impressed with the alleged expertise of the Bar in advocacy matters, pointing out the high number of returned briefs in criminal matters and the comparative inexperience of the junior Bar.[25]

E. RELATIONSHIPS WITH UNREPRESENTED PARTIES

Where the other party is not represented by a solicitor, how should the solicitor deal with him or her? Solicitors tend to dislike dealing with laypersons, fearing that they will delay matters or not understand what to do. Do-it-yourself conveyancers often encounter this attitude. But unrepresented parties must be dealt with fairly under the obligation imposed by Principle 17.01. A solicitor may even be inclined to deal with an unrepresented person helpfully. In such a case he or she must beware, says the Law Society that "no retainer arises by implication". They may amend documents coming from unrepresented parties if this can reasonably be done and it is in the client's interests to do so.

If the other party is represented or helped by an unqualified person, then the solicitor may decline to communicate with that representative if he or she is undertaking prohibited acts, and should report him or her to the Law Society. Prohibited acts are the provision of litigation, probate and conveyancing services whilst unqualified.[26] A fine line will have to be drawn between communicating with someone who is lawfully assisting another with advice to help them represent themselves, such as a *McKenzie* friend[27] or advice workers, and unlawful practice. However, lay representatives now do have full rights of audience in the Small Claims Court, the Lord Chancellor having granted this right under section 11 of the Courts and Legal Services Act 1990, and also in tribunals. Where relevant, these lay representatives can obtain the costs of representation. Such activity must be distinguished from acting as a solicitor. As Lord Justice Potter put it, "[t]he words 'acting as a solicitor' are limited to the doing of acts which *only* a solicitor may perform and/or the doing of acts by a person pretending or holding himself out to be a solicitor. Such acts are not to be confused with the doing of acts of a kind *commonly* done by solicitors but which involve no representation that the actor is acting as such."[28]

---

[24] *Rights of Audience and Rights to Conduct Litigation in England and Wales: The Way Ahead* (Lord Chancellors Consultation Paper, June 1998) para. 2.9.

[25] Up to 75% of CPS instructions had been returned in a recent survey of 9 Crown Court Centres, *ibid.*, para. 2.11.

[26] Solicitors' Act 1974 s.22 and Courts and Legal Services Act (CLSA) 1990 s.70.

[27] *McKenzie* v. *McKenzie* [1970] 3 All ER 1034. A *McKenzie* "friend" is a person who accompanies a litigant in court and gives them advice. Such a representative has no general right to address the court unless the court allows this. See also *R.* v. *Leicester City Justices* [1991] 3 All ER 935; *Re H* [1997] 2 FLR 423; and *Re Pelling* [1997] 2 FLR 458. Members of ILEX have had advocacy rights in the lower courts in civil and family proceedings since the spring of 1998 (The Institute of Legal Executives Order 1998, SI. No. 1077).

[28] Potter J in *Piper Double Glazing Ltd.,* v. *AC Contracts* Ltd. [1994] 1 All ER 177 at 186, emphasis added.

Individuals Owed a Duty

A solicitor normally owes no professional duties, other than those of courtesy and fairness, to persons who are neither clients nor the other side, but who may be affected by the transaction, such as the beneficiaries of wills or trusts. There may, however, be liability in negligence to such third parties in certain circumstances. In *White* v. *Jones*[29] the House of Lords held that a beneficiary could sue the deceased's solicitor in negligence. The case concerned the deceased's instructions to draw up a will. The matter was negligently delayed by the solicitors and the testator died before executing the will. As a result the beneficiary lost the bequest. It was held that it was reasonably foreseeable that the negligence would cause such a loss and neither the testator nor the estate had a remedy against the solicitor. The only way a remedy for the loss could be granted was to allow the intended beneficiary to make a claim.

The House of Lords recognised that there were difficulties in reaching this decision (and two of their Lordships dissented). A solicitor normally owes a duty of care to clients only; no duty is owed to opponents in litigation or to the other side in conveyancing matters for example. Nor is there a duty of care to a prospective beneficiary of a client's disposition during that client's lifetime.[30] However where the client is unable to obtain a remedy for the solicitor's negligence, as in *White* v. *Jones*, a remedy should be provided for the beneficiary on the basis that "the assumption of responsibility by the solicitor towards his client should be held in law to extend to the intended beneficiary".[31] There is no conflict of interest in this type of case between the client and the third party; arguably, by allowing the action by the beneficiary, the duty of care owed to the testator is reinforced.

Where a solicitor accepts responsibilities to a third party by giving an undertaking, he or she may also be liable in negligence to that third party. An example of this arose in the matrimonial case of *Al-Kandari* v. *Brown*.[32] The solicitor for the husband undertook not to release the husband's passport to him. On this basis the husband was granted access to the children of the family. Due to the solicitor's negligence the husband obtained the passport and managed to take his children out of the country. The wife sued in negligence and succeeded. The solicitors, in giving the undertaking, had "stepped outside their role as solicitors for their client and accepted responsibilities towards both their client and the

---

[29] [1995] 1 All ER 691.

[30] See generally *Gran Gelato Ltd.* v. *Richcliff Ltd.* [1992] 1 All ER 865; *Clark* v. *Bruce Lance* [1988] 1 All ER 364; *Al-Kandari* v. *Brown* [1988] 1 All ER 833.

[31] *White* v. *Jones* [1995] 1 All ER 691 at 710. See now *Carr-Glynn* v. *Fearsons* [1998] 4 All ER 225 where a beneficiary under a will recovered from the deceased's solicitor even though the estate also had a remedy against them.

[32] [1988] 1 All ER 833.

plaintiff and the children".[33] Another route which might result in liability in negligence to a third party relates to a possible duty to warn such a party of a threat to life or injury. It would be a justifiable breach of the duty of confidentiality to a client to reveal information of this kind. Could a solicitor be held liable in negligence for a failure to warn an intended victim?[34]

Duties to the Public

The issue of the extent to which lawyers should be responsible to "the public" or the state, except in clearly identified circumstances such as those presented by legal aid or money laundering, is a hotly contested issue. What are lawyers' responsibilities where they hold client information which may prevent environmental, public health or financial disasters?[35] The last of these hypothetical issues was thrown into sharp relief by a case in the United States in the Savings and Loan scandal. This raised significant questions about the balance to be struck between duties to clients and wider duties to the public. The specific issue was whether a duty of candour is or should be owed to third parties, here represented by government administrative agencies, on matters of public importance and the implications of substituting such a duty for the duty of confidentiality owed to clients. Although much has been written about the case in general, the following discussion is based on an article by William Simon and several articles written in response to Simon's views.[36]

The background to the case is complex but an outline is sufficient to set the scene. Lincoln Savings and Loan was liquidated with a loss of $3.4 billion to the United States federal banking and insurance system. Banking agencies, sifting through the confidential records of the defunct bank, found documents which suggested that its lawyers, Kaye, Scholer, Fierman, Hays and Handler ("Kaye Scholer"), had systematically misled the regulatory authorities about the activities of its client bank over a three-year period. Had it not done so, numerous dubious transactions and substantial losses of publicly underwritten insurance money would probably have been prevented. Simon's analysis of the conduct of the lawyers was based on allegations made in the pleadings.[37]

---

[33] *Ibid.*, at 836.

[34] In the USA a psychiatrist was held to be negligent for failing to warn a murder victim of the murderous intentions of his patient, her former boy friend: *Tarasoff* v. *Regents of the University of California* (1976) 131 Cal. Rpter. 14. See further Chap. 10, on confidentiality.

[35] In relation to the environment, a European Union convention is likely to impose obligations on public authorities to disclose environmentally sensitive information during the next five years: see A. Osborn, "Environmental Law in Public Hands", (1998) *The Lawyer*, 20 Oct. 11. This would create the circumstances in which in-house and external lawyers employed by corporations could be subject to considerable conflicts in advising clients.

[36] W. H. Simon, "The Kaye Scholer Affair: The Lawyer's Duty of Candor and the Bar's Temptations of Evasion and Apology" (1998) 23 *Law and Social Inquiry* 243.

[37] *Ibid.*, at 247–51.

These showed active participation by the lawyers, including the provision of misleading information to the regulator, in many of the transactions.

To Simon the key ethical issue raised by the case was whether a lawyer, who knows that he cannot act for a client without furthering a client's fraud, should withdraw.[38] This begs a number of questions, including the definition of "fraud", what the lawyers knew about it and about the respective responsibilities of government and bureaucrats for the debacle. At the ethical level, a major issue is how the lawyers perceived what was happening and their obligations.[39] What was the obligation of the lawyers to disclose information to third parties, here the regulatory body? Were the lawyers subject to a minimal obligation, for example an obligation not explicitly to mislead, or a more onerous obligation to fulfill the client's obligation of full disclosure under the banking regulations or, at least, to withdraw from representation if the client refused to authorise them to do so?

The regulator's first argument for the higher duty was based on the fact that the firm had actively "interposed" itself between the regulator and the client by insisting that the regulator should deal directly with the firm. The second argument was based on the alleged existence of a general duty to disclose regulatory evasion by clients. Simon agrees with the first argument but regards the second as less plausible, even in the context that the strict regulatory regime covering banks clearly operated in the public interest to ensure the probity of the financial system. Because of the difficulty in drawing general principles from the case Simon suggests that an intermediate standard should be applied, whereby the lawyer would be prohibited from directly or indirectly misleading conduct and "from providing any services substantially related to active unlawful client conduct".[40]

Simon accuses the legal establishment of defending Kaye Scholer on the ground that its lawyers were bound not to disclose details of their client's actions by a duty of confidentiality. It was argued that not only was the duty of confidentiality more binding because the firm was instructed in anticipation of litigation instigated by the regulator, but that assertions made to the regulator were in the nature of argument rather than statements of fact. Simon offers a compelling demolition of these arguments,[41] and particularly that relating to confidentiality. One of the key arguments for confidentiality is that it encourages clients to disclose planned wrongful conduct *so that the lawyer can dissuade them from the proposed course of action*.[42] For Simon, the failure of the Kaye Scholer lawyers to do this, and the nature of the arguments raised by the legal establishment in their defence, raises serious questions about the profession's ethics and, hence, its capacity to regulate itself.[43]

---

[38] *Ibid.*, at 244.

[39] D. C. Langevoort, "What Was Kaye Scholer Thinking?" (1998) 23 *Law and Social Inquiry* 297.

[40] Simon, n. 36 above, at 255.

[41] *Ibid.*, at 270–3.

[42] *Ibid.*, at 281.

[43] The New York Sup. Ct., the disciplinary authority, found no grounds for professional discipline. Nevertheless, judgments worth billions of dollars are outstanding against the key figure at the

There are disagreements with Simon on points of detail. For example, in relation to confidentiality, clients sometimes legitimately need to explore the limits of legality.[44] It was said that Simon's expectation that the ABA, and other bar institutions, would do other than defend Kaye Scholer, was naïve; lawyers had long ago abandoned all but a pretence of serving any wider interest than that of clients.[45] The behaviour of the lawyers and their organisations was, therefore, outrageous but not surprising. The debate rumbles on, both the issues and their wider implications being in considerable dispute. This debate illustrates the inherent difficulty of establishing a clear standard for the disclosure of information which may cause wrongful and avoidable loss to others.[46]

What Kay Scholer and the reaction to it also illustrates is the wider problem of squaring the client-focused ethics of lawyers with expectations of virtue associated with professionals. Gordon, for example, blames the Kaye Scholer affair, and the Bar's response, on the:

> "uncontrolled expansion of libertarian ideology into lawyers' common consciousness —to the point where lawyers have come to feel genuinely affronted and indignant when any authority tries to articulate a public obligation of lawyers that may end up putting them at odds with clients. We have no public obligations, they claim; we are private agents for private parties (though at the same time they claim privileges and immunities that ordinary citizens don't have); our loyalties to clients must be absolute and undivided. In this libertarian mood, they tend to characterize the framework of law as some alien other —'the government,' the 'cops' the 'regulators'— an adversary that they are entitled to outwit and frustrate with every trick in the book."[47]

G. OBLIGATIONS TO A THIRD PARTY PAYING THE CLIENT'S FEES

The payment of fees by a third party used to be illegal under the old laws of maintenance. As is noted in Chapter 12 on fees and costs, there were a number of reasons for this. One of them, however, relates to the primary duty of the

bank and his associates. Kaye Scholer have themselves been subject to injunctions and compensation orders for over $40 million in an out-of-court settlement of the regulatory authority's claim.

[44] S. Pepper, "Why Confidentiality" (1998) 23 *Law and Social Inquiry* 331.

[45] J. R.Macey, "Professor Simon on the Kaye Scholer Affair: Shock at the Gambling at Rick's Palace in Casablanca" (1998) 23 *Law and Social Inquiry* 323.

[46] Miller argues that Simon's "onerous standard" is that which currently applies and that the difficulty with the case is the unproven nature of the allegations. Even the payment by Kaye Scholer to settle the case is not suggestive because the regulatory body obtained an order freezing the firm's assets and effectively stopped them from trading. Setttlement, he argues, could therefore be seen as the only prudent course for the firm: G. P.Miller, "Kaye Scholer as Original Sin: The Lawyer's Duty of Candor and the Bar's Temptations of Evasions and Apology" (1998) 23 *Law and Social Inquiry* 305, and arguably an oppressive and unethical tactic by government lawyers doubtful about their ability to prove the charges: see K. R.Fisher, "Neither Evaders nor Apologists: A Reply to Professor Simon" (1998) 23 *Law and Social Inquiry* 341 and Macey, n. 45 above, and Simon's comment, "Further Thoughts on Kaye Scholer" (1998) 23 *Law and Social Inquiry* 365.

[47] R. W. Gordon, "A Collective Failure of Nerve: The Bar's Response to Kay Scholer" (1998) 23 *Law and Social Inquiry* 315.

lawyer to the client and the possible conflict that may arise where the fees are paid by another. The lawyer may feel that a duty is owed to the fee payer which conflicts with the interests of the client. Now there is no legal or ethical objection to the payment of fees by a third party. Common third party supporters of litigation include insurance companies, trade unions or other professional bodies, associations like the AA or RAC, charities and pressure groups. Not only is there now no objection to such support, there are provisions under the Solicitors' Act 1974 section 71 for such third parties to apply for taxation of costs.

The Solicitors' Introduction and Referral Code (1990), considered in Chapter 7, provides general guidance and, in particular, stresses that solicitors should "never permit the requirements of an introducer to undermine . . . their ability to advise their clients fearlessly and objectively".[48] The Law Society provides guidance to solicitors on their duties in the case of one specific type of third party funder—the legal expenses insurance company. Solicitors who accept a referral from an insurance company to act for a particular insured client must remember that it is the insured who is the client and not the company.[49] The insured client will have a contractual obligation to inform the insurance company of the progress of the action. It is the duty of the solicitor to "remind" him of this and not make the report on his own initiative and thereby break the duty of confidentiality to the client.[50] Solicitors cannot in general enter into agreements with insurance companies giving them the right to act for a particular client. The *Guide* states that the client's freedom of choice may be not be restricted unless terms of the policy fall within the Insurance Companies (Legal Expenses Insurance) Regulations 1990.

These regulations appear to allow restrictions on freedom of choice of solicitor except where there is a conflict of interest between company and insured or in relation to an inquiry under the policy.[51] This, however, may be an inaccurate interpretation of the Insurance Companies (Legal Expenses Insurance) Regulations 1990. Clause 5(4) of these Regulations states that "[t]he company shall . . . afford the insured the right to entrust the defence of his interests from the moment that he has the right to claim from the insurer under the policy, to a lawyer of his choice . . .". Clause 6 then goes on, rather unnecessarily, to state that the insured shall have freedom of choice of a lawyer "to defend, represent or serve the interests of the insured *in any inquiry or proceedings*".[52] Clause 6(2) makes clear that the insured always has a free choice of lawyer where a conflict of interest arises, a statement that is otiose if Clauses 5(4) and 6(1) mean what they say.[53] It is very difficult to make sense of these Regulations, which were enacted to give effect to European Directive 87/344. That they are confusing,

[48] *Law Society Guide*, n. 4 above, at 205, r. 1.1.
[49] *Ibid.*, r. 6.01.
[50] *Ibid.*, r. 6.02, para. 2.
[51] *Ibid.*, r. 6.01, para. 3.
[52] Emphasis added.
[53] There are other exceptions to these rules laid down in reg. 7.

and that no clarification has been forthcoming, is perhaps a sign of how little legal assistance is funded by insurance in this country.[54] It should be noted that a solicitor employed by an insurance company as an employed solicitor can act for an insured person, provided the latter consents, if the claim comes within the County Court small claims limit (£5,000 from April 1999) and does not concern personal injuries.[55]

One piece of guidance that may cause some puzzlement to solicitors and clients alike is contained in paragraph 6.01, note 5, which requires solicitors to make clear to insured clients that they have the ultimate responsibility for the costs if for any reason the insurance company refuses to pay. This guidance is, of course, consistent with the premise that the retainer is with the client and not with the insurance company. However, this paragraph may also owe its origin to the rule laid down in *Adams* v. *London Improved Motor Co.*,[56] which states that, unless the successful insured party (or in this case union member) retains a liability, however residual or theoretical, to pay the costs personally, no order for those costs can be made against the losing party.[57]

In many cases which are funded by insurance companies the insured client is a purely nominal client. For all practical purposes the case is managed by the insurance company and the client has little personal interest in its progress. Nevertheless, the theory is still that the solicitor should receive instructions from the insured client and is therefore responsible only to him or her. This theory is strained and will become further strained in the light of the recent decision in *Chapman* v. *Christopher*,[58] which held that the insurance company's liability for the costs of the other side where the case is lost cannot be limited by the terms of the insurance contract with the nominal plaintiff where the company, in effect, managed and conducted the plaintiff's litigation. It was recognised in this case that the solicitor for the plaintiff was, in reality, being instructed by the insurance company. Where this is the situation it may be arguable in a future case that the solicitor should owe certain duties to the insurance company, such as providing them directly with information on the progress of the litigation, in particular in relation to their liability for costs.

H. OBLIGATIONS TO THE LEGAL AID BOARD

Legal aid is, of course, a specific example of the payment of the client's fees by a third party, in this case by the state in the guise of the Legal Aid Board. As such it raises similar ethical issues as arise in the case of insurance, namely the

---

[54] Little help is to be found in J. A. Holland (ed.), *Cordery on Solicitors* (London, Butterworths, 1995), which simply states that any restriction on the freedom to chose a solicitor is unenforceable (para. K 1088).

[55] *Law Society Guide*, n. 4 above, para. 6.04.

[56] [1921] 1 KB 495.

[57] See also on this *R* v. *Miller* [1983] 3 All ER 186; *Davies* v. *Taylor* [1973] 1 All ER 959; and *Lewis* v. *Avery* [1973] 2 All ER 229.

[58] [1998] 2 All ER 873.

possibility of a conflict of interest between the interests of the client and the interests of the Legal Aid Board. Issues arise relating to the restriction on the client's right to free choice of solicitor and possible breaches of client confidence where the solicitor makes reports on the progress of the case, or changes in the client's circumstances, to the Board. Indeed, these ethical considerations were raised by opponents of legal aid when it was first introduced. Notwithstanding these objections, where the overall best interests of the client were concerned, the balance lay in favour of the legal aid scheme. Apart from these restrictions on the solicitor, the basic principle is that the legally aided client should be treated in the same way as a privately paying client, subject to the specific provisions of the Legal Aid Act 1988. This principle is not statutory but is contained in note 6 to paragraph 5.01 of the *Law Society Guide*.[59] In reality, however, there are considerable differences between the legally aided and the privately paying client because of the control the Board can exercise over the conduct of the case and the duties of the lawyers towards the Board.

There are three main constraints on the solicitors' freedom of action on behalf of the legally aided client. First, the solicitor can act for the client only within the scope of the Legal Aid certificate and is therefore not able freely to accept a client's instructions. Moreover, the client cannot agree to pay privately for work that the certificate does not cover.[60] Secondly, although the client does have a free choice of solicitor (provided he or she operates under the scheme), there are restrictions on changing the solicitor once the certificate is in force. In civil cases the certificate will have to be amended by the Board in favour of the new solicitor. It will not agree to do this if the reason for the change is that the client dislikes the solicitor's advice. A similar application has to be made in criminal cases. Also in criminal cases, there are occasions where the client has to accept an assigned solicitor, for example in the case of co-defendants whose cases are to be heard together. Thirdly, a solicitor acting under the legal aid scheme is under a duty to make reports to the Legal Aid Board of information that would otherwise be confidential to the client. This includes suspected abuse of the fund by the assisted person, reasons for doubts that the action should be continued and information on the conduct of the assisted person.

The Bar also has duties to the Legal Aid Board where acting for legally aided clients. In giving an opinion on an applicant's case, a barrister clearly has to act both for his client and the Legal Aid Board, according to the guidance issued by the Bar. Counsel should set out any rival accounts of the facts so that the Board can estimate the strength of the applicant's case. He must state whether a conference has been held to estimate the applicant's reliability as a witness, and suggest any limitations that should be imposed on the grant of a certificate.[61]

---

[59] See also, on solicitor's duties, O. Hansen, *Legal Aid in Practice: The Guide to Civil and Criminal Proceedings* (London, Legal Action Group, 1993), at 11. The *Legal Aid Handbook* says nothing on this.

[60] Legal Aid Act 1988 s.15(6).

[61] *Bar Code*, n. 16 above, para. 3; *Legal Aid Handbook* (1994), at 530.

The *Law Society Guide* imposes a duty on all solicitors to consider and advise all clients on the availability of Legal Aid.[62] It warns that failure so to do could amount to "unbefitting conduct" and a claim for negligence by the client. Solicitors are not permitted to act on a private basis for clients who are entitled to Legal Aid unless that client makes an informed decision to that effect. This also applies to acting on a conditional fee basis where Legal Aid is available to the client. The latter problem will disappear when legal aid is withdrawn from cases capable of being dealt with under a conditional fee arrangement.

Legal aid in its conventional form—the funding of litigation through private practitioners on a case-by-case basis—is due to be abolished under the Accesss to Justice Bill 1998. In its place a Legal Services Commission will be responsible for block funding legal services, both civil and criminal, to both solicitors' firms and other community legal services agencies, including a criminal defence service. This will profoundly affect the relationship of the client with the solicitor. The solicitor will be concerned to obtain a reasonable return for the work done under the block contract; the client will, in effect, be competing for scarce resources with the other clients funded by the Commission. The ethical implications of this have as yet been largely unexplored by the government and the profession. If the Bill becomes law, a gradual introduction of the new scheme is envisaged.

I. LIABILITY FOR WASTED COSTS

A jurisdiction which has developed rapidly over the past few years is the wasted costs jurisdiction under the Rules of the Supreme Court. Under it the lawyer may be ordered *personally* to pay the costs of either the opponent or his own client. In so far as it requires the lawyer to pay the costs of the other side, it provides a stark example of the solicitor (or barrister) having a duty to consider the interests of the other side as well as those of his or her own client. This creates a classic conflict between the lawyer's duty to the client, to the other side and to the court and the proper administration of justice. This conflict is clearly illustrated in the decided cases under this jurisdiction.

The wasted costs jurisdiction now comes under the Supreme Court Act 1981 section 51(6) as amended by the 1990 Courts and Legal Services Act.[63] The latter Act was specifically directed at providing a remedy for people affected by unsatisfactory work by making lawyers pay personally any costs that they have run up as a consequence of that work. Under the Act the court may, at the instigation of either the client or the other side to the litigation, order the lawyer to pay the whole or any part of any wasted costs. Wasted costs are defined as costs incurred by a party as "a result of any improper, unreasonable or negligent act or omission on the part of any legal or other representative or any employee of such representative".[64] At the time that the 1990 Act was being debated, the Law

---

[62] *Law Society Guide,* n. 4 above, r. 5.01.
[63] See ss.4, 111, 112.
[64] Supreme Court Act 1981 s.51(7).

Society was very concerned that the jurisdiction would be used by the opposing side to intimidate or prevent a solicitor from acting properly for his client; in other words, that the ethical duty to the court and to the administration of justice would be used as a tactical weapon in the litigation process. As can be seen from the cases, this is exactly the issue with which the courts have had to grapple in exercising the wasted costs jurisdiction.

The leading case is *Ridehalgh* v. *Horsefield*.[65] This was a consolidated appeal in six actions where the judge at first instance had made wasted costs orders against the solicitors and, in one case, a barrister. The facts of the six cases were very varied. They included a failure by a solicitor to ascertain that the workplace of the plaintiff suing for noise-induced hearing loss was not dangerously noisy, and a failure to inform the other side that legal aid had been granted, which could have resulted in early settlement. The Court of Appeal, which allowed all the appeals, was therefore in a position to give general guidance on the jurisdiction. The court decided that "improper" conduct is constituted by a significant breach of a substantial duty imposed by a code of professional conduct, or by conduct which would be considered improper according to the consensus of professional opinion. "Unreasonable" conduct is vexatious conduct designed to harass the other side rather than advance the resolution of the case. "Negligent" conduct is a failure to act with the competence reasonably expected of a member of the profession.

The court was anxious that the wasted costs jurisdiction should not be used to require lawyers to "filter out" unmeritorious cases. It is said that "[a] legal representative is not to be held to have acted improperly, unreasonably or negligently simply because he acts for a party who pursues a claim or defence which is plainly doomed to fail".[66] It was argued that any other approach would conflict, in the case of barristers, with the cab-rank rule. It would also discourage solicitors who respect the policy underlying that rule from "affording representation to the unpopular and the unmeritorious".[67] This argument represents a confusion concerning the purpose of the cab-rank rule. It is aimed at ensuring that unpopular *people* or causes receive representation, not that unmeritorious *litigation* should be pursued. Sir Thomas Bingham recognised that it is not always easy to distinguish the case which is hopeless from the case which is an abuse of the process of the court, but stated that any doubt should be resolved to the benefit of the legal representative. A general statement from the Court of Appeal that *bona fide* actions aimed at bringing about a change in the law would not fall foul of the wasted costs jurisdiction would have been welcome but was not made.[68]

---

[65] [1994] 3 All ER 848.

[66] *Ibid.*, Sir Thomas Bingham at 863a. See similarly *Locke* v. *Camberwell HA* [1991] Med. LR 249 and *C* v. *C* [1994] 2 FLR 34.

[67] *Ibid.*, at 863f.

[68] The ruling in *Ridehalgh* v. *Horsefield* reflects that in *Orchard* v. *SE. Electricity Board* [1987] 1 All ER 95 under the old costs jurisdiction.

The court was also well aware of another danger, originally pointed out by Lord Justice Balcombe in *Symphony Group* v. *Hodgson*,[69] that an application to make the solicitor pay wasted costs may be used as a way of getting round the fact that many successful unaided parties will not, at first instance, be able to get a costs order against a legally aided party or against the Legal Aid Fund.[70] It would, said Sir Thomas Bingham, "subvert the benevolent purposes of [the legal aid] legislation if such representatives were subject to any unusual personal risk".[71] A number of the six cases in *Ridehalgh* involved legally aided parties who lost their actions. In the actual case of *Ridehalgh* the issue involved complex landlord and tenant legislation which both sides' solicitors had misconstrued, as indeed had the judge at first instance. Unsurprisingly, therefore, it was held that the solicitors had not been negligent or careless in coming to their mistaken conclusions on the meaning of the legislation.

An example of a case where a wasted costs application was successful is *Tolstoy* v. *Aldington*.[72] This case involved a lengthy and successful libel action brought by Lord Aldington against Count Tolstoy. Tolstoy sought to get the judgment set aside on the ground of fraud. His solicitors acted for him without fee, without having applied for Legal Aid[73] and without sending a letter before action. Tolstoy himself had been declared bankrupt and so, obviously, could not pay any costs awarded against him. The court found that the case was hopeless and struck it out as an abuse of process. Aldington therefore applied for a wasted costs order against the solicitors. He succeeded. In his judgment Lord Justice Rose stressed that acting without fee, even in a hopeless case, was not sufficient to justify an order. The circumstances in this case however were "at least potentially vexatious"[74] and were a collateral attack on the judgment of a court of competent jurisdiction. He concluded that no solicitor could "reasonably have instituted these proceedings". In this case counsel had signed the statement of claim. This astonished Lord Justice Rose, but no case against counsel was before the court. His Lordship stressed, however, that counsel's involvement did not exonerate the solicitors from their duty to exercise their own independent judgement in relation to the case.[75] Lord Justice Ward likewise concluded that the "solicitors allowed themselves to be dragged outside that

---

[69] [1993] 4 All ER 143.
[70] See on this s.18 of the Legal Aid Act 1988. In a recent case, *Kelly* v. *South Manchester HA* [1997] 3 All ER 274, the court made a costs order against the Legal Aid Board under its discretionary powers in the Supreme Court Act 1981 s.51(1), holding that s.18 of the Legal Aid Act 1988 was not a "complete code" in relation to costs orders against the Board. This jurisdiction would be exercised in exceptional circumstances only. This is a first instance decision and may well be appealed. Orders for costs against third party funders of litigation are frequently applied for but seldom awarded. For a comprehensive survey of recent cases, see C. Passmore (1997) 147 *New Law Journal* 1465, 1521.
[71] *Ridehalgh* v. *Horsefield* [1994] 3 All ER 848 at 864c.
[72] [1996] 2 All ER 556.
[73] Which would have provided a screening process on the merits of the case.
[74] [1996] 2 All ER 556 at 567c.
[75] See also *Davy Chiesman* [1984] 1 All ER 321; *Locke* v. *Camberwell HA* [1991] Med. LR 249.

broad province where their actions could reasonably be said to further the ends of justice".[76]

Another example where a wasted costs order was made is *C* v. *C*.[77] Here a husband and wife, who were in dispute over financial provision on divorce, both applied for a wasted costs order against the wife's solicitor. The solicitor had failed to reconsider the case after it had become clear that the husband's assets were much less than originally thought. Expensive further investigations were made and information required of the husband. A Calderbank offer of £50,000 was rejected. The wife was eventually awarded £20,000, by which time her costs amounted to £60,000 and the husband's £70,000. A wasted costs order was made in respect of some of these costs on the grounds of unreasonableness and negligent conduct on the part of the solicitor.

Clearly, the wasted costs jurisdiction in civil cases shows that lawyers must not simply act as hired guns, but neither are they expected to act as a filter and ensure that only cases with a better than even chance of success are taken on. This is not always an easy distinction to make, but lawyers can take some comfort from the fact that comparatively few applications for wasted costs appear to have succeeded.[78] However, it is still not totally clear what is the main purpose of the jurisdiction. Is it to punish solicitors for unreasonable or negligent conduct of the case, or to compensate the other side (or the client) for having incurred unnecessary or excessive costs which cannot be recovered from any other source? It seems that the courts are primarily concerned with the former aim but the latter also sometimes seems to be a consideration.[79]

CONCLUSION

As will be clear from this chapter, in general a lawyer's obligations to third parties are severely limited. While there are rules which impose such obligations these tend to be designed to facilitate legal transactions. The most notable exceptions, duties to the Legal Aid Board and the wasted costs jurisdiction, can be seen as attempts, not to boost the ethical responsibility of lawyers to third parties as such, but to ensure the protection of public funds and to prevent frivolous litigation respectively. This underlines the argument that, recent protestations in the *Law Society's Guide* notwithstanding, lawyers have considerable freedom in determining what they will do for clients.

[76] *Tolstoy*, n. 15 above, at 572c.

[77] [1994] 2 FLR 34.

[78] See also *Re O (A minor)* [1994] 2 FLR 842; *Horsham DC* v. *West Sussex CC* (1993) *New Law Journal* 22 Oct. 1477; *R.* v. *M* [1996] 1 FLR 750; *Re A Solicitor* [1996] 2 All ER 416; and *Neill* v. *DPP* (1997) *New Law Journal* 31 January 136.

[79] See further P. Jones and N. Armstrong, "Living in Fear of Wasted Costs" [1994] *Civil Justice Quarterly* 208.

9

Public Service

"It is demonstrably true that today the sharpest critics of the legal profession and the administration of justice are judges, lawyers, and teachers of law. It is historically true that the great legal reforms of the twentieth century have been devised, fought for, and established by lawyers. Often they have been opposed by too many members of the profession; often they have won the day only by securing public support; but the fact remains that the constructive leadership came from within the profession itself."[1]

"It is pretty hard to find a group less concerned with serving society and more concerned with serving themselves than the lawyers".[2]

A. INTRODUCTION

A key determinant of professional status has, in the past, been an orientation to the community interest, as opposed to individual self-interest. Although the notion of public service is still central to the professional ideal[3] what is meant by public service is unclear. Pound's analysis of the public service contribution of professions reflected the view, prevalent at the time, that by their very nature, professions were a force for the good. In his view, public service is inherent in the definition of a profession; "a group of men pursuing a learned art as a common calling in the spirit of public service—no less a public service because it may incidentally be a means of livelihood".[4] The fact that pecuniary considerations were secondary was manifest from the fact that professionals do not strike and, if a lawyer discovered something "useful to the profession and so to the administration of justice through research or experience he publishes it in legal periodicals . . . It is not his property".[5]

Pound's analysis of the declared aims of the various bar associations in the United States during their formative period suggests a number of ways in which

---

[1] R. Pound, *The Lawyer from Antiquity to Modern Times: With Particular Reference to the Development of Bar Associations in the United States* (St. Paul, Minn., West Publishing 1953), X.

[2] F. Rodell, "Goodbye to Law Reviews" (1936) 23 *Virginia Law Review* 38 at 42.

[3] See, e.g., A. T. Kronman, "Living in the Law" in D. Luban (ed.), *The Ethics of Lawyers* (Aldershot, Dartmouth Publishing Co., 1994), at 835. The deployment of skill without concern for public interest makes a person a legal technician, not a good lawyer: see N. Strosen, "Pro bono Legal Work: For the Good of not Only the Public but also the Lawyer and the Legal Profession" (1992–3) 91 *Michigan Law Review* 2122. See also H. T. Edwards, "A Lawyers' Duty to serve the Public Good" (1990) 65:4 *New York Law Review* 1148.

[4] Pound, n. 1 above, at 5.

[5] *Ibid.*, at 6 and 10.

associations of lawyers might contribute to the public good, i.e. by advancing the science of jurisprudence, promoting the administration of justice, upholding the honour of the profession of law and establishing cordial relations among the members of the bar.[6] Pound did not state, but clearly thought, that defending or advancing the profession of law was a public good. This was because, in all instances where there had been a policy of discouraging lawyers or where had been weak organisation of those calling themselves lawyers, from ancient Rome to the American frontier, abuse had been rife.[7] Although strong legal professions were desirable, however, Pound knew that lawyers as a group are seldom popular with the general population, and therefore they should give no reason which justifies or feeds these feelings.

This chapter explores other ways than those suggested by Pound in which service to the community may be manifested in professional life. In setting out these possibilities there is a significant difference between specific rules of conduct and ethical obligations. While conduct rules often prescribe minimum standards, ethics involve obligations which go beyond the minimum. Practice rule 1 of the Solicitors' Practice Rules states, *inter alia*, that a solicitor shall not do anything that *injures* the good reputation of the solicitor or of the profession. This obligation, in common with the other obligations set out in practice rule 1, is expressed negatively. Yet, to the extent that society places trust in professions, it is because their members are assumed to be able to "elevate the social good" above the narrow interests of their practitioner members and their clients.[8] This raises a number of questions. How broad, or narrow, is the ethos of public service at the core of legal professionalism?[9] How can lawyers, engaged in the practice of law as a commercial enterprise, be public-spirited? How can they be said to be engaged in public service?

Public service by facilitating access to justice is the aspect of the public service commitment which is dealt with in this chapter. The classic example of this is legal work performed *pro bono publico*, or for the good of the community, which work the Bar Council has asserted, 'is a vital ingredient of any profession worthy of that title'.[10] There is no professional requirement that lawyers perform such work although they are often encouraged by their professional body to do so. By undertaking such work lawyers can also promote the reputation of themselves and their firm for their own commercial benefit. Does public service work carried out for commercial reasons, marketing a firm's expertise for example, cease to be an ethical activity? Does it, indeed, become unethical? If there is

---

[6] Pound, n. 1 above, at 14.

[7] *Ibid.*, at XXV and 40.

[8] R. Abel, *The Legal Profession in England and Wales* (Oxford, Blackwell, 1988), at 27.

[9] A. Flores, "What Kind of Person Should a Professional Be" in A. Flores (ed.), *Professional Ideals* (Belmont, Calif., Wadsworth, 1988), at 1.

[10] The General Council of the Bar 'The Quality of Justice: The Bars Response' (London, Butterworths, 1989) para. 9.26. Bellacosa suggests that *pro bono* work is performed for the good of the state not for the good of the public as is commonly believed: J. W. Bellacosa, "Obligatory *Pro Bono* Legal Services: Mandatory or Voluntary? Distinction without a Difference" (1991) 19 *Hofstra Law Review* 744.

this risk, should promotion of a profession's public service efforts be placed in the hands of the professional body or should it be otherwise subject to regulation? These issues will be considered in the course of this chapter.

B. CONCEPTIONS OF PUBLIC SERVICE

The meaning of public service is often ill defined.[11] This section looks at three ways in which the legal profession may be said to be committed to public service. They are, first, placing the interests of clients before those of the lawyer, secondly, the defence of legal processs, and thirdly, the facilitation of access to justice. This is not intended to be an exhaustive list of possible public service.

Prioritising the Interests of Clients

Mungham and Thomas suggest that wider notions of public service gave way to an ethic of dedicated service to individual clients with the advent of legal aid.[12] This is a dangerously fragile platform on which to base a claim to act in the public interest. Unlike some other professions, the services lawyers provide are not easily subject to evaluation.[13] In 1967–8 a survey of respondents using a number of agencies in three London boroughs revealed a mixed but broadly positive perception of lawyers. The majority thought lawyers charged fair prices,[14] that they were honest,[15] and gave both rich and poor equal attention. Slightly more ambiguously in terms of approval it was thought that "for a price lawyers will use every trick in the book to help their clients".[16] The one clear criticism was that lawyers were thought to "often overcharge".[17] With the growth of consumerism, the seeds of doubt about commitment to individual clients began to sprout and grow.[18] More recently the Law Society's own research showed that,

---

[11] See further R. L. Nelson and D. M. Trubeck, "Arenas of Professionalism: The Professional Ideologies of Lawyers in Context" in R. L. Nelson, D. M. Trubeck and R. L. Solomon (eds.), *Lawyer's Ideals/Lawyer's Practices* (Ithaca NY, and London, Cornell University Press, 1992), 177 at 190.

[12] See G. Mungham and P. A. Thomas, "Solicitors and Clients: Altruism or Self Interest?" in R. Dingwall and P. Lewis (eds.), *The Sociology of the Professions: Lawyers Doctors and Others* (Basingstoke, Macmillan Press, 1983).

[13] A surgeon can perform an autopsy to check the accuracy of a diagnosis but lawyers cannot guarantee that their clients will receive equal treatment before the law: M. J. Saks, "Enhancing and Restraining Accuracy in Adjudication" (1988) 5 *Law and Contemporary Problems* 243 at 246.

[14] 34% agreed or strongly agreed with this proposition while 19% disagreed or strongly disagreed: B. Abel-Smith, M. Zander and R. B. Ross, *Legal Problems and the Citizen: A Study in Three London Boroughs* (London, Heinemann Educational, 1973), at 249.

[15] 55% against 12%: *ibid*.

[16] 54% agreed and 19% disagreed: *ibid*.

[17] 39% thought they did and 13% that they did not: *ibid*.

[18] S. Jenkins, E. Skordaki and C. F. Willis, *Public Use and Perception of Solicitors* (London, The Law Society, 1989). Note however, that public support in institutions is strongly influenced by knowledge of those institutions. See A. Sarat, "Support for the Legal System" in W. M. Evan (ed.), *The Sociology of Law: A Social-Structural Perspective* (New York, Free Press, 1980), at 167.

compared with accountants, bank managers and estate agents, solicitors were only thought to be more honest and less "after your money" than estate agents.[19] This loss of confidence in lawyers seems to be widespread. The legal profession in the USA, for example, was held in equally low public esteem. It was subject to stinging rebukes by the President and Chief Justice. Much of the problem was attributed to the perception, revealed in reliable opinion polls, that the profession was "greedy and self serving".[20]

Luban argues that one way by which the legal profession fulfils its obligation to secure justice is by striving to redress imbalances in power between the parties. This suggests that acting for disadvantaged clients may give rise to an ethical obligation to put extra effort into cases, which may be less generously remunerated than privately funded cases.[21] Unfortunately, this is unlikely to happen. When legal work becomes high volume and low value the interests of the lawyer lie in the smooth processing of work. The need to achieve a high rate of turnover produces a pressure to be less adversarial than traditional ethics demand and to prioritise relationships with those who facilitate smooth processing over the interests of the client. This is a pattern which has been detected in criminal cases, particularly in plea bargaining,[22] and in a range of civil contexts.[23] The lawyer must be extraordinarily committed and energetic to both make a living from low value work, like most legally aided criminal work, and give adversariality its due. It is a testimony to some lawyers that they achieve this. Regrettably, the likelihood is that most will not.[24] The spirited defence of rights thrives on incentive, an argument made in favour of conditional fee agree-

[19] Jenkins *et al.*, n. 18 above, at 10.

[20] H. C. Petrowitz, "Some Thoughts About Current Problems in Legal Ethics and Professional Responsibility" (1979) 6 *Duke Law Journal* 1275.

[21] O. Hansen, "A Future for Legal Aid" (1992) 19 *Journal of Law and Society* 85.

[22] Blumberg's analysis of criminal proceedings in the USA suggests that all court personnel, including defence attorneys, are co-opted to become agents and mediators in the criminal process. They preserve future relations with those involved in the process, particularly the "lawyer regulars" or repeat players. Clients therefore become "secondary figures" who are induced by pressure, such as the possibility of a harsh sentence, to enter a guilty plea. Lawyers stage-manage the relationship. The lawyer must arrange for payment of fees, "cool out" his client to accept the possibility of conviction and satisfy the organisation that he has adequately negotiated a plea so as to avoid outside scrutiny. "[L]awyers keep their clients in a proper state of tension, and arouse in them the precise level of anxiety which will encourage prompt fee payment": A. S. Blumberg, "The Practice of Law as a Confidence Game" (1967) 1 *Law and Society Review* 15, and see M. Heumann, "A Note on Plea Bargaining and Case Pressure" (1975) *Law and Society* 515 and M. McConville, J. Hodgson, L. Bridges and A. Pavlovic, *Standing Accused: The Organisation and Practices of Criminal Defence Lawyers in Britain* (Oxford, Clarendon Press, 1994).

[23] Sarat and Felstiner's study of divorce lawyers in California and Massachusetts taped and observed 115 conferences: A. Sarat and W. L. Felstiner, "Law and Strategy in a Divorce Lawyer's Office" (1986) 20 *Law and Society Review* 93). Lawyers and clients each set out to fulfil their own agendas. Lawyers tended to provide information only in response to the client's specific demands see also J. Griffiths, "What do Dutch Lawyers Actually do in Divorce Cases?" (1986) 20 *Law and Society Review* 135. Clients typically believed in "formal justice" but the lawyers attempted to create an impression that justice was uncertain and arbitrary. Lawyers emphasised the client's dependence on the lawyer for dealing with the uncertainties of the system. This justified the lawyer's argument about the best way to deal with the case.

[24] McConville *et al.*, n. 22 above.

ments. "Spirited advocacy" and the appearance of spirited advocacy are, however, in the public interest in *all* cases. We must assume they affect the outcome
of cases and therefore, and importantly, they build trust in the fairness of the
legal system.[25]

Protecting Third Parties

In the previous chapter we saw that ethical obligations to third parties are currently limited. Nevertheless, notions of public service are often associated with
increasing obligations owed to third parties. The conception of the lawyer as
aristocrat is associated with the idea that a lawyer should not be dominated by
the anti-social demands of clients,[26] a notion threatened by competition in the
legal services market. Competition makes it difficult, even for elite lawyers, to
infuse "higher", non-commercial values into a commercial society.[27] And yet
the aristocratic ideal of the professional ethic, adapted by the democratic notion
of service to new social groups, is that most often proposed as an antedote to the
unrestrained growth of the client based ethic.

The Defence of Legal Process

As we saw in Chapter 1, lawyers are the natural defenders of the rule of law and
of legal process. This cuts across attempts to make access to dispute resolution
easier and cheaper. Legal aid has become a mainstay of litigation and provides
the bedrock income of some lawyers. This creates a tension between the
lawyer's role in defence of rights and responsibility for the use of public funds.
We have seen how public confidence that legal traditions operated in the public
interest was undermined.[28] The legal profession made many concessions, offering to eliminate professional restrictive practices which were perceived to be
against the public interest.[29] But it was not enough. The spiralling cost of Legal
Aid is considered to be the consequence of supplier (i.e. lawyer) induced

[25] P. D. Carrington, "The Right to Zealous Counsel" (1979) 6 *Duke Law Journal* 1291.

[26] W. Simon, "Ethical Discretion in Lawyering" (1988) 101 *Harvard Law Review* 1083; R. W.
Gordon, "The Independence of Lawyers" (1988) 68 *Boston University Law Review* 1; and M. J.
Osiel, "Lawyers as Monopolists, Aristocrats and Entrepreneurs" (1990) 103 *Harvard Law Review*
2009.

[27] Osiel, n. 26 above, at 2014.

[28] See generally on the legal aid proposals T. Goriely, "The English Legal Aid White Paper and
the LAG. Conference" (1996) 3:3 *International Journal of the Legal Profession* 353.

[29] In response to *The Work and Organisation of the Legal Profession* the Bar stated that "only
those rules of the Bar which are necessary for the maintenance of its independence, the 'cab-rank'
rule and the consultant nature of the profession should be retained. The Bar Council will move to
change its rules with despatch, taking full account of the interests of the public which must be paramount": General Council of the Bar, *The Quality of Justice: The Bar's Response* (London,
Butterworth, 1989), hereafter *Quality of Justice*, at paras. 2.3–2.4.

demand. In civil litigation the responsibility for the conduct of actions was in the hands of the parties and lawyers were remunerated according to steps taken in an action. In independent research conducted for Lord Woolf's inquiry into civil justice, Zuckerman argued that "the cause of excessive costs lies not in the complexity of our procedure, but in the incentives that lawyers have to complicate litigation"[30] and Lord Woolf concluded that "the present system provides higher benefits to lawyers than to their clients".[31]

Here we see a clear conflict between two aspects of the ethic of lawyers; lawyers' duty to their clients and their wider duty to the public as taxpayers and to defend the legal process. Lawyers have always assumed that their obligations in an adversarial system demand that they pursue every avenue on behalf of clients, including their legally aided clients. This escalates costs. In a House of Lords debate on large increases in court fees, the new Lord Chancellor, Lord Irvine, focused on the fact that some QCs earned as much as £1 million a year. It was the high cost of lawyers' fees rather than court fees which were the largest impediment to access.[32] He said that "[t]o argue that court fees act as a deterrent to litigants is rather like arguing that people are deterred from buying a new motor car by an increase in vehicle excise duty. Fat cat lawyers railing at the inequity of court fees do not attract the sympathy of the public". Lord Irvine also revealed that 55 barristers were each paid between £270,000 and £575,000 from the Legal Aid fund in 1996–7 and that, over the same period, 1,000 barristers had earned more from Legal Aid than hospital consultants are paid.[33] The relevance of this is, perhaps, that in the modern state more people value access to medical services more than access to legal services.

Current proposals, such as those of Lord Woolf, aim to reduce the complexity, and therefore the cost, of dispute resolution. This creates a basic conflict for the profession; whether to embrace change or to defend its conception of "due

---

[30] In his view three factors contribute to excessive costs. The first is remuneration on a hourly rate which rewards lawyers for making litigation complex and long-winded. The second is the indemnity rule, whereby the loser pays the winner's costs, which encourages a "competition of investment" in litigation. The third is the availability of almost limitless Legal Aid funds, which, in tables annexed to the report, proved to be the variable most likely to be associated with cases of excessive duration: A. S. Zuckerman, "Lord Woolf's Access to Justice: Plus ça Change . . ." (1996) 59 *Modern Law Review* 773.

[31] Only in cases where the claim value is over £50,000 does the average combined costs of the parties fall to below the value of the claim: *Final Report*, para. 1.11, at 17.

[32] It was widely speculated that this level of earning was only true of top commercial silks although it was said that top criminal silks, particularly those specialising in fraud, and those conducting childcare cases, could earn £200,000 to £300,000 *per annum*, largely from legal aid: *The Guardian*, 15 July 1997, at 1.

[33] C. Dyer, "Law Chief Fires Fresh Volley on 'Fat Cat' Lawyers", *The Guardian* 10 Dec. 1997. In June 1998 the Clerk to the Parliaments refused to sanction Legal Aid bills presented by QCs for work in the House of Lords, the first time this had ever happened: C. Dyer, "On Trial: A System that Makes QCs Rich", *The Guardian* 3 June 1998. An enquiry conducted by the Lord Chancellor's Department forced the Bar Council to accept that barristers claiming excessive fees should be disciplined. (S. Pye, "Bar memo admits ludicrous fees", *The Lawyer*, 11 August 1998 at 1 and at 16).

process".[34] By defending the existing system, lawyers risk being seen to be defending their self-interest. An example is Lord Woolf's proposal to restrict party control over the process of litigation by creating "a managed environment governed by the courts and by the rules which will focus effort on the key issues rather than allowing every issue to be pursued regardless of expense and time".[35] Lord Woolf thought that the resistance of personal injury lawyers to these proposals could not be justified in the public interest. He told them:

> "If the profession is not willing or able to meet this challenge, then it should not imagine that the status quo can be retained. More fundamental measures, possibly involving the removal of at least moderate-sized injury claims from the litigation system, would have to be envisaged."[36]

Responding to suggestions that insurers generally paid the cost of personal injury litigation Lord Woolf asserted that "a system which fails to maintain the principle of proportionality [between damages and costs] simply fails to command public confidence".[37] He rejected arguments that the high cost of defending claims was an incentive to safety in the workplace. He argued that the costs of insurance were ultimately borne by society generally and that "the pattern of high spending on personal injury contaminates other areas of litigation where the costs are less likely to be borne by insurers".[38]

Although Lord Woolf did not expressly deal with Legal Aid in his report[39] the need to contain public expenditure informed his conclusions. He urged that the reform of Legal Aid should take account of and support his recommendations.[40] In 1997 the new Labour government made proposals to reduce the £800 million Legal Aid bill by £300 million by extending conditional fees to all damages claims and by limiting the availability of Legal Aid to criminal, family and social welfare cases.[41] Conditional fees and legal expenses insurance, both supported by Lord Woolf,[42] would enable lawyers to replace Legal Aid work with private funding sources. The risk that lawyers will continue to overcharge their clients remains.[43] Lord Woolf underestimates the capacity of lawyers to circumvent

---

[34] An example arises from a section of the Woolf report (Lord Woolf, *Access to Justice: Final Report to the Lord Chancellor on the Civil Justice System in England and Wales* (London, HMSO, 1996), hereafter *Final Report*) dealing with personal injury cases. The Law Society supported the proposal for a fast track procedure, using fixed timetables and governed by the principle of proportionality between costs and procedures and the damages in issue. This cut across the Association of Personal Injury Lawyers' arguments, which included the prediction that small-scale personal injury work would become so unprofitable that experienced solicitors would give up the work: *Final Report*, paras. 1.9 and 1.20.

[35] *Ibid.*, at paras. 1.3 at 14.

[36] *Interim Report*, chap. 7, paras. 24–25 and *Final Report*, n. 34 above, 1.21 at 25.

[37] *Ibid.*, para. 1.23.

[38] *Ibid.*, para. 1.24.

[39] *Ibid.*, para. 10 at 9.

[40] Including by providing legal aid for pre-litigation resolution and ADR (*ibid.*, para. 11 at 9).

[41] C. Dyer, "Poor Pay Price as Irvine Wields Reform Axe on Legal Aid Bill", *The Guardian*, 18 Oct. 1997.

[42] *Final Report*, n. 34 above, para. 12.

[43] P. Abrams, A. Boon, and D. O'Brien, "Access to Justice: The Collision of Funding and Ethics", (1998) 3:1 *Contemporary Issue in Law* 59.

measures to prevent the running up of unnecessary costs.[44] It seems a forlorn hope that any future government will significantly expand legal aid in an age where the containment of public expenditure has become a cornerstone of the policy of the main political parties.[45] Indeed, one result of the failure of measures to control public expenditure and increase access to justice is the proposed creation of a community legal service, using qualified lawyers in the service of the state as an alternative to legal aid.[46] For lawyers employed by this service the pursuit of "justice as process" as a public good will give way to the need to promote the good of access to justice.

Facilitating Access to Justice

A prerequisite of access to justice in an adversary system is access to lawyers and legal advice. This requires legal services to be conveniently located, user friendly and reasonably priced. The Marre Report recognised that several factors contributed to the perceived problem of unmet legal need including ignorance of the work of advice agencies, low public awareness of services offered by solicitors, fear of lawyers, dissatisfaction with lawyers and unavailability of lawyers.[47] This demonstrates that lawyers are at a considerable disadvantage in comparison with, for example, the medical profession in demonstrating that the distribution of legal services is in the public interest. The welfare state decides as an issue of public policy where medical services, e.g. major hospitals, are located. Lawyers in private practice must respond to the market for their services and they are usually drawn to profitable locations. Lawyers in private practice do not enjoy the comfort of secure incomes paid directly by the state. As a result, legal services are often distributed unevenly among the population. Advice agencies, which serve economically deprived areas, attempt to remedy this

---

[44] Zuckerman, n. 30 above.

[45] The overall net cost of legal aid for 1997 was £1,177m (excluding criminal cases in higher courts and administrative costs): *Legal Aid Board Annual Report 1997–8*. See *Striking the Balance: The Future of Legal Aid in England and Wales*, Cm 3305 (London, The Lord Chancellor's Department, 1996). The Lord Chancellor, Lord Mackay, is quoted as saying "legal aid is not, and cannot be, an unconditional blank-cheque for the taxpayer": T. Goriely, "Rushcliffe Fifty Years On: The Changing Role of Civil Legal Aid Within the Welfare State" (1994) 21 *Journal of Law and Society* 555 at 561.

[46] *A Time for Change: Report of the Committee on the Future of the Legal Profession* (London, The General Council of the Bar and the Council of the Law Society, 1988), hereafter the Marre Report, rejected proposals for the establishment of a national legal service or the creation of the office of Public Defender on the grounds of the cost of the former and the potential loss of independence of lawyers employed by such services: paras. 9.26–9.36. The Report considered that the cost of a national legal service would exceed the cost of Legal Aid which would be diverted to pay for it. The proposal for a Public Defender, emanating from a Justice Report in 1987 which argued that this would facilitate investigation, was rejected on similar grounds.

[47] *Ibid.*, para. 7.15. The report also proposed the establishment of Community Legal Services. This idea is currently being promoted by the Labour Lord Chancellor, Lord Irvine, in the White Paper *Modernising Justice* Cm 4155, 1998 and the Access to Justice Bill 1998.

uneven distribution. The relationship between advice agencies and the legal profession therefore becomes an issue. The public good of access to justice is served by collaboration between advice agencies and the legal profession.

The relationship between the legal profession and independent para-legal services has always been ambivalent. Before the advent of the welfare state, the legal profession was unconcerned about low paying work. The changes introduced by the welfare state reflected ambivalence towards lawyers. They were paid to expand access to courts[48] but, in other areas, tribunals for example, lawyers were deliberately excluded. The gaps intentionally created by government, or left by lawyers because they were not profitable, were filled by advice agencies and law centres. In the 1970s law centres alarmed the profession. Initially they provided "sympathetic lay advice" and yet were seen to herald deprofessionalsiation.[49] By 1977 an agreement had been reached that, provided they did not encroach on areas such as personal injury and crime, the Law Society would grant waivers to law centres from certain practice rules. Anxiety was further allayed when it was recognised that advice agencies actually expanded and improved the work of the profession by providing points of access and by screening cases.[50] By the late 1980s advice agencies actually had gained superior knowledge of social security law at a time when declining legal aid eligibility rates were forcing many lawyers into the same welfare field, and competition again arose.[51]

Despite the tension in the relationship, the legal profession has come to regard advice agencies as a complementary service to solicitors in terms both of expertise and locations.[52] The Marre Report acknowledged that "'[i]t is no longer possible to consider only the two branches of the legal profession when considering the supply of legal services".[53] Advice agencies not only relieved the profession of an obligation to offer accessible legal services, they often operated in tandem with local solicitors in terms of arranging free legal advice sessions by lawyers and by referral. One anxiety is that, as the agencies themselves were

---

[48] The Law Society had successfully resisted the establishment of state employed and salaried lawyers: T. Goriely, "Law for the Poor: The Relationship Between Advice Agencies and Solicitors in the Development of Poverty Law" (1996) 3:1/2 *International Journal of the Legal Profession* 215 at 224 and J. S. Auerbach, *Unequal Justice: Lawyers and Social Change in Modern America* (New York, Oxford University Press, 1976).

[49] *Ibid.*, at 220–1.

[50] *Ibid.*, at 233–7.

[51] Green form bills for areas of "social welfare" law for 1975–6 were £27,000 or 11% of the total. By 1994–5 this has risen to £468,000 or 30% of the total.

[52] Advice agencies tend to provide advice to low income groups particularly on social security, housing, family and consumer law. A 1986 survey by the Advice Services Alliance recorded that, nationwide, there were 896 CAB service points, 354 generalist independent advice services, 142 generalist advice agencies serving specific groups (e.g. young people), 55 independent housing advice service points, 25 money advice service points and 14 immigration advice service points: *The Recruitment Crisis* (London, The Training Committee of the Law Society, 1988) at 17.

[53] The Marre Report, n. 46 above, para. 5.28. See also B. Abel-Smith, M. Zander, and R. Brooke, *Legal Problems and the Citizen: A Study of Three London Boroughs* (London, Heinemann Educational, 1973) at 217.

usually funded centrally or by local authorities, their independence was in doubt.

Effective representation is a prerequisite to the satisfactory enforcement of rights.[54] Although the numbers consulting lawyers is relatively high,[55] it is often suggested that there is a deficit of services available in the area broadly defined as welfare law.[56] Despite the existence of advice and law centres, there is reason to suspect that unmet legal need is huge.[57] As eligibility rates for legal aid have declined, those just above the poverty level and those in the middle income range have found it increasingly difficult to finance cases.[58] The corresponding failure of legal services to match legal need is reflected in the rise in the number of litigants in person. A working party chaired by Lord Justice Otton in July 1995 indicated that in March 1995 alone there were 4,258 litigants in person involved in actions in the High Court, representing an increase from one in ten cases in 1989/90, to one in three. Litigants in person absorbed a disproportionate amount of the time of the courts and court staff, and were less successful than represented parties.[59] The profession's plea for "adequate" legal aid having failed, the only alternative is for the legal profession to provide free legal advice and representation.[60] Despite the increasingly commercial orientation of legal practice the profession is beginning to recognise that enlightened self interest requires this. For, "[t]o provide legal services for the poor is to assert the universality of law. It legitimises the product lawyers sell."[61]

---

[54] H. Genn, "Tribunals and Informal Justice" (1993) 56 *Modern Law Review* 393.

[55] A survey conducted by the NCC in 1995 suggested that 13% of the adult population had been involved in a civil dispute in the previous three years: *Seeking Civil Justice: A Survey of People's Needs and Experiences,* a report by the National Consumer Council of a survey of people in England and Wales, commissioned by the NCC and the BBC. "Law in Action" programme (London, National Consumer Council, 1995), at 5.

[56] The Marre Report, n. 46 above, paras. 7.9–7.14.

[57] The assessment of unmet legal need is problematic because the process by which misfortunes are experienced as grievances and become disputes is complex and culturally determined: W. Felstner, R. L. Abel and A. Sarat, "The Emergence and Transformation of Disputes: Naming, Blaming and Claiming" (1980–1) 15:3/4 *Law and Society Review* 631. Estimates in the USA suggest that 10 times the current level of resources would be necessary in order to make available to all the legal services currently enjoyed by the affluent. In the UK it has been suggested that in a survey of three local authorities, only one quarter of callers at CABx etc. who needed legal advice saw an independent lawyer: Abel-Smith, *et al.,* n. 14 above, at 219.

[58] Goriely, n. 48 above, citing (at n.9) J. Plotnikoff and R. Woolfson, *Report of Study into Reasons for Refusal of Offers of Legal Aid* (Legal Aid Board, 1996); T. Ingman, *The English Legal Process* (London: Blackstone Press, 1996), at 64; G. Slapper and D. Kelly, *English Legal System* (London, Cavendish Press, 1995), at 359; see also Hansen, n. 21 above, and Goriely, n. 48 above.

[59] *The Times,* 7 July 1995. See also J. Ames, "Rescuing DIY. Litigants", *Law Society's Gazette,* 26 July 1995.

[60] *Quality of Justice,* n. 29 above, para. 2.20.

[61] Goriely, n. 48 above, at 242.

C. PRO BONO PUBLICO

Legal work performed *pro bono publico* is work performed free and without any expectation of payment.[62] It is sometimes argued that true *pro bono publico* is limited to the provision of litigation services, a proposition considered below. The roots of the *pro bono* tradition run deep, with examples of legal representatives being prohibited from accepting fees in ancient Rome and dark age Europe.[63] In the Middle Ages the Roman law forbidding advocates from receiving a fee, but permitting them to accept a gift, was often adopted.[64] Both the medical and legal professions assumed responsibility for their areas of expertise from the clergy and, with them, the Christian responsibilities for the poor and the dispossessed. The professions, medicine and law, established their distinctiveness from other professional groups by offering free services to the poor.[65]

Charitable aid for the poor developed via a limited right to sue *in forma pauperis*, whereby the court could assign lawyers to act for litigants without a fee.[66] Not surprsingly, these and similar procedures were not popular with lawyers. In the seventeenth and eighteenth centuries, these early altruistic inclinations of the legal profession declined. Free representation by lawyers was so restricted by judges that by the early twentieth century, it was rare.[67] Worse, as part of the professionalisation project of the 1800s, the profession sought to surrender "low grade" work, including low value litigation[68] and discouraged practitioners from pursuing it. By the nineteenth and twentieth centuries the provision of free services was not widespread. Even the dock brief was not much used. Attempts to introduce limited Legal Aid in the early twentieth century were obstructed by the professional bodies and received inadequate support from practitioners.[69]

---

[62] Legally aided work and work performed under conditional fee arrangements, therefore, does not satisfy this strict definition. Lawyers may be underpaid under Legal Aid certificates, but they are paid. Lawyers may not be paid under conditional fee arrangements but they fully expect to be paid. They also receive an uplift of their profit costs if they are successful to reflect the risk that they would lose and not be paid.

[63] R. Pound, *The Lawyer from Antiquity to Modern Times: With Particular Reference to the Development of Bar Associations in the United States* (St. Paul, Minn., West Publishing 1953), at 52.

[64] *Ibid.*, at 55 and 68.

[65] J. A. Brundage, "Legal Aid for the Poor and the Professionalisation of Law in the Middle Ages" (1988) 9 *Journal of Legal History* 169.

[66] W. R.Prest, *The Rise of the Barristers: A Social History of the Bar 1590–1640* (Oxford, Clarendon Press, 1986), at 22.

[67] Goriely, "Law for the poor" n. 48 above, at 217.

[68] In the late sixteenth and seventeenth centuries, for example, litigation was more widespread than at any time until the 1970s and probably over 75% of litigants were "non-gentlemen". Litigation however, was apparently not encouraged by the profession M. Burrage, "From a Gentleman's to a Public Profession: Status and Politics in the History of English Solicitors" (1996) *International Journal of the Legal Profession* 45 at 47)

[69] See B. Abel-Smith and R. Stevens, "Legal Services for the Poor" in *Lawyers and the Courts: A Sociological Study of the English Legal System 1750–1965* (London, Heinemann, 1967), at 135–164, 146 and 158 and Goriely, n. 48 above, at 218 (a poor persons procedure was instituted in 1914 to deal with divorce and was administered by the Law Society from 1926 but, frequently, insufficient solicitors could be found to do the work).

Despite the antipathy to *pro bono publico* in that apparently golden age of legal professionalism, in 1925 the Lawrence Committee on Poor Persons Rules recognised a moral obligation, in return for the monopoly in the practice of law, to offer legal services to those who could not afford to pay, provided this did not place an unnecessary burden on individual members of the profession.[70] This obligation was very much against the spirit of the times. Hoggart notes that the incidence of public service work has been declining and that negative attitudes towards it:

> ". . . have been growing since at least the turn of the century, as the rise of relativism and populism gradually made proconsular activities or even modest activities pro bono publico seem patronising or pompous. Yet they survived fairly well into the Sixties. It has been shown that in the last couple of decades the rejection of them has strengthened as consensual political attitudes turned into the confrontational."[71]

Although the tradition of *pro bono publico* did not completely die out, and may even have revived recently with the arrival of advice agencies, little is known about the volume of such work performed by lawyers.[72] The profession consistently claims that its record is good.[73] Surveys paint conflicting pictures. In 1976 the Royal Commission on Legal Services estimated that 3,300 solicitors supported advice agencies by offering free services.[74] In a Law Society survey of solicitors in 1989, 41 per cent claimed to carry out "public service work for which [they did] not charge fees" but the majority performed one hour or less work a week.[75] An independent survey of 59 Law Centres found 369 wholly or partly qualified lawyers, less than one per cent of the solicitors then holding practising certificates, offering voluntary services.[76] In November 1993 the Law Society's' Pro Bono Working Party undertook a survey of 123 local Law Societies to determine the extent of work undertaken. Thirty two responses were received. "None of the local Law Societies which responded to the survey held formal records of the work their members did or monitored it in any way. Many were "aware" that local practitioners were fairly active in the voluntary sector, particularly in assisting Citizens Advice Bureaux on a rota basis."[77]

---

[70] A. A. Paterson, "Professionalism and the Legal Services Market" (1996) 1/2 *International Journal of the Legal Profession* 137 at 160 n.19.

[71] R. Hoggart, *The Way We Live Now* (London, Chatto and Windus, 1995).

[72] Surprisingly, this is also true of the USA where the American Lawyers Annual Survey of large firm contributions, dates only from 1990. See M. Galanter and T. Palay, "Public Service Implications of Evolving Firm Size and Structure", in R. A. Katzmann (ed.), *The Law Firm And The Public Good* (Washington, The Brookings Institute, 1995) at 41.

[73] A. Bradbury, "Solicitors Rally for UK *Pro Bono* Scheme", *The Lawyer* 15 October 1996 at 1, claimed "the legal aid factor is largely responsible for the fact that there is no national *pro bono* scheme, even though 75 per cent of firms do *pro bono* work".

[74] The Royal Commission on Legal Services Report, Cmnd 7648, 1979 para. 2.21.

[75] G. Chambers and S. Harwood, *Solicitors in England and Wales: Practice, Organisation and Perceptions* (London, The Law Society, 1990).

[76] L. Hiscock and G. Cole, "The Motivation, Use and Future of Volunteer Lawyers in Law Centres" (1989) *Journal of Social Welfare Law* 404.

[77] Report of the Law Society's *Pro Bono* Working Party (London, The Law Society, 1994) Annex C, para. 1.

In 1997 the Law Society published some details of one of its panel surveys based on responses from 460 firms. The definition of voluntary work covered work charged at a rate substantially below that normally charged. Seventy per cent of firms claimed to provide legal advice to private individuals whose cases fell outside the scope of legal aid and only eleven per cent of firms admitted to providing no such services. As the table following shows, eighty five per cent of firms responding agreed that providing voluntary services enabled the firm to contribute to the public good.[78]

Table 9: Effect on solicitors' firms of providing voluntary legal services.

Providing Voluntary Services	No. of Firms (weighted base)	Proportion Agreeing	Proportion Neither Agreeing or Disagreeing	Proportion Disagreeing
Enables the firm to contribute to the public good	413	85%	14%	1%
Enhances the reputation of the firm	410	68%	28%	5%
Promotes the loyalty and goodwill of clients	397	58%	31%	11%
Leads to referrals and work for the firm	407	57%	31%	12%
Provides training opportunities for legal staff	357	32%	35%	33%
Produces little or no benefit to the firm	406	25%	32%	43%
Reduces the productivity of the firm	404	29%	33%	38%

Finally, a survey conducted for the Law Society Research Unit in October 1997 suggested that solicitors in private practice may contribute an average of 37 hours of services per year "free of charge or at a rate substantially below that normally charged either during the firm's time or during your own".[79] The Law Society issued a press release claiming that "value of pro bono work by solicitors is the equivalent to a cash gift to good causes of at least £124 million a year".[80]

---

[78] Research and Policy Planning Unit Panel Study of Solicitors' Firms (London, The Law Society, 1997).

[79] J. Jenkins, *Law Society Omnibus Survey 2: Report 5: Pro Bono Activities Conducted by Private Practice Solicitors* (London, The Law Society, 1997).

[80] News Release, "Solicitors Give at Least £124 Million of Free Legal Help a Year", Law Society 27 January 1998.

A number of reasons may explain the discrepancies in the results of the surveys. The Law Society data in this last survey was based on self reporting by 1,113 interviewees and was multiplied by a notional charging rate, which was unspecified, to produce a global figure. It was not clear what was meant by "charging a rate substantially below that normally charged". Nor was it clear for whom the work was conducted; solicitors working in advice agencies appeared to be considerably fewer than the 73% providing services for "individuals or families", a category which could include substantial numbers of friends, acquaintances or existing clients.

D. THE POLICY OF PROFESSIONAL BODIES

England and Wales

In 1989, in response to the Green Papers, the Bar undertook to encourage barristers to do *pro bono* work and to expand the Free Representation Unit both in London and in other major centres. At the same time it warned that the implementation of the government's proposals would *diminish* the public service work performed by solicitors and barristers.[81] In 1992 the Bar Council established a pro bono scheme as an independent charity called the Pro Bono Unit. This was an addition and complementary to existing schemes, especially the strong regional schemes run on the Northern Circuit, Western Circuit and Wales and Chester Circuit, and the schemes run by subject area Bar Associations.[82] Barristers were asked to donate two or three days a year to free work, a commitment one commentator described as "far too modest".[83] In 1997 it was reported that 720 barristers of differing levels of seniority, including 120 QCs, had agreed to provide at least three days a year to *pro bono publico* work. This represented less than 10% of the practising bar. It was reported that the Bar's pro Bono Unit took on 44% of the cases referred to it and, in half the cases, advice only was given. Some significant cases have been dealt with, including a challenge by pensioner to the National Grid over the alleged use of £47 million of pension fund money to make redundancy payments.[84] By 1998 it was reported that the number of participating barristers had increased to 800, including 130 QCs, of which almost 600 were based in London. Fifty legal specialisms were represented. The major areas of work are set out in Table 10.

It was noted, however, that in cases where a solicitor's assistance was required the case was likely to be refused. In some cases, and "exceptionally"

[81] *Quality of Justice,* n. 29 above.

[82] E.g., the Employment Law Bar Association Scheme, the Planning Bar Association's Free Advocacy Scheme and Environmental Legal and Mediation Service, V. Sims, "Pro Bono at the Bar" (1998) 4 *Amicus Curiae: Journal of the Society for Advanced Legal Studies* 21.

[83] M. Phelam, "Effective Access to Justice", *Counsel* April 1996 at 16.

[84] C. Dyer, "On the Lawyers Who Work for Free", *The Guardian* 15 July 1997 at 17.

Table 10: Participation of Barristers in Pro Bono Publico

Area of work	No. of barristers	Including QCs
Commercial	190	46
Criminal	210	38
Employment	150	17
Family	170	11
Housing	130	7
Professional negligence	240	46
Personal injury	205	37

solicitors have been found to help.[85] This suggests a need for greater co-operation between the branches of the profession.

In contrast to the position taken by the Bar, the Law Society has been ambivalent regarding free legal work. In the 1900s the Law Society was concerned to limit competition, even in relation to those clients who could not otherwise go to law, and to stamp out "a black market in legal aid" conducted on a contingency basis.[86] Subsequently, fears that free work amounted to advertising and unfair attraction of business led to the imposition of restrictive rules governing solicitors acting in free legal advice centres.[87] Encouraging solicitors to conduct more free work ran counter to this policy and fell foul of the measures put in place to counter these "threats". The Report of the Law Society's Pro Bono Working Party, published in 1994,[88] changed the policy and made a number of proposals intended to stimulate the involvement of solicitors in *pro bono* activity.[89] The Working Party sought to avoid the term *pro bono publico*, preferring "voluntary legal services" which expanded the meaning of what was, arguably, a historically specific concept. The report concluded, however, that solicitors should not be subject to a mandatory professional obligation to provide free legal services.

The Working Party recognised that the timing of its report was inauspicious. There was the threat to the profession's monopoly in the provision of legal services, the decreasing profitability of practice and the argument that the

[85] Sims, n. 82 above.

[86] Abel-Smith and Stevens, n 69, at 138 (the authors use the word "commission", but it is clear that what the Law Society were seeking to abolish was contingency and speculative work by solicitors).

[87] M. Zander, "Restrictions on Lawyers Working for the Poor" in *Lawyers and the Public Interest: A Study of Restrictive Practices* (Weidenfeld and Nicolson, 1968), 238.

[88] Report of the Law Society's *Pro Bono* Working Party, 1994 (and see *The Times* 9 October 1995)

[89] R. Abbey and A Boon, "The Provision of Free Legal Services by Solicitors: A Review of the Report of the Law Society's Pro Bono Working Party" (1995) 2 *International Journal of the Legal Profession* 261.

profession should not ameliorate or redress, by the provision of free services, the growing legal need created by declining legal aid budgets. The Law Society moved very slowly on the constructive proposals made by the Working Party. By November 1996, of the Working Party's six other recommendations, progress was reported on only one; representation at tribunals.[90] No mention of *pro bono publico* is made in either the Bar's or the Law Society's codes of conduct.

Following the publication of the report the Law Society was keen to reinforce the message that *pro bono publico* must not be seen as a substitute for legal aid.[91] This may reflect the concern of its membership, the vast majority of which are in small to medium practices, at the decline of "high street practice".[92] While solo practitioners and small units must respond to the demands of the market, elite lawyers "are more concerned with the image and status of the profession and with the character and organisation of the legal system".[93] Neither the Bar nor the Law Society has collected or published comprehensive data on the provision of services pro bono publico.[94] With modern office systems it would be fairly easy to require firms to keep a detailed record of work performed and to audit the results. The Bar's recent decision to publish details of its efforts is to be welcomed.

A Comparison with the USA

The policy of the American Bar Association (ABA) is markedly different and, because of this, instructive. Because of its roots in the English common law, *pro bono publico* is a strong tradition in the USA. The ABA has, throughout history,

---

[90] These included: the publication of a policy statement encouraging solicitors to conduct more *pro bono* work; a free representation advice agency and the establishment of a Trust Fund to receive voluntary funds to support *pro bono* activities.

[91] John Buckingham, head of litigation at Shakespears said ". . . any government should be making sure that the rates of the legal aid fund are in good order, not telling lawyers what they should be doing" (J. Smerin, "For Love Not Money" (1995) 92/38 *Law Society's Gazette* 1). In a public row between Martin Mears (former president of the Law Society) and Paul Boateng (of the Labour Party), regarding Labours plans, Mears pointed out that "far from enjoying a "gravy train" 25 per cent of small firms earn less than ten thousand a year".

[92] The Law Society's *Pro Bono* Working Party's Report (May 1994) argued that any obligation to provide voluntary legal services to the poor had been reduced by the suffering wrought on "high street" firms by declining levels for legal aid and by the decline of conveyancing. The Working Party argued that firms performing legal aid work made a significant contribution to the performance of any *pro bono publico* obligation which the profession might have. The position taken by the Working Party has been repeated since the report. See also N. Maley, "Bar and Law Society Warn *Pro Bono* Work is 'No Substitute' for Legal Aid", *The Lawyer* 10 October 1995 at 2 and R. Abbey, and A Boon, n. 89. The Bar Council has also assented to the need to maintain a proper system of legal aid (*Quality of Justice*, n. 29 above, paras. 2.28 and 2.32.

[93] *Ibid.*, 363.

[94] The Law Society's panel survey found that 68% of firms kept no record of time spent (Research and Policy Planning Unit Panel Study of Solicitors' Firms (London, The Law Society, 1997).

expected practitioners to offer voluntary legal services to the poor.[95] Since 1908 the American Bar Association's model code of conduct has recommended that lawyers work *pro bono publico*. In 1972 the ABA proposed "drafting or socialising a percentage of lawyers time for professional public interest work".[96]

In 1980 the Kutak Commission (The ABA Commission on the Evaluation of Professional Standards) recommended, along with many other radical reforms, that a mandatory obligation to perform *pro bono publico* work be included in a revision of the 1969 Code of Professional Responsibility.[97] This was to cover contributions to Welfare Law, Civil Rights, Public Rights, Charitable Organisation Representation and Administration of Justice Activity.[98]

State bars were encouraged to implement schemes setting guidelines on the number of hours to be performed. There have been various proposals for the number of hours from the ABA and others. These have varied from 20 to 50 hours per annum.[99] The Commission also recommended a national rule, enforceable by disciplinary action, that "a lawyer should render unpaid public interest legal service". After much political infighting this was replaced, in 1981, by a draft which diminished the mandatory nature of the obligation.[100] Despite a few localised programmes, notably in Florida, most of the initiatives stimulated by the draft were "ambitious and abortive".[101] In 1989 the ABA launched a Law Firm Pro Bono Project followed by a "pro bono challenge" to the 500 largest US law firms to make a commitment to contribute, by the end of 1995, either three or five per cent of the firm's total billable hours to *pro bono* work.[102] The results are currently being collated but there are some indications that it has been successful.[103]

---

[95] In *US* v. *Dillon* 382, US 978 (1965) the obligation to provide *pro bono publico* services in both criminal and civil cases, was traced at least to the fifteenth century, when sergeants at law in England could be required by the courts "to plead for the poor man", S. B. Rosenfeld, "Mandatory *Pro Bono*" (1981) 2 *Cardozo Law Review* 255 citing W. Holdsworth, *A History of English Law* (London, Sweet & Maxwell, 1923) at 491.

[96] R. H. Silverman, "Conceiving a Lawyer's Legal Duty to the Poor" (1990–91) 19 *Hofstra Law Review* 885

[97] See Chap. 4.

[98] Rosenfeld, n. 95 above.

[99] The American Bar Association suggested that every US attorney should perform a minimum 50 hours per annum. This proposal was fiercely resisted. Volunteers of Legal Services, a public service organisation encouraging the *pro bono* efforts of New York law firms, recommended a 30 hour average commitment by firm members. Various firms advertise their achievements on the World Wide Web, including Kramer Levin who averaged 39 hours per attorney during 1994 (http://www.kramer-le vin.comm/probono.html).

[100] Silverman, n. 96 above, at 892.

[101] *Ibid.*, at 893–894.

[102] E. F. Lardent, "Structuring Law Firms Pro Bono Programmes: A Community Service Typology", in Katzmann, n. 72 above, at 59, observes that 171 firms agreed to participate, but more have implemented a truly mandatory programme. See also B. D. Parker, "Monitoring Compliance With the ABA Law Firm *Pro Bono* Challenge" in Katzmann, *ibid.*, at 158.

[103] M. Galanter and T. Palay, "Large Law Firms and Professional Responsibility" in R. Cranston (ed.) *Legal Ethics and Professional Responsibility* (Oxford, Clarendon Press, 1995).

The Free Representation Unit

The Free Representation Unit (FRU) was established in 1972 by a group of Bar students who set out to represent welfare benefit claimants but has been claimed by the Bar as one of its 'best initiatives'.[104] It has expanded its work to embrace a range of tribunals for which legal aid was not available, and aims to provide a standard of representation which clients would receive if legally aided.[105] In 1992, 2,063 cases were referred to FRU by Citizens Advice Bureaux and Law Centres and representation was provided in 1200 cases.[106] FRU employs a number of administrators and a solicitor to prepare more complex cases for barristers.[107] In 1993 FRU appealed to barristers in London and the South East to assist by launching its "Chamber Scheme".[108] This was enthusiastically supported by the Bar Council, whose Chairman took cases himself, providing a lead to senior barristers to supplement volunteers from the Inns of Court School of Law and pupils.[109] In 1996, however, it was noted that the number of cases for which representation could be found had declined.[110]

Large Firms of Solicitors

Large firms are well placed, both organisationally[111] and economically,[112] to develop *pro bono* services. Their everyday legal experience however, has nothing

---

[104] FRU pamphlet (undated) at 1 and 'The Quality of Justice', n. 10, above, at para. 9.25.

[105] FRU is authorised by the Bar Council in relation to each of the tribunals in which its representatives appear. In 1991–2 55% of FRUs representation was provided in Industrial Tribunals (55%), Social Security Tribunals (23%), Criminal Injuries Compensation Board (8%), Medical Appeals Tribunals (4%), and other tribunals (10%) *ibid.*, at 4.

[106] *Ibid.*, at 2.

[107] Funding is provided by the Bar Council (33%), the Inns of Court (26%), covenants from individual barristers (20%) subscriptions from referral agencies and income from training days. (See Counse, "FRU—The Bars Contribution", *Counsel*, April 1994) at 23.

[108] D. Conn, "A matter of principle" *Counsel*, July 1993 at 18, notes that by 1993 FRU had 2,400 clients an increase of 25% over the previous year.

[109] The Inns of Court Law School provides a Bar Vocational Course option for those wishing to work at FRU. See N. Duncan, "FRU and the Bar Vocational Course", *New Law Journal* 5 November 1993.

[110] From 1,682 in 1994 to 1,394 in 1995, M. Phelan, "Effective Access to Justice", *Counsel* April 1996 at 16.

[111] E. F. Lardent, n. 102 argues that the "oral tradition" of induction into *pro bono* work is replaced in large firms by reliance on structure and formalism.

[112] Silverman, n. 96 calculates that ambitious mandatory *pro bono* proposals would impose a "relatively modest burden" on the top firms in New York. See R. A. Katzmann, "Themes in Context" in Katzmann, n. 72 above, at 1. The earnings of partners in the top 25 firms exceed £200,000 per annum and in firms towards the top of the income league table they are almost double that. Yet Lee suggests that only the top six law firms in the UK are financially secure from merger pressure, R. G. Lee "From Profession to Business: The Rise and Rise of the City Law Firms" in P. Thomas (ed.) *Tomorrow's Lawyers* (Oxford: Blackwell, 1992), at 31.

to do with welfare advice and assistance.[113] A former President of the Law Society, hearing that large firms were performing pro bono work said ". . . if a big City firm is doing a certain amount of pro bono work this has far less value for ordinary people than pro bono work by High Street practices which are geared up for everyday problems."[114] Galanter and Palay's qualitative study, conducted in large London law firms between 1990 and 1994, suggested that individuals in these firms were unconcerned at the commercialisation of legal practice, the poor image of the profession or the attacks on its power. There was ". . . hardly a glimmer of interest in expansive pro bono activity, although inquiry revealed that several of the firms visited had "substantial pro bono programmes".[115]

In a survey of the 100 largest national firms in 1994, 46 respondents from 61 firms provided details of their pro bono work.[116] Advisory work at Citizens' Advice Bureaux and Law Centres conducted by trainees was the major area of activity. Senior personnel tended to deal with appeals to the Judicial Committee of the Privy Council in capital cases or with cases from organisations such as Business in the Community or Liberty. Only six firms had a policy on pro bono work conducted by the firm and only four claimed to formally assign work to firm members. Twenty seven firms claimed to perform work which exceeded £10,000 in value per annum. More significant than the volume of the work performed is the conclusion that this is a growing commitment by large firms[117] as is evidenced by the fact that at least four have appointed their own in-house *pro bono* co-ordinators.

Trainees and young lawyers working in large firms are the most likely to suffer as a result of their specialisation and client centredness. They may work in narrow fields and have little direct responsibility for clients until they have been qualified for a few years. It is therefore arguable that *pro bono publico* is not only in the interest of the client, it is in their interest also. Providing voluntary legal services allows them to develop skills[118] and to grow as a professional.[119]

---

[113] See para. 22 of The Law Society's *Pro Bono* Working Party Report which suggested that the imposition of a requirement for *pro bono publico* work was counter to the Law Society's role in promoting ". . . high standards of integrity, a high quality of work and guaranteed compensation when things go wrong."

[114] Smerin, n. 91. The present senior personnel of the Law Society may be more sympathetic to the contribution which can be made by large firms, and are maintaining contact with the new Solicitors' *Pro Bono* Group.

[115] Galanter and Palay, "Large Law Firms and Professional Responsibility" in Cranston, n. 103 above, at 201.

[116] Of the remainder seven did some work but were unable to provide any details and eight said they undertook no *pro bono publico* work whatsoever.

[117] A. Boon and R. Abbey, "Moral Agendas: *Pro Bono Publico* in Large Law Firms in the United Kingdom" (1997) 60 *Modern Law Review* 630.

[118] See generally D. W. Hoagland, "Community Service Makes Better Lawyers", in Katzmann, n. 72 above, at 104, who argues that working for the poor with limited resources sharpens decision making powers and increases sensitivity to the human dimension of complex problems.

[119] Galanter and Palay, suggest that, because the clients of large firms are "the firm's clients", non partner fee earners become anonymous employees whose time is monopolised by more senior staff. Their names acquire "none of the value which seems to constitute the chief capital of a professional man", n. 103.

Public service can "infuse" professional life with more immediacy, reducing the sense of isolation lawyers experience in large firm practice. It has also been suggested that the opportunity to conduct *pro bono* work may influence graduates' decisions on which firm to join.[120]

The Solicitors' *Pro Bono* Group

Late in 1996 a "Solicitor's *Pro Bono* Group" was formed. The group aims to promote pro bono work among solicitors and a small, full-time unit has been set up in order to achieve this.[121] Despite the fact that the initiative was backed by "many City firms", the group recognised that, to be successful, it had to appeal to the whole profession. A full-time director has been appointed who is establishing links with local law societies, umbrella organisations and others interested in the field. Many local law societies have expressed a desire to stimulate greater *pro bono* contributions in their local areas. An initial hope was that this initiative would be taken over by the Law Society. At present there is no sign of this happening.

F. PUBLIC SERVICE OR PUBLIC IMAGE?

The growth of interest in *pro bono publico* exists throughout the common law world. Although there appears to be a relatively high level of commitment to the idea of *pro bono publico,* there is typically uncertainty as to how it should be defined and a lack of clear mechanisms for co-ordinating or quantifying the work.[122] Despite this, professional bodies are inclined to make exaggerated claims for the work done. An economic explanation for the perceived growth in *pro bono* work is unlikely, because of the lack of direct economic benefits flowing to any of those involved in the schemes described above. Economic analysis may however be relevant where *pro bono* work reflects an attempt to pre-empt measures to tackle the inequalities in access to justice, which, for example the presence of large firms in the market place accentuate,[123] and to pre-empt exter-

---

[120] This was the case in the USA in the 1960s the expansion of law firms was followed by a period in the 1970s in which recruitment was difficult. Large corporate law firms therefore permitted attorneys to spend substantial time conducting "non-commercial work" as a "life-style reward". It was widely predicted that the shape of legal practice in the future might include "pecuniary" and "life-style" rewards in order to attract and keep staff (Galanter and Palay, n. 103 at 127).

[121] The meeting, held on 2 November 1996 at the Law Society, followed an open invitation to the profession to attend. It attracted representatives from some regional Law Societies and several large firms (The Lawyer, "Solicitors vote for boost to *Pro Bono*", *The Lawyer* 12 November 1996 at 1. A further meeting in December 1996 proposed electing an executive committee and appointing an organiser to promote further work in the field.

[122] See above and Law Foundation for New South Wales/Centre for Legal Process, *Future Directions for Pro Bono Legal Services in New South Wales* (Sydney, Law Foundation for New South Wales, 1998), hereafter *Future Directions for Pro Bono*.

[123] Galanter and Palay, n. 103 above, at 40.

nal regulation.[124] Concern for the image of the profession is also a reason for such initiatives. It may, therefore, have an indirect economic motive; that of strengthening the profession's "side of the bargain" with the state.[125]

Research in the USA shows a strong correlation between the success of large firms, particularly in terms of size, number of associates and gross revenue, and the performance of *pro bono publico* work.[126] The larger the firm, and its gross revenues, the more likely it is to encourage or permit this activity.[127] There are several explanations for this. Elites have the most to gain from the preservation of the profession's reputation in terms of their own status and prestige. Elite lawyers are perhaps more likely than other lawyers to espouse high ethical standards but, in relation to pro bono work, they have a problem. While their professional status derives from the purity of the problems on which they work, their absence from the front line of practice causes problems of integration.[128] Another reason why elite firms may become more involved in offering voluntary legal services is that they have greater opportunity to do so. Organisations like the Liberty Pro Bono Panel, Business in the Community and the London Panel, which finds lawyers to handle appeals to the Judicial Committee of the Privy Council in Capital Cases, are all fairly recent innovations.[129] They provide a link between "deserving cases" and lawyers willing to provide help. They match the skills of senior staff in large firms to projects which require their specialist expertise and which are consistent with their status.[130] These senior staff can perform *pro bono publico* work, suited to their skills and preferences. This admits them to the rank of "front-line" professionals admired by the public[131] and produces innovations which others can develop or follow.[132]

Pro bono activity currently contributes in a small way to access to justice, but it should be further developed by the professional bodies. Failure to regulate it

---

[124] The Labour Party plans to stimulate *pro bono* activity among lawyers. See for example; "Labour Suggests Levy to Support Legal Assistance", *The Lawyer* 27 September 1994 at 3, "Labour Eyes US *Pro Bono* Model", *The Lawyer* 8 November 1994 at 2, "Labour Creates Future Vision", *Law Society's Gazette* 22 February 1995 at 68.

[125] Paterson, n. 70 above, at 155.

[126] Galanter and Palay, n. 103 above, at 43.

[127] *Ibid.*, at 46.

[128] A. Abbott, "Status and Status Strain in the Professions" (1981) 86 *American Journal of Sociology* 819. See Galanter and Palay, n. 103, and Boon and Abbey, "Moral Agendas", n. 117 above.

[129] All of these organisations, with the exception of the London Panel, are of fairly recent origin. Business in the Community Professional Firms Group was established in 1989 and the Liberty *Pro Bono* Panel in 1993. The London Panel of solicitors was formed in the early 1980s by Bernard Simons of Simons Muirhead and Burton. He approached friends in large City firms for assistance in 1987. From that time stronger links were developed with the Jamaican Council for Human Rights and the Panel became much more strategic in its' approach to death penalty appeals. G. Huntley, "The Panel", in *Caribbean Commonwealth: A Review of the Appeals Process for Death Row Inmates* (London, Deathwatch, 1995).

[130] It is recognised in the USA that the development of new mechanisms for delivering *pro bono publico* may encourage more senior lawyers to participate. See E. L. Noel, A. F. Earley and L. F. Powell, "Community Service and *Pro Bono* work" in Katzmann, n. 72.

[131] A. Abbott, "Status and Status Strain in the Professions" (1981) 86 *American Journal of Sociology* 819 at 819.

[132] Katzmann, n. 72 above, at 12, and Lardent, n. 102 above, at 87.

could lead to a number of problems. Much of the effort expended in the name of *pro bono* may not expand access to justice. There will be pressure from within the profession to define *pro bono publico* in terms of *any* professional legal services, without reference to access to justice, and to include services provided for reduced fees or on a speculative basis.[133] Careful thought must be given to whether or not these extensions of the meaning of *pro bono* would devalue the idea that *pro bono publico* evidences a public service commitment.

There is another risk; that *pro bono publico* could also be devalued by being used to promote firms and attract business. Thus, a spokesman for Freshfields on the selection of the firm as legal consultants to Green Globe, an environmental pressure group said "We are happy to provide the service on a *pro bono* basis because it is a very good way of accessing a huge market which we think we are uniquely well placed to serve".[134] Whilst this may appear to be an unethical motive for offering *pro bono publico* services[135] it is arguable that what is important is that the work is done.[136] One reason for more active involvement by the Law Society is that more effective promotion and policing by the profession could mitigate the tensions created by the need to integrate altruistic and competitive pressures.

CONCLUSION

The legal profession's commitment to public service is ambiguous. It is unclear what public service means and, in relation to some very obvious means of contributing to the public good, the profession has a patchy record. It is clearly not accessible to all groups in society, it often opposes moves designed to make justice more accessible or procedures more simple and its *pro bono publico* activity is in its infancy. Recent years have seen calls for a re-evaluation of the profession's obligations in this area. In the UK, the wide availability of legal aid fostered the view that access to justice was a matter for the state, not the profession, and many legal aid lawyers considered—and still consider—that, by undertaking legal aid work, they fulfilled the professions' commitment to public service. This may well have been true, but legal aid is now declining. Will conditional fee arrangements fill the gap and, if not, should the profession undertake more *pro bono* work? Should it expand this kind of work in any event? Whilst the profession may not feel it can afford to do this, its long term interests may well depend on such willingness. By voluntarily providing free legal services, the

---

[133] *Future Directions for Pro Bono*, n. 122 above.

[134] "Freshfields to do free work for Fresh Fields", *The Lawyer* 22 November 1994 at 3.

[135] See E. Nosworthy, "Ethics and Large Law Firms" in S. Parker and C. Sampford. (eds.), *Legal Ethics and Legal Practice* (Oxford, Clarendon Press, 1995), at 71 and C. S. Rhee, "*Pro Bono*, Pro Se" (1996) 105 *Yale Law Journal* 1719 at 1724.

[136] For further discussion see M. Ridley, *The Origins of Virtue* (Harmondsworth, Middlesex, Penguin, 1997) at 21, and M. Waters, "Collegiality, Bureaucratization, and Professionalization: A Weberian Analysis" (1989) 94 *American Journal of Sociology* 945.

demand for more external controls over the profession may be quietened. Moreover, paying clients may have greater trust and respect for a lawyer who can commit him or herself to a cause without personal benefit.

Lawyers need to accept positive obligations to promote the public good. They can do this, not only by undertaking *pro bono* work, but also by actively promoting improvements to access to justice, such as the reforms advocated by Lord Woolf, promoting ADR or controlling their fees. Their failure to do the latter has had the detrimental result that the public blame lawyers for increasing the cost of legal aid, thereby precipitating cutbacks which have reduced access to justice. Methods of inculcating the public service ethic, such as *pro bono* work, may also offer one way to arrest the diffusion of a common legal culture. Elite lawyers could, for some of their working week work alongside high street lawyers and employed lawyers. But the enthusiasm of lawyers outside the professional elite for unpaid work is understandably muted. Some have experienced a substantial reduction in their autonomy and their capacity to cross-subsidise unprofitable with profitable work.[137] In professions, as elsewhere, there is a critical relationship between economic welfare and gratuitous commitments; "in a house without bread, ethics is not an appropriate topic of conversation".[138]

[137] Paterson, n. 70 above, at 155–7.
[138] J. Weinstein, "On the Teaching of Legal Ethics" (1972) 72 *Columbia Law Review* 452.

PART IV
Duties to Clients and Potential Clients

Introduction

In the next three chapters we consider the ethical principles and rules of conduct which relate to a lawyer's duties to the client in specific contexts. This theme is also further developed in Part V in the specific context of advocacy and dispute resolution. In this part we are concerned with the general principles that govern the duty to the client and the conflict that may arise between the client's interests and those of the lawyer (for example in relation to fees), and also any conflict between the client's interests and those of the court. In addition to an examination of the detailed rules and guidance, we also consider in greater detail a fundamental question raised in Part I and in Chapter 7. How far can, or should, a lawyer depart from his or her own standards of morality, or those standards generally accepted, in advancing the interests of the client? This issue also clearly arises in the context of the lawyer's advocacy role.

In examining these issues it can be seen that there is a complex interrelationship between the operation of rules of law, both statutory and case law, professional principles, professional guidance and general ethical precepts. The divisions between all these sources are fluid. Some ethical principles, which at one point in time are barely articulated, later become embodied in professional principles. Principles are sometimes referred to in judicial decisions and may become rules of law. Statutory changes can, of course, cut a swathe through all these principles and rules, as is the case with the money laundering provisions described in chapter 10, but may fail to articulate precisely what ethical or other principles form their basis. In turn, the new rules may lead to the formulation of new professional principles.

We also see in these situations the tension between professional rules and basic ethical principles. If, for example, the promotion of justice is the fundamental basis for lawyers' ethics, how can the rules on confidentiality be justified where they appear to promote injustice? If it is a fundamental principle that lawyers should act in the best interests of their clients, how can rules relating to fees be justified where they operate against those best interests?

10

Confidentiality

"This principle we take to be this; that so numerous and complex are the laws by which the rights and duties of citizens are governed, so important is it that they should be permitted to avail themselves of the superior skill and learning of those who are sanctioned by the law as its ministers and expounders, both in ascertaining their rights in the country, and maintaining them most safely in courts, without publishing those facts, which they have a right to keep secret, but which must be disclosed to a legal advisor and advocate, to enable him succeessfully to perform the duties of his office, that the law has considered it the wisest policy to encourage and sanction this confidence, by requiring that on such facts the mouth of the attorney shall be for ever sealed".[1]

A. INTRODUCTION

A fundamental ethical duty imposed on the legal profession is to keep client affairs confidential. Most other professionals also adopt this rule. On the face of it this duty seems easy to justify. It embodies a respect for privacy—a "right" which many would argue is currently inadequately protected elsewhere in English law. In purely professional terms, clients will be loath to consult a lawyer who gossiped about their affairs in the pub or at the PTA meeting, or who wrote a best seller about clients' cases. Such conduct would run counter to other general principles, for example, to act in the client's best interest and not to profit personally from client information. It would also amount to a breach of contract. This confidentiality "belongs" to the client and not the lawyer; only the client can waive it, either expressly or, sometimes, impliedly. Lawyer confidentiality is sometimes justified on the more fundamental basis that it safeguards both access to justice and the protection of individual legal rights.[2] In a complex modern society these "goods" can be delivered to individuals only with the assistance of a lawyer. Unless the client is confident that the information he or she provides for the lawyer will remain confidential, then the client will not be frank and the lawyer will be unable to do the job of advising or representing the client. Where the client is accused of a crime this is particularly important; without confidentiality the right to silence and the protection from self-incrimination would be negated.

---

[1] *Hatton* v. *Robinson*, 31 Mass. (12 Pick.) 416, 422 (1834).
[2] As can be seen in the case of *R.* v. *Derby Magistrates' Court, ex parte B* [1995] 4 All ER 526, discussed below at 250 below. See also *D* v. *NSPCC* [1977] 1 All ER 589 at 606.

Yet there are those who express doubts about the value of the concept of confidentiality and its colleague, legal professional privilege. To Jeremy Bentham the privilege could only protect the guilty, the innocent had nothing to fear, a surprisingly sanguine view of the operation of the legal system given Bentham's generally more critical view.[3] Certainly both the lay public and philosophers have queried the proposition that, for example, lawyers should never tell the police if a client confesses to having committed a crime. Equally, in civil proceedings, is it in the public interest to suppress an expert's report which indicates that the other side is correct? Suppose a client admits that he is abusing his child or is unlawfully syphoning off money from a pension fund he controls? Why should the ethical rules relating to legal practice prefer to protect the "guilty" client rather than seek to protect an "innocent" third party from injury or injustice?[4] There is a danger that the claim to confidentiality can become "ritualistic and universal" resulting in "a kind of moral blindness to the real issues of potential conflict and abuse that a broad and unqualified claim to confidentiality can mask".[5]

Others doubt whether "empirical evidence would lend any support to the rationale of encouraging client disclosure".[6] Few clients will be aware of all the qualifications that attend the rules on confidentiality. Also many are sceptical of lawyers' claims that the privilege and the confidentiality belong to the client and not the lawyer, because legal privilege is a "valuable product" that lawyers, and no other professionals, can sell.[7] This suspicion seems justified as the rhetoric of confidentiality is abandoned when it "rubs hard against lawyer self-interest", as when they are sued by their clients for malpractice.

B. CONFIDENCE AND LEGAL PRIVILEGE

In considering these issues it is neccessary to distinguish between the general professional duty to keep confidences and the narrower concept of legal professional privilege. Much of the criticism is addressed to the latter rather than the former. The general duty of confidentiality is expressed in the *Law Society Guide* in the following terms: "[a] solicitor is under a duty to keep confidential to his or her firm the affairs of clients and to ensure that the staff do the same".[8]

---

[3] J. Bowring (ed.), *The Works of Jeremy Bentham* (New York, Russel & Russel, 1962), vii, 474–5.

[4] See R. Wasserstrom, "Lawyers as Professionals; Some Moral Issues" (1975–6) 5 *Human Rights* 1; W. Simon, "Ethical Discretion in Lawyering" (1988) 101 *Harvard Law Review* 1083 at 1142.

[5] C. Wolfram, *Modern Legal Ethics* (St. Paul, Minn., West Publishing, 1996), at 246.

[6] R. Cranston (ed.), *Legal Ethics and Professional Responsibility* (Oxford, Clarendon Press, 1995), at 9. Equally there is little evidence the other way. Cranston's claim that most clients are ignorant of the privilege seems doubtful especially of criminal clients; if they are then their solicitors should tell them of it.

[7] Wolfram, n. 5 above, at 247.

[8] N. Taylor (ed.), *The Guide to the Professional Conduct of Solicitors* (London, The Law Society, 1996), r. 16.01, hereafter the *Law Society Guide*.

Legal professional privilege, on the other hand, is a rule of evidence under which neither the lawyer nor the client can be ordered to give evidence in court, or elsewhere, of communications between them or of work done by the lawyer in giving advice to the client or in preparing for litigation. We now have a statutory definition of this privilege in the Police and Criminal Evidence Act (PACE) 1984, section 10. "Items" protected by legal privilege are:

(a) communications between a lawyer and his client or person representing his client in connection with giving the client legal advice;
(b) such communications, including communications with "any other person", made in connection with or in contemplation of legal proceedings; and
(c) items referred to or enclosed with such advice or proceedings in the possession of anyone entitled to them.

"Items held with the intention of furthering a criminal purpose are *not* items subject to legal privilege".[9]

It will be noted from this definition that *all* communications between solicitor and client are privileged if they concern giving legal advice, whether or not they relate to litigation. Communications between solicitors and third parties, on the other hand, are privileged only if they relate to litigation. Indeed, a witness who has prepared a report for the solicitor on one side can be subpoenaed to give evidence by the other side, there being no property in a witness. The solicitor could not, however, be required to produce or give evidence of the report.[10] Despite the statutory definition in PACE, the case law in this field is often ambiguous or confused. The probable reason for this is that the extent of professional privilege involves important and conflicting issues of public policy. The issues have not been subjected to sophisticated analysis by either the judiciary or the legal profession. Guidance is therefore very thin on the ground.

An illustration of the operation of professional privilege, and a justification for it, can be found in the House of Lords decision in *R. v. Derby Magistrates' Court, ex parte B*.[11] On arrest B had admitted to the murder of a girl. Before the trial he retracted his confession and implicated the girl's stepfather in the murder. B was acquitted. He later again admitted the offence and subsequently retracted the confession. Eventually the stepfather was charged with the murder. B was called as a witness for the Crown. Counsel for the stepfather sought to obtain evidence from him, and also from his solicitor, of his previous inconsistent instructions relating to his defence to the murder charge.[12] At first instance the court ordered disclosure. The reasoning was that the public interest in ensuring that all relevant evidence was available to the defence out-

---

[9] S.10(2) of the Police and Criminal Evidence Act 1984.
[10] *Harmony Shipping Co. SA v. Saudi Eutope Line Ltd.* [1979] 3 All ER 177.
[11] N. 2 above.
[12] Under the Criminal Procedure Act 1965 ss.4 and 5 and the principles laid down in *R. v. Barton* [1972] 2 All ER 1192 and *R. v. Ataou* [1988] 2 All ER 321.

weighed the interest of confidentiality as B no longer had any recognisable interest in the privilege. (Having been acquitted of the murder he could not be tried again and a prosecution for perjury was unlikely.) It was held by the Lords, however, that B's statements were protected by professional privilege and so immune from production.

In a comprehensive judgement, Lord Taylor, the then Lord Chief Justice, examined the history of, and previous cases on, legal privilege. He concluded, "[t]he principle which runs through all these cases . . . is that a man must be able to consult his lawyer in confidence, since otherwise he might hold back half the truth. The client must be sure that what he tells his lawyer in confidence will never be revealed without his consent. Legal professional privilege is thus much more than an ordinary rule of evidence, limited in its application to the facts of a particular case. It is a fundamental condition on which the administration of justice as a whole rests."[13] Lord Taylor concluded that legal privilege "*once established*" should be absolute. No exception should be allowed.[14] Were this not to be the law then solicitors would have to tell their clients that their confidence would be broken if "in some future case the court were to hold that [they] no longer had 'any recognisable interest' in asserting it".[15]

Lord Nicholls, agreeing with Lord Taylor, considered that if the court were to have a discretion to override privilege it "would be faced with an essentially impossible task". What criteria would it use? Would the public interest in the conviction of the guilty always override it? Would the need for evidence in a serious civil claim be a sufficient cause, "say where a defendant is alleged to have defrauded hundreds of people of their pensions or life savings"?[16] Many would, unlike Lord Nicholls, answer yes to both of these questions and point out that such balancing acts—deciding in individual cases which of two competing public interests (or private interests) should prevail—is just what the courts should be doing.

In a subsequent House of Lords case, *Re L*,[17] concerning childcare proceedings, a distinction was drawn between communications between solicitor and client to which absolute privilege applied, and "other forms of legal privilege" such as reports made by expert third parties on a party to the litigation. In *Re L* it was held that in cases under the Children Act 1989 no privilege attached to such reports and therefore a report made for the mother in care proceedings could be revealed to the police with a view to investigating whether she should be prosecuted. This case probably applies only to Children Act proceedings, though even on this basis it is not easily reconciled with the *Derby Magistrates* case (and Lord Nicholls and Lord Mustill considered it could not).

[13] [1995] 4 All ER 526 at 540–1.

[14] *Ibid.*, at 542d. See *Saunders* v. *Punch Ltd.* [1998] 1 All ER 234 at 244 for a more sceptical judicial view on the need to rule out any exceptions to legal professional privilege.

[15] [1995] 4 All ER 526 at 541g.

[16] *Ibid.*, at 545.

[17] [1996] 2 All ER 78. Lord Nicholls, who sat in the *Derby Magistrates* case, n. 2 above, was one of two dissenters in *Re L*. See below at 254–5 for further details of *Re L*.

It should be emphasised that the *Derby Magistrates* case concerns privilege, not the general duty of confidence to which there are recognised exceptions. It also states that the doctrine of privilege is absolute *once established*. So, much depends on defining when it is so established and when it is not.

C. ESTABLISHING LEGAL PRIVILEGE

The definition of legal privilege under the Police and Criminal Evidence Act 1984 has been noted above. This definition is regarded as embodying the existing common law definition and covers both solicitor and client communications and third party communications made in connection with litigation, such as experts' reports.[18] The statute confers privilege on communications between solicitor and client in connection with giving legal advice. However the courts have adopted a wider definition. For example in *Nederlandse Reassurantie Groep Holding NV* v. *Bacon & Woodrow*[19] assistance provided for the client included advice given by solicitors on the commercial wisdom of a proposed transaction. This information was held to be covered by privilege provided it was given in the context of acting as a legal advisor. Privilege extends to clients' instructions to the solicitor, instructions to a barrister and the barrister's opinion, documents, and copies of them, created in order to obtain legal advice and which "betray the trend of the advice which [the solicitor] is giving the client".[20] The privilege extends to employed lawyers and also to patent agents, licensed conveyancers and "authorised advocates and litigators".[21]

The definition in the PACE section 10(2) denies privilege to items held with the intention of furthering a criminal purpose, as in the old case of *R* v. *Cox & Railton*.[22] This issue was considered by the House of Lords in *Francis & Francis* v. *Central Criminal Court*.[23] Mrs G retained a solicitor to assist her in purchasing a house. Unknown both to her and the solicitor, the money for this purchase allegedly came from drug trafficking by a member of Mrs G's family. The police applied for an order requiring the solicitors to deliver up all the files in their possession relating to the transaction. They considered that they fell within PACE section 10(2). The House of Lords agreed. It did not matter that neither the solicitor, as holder of the records, nor the client of the solicitor, intended to fur-

---

[18] It was held at first instance in *R.* v. *Egdell, The Times*, 14 Dec. 1988, that legal professional privilege did not extend to experts' reports, which is not consistent with PACE s.10. For criticism of this see J. V. McHale, "Confidentiality, an Absolute Obligation" (1989) 52 *Modern Law Review* 715.

[19] [1995] 1 All ER 976.

[20] See A. Keane, *The Modern Law of Evidence* (London, Butterworth, 1996), at 520–1. See also *Re Barings Plc.* [1998] 1 All ER 673 for a comprehensive review of the law by Sir Richard Scott V-C.

[21] Courts and Legal Services Act 1990 s.63.

[22] (1884) 14 QBD 153.

[23] [1988] 3 All ER 775.

ther a criminal purpose. As long as someone had a criminal intention in relation to the documents they fell within section 10(2).[24]

There must be *prima facie*, and probably strong, evidence of a criminal purpose, and criminal purpose probably includes civil fraud or "iniquity" which might not constitute a crime. In *Barclays Bank* v. *Eustice*,[25] it was held that documents created by the client's solicitors for the "dominant" purpose of prejudicing the interests of the creditor bank were not privileged in subsequent civil proceedings by the bank under the Insolvency Act 1986. It was stressed that there was clear *prima facie* evidence that this was the intention, and also that the purpose of seeking legal advice was not to explain what had been done (or prepare a criminal defence on that basis), but to "enter into transactions at an undervalue the purpose of which was to prejudice the bank".[26] Lord Justice Schiemann regarded this purpose as being "sufficiently iniquitous for public policy to require that communications between [the client] and his solicitor in relation to the setting up of these transactions be discoverable".[27] How far this decision is consistent with the *Derby Magistrates* case (it was decided at about the same time and not discussed in it) is clearly debatable. It may be that the same rules do not (or should not) apply in civil as in criminal cases, though their Lordships in the *Derby* case clearly thought that they did. In *Barclays Bank* v. *Eustice*, Lord Justice Schiemann was more than happy to carry out what Lord Nicholls in the *Derby* case considered to be the "impossible task" of evaluating the balance of public interest. He commented:

> "I do not consider that the result of . . . the order in the present case will be to discourage straightforward citizens from consulting their lawyers. Those lawyers should tell them that what is proposed is liable to be set aside and the straightforward citizen will then not do it and so the advice will never see the light of day. In so far as those wishing to engage in sharp practice are concerned, the effect of the present decision may well be to discourage them from going to their lawyers. This has the arguable public disadvantage that the lawyers might have dissuaded them from the sharp practice. However, it has the undoubted public advantage that the absence of lawyers will make it more difficult for them to carry out their sharp practice."[28]

In the light of recent notorious city frauds and sharp financial practices, such as those perpetrated by Robert Maxwell and BCCI, this is a timely warning for both city financiers and their solicitors.

---

[24] For a criticism of the correctness of this decision see L. Newbold, "The Crime/Fraud Exception to the Legal Professional Privilege" (1990) 53 *Modern Law Review* 472.

[25] [1995] 4 All ER 511.

[26] *Ibid.*, at 524f. The case was followed in *Nationwide Building Society* v. *Various Solicitors* (1998) 148 *New Law Journal* 241, which held that procuring a loan by deception fell within the exception to professional privilege where the solicitor's advice furthered the deception, even though the solicitor was unaware of the deception.

[27] See also *Derby & Co. Ltd.* v. *Weldon (No 7)* [1990] 3 All ER 161 and *Re Konigsberg* [1989] 3 All ER 289.

[28] N. 25 above, at 525c.

Privilege in Cases Involving Children

A controversial field in which legal professional privilege has been considered recently relates to proceedings under the Children Act 1989. Here too the case law is either vague or conflicting. Debates may be had on whether privilege exists at all in Children Act cases [29] or whether they constitute an exception to the normal operation of privilege, and, if the latter, the extent of that exception. The issue has arisen in a number of cases starting with *Re A*,[30] in which the effect of the 1991 Family Proceedings Rules, rule 4.23, came to be considered. This provides that, with the leave of the court, documents normally confidential can be disclosed to all parties, guardians ad litem (GALs) and welfare officers. In addition, the general policy of the Children Act that the welfare of the child is paramount, has encouraged the courts to take the view that expert reports, whether prepared for the parents, the local authority or any other party and whether or not actually used in evidence, should all be disclosed to the parties and the court. Children proceedings are considered not to be adversarial, and therefore there is no scope for claiming legal privilege for these reports. This reasoning makes two rather sweeping assumptions: first, that the proceedings are not experienced in reality as adversarial by the parties, especially the parents, and secondly, that privilege is justified only by reason of adversariality.

In general, the justification for privilege is based only partly on adversariality. It is also based on the need to allow free and frank access by a client to his or her lawyer. The need for such access, and the privilege, covers both litigation and non-litigious matters. The courts have, however, created a general rule which denies the protection of legal privilege to experts' reports in Children Act proceedings, though the precise extent of this rule is not clear. In 1996 in *Re L* the House of Lords had an opportunity to consider the issue. The mother, a drug addict, had, via her solicitor, commissioned a report by a consultant on how her child had come to take methadone. Clearly the consultant thought that it had been administered by the mother, whereas her story was that the child had swallowed it accidentally. The report was disclosed to all parties in the care proceedings under the normal procedures noted above. When the police heard of the report's existence (at a case conference) they sought a copy of it with a view to instituting criminal proceedings against the mother. The police were not parties to the care proceedings. The mother claimed that the report was covered by legal professional privilege, and also the privilege against self-incrimination. She failed. The House of Lords held by a majority that there was a difference

---

[29] See R. Cross and C. Tapper, *Cross and Tapper on Evidence* (London, Butterworths, 1995), at 494, for a rather sweeping view.

[30] [1991] 2 FLR 473. See also *Essex CC v. R.* [1993] 4 All ER 702; *Oxfordshire CC v. M* [1994] 2 All ER 269.

between the privilege attatching to solicitor and client communications and to reports by third parties for the purposes of litigation. The former was absolute, but the latter were not covered by privilege in care proceedings under the Children Act which were non-adversarial and investigative. Moreover, because the documents were not covered by privilege, there was no need for a judge to undertake a balancing act in order to decide whether it was in the public interest to order their disclosure.[31]

Does this mean that a court order is needed *at all* before such disclosure? Logically it should not be, but their Lordships were not clear on this point. However Lord Jauncy considered whether solicitors have what he called a "duty" to make a "voluntary" disclosure of "all matters likely to be material to the welfare of the child".[32] There are cases that indicate that no court order is needed,[33] but Lord Jauncy did not find it necessary to decide the issue. He did, however, say that "this further development of the practice in cases where the welfare of children is involved [may well be] welcomed".[34] Here he did not appear to be confining himself to reports by third parties but included communications between solicitor and client also.

If it is argued that there is a duty to disclose in these circumstances what penalty for non-disclosure is proposed? Non-disclosure could be contempt of court only where there was a breach of a court order. Would failure by the solicitor or barrister to disclose amount to professional misconduct? Clearly there are issues here which have not been explored by their Lordships in *Re L* and the law is in need of systematic clarification.

Lord Jauncy gave the sole judgment for the majority in *Re L*. A powerful dissenting judgment was given by Lord Nicholls with which Lord Mustill agreed. Lord Nicholls' basic point was that it is nowhere clearly spelled out in the Children Act that legal professional privilege is abrogated and its abrogation cannot be implied from the welfare principle in section 1. This principle, in any case, considerably predates the passing of the Act in 1989 and it had not been suggested that the privilege did not apply before 1989. If the Children Act had abrogated privilege, then the Family Proceedings Rules 1991 rule 4.23, on disclosure of evidence would not have been required. Lord Nicholls denied that privilege can be split into solicitor and client privilege (which he calls legal advice privilege) and "litigation privilege" covering third party reports. Both are equally privileged. The decision of the majority in *Re L* was contrary to the decision of the House in the *Derby Magistrates* case. But the most fundamental reason for Lord Nicholls' dissent is the importance of the doctrine of legal professional privilege. Parties to family proceedings are also entitled to a fair hearing and the same safeguards enjoyed by parties to other proceedings and "it must be doubtful whether a parent who is denied the opportunity to obtain legal

---

[31] See Lord Jauncy in *Re L*, n. 17 above, at 87j.
[32] *Ibid.*, at 86e.
[33] E.g. *Re R* [1993] 4 All ER 702; *Re DH* [1994] 1 FLR 679.
[34] *Re L*, n. 17 above, at 97b.

advice in confidence is accorded the fair hearing to which he is entitled under Article 6(1), read in conjunction with Article 8, of the European Convention of Human Rights".[35] This is, of course, a dissenting judgment but it clearly illustrates the competing issues of public policy that have to be considered.

What advice is given to solicitors by the Law Society on this matter? In *Disclosure of Reports in Children's Cases* (1994) the Law Society advises solicitors to consider carefully with their client whether or not to commission an expert's report in the light of the duty to disclose it and the possibility that it might be adverse. It is essential that solicitors obtain all existing medical reports and information before deciding to commission another report, and also ensure that the expert instructed is fully informed. The general duty of confidentiality remains, as the rule in *Re L* covers only experts reports. Whether the rule in *Re L* covers private, as well as public, proceedings involving children is not clear, but the Law Society thinks it probably does. Certainly the justification for the *Re L* rule, that the proceedings are not adversarial, can also be used in private cases. What the Law Society does not address is what to tell the client about confidentiality in child cases. Arguably the client should be told at the outset that experts' reports may well be revealed to all parties and to the police even if not used in the litigation by the client. In other words, an expert's report cannot be kept private.

Disclosure in the Public Interest

Here we are concerned with an exception to the duty of confidence, not to privilege. Most professional codes relating to confidence permit breaking it where it would be in the public interest. For example, doctors can breach confidentiality under this head where secrecy would cause serious harm to anyone.[36] The main problem is defining public interest. In an English case concerning a doctor, *W v. Egdell*,[37] the need to protect public safety prevailed over the public interest in confidentiality. The case concerned a report prepared on the instructions of W's solicitor for the purposes of a hearing before a Mental Health Review Tribunal (MHRT) by Dr Egdell, a consultant psychiatrist. Dr Egdell strongly opposed W's release from a mental hospital because he considered him to be a danger to the public. W decided to abandon his application to the MHRT in the light of this report and accordingly it was not revealed to the tribunal. Dr Egdell was concerned that the hospital had not been given his report and sent it to it, and also the Secretary of State. W applied for an injunction to restrain further disclosure of the report and also for damages for breach of confidence. He lost. The

---

[35] *Re L,* n. 17 above, at 90h.
[36] General Medical Council, *Confidentiality* (General Medical Council, 1995). See also the American case of *Tarasoff* v. *Regents of the University of California* (1976) 131 Cal. Rpter. 14.
[37] [1990] 1 All ER 835.

Court held that the public interest required disclosure.[38] It should be noted that this was a case of a mental patient who had already committed murders and the authorities needed to be sure, before releasing him, that the "risk of repetition is so small as to be acceptable". A doctor who fears that such a decision will be made on the basis of inadequate information is justified in breaking a confidential relationship.[39]

It has long been accepted that a lawyer can break a client's confidence in order to prevent the commission of certain serious crimes. The Law Society advises that where the solicitor is being "*used* by the client to facilitate the commission of a crime or fraud" the solicitor is not bound by confidentiality.[40] This is, of course, consistent with the principles set out in PACE. Solicitors are also advised that they can reveal information to prevent the client "or a third party" from *committing* a crime which the solicitor has reasonable grounds for believing will lead to "serious bodily harm". Solicitors, therefore, are advised that they may *not* break confidence and reveal anticipated crimes which do not involve serious bodily harm.[41] The guidance is not totally clear: would it be sufficient, for example, if bodily injury was not the intended purpose of the crime but an incidental risk, e.g. in an armed robbery? The solicitor is bound by confidentiality where the client reveals past criminality, however heinous, but is of course restricted in the way he or she may represent that client in relation to that crime.[42] This guidance does not extend to material covered by legal privilege. A solicitor would therefore be in breach of privilege if he or she revealed privileged information in order to prevent serious harm to another (e.g. to prevent an innocent person serving a term of imprisonment). However it must be remembered that if the anticipated harm amounts to furthering a criminal purpose then privilege does not exist.

Does the above advice on confidentiality extend to the situation where what is feared is a public danger which may *not* involve the commission of a crime? The Law Society gives no hint that such a breach of confidence might be justifiable. Suppose, for example, a client tells a solicitor that he knows that a building owned by his adversary is seriously unsafe but he does not want the information revealed to anyone for tactical reasons connected with the litigation. Should, or may, the solicitor reveal this information in the interest of public safety? The *Derby Magistrates* case, which, as we have seen, takes a robust "no exceptions" approach to legal privilege, would suggest that the information should not be revealed. But if the principle of *Egdell* applies to solicitors, then

---

[38] It was accepted by counsel that legal professional privilege did not arise in this case (*ibid.*, at 846b). The question had been argued in the court below and Scott J had found that expert evidence is evidence of fact and therefore not subject to legal professional privilege. For a criticism of this finding see McHale, n. 18 above, at 719.

[39] See *R* v. *Egdell*, n. 18 above, *per* Bingham LJ at 852–3.

[40] *Law Society Guide*, n. 8 above, r. 16.02, para. 1.285.

[41] The US. Model Rules extend this to "substantial injury to the financial interests or property of another": see r. 1.6.

[42] See Chap. 11 on this issue in relation to advocacy.

the courts might well accept the argument that "as a matter of public policy . . . the solicitor ought to be entitled, without either being liable to action by his client or to a charge of professional misconduct, to take the necessary steps in the public interest to prevent death or serious injury".[43]

Except in certain money laundering situations (see below), the solicitor does not have an *obligation* to reveal information to prevent the commission of a crime; he or she *may* do so, according to the *Law Society Guide*.[44] The *Guide* does not indicate to whom the information may be revealed. Normally confidences can be revealed only to those having a legitimate interest in receiving the information, which would include the police or other relevant enforcement authority, and also the intended victim. Gossiping in the pub about it or informing a tabloid newspaper would not be a disclosure in the public interest. Where a third party, such as the police, asks the solicitor for information then, unless the solicitor has "strong prima facie evidence that he or she has been used by the client to perpetrate" the crime, the solicitor should insist on a witness summons or subpoena.[45] This does not apply where the solicitor decides to inform in order to prevent a crime from being committed.

The *Guide* also considers the position relating to child abuse at some length. Many jurisdictions in the United States have "reporting" statutes in relation to child abuse which require professionals, including lawyers, to break confidence and inform the authorities where they have reason to suspect child abuse. There are no such statutory provisions in this country. The Law Society guidance advises that in "exceptional circumstances" the solicitor may reveal information concerning child abuse to the police or local authority if there is a risk to the child's health. The guidance states, "[o]nly in cases where the solicitor believes that the public interest in protecting children outweighs the public interest in maintaining the duty of confidentiality could the solicitor have a discretion to disclose confidential information". The guidance is concerned with current or future abuse, not past abuse. As such this guidance in relation to child abuse is on all fours with the general principle that confidentiality can be breached to prevent the commission of a crime involving serious bodily harm. Solicitors are referred by the *Guide* to the *Egdell* case noted above. But the Law Society is very anxious to stress that there is a normal duty of confidentiality and that all routes other than its breach should first be explored. For example, the client may be persuaded to approach social services or the police. The client has a right to know that the confidence has been or might be breached and, if it is, the termination of the retainer will be "almost inevitable".[46]

---

[43] M. Brindle and G. Dehn, "Confidence, Public Interest and the Lawyer", in Cranston (ed.), n. 6 above, at 122.

[44] In the USA the failure by the pschiatrist to reveal to the intended victim that his patient had threatened to murder her led to a successful action for negligence when the murder occurred: *Tarasoff* v. *Regents of the University of California*, n. 36 above.

[45] *Law Society Guide*, n. 8 above, r. 16.02, para. 7, which suggests that the solicitor should not assist the police, but may give the evidence under oath if so directed by a judge.

[46] See *Law Society Guide*, n. 8 above, Annex 16A, para. C.

Money Laundering

Money laundering is described by the Law Society as the process by which "dirty money"—the proceeds of crime—is changed so that the money appears "to originate from a legitimate source".[47] The most infamous example is that of Michael Renton, a partner in a South London criminal practice convicted of laundering some of the £30 million stolen in the Brinks Mat gold bullion robbery. Overseas accounts were used to launder the money and produce profits from property transactions.[48] Concern that sophisticated criminal clients were able to make use of lawyers, and the protection afforded by the rules on confidentiality and legal privilege, to make arrangements for laundering the proceeds of crime, in particular the proceeds of drug trafficking and terrorism, has led to the creation of a major statutory inroad into the duty of confidentiality and privilege. The provisions are contained in the Criminal Justice Act 1988 section 93A,[49] the Drug Trafficking Offences Act 1994 and the Prevention of Terrorism (Temporary Provisions) Act 1989. Money laundering is an international problem and the provisions of the Criminal Justice Act and the accompanying Money Laundering Regulations were enacted partly as a response to the European Council Directive 91/308/EEC, which requires disclosure of suspicious transactions by credit and financial institutions.

It is a criminal offence for anyone, including a solicitor, "knowing or suspecting" that a person is or has been engaged in certain criminal conduct, to assist that person to launder the proceeds of crime. Proceeds of crime are broadly defined as property which "in whole or in part directly or indirectly represent the proceeds of that person's criminal conduct".[50] The section applies to indictable offences in the Crown Court or Schedule 4 offences in the magistrates' court.[51] It is a defence to disclose suspicions of money laundering to the police.[52] Where a solicitor makes the disclosure *after* doing any act in contravention of section 93A, then it must be shown that the disclosure was made on the initiative of the solicitor and as soon as reasonably possible.[53] It is also a defence to show that:

1. the solicitor did not know or suspect the property to be the proceeds of crime,
2. that he did not know or suspect money laundering, or
3. that he intended to make a disclosure but had a reasonable excuse for failure to do so.[54]

[47] *Law Society Guidance 1993*, para. 2 reproduced in J. A. Holland (ed.), *Cordery on Solicitors* (London, Butterworths, 1995).
[48] P. Lashmar, "Grassing on the Client", *The Guardian*, 29 Mar. 1994.
[49] Inserted by the Criminal Justice Act 1993 s.29.
[50] Criminal Justice Act 1988 s.93A(2).
[51] Criminal Justice Act 1988 s.93A(7).
[52] Disclosure can be made to the National Criminal Intelligence Service.
[53] 1988 Act, s.93A(3)(b)(ii).
[54] 1988 Act, s.93A(4).

Most important for our purposes is section 93A(3)(a) of the 1988 Act which provides that the disclosure "shall not be treated as a breach of any restriction upon the disclosure of information imposed by statute or otherwise". In other words a disclosure by the alleged offender's lawyer will not amount to an unlawful breach of confidence or of legal professional privilege, whether that obligation arises as a result of statute, common law, professional rules or contract.

What should a solicitor who is considering reporting a suspicion of money laundering tell the client, if anything? Under section 93D of the Criminal Justice Act 1988 it is an offence to tip off a suspect if a person "knows or suspects" that a money laundering investigation is likely, or that the tip-off is likely to prejudice the investigation. However, subsection 4 states that these provisions do not make it an offence for a "professional legal advisor" to disclose information to a client in relation to giving him or her legal advice or to anybody (i.e. not just the client) in connection with legal proceedings. But the offence is still committed if this information is given "with a view to furthering any criminal purpose".[55] Again there is a general defence that the informer did not know or suspect that the disclosure to the alleged offender would prejudice the money laundering investigation. Clearly solicitors may find themselves making some difficult and fine distinctions in this context.

Similar provisions to the above are also specifically contained in the drugs and terrorism legislation. In one respect this latter legislation goes further and makes it an offence not to give information of money laundering to the police even though the solicitor is in no way involved, or has been asked to help with, the laundering. Under section 26B of the Drug Trafficking Offences Act 1986,[56] it is an offence for someone who knows or suspects drug money laundering, and who acquired that information "in the course of his trade, profession, business or employment", not to report the information to the police as soon as is reasonably practical. However no offence is committed if the information came to a lawyer in "privileged circumstances" which, of course, is a category narrower than confidential circumstances.[57] A similar provision applies to information on financial assistance for terrorism.[58] Under the drug trafficking and terrorism legislation, the offences are committed if they took place outside England and Wales and would constitute an offence had they taken place within the jurisdiction.

In addition to the above law, the Money Laundering Regulations 1993, which apply only to firms conducting investment business within the Financial Services Act 1986, require that staff be trained to recognise and handle suspicious transactions, that internal reporting procedures are set up and that certain records of

---

[55] 1988 Act, s.93D(5).

[56] As amended by the Criminal Justice Act 1993 s.18.

[57] Drug Trafficking Offences Act 1994 s.26A(2) and (9).

[58] Prevention of Terrorism (Temporary Provisions) Act 1989 s.18A, inserted by the Criminal Justice Act 1993 s.51.

transactions are maintained for five years. Firms must verify the client's identity before proceeding with any financial transaction.[59] This applies even to what may appear to be mundane transactions, such as house purchase as the solicitor in *Francis and Francis* v. *Central Criminal Court*, discussed previously, discovered. The aim, obviously, is to encourage detection and render excuses such as "I didn't know or understand what was going on", or "it wasn't me, it was my staff" less sustainable. The requirement to keep records is to enable an audit trail of transactions to be followed.

How, therefore, should a solicitor react if asked by the police for disclosure of files in connection with a money laundering investigation? The *Law Society Guide*[60] reminds solicitors of the normal duty of confidentiality. If the solicitor does not suspect the client of laundering or of using the solicitor to further a criminal purpose, then the information should not be given. It is then up to the police to apply for a court order, with which the solicitor must then comply. If the solicitor has given information under the statutory provisions and without a court order, should he or she continue to act for the client he has reported? According to the *Guide* "there is no necessary objection to a solicitor continuing to act".[61] The client may, of course, take a different view.

Solicitors are under a cloud in the context of money laundering. Few firms report suspicions; in 1996 it was 300 and this dropped to 236 in 1997. Six big city law firms are allegedly under police investigation for laundering drug proceeds by setting up off shore companies for drug barons. The Home Office plans to extend the law making it an offence to fail to give information about laundering to all crimes, not just drugs and terrorism crimes as now.[61a]

Client/Solicitor Litigation

Where the client sues the solicitor, then confidentiality vanishes from the client's point of view. A solicitor may reveal confidential information in so far as it is necessary to establish a defence. This also covers the investigation of a complaint against the solicitor and proceedings of the Solicitors Disciplinary Tribunal.[62] A justification put forward for this is not that it constitutes an exception to confidentiality or privilege, but that the client has impliedly waived them.[63] This justification could not therefore apply where the solicitor initiated the proceedings against the client, as where the client is sued by the solicitor for fees.

---

[59] For full details see the guidance published by the Law Society.
[60] N. 47 above, at para. 10.2.
[61] *Ibid.*, r., para. 7.
[62] *Ibid.*, r. 16.02, para. 10.
[61a] See *The Lawyer*, 17 and 24 November 1998 and, December 1998. See also guidelines on the issue related to litigation laid down in *C v S, New Law Journal*, 20 November 1998 at 1723.
[63] See Keane, n. 20 above, at 538.

An example of the operation of these rules is *Lillicrap* v. *Nalder & Son*.[64] The plaintiffs were property developers for whom the defendant solicitors had acted in a number of purchases. In relation to one of them the plaintiff alleged that the solicitors had been negligent in failing to tell them of a right of way over the land. The solicitors admitted negligence but maintained that the plaintiffs would have gone ahead with the purchase anyway. They sought to base this contention on evidence that in six other transactions in which they had acted for the plaintiffs, they had bought property despite having been told of various risks. The plaintiffs considered that this evidence was covered by legal privilege and sought delivery up of the relevant documentation. On appeal it was held that, once the client had instituted proceedings against the solicitors, they had impliedly waived privilege in relation to all documents relevant to the suit.

Waiver of Privilege

It follows from the previous section that the client can waive his or her right of confidentiality or privilege. The *Law Society Guide* requires "express" consent to this, but it is also clear from the last section that implied consent is sufficient at common law. Where the other party provides privileged documents to a solicitor, then the privilege will normally have been waived. However, if the documents have been provided by accident or mistake there is no implied waiver. If, therefore, a solicitor acquires information from the other side which is clearly confidential and came by mistake, then the information must be returned and cannot be used in litigation.[65] This rule must also extend to confidential information which was unlawfully acquired by the client, for to use it would be to profit from the commission of a crime. A case currently under review by the Law Society involves the solicitors who advised Andrew Regan in his attempt to take over the Co-operative Wholesale Society in April 1997. Stolen documents which were privileged were allegedly used by the solicitors in preparing the predatory take over. This is not only unethical but probably unlawful.[66]

The law on waiver of privilege is complex and reference should be made to texts on evidence for the detail. In general, once privilege in relation to a document is waived, the privilege in relation to the whole document is waived; the client cannot "edit" it.[67] A client can decide to waive privilege over some documents but not others, but this is subject to a general condition that such partial waiver must be fair. For example, where the documents relate to the same issue, and are not severable, then waiver of one may lead the court to order the dis-

---

[64] [1993] 1 All ER 724 (CA).

[65] *Law Society Guide*, n. 47 above, para. 16.06, n. 6. Note also that waiver cannot be implied where documents are handed to the police in order to assist a criminal investigation: *British Coal Corp.* v. *Dennis Rye Ltd*. [1988] 3 All ER 816.

[66] See *The Lawyer*, 6 May 1997, at 7.

[67] See Keane, n. 20 above, at 537. See also Cross and Tapper, n. 29 above, at 474.

covery of the other; "to allow an individual item to be plucked out of context would be to risk injustice through its real weight or meaning being misunderstood".[68] Where a report of an expert witness has been given to the other side, and the litigation privilege in it thereby waived, then privilege in any background material referred to in the report is also waived. This was held to be the case in *Clough* v. *Thameside and Glossop Health Authority* where Mrs Justice Bracewell stressed that her decision was also based on the need to make the litigation process more open, in the light of the Woolf Report. "Although civil litigation is adversarial, it is not permissible to withhold relevant information, nor to delete nor amend the documents of a report before disclosure, as was submitted . . . to be the practice of some firms of solicitors."[69]

At what point in the proceedings is the other party entitled to the additional related documents where there has already been partial disclosure? There is some confusion here. Some authorities consider that the additional documents are not discoverable until those originally waived have been used in court. Others consider this rule illogical. The most recent decision follows the latter line. In *R.* v. *Secretary of State for Transport, ex parte Factortame and Others*, Lord Justice Auld decided that the additional discovery could be ordered as soon as the documents in relation to which privilege was waived were disclosed.[70]

Information to the Legal Aid Board

Certain confidental information must be provided to the Legal Aid Board by solicitors acting for legally aided parties.[71] The regulations specifically override confidentiality and privilege here. Solicitors must give information on the progress of the case to the Area Director when asked. They must also volunteer information where they believe the case is being conducted unreasonably by the client, such as where a settlement is unreasonably declined, or where there is fraud or a failure to comply with provisions under the Legal Aid Act.

Joint Retainers

Where two or more clients jointly instruct a solicitor then all information must be given to all of the clients; one cannot claim confidentiality in respect of the other. This is not strictly an exception to the doctrine of confidentiality, but may appear to be so to the client. In some circumstances he or she may regret

---

[68] Mustill J, in *Nea Kateria Maritime Co. Ltd.* v. *Atlantic and Great Lakes Steam-Ship Corp.* [1981] Comm. LR 138. See C. Passmore, "The Dangers of Waiving Privilege" (1997) 147 *New Law Journal* at 931.

[69] *Clough* v. *Thameside and Glossop Health Authority* [1998] 2 All ER 971 at 977.

[70] Passmore, n. 68 above, no other report of the case available at time of writing.

[71] See also on this, Chap. 8.

information being given to a co-client, as in *Re Konigsberg*, discussed below. As is noted in Chapter 11 in relation to conflict of interest, there have been a number of recent cases on the duty of solicitors to inform a mortgagee of a change in the mortgagor's circumstances where both are being represented by the same solicitor. All clients must waive their rights before any confidential information is given to a third party.[72]

Insolvency and Bankrupcy

The problem of precisely who is the client, and therefore to whom the duty of confidentiality is owed, can be confusing in the case of corporate or other group clients. Where the solicitor acts (or has acted) for a company, as opposed to an individual director, and the company becomes insolvent, how much information should the solicitor give to the liquidator or similar person? The liquidator has extensive duties and powers to collect information about the company's business dealings and is, in effect, in the same position as was the company itself in relation to this information. Therefore, the solicitor for the company should provide all the information in his or her possession to the liquidator. As the *Law Society Guide* notes, this "includes information in the possession of the solicitor which would otherwise have been protected by confidentiality or privilege".[73] This is not, in theory, an exception to these doctrines because of the special status of the liquidator.

Similarly where an individual client becomes bankrupt, there is an obligation to hand over all the bankrupt's property, including papers and records relating to his estate and affairs, to the trustee in bankruptcy. This applies to privileged communications with a solicitor.[74] Again, this does not amount to an exception to confidence or privilege because the trustee in bankruptcy is in the position of the bankrupt. However this represents theory rather than practice. In reality the bankrupt and the trustee often do not have identical interests. The rules in the Insolvency Act are therefore better thought of as exceptions to confidentiality. This reality is clearly illustrated in the case of *Re Konigsberg*.[75] Mr and Mrs Konigsberg jointly consulted a solicitor in order to transfer property from the husband to the wife. The husband subsequently became bankrupt and the trustee sought to set aside the transfer as being a voluntary settlement and therefore void as against the trustee under the Bankruptcy Act. Mrs Konigsberg objected to the solicitor giving evidence to the trustee on the nature of the transfer on the ground that this information was a communication between solicitor and client and therefore covered by legal privilege. It was held that the communication was properly available to both clients as the solicitor was jointly

---

[72] *Buttes Gas & Oil Co. v. Hammer (No 3)* [1981] QB 223 (CA).
[73] R. 16.02, para. 2. See also the Insolvency Act 1986 s.234, 236.
[74] See *Law Society Guide*, n. 47 above, para. 16.03 n. 6 and Insolvency Act 1986 s.311.
[75] [1989] 3 All ER 289.
[76] *Ibid.*, at 297a.

retained by them. The trustee in bankruptcy had to be treated as being in the same position as the bankrupt client and therefore no assertion of legal privilege could be made to prevent his receipt of the communication. A trustee in bank-ruptcy, said Mr Justice Peter Gibson, "is no ordinary third party". All the assets of the bankrupt are vested in him and, as a successor in title he "stands in the predecessor's shoes".[76]

The Law Society notes that there is little guidance on how far this rule and the statute can be taken. There are at least three kinds of information relating to a client which a trustee in bankruptcy may not be entitled to. A solicitor may have information about a client that does not relate to financial matters. He may relate the advice sought by the bankrupt in relation to resisting the bankrupcy or its conduct or the information may incriminate the bankrupt. In such cir-cumstances the solicitor is advised to refuse to disclose the information to the trustee in bankruptcy in the absence of the client's consent or an order of the court. If an order is sought, "it is not the solicitor's duty to bear the cost of opposing the trustee, or the risks of a costs order, without the client's instruc-tions and funding".[77] Therefore, by doing nothing the solicitor becomes subject to an order *requiring* that the client's privilege or confidence is abrogated.

CONCLUSION

Legal professional privilege, and some aspects of the doctrine of confidentiality, is under increasing attack. Two main justifications for the attack are put for-ward. The first, made in proceedings relating to children, is that, where the pro-ceedings are not really adversarial, there is no need to maintain legal privilege. If the non-adversariality of the proceedings alone justifies an abandonment of legal privilege, then it could also apply to many other types of proceeding, for example some tribunal cases, mediations or arbitrations. Lord Woolf's propos-als in relation to ordinary civil litigation are aimed at reducing the adversarial ethos. If adopted, will these reforms lead to further reduction in the scope of professional privilege?

The second justification is the need to protect the public interest. Privilege may in some cases have to give way to the need to protect the welfare of a child or the prevention or detection of crimes such as drug dealing or terrorism. But how far should this be extended? In the case of the money laundering provisions there is an additional matter to be taken into account. Money laundering can often be effected only if "the launderer" engages the services of a lawyer, under the cloak of secrecy provided by professional privilege. The privilege is therefore being used to allow the perpetrator to benefit from the proceeds of his or her unlawful acts and not simply to allow the client who is accused of such an act to prepare a defence by being frank with his or her lawyer. How far should this

[77] *Law Society Guide*, n. 47 above, r. 16.03, para. 12.

idea be extended? Should it apply where a client asks the solicitor to undertake acts which are civil wrongs, such as transferring funds from a pension fund in circumstances which may constitute a tort or breach of trust?

As we have seen, professional privilege, although it may "belong" to the client, is in fact a valuable commodity that only a lawyer can deliver to a client. It is arguable that society allows this in return for a guarantee of high professional and ethical standards from lawyers when advising clients. If it is successfully argued that lawyers are now simply commercial entrepreneurs and should not be expected to adhere to professional or ethical norms, then the justification for this privilege begins to look very thin. Yet, put it at its lowest level, the commercial interests of the profession may themselves require that every effort is made to behave ethically. Otherwise, this valuable commodity, legal professional privilege, will be lost. This, then, is perhaps a prime example of why the legal profession cannot afford to surrender a claim to ethicality.

11

Conflict of Interest

A. INTRODUCTION

As discussed in Chapter 1, a central tenet of professional practice is that a lawyer should promote the interests of the client and avoid situations where those interests conflict either with the lawyer's own interests or with those of another client. Thus, in Practice Rule 1, it is stated that a solicitor must not do anything which compromises, or is likely to compromise, his "duty to act in the best interests of the client".[1] This principle is often said to derive from the adversary nature of common law systems, which requires that each party to a dispute should have someone on its side, and its side alone, whose duty it is "to advocate its own case and to assault the case of the other" irrespective of the moral or other merits of that client or the case.[2] Whilst the conflict of interest rules, and also the related rules on confidentiality discussed in the previous chapter, are closely connected with the adversary process, they can also be justified independently of it.

The main justification is that rules on conflicts of interest protect client autonomy. A lawyer is retained by a client in order to do what the client would have done for him or herself had he or she the knowledge, skills or time. The lawyer thus provides access to the law and increases the ability of the client to act autonomously.[3] Unless the client can confide absolutely freely in the lawyer, confident that the information will not later be used to his disadvantage and confident that any proposed action will not be tainted by a contrary interest of the lawyer, then the lawyer will not be able to act effectively for the client. This justification applies as much to non-contentious business, such as making wills or drafting contracts, as to contentious business. The need for the lawyer to act disinterestedly in the interests of the client alone, is as important in such transactions as it is in litigation.

---

[1] Note the use of the word "best" in this context, which raises the issue of what should happen if the lawyer's and the client's notions of the best interest conflict. This is discussed further in Chap. 7.

[2] D. Luban, *Lawyers and Justice: An Ethical Study* (Princeton, NJ, Princeton University Press, 1988), at xx and 57.

[3] See S. L. Pepper, "The Lawyer's Amoral Ethical Role: A Defense, A Problem, and Some Possibilities" [1986] *American Bar Foundation Research Journal* 613 and the response by D. Luban [1987] *American Bar Foundation Research Journal* 637.

B. THE NATURE OF INTERESTS

By interests we mean benefits or positions which a person may wish to defend or promote, including those relating to personal or business relationships, financial or property interests or interests in maintaining certain public offices. Conflicts of interest relating to lawyers' fees, in particular conditional and contingency fees, are dealt with in the next chapter. In reality, of course, it is not possible to eliminate all conflict of interest, and in certain circumstances it may not be desirable to do so. As is discussed in Chapter 7, it may not always be desirable that a lawyer should disregard his own moral standards in favour of those of the client. Can, or should, the lawyer act on behalf of the client in a way which would be regarded as immoral if such actions were done in a personal capacity? This type of conflict is implicitly recognised in Practice Rule 1, which requires solicitors not to compromise their duty to the court and to the good repute of the profession. Quite apart from the more obvious conflicts, however, it is obvious that no human being can be totally or exclusively concerned with the interests of another. A lawyer always has considerations to take into account other than the interests of clients. These include the exigencies of running an efficient or profitable practice, relationships with partners or other clients and the lawyer's own conception of the morally acceptable way to behave. It is naïve for any professional—whether doctor, lawyer or social worker—to maintain that that they *always* put the interests, or the best interests, of the patient, client or child first.

So far we have assumed that we know who the client is—an individual with interests he or she can articulate. In reality, however, many clients are not individuals but are institutions made up of many interests. In the case of prosecution lawyers, it is difficult to identify a client at all. Is it the Crown? The Crown Prosecution Service? Do either of those bodies have an "interest" in maximising convictions or in obtaining a particular sentence? If not, what are their interests?[4] Similarly where a lawyer represents a child or an incompetent person, who decides what the best interests of the client are?

These problems are faced daily by practising lawyers and guidance is often needed. A code of professional ethics should advise and also seek to control any avoidable, unacceptable or unreasonable conflicts of interest between lawyers and their clients.[5] It should also indicate the limitations on what clients can expect from their lawyers, such as when the lawyer can refuse to act in a morally repugnant (though legal) manner on behalf of the client. Finally the Code should be realistic, not promise what cannot be delivered and ensure that the client

---

[4] Sir Herbert Stephen wrote that the role of the prosecutor was "not to get a conviction without qualification, but to get a conviction only if justice requires it". The CPS *Statement of Purpose and Values* 1993 requires prosecutors to treat defendants "fairly". See A. Ashworth, "Ethics and Criminal Justice", in R. Cranston (ed.), *Legal Ethics and Professional Responsibility* (Oxford, Clarendon Press, 1995), at 172.

[5] C. Wolfram, *Modern Legal Ethics* (St. Paul, Minn., West Publishing, 1996), at 313.

knows what he can expect. Whether the Law Society guidance (or the minimal guidance given by the Bar) meets these criteria will be considered in the light of the rules and principles described below.

Conflicts Between Existing and Proposed Clients

Obviously a lawyer cannot represent one client whose interests conflict with those of another. The *Law Society Guide* requires a solicitor to refuse to accept instructions where there is a "significant risk" of such conflict. A major area of possible conflict in this situation is a breach of confidentiality. If a solicitor acts for a client who is suing a former client of the firm, then the solicitor may have access to useful confidential information about the latter. If this is the case, the solicitor should not act for the new client unless the firm can successfully erect a "Chinese wall" which prevents all possibility of leakage of confidential information taking place. For example, it may be that no currently employed member of the firm worked on the old case. There may be no documents in the firm's files about the case containing any relevant confidential information. The *Bar Code* similarly tells barristers not to accept a brief which would profession- ally embarrass them because there is a conflict of interest between the clients. In the case of solicitors, this prohibition survives even if all clients are fully informed of the conflicting interest and consent to the solicitor acting.[6]

The *Guide*'s phrase, "significant risk," leaves room for interpretation. In *Re A Firm of Solicitors* (1992)[7] a large firm of City solicitors wished to represent a client bringing an action against a company which, some years previously, had been, in effect, a client of the firm. The solicitors went to some trouble to erect a "Chinese wall" between the staff working on the current case and those on the previous case. Nevertheless, the Court of Appeal upheld the grant of an injunc- tion prohibiting the firm from representing the new client. There was, held the court, no general rule that a solicitor could *never* act against a former client. But it could not do so if the reasonable man would reasonably anticipate a breach of confidentiality or some likelihood of mischief. In this particular case, it was found that the Chinese wall could not provide an effective barrier against such a risk.

Conflicts of this kind can also arise in the increasingly common situation where firms of solicitors merge or where solicitors move firms. Solicitors may

---

[6] N. Taylor (ed.), *The Guide to the Professional Conduct of Solicitors* (London, The Law Society, 1996), r. 15.01, para. 2, hereafter the *Law Society* Guide. This does not seem to be the case with the Bar: see *Code of Conduct of the Bar of England and Wales* (London, The General Council of the Bar of England and Wales, 1990), para. 504, hereafter the *Bar Code*.

[7] [1992] 1 All ER 353 (CA). See also *Rakusen* v. *Ellis Munday and Clarke* [1912] 1 Ch 831; *Supasave Ltd.* v. *Coward Chance* [1991] 1 All ER 668; *David Lee & Co.* v. *Coward Chance* [1991] 1 All ER 668.

find that their new firm is acting against their own former clients. Again, the firm must cease to act if there is likely to be a leakage of confidential information. In *Re a Firm of Solicitors* (1995)[8] a solicitor who had been employed by a firm acting for a plaintiff in patent litigation moved firms. Some two and a half years later the new firm was retained to act for the defendants in the patent litigation. The individual solicitor had never been involved in the case against these defendants in his previous employment. Moreover, he managed to establish that he had no information relating to the previous litigation that would now be recallable, confidential or relevant, bearing in mind the lapse of time and the complexity of the issues. The injunction to prevent him from acting was refused. The judge held, however, that it was for the *solicitor* to prove that there was no reasonable prospect of a conflict between the two clients, not for the complainant to prove that there was a conflict. He also acknowleged that the American-based plaintiffs in the action were "genuinely aghast" at the turn of events, since in the USA there would be no question of the solicitor continuing to act. However the court had to balance two conflicting principles, namely the protection of client confidence and the freedom of the client to instruct a solicitor of its choice.[9]

This case was followed in *Re Schuppan (A Bankrupt)*,[10] the facts of which would cause even greater incredulity amongst American lawyers. The solicitor for the petitioning creditor had also acted for that creditor in litigation against the bankrupt. The solicitor was retained by the trustee in bankruptcy to advise in the administration of the bankrupt's estate. The bankrupt objected on the ground of conflict of interest. The court disagreed. It was held that it was not unreasonable for the trustee to retain the creditor's solicitors who would already be aware of difficulties relating to the tracing of the bankrupt's assets. Separate solicitors had been retained by the creditors to deal with issues that remained to be settled in relation to the litigation, such as a wasted costs application. In relation to an outstanding slander action brought by the bankrupt against the creditor's solicitors, any conflict of interest that might arise by virtue of the fact that they, in their capacity as the trustee's solicitors, might have access to the debtor's documents relating to this litigation could be resolved. One solution would be for the solicitor to give an undertaking not to use those documents without leave of the court. This decision seems to stretch the criteria laid down in *Re a Firm of Solicitors* (1995) much too far. In particular it fails to apply the criteria that it is for the *solicitors* to prove that there is no reasonable prospect of conflict.

Maintaining a balance between protecting confidence and the freedom to instruct a lawyer of choice is difficult. To permit such conflicts of interest undermines client confidence in the integrity of the profession. On the other hand, there is an increasing tendency in some commercial cases to use these ethical

---

[8] [1995] 3 All ER 482.
[9] The court considered that the same rule applied to barristers.
[10] [1996] 2 All ER 664.

principles cynically as a litigation tactic. There are instances where litigants have sought to deny an opponent access to the lawyer of his choice and run up the costs by initiating such actions where he risk of conflict is very remote. This problem is prevalent in the USA[11] and was also noted as an emerging phenomenon in England in the *Report of the Solicitors' Complaints Board* for 1994.

In criminal proceedings also, lawyers are generally precluded from acting against former clients. The criminal courts have not, however, been so particular about spelling out the way the rules should operate in this context. For example, in *R. v. Ataou*[12] the court stated merely that it was "at least doubtful" whether a solicitor should continue to act for either client in a case where a conflict might arise between an existing and a former client (the conviction was however quashed in this case because of such a conflict). Slightly stronger guidance was given by Lord Donaldson in *Saminadhen* v. *Khan*,[13] who said, "I can conceive of no circumstances in which it would be proper for a solicitor who has acted for a defendant in criminal proceedings, the retainer having been terminated, to then act for a co-defendant where there is a cut throat defence between the two defendants".

Where Conflict Arises Between Existing Clients

The rule here is clear. If a dispute arises between two parties both of whom are clients, then the solicitor must refuse to act for both; he or she cannot choose between them.[14] However the *Law Society Guide* does allow an exception. A solicitor can continue to act for one client if he is "not in possession of any relevant confidential information concerning the other obtained whilst acting for the other". In such a case, however, it would be "prudent" to check that the other party does not object. As this will mean that the other party alone will have to find another solicitor, it is likely that he or she will object. This situation frequently arises in relation to matrimonial proceedings where a solicitor may have previously acted for either or both spouses in relation to house purchase or making a will. Again the *Guide's* advice[15] is to act for neither if the solicitor has confidential information about one of them which is unknown to the other. On the basis of *In Re a Solicitor* (1995) it is clearly for the *solicitor* to establish that there is no reasonable prospect that this is so. This is likely to be almost

---

[11] See, e.g., L. Crocher, "The Ethics of Moving to Disqualify Opposing Counsel for Conflict of Interest" (1979) 6 *Duke Law Journal* 1310.

[12] [1988] 1 QB 798.

[13] [1992] 1 All ER 963.

[14] *Law Society Guide*, n. 6 above, r. 15.03.

[15] At r. 15.02, para. 2. The *Law Society Guide* refers to confidential information "received in the course of the joint retainer" which is unknown to one of the spouses. This, of course, should not happen. Where a solicitor acts for co-clients there should be no confidential information on one which is witheld from the other. See Chap. 10 at p. 263 on joint retainers.

impossible in the case of small firms of solicitors who normally deal with family matters.[16]

It is arguable that the above guidance is not strict enough, even though the burden of proving the absence of conflict of interest rests on the solicitor. Private clients are normally most upset if "their" solicitor acts for their opponent. The solicitor will obviously know them, their character, the way they are likely to act under stress, etc. This information cannot be categorised as confidential but it will be useful to an opponent. It is arguable that the solicitor should not be allowed to act against a former client in these circumstances. A similar case could be made in relation to acting against an organisation that was a former client. A general knowlege of the culture of a company or public authority, and of the way it works, will often be very useful in conducting litigation or negotiations with it.[17] Finally, there is the problem which arises where information provided by one client could assist another client, e.g. one who has been convicted of a crime he did not commit. The obligation of confidentiality prevents the lawyer from revealing the confession and releasing the innocent person, and only the death of the guilty party can release the lawyer from his obligation of silence.[18]

Acting for Organisations

In acting for a company, partnership or other organisation, a solicitor must be clear who gives the instructions. There is a danger that the solicitor might become involved in conflicts within the organisation, e.g. between shareholders and the Board of Directors or between partners. The *Law Society Guide* provides no guidance. From whom should the solicitor accept instructions where the client is an organisation? Presumably the solicitor should make sure that the relevant governing body, e.g. board of directors, has lawfully approved the instructions or authorised someone to give them. Where the solicitor has acted for the company and has also acted for the directors in a personal capacity then, if there is subsequently a dispute between directors and shareholders which leads to litigation, the Law Society considers it unlikely that the solicitor will be able to act for either party. A solicitor who has acted for a partnership may act against a partner only if he or she had no confidential information relating to

---

[16] In *Royal Bank of Scotland* v. *Etridge*, [1998] 4 All ER 705, the court said it was a matter of "professional judgement" for a solicitor to decide whether to continue to represent both a husband and a wife where the home was to be charged.

[17] In the Peggy Wood case (1993), the Law Society saw no conflict of interest where a solicitor arranged a loan between clients, even where the solicitor had a substantial personal interest in the loan company. It is doubtful that the Law Society could arrive at the same conclusion today. See on the case *Legal Action*, Sept. 1993, at 8.

[18] For examples of these and similar conflicts see S. Nathanson, *What Lawyers do: A Problem Solving Approach* (London, Sweet & Maxwell, 1997), Chap. 9.

[19] *Law Society Guide*, n. 6 above, r. 15.02, paras. 5 and 6.

that partner.[19] Again, it follows from the previous section that it is for the solicitor to prove that there is no conflict of interest.[20] In acting for a club or other informal organisation, the solicitor is reminded[21] that conflicts of interest may arise and that a member may need to be advised that separate representation should be sought.

Acting for Buyer and Seller or Lender and Borrower

The conflict of interest arising from acting for both sides in a conveyancing matter is so manifest it might be thought that no such joint representation would ever be allowed. This is not the case, although there are current moves to change the Law Society's official position on this. This is largely because of the high level of default related to mortgage frauds in cases where the solicitor acted for both lender and borrower.[22] There are a number of specified situations under the Solicitors' Practice Rules 1990, rule 6, where the solicitor *can* act for both buyer and seller. First if the transaction is *not* at "arm's length" then the solicitor can act, though not if there is in fact a conflict of interest. In this context a transfer is regarded by the Law Society as being not at arm's length if it is between related persons, settlor and trustee, trustee and beneficiary and associated companies.[23]

Even where the transaction *is* at arm's length, the solicitor who acts for the *buyer* may also act for the seller in certain exceptional cases, providing no conflict of interest arises. The parties must consent to the joint representation, and the solicitor must not be involved in negotiating the sale of the property, nor in representing the developer of the property. If these conditions are satisfied then the solicitor can represent both sides to the transaction in the following cases:

- where both parties are established clients, or
- where the consideration is less than £10,000 , or
- where there is no other solicitor in the vicinity that the client can reasonably be expected to consult, or
- where the parties are represented by two associated offices or practices in certain conditions.[24]

Where the transaction is at arm's length and a solicitor acts for the *seller* of the property, then he or she can also act for the buyer provided both parties

---

[20] *Re a Solicitor* [1995] 3 All ER 482.

[21] In r. 11.06 in the chap. on obtaining instructions.

[22] See e.g. *R. v. Law Society, ex parte Mortgage Express Ltd.* [1997] 2 All ER 348, dealt with in Chap. 5.

[23] *Law Society Guide*, n. 6 above, para. 25.01, which embodies the Solicitors' Practice Rules 1990, r. 6. These have now been amended by the Solicitors' Practice (Joint Property Selling) Amendment Rules 1997 to take into account solicitors who operate a joint estate agency (SEAL). A firm participating in such an agency can, in certain circumstances, undertake conveyancing for a buyer or a seller who was also a client of the SEAL. See *Law Society Gazette*, 29 Oct. 1997, at 30.

[24] For full details see *Law Society Guide*, n. 6 above, at 393.

consent, no actual conflict arises and the seller is not a builder or developer. In addition the following conditions must be complied with:

- the solicitor must not do the actual conveyancing (i.e. the solicitor can act in relation to the mortgage or in other ways short of doing the conveyancing);
- if the solicitor provides a selling service to the seller it must be through a SEAL;[25]
- the solicitor can act for both in relation to a mortgage provided the mortgage service is provided through a SEAL;
- different persons in the firm must actually conduct the work for the buyer and the seller;
- the seller must be informed of any services that are being offered to the buyer;
- the buyer must be given the information listed in regulation 6(3)(vi).

In relation to mortgages, the solicitor can act for both the borrower and an *institutional* mortgage lender provided there is no conflict of interest. Consent is not mentioned in this context. In the case of a *private* mortgage a solicitor can act for both, provided the transaction is *not* at arm's length.[26] From June 1999 additional conditions for such joint representations come into force in relation to institutional mortgages. Solicitors will be able to act for lender and borrower provided their instructions from the lender are limited to those specified in the new rule 6 (3) (c) and (e). These model instructions are designed to ensure that the duties to the lender are restricted to reporting on title, advising on other legal issues affecting the property and undertaking the necessary steps to complete the transaction. The solicitor must not receive instructions to report on the credit worthiness of the borrower or on the real value of the property to be mortgaged. These new rules are designed to overcome the problems exemplified in the cases discussed below.[26a]

It can be seen from the above that there is, in fact, considerable scope for acting for both buyer and seller or borrower and lender, and that this has recently been extended by the introducion of SEALs. Much depends on identifying when a conflict of interest arises and, also, where acting for a buyer and seller is concerned, on the consent of the client. This is an issue on which clients may well not be fully informed. Again, it is likely that the criteria laid down in *Re a Firm of Solicitors* (1995) will apply, namely that the burden of proving the absence of a conflict of interest is on the solicitor. The *Guide* itself mentions one situation of conflict—where the solicitor is required to advise the borrower client of the suitability of the mortgage deal on offer. In such circumstances the solicitor

---

[25] A SEAL is a company consisting of at least 4 solicitors' practices which undertakes property selling services.

[26] Rr. 6(3),(4); *Law Society Guide*, n. 6 above, para. 25.01.

[26a] Solicitors' Practice (Lender and Borrower) Amendment Rule 1998, inserting new provisions in the Solicitors' Practice Rules 1990, rule 6. See the *law Society Gazette*, 21 Oct. 1998 at 42 for the full text of the amendment.

should not continue to act for both parties and should refuse the instructions from the *lender*.[27]

The incredible, and probably unworkable, complexity of the rules summarised above is a consequence of the desire of the profession to retain as much valuable conveyancing work as it can, and add to it valuable estate agency work. This is despite the obvious problems it raises relating to conflict of interest, the possibility of fraud and heavy calls on the compensation fund. Representation of both borrower and lender has recently led to considerable litigation against solicitors by lenders whose borrowers have defaulted on the repayments. As Lord Justice Peter Gibson notes in *National Home Loans Corporation* v. *Giffen Couch & Archer*, "the recession and the collapse of the housing market at the beginning of this decade, left mortgage lenders, who had vied with each other to obtain business in the 1980's, with defaulting mortgagors and substantial losses which they were unable to recover out of the security they had taken. This has led mortgage lenders to seek ways to recover their losses from others, and actions in negligence against their professional advisers have become only too common."[28]

In this case, the loan company had lent the borrower over £92,000 on the security of a home which was already subject to another mortgage. On default of repayment the property was sold for £70,000. The loan company sued for its loss. The company and the borrowers had both been represented by the same firm of solicitors, Giffen Couch & Archer. The company maintained that the solicitors should have told it that the lenders were in arrears with their existing mortgage and had been threatened with legal proceedings. It succeeded at first instance. On appeal, however, it was held that, in the circumstances of the case, there was no duty on the solicitors to pass this information about the borrower to the lenders. The solicitors' duties depended heavily on what they were instructed to do (and were paid for) by the client. In this case they were instructed to report on title and to certify whether there had been a change in circumstances since the loan had been offered. They had to undertake a bankruptcy search. They were not asked to report on the personal creditworthiness of the borrowers.

The instructions from the lender in this case were very specific. It had provided a set form on which the solicitor was asked to advise it. Moreover it was an experienced commercial lender which admitted in evidence that it considered that, as it was lending only up to 75 per cent of the value of the property, it did not expect to make a loss in the event of a forced sale. Indeed it already knew that the borrower had a county court judgment against him (despite his failure to reveal this) and yet continued with the loan. In other words, the lender had calculated that the continuing rise in property prices would protect its investment and had been caught out by the recession. It was seeking to impose a duty

---

[27] See *Law Society Guide*, n. 6 above at r. 25.02, para. 4.
[28] [1997] 3 All ER 808 at 810.

on its solicitors to report on the borrower's creditworthiness retrospectively. It is unsurprising that the court was unsympathetic to its claim against the solicitor. However, it is also the case that such clients would normally expect their solicitor to tell them if he or she received information about the creditworthiness of proposed borrowers. The case shows how unsatisfactory it is for solicitors to represent both sides in such transactions. They cannot act in the best interest of both clients simultaneously. Now under the new rules noted above, the solicitors in this case would not have been able to represent both parties on the basis of such instructions.

The case should be contrasted with that of *Mortgage Express* v. *Bowerman*.[29] In this case a solicitor acting for both lender and borrower became aware that the lender had been told that the value of the property was £220,000, whereas in fact the purchaser was buying it at £150,000. In the report on title to the lender the solicitor did not mention this discrepancy. The borrower eventually defaulted on the loan and the property was repossessed and sold for only £96,000. It was held that the solicitors *did* have a duty to pass on information which had a bearing on the value of the lender's security. Their duty was not confined to advising on title alone. The instructions to the solicitors required them to undertake "the normal duties of a solicitor when acting for a mortgagee".[30] Lord Bingham considered that "if, in the course of investigating title, a solicitor discovers facts which a reasonably competent solicitor would realise might have a material bearing on the valuation of the lender's security or some other ingredient of the lending decision then it is his duty to point this out".[31] This does not, however, apply to confidential information unless the borrower consents.[32] This qualification again shows how problematical this can be. How realistic is it for a client to expect any information relating to the transaction to be confidential where the solicitor is representing both sides? Again, the new rules noted above will prevent a joint representation on the basis of the instructions given by the lender in this case.

Acting for Spouses and Children

As has already been noted above, where both spouses have been clients, a solicitor should not normally agree to act for one spouse against the other. Certainly this is the case where the solicitor has confidential information, unknown to one of the spouses, which was acquired during the course of the retainer.[33] But can

---

[29] [1996] 2 All ER 836 (CA). See also *Bristol & West BS* v. *Fancy and Jackson and others* [1997] 4 All ER 582.

[30] It will be noted that no such general instruction had been included in the case of *National Home Loans Corporation* v. *Giffen Couch & Archer*, n. 28 above,

[31] *Ibid.*, at 842.

[32] However legal professional privilege does not protect purchasers where their solicitors' advice was used to "further iniquity" by procuring a loan by deception: *Nationwide Building Society* v. *Various Solicitors* (1998) 148 *New Law Journal* 241.

[33] *Law Society Guide*, n. 6 above, r. 15.02, para. 2.

the solicitor act for *both* spouses in matrimonial matters where the parties agree to it and wish for a non-contentious divorce settlement? This does not appear to be prohibited, provided there is no conflict of interest or significant risk of it. In reality it will be virtually impossible to show that there is no such conflict, especially if, later on, one of the parties alleges that there was a conflict. One spouse may use this as a reason to renege on an agreement on the grounds either that its implications were not fully understood or that some form of undue influence was exerted. It seems that the Law Society, solicitors themselves and the courts are insufficiently aware of these conflicts.

This proposition is illustrated by a number of cases where charges on matrimonial homes were made as security for a husband's business debts. In one of the most recent, *Barclays Bank* v. *Thomson*,[34] the bank obtained such a charge over the home, which was owned by the wife. The solicitors acted for the husband's business, for the wife in relation to the transfer of the home into her name and for the bank in registering the charge. They were also asked by the bank to ensure that the wife fully understood the nature of the charge. In resisting a possession order when the loan repayments were in arrears, the wife attempted to negate the validity of the charge on the ground, *inter alia*, that she had not been properly advised by the solicitors of the extent of her potential liability under the charge. She maintained that the bank had constructive knowlege of this deficiency because the solicitors were acting for it. She lost her case on the ground that the bank was entitled to rely on its solicitor's advice that they, the solicitors, had discharged their duty to the wife to warn her of the nature of the charge. Significantly, there was no comment in the judgments of the Court of Appeal on the wisdom or the propriety of one firm of solicitors acting for all the parties despite an obvious conflict of interests.[35]

Solicitors can also act as mediators between the parties in family matters, but should not thereafter act as solicitors for one of them "in relation to the subject matter of the mediation". The mediator's role is to help the parties to reach their own solution to the dispute, not to impose a solution apon them. The mediator should be impartial and the process confidential. In its guidance on mediation the Law Society stresses that a mediator "does not give professional advice to the parties, individually or collectively". This must be difficult to avoid in cases where one or both of the parties do not have a solicitor.[36] Nevertheless, some have argued for further reduction of the constraints of the conflict rules, for example, there are lawyers who feel that the rules against acting for both spouses are unduly restrictive. Thus, R. H. Tur argues that "some reformulation of the conflict-of-interest rules of professional conduct is highly desirable in

---

[34] [1997] 4 All ER 816. See also *Royal Bank of Scotland v Etridge* [1998] 4 All ER 705.

[35] The solicitor's fee in this case was paid initially by the bank, but would be added to the borrower's total liability. See also the following similar cases: *Banco Exterior Internacional* v. *Mann* [1995] 1 All ER 936 and *Bank of Baroda* v. *Rayarel* [1995] 2 FLR 376. In these two cases the court advised the solicitors not to act for the complaining wife if they thought there was a conflict of interest.

[36] See further Chap. 13 on mediation generally.

order to permit family lawyers to act, where appropriate, for and in the best interests of the family rather than solely for one individual member".[37] There is talk of being a "lawyer for the family" rather than a representative of an individual member of the family. This cannot be appropriate, however, unless all parties consent and that consent is fully informed. How can the latter be achieved by one lawyer who also has his or her own interest in retaining the rest of the family as a client? The notion seems to be simplistic and dangerous, especially for the members of the family with the least power.

In representing children, the solicitor must be clear who gives instructions. In ordinary litigation, such as personal injuries, a minor cannot initiate litigation except by a next friend or guardian ad litem (GAL).[38] A parent has the right to act as a next friend. It is for the next friend to instruct the solicitor in the best interests of the child and he or she must not have any interest adverse to that of the child. The solicitor acts for the next friend but must be concious of any conflict of interest between the child and the next friend. The solution, if such a conflict does arise, is for the next friend to be removed by the court on the application of the solicitor or other interested person.[39]

In family proceedings there is provision for a child to initiate or defend litigation, such as an application under section 8 of the Children Act 1990 in relation to care or contact, without a next friend or GAL. The solicitor must ascertain if the child has both a sufficient understanding of the issues and the ability to give instructions.[40] If this is the case then the solicitor can act directly for the child. Similarly if a GAL has already been appointed but a conflict arises between the instructions of the child and the GAL, then the solicitor should accept the instructions of the child if capable of instructing. It is the duty of the GAL to inform the court of the conflict and carry on with all the Children Act duties of a GAL except instructing the child's solicitor.[41] A solicitor representing a child without a GAL, where the child is not in the view of the solicitor capable of giving instructions, must act in the best interests of the child.[42]

The court has power to appoint a GAL if necessary. This raises the issue of what is in the best interests of the child in these circumstances. Should the solicitor take a view on the best way to dispose of the issue in dispute and press that view on the court? Alternatively, should he or she take the view that the best

---

[37] R. H. Tur, "Family Lawyering in Legal Ethics" in S. Parker and C. Standford (eds.), *Legal Ethics and Legal Practice: Contemporary Issues* (Oxford, Clarendon Press, 1995).

[38] RSC. Ord.80, r.2.

[39] See RSC, Ord.80, n. 3 and *Re Taylor's Application* [1972] 2 All ER 873.

[40] I.e., is the child Gillick competent: *Gillick v. West Norfolk etc. AHA and DSS* [1986] AC 112. See also Law Society guidance reproduced in J. A. Holland (ed.), *Cordery on Solicitors* (London, Butterworths, 1995,) ii, para. 4–1071.

[41] Family Proceedings Rules 1991 r.11(3). See also *Re T* [1993] 4 All ER 518 in which the court stressed that while it is basically for the solicitor to determine whether a child is capable of giving instructions, nevertheless the court has the ultimate right to decide the issue either of it own motion or on the application of another because "there are bound to be some cases . . . where a maverick assessment might be made by a solicitor": Waite LJ at 529.

[42] Family Proceedings Rules rule 12(1) and see *Re H* [1993] 1 FLR 440.

interests of the child are advanced by ensuring that the court has all relevant information on all options? In short, is it the solicitor's or the court's role to arrive at a well informed decision? A full discussion of this issue is beyond the scope of this chapter's concern with conflicts of interest, but it is clear that a solicitor in this position must be wary of presenting the court with his or her own personal views on the best way to bring up children. In the absence of instructions from either a GAL or a competent child, it is probably best that the solicitor relies on the court rather than his own opinions. Such opinions are not expert in the field of family welfare and may even be quixotic or inappropriate to the particular child and his family.

Acting for Groups and Representative Actions

Major disasters, such as air crashes, adverse reactions to drugs or environmental problems, can affect large groups of people, all or some of whom may want to seek compensation. There may be conflicts of interest between the victims and also between them and their lawyers. Some victims may not be aware that litigation is under way or, if they are, will not understand what is happening. The majority of the victims may leave the matter to a small group of plaintiffs or even to the lawyers alone. The litigation is therefore often characterised by a "relative absence of client control"[43] which can leave the lawyers free to follow their own inclinations rather than the instructions of the client.

　Two frameworks exist for litigating such group actions. First, all the parties may sue as a group. This requires leave of the court to join all of them as parties and, in theory, all are equally involved in the progress of the case. Secondly, some of the group may bring the action as representatives of the others. This avoids the need to join large numbers of people as plaintiffs, but every person represented is bound by the outcome of the litigation.[44] Representative actions are comparatively rare; the multi-party action is more usual. Examples of multi-party actions include litigation arising in relation to abestosis, the Dalcon Shield and Opren.[45] The Opren case concerned the alleged side effects of the anti-arthritis drug, Opren. Two group actions, involving about 1,500 plaintiffs, were launched against the manufacturers, Eli Lilly & Co and were co-ordinated by a group of solicitors known as the Opren Action Group (OAG). The clients set up an Opren Action Committee (OAC), and the Law Society set up a register of solicitors acting for Opren victims. The management of the case was difficult and fraught with the possibility of conflict between the different groups. In the event, a settlement was reached

---

[43] Lord Woolf, *Access to Justice: Final Report to the Lord Chancellor on the Civil Justice System in England and Wales* (London, HMSO, 1996), at 243, para.72, hereafter *Final Report*.

[44] See for the procedures, RSC, Ord. 15, r. 12 and Ord.15, r. 4.

[45] M. Day and S. Moore, "Multi-party Actions: A Plaintiff View", in R. Smith (ed.), *Shaping the Future New Directions in Legal Services* (London, Legal Action Group, 1995), at 188.

whereby a lump sum payment was agreed with the defendants and was distributed between the various plaintiffs by the solicitors in ORG, subject to an appeal to a judge as arbitrator. However it seems that the solicitors did not discuss the terms of the settlement with OAC and, moreover, told their clients that if the settlement were not agreed they would cease to act.[46] The case had been further complicated by Legal Aid. The court ordered that, despite the fact that the action had been brought only by plaintiffs entitled to Legal Aid, the costs of the action should be shared equally by all of the group involved, including those not legally aided. The unaided parties naturally had a different attitude to the risks of the litigation than the legally aided, the latter being unlikely to face any personal liability for the costs of the action.[47]

The actual and potential conflicts inherent in litigation such as the Opren case are obvious, but there is little guidance on this to be found in the *Law Society Guide*. It warns solicitors that they should be alive to possible conflicts and that they "might need to warn the prospective clients that at some later stage it may be neccessary that each person is separately represented".[48] The situation can be helped by the involvement of professional bodies in the proceedings.[49] In multi-party actions the parties clearly have to sacrifice some of the protection provided by the conventional conflict of interest rules in order to obtain the benefits, in terms of finance and expertise, that can come from a multi-party action. Without the group they would probably be unable to get any redress, bearing in mind the complexity and costs of the litigation. The Opren case, for example, involved investigations and scientific research costing millions of pounds. However, these inherent conflicts must be appropriately managed if justice is to be done equally to all the parties. Lord Woolf addressed some of these issues in his *Final Report*.

Lord Woolf recommended special procedures for managing group actions. He thought that an application should be made to the court at the outset to certificate a multi-party action and a managing judge appointed to control the proceedings. The judge would make decisions about lead lawyers, notify possible plaintiffs and allocate costs. Lord Woolf proposed dealing with the "relative absence of client control" in such actions, and the consequent tendency of the lawyers to undertake more work than necessary, by appointing a taxing master to monitor the case as it progressed. The role of the informed client could be taken by an action group or, where there is no such group, by the appointment of a trustee to undertake this role. All settlements would have to be approved by the court so as to ensure that "the lawyers do not benefit themselves while

---

[46] See G. Dehn, "Opren: Problems, Solutions and More Problems" (1989) 12 *Journal of Consumer Policy* 397.

[47] *Davies* v. *Eli Lilly & Co.* [1987] 1 WLR 1136. Another successful multi-party action was that against British Coal in respect of miners' lung disease. See for details of how this was handled, *The Lawyer*, 10 Feb. 1998.

[48] *Law Society Guide*, n. 6 above, r. 11.06, para. 3.

[49] The Law Society can help to co-ordinate multi-party actions, as it did in the Opren case.

obtaining minimal benefits for their clients". Finally, Lord Woolf recommended that the Bar and the Law Society "give special attention to the ethical problems involved in multi-party litigation".[50]

Such ethical guidance must, at the very least, ensure that all the parties are fully informed in writing of the nature of the group action and the constraints within which is is being conducted, in particular the limited possibilities for the client to give personal instructions. He or she should have a right to a regular progress report, either in person or in writing, and be informed of the terms of any proposed settlement and how it would affect him or her. It is essential to inform the client fully from the outset what can be expected from the lawyer because the relationship between lawyer and client in multi-party actions is not the same as in one-to-one relationships.

D. CONFLICTS WITH THE SOLICITOR'S OWN INTERESTS

Principle 15.04 of the *Law Society Guide* states that a solicitor must not act for a client if his or her own interests conflict with those of the client. A startling recent example of this arose in relation to the trial of Frederick West for multiple murder in 1994. His solicitor was alleged to have been commissioned by a publisher to write a book about the case when it was concluded. The *Law Society Guide* states firmly that "a solicitor should not enter into any arrangement . . . with a client or prospective client *prior to the conclusion of the matter* giving rise to the retainer by which the solicitor acquires an interest in the publication rights with respect to that matter".[51] There seems to be no problem about such agreements for publication once the case has finished, though a solicitor cannot reveal confidential information about a client without the client's consent, and in obtaining that consent the solicitor must ensure that the client has independent advice under the guidance noted below. Equally tempting, and increasingly common in notorious cases, may be the possibility of negotiating with the press on behalf of the client for exclusive interview rights. Again, the solicitor must avoid any conflict of interest which might arise, for example where the solicitor obtains a commission from one or two competing newspapers. In advising the client which offer to accept, the lawyer would not be able to avoid the suspicion of personal interest.

More conventional conflicts arise where the solicitor, or his firm, personally buys from or sells or lends to the client, or has a personal interest in any transaction which the client is undertaking.[52] In these cases the solicitor must reveal

---

[50] See the *Final Report*, n. 43 above, chap. 17. See also Law Society Report of the Civil Litigation Committee, *Group Actions Made Easier* (Sept. 1995). The latter does not, however cover the ethical issues involved.

[51] R. 15.04, para. 2, emphasis added.

[52] See Chap. 12 in relation to commissions.

the interest to the client with "complete frankness"[53] and the client must receive independent advice from another solicitor or other appropriate advisor such as a surveyor. Only if the client gets such advice can the solicitor continue to act in relation to the transaction. Again it might be thought that the Law Society guidance here is too lenient. A rigid rule that a solicitor should never act for a client where the solicitor has a personal interest in the transaction would eliminate all suspicion of conflict of interest.

Are solicitors prohibited from acting for a client with whom they have some personal relationship? Clearly there could be a conflict of interest in such circumstances as neither the solicitor nor the client may always wish to be frank in his or her professional dealings if this would compromise their personal relationship. The Law Society states that solicitors must "consider" whether any personal relationship inhibits the giving of impartial advice to the client, and the same vague and ambiguous wording is used where the solicitor is involved in a sexual relationship with a client.[54] This guidance seems rather thin. It fails to deal adequately with the risk of abuse of power where personal relationships are mixed with solicitor–client relationships and the risk that the reputation of all lawyers will be undermined when, as sometimes happens, sordid allegations are made in the press. Normally the solicitor will be in the more powerful position and there may be a risk that the help or advice given may be influenced by the prospect of sexual favours. Arguably professionals must adhere to higher standards than are the norm, and it should be a rule that solicitors and barristers never act for their spouses, cohabitants or lovers. Any other rule risks compromising the value that should be at the root of the solicitor–client relationship. Lawyers must be free to give completely disinterested advice and representation to the best of their ability in order to advance the lawful interests of the client.

There are also other situations where a close relationship between the solicitor and a particular person or body may lead the client to suspect that the solicitor will not act energetically in his or her best interests. An example of this is a firm of solicitors which had close ties with the local police, one of their partners being an ex-policeman, and which habitually handled divorces and the conveyancing of officers working in the local police station. Arrested suspects who found a member of that firm advising them under the Police Station Advisors' Scheme might well be concerned that conflicting loyalties would inhibit the assistance given to them. However, it is not clear that this is an example of conflict of interest which is covered by principle 15.04 of the *Law Society Guide*, and the firm in question was unconcerned by the possible conflict.

Finally, a solicitor must decline to act for a client where the solicitor, or a partner, employee or relative holds an office which gives rise to a reasonable risk of a conflict of interest.[55] A number of examples are given in the *Law Society*

---

[53] *Law Society Guide,* n. 6 above, r. 15.04, para. 4.
[54] *Law Society Guide,* n. 6 above, r. 15.04, paras. 9 and 10 which also refer to r. 12.07: A solicitor must not take advantage of the client.
[55] *Ibid.,* r. 15.06.

Guide. A solicitor must consider whether he or she can act for or against the local authority if the solicitor is a councillor. It will be noted that, again, the obligation to "consider" is weak, since it may be discharged by putting a moment's thought to a problem. A solicitor, whilst a member of a Police Authority, "should not" appear as an advocate in prosecutions brought by the CPS in the Authority's area. A solicitor who is a recorder, deputy judge or registrar must not sit in a court in which he, she, a partner or an employee regularly practises. Similarly a solicitor magistrate cannot act for a client appearing before the justices in the area in which he or she is a JP.[56] Similar rules should govern circumstances where a solicitor acts as a tribunal chair or coroner.

CONCLUSION

No lawyer can guarantee that there will be no conflict between the interests of the client and other interests. However, one of the most valuable services that a lawyer as contrasted with many other commercial advisers, can offer, is disinterested and confidential advice. The client needs to know what this entails and, in particular, what the position is where a conflict can or does arise. This is particularly important where the lawyer is working outside the context of a one-to-one lawyer–client relationship, as where the lawyer is representing an institution or a group, or is undertaking mediation, conciliation or other non-conventional work. If civil procedures do become less adversarial as a result of the Woolf reforms, it may be that the rules and principles on conflict of interest will have to be radically revised in order to accommodate a more co-operative and facilitative ethos. This is already apparent in many family cases, especially where children are involved. Hence R. H. Turr's proposal that there should be lawyers for the family, rather than for individual members of it. But care needs to be taken to prevent the cynical use of the conflict rules in order to play tactical litigation games.

The litigation that has arisen in relation to the joint representation of buyer and seller or mortgagor and mortgagee, instituted with a view to allowing solicitors to offer an efficient and less costly service in a non-contentious situation, should lead to caution. It may be asking too much of anyone that they represent different interests at the same time and are also constantly alive to the possibility of conflict of interest arising. The risk is that the lawyer who is required to warn a client will possibly lose his or her business and, in addition, will upset the arrangement or progress already made on the issue.

[56] Solicitors' Act 1974 s.38.

12

Fees and Costs

"There are three golden rules in the profession [criminal law] . . . the first . . . thoroughly terrify your client. Second, find out how much money he has and where it is. Third, get it. The merest duffer can usually succeed in following out the first two of these precepts, but to accomplish the third requires often a master's art. The ability actually to get one's hands on the coin is what differentiates the really great criminal lawyer from his inconspicuous brethren."[1]

A. INTRODUCTION

Central to the relationship of lawyer and client are the fees paid by, or on behalf of, the client and the conditions under which those fees are negotiated and charged. In most professional relationships the client is often unable to evaluate the amount or type of work that needs to be done. It is essential, if the client's interests are to be protected and prioritised, that there is effective control against overcharging. A separate issue is that of overworking, that is, doing more work than is necessary, bearing in mind the nature or value of the case. Even the sophisticated corporate client may find this difficult to control. These issues cannot be left to the operation of the market. Fees are an ethical issue because, in Schaffer's words, "[t]he distinctive feature of ethics in a profession is that it speaks to the unequal encounter of two moral persons. Legal ethics . . . becomes the study [for lawyers] of what is good . . . for this other person, over whom I have power."[2] In the context of charging fees, the lawyer has power because he or she has the knowledge regarding the likely costs and benefits of any proposed course of action and the client is, at least relatively, ignorant of this.

Fees and costs are also a major barrier for the ordinary client in getting access to justice, as Lord Woolf has constantly reiterated in his 1996 report on civil litigation.[3] Indeed, access to the courts has now been recognised by the Divisional Court as a basic constitutional right which can be abrogated only by express provision in an Act of Parliament.[4] As we saw in Part 1, promoting access to

---

[1] A Train, *The Confessions of Artemas Quibble* (New York: Scribner's 1911), at 77.

[2] T. L. Schaffer, "Legal Ethics and the Good Client" (1987) 36 *Catholic Universiy Law Review* 319.

[3] E.g., Lord Woolf, *Access to Justice: Final Report to the Lord Chancellor on the Civil Justice System in England and Wales* (London, HMSO, 1996), at 78,. hereafter *Final Report*.

[4] R. v. *Lord Chancellor, ex parte Witham* [1997] 2 All ER 779, where the Lord Chancellor's order withdrawing exemption from court fees to those on income support was declared *ultra vires* because there was no specific provision in the relevant enabling Act permitting this.

justice and the courts is arguably the distinctive purpose of the legal profession. This ideal is seriously undermined if the profession itself, through doing unnecessary work and overcharging, makes litigation unaffordable both for the privately paying client and even for the state in funding the Legal Aid scheme. Lord Woolf is clearly influenced by this ideal when he concludes that, "the present system provides higher benefits to lawyers than to their clients".[5]

Complaints about lawyers' charges are the most common of all complaints received by the Law Society and the Legal Services Ombudsman. The latter, in his report for 1995, specifically noted that legal fees were soaring and that clients generally lacked adequate information. As an example he gave the case of a builder who lost an action to recover £9,800 and in so doing incurred costs of £26,000 including an expert's fee, to which he had not agreed, of £5,000.[6] In his 1996 Report the Ombudsman noted "almost wistfully" that he had dealt with solicitors' costs in every annual report since 1991 and that, six years later, "lack of adequate costs information remains a staple of my work diet".[7]

Despite their centrality to the role of the lawyer, remarkably little attention has been given to fees in texts on legal ethics other than in relation to the perennial debate over contingency fees.[8] The chapter on professional fees in the *Law Society Guide* is a fairly brief 40 pages including all annexes. It contains little that can be described as general principles of an ethical nature. Significantly, the first "general principle" dealt with in the chapter (14.01) concerns the power of solicitors to "require" payments on account from clients! Similarly, the Bar Code says little about fees in relation to clients except to state that a barrister may charge on any basis or by any method he thinks fit.[9] In reality both the law and the guidance are more complex than is implied by the above, but the literature contains little or no commentary or analysis of this material from the ethical point of view, and no clear statement or explanation of the principles underlying it.

In relation to fees there is an inherent conflict of interest between lawyer and client. The lawyer normally, and probably naturally, wishes to charge more than the client wants to pay. Since there is usually a power imbalance in favour of the lawyer, what general principles should underlie the regulation of fees?

---

[5] Lord Woolf, *Access to Justice: Interim Report to the Lord Chancellor on the Civil Justice System in England and Wales* (London, Lord Chancellor's Department, 1995), at 13. See also P. Abrams, A. Boon and D. O'Brien, "Access to Justice: The Collision of Funding and Ethics" (1998) 3:1 *Contemporary Issues in Law* 59.

[6] Fees were the problem in relation to a major scandal known as the "Glanville Davies affair" in which the Law Society complaints machinery failed for a long time to deal with an overcharge by the solicitor of £130,000. This was dealt with only after much litigation, a report by the lay observer and also by the Law Society (the Ely Report) in 1984.

[7] 1996 *Report of the Legal Service Ombudsman*, HC. Paper 24, at 14.

[8] Deborah Rhode's recent text, *Professional Responsibility: Ethics by the Pervasive Method* (Boston, Mass., Little Brown, 1994) barely mentions fees, for example.

[9] *Code of Conduct of the Bar of England and Wales* (London, The General Council of the Bar of England and Wales, 1990), at para. 308, hereafter the *Bar Code*. Barristers may not change a fixed fee over a fixed period of time irrespective of the amount of work done.

The following principles suggest themselves. First, most obviously, the level of the fees cannot be left solely to market forces or individual agreement. Secondly, the imbalance of power between the parties in negotiating fees should be countered by ensuring that the client gives an informed and unpressured consent to any proposal made by the lawyer. Thirdly, the client should be clearly informed by the lawyer of any actual or potential conflicts that may arise in relation to any particular funding mechanism, such as conditional fees or costs insurance. Fourthly, the client should be regularly updated on his or her liability for fees and the amount owed. Fifthly, there should be effective, fair and accessible procedures for reviewing fees so as to rectify overcharging or any failure by the lawyer to abide by the above principles. The law and rules of professional conduct relating to lawyers' fees are examined in this chapter in the light of these principles.

B. WHAT KIND OF FEE IS CHARGEABLE?

Some of the oldest and most arcane rules of legal professional conduct relate to the prohibition of certain types of fee arrangements in relation to contentious matters. Thus the contingency fee (under which the lawyer is not paid if the case is lost, but gets a percentage of the damages if it is won) has always been prohibited in the UK under the common law relating to champerty.[10] Speculative fees and arrangements whereby a client's fees are paid by third parties, or even the solicitor himself, were prohibited or affected by the common law prohibiting maintenance.[11] These rules also applied in America and, traditionally, American texts on legal ethics confined their discussion of the ethical implications of fee arrangements to these issues. In the words of Charles Wolfram, "[n]ot so long ago, a considerable area of the law of legal ethics was given over to the mysteries of the Macbethian witches of the common law who stirred the law of despised litigation—maintenance, champerty and barratry".[12] In the UK these three were not only regarded as unethical, they were criminal until the passing of the Criminal Law Act 1967 though this had been rendered obsolete by case law long before 1967. However these rules still affect the fee arrangements that can lawfully be made between solicitor and client. It is therefore

---

[10] For a recent statement of the rule see *Aratra Potato* v. *Taylor Joynson Garrett* [1995] 4 All ER 695, and see *Thai Trading Co.* v. *Taylor* [1998] 3 All ER 65, which makes lawful speculative fees.

[11] The latter is urging others to litigate. See *Hill* v. *Archbold* [1967] 3 All ER 110 and *Shah* v. *Karanjia* [1993]4 All ER 792

[12] C. W. Wolfram, "Modern Legal Ethics" (St. Paul, Minn., West Publishing Co., 1986), at 489. It is suggested by Luban that the strict control of contingency fees in ethics codes in the USA reflects the disdain with which high status lawyers regarded the methods used by low status lawyers to get access to clients and the courts: see D. Luban, "Speculating on Justice: The Ethics and Jurisprudence of Contingency Fees" in S. Parker and C. Sampford (eds.), *Legal Ethics and Legal Practice: Contemporary Issues* (Oxford, Clarendon Press, 1995), at 114.

important to understand the basic ethical concerns which underpinned maintenance, champerty and barratry.

The laws against the maintenance of litigation by third parties and also
against barratry were justified on the basis that persons with no direct interest
in a dispute should not intermeddle in it and thereby encourage spurious litigation, causing grief and possible financial loss to the other side. The same justification was applied to the law on champerty, because lawyers who handled cases
on a no-win, no-fee basis, or who were paid a proportion of the winnings,
would have a personal interest in stirring up another's litigation. Nowadays,
few people consider that maintenance is unethical. Indeed, many organisations
are devoted to the task of encouraging and enabling others to take legal action,
including charitable organisations, pressure groups and bodies like insurance
companies, motoring organisations or trades unions. The state is the largest
maintainer of litigation through the Legal Aid Fund. Participating in such public service provision, *pro bono publico,* is a mark of professionalism, as has been
argued in Chapter 6. Encouraging litigation is no longer seen to be a problem:
the denial of access to the courts because of lack of funds is.

The law against maintenance and champerty was also based on two additional ethical principles. The first relates to conflict of interest between a lawyer
and client. A lawyer who has a personal interest in the proceeds of the client's
litigation has, it is argued, an interest of his own, an interest other than the best
interests of the client. At first sight this may seem to be a curious view. Surely, it
may be argued, the contingency fee arrangement ensures that the lawyer and the
client have the *same* interest, namely, winning the case and maximising the damages recovered. In some cases this will be the position. However, in others it may
not be so. For example, where the issue of liability is clear, it may be in the
client's interest to maximise the amount of damages by negotiating long and
hard. The lawyer, however, might want to settle quickly for less because the
extra amount that he or she could recover for the client by hard bargaining
would not compensate for the money earned in the extra hours of work that had
to be put in to achieve it.[13] Should the lawyer in this situation be able to withdraw from the case if the client refuses to authorise the settlement? Conflict of
interest also arises in relation to maintenance. If the lawyer is being paid by a
third party then he or she might owe some allegiance to, or be instructed by, that
third party rather than by his client. The profession's resistance to the growth
of trades union organised legal expenses insurance plans in the USA was publicly justified on this basis. In England some lawyers resisted the introduction of
Legal Aid in the 1940s and 1950s on the ground that the independence of lawyers

---

[13] The empirical evidence on this in the USA seems to indicate that in the smaller cases this is
what actually happens: see H. M. Kritzer, *The Justice Broker: Lawyers and Ordinary Litigation*
(New York, Oxford University Press, 1990), at 108 ff.; P. Danzon, *Contingency Fees for Personal
Injuries Litigation* (US. Department of Health, 1981); Swartz and Mitchell, "An Economic Analysis
of the Contingent Fee in Personal Injuries Litigation" (1970) 22 *Stanford Law Review* 1125.

to act in their clients' best interests would be compromised by their responsibilities to the Legal Aid Fund.[14]

An ethical objection aimed at champerty relates to the need to promote the integrity of the legal process and the principle that the lawyer is an officer of the court. A personal interest in the outcome of a client's litigation might induce the solicitor to encourage perjury, corruption or attempt sharp practices, which would corrupt the legal process. Moreover, the higher the percentage taken by the lawyer, the higher the damages that are likely to be awarded, it is alleged, and this is unjust to the losing party. In addition, contingency fees in the USA are held responsible for a litigation explosion, and defensive practices by manufacturers and service providers, which are assumed to have negative social consequences, such as driving up the cost of goods and services.[15]

The problem with all these arguments is that it is never convincingly explained why the hourly paid lawyer does not also have a personal incentive to take on spurious cases, or to seek to win them by sharp practices. Not only does the lawyer, thereby, increase his income from the case, he pleases his client, who may then be prepared to pay him larger fees, employ him again and recommend him to friends. Whilst contingency fees may sometimes encourage lawyers to minimise the work they do in order to maximise their gain when the case is settled or won, at least such lawyers have an interest in winning their cases. Hourly paid fees can encourage the lawyer to do unnecessary work in order to increase fees, or simply to work more slowly and inefficiently, confident that he or she will be paid whatever the outcome. "Experience shows that, given a free reign, lawyers (who are normally paid by the hour) will tend to do too much rather than too little work with not always sufficient regard to the relevance of what they are producing".[16] The client, presented with a choice of between these two types of conflict of interest, might well choose that inherent in the contingency fee system, which at the very least offers an incentive to the lawyer to win the case and obtain a reasonable amount in damages because his fees depend on that.[17] The main constraint on overworking in the English system is taxation of costs after the event, which is explained in more detail below. This constraint is not adequate in itself, particularly in relation to the vast majority of cases which settle with the fees being agreed between the lawyers. This is because the lawyers advising the client who is paying the other side's costs have an incentive to recommend payment of high fees so that they can justify charging a similarly high fee for their own work.

[14] B. Abel-Smith and R. Stevens, *Lawyers and the Courts: A Sociological Study of the English Legal System, 1750–1965* (London, Heinemann, 1967), chap. 5, n. 343. The block funding and franchising of Legal Aid proposed by the Conservative and Labour governments has led to the same allegations: see Abrams, Boon *et al*. n. 5 above.

[15] Against which argument see M. Galanter, "The Day After the Litigation Explosion" (1986) 46 *Maryland Law Review* 3, and also Luban, n. 12 above, at 89–126.

[16] Stated, admittedly in a slightly different context, in the Report of the Law Society's Civil Litigation Committee's on Multi Party Actions, *Group Actions Made Easier* (1995), at 3.

[17] In the USA this is exactly the choice made by both individual and institutional plaintiffs: see Wolfram, n. 12 above, at 526.

As we shall see, the continued prohibition in England of contingency fees is becoming increasingly difficult to justify, especially in the light of the introduction of conditional fees in 1995, their expansion in 1998[18] and the decision of the Court of Appeal in *Thai Trading Co. v. Taylor*[19] which legalises speculative fees. The rest of this section therefore looks in more detail at the types of fee arrangement that are currently lawful, and considered to be ethically acceptable, and the conditions relating to them. The way fees may be negotiated with the client and the information to be given to the client is dealt with in the next section .

Hourly or Fixed Fees

These are currently the normal fee arrangements in the UK. The solicitor is paid by the hour for the actual work done, or, as is common in fairly routine transactions like conveyancing or making wills, a fixed fee. There is evidence that large commercial clients now prefer a fixed fee for a particular piece of work, rather than hourly rates, as the client is thereby enabled to maintain more control over the work done for him or her.[20] Barristers normally quote a fixed fee for a particular advice or piece of drafting and a daily rate for court work. Barristers have traditionally attempted to avoid the problems of conflict of interest inherent in fixing fees by denying any interest in the issue. Their fees are negotiated by their clerks and are regarded as "honoria" which give rise to no legal liability on either side. This has been used, *inter alia*, to justify the immunity of barristers for liability in negligence for court work.[21] Now, under the Courts and Legal Services Act 1990 section 61, barristers can legally enter into binding contracts. The General Council of the Bar can, however, make rules prohibiting this, which they have done.[22] Whether this was in the public interest seems not to have been debated.

An issue that often causes surprise to clients whose bills are larger than they expected is the treatment of disbursements. These are the payments made by solicitors to third parties on behalf of their clients, such as stamp duties, registration fees, court fees and witness fees, which are added to the final bill. Most clients would accept that such items should be separately charged. But what about postage, printing costs, travel? Are these disbursements or simply overheads that should be absorbed in the fee agreed with the client? Often this will not be made clear to the client. There is no guidance from the Law Society on how such overheads should be treated.

---

[18] These were introduced in 1995 after the publication of the Government Green Paper, Contingency Fees, Cm. 571 (London, HMSO, 1989). This rejected US-style contingency fees on the ground that the litigant would be unable to negotiate meaningfully with the lawyer on them: see para. 4.9.

[19] [1998] 3 All ER 65. A subsequent decision of the Divisional Court refused to follow this case: *Hughes v Kingston upon Hull City Council* 9 November 1998 LAWTEL and p. 295 below.

[20] See e.g. G. Hanlon, "A Profession in Transition" (1997) 60 *Modern Law Review* 798 at 813.

[21] See Abel-Smith and Stevens, n. 14 above, at 231 for the debate between the professions in 1876 on this issue.

[22] See *Bar Code*, n. 9 above, Annex D paras. 25, 26.

However the bills are made up, there are now no professional rules restraining lawyers from undercutting each other, as existed in the mid 1930s for solicitors. In 1996, Martin Mears, a past President of the Law Society, wanted these rules restored in relation to conveyancing charges, but the Law Society Council managed to avoid making a decision on his proposal.[23] Clearly undercutting is not really an ethical issue but relates to the desire of the profession to maximise its income. Some lawyers claim, however, that the possibility of undercutting encourages "fee shopping". This in turn is said to encourage low standards of work by lawyers and is therefore brought within the realm of the professional codes of conduct.

Overcharging is, however, a problem. As has already been noted, there is now considerable pressure from commercial clients and also institutional funders of legal services, such as the Lord Chancellor in relation to legal aid, and insurance companies, towards fixed fees rather than hourly fees. This is aimed at controlling both overwork and overbilling which many institutions, including the judiciary, see as endemic.[24] Hourly charging encourages inefficiency as well as overcharging. Richard Susskind has even suggested that lawyers will be "reluctant to become too efficient with technology until there is a move beyond the billable hour".[25] The reluctance of lawyers to abandon the billable hour was illustrated in 1993 when the Law Society challenged, by judicial review, the decision of the Lord Chancellor to introduce standard fees in legally aided criminal cases. The case was lost. Fees can, of course, be controlled—by taxation and the other mechanisms dealt with below—but these mechanisms can in themselves be costly and uncertain.

Conditional and Contingency Fees

Contingency fees are arrangements whereby the lawyer is paid a fee by the client only if the case is won, in which case the fee will be a proportion of the amount recovered. As already noted, such arrangements, in relation to contentious business, are still unlawful under the common law against champerty, section 59(2) of the Solicitors' Act 1974, rule 8 of the Solicitors Practice Rules 1990 and the

---

[23] See *The Lawyer*, 19 Mar. 1996, at 2.

[24] See e.g. *The Guardian*, 18 Nov. 1996, and as long ago as 1993 a solicitor in a legal expenses insurance group made a plea for more fixed fees in litigation: *The Lawyer*, 18 May 1993 at 12. Lord Woolf also sees fixed fees as essential to the success of his proposed "fast track" procedure for civil cases up to £10,000. There are already many fixed fees in relation to criminal work, introduced in the teeth of lawyer opposition during the 1980s and 1990s. Large corporate clients now produce detailed codes regulating their relationship with their lawyers. See e.g. Lloyd's of London whose code requires the lawyers to justify their fees and give advance warning of bills. Lloyds Underwriters are concerned about overmanning in solicitors' firms. See *Law Society Gazette*, 1 July 1998, at 9.

[25] R. Susskind, *The Future of Law: Facing the Challenges of Information Technology* (Oxford, New York, Clarendon Press, 1996), at 173.

professional codes of both professions.[26] As also noted above, the ethical principle advanced for this rule is the prevention of conflicts of interest between lawyer and client and to uphold probity in court proceedings by lawyers.[27]

What are the possible consequences of charging an unlawful contingency fee? First the solicitor will be unable to recover the fee, or even disbursements, from the client.[28] If, however, the client has already paid money over to the solicitor, it cannot be reclaimed, the agreement being unenforceable rather than void or voidable.[29] The loss of champertous fees is not insurable.[30] More serious for solicitors is that they may find themselves liable for the costs of the other side if the case is lost, as occurred in the case of *McFarlane* v. *EE Caledonia*.[31] If the case is won, the question of a costs order against the loser arises. Here there is no direct authority, but it is arguable that, if the liability for costs between solicitor and client is unenforceable, then there is no basis for ordering the losing party to pay such costs, unless they have already been paid by the client as in the *Aratra Potato* case cited above. In addition, the solicitor could be subject to disciplinary proceedings, but there is little evidence of such cases having been pursued.

The most significant exception to the rules forbidding contingency fees is contained in the Courts and Legal Services Act 1990 section 58, which legalises conditional fees and came into force in July 1995.[32] Under a conditional fee agreement solicitors and barristers can agree with the client that a fee will be payable only if the case is won. But, if the case is won, the fee may be uplifted by up to 100 per cent of the normal fee, excluding disbursements. Initially these agreements could be made in three types of cases only: actions for personal injury; actions relating to winding up companies or in bankruptcy proceedings and actions before the European Commission or Court of Human Rights.[33]

---

[26] Contingent fees are allowed in respect of non-contentious business, including debt collecting. They are also allowed in employment cases before employment tribunals. They may be allowed in some arbitrations. See J. Levin, "Solicitors Acting Speculatively and Pro Bono" (1996) 15 *Civil Justice Quarterly* 44 at 47 and *Bevan Ashford* v. *Yeandle* [1998] 3 All ER 240. Speculative fees are now probably lawful in England and Wales: *Thai Trading* v. *Taylor* [1998] 3 All ER 65. For a recent case on an illegal agreement by a solicitor to share fees by paying for introductions from the fee charged to the client, see *Mohamed* v. *Alagra* [1998] 2 All ER 720.

[27] In the USA the term "contingency fee" also covers percentage uplifted fees (our conditional fee) and speculative fees; a US contingency fee is a no win no fee arrangement.

[28] *Re Trepca Mines* [1962] 3 All ER 35; *Wild* v. *Simpson* [1919] KB 544. For further detail see Levin n. 26 above.

[29] *Aratra Potato Co.* v. *Taylor Joynson Garrett* [1995] 4 All ER 695.

[30] *Haseldine* v. *Hoskin* [1933] All ER 1.

[31] [1995] 1 WLR 366.

[32] For a fuller analysis of the new law see J. Levin, "Conditional Fees, the New Law" (1996) 3 *Personal Injury* 35 and M. Napier and F. Bawdon, *Conditional Fees, A Survival Guide* (London, Law Society, 1995).

[33] Conditional fees cover court proceedings and litigation services generally. The Courts and Legal Services Act 1990 s.58 does not extend to arbitrations, but it has been held in *Bevan Ashford* v. *Geoff Yeandle* [1998] 3 All ER 238 that there is no public policy objection to conditional fees in arbitrations in cases similar to those covered by the Act and the regulations made under it.

From July 1998 conditional fees were extended to all civil actions other than matrimonial cases.[34] It is planned that legal aid will be withdrawn from personal injury cases, with the exception of medical negligence,[35] but this has not yet been implemented.

Where the case is lost the client will not pay a lawyer's fee but will normally have to pay the disbursements—which can be considerable, especially where expert witnesses are used. The Law Society, therefore, does not like to use the expression "no win, no fee" to describe conditional fees. It would be possible for the solicitor to agree to pay the disbursements arising under a conditional fee agreement, though the model agreement promoted by the Law Society does not provide for this. There is currently under discussion a plan to fund loans to clients to cover disbursements, including the Accident Line Insurance premium noted below.[36] If the client wins the case and gets costs then the client will be in funds to pay off the loan.

More significant than disbursements, from the client's point of view, is liability for the other side's costs if the case is lost. In most personal injury cases this can be dealt with by insurance. The Law Society-sponsored Accident Line insurance, applicable only to solicitors on the Law Society Personal Injuries Panel, will cover the client for the costs of the other side in personal injury actions (with some exceptions, e.g. medical negligence cases), and other insurance companies can provide a variety of cover in conditional fee cases. The Accident Line premiums in 1997 were £95.68 per case in road traffic cases and £161.20 in other personal injury cases. One other insurance company, Litigation Protection, offered cover generally at £182 for each £10,000 of cover.[37] The extension of conditional fees to all civil cases will succeed only if insurance cover is available for opponents' costs.

One issue relating to conditional fees that was uncertain concerned the possible liability of solicitors for the costs of the opposing side where the case was lost. It was argued that they might be liable on the ground of unlawful maintenance and the legislation did not deal with the point. It has now been decided in *Hodgson* v. *Imperial Tobacco Ltd.*[38] that the existence of a conditional fee agreement makes no difference to the relationship of the solicitor with the other side. Solicitors will be personally liable for costs only under the normal wasted costs rules or under the inherent jurisdiction of the court under the Supreme Court Act 1981 section 51. The position of the lawyer under a conditional fee agreement was held to be the same as that of the Legal Aid lawyer where there is a similar risk that the defeated legally aided party will be unable to pay the costs of the successful unaided party. The conditional fee agreement is, how-

[34] Conditional Fees Order 1998, SI 98/1860.
[35] Consultation Paper, Lord Chancellor's Department, *Access to Justice with Conditional Fees* (London, Lord Chancellor's Department, 1998) and Access to Justice Bill 1998, clauses 27, 28 and schedule 2.
[36] *Law Society Gazette*, 20 Nov. 1996, at 4.
[37] See (1997) 147 *New Law Journal* 1559.
[38] [1998] 2 All ER 675.

ever, covered by professional privilege. Contrary to the position with legally aided parties, therefore, there is no obligation to disclose the conditional fee agreement to the other side, except possibly after the litigation has come to an end.

Bearing in mind the intense opposition on ethical grounds that these new provisions faced from many lawyers, it might be thought that they would be smothered in professional practice rules designed to ensure, as far as possible, that any conflict of interest between the solicitor and client was resolved in favour of the client. In fact this is not the case. The accompanying rules, largely concerned with the amount of information to be given to the client, are brief. There are no binding provisions limiting the amount recoverable by the solicitor, other than the statutory 100 per cent uplift limit. Taxation by the court is relied on to control excessive uplifts.[39] In the *Law Society Guide*[40] it is noted that the Law Society Council takes the view that, as yet, no new practice rules or formal guidance is necessary, but that the matter will be kept under review.

The Law Society is, however, very keen to promote the use of conditional fees. It has organised a means of providing insurance cover for the other side's costs. This is, however, confined to personal injury cases and also applies only to solicitors who are members of the Accident Line scheme in order to ensure that they have some specialised expertise in the field. The Law Society has also produced a model contract for solicitors to use and also a detailed guide to the new law. It also recommends that solicitors should not charge *an uplift* which exceeds 25 per cent of the amount recovered by the client. This does not, of course, mean that the *total fee* recovered by the solicitor will not exceed 25 per cent of the sum recovered. The model contract has been drafted using direct and untechnical language which the Law Society hopes is comprehensible to the lay client. It requires solicitors to state clearly their normal hourly rates and liability for disbursements as well as the success fee which will be charged.

It the client terminates the agreement before the case is completed then basic costs will become payable to the solicitor. If the client continues with the case and is successful then the success fee also is payable. The solicitor can terminate the agreement where the client fails to discharge his or her obligations under it. These obligations are to give instructions, not to mislead the solicitor, to be cooperative, submit to any necessary medical or other examinations and to pay disbursements as the case proceeds. The solicitor, on termination, can then require the client to pay basic costs and disbursements and also the success fee if the client goes on to win the case. The solicitor can also end the agreement if the client rejects advice on the likelihood of success or on accepting a settlement. In the latter case costs, disbursements and, in certain circumstances, the success fee are payable by the client. As can be seen from these terms, the client will face a considerable costs penalty if he or she terminates the agreement or disagrees

---

[39] See RSC, Ord. 62, r. 15A.
[40] At 264.

with the solicitor. The definition of being unco-operative or misleading the solicitor could be a cause of dispute in which the client will be at a considerable disadvantage in predicting the outcome.

In March 1998 the total number of conditional fee agreements made was about 34,000, with between 1,300–1,500 cases being dealt with each month. Initial research into conditional fee agreements published in the September 1997, indicated that the average uplift charged was 43 per cent. Nearly all agreements used the Law Society's model and limited the uplift fee to 25 per cent of the damages recovered.[41]

Speculative Fees and *Pro Bono* Work

A solicitor might wish to agree to undertake a case on a speculative basis—that is to agree with the client that a fee will be payable only if the case is won, knowing that either the client will be in funds in that event or, more likely, that costs, including the solicitor's fees, will be ordered against and paid by the losing party. Such an agreement does not involve any uplift or percentage of the damages as in conditional or contingency fees. This is known as a speculative fee. It has been legal for years in Scotland, although the extent to which it has been used is unknown.[42] Conventional wisdom regarded such fee arrangements as unlawful and professionally unacceptable in England. It was thought that they amount to unlawful maintenance by the solicitor and that they smack of ambulance-chasing. Nevertheless many solicitors were prepared to undertake certain work on this basis, especially personal injury work for clients ineligible for legal aid on financial grounds.[43]

The *Law Society Guide* did not provide much help on the ethicality of such arrangements. Under the Solicitors' Practice Rules 1990, rule 8, speculative fees were proscribed—the rule prevented a solicitor from entering into any arrangement to receive a fee payable only on the success of the action. However it has always been arguable that at common law speculative fees are lawful, and should therefore be regarded as professionally acceptable.[44] A number of early twentieth century cases indicate that acting speculatively is not only acceptable but desirable, as is illustrated in the following comment of Lord Russell in *Ladd v. London Road Car Co.*: "[i]t is perfectly consistent with the highest honour to take up a speculative action in this sense, *viz.*, that if a solicitor heard of an injury to a client and honestly took pains to inform himself whether there was a *bona fide* cause of action, it was consistent with the honour of the profession

---

[41] S. Yarrow, *The Price of Success* (London, Policy Studies Institute, 1997).

[42] In the debates in the HL on conditional fees, it was said by Lord Allen that speculative fees are frequently used in Scotland: *HL Debs*, 12 June 1995, col.1573.

[43] See H. Genn, *Hard Bargaining: Out of Court Settlement in Personal Injury Actions* (Oxford, Clarendon Press, 1987), and J. Levin, supra n. 26.

[44] *Ibid.*

that the solicitor should take up the action".[45] This is the law in Australia[46] and New Zealand,[47] based on English case law.[48]

The legality of speculative fees was recently accepted by the Court of Appeal in England. In *Thai Trading Company* v. *Taylor*[49] it was held that "there is nothing unlawful in a solicitor acting for a party to litigation agreeing to forgo all or part of his costs and disbursements if he wins". Such costs can be recovered from the other side and statements to the contrary in *BWB* v. *Norman*[50] are overruled. The court considered that a speculative fee should not "be regarded as contrary to public policy today, if indeed it ever was" and that rule 8 of the Solicitors' Practice Rules 1990 would have to be reconsidered. The court considered it to be "fanciful" to suppose that a solicitor would be tempted to behave improperly because he would be unable to recover his costs in a small case when he lost; there were far greater incentives to impropriety, such as the knowledge that losing a case will result in the loss of a valuable client. There was a countervailing issue of public policy—that of making justice accessible to those of modest means. Under the Access to Justice Bill 1998 speculative fees are treated in the same way as conditional fees and will be permitted if the agreement is in writing.[51]

Acting *pro bono* is not now regarded as illegal maintenance and is positively encouraged by the Law Society and the Bar.[52] The main problem is, as noted above in *BWB* v. *Norman*, that the successful party's costs may not be recoverable from the other side. There is however another risk associated with acting *pro bono*. Where the case is lost liability for the costs of the winning side might be imposed by the court on the losing party's lawyers personally. Certainly, some old cases indicate that a solicitor acting without fee might be personally liable for the costs of the other side if he had not satisfied himself that the client had a reasonable case.[53] The law here has recently been clarified in the case of *Tolstoy-Miloslavsky* v. *Aldington*.[54] In this case it was held, first, that the court had no jurisdiction to make a costs order against a solicitor solely on the ground that he acted without a fee. Secondly, when so acting, a solicitor is not under an obligation to protect the other side from a hopeless case. He does not have to "impose a pre-trial screen through which litigants must pass" before receiving free representation.[55] The only way in which a

---

[45]   (1990) 110 LT. Jo. 80.

[46]   *Clyne* v. *NSW Bar Association* (1960) 104 CLR 186.

[47]   *Sievwright* v. *Ward* (1935) NZ LR 43.

[48]   Such as *Ladd*, n. 46 above, and *Rich* v. *Cook* (1900) 110 LT. Jo. 94.

[49]   [1998] 3 All ER 65 (CA). This case may be appealed to the Lords. The Divisional Court in *Hughes v Kingston upon Hull City Council*, n. 19 above, has refused to follow this case on the ground that Practice Rule 8 forbids them and must be regarded as having the force of subordinate legislation under the House of Lords decision in *Swain v The Law Society* (1975) AC 598.

[50]   [1993] 26 HLR 232 (Div Ct.).

[51]   See Access to Justice Bill 1998, clause 27.

[52]   See Chap. 6.

[53]   See cases cited in n. 20 above.

[54]   [1996] 2 All ER 556.

[55]   See also *Orchard* v. *SE. Electricity* [1987] QB 565 at 572.

solicitor might be held personally liable for the other side's costs is under the wasted costs jurisdiction. This risk applies to all cases, whether the lawyer acts without charge or for a fee.[56]

Commissions

Where a solicitor arranges an insurance policy, pension, the purchase of shares or similar transaction for a client, should he or she be allowed to receive commission from the insurance company or other financial institution in the same way as other brokers? The prospect of commission for the solictior introduces a clear conflict between the duty to promote the client's best interests and the solicitor's interest in successfully selling something to the client. In view of the firm statement contained in principle 15.04,[57] that a solicitor must not act where his or her interests conflict with those of the client, it might be thought that solicitors should be barred from receiving such commission. This, however, is not the case; practice rule 10[58] allows commission provided the following conditions are met. Solicitors must account to their clients (i.e. pay to them) all commission of over £20. But, if the solicitor discloses in writing the amount of the commission or how it is calculated, and the client consents, then it can be retained by the solicitor. The client's consent, it appears, does not have to be in writing under the Rules, but the Law Society recommends this in its detailed guidance on the rules.[59] Any material excess on the original written calculation of the amount must be handed over to the client. This rule is in accordance with the normal law that a fiduciary or trustee shall not make a secret profit from his trust.

There is no specific requirement in either practice rule 10 or the Law Society's guidance thereon, contained in Annex 14G, that the client should be advised to take independent advice, for example where the commission is particularly significant in amount. However, elsewhere in the *Guide*, in principle 15.04, which deals specifically with conflict of interest, the Law Society does stress the need to advise a client to obtain independent advice in cases where, for example, a solicitor sells something to a client. Indeed, in this circumstance, the Law Society advises the solicitor not to go ahead with the transaction if the client refuses to take such advice.[60] There is no obvious reason why this advice should not also apply to large commissions. This principle is one of general professional practice, and perhaps of the law of equity, within which the specific provisions of the Solicitors' Practice Rules must be read.[61]

---

[56] See Chap. 8, below on wasted costs.

[57] N. Taylor (ed.), *The Guide to the Professional Conduct of Solicitors* (London, The Law Society, 1996) at 276, hereafter the *Law Society Guide*.

[58] *Ibid.*, at para.14.14.

[59] *Ibid.*, at 269 and paras. 4 and 5.

[60] See paras. 1 and 4 of the guidance on principle 15.05.

[61] It may be argued that these rules on commission are not in accord with the ordinary law on the duties of fiduciaries, in which case the law would prevail over the Rules. See A. Crawley and

It might be argued that these rules are not necessarily contrary to the interest of the client because, if the solicitor receives commission in respect of the transaction, then his bill to the client may (but not must) be reduced. Nevertheless, many scandals in the financial services industry have, at their root, the desire of commissioned agents to represent that they are giving a client disinterested advice when in fact their advice is influenced by the commission available. Disinterest is supposed to be the gold standard which distinguishes the advice of the professional lawyer from that of other types of agent. Allowing such commission may therefore be regarded as dangerous to the long-term interest of the profession, that it be seen too offer disinterested advice, as well as to clients.

C. NEGOTIATING THE FEE WITH THE CLIENT

Except where the fees are fixed, as is the case with much legally aided work and some litigation, it is for the solicitor and client to agree, subject to the possibility of taxation, the amount to be paid for the work. How should this be done? Does the legislation or *The Guide to Professional Conduct* lay down any special rules, or is this matter left to the parties under the normal rules of contract?

General Rules on Negotiating Fees

First, what information does the solicitor have to provide for the client before finalising the financial terms of the retainer? There are no rules or specific legislation on this. However, in 1991 the Law Society promulgated written professional standards on information on costs, to supplement the introduction of Rule 15 of the Solicitors' Practice Rules 1990. This rule requires solicitors to ensure that clients are given appropriate information on the progress of their case and that each practice sets up a complaints procedure for clients.[62] The Standards, which are reproduced in the *Law Society Guide* in chapter 13 on client care (and, surprisingly, are not mentioned in chapter 14 covering fees) are simply guidance and not binding rules.[63] They are, notoriously, frequently disregarded.[64] Solicitors are constantly reminded of their importance by the Law Society, the OSS and others as can be seen in the publication, *Client Care*. They point out that cost quotations are expected from all others who do work for us,

C. Bramall, "Professional Rules, Codes and Principles Affecting Solicitors" in R. Cranston (ed.), *Legal Ethics and Professional Responsibility* (Oxford, Clarendon Press, 1995), at 104.

[62] See further on complaints Chap. 5.

[63] In May 1997 the Law Society issued a Consultation Paper proposing that information on costs should be contained in a new code of written professional standards attached to a new practice rule 15: see *Law Society Gazette*, 14 May 1997, at 26.

[64] See Research and Policy Planning Unit, *Quality of Solicitors' Practice Management*, Research Study No. 10 (London, Law Society, RPPU, 1993); NACAB Report 1995; Ombudsman Annual Report 1995 and National Consumer Council Report, *Solicitors and Client Care* (NCC, 1994).

so why not solicitors? More recently Lord Woolf has firmly recommended that it should be a professional obligation for solicitors to explain their charges to clients.[65]

Solicitors are advised in the Standards to "consider with clients whether the likely outcome will justify the expense or risk involved".[66] Solicitors, on taking instructions, are required to "give the best information possible" about likely costs, how the fee will be calculated, and when and how it will be paid. This information need not be given in writing. However, on confirming instructions, the solicitor should in writing "record whether a fee has been agreed" and whether it includes VAT and disbursements, and also confirm oral estimates. Non-contentious business agreements and agreements on costs in contentious matters must, in any case, be in writing under the Solicitors' Act 1974 sections 57 and 59. The solicitor should also discuss the possibility of legal aid, and insurance cover for costs, with the client.[67] This does not have to be in writing. Further the solicitor should inform private clients that they may set a limit on costs, as well as explain that it is often not possible to estimate costs in advance.

Once the matter is under way, the Professional Standards advise that the solicitor should inform clients every six months "in appropriate cases" of the "approximate" costs to date and /or deliver an interim bill. In contentious matters the solicitor should tell the client the rules on liability for costs, both where the case is won or lost, for example that even if the case is won they may not recover all or, indeed, any of the costs for which they will be personally liable. Legally aided clients should be told of the effect of the statutory charge, of their obligation to pay any contribution and other information on their possible liability for costs. Again it is not specified that any of this information should be in writing. Solicitors can advertise their fees provided they comply with the Solicitors' Publicity Code 1990. Such publicity must not be misleading, nor must it make direct comparison with the charges of any other identifiable solicitor.[68] Statements in relation to fees must be clear, for example on whether VAT and disbursements are included. Solicitors cannot advertise that their fees start from a certain figure, nor can they quote composite fees.

As noted above, barristers negotiate their fees with solicitors through their clerks. Their Code simply states that barristers may charge on any basis they think fit, subject to the general prohibition on unlawful contingency fees and on working for a fixed salary. A barrister may refuse a brief, despite the cab-rank rule, if the proposed fee is other than "proper" having regard to the complexity, length or difficulty of the case and the experience of the barrister. Barristers may also stipulate that their fee shall be paid in advance.[69] Barristers may advertise

---

[65]   *Access to Justice Final Report*, n. 3 above, at 79.

[66]   *The Law Society Guide*, n. 57 above, at 282. Lord Woolf recommends that if this is not done the court should take this into account when awarding costs: *ibid.*, at 80.

[67]   Not to advise about legal aid in appropriate cases would amount to negligence.

[68]   *Advertising Code*, para. 2(d).

[69]   *Bar Code*, n. 9 above, para. 502.

their fees but, like solicitors, must not compare themselves with other barristers.[70]

Negotiating Conditional Fees

Conditional fees are subject to a greater amount of legislative control than other fees. The Conditional Fee Agreement Regulations[71] require the solicitor to draw the client's attention to certain information. Any conditional fee agreement made between them (which must be in writing) must state that this has been done. It need not, however, set out the detail of the information actually given. The solicitor must give information on:

(i)   whether the client might be entitled to legal aid and under what conditions;

(ii) the client's liability for any fees and disbursements (for example, if either or both will be charged only if the case is successful, how success is defined);

(iii) the circumstances in which the client may have to pay the other side's costs;

(iv) how costs are calculated (for example, what the basic hourly rate is and what percentage uplift will be charged as a success fee) and whether they are limited by reference to the amount of damages recovered;

(v)   the availability of taxation of costs.[72]

Note that the solicitor does not have to give the client information which will enable the client to compare the likely costs under a conditional fee arrangement with those under a conventional fee arrangement. Although the uplift charged cannot exceed 100 per cent, there is no statutory provision preventing the fees charged from exceeding either the amount recovered or any fixed percentage of that sum. Strong views were expressed in favour of such limitations in the House of Lords when approving the regulations. As noted above, the limited research published on conditional fees indicates that in fact solicitors do comply with Law Society advice and limit the success fee to 25 per cent of the sum recovered.[73]

D. CONTROLLING THE AMOUNT CHARGED

Lord Woolf, perhaps optimistically, suggests that there are eight requirements that clients should impose on solicitors to control fees including preventing major litigation strategies without instructions, preventing meetings when

---

[70] *Ibid.*, paras. 307.1 and 2.
[71] SI 1995 No.1675.
[72] Conditional Fee Agreements Regulations 1995, cl. 3.
[73] Yarrow, n. 42 above.

telephone calls will suffice and emphasising that the case belongs to the client.[74] Usually , however, control comes *after* the event, in the form of a challenge to fees.

There are a number of ways in which the amount charged by a lawyer can be challenged, quite apart from the general procedures for complaints and discipline dealt with in Chapter 5. Fees may be taxed by the court, reviewed by the Law Society, controlled by the court via the wasted costs jurisdiction and also, in legally aided cases, controlled by the Legal Aid Board. In the context of this book it is possible only to outline these controls. The central question to be considered is how far is it possible for the client, or the losing party, who may in fact be paying the other side's lawyer, to challenge the amount charged under the retainer. In other words, how far is it possible to ensure that the lawyer does genuinely act in the client's best interests, or in the interests of justice, in relation to charging fees?

Taxation by the Court

Court control of the costs that lawyers charge is achieved through the taxation procedure. There are two types of taxation:

(i)   the taxation of the winner's costs where they are to be paid by the loser as a result of a costs order at the end of the litigation; these are known as party and party costs.

(ii) the taxation of the lawyer's costs that are to be paid by his or her own client. These are known as solicitor and client costs. This taxation can be applied for by the client in both contentious and non contentious business.[75]

The principles applied differ in the two types of taxation. When taxing party and party costs the taxing officer is concerned to allow only such costs as were reasonably necessarily incurred in the conduct of the litigation. In the taxation of solicitor and client costs, much will depend on the terms of the solicitor's retainer and what the client instructed the solicitor to do. In both cases the court will concern itself only with the costs that are specifically challenged and not evaluate the solicitor's bill as a whole unless this is asked for. In practice, taxation of solicitor and client costs is rare. The mechanism does not, therefore, provide much control over escalating costs. A major reason for this is that the client must pay the costs of taxation unless the bill is reduced by more than one fifth.[76] Moreover the solicitor must tell the client of the availability of taxation only before *suing* for the costs. The exception is the case of conditional fee arrangements, when such information must be contained in the agreement itself. Of course, party and party taxation, which is almost invariably applied for by the

---

[74] Final report, Ch. 7 para.30.
[75] Solicitors' Act 1974 ss. 68 and 70.
[76] *Ibid.*, s.70(9).

loser at the end of litigation, will often also act as a protection for the winning client. Few solicitors are happy to present their client with an enormous bill for work which the taxing officer considered unnecessary. A third party who has paid, or is liable for, the costs can also apply for taxation but cannot apply for a remuneration certificate from the Law Society.[77]

A number of issues about court taxation of costs concerned Lord Woolf. First, in contentious matters, it is available only in the context of litigation. Where the case is settled—the vast majority of cases—the court has no jurisdiction. He recommends that the court should have jurisdiction over unlitigated settlements in order to facilitate the economic settlement of cases without litigation. Secondly, the costs of interlocutory matters are usually postponed until the end of the case. At that stage the loser may face a bill inflated by purely tactical interlocutory proceedings. Lord Woolf considers that such costs should be awarded at the conclusion of the interlocutory proceedings and paid forthwith. Finally he argues that the order should reflect the real need for the proceedings and be proportionate to the value of the issue being litigated.[78]

Review by the Law Society

A costs review by the Law Society is available only in relation to costs in non-contentious matters where no non-contentious business agreement has been entered into.[79] As noted above, clients rarely apply for taxation of their solicitors' bills, probably because of the risk of incurring further costs in so doing. The Law Society has long provided a free service for clients reviewing bills under £50,000 in non-contentious matters.[80] It is for the *solicitor*, at the request of the client, to apply for a review by the Law Society, which will result in the issue of a remuneration certificate. The certificate will state what would be a fair and reasonable charge for the work covered by the bill. It will not increase the bill. A solicitor must inform his client of the right to apply for a remuneration certificate before suing or threatening to sue his client for the fees. He need not do this before sending the bill (or even making a further demand for payment). Similarly, where the solicitor deducts the costs from money held on behalf of the client, and the client objects to the costs in writing within three months of

---

[77] For details of such certificates see below.

[78] See *Final Report*, n. 3 above, at 83. This view is increasingly being reflected in judicial decisions. For a recent example see *Bailey* v. *IBC. Vehicles Ltd*. [1998] 3 All ER 570 at 575.

[79] Under the Solicitors' Act 1974 s.57. See Solicitors' (Non-Contentious Business) Remuneration Order, cl. 9(c). A non-contentious business agreement is an agreement made in writing between solicitor and client on non-contentious business remuneration. It must be signed by both. It may be sued upon and, as such, is subject to review on taxation of costs. A client may be induced into making such an agreement without realising that by doing so he or she forfeits the right to use the remuneration certificate procedure. This rule was criticised by the Legal Services Ombudsman in his *Annual Report* (1996) at 15.

[80] This limit was first introduced in 1994 by the Solicitors' (Non-contentious Business) Remuneration Order, n. 79 above.

delivery of the bill, the solicitor must inform the client of his right to apply for a remuneration certificate.[81] A major condition, first introduced by the 1994 Order, clause 11, requires the client requesting a remuneration certificate to pay 50 per cent of the costs plus VAT and disbursements. The Law Society does have power to waive this requirement. The client cannot get a remuneration certificate after the expiry of the time limits nor, most importantly, where the bill has already been paid. The exception is where the payment was made by deduction from client money held by the solicitor. Nor can a remuneration certificate be obtained where a court has ordered taxation of the bill.[82] Failure by the solicitor to comply with the certificate may result in disciplinary proceedings.

The Law Society review procedure has obvious limitations and is little used by clients compared to the numbers who, in surveys, express concern about solicitors' costs. About 2,000 bills are reviewed each year. This small number may be due to the procedure being little known to clients. It may also be due to the feeling that the Law Society is unlikely to disagree with the solicitor on the matter of costs. Lay clients have obvious difficulties in estimating the work that has to be done and therefore the reasonableness of the fee. In fact, about 56 per cent of bills considered under the Law Society procedure were reduced in 1996, a percentage that has been rising in recent years.[83]

Wasted Costs

The wasted costs jurisdiction under the Supreme Court Act 1981 section 51(6), as amended by the Courts and Legal Services Act 1990, is another method by which solicitors' and barristers' costs can be controlled at the behest of both their clients and the other side. This jurisdiction has greatly expanded in recent years. It is dealt with in detail in Chapter 8.

Legally Aided Cases

The control of costs in legally aided cases rests, to a large extent, with the Legal Aid Board. This control is achieved partly by limiting certificates, for example, to obtaining counsel's opinion before issuing proceedings, or by the increasing use of standard fees. This is designed to protect both the public purse and the other side, who will be less likely to have to respond to unmeritorious actions. It will also protect assisted clients if they are paying a contribution or will be liable under the statutory charge. In some cases, however, it may prevent lawyers from undertaking work that both they and clients consider necessary.

---

[81] *The Law Society Guide*, n. 57 above, at 254.
[82] Solicitors' (Non-contentious Business) Remuneration Order, n. 79 above, cl. 9.
[83] See *Report of the SCB 1996*, at 10. The *Royal Commission on Legal Services*, Vol.II at 545 reported in 1979 that only 20% of bills were reduced.

The same process of taxation by the court applies to legally aided cases as to those that are privately funded. The legally aided client can take part in the taxation process if he or she has an interest in the outcome. Such an interest may arise if the client is liable for a contribution or because the client is affected by the statutory charge.[84] The costs of the taxation will be covered by the legal aid certificate. Where the costs are under £1,000 the solicitor can opt for the Legal Aid Board to assess the bill rather than the court.

E. RECOVERING THE FEE FROM THE CLIENT

Having negotiated the fee and dealt with any review or taxation, are there any special rules or guidance on enforcing the payment of the fee?[85] In relation to solicitors, the relationship between lawyer and client is basically contractual and the general rules of contract normally apply. The contract can stipulate for payments on account for example[86] and solicitors are free to sue if fees are not paid. There are, however, some special provisions, in particular relating to contentious business agreements.[87] Certain general rules are also more significant in lawyer–client relationships than in other relationships. Two in particular should be noted: first, the rules conferring a lien over papers and property held by the solicitor where the fee is not paid; secondly, the rules permitting a solicitor to refuse to do further work until he or she has been paid.

Billing

Bills must be sent to clients within a reasonable time of the conclusion of the matter, but no guidance is given on what is reasonable.[88] The bill should be reasonably detailed and must distinguish between fees and disbursements. In contentious matters the client has a right to demand a detailed bill under the Solicitors Act 1974, section 64.

The Solicitor's Lien

The solicitor's lien enables the solicitor to retain papers and property belonging to the client pending the payment of the bill. The lien does not arise until a

---

[84] Legal Aid (General) Regulations, para. 11.

[85] As already noted, the Bar still adheres to the notion that there is no legally binding contract between barristers and solicitors, and therefore suing for the fees is not possible. See *Bar Code*, n. above,, Annex D, paras. 25, 26. If a solicitor fails to pay a barrister, the ultimate sanction is that the Chair of the Bar instructs members of the Bar not to accept work from that solicitor: see Annex D, para. 17.

[86] A contractual stipulation is not needed for payments on account in contentious matters. See *The Law Society Guide*, n. above, principle 14.01.

[87] Solicitors' Act 1974 ss.57(4), 60(2).

[88] See *The Law Guide,* n. 57 above, at 237.

properly itemised bill has been delivered to the client. It applies to all papers, in the view of the Law Society, not simply those relating to the unpaid bill.[89] This power is not of course unique to solicitors; any person who has done work for another may retain the property on which the work has been done pending payment. Solicitors also frequently have possession of large sums of client funds. But holding on to papers until a bill is paid will make it difficult for the client to instruct another solicitor. This is a particular problem for clients who, without first paying the bill, want to pursue a negligence claim against the first solicitor. The Law Society recommend that, where a solicitor is discharged by his client, that solicitor should release the papers to the successor solicitor if an undertaking is given to pay the outstanding costs on the conclusion of the matter. However there is no obligation to accept such an undertaking.[90] The Court has a general jurisdiction and discretion to order a solicitor to deliver up any documents in his custody.[91] It will normally do this where the client needs the documents for continuing litigation. An undertaking to restore the documents to the solicitor at the end of the litigation would normally be ordered. Further conditions might be imposed by the court, depending on the circumstances of the case. For example, in *Ismail v. Richards Butler* the ex-client was required to provide further security for the payment of the outstanding bills.[92]

Suing for Fees

In both contentious and non-contentious matters the solicitor cannot sue on the bill before one month has elapsed from its delivery to the client, unless the court gives him permission so to do. Where the bill relates to a contentious matter the solicitor must always seek the leave of the court to sue.[93] Obviously the client can ask for the bill to be taxed. The court has powers where the solicitor sues on the bill in contentious matters to set aside the agreement on fees with the client if it is unfair or unreasonable, and order the bill to be taxed.[94] In non-contentious matters the solicitor cannot sue unless he has first informed the client of the right to apply for a remuneration certificate and the right to seek taxation. It can be seen from this that solicitors are not as free as other business people to sue for their fees. This follows from the fact that the amount of their fees is not simply a matter of free negotiation with the client.

---

[89] See *Law Society Gazette* answer to an ethics problem in Aug. 1996. See also *Ismail* v. *Richards Butler* [1996] 2 All ER 506.
[90] The *Law Society Guide*, n. 57 above, at 12.12, n. 5.
[91] Solicitors' Act 1974 s.68.
[92] [1996] 2 All ER 506.
[93] Solicitors' Act 1974, s.61.
[94] *Ibid.*

Terminating the Retainer

In general the solicitor can terminate the retainer with the client only for good reason. Is the client's failure to make a payment on account a good reason? In general it is, though in non-contentious matters there must be an agreement with the client to make such payments in relation to fees but not disbursements. In contentious matters a specific agreement is not required and a failure to make a payment on account is an acceptable reason for terminating the retainer on reasonable notice.[95]

Collecting Fees and Confidentiality

The duty of confidentiality and legal privilege are not waived where the solicitor sues the client for fees.[96]

F. LOOKING AFTER CLIENT FUNDS

Introduction

The rules on solicitors' accounts and the management of client funds have traditionally occupied most of the pages of the *Professional Practice Guide*. Until very recently, this area was also the only aspect of professional ethics forming a compulsory part of professional training. The rules, together with those on investment business, still occupy nearly 250 pages of the current issue of the *Guide*. This is not really surprising; it is vital that clients should have absolute confidence that solicitors will deal properly with their funds and that they will receive compensation if something unlawful happens which causes loss. The professional relationship would otherwise be jeopardised. It is significant that this area of professional practice is almost entirely based on binding rules made under the Solicitors' Act 1974; it is not left to discretionary guidance. There are five sets of rules, the most important being the Solicitors' Accounts Rules 1991. It is not intended to deal with them in detail in this book.[97] The aim here is to consider the ethical principles behind the rules and to examine the way in which these principles are given practical effect.

Accounting rules are needed both to ensure that solicitors act in the best interests of the client and to prevent solicitors acting fraudulently or making a secret profit from a fiduciary relationship. They are also needed in purely practical terms to ensure that client funds are not confused with those of the solicitors' practice.

[95] The *Law Society Guide*, n. 57 above, at para. 14.01.
[96] See Chap. 10 on confidentiality.
[97] The detail can be found in the *Law Society Guide*, n. 57 above, and in J. A. Holland, *Cordery on Solicitors* (London, Butterworths, 1995).

This protects clients in the event of the solicitors' insolvency or other indebtedness. Finally, they are needed to ensure efficient and proper book-keeping systems in solicitors' offices. The Law Society stresses that responsibility for adhering to the rules lies with all the partners of a firm; it cannot be delegated to one partner.[98]

The Basic Accounting System

The system laid down by the rules relies on the requirement to maintain two separate sets of accounts, the client account and the office account. In addition there must be a controlled trust account to hold money that the solicitor receives as a sole trustee. Separate accounts ensure that neither the bank, building society or solicitor can use the monies in one account for the purposes of the others, i.e. funds in a client account cannot be used to satisfy the debts or expenses of the firm. The rules then lay down precisely what monies must go into the client account and what into the office account, and what withdrawals may legitimately take place from both. Any money held or received by the solicitor on account of his client must be paid without delay into the client account, unless the client instructs otherwise. This includes money paid by the client for disbursements and payments on account of costs.[99] Where a single cheque consists of a mixture of client and office monies, the payment may be divided into each account or, if not, all of it must be paid into the client account.

Compliance Rules

There are also rules designed to ensure compliance with the accounts rules. First, the Law Society has the power to order that the books be inspected at random and without giving any reason for the inspection.[100] Secondly, annual accounts prepared by an accountant must be delivered to the Law Society by the firm within six months of the end of the accounting period. Failure to do so, or lateness in doing so, may result in the refusal of a practising certificate.[101] The rules governing accountants' annual reports are the Accountants Reports Rules 1991, which have been tightened up by the Accountants Report (Role of Reporting Accountant) (Amendment) Rules 1995. These came into force in September 1998 but will, of course, relate to the financial year 1997–8. Under the new rules all reporting accountants must be registered auditors. Their terms of

---

[98] The *Law Society Guide*, n. 57 above, at para. 28.03.

[99] There are some exceptions to this rule and payment for certain disbursements already paid from the office account can be paid into the office account. See *ibid.*, chap. 28.11, n. 3.

[100] Solicitors' Accounts Rules 1991, r. 27. The books can also be inspected as a result of third party complaint in which case the Society requires *prima facie* evidence of a ground of complaint: cl. 27(4). There were 1,266 such Accounts Rules visits in 1995. They are conducted by the Chartered Association of Certified Accountants.

[101] Solicitors' Act 1973, s.12.

engagement, which must be in writing, must incorporate the Law Society's standard terms. The accountant *may* inform the Law Society if his employment is terminated following a qualified report or after raising concerns with the Law Society. The accountant now has to complete a standard-form checklist for the Law Society as well as producing a report. This is to provide the Society with greater assurance that the audit work has actually been done. Thirdly, breaches of the accounts rules may result in disciplinary proceedings. Indeed such breaches are the most common reasons for disciplinary complaints and penalties. Protection for the client who suffers as a result of any breach of these rules is assured via the Solicitors' Indemnity Fund, established under section 37 of the 1974 Act, on which see Chapter 5.

Interest on Client Accounts

One issue relating to accounts has, in the past, been the subject of considerable controversy. What should be done with the interest earned on client accounts? In the absence of specific instructions to the contrary, most solicitors maintain one client account where all client funds are lodged. Individual clients may not have a large sum deposited with the solicitor, or sums may be in the account for a short period of time only. But the total amount in the account at any one time may be considerable, and interest will accrue on this balance. If the solicitor takes this interest, then he is unlawfully profiting at the expense of the clients. This was clearly held in *Brown* v. *IRC.*,[102] a case where the Inland Revenue wanted to charge a solicitor tax on interest in client accounts. The court pointed out that this money did not belong to the solicitor, to the surprise of solicitors in general. The Law Society, citing administrative difficulties produced by *Brown,* got section 33 inserted into the Solicitors' Act 1974 under which, *except as defined in the rules*, a solicitor is *not* liable to account to the client for interest on client accounts.[103]

Rule 20 of the Solicitors' Accounts Rules 1991, made under section 33, appears to reverse the thrust of the section by stating that solicitors *shall* account to clients for any interest earned on deposits, whether that interest is earned in a separate designated account for that client, or in a general client account. This rule is subject to exceptions. Where the sum held is small, or is held for only a short time, then no accounting is required. Thus, under rule 21, the solicitor need not account where he holds £1,000 of client's money for under eight weeks, £2,000 for under four weeks, £10,000 for under two weeks and £20,000 for under one week. Even where the solicitor holds more than £20,000 for under one week, he need account only if it is "fair and reasonable" in all the circumstances.[104] Where the solicitor holds funds as a stakeholder, for example

---

[102] [1964] 3 All ER 119.
[103] See Act s.33(3).
[104] R. 21, para. (ii).

a deposit in relation to a house purchase, then he must account for the interest to the person to whom the stake is paid.

These rules do not apply if a contrary arrangement is made in writing between the solicitor and client.[105] Theoretically, therefore, the solicitor could ask the client to agree that all the interest earned in the client account should belong to the solicitor. However the Law Society counsels against such an arrangement in its *Guide*. It points out that the client in such a case will probably be in no position to give an informed consent. The Law Society advice concludes "contracting out would never be appropriate where it is against the client's interests".[106] The basic assumption that the solicitor will benefit from interest on client accounts is underlined by another rule. This states that the bank holding the account must be instructed by the solicitor to credit the interest earned on the general client account, or an individual client account where the interest goes to the solicitor, to the office account.[107]

The Law Society justifies the rules on client account interest by reference to the *de minimis* principle that applies to commission (see above), under which a solicitor should not have to account to the client for sums around £20. However, of course, an amount which is *de minimis* to an individual client may not be *de minimis* when all clients are added together. It is not known how much solicitors benefit from interest on client accounts. In 1984 the Consumer Council issued a discussion paper on the issue.[108] It estimated, conservatively, that it amounted to over £40 million a year. Since 1984, the rules have been tightened up in favour of clients, interest rates have declined and more use is now made of electronic money transfers. This means that less money is in fact held in client accounts in many transactions. However, client interest is still being retained by solicitors. If it is still not feasible to account to each client because of the costs of identifying and paying over such small amounts, what should be done with it? In some jurisdictions, for example, in Australia and in Ontario, Canada, a proportion of this interest is paid into a Foundation managed by the Law Society and devoted to supporting a wide variety of charitable and *pro bono* legal activities, such as educational scholarships, supporting law centres or libraries, research into the justice system and public interest advocacy centres. This was suggested for England and Wales by the Consumer Council in 1984 but nothing has come of it. This is not surprising in view of the recession which hit the profession in the late 1980s, from which it has not yet fully emerged. More controversially, in some jurisdictions, for example, in Victoria, Australia, client interest is used to finance compensation funds for the clients of fraudulent lawyers. Modern computing makes it possible and simple to calculate client

---

[105] R. 26(a).

[106] The *Law Society Guide*, n. 57 above, Annex 28E, para. 22 at 637.

[107] Accounts Rules 6.

[108] National Consumer Council, *Whose Interest?: Soclicitors and their Clients Accounts: A Discussion Paper* (London, National Consumer Council, 1984).

interest and pay it to each individual client.[109] This is clearly in the client's best interest and it is therefore troubling that the rules have not been amended to reflect this.

CONCLUSION

Ensuring effective and fair control by clients over the fees charged by lawyers is difficult. Even the government, in the context of legal aid, and corporate clients experience this problem. This may be exacerbated by the introduction and extension of conditional fees. As already noted, complaints on costs form the majority of those made to the OSS and the Legal Services Ombudsman. This is not surprising. There is an essential conflict of interest between a lawyer and client on the issue of the fee charged which cannot be resolved by high-sounding rhetoric in codes of conduct. Moreover, the high cost of access to justice is now a key political issue, at least in relation to litigation. The introduction of the wasted costs procedure is one response to this. Another solution which is gaining ground, and which lawyers find threatening, is delegalisation. This can be seen in the family law field, for example where the use of various types of conciliation and mediation is increasing. Alongside these developments the imposition of standard or fixed fees is likely to increase. They already exist in relation to much legal aid work. They will be extended to the "fast track" litigation procedure for cases under £15,000 once Lord Woolf's proposals are enacted. The advantage of this type of proposal is that the control of costs becomes automatic and ceases to be the responsibility of the client.

There is no doubt that the extension of conditional fees to most civil cases and the proposed cuts in Legal Aid for such cases both exacerbate the tensions outlined in this chapter and present new ethical challenges for lawyers. Disapproval of conditional (and contingency) fees is still voiced by many senior lawyers. For example Lord Ackner in the debate in the House of Lords on conditional fees stated:

> "The lawyer with a financial stake in the outcome of litigation has a concern to win the case which may distort the advice he gives and may even tempt him into unethical conduct."[110]

However, a non-lawyer, Lord Allen, put the contrary view. Conditional fees looked "rather different if one is just an ordinary person who is not poor enough for legal aid and not rich enough to embark upon litigation with equanimity . . . To people like me it seems that at last there is some prospect of access to justice becoming more open".[111]

---

[109] See A. Evans, "Professional Ethics North and South: Interest on Clients' Trust Funds and Lawyer Fraud. An Opportunity to Redeem Professionalism" (1996) 3:3 *International Journal of the Legal Profession* 281.
[110] *HL Debs.*, 1613, 1 Nov. 1994, col.789.
[111] *HL Debs.*, 12 June 1995, col. 1560.

The use of conditional fees should be closely monitored, both independently and by the Law Society, and the incidence of ethical problems noted. The temptation for solicitors to overestimate the risk, and therefore the level of the success fee, is obvious and clearly contrary to the best interest of clients. But it seems that the government is more interested in reducing legal aid expenditure. There is a substantial risk that it will not monitor conditional fees closely because it will not want its initiative to be seen to have failed. The profession should ensure that it is done, in the interest of clients.[112]

---

[112] See views of Lord Ackner in (1998) 148 *New Law Journal* 477.

PART V
Dispute Resolution

Introduction

In Part 1 an it was argued that the distinctive social purpose of the legal profession was to assist clients in gaining justice and, in doing so, to support the legitimacy of the democratic state. In common law systems the idea of justice has been identified with the adversary system. A characteristic of adversary systems is not that trials are frequently held but the large number of settlements without trial. Settlement can be viewed both positively and negatively. Consensual dispute resolution may be preferred to adversarial proceedings. Open conflict is thereby apparently reduced and costs avoided. But when pressure to settle is produced by excessive cost, delay in getting cases to court and unduly lengthy hearings, the value of settlement is put in doubt. Unfortunately these are endemic features of adversarial justice. The identification of lawyers with adversarial justice, and therefore with cost, delay, and other arguably systemic defects, ensures that the weaknesses of adversarial justice are also weaknesses in attempts to legitimise the lawyer's role and ethic.[1]

Government has become increasingly sensitive to the allegation that citizens are obtaining more rights but that access to justice is becoming less affordable. How can access to justice be expanded without placing additional burdens on the exchequer? A number of enquiries down the years have made proposals which address procedural problems in the adversary system. The core problems, however, remain. The most recent policy reviews, comprising Lord Woolf's Report on civil justice, the Green and White Papers on legal aid and Lord Irvine's consultation paper on conditional fees, challenge aspects of the adversary system and, therefore, those ethics of lawyers based on adversarial assumptions. If implemented, these proposals would:

(a) diversify dispute resolution mechanisms, making them more appropriate to the kind of dispute and increasing the congruence between the procedure used and the costs recoverable[2];

(b) expand the providers of legal services so as to reduce cost through competition;

(c) substantially limit the scope of legal aid; and

(d) permit methods of funding litigation which shift the expense and risks onto lawyers, through conditional fees, or spread it more widely through legal expenses insurance.

[1] Despite differences in the legal systems in the USA and the UK, the concerns of "the cost, delay and inaccessibility of the legal process, the high level of unmet legal need, the range of unprotected interests, the frequency of professional incompetence, neglect, incivility and adversarial abuse and the inadequacy of institutional response" (D. L. Rhode, "Ethics by the Pervasive Method" (1992) 42 *Journal of Legal Education* 31) are common to both.

[2] Lord Woolf, *Access to Justice: Final Report to the Lord Chancellor on the Civil Justice System in England and Wales* (London, HMSO, 1996), hereafter *Final Report*.

As a consequence the role of lawyers in dispute resolution could change significantly. The implications for the ethics of lawyers are profound.

The implementation of the Woolf Report may also herald a more co-operative ethic for the resolution of civil disputes. This has been accepted by the professional bodies, who have suggested that the Bar's and solicitors' work in conciliation and out-of-court settlement needs to be developed further. Moreover, the profession has itself proposed that working parties of judges, barristers and solicitors should lay down effective means for bringing to an early conclusion civil and criminal cases which do not need to be fought at trial.[3] The aim of making the processes of dispute resolution cheaper is to increase access to justice. But there is little concrete evidence that this is achieved in fact. Legal practitioners "in the field" remain suspicious of new methods of dispute resolution.[4]

Chapter 11 explores in greater detail the lawyer's role in achieving the vast numbers of annual settlements of actions and, in particular, strategy and tactics in litigation and negotiation. Chapter 12 looks at the duties and role of the advocate. The final chapter in Part V explores one of the growing areas of work in which lawyers are competing with other professionals, ADR. Roberts reminds us that ways of resolving disputes are culturally and socially determined.[5] Our familiarity with adversarial justice may have blinded us to some of its failings. The fact that lawyers are often the strongest advocates of features of the present system reinforces this point. But are lawyers being myopic or self-serving when they support the adversarial system? Could it be that the adversarial trial really is the best way we have of discovering the truth? The growth of interest in Alternative Dispute Resolution (ADR) in the UK is partly as a result of a generally positive reaction in the USA,[6] and partly because ADR is perceived to be cheaper and quicker than adjudication. Arbitration, expert determination, mediation and conciliation are all gaining ground as alternatives to trial in different areas of legal activity. In the longer term, they may become preferred methods of dispute resolution in the vast majority of cases or they may remain adjuncts to the litigation process. The chapter considers the broader frameworks of dispute resolution and the ethical issues for the profession which spring from the involvement of lawyers in ADR.

---

[3] General Council of the Bar, *Quality of Justice: The Bar's Response* (London, Butterworth, 1989), para. 2.29.

[4] Solicitors were found to be "generally unenthusiastic" or "positively hostile" about a mediation pilot scheme operating from the Central London County Court since 1996, although many had not actually tried the scheme: L. Tsang "Research finds Solicitors are Hostile to Mediation Scheme" (1998) *The Lawyer*, 4 Aug., at 2.

[5] S. Roberts, *Order and Dispute* (Harmondsworth., Penguin, 1979).

[6] Lady Marre CBE, *A Time for Change: Report on the Committee on the Future of the Legal Profession* (London, The General Council of the Bar, The Law Society, 1988). The Report noted that over half of law schools in the USA offered courses: para. 11.7.

13

Litigation and Bargaining in an Adversarial System

A. INTRODUCTION

Since the war the volume of litigation has increased substantially. For the population at large the advent of legal aid substantially increased access to justice. In the 1960s there was a growth of legal services programmes for the poor and an increase in Legal Aid.[1] During and after the 1970s a burgeoning paralegal sector, located in Citizens Advice Bureaux and Law Centres, began to provide significant services, particularly in the area of welfare law.[2] The increase in crime and the increase in commercial activity have both led to increases in litigation. In recent years a crisis in the system of civil justice has arisen. Litigation has become more complex and unpredictable. The cost of litigation has also increased. Unpredictability and cost affect litigation decisions made by clients, particularly when, as in the English system, the losing litigant pays the winner's costs. What responsibility do lawyers have for either exploiting unpredictability and cost or mitigating the impact of these factors on the outcome of disputes?

Unpredictability, delay and cost can be used by lawyers as litigation tactics. Some clients, large organisations for example, are often said to be neutral about litigation risks; they are able to absorb the costs. Individuals, particularly those funding litigation themselves, are more likely to be risk-averse; they are anxious about the cost, trouble and risks inherent in litigation.[3] Clients receiving Legal Aid are doubly fortunate. Win or lose, their own costs are paid and their opponents in litigation are unlikely to recover any costs.[4] A non-legally aided party involved in litigation with a legally aided party has a massive incentive to settle. Imbalances in the positions of the parties produce different pressures towards

---

[1] The first Law Centre was established in the UK in 1970. During a similar period there was an increase in public interest law centres in the USA: See National Consumer Council, *Ordinary Justice: Legal Services and Courts in England and Wales: A Consumer View* (London, HMSO, 1989) and M. Galanter, "Law Abounding: Legalisation Around the North Alantic" (1992) 55 *Modern Law Review* 1 at 12.

[2] Lady Marre CBE, *A Time for Change: Report on the Committee on the Future of the Legal Profession* (London, The General Council of the Bar, The Law Society, 1988), chap. 9, hereafter the *Marre Report*.

[3] Galanter, n. 1 above, at 20.

[4] See H. Genn, *Hard Bargaining: Out of Court Settlement in Personal Injury Actions* (Oxford, Clarendon Press, 1987), at 85–96. Some legally aided clients have to pay a contribution, however, and the statutory charge can create problems.

settlement which may have little to do with the legal merit of a case. This has a considerable social cost. People with modest incomes may be unable to afford to pursue their legal remedies. Commercial enterprises may consider non-litigation alternatives, negotiating terms or declaring bankruptcy, for example.[5] While the search for better ways of processing claims, of reducing costs, present substantial political problems, "an effective system of redress is essential to the smooth operation of the market-place. Such a system is needed if people are to have respect for, and confidence in, the law.[6]

These criticisms of adversarial justice suggest the need for cheaper and quicker procedures. But even this would not produce an ideal system of dispute resolution. An example is the incremental exclusion of lawyers from disputes by raising of small claims limits in the county courts. In theory this reduces the burden of costs and therefore removes a considerable source of anxiety from the parties. But Baldwin found that raising the small claims arbitration limit has not led to increased usage, partly due to the unfavourable image of the civil courts.[7] The introduction of cheaper procedures, or even no cost rules, can be used tactically. Small businesses, for example, which may wish to sue chronic debtors, can find that low costs encourages the debtor to defend the action.[8] Tighter timetables favour larger firms which can mobilise resources quickly.[9] Where individuals run no risk of a costs penalty they may try to extract "nuisance" payments for dubious claims. Measures which might reduce cost may also exclude lawyers, to the detriment of those who really need them.[10]

The lawyer's duty in dealing with litigation is complex. It can be construed as a purely technical exercise, one in which the only constraint is whether a claim or defence is "arguable". It can be seen as a deeply ethical exercise; one in which lawyers shoulder responsibility for "justice" by deciding whether or not it is right in the circumstances to bring a particular claim or offer a particular defence. But there are many ways of interpreting such an ethic when there is no clear guidance. Lawyers who pursue an arguable point may argue that their efforts enhance the legitimacy of the system. Everyone is entitled to his or her day in court and to representation if he or she wishes it. Does this argument extend to settlement? Here, the ethical questions become more even more complex. Does achieving a fair, consensual settlement override the lawyer's obligation of fairness or honesty? How co-operative or combative should a lawyer be

[5] See R. E. Kagan, "The Routinization of Debt Collection: An Essay on Social Change and Conflict in the Courts" (1984) 18 *Law and Society Review* 323.

[6] R. Thomas, "A Code of Procedure for Small Claims: A Response to the Demand for Do-It-Yourself Litigation" (1982) 1 *Civil Justice Quarterly* 52, which discusses the small claims procedures of the county courts and the extent to which they meet the demand for access to justice in relation to small claims.

[7] J. Baldwin, *Monitoring the Rise of the Small Claims Limit: Litigant's Experiences of Different Forms of Adjudication* (London, Lord Chancellor's Department), at 74.

[8] T. Aldridge, "Downside of Procedural Reform", *Solicitors Journal*, 29 Nov. 1996, at 1142.

[9] C. Glasser, "Civil Procedure a Time for Change" in R. Smith (ed.), *Shaping the Future: New Directions in Legal Services* (London, Legal Action Group, 1995).

[10] R. Smith, "The Changing Motive of Legal Aid", in *ibid.*, at 209.

in settlement negotiations? How unfair to other parties and other lawyers can a lawyer be before it affects their reputation? One way of analysing these questions lies in theories of bargaining. Such theories also provide insight into the advantages and disadvantages of adversarial adjudication[11] and ADR, both of which are considered in later chapters, and the ethical issues involved in a shift from one paradigm of dispute resolution to the other. Before considering such theories, however, it is necessary to outline the context in which dispute bargaining takes place.

B. CRIMINAL LITIGATION

Much of the rationale for the current ethics of lawyers is based on criminal representation. A criminal justice system is the arena where we find the commitment to treat all citizens equally, and to evolve principles that can achieve this aim. It is, therefore, a fine testing ground of ethical principles, not just of lawyers but of the system as a whole. Although people may be guilty of horrible crimes, it is important to maintain the notion of an adequate defence, not least because a proper assessment of the facts increases the chances of correct verdicts and, where conviction results, enables a sentence which is *proportionate* to the crime to be imposed.[12] Research in both the USA and UK raises serious questions about the role of lawyers in criminal defence and whether they provide the level of service necessary to justify faith in adversarial justice. A recent study of criminal defence lawyers in the UK suggests that defendants often receive discontinuous representation, that is, different staff are assigned to deal with different stages of a case.[13] Solicitors specialising in criminal defence often spend most of their time in the magistrates' court while unqualified staff deal with other stages of the case. More serious cases, or those containing elements of difficulty, usually involve barristers. This assists the processing of cases and maximises profitability for the solicitors' firm. McConville *et al.* conclude that:

> "Almost all our respondents came to see criminal defence practices as geared, in co-operation with the other elements of the system, towards the routine production of guilty pleas. A minority of them found this to be a source of injustice for clients and of disillusionment for themselves, given their earlier expectations of the defence solicitors' role in an adversarial system."[14]

In criminal defence it seems that it is all too easy for lawyers to develop a view that clients tend to be guilty. This view can become an ideological assumption

[11] Note that adjudication is sometimes used to describe a method of expert determination in construction contracts: see generally chap.15 and J. Kendall, "Simpler Dispute Resolution" *Solicitors' Journal* 29 November 1996, 1152 and *Export Determination* (London, Longman, 1992).

[12] A. Ashworth, "Ethics and Criminal Justice" in R. Cranston (ed.), *Legal Ethics and Professional Responsibility* (Oxford: Clarendon Press, 1995) at 146.

[13] M. McConville, J. Hodgson, L. Bridges and A. Pavlovic, *Standing Accused: The Organisation and Practices of Criminal Defence Lawyers in Britain* (Oxford, Clarendon Press, 1994), at 41.

[14] *Ibid.*, at 71.

that displaces, in the lawyer's mind, the need to construct a defence or set out to test the prosecution evidence.[15] These broad generalisations relate to the handling of minor criminal cases. In more serious cases, the defendants' interests are more likely to be rigorously pursued. Nevertheless, the research suggests that, over large parts of the system, adversarialism consistently fails criminal defendants. This is not a failure of technique as, prior to the LPC, might have been the case.[16] This is a failure of the culture of criminal defence. It is a failure to recognise that the rationale of the adversarial system and the ethics of lawyers built around that system require that, guilty or not, defendants must be given diligent representation.

C. CIVIL LITIGATION

The majority of civil actions involve minor issues and ordinary people. A recent survey suggested that approximately half of civil disputes involved damage to vehicles, divorce, accident or injury and unpaid debts.[17] As we have seen, most civil cases are settled; indeed, with some exceptions, most commentators see the eventuality of a trial as the failure of the settlement process. Unless there is a political motive or desire to set a precedent, a trial only occurs because one of the parties, or its lawyers, or all of them, have miscalculated the risks or because the lawyers have engaged in a litigation or negotiation strategy which has misfired.[18] This view, however, disguises the complexity of negotiation and settlement decisions, the difficulty in calculating risk and the different assumptions of parties and their advisers. A plaintiff's lawyer in a money claim may, for example, calculate that she only has a 20 per cent chance of winning at trial. That lawyer may be prepared to accept only 20 per cent of the damages payable if the plaintiff succeeds in full. The defendants' lawyer may, on the same calculation, conclude that the litigation risk is not viable from the plaintiff's point of view and refuse to pay anything. In fact the defendant may not be prepared to pay anything in recognition of the litigation risk unless the plaintiff has at least a 50 per cent chance of winning. The difficulty of reconciling these approaches to calculating and responding to risk is compounded when risk assessments differ.

This crude example of risk assessment exemplifies the danger of generalising about litigation strategy.[19] The factors which determine the strategy of lawyers

---

[15]   M. McConville, J. Hodgson, L. Bridges and A. Pavlovic, *Standing Accused: The Organisation and Practices of Criminal Defence Lawyers in Britain* (Oxford, Clarendon Press, 1994), at 137 and for a consideration of the ethics and practice of plea bargaining, M. McConville, "Plea Bargaining: Ethics and Politics", (1998) 25 *Journal of Law and Society* 562.

[16]   A. Sherr, "Lawyers and Clients: The First Meeting" (1986) 49 *Modern Law Review* 323 and discussion by McConville *et al.*, n. 15 above, at 136, 142–9, which suggests that elementary interviewing skills would avoid some of the problems identified.

[17]   National Consumer Council and the BBC Law in Action Programme, *Seeking Civil Justice: A Survey of People's Needs and Experiences* (London, National Consumer Council, 1995), at 15.

[18]   S. R. Gross and K. D. Syverud, "Getting to No: A Study of Settlement Negotiations and the Selection of Cases for Trial" (1991) 90 *Michigan Law Review* 319.

[19]   For a more detailed exposition of this kind of analysis see *ibid.*, at 322–6.

could vary substantially between fields of litigation, reflecting the interplay of these factors.[20] It may also vary within a field, depending on context. The relevant factors may include the parties' relationship, the funding arrangements and the likely incidence of costs, the availability of insurance or other means of offsetting liability for damages and costs, and the distribution of authority to settle as between claimants and, for example, insurers.[21] The identity of the party who is shouldering the risk can be crucial to the way litigation is conducted. If legal aid is paying, the plaintiff and the plaintiff's lawyer are more likely to be bullish in pursuing the claim. Where lawyers shoulder the risk as to costs, as with conditional fees, they will be more cautious about which claims they sponsor and how those claims are pursued.[22] The contextual differences between fields may also be significant; negotiations in family disputes, for example, may be particularly sensitive to disruption because of the pre-existing relationship between the parties and the strategic behaviour of the parties in the dispute process.[23]

In each area of work, different factors determine how lawyers handle litigation and bargaining on behalf of clients. A lot depends on the predisposition of the lawyer; his or her attitude to the work. Thus, it is possible that different lawyers will approach contentious issues with different assumptions about the purpose and process. In one study a solicitor said:

> "When I specialised in matrimonial . . . I would give them [clients] my best advice based on the law and a reasonable approach to a family problem. I would try and reach an understanding with the other solicitor. Quite a lot seemed to think war had broken out; you couldn't send their letters to your client. Some lawyers think what their client wants must be right. Invariably the case is settled on a compromise which could have been reached nine months earlier . . . too often its because the client is calling the tune rather than the lawyer advising them what is reasonable. This is especially important in family situations; you want the relationship to continue even if the marriage has failed—the solicitor's job is not to exacerbate the situation."[24]

Family work, however, is an increasingly specialised area where a special consideration, the welfare of children, should be dominant. Personal injury litigation, which is considered in more detail in the next section, can be regarded as

---

[20] Although previous research had shown that plaintiffs were, in the aggregate, successful in 50% of cases, Gross and Syverud showed, in their sample of jury verdicts in the California superior courts, that the success rates at trial varied greatly between and within "fields". So, e.g., the plaintiff's success rate for road traffic cases based on negligence was 42.1% and in medical negligence 29.2%. In contrast, in the commercial sphere, 92% of employment cases were successful and 71.4% of real estate cases. The average success rate of 50% concealed these differences, which were in part attributable to the factors determining *which* cases were brought to trial: *ibid.*, at 338.

[21] *Ibid.*

[22] *Ibid.*

[23] *Ibid.*, and see R. H. Mnookin and L. Kornhauser, "Bargaining in the Shadow of the Law: The Case of Divorce" (1979) 88 *Yale Law Journal* 950.

[24] A. Boon, "Assessing Competence to Conduct Civil Litigation: Key Tasks and Skills" in P. Hassett and M. Fitzgerald (eds.), *Skills for Legal Functions II: Representation and Advice* (London, Institute of Advanced Legal Studies, 1992).

more representative of the mainstream litigation work of lawyers outside the commercial sphere. It must be remembered in relation to civil litigation that one of the recurring debates, certainly in the United States, has been whether it is necessary or desirable to have ethical rules in addition to rules of litigation which explicitly govern the process of litgation. One of the arguments against increasing the ethical dimension of the civil litigation process is that the court should exercise effective oversight of litigation. By adding ethical obligations in relation to that process, one may encourage the use of ethics as a tactic in litgation.[25]

Personal Injury Litigation

Rather than describe strategies and tactics in general we focus on personal injury. This is one of the most numerically significant areas of civil litigation[26] and one of the few areas of practice which has received sustained academic attention.[27] A number of factors invest the work of personal injury lawyers with particular ethical significance. First, at the policy level, the large numbers of personal injury victims and the expense of litigation raise an issue of access to law of the most fundamental kind. The ways in which personal injury lawyers have reacted to threats to their jurisdiction illustrates the fine balance between protecting professionalism and protectionism (see Chapter 7 and below). Secondly, the relative naïveté of most personal injury victims, and the lack of control they are able to exercise over their lawyers[28] reveal how lawyers act when they have a relatively free hand. This is an area where lawyers are often accused of incompetence and the manipulation of the system for their own advantage.[29] Thirdly,

---

[25]   T. Schneyer, "Professionalism as Politics: The Making of a Modern Legal Ethics Code", in R. L. Nelson, D. M. Trubek and R. L. Solomon (eds.), *Lawyers' Ideals/Lawyers' Practices: Transformations in the American Legal Profession* (New York, Cornell University Press, 1992), 95 at 119.

[26]   There are over 3 million accidents a year and, although 95% of the cases brought are settled by negotiation, personal injury trials remain one of the most significant areas of work of the high court.

[27]   Empirical studies have been conducted in both the USA and UK: Genn, n. 4 above,, at 19–138; H. L. Ross *Settled Out of Court: The Social Process of Insurance Claims Adjustment* (Chicago, Ill., Aldine, 1970 (see n. 65); and D. Rosenthal, *Lawyer and Client: Whose in Charge?* (New York, Russell Sage Foundation, 1974).

[28]   T. M. Swanson, "A Review of the Civil Justice Review: Economic Theories Behind the Delay in Tort Litigation" [1990] *Current Legal Problems* 185 at 202–4; D. R. Harris, M. Maclean, H. Genn, S. Lloyd-Bostock, P. Fenn, P. Corfield and Y. Brittan, *Compensation and Support for Illness and Injury* (Oxford, Clarendon Press, 1984), at 124; Genn, n. 4 above, at 7 and Rosenthal, n. 27 above.

[29]   *The Report of the Committee on Personal Injuries Litigation* (Cmnd. 3691, 1968): the Winn Committee found that firms underestimate complexity of personal injury work; *Report of the Personal Injuries Litigation Procedure Working Party* (The Cantley Report, Cmnd. 7476, 1979): problems of delay laid at door of inexperienced solicitors; *Report of the Royal Commission on Civil Liability and Compensation for Personal Injury* (The Pearson Report, Cmnd. 7054, 1978); *Report of the Review Body on Civil Justice* (Cmnd. 394, 1988) found that personal injury litigation is a major cause of public concern because delay saps the morale of plaintiffs and causes them to accept low sums. See also J. Phillips, and K. Hawkins, "Some Economic Aspects of the Bargaining Process: A Study of Personal Injury Claims" (1976) 39 *Modern Law Review* 497; Genn, n. 4 above; M. Joseph, *Lawyers Can Seriously Damage Your Health* (London, Michael Joseph, 1985).

what level of co-operation is desirable or permissible between the plaintiff's lawyers and insurance companies' representatives, who often negotiate the settlement of claims, or their lawyers? This is a particularly important issue where there is a likelihood of "repeat encounters" between specialist lawyers and insurers out of which personal relationships will inevitably develop. The client, however, is unlikely to be a repeat player.

The main factor in determining litigation strategy is uncertainty. Will liability be established? How high will the damages be? Will there be deductions for contributory negligence? The plaintiff's lawyers have the initiative and they can control the pace of litigation. Costs operate as a constraint, and can be used as part of the tactical armoury of the litigation solicitor. Costs are also the main way in which lawyers generate income; lawyers may therefore be seen to have an incentive to increase costs. The heaviest costs are usually incurred at trial. Costs follow the event, but the exception to the rule that the loser pays the winner's costs arises where the plaintiff has refused to accept a payment into court by the defendant and then fails to recover damages which exceed that sum. Payment into court therefore is one of the tactical options available to defendants because it increases the risk for the plaintiff and, therefore, the pressure to settle.

Two main choices face a defendant in deciding how to handle litigation. One is to settle early and avoid further costs accumulating. The other is to try and delay the conduct of the matter as long as possible. This tests the plaintiff's resolve and financial backing. It can also lead to the weakening of evidence, since witnesses may disappear or their memories fade. Mistakes may be made by the plaintiff's lawyers early in the case which, with the passage of time, cannot be rectified. In general, therefore, delay favours the defendant. However, when the potential damages are small, defendants, particularly institutions, have little incentive to delay settlement. It is cases involving large sums of damages which are most likely to be keenly fought because this is where the largest savings may be made.[30]

Litigation Strategy: "Litigation First"

From the plaintiff's point of view, litigation should generally proceed as quickly as possible.[31] This has two main advantages. First, it reduces the pressure on the

[30] These ideas were explored in A. Boon, "Cooperation and Competition in Negotiation: The Handling of Civil Disputes and Transactions" (1994) 1 *International Journal of the Legal Profession* 109 (hereafter referred to as "Cooperation and Competition") and "Ethic and Strategy in Personal Injury Litigation" (1995) 22 *Journal of Law and Society* 353 (hereafter referred to as "Ethics and Strategy").

[31] Genn, n. 4 above, and, of course, it may also be in the defendant's interest where the defendant is a private individual because litigation causes anxiety to all parties to litigation, hence the application of striking out rules when the plaintiff delays: see further R. James, "Delay and Abuse of Process" (1997) 16 *Civil Justice Quarterly* 289.

plaintiff to settle in order to avoid the anxiety of proceedings.[32] Secondly, it gives the plaintiff's lawyers some "bargaining leverage".[33] The longer the defendant delays settlement the more costs he or she will eventually have to pay.[34] Early settlement, even on terms favourable to the plaintiff, may be preferred to the costs incurred as a result of late settlement.[35] Research conducted in the 1980s strongly endorsed this "bulldozing", or "litigation first" strategy as the best means of representing personal injury victims. Insurers, as institutional "repeat players" in the litigation of claims, were widely believed to use tactics of delay as a way of increasing psychological pressure on the plaintiff to accept less than full damages.[36] Moreover there were large numbers of general practice solicitors who "dabbled" in personal injury work, making such tactics even more effective.

This led to the denigration of co-operative strategies between the parties' representatives in order to settle litigation. In an influential book Genn criticised an "orientation to claims management which stresses negotiation and settlement as an alternative to litigation rather than as the product of preparing for litigation"[37]:

> "a common response to the problems of uncertainty, lack of expertise in personal injury work, and concern about legal costs is to adopt an approach to claims settlement based on co-operation with the opponent rather than confrontation: reasonable negotiation, without the commencement of proceedings, rather than litigation."[38]

Expert plaintiffs' solicitors, it was said, did not regard the cultivation of a co-operative, reasonable relationship with insurers or their solicitors as vital to their work.[39] This kind of criticism justified the creation of the Law Society Personal Injury Panel by leading personal injury firms.[40] To gain membership solicitors were required to provide extensive details of their experience of the field[41] and were also required to be committed to "the expeditious pursuit of proceedings and the readiness to go to trial if need be".[42] The guidance notes

---

[32] Swanson, n. 28 above, at 198 n. 24 and at 200 n. 13.

[33] Genn, n. 4 above, at 97–123.

[34] If, as a defendant, I think your claim is probably worth £25,000 to £30,000, I may as well pay you £30,000 now, when your costs are £1,000, rather than £27,500 later when your costs are £10,000.

[35] Swanson, n. 28 above, at 197 n. 24.

[36] E.g., S. MaCaulay and E. Walster, "Legal Structures and Restoring Equity" (1971) 27 *Journal of Social Issues* 173.

[37] Genn, n. 4 above, at 106–8.

[38] *Ibid.*, at 166.

[39] *Ibid.*, at 113.

[40] Delay, incompetent claims-handling and the risk that inexperienced solicitors would be exploited by experienced opponents were all cited as reasons for establishing the panel, and it was noted that personal injury cases accounted for 10% (£17.8 million) of the total paid under the solicitor's indemnity fund in 1991: E. Gilvarry, "Council Backs PI Panel" (1992) 27 *Law Society Gazette* 4.

[41] The Panel's initial criterion, that an applicant was required to have taken 5 cases to trial in the 5 years preceding the application, was dropped in Feb. 1995.

[42] D. Skidmore, *Drawing the Line: A Report on the Law Society's Personal Injury Panel* (1993), an explanatory note by the Personal Injury Panel Chief Assessor accompanying the applicants' questionnaire.

sent out to prospective members of the panel by the Law Society asserted that:

> "It is essential that personal injury specialists approach the majority of their personal injury cases on the basis that the case will reach trial and not be settled. Panel applicants are expected to demonstrate a commitment to take appropriate cases to a full hearing".[43]

Members of the panel obtained advantages which went beyond the "kite mark" of expertise. Only firms with members on the Panel were able to take cases referred from the Law Society's "Accident Line" service. Only panel members handling cases on a conditional fee basis had the right to participate in the Law Society-organised insurance scheme covering any plaintiff's liability for costs.

The panel sought to establish powerful practice norms. Indeed, by using the power of exclusion the Panel set up norms which were arguably more powerful than the ethical rules of the Law Society. In effect the Panel supported the adversarial ethic and the litigation first strategy as its practical manifestation. It also endorsed an approach which had the likely result of increasing costs in the average action.[44] It may be coincidental that this was in the interests of these specialist lawyers who were geared up to process claims quickly. Although the vast majority of claims continued to settle, the lawyers were able to make the work, which was often routine, highly profitable. Their strategy, however, ran counter to the government's policy, now fully matured in the Woolf proposals, of limiting the cost of litigation.[45] Lord Woolf's report attacks this particular manifestation of adversariality with proposals which will force lawyers to disclose more information early on so as to facilitate settlement[46] and to subject more claims to pre-action mediation. His vision of a new landscape for "procedural justice, operating in the traditional adversarial context" assumes "[p]eople will be encouraged to start litigation only as a last resort"[47] and that "litigation will be less adversarial and more co-operative".[48] He envisages new processes incorporating limited procedures and fixed timetables. Civil litigation would be less complex, less prolonged and less expensive. There was to be a "fast track" for cases valued at less than £10,000[49] (now £15,000) and a multi-track, including variable procedures for those cases valued at over £10,000. Central to Lord

---

[43] The Law Society, *The Personal Injury Panel—Notes for Guidance* (London, Law Society, undated): applicants will normally be expected, *inter alia*, to have "actively supervised at least sixty personal injury instructions in the five years prior to the application or at least thirty six personal injury instructions in the three years prior to application": *Rules and Procedures for the Law Society's Personal Injury Panel* (London, Law Society, undated).

[44] This issue is considered generally by P. Cain, *Atiyah's Accidents Compensation and the Law* (London, Dublin, and Edinburgh, Butterworths, 1993); Genn, n. 4 above, at 83–96.

[45] Lord Mackay of Clashfern, "Access to Justice: The Price" (1991) 25 *The Law Teacher* 96.

[46] See the proposals for pre-action protocols in chapter 10 of the Woolf Report, Lord Woolf, *Access to Justice Final Report to the Lord Chancellor on the Civil Justice System in England and Wales* (London, HMSO, 1996), hereafter *Final Report*.

[47] *Ibid.*, paras. 8 and 9 at 4.

[48] *Ibid.*, at 5.

[49] *Ibid.*, para. 9 at 4–9.

Woolf's aim, expanding access to justice without expanding public expenditure,[50] was transferring control of litigation from lawyers and placing primary responsibility for case management in the hands of judges.[51].

Is the criticism of lawyers expressed in Lord Woolf's report, and implied in his proposals, justified? Does the adversarial system demand that a "litigation first" strategy is pursued in the interests of clients? In order to consider this further it is necessary to consider an alternative approach to litigation-first strategy.

An Alternative Paradigm: Conditional Co-operation

There is, in fact, little evidence that litigation-first strategies are associated with success, however this is defined, in personal injury cases.[52] A number of elements produce this conclusion. While it may be true in general that inexperienced personal injury litigators delay proceedings and achieve less in damages, and that some experts favour litigation-first, this is insufficient to establish a link between either expertise or the recovery of higher damages and non-co-operation. Moreover, there is little concrete evidence that all insurers, as a matter of practice, attempt to delay proceedings. The bad-faith tactics of insurers in general may have been overstated.[53] Obviously, if Lord Woolf's accusation that lawyers sometimes generate costs unnecessarily is correct, then litigation-first is consistent with that pattern. It is, however, also consistent with the adversarial ethic. Does it produce better results for clients as is often assumed?

This assumption was called into question by Robert Axelrod's work on strategic co-operation,[54] based on the famous "prisoners dilemma". This is a simple game in which two accomplices (the prisoners) have to decide whether or not to co-operate with the authorities and implicate each other or remain silent and hope that their co-defendant does likewise. Their decisions are, therefore, to co-operate (i.e. with each other, by remaining silent) or to defect (i.e. to implicate their accomplice). There is a complicated reward structure. If they co-operate with each other they share six points (i.e. three each). If one defects and the other does not the defector gets five points and the co-operator nil. If they both defect they get one point each. They each make their decision without knowing what the other is going to decide. Obviously, if the game is played for

---

[50] *Ibid.*, para. 5 at 3 (and note the "substantial risk" that the existing system undermines "our competitive position in relation to other jurisdictions").

[51] *Ibid.*, para. 3 at 2–3.

[52] In particular, it is noteworthy that it is not delay, *per se*, which distinguishes experts from the non-experts, but the strategy, or lack of strategy, behind delay. See R. Dingwall, T. Durkin, and W. L. F. Felstiner, "Delay in Tort Cases: Critical Reflections on the Civil Justice Review" (1990) 9 *Civil Justice Quarterly* 353 at 363.

[53] The fact that solicitors do not hold insurers responsible for "bad faith" tactics, such as litigation delay, undermines the force of this argument: Lord Chancellor's Department, *Civil Justice Review: Personal Injury Litigation* (London, Lord Chancellor's Department, 1986), at para. 67.

[54] R. Axelrod, *The Evolution of Co-operation* (London, Penguin, 1984).

one round only, the rational decision, given the reward structure, is to defect.[55] If, however, the game is repeated many times between the same parties, defection would not be the rational strategy. By co-operating the competitors share the maximum points available i.e. three each. A pattern of defection, however, gives each side only one point from each exchange. The problem, therefore, is to design a strategy which encourages consistent co-operation so as to maximise the points available to both parties.

Axelrod organised a competition in which computer programs played each other. Each program repeated the co-operate/defect decision 100 times against other computers and their accumulated scores were listed in a league table. The most successful program was extremely simple and predictable. Called "tit for tat", its strategy was to co-operate until the other player defected. On the next exchange "tit for tat" defected. "Tit for tat" then continued to mirror the move of the other program in the previous exchange. If the other program continued to defect so did "tit for tat". "Tit for tat" would not randomly return to co-operation. Unless the original defector returned to co-operation, i.e. while "tit for tat" defected (i.e. the defector "apologised" to "tit for tat" for the original defection), both sides were condemned to gain one point a round for the rest of the game. Most of the programmes were intelligent enough to realise that this would produce a poor result and returned to co-operation. Against a number of programmes, some based on the idea of picking up five points here and there for random defection, "tit for tat" was clearly the most successful. In "round robin" competition, as weaker programmes were eliminated, its scores became stronger.

The prisoners' dilemma is only a *model* of strategic decision-making. It cannot capture all the nuances of real-life interactions. Nevertheless, game theory has been a fruitful source of theorising in many academic disciplines. Axelrod's work in particular led to renewed thinking about the roots of social competition and co-operation.[56] Some of the implications of this thinking relate to bargaining and are considered below. How could it apply to the conduct of litigation? In personal injury litigation, lawyers deal with each in different matters over a period of time. To what extent can they co-operate? If, for example, a defendant's solicitor has failed to file a notice of appearance to a legal action, should the plaintiff's solicitor warn his or her opponent that he or she are about to enter judgment or should he or she just go ahead and do it? The decision to warn is often referred to as "professional courtesy".[57] The decision to enter judgment is perhaps more consistent with the adversarial ethic. Either course of action may be justified; the decision to enter judgment is in the interests of the client and the

---

[55] This guarantees one point. There is no way of retrieving unreciprocated co-operation and, on an isolated occasion, there is no way of predicting how the other accused will react.

[56] M. Ridley, *The Origins of Virtue* (Harmondsworth, Penguin, 1997), chap. 3.

[57] In research into the conduct of asbestosis litigation expert plaintiffs' lawyers were found to offer "reasonable opposition", rather than fierce competition, so that they were able to give and receive the benefits of "professional courtesy" from those defendants' representatives they dealt with regularly. See Dingwall *et al.*, n. 52 above, at 363.

decision to warn are in the interests of justice. But could the solicitor who took such an unforgiving course of action expect professional courtesy if he made a similar mistake?

Plaintiffs' solicitors who adopt litigation-first strategies in all their cases must expect that their opponents will treat this as defection and punish them if they can. The battle of the courtroom is transposed to the legal office, undermining the litigator's ability to achieve the best results for future clients. Defendants may rightly conclude that "you cannot negotiate with X and Co.; pay the money into court". Such attitudes inevitably increase the use of legal processes and increase the volume of costs in the system. One of the benefits of co-operation between repeat parties to litigation could, therefore, be a higher number of timely and reasonable settlements. An alternative to litigation first could be called conditional co-operation. Following a strategy based on tit-for-tat, a lawyer representing a large volume of personal injury victims would not routinely issue proceedings. But if the insurer took advantage of this, by unreasonably delaying settlement or trying to strike out a claim for delay, a conditional co-operator would, in future, adopt a litigation-first strategy with that insurer. The rational response for an insurer is to try and restore co-operation[58] because this is the best way of settling future cases cheaply. In this way, like tit-for-tat, the conditional co-operator develops a reputation which evokes co-operation from all he or she deal with: "Y and Co. are firm but fair".

There is evidence that some experts use conditional co-operation in handling litigation. If they know and trust an insurance company they are prepared to wait a reasonable time for an offer to be made rather than rush into proceedings. They judge the offer on the basis of whether it is "fair and reasonable" and, if it is, they advise the client to accept. In doing so they are not "competing" on every claim and, consequently, they may sacrifice the possibility that they can maximise gain for clients in individual cases. This is a problem where litigators have strategic advantages, such as where they represent a client of limitless wealth against someone of limited means. They may feel obliged to press home this advantage.[59] Since the strategy of conditional co-operation depends on a reputation for fair dealing a litigator with such advantages would need to think carefully about the implications of such actions.[60] But would it be unethical to do so? Does it run counter to the obligation to act in the best interests of clients? Logically, a lawyer cannot act in the best interests of *a particular* client if she fails to exploit the situation and, instead, accepts what is fair and reasonable. If this is right, it must also be in the best interests of the client to try and gain bargaining leverage by the use of litgation strategy. On the other hand, general ethical principles recognise an obligation to achieve fairness *between* clients.[61]

---

[58] Discussed by R. J. Condlin, "Bargaining in the Dark: The Normative Incoherence of Lawyer Dispute Bargaining Role" (1992) 51 *Maryland Law Review* 1 at 57.
[59] *Ibid.*, at 64; and see Axelrod, n. 54 above, at 152.
[60] Condlin, n. 58 above, at 80–1.
[61] *Ibid.*, at 88–95.

This may be difficult to achieve when a lawyer acquires a reputation for defection which invites both punishment and pre-emptive strikes.

Codes of ethics are understandably silent in relation to these grey areas. There are arguments for both points of view. If lawyers should pursue substantive justice, conditional co-operation is more likely to achieve this in more cases. If lawyers are merely partisan respresentatives whose obligation is to do the best for every client, then any action permitted by law and conduct code is open to them. This seems a negation of professional responsibility which renders professional ethics meaningless. Surely, lawyers must pursue substantive justice and exercise discretion in deciding how that is best achieved. To conclude otherwise places technical possibilities above ethical considerations. It is in the realm of bargaining, however, that ethical choice between co-operation and defection are most starkly illustrated.

D. BARGAINING: THE LAWYER'S ROLE IN AN ADVERSARIAL SYSTEM

Negotiation Problems

"Negotiating deals" of various kinds is a central part of most lawyers' work, in the context of transactions (non-contentious proceedings) or disputes (contentious proceedings).[62] A voluminous literature on the theory of dispute bargaining[63] suggests that, while certain patterns may be universal[64] in both transactions and disputes, the difference between distributive and integrative problems is fundamental.[65] Distributive problems involve bargaining over a fixed resource: a gain for one side implies loss for the other. Integrative problems contain the possibility of satisfying, to a greater or lesser degree, both parties' interests. A classic illustration of the distinction between distributive and

---

[62] See generally on this distinction D. G. Gifford, *Legal Negotiation: Theory and Applications* (St. Paul, Minn., West Publishing Co., 1989), at 38–42 and M. A. Eisenburg, "Private Ordering Through Negotiation: Dispute Settlement and Rulemaking" (1976) 89 *Harvard Law Review* 637.

[63] Summaries of much of the theoretical work can be found in G. T. Lowenthal, "A General Theory of Negotiation Process, Strategy and Behaviour" (1982) 31 *Kansas Law Review* 69; C Menkel-Meadow, "Toward Another View of Legal Negotiation: The Structure of Problem Solving" (1984) 31 *UCLA Law Review* 754 (and see Condlin, n. 58 above, for criticisms of the theory applied to practice). Empirical work includes G. Williams, *Legal Negotiation and Settlement* (St. Paul, Minn., West Publishing Co., 1983); Gross and Syverud, n. 18 above; M. Heumann and J. M. Hyman, "Negotiation Methods and Litigation Settlement in New Jersey: 'You Can't Always Get What You Want' ", paper prepared for the International Conference on Lawyers and Lawyering (Lake Windermere, UK, 1993); divorce (e.g., A. Sarat and W. L. F. Felstiner, "Law and Strategy in the Divorce Lawyer's Office" (1986) 20:1 *Law and Society Review* 93; J Griffiths, "What Do Dutch Lawyers Actually Do in Divorce Cases?" (1986) 20 *Law and Society Review* 135) and plea bargaining (e.g., M. Heumann, "A Note on Plea Bargaining and Case Pressure" (1975) 9 *Law and Society Review* 515).

[64] P. Gulliver, *Disputes and Negotiations: A Cross-Cultural Perspective* (New York and London: Academic Press, 1979).

[65] Gifford, n. 62 above. See also Ross, n. 27 above.

integrative problems is that of a parent mediating in a dispute between two children over an orange. A distributive solution is to divide the orange. However, if the parent identifies the underlying interests of the children in the orange a better solution may be discovered; one child wants the skin for a cake and the other wants the fruit to eat. The problem is integrative; both can have what they want. Even where interests may appear to be opposed it may be possible to improve outcomes by understanding the different values which the parties place on the subject matter.[66] Some areas of legal dispute may be expected to lean towards one or other of these models. Personal injury actions are more likely to centre around distributive problems (how much damages), whereas child custody disputes are more likely to have integrative features.

Negotiation Strategies

A common strategy used by lawyers is positional bargaining. This involves each side taking a position and moving, by a process of concessions, to the point where agreement is reached.[67] Positional bargaining may be particularly suited to the swift resolution of distributive problems.

A positional strategy is, however, less likely to produce a satisfactory solution to integrative problems because it assumes a limited number of outcomes. For integrative problems a "problem solving" orientation is preferable. This "depends on two structural components: (1) identifying the parties' underlying needs and objectives, and (2) crafting solutions, first by attempting to meet those needs directly, and second, by attempting to meet more of those needs through expanding the resources available".[68]

William's identifies two styles of bargaining used in legal negotiation which may be consistent with these strategies; competitive and co-operative. Co-operative negotiators seek "fair" agreements and "communicate a sense of shared interests, values and attitudes using rational logical persuasion as a means of co-operation".[69] The competitive[70] or "adversarial"[71] style is characterised by the pursuit of one-sided gains and attempts to dominate the negotiating relationship. Condlin observes that:

> "co-operative argument consists of non-coercive rational analysis in which the objective is to teach another about the truth of one's substantive claims. This effort stops when the listener understands, or when the claims have been shown to be false . . .

---

[66] Menkel-Meadow, n. 63 above, at 795.

[67] Rigid commitments at or near the other side's minimum settlement point is a basic tenet of competitive negotiation and the discovery of that point is the fundamental aim of competitive strategy: Lowenthal, n. 63 above. Condlin, n. 58 above, argues that the objection to this kind of bargaining is not the taking of positions but the manner in which positions are advanced.

[68] Menkel-Meadow, n. 63 above.

[69] Williams, n. 63 above, at 53.

[70] Gifford, n. 62 above, at 8.

[71] Menkel-Meadow n. 63 above, at 756 n. 3.

Competitive argument consists of rhetorical psychological manoeuvring designed to coerce an adversary, sometimes subtly and sometimes not, into deferring to one's view when, if fully informed he would not or should not. The objective is manipulation not understanding. Efforts to persuade stop when the adversary agrees to do as one wishes."[72]

A competitive style is suited to positional bargaining because it may allow a bargainer to exploit the personal weaknesses of the other bargainer, e.g. his or her aversion to conflict, or the weaknesses of his or her bargaining position. A co-operative approach is virtually essential to problem solving because it allows bargainers to explore a range of solutions without forming premature conclusions.

Positional bargaining appears to satisfy the demand for an exchange which appears to be adversarial. But positional bargaining must be conducted using both demands and concessions. It is sometimes difficult to know whether one has demanded too much or too little. The only yardstick is what would be a fair and reasonable settlement, a view which must be informed by an assessment of the likely outcome of the case. So, how should lawyers conduct themselves in an environment where they may or may not know what the disposition of the other side is likely to be? Here, again, Axelrod's work offers some food for thought. The qualities of "tit for tat" which made it such a robust negotiating strategy in an environment of potential co-operation *and* exploitation, can be translated into human qualities. First, it is "nice"; it is never the first to defect. Secondly, it is provocable; it does not suffer betrayal by the other side without a reprisal. Thirdly, it is forgiving; it returns to co-operation when the other side indicates a willingness to do so. Finally, it is transparent. There is nothing concealed or unpredicatable about the tit-for-tat strategy. Indeed, it works *because* it is predictable. This suggests that a lawyer should attempt to conduct negotiation co-operatively so as not to jeopardise the advantages which co-operation may bring.

A method of negotiation which operationalises many of the features of "tit-for tat" is Fisher and Ury's influential "principled negotiation". Their method incorporates co-operative style and a problem solving orientation but, unlike "tit-for-tat", does not immediately respond to provocation. Rather, "principled negotiators" focus on interests rather than positions, seek creative solutions, resolve distributive problems by identifying appropriate objective criteria and reduce the interpersonal friction which sometimes accompanies competitive approaches. Agreement is more likely because both negotiators recognise an obligation to consider the other side's interests and, by their joint efforts, to produce an agreement which maximises the advantages of the interaction for both sides. The assumptions underlying this style of negotiation are that the aim is a fair and reasonable agreement, efficient in expression and operation which

[72] See R. J. Condlin, "Cases on Both Sides: Patterns of Argument in Legal Dispute-Negotiation" (1985) 44 *Maryland Law Review* 65.

improves, or at least does not harm, any continuing relationship between the parties.[73] Principled negotiation is unlike "tit-for tat", in that it is not provocable, at least on the surface. Principled negotiators are encouraged to try and model the behaviour they want from an opponent who defects. Eventually, however, even principled negotiators must walk away from a deadlocked negotiation.

Which method of negotiation should a lawyer use? If the best interests of the client is the yardstick, the subject matter of the negotiation should determine which strategy is used. In personal injury litigation, for example, the principal focus of bargaining is monetary, there being far fewer integrative features than may be found, for example, in negotiation over a broken commercial agreement.[74] Indeed, personal injury bargaining has been described as relatively crude[75] or "horse trading".[76] But research in both the USA[77] and the UK[78] suggests that most of the bargaining conducted by lawyers is positional. Heumann and Hyman found that US litigation lawyers used positional bargaining in 71 per cent of cases and a "problem solving" approach was used in only 16 per cent of cases. Therefore, although Williams found that the vast majority of lawyers in his study had a co-operative orientation to bargaining there is little evidence that co-operation was allied to problem solving.[79] This is problematic because sensitivity to problem solving potential is one of the main justifications of not using a positional strategy. There may be a number of reasons why positional strategies are pervasive. First, the integrative potential of all problems varies and the fact that lawyers often enter disputes at a late stage, when clients have adopted positions, may reduce the lawyer's room for manoeuvre.[80] The demands of clients and their desire to use any bargaining leverage present in the situation may further reduce the scope for problem solving. Certain business

---

[73] R. Fisher, W. Ury and B. Patton, *Getting to Yes: Negotiating Agreement Without Giving In* (London, Century Business, 1992).

[74] The only incentive for plaintiffs' lawyers to co-operate with insurance companies is a desire for early settlement or structured settlement.

[75] See Genn, n. 4 above, at 134.

[76] Ross, n. 65 above (but see Fisher *et al.*, n. 73 above, and Menkel-Meadow, n. 63 above).

[77] M. Galanter, "The Federal Rules and the Quality of Settlements: A Comment on Rosenburg's, The Federal Rules of Civil Procedure in Action" [1989] *University of Pennsylvania Law Review* 2231 at 2236.

[78] M. Murch, "The Role of Solicitor's in Divorce Proceedings" (1977) 40 *Modern Law Review* 625 for solicitors and J. Morison and P. Leith, *The Barrister's World and the Nature of Law* (Milton Keynes and Philadelphia, Open University Press, 1992).

[79] Williams, n. 63 above. But see Heumann and Hyman, n. 63 above; A. Boon, "Competition and Cooperation in the Handling of Disputes and Transactions" [1994] *International Journal of the Legal Profession* 109; Morison and Leith, n. 78 above, at 121.

[80] Even if we accept that legal problems are rarely purely distributive or purely integrative do they ever have integrative features which can place distributive issues in a subsidiary role? We may, for example, see marital breakdown as a complex and potentially integrative problem. However, an analysis of the issues suggest that they are substantially distributive: see Mnookin and Kornhauser, n. 23 above.

practices, such as the use of standard-form contracts, may further limit scope for innovation.[81]

Although competitive positional bargaining may appear to satisfy the assumed obligation to be adversarial, a number of ethical issues are raised. First, is this a situation in which the client's best interests should be the determining factor? For example, is it ethical that lawyers should use advantages, such as superior bargaining strength or superior competence, to achieve settlements that are unfair or unreasonable? It would certainly appear to be inconsistent with the notion of co-operative litigation espoused by Woolf. The second concern is that the use of positional bargaining can be conducted both competitively and co-operatively. The use of positional bargaining has a deceptive feel of competition to it; lawyers may appear to be adversarial without being so competitive that bargaining is deadlocked. Thirdly, because positional bargaining is so quick and simple it saves time; a particular virtue when a legal problem is large and complex.[82] Positional bargaining can therefore be seen to be in the interests of lawyers; it allows them to return to their other cases more quickly. If it is true that positional strategies dominate lawyers' negotiations, lawyers may fail to act in the best interests of their clients. Although problem solving may not be required in every situation there must be many occasions when the interests of clients are better served by a problem solving strategy than by competitive or positional strategies.[83] These concerns are exacerbated by the fact that negotiation strategies tend not to be discussed with clients.

Bargaining Standards

The prevalence of positional bargaining in legal culture is one of the major problems of ethics generally ignored by professional codes. Condlin and others have pointed out the basic incoherence of the lawyer's role in litigation and

[81] J. Flood suggests that "[l]awyers will often modify an existing document rather than draft a new one. The uncertainty of putting deals together is reduced by relying on something that has proved successful before": "Doing Business: The Management of Uncertainty in Lawyers' Work" (1991) 25 *Law & Society Review* 41 at 57.

[82] Critics suggest that "principled negotiation" has less value when there are no continuing relationships to consider, that objective criteria are persuasive rationalisations for positions and warnings of the consequences of failing to reach agreement are just subtle threats: see J. J. White, "The Pros and Cons of Getting to Yes" (1984) 34 *Journal of Legal Education* 115. R. Fisher, in his response to this review ("Fisher's Response to Jim White" [1984] *Journal of Legal Education* 120), and Menkel Meadow (n. 63 above, at 829) acknowledge the limitations on a problem solving strategy when dealing with negotiators who have the leverage to achieve their goals by the exercise of power.

[83] Roger Fisher (n. 82 above), commenting on criticisms of "Getting to Yes" says "[s]tudents have now taught me that there are categories of negotiations where positional bargaining is the best way to proceed. On single issue negotiations among strangers where the transaction costs of exploring interests would be high and where each side is protected by competitive opportunities, haggling over positions may work better than joint problem solving. A typical case would be negotiating a sale on the New York Stock Exchange". Menkel-Meadow (n. 63 above,) argues that competitive approaches encourage rigidity and potential stalemate and allow for "closed or limited problem solving".

settlement.[84] The rules of litigation, which support substantive competitiveness, are often taken by practitioners to support "stylistic competitiveness"; behaviour not supported by rules of litigation and ethically dubious.[85] Analysts of the role of lawyers in disputes are divided on whether there are any limits on competitiveness. After all, in an adversarial system the outcome of bargaining should be the same as would be produced at trial, but at a fraction of the cost. In some circumstances lawyers may be expected to be tough, to test the evidence in an adversarial fashion, in order properly to evaluate the claim. What are the limits of this? If, in the course of the negotiation, a lawyer detects weakness or uncertainty, should she take advantage of weakness or incompetence in other representatives? If it is acceptable to take advantage in this way, is there any logical reason why she should not conceal information from the other side, or even lie, if it is in the best interests of her clients that she should do so? Many observers have argued that to seek high standards of bargaining is pointless. Therefore, because of the danger presented if the norms are widely and routinely violated, the drafters should err on the conservative side and must sometimes reject better and more desirable rules for poorer ones simply because the violation of the higher standards would cast all the rules in doubt.[86]

The answers to such questions are not obvious. In the USA it has been argued that lying on behalf of clients is consistent with the client-centred approach promoted by the ABA's model code.[87] Indeed, it has been suggested that "effectiveness in negotiations is central to the business of lawyering and a willingness to lie is central to one's effectiveness in negotiations".[88] This contradicts the ABA's model rules which specifically require that negotiators have honest dealings with others. These rules are subject to exceptions based on the ordinary conventions of negotiation, for example, concealing estimates of value and a party's intentions as to acceptable settlement. It has been argued that the exceptions should be abandoned as they are likely to lead to unintended violations, compromise the position of lawyers as officers of the court or lead to a decrease in necessary levels of trust and co-operation.[89] As we have seen, it is only recently that the long-term effectiveness of such "defections" has been queried.[90] The

---

[84] Condlin, n. 58 above.

[85] See generally Lowenthal, n. 63 above.

[86] J. J. White, "Machiavelli and the Bar: Ethical Limitations on Lying in Negotiation" [1980] *American Bar Foundation Research Journal* 926 at 938.

[87] There is considerable literature in the USA on whether the lawyer's duty to her client obliges her to take a partisan, and therefore competitive, stance in negotiation. Much of this work is reviewed by Condlin, n. 58 above. See also Rosenthal, n. 27 above; W. H. Simon "Visions of Practice in Legal Thought" (1984) 36 *Stanford Law Review* 469; J. P. Heinz, "The Power of Lawyers" [1983] *Georgia Law Review* 891; and C. Fried, "The Lawyer as Friend: The Moral Foundations of the Lawyer-Client Relationship" (1976) 85 *Yale Law Journal* 1060.

[88] G. B. Wetlaufer, "The Ethics of Lying in Negotiation" (1990) 76 *Iowa Law Review* 1219.

[89] See generally S. Bok, *Lying: Moral Choice in Public and Private Life* (London, Harvester Wheatsheaf Press, 1978); R. F. Thurman, "Chipping Away at Lawyer Veracity: The ABA's Turn Towards Situation Ethics in Negotiations" [1990] *Journal of Dispute Resolution* 10.

[90] See generally R. A. Johnson, *Negotiation Basics: Concepts, Skills and Exercises*" (Berkeley, Calif., UK and New Delhi, Sage Publications, 1993), at 77 and Condlin, n. 58 above.

expression of doubt as to whether a profession should explicitly sanction lying on behalf of clients is also recent.[91] This may explain why neither the Bar nor the Law Society deals explicitly with standards in bargaining in its guidance to the profession. Principle 19.01, of the *Guide*, which deals with duties owed to other solicitors, states that:

> "A solicitor must act towards other solicitors with frankness and good faith consistent with his or her overriding duty to the client."[92]

The solicitor's obligation of frankness and good faith is therefore qualified, in bargaining as in other contexts, by "the overriding interests of clients".[93] This could be read so as to permit, or even to require, dishonesty in the conduct of negotiations. However, this is unlikely because lawyers can be held liable for misrepresentations made in settlement negotiations. Indeed, note 1 to Principle 19.01 reminds solicitors that "any fraudulent or deceitful conduct by one solicitor to another will render the offending solicitor liable to disciplinary action in addition to the possibility of civil or criminal proceedings". If, as the *Guide* asserts, ethics follow the common law, to conclude that Principle 19.01 condones misrepresentation would be perverse. The problem in reality is more practical—the other side will often not discover the deception. Ethical norms can therefore "be violated with . . . confidence that there will be no discovery and no punishment".[94] Negotiation, more than any other area, presents a fundamental problem for professional ethics. For, whereas other important activities, litigation and advocacy for example, are subject to sophisticated rules of procedure, "negotiators operate under primitive and obtuse rules of professional responsibility".[95]

The voluminous literature on the ethics of bargaining in the USA springs from the tensions produced by the obligation of partisanship. This has been interpreted to mean that lawyers should act on a client's instructions, even where

---

[91] *Ibid.*, at 68–86 and L. E. Fisher, "Truth as a Double-Edged Sword: Deception, Moral Paradox, and the Ethics of Advocacy" (1989) 14 *The Journal of the Legal Profession* 89.

[92] 1996 edn. at 322.

[93] "Frank" means straightforward, sincere, open or candid: R. E. Allen (ed.), *The Concise Oxford Dictionary of Current English* (Oxford, Clarendon Press, 1990). "Candour" is an obligation to provide full and accurate information. "Good faith" "is an intangible and abstract quality with no technical meaning or statutory definition" but that it encompasses "an honest belief [and] an absence of design to seek an unconscionable advantage . . .": H. C. Black, J. R. Nolan and J. M. Nolan-Haley, *Black's Law Dictionary Definitions of the Terms and Phrases of American and English Jurisprudence, Ancient and Modern* (St. Paul, Minn., West Publishing Co., 1990), at 693: "honestly and with no ulterior motive": *Central Estates (Belgravia) Ltd.* v. *Woolgar* [1971] 3 All ER 647 at 649, *per* Lord Denning MR, quoted in J. B. Saunders, *Words and Phrases Legally Defined* (London, Butterworths, 1989) ii, at 321. "Good faith bargaining" is a labour law concept meaning coming to the table with an open mind and sincere desire to reach agreement: Black, *et al.*, above.

[94] C. B. Craver, *Effective Legal Negotiation and Settlement* (Charlottesville, Va., Michie Co., 1993). See also the *Law Society Guide: Professional Conduct of Solicitors*, 6th Edition (1990) which contains statistics showing that only 33 allegations of impropriety were made by solicitors against fellow solicitors in 1986 and 45 in 1987. It is not clear whether any of these complaints arose from bargaining.

[95] W. W. Steele Jr., "Deceptive Negotiating and High-Toned Morality" (1986) 39 *Vanderbilt Law Review* 1387.

they appear to be contrary to other professional or social norms.[96] A fundamental barrier to developing "ethical bargaining" is the fact that adversarial litigation encourages adversarial bargaining. At the heart of positional bargaining
is the need to mislead the other side. The most obvious example of information
to which this relates is the "bottom line"; only a fool would begin bargaining by
telling the other side the minimum payment he would accept. But once one
accepts the legitimacy of misleading information on estimates of price or value
it can easily be extended to validate a range of bargaining tactics which are more
obviously dishonest.[97] An officially sanctioned "culture of dishonesty" can too
easily contaminate other aspects of lawyers' work. Further, there is concern that
unethical decisions are more likely to occur in circumstances where *some deception is recognised as legitimate*. The "bright line" between the ethical and unethical becomes blurred leading to larger and larger infractions.[98]

In the USA there have been periodic calls for revised standards of bargaining
and heavier regulation.[99] Thurman argues that ambiguity in the Model Rules
should be eradicated:

> "Maintaining moral sensitivity and awareness is crucial to the practice of law. The
> profession must resist inroads on the lawyer's commitment to the truth, and take steps
> to correct rules that lessen this commitment. The unique role lawyers occupy in our
> society and their position as officers of our judicial system require that their word be
> trusted. More is required of a lawyer than the custom of the marketplace, than bar-
> gaining in a bazaar, or in playing poker. Lawyers must feel that theirs is a worthy role
> and an honourable profession."[100]

Given that the profession in the UK has a weaker commitment to partisanship
and the obligation of zealous advocacy,[101] we might expect that it would be less
willing to endorse the bargaining practices which are the source of so much
adverse comment in the USA. It is therefore surprising that the bargaining obligations of lawyers are so imprecise and ambiguous. It would be possible to draft
a principle of conduct which broadens the obligation of honesty in bargaining.
The crucial requirement is that any duty to third parties is not qualified by an

---

[96] Condlin n. 58 at 72.

[97] E.g. the argument that lawyers need not be truthful where deception is a norm of bargaining
or where there is a power imbalance between the parties and the deceitful lawyer acts for the weaker
side. W. H. Simon, "Ethical Discretion in Lawyering" (1988) 101 *Harvard Law Review* 1083, calls
this the test of relative merits (and see Gifford, n. 62 above, at 134 and R. B. McKay, "Ethical
Considerations in Alternative Dispute Resolution" (1990) 45 *The Arbitration Journal* 15, noting
that although the ABA's Model Rules of Professional Conduct (Rule 4.1) prohibit making a false
statement of material fact estimates of value are not treated as material facts (at 19).

[98] D. J. Luban, "Milgram Revisited" (1998) 9 *Researching Law: An American Bar Foundation
Update* 1 at 4.

[99] R. R.Perschbacher, "Regulating Lawyers' Negotiations" (1985) 27 *Arizona Law Rev.* 75–138;
A. R. Rubin, "A Causerie of Lawyer's Ethics in Negotiation" [1975] *Louisiana Law Review* 577;
Steele n. 95 above.

[100] R. F. Thurman, "Chipping Away at Lawyer Veracity: The ABA's Turn Toward Situation
Ethics in Negotiations" [1990] *Journal of Dispute Resolution* 103 at 115.

[101] D. Luban, *Lawyers and Justice: An Ethical Study* (Princeton, NJ, Princeton University Press,
1988).

overriding duty to clients. This may be thought unworkable but it is not. It would merely mean that a solicitor would have to adopt methods of bargaining, like principled negotiation, which seek solutions in both parties' interests. It would also require that they give reasons for not revealing particular information rather than giving misleading information on that point. If the practicality of such a principle is doubted, it should be noted that the solicitor's existing obligation of honesty to non-solicitor third parties, including professional bargainers such as insurance company representatives, is not qualified by the overriding interests of clients. Principle 17.01 of the *Guide* states that:

> "Solicitors must not act, whether in their professional capacity or otherwise, towards anyone in a way which is fraudulent, deceitful or otherwise contrary to their position as solicitors. Nor must solicitors use their position as solicitors to take unfair advantage either for themselves or another person."[102]

There appears to be no reason in principle why this formulation should not apply to dealings between solicitors. There are also strong arguments for adopting a principle of conduct which explicitly governs the obligations of lawyers in bargaining. This could marry the obligations of frankness and candour in relation to material facts with:

- an obligation to explore with clients their perceptions of their interests, and
- to seek a settlement where that is in the client's best interests, and
- to seek a settlement which satisfies the client's interests as far as possible and which is fair and reasonable to both sides.

This would shift the solicitors' focus from the pursuit of litigation to the pursuit of settlement. Since this is likely to be successful only if it is also financially rewarding it is necessary to recognise that the work which goes into achieving settlement is at least as valuable and skilled as that which goes into litigation. This would need to be reflected in the costs which a solicitor is allowed for pursuing settlement, either by agreement with the other side or on taxation of costs.

E. OVERVIEW OF STRATEGIES OF LITIGATION AND BARGAINING

It will be clear from the discussion so far that there are links between the conduct of litigation and the bargaining strategies which are used. These can be represented as overarching strategies of litigation and bargaining. Some of the possibilities which arise from the previous discussion are now summarised.

Strategic Defection

This is the strategy of "litigation-first". Lawyers using this strategy seek to avoid bargaining and settlement until late in the action and to build up costs. The

[102] At 308.

desired outcome, so far as the plaintiff's lawyer is concerned, is to reach trial without being forced to accept a settlement. The aim is to reduce the chance that the defendant will make an accurate payment into court.

Deceptive Defection

This strategy involves *appearing* to use a litigation-first strategy. The lawyer increases bargaining leverage by evincing determination to go to trial. In order to avoid the risk of trial and its considerable costs, the insurers have an incentive to make a generous offer. The desired outcome is that the insurer makes an early offer and is open to negotiation. Having achieved that position any form of bargaining can be used.

Deceptive Co-operation

Deceptive co-operators are not committed to the litigation-first strategy, although it may be used sometimes. Their preference is to settle as many cases as possible on favourable terms. They encourage settlement discussions and manipulate the process of bargaining to achieve their goal. A variety of deceptive tactics are used, including aggressive behaviour, "inflating" schedules of damages and concealing material information, such as the fact that a client has, in fact, recovered faster than her last medical report suggested she would.[103] Lawyers using such a strategy may convince themselves that it is, in fact, insurance companies which manipulate the bargaining process.[104] This justifies plaintiffs' lawyers asking "for considerably more than the case is worth, on the assumption that they will then offer much less, and it may be possible to settle the case for its true value with the insurers feeling they have managed to negotiate a low settlement".[105] Typically, therefore, the plaintiff's lawyer makes a high initial demand and, if resistance is encountered, there is a credible retreat,[106] through concessions, to settlement. In one study a solicitor said:

> "if it's worth £1000 it's worth £1200. If it's worth £100,000 it's worth £120,000. There's no difference in percentage. Your client may at the end of the day not care but you have to know you"ve done a good job. You want to be able to say 'that was worth £1,000 and I got £1,200'."[107]

---

[103] It could be argued that a defendant's representative should obtain his or her own up-to-date medical report before settling a case on the basis of the plaintiff's medical evidence; that is the nature of adversarial justice. If, however, it is accepted that bargaining should produce the outcome which a court would come to, this concealment would produce an obvious distortion.

[104] Genn observes that insurers are almost always competitive: Genn, n. 4 above, at 132.

[105] *Ibid.*, at 141.

[106] Ross, n. 65 above.

[107] A. Boon, "Ethics and Strategy in Personal Injury Litigation" (1995) 22 *Journal of Law and Society* 353 at 362.

Unconditional Co-operation

Unconditional co-operation has no role in the context of adversarial litigation. It leaves the person who uses it open to exploitation and his or her client at risk. There are times when proceedings must be issued or steps taken. Further, lawyers involved in bargaining must be able to be tough; to be provocable. It is the question of how toughness manifests itself, whether in a principled or unprincipled way, which is the issue.

Conditional Co-operation

It is clear from the above that a strategy of conditional co-operation is, in our view, the most ethical way for litigators to proceed in both litigation and bargaining. By maintaining reasonable relations with insurers and other lawyers, litigators are able to settle appropriate cases speedily. It is in the interests of insurance companies and others to treat them fairly, because failure to do so may result in legitimate reprisals. Conditional co-operators do not evoke the hostility which may prejudice reasonable settlements in later cases, and they are not open to accusations that they start proceedings in order to run up costs. The strategy marries the values of honesty and integrity to the technical skill of the litigator. The litigator must be highly expert in order to operate such a strategy and consistently obtain good results for clients. Conditional co-operation calls for a high level of strategic decision making and, because of this element of discretion, conditional co-operation is consistent with high traditions of professionalism. Of all the litigation and bargaining strategies, those which are most consistent with ethical conduct are (a) strategic defection and (e) conditional co-operation. The main problem with conditional co-operation is that it is not designed to take advantage of any weakness of the other side or mistakes made by it. By failing to take advantage the lawyer may not be acting in the best interests of the client. This provides at least some justification for the preference of the legal profession for strategic defection, a strategy of dubious effectiveness and relatively doubtful ethics, as a foundation for civil litigation.

CONCLUSION

There have been more changes in the profession's ethical stance in relation to litigation in the USA than in the UK. The 1936 ABA Canons of Professional Ethics were essentially hostile to litigation providing that "[w]henever the controversy will admit of fair adjustment, the client should be advised to avoid or to end the litigation"[108] and that "[i]t is unprofessional for a lawyer to volunteer advice to

---

[108] Canon 8 (see G. C. Hazard, "The Future of Legal Ethics" (1991) 100 *Yale Law Journal* 1239).

bring a lawsuit, except in rare cases where ties of blood, relationship or trust make it his duty to do so".[109] The 1983 Model Rules of Professional Conduct abandoned these admonitions and imposed no constraints on litigators going beyond those imposed by the law itself for the conduct of litigation.[110] The rules adopted a neutral stance which neither encouraged nor discouraged a particular strategy of negotiation. This difference in experience may, in part, be explained by the different methods of funding employed in the USA and the UK. Private-practice lawyers in the USA, whose costs are paid by their clients, place no demands on public funds; the costs of adversarialism are distributed between parties, insurers and society. The criticism which lawyers have attracted in the civil sphere in the UK may dissipate if the introduction of conditional fees proves to be a success.

Whether or not the current mistrust of the adversarial ethic continues, it is troubling that lawyers can develop norms which so clearly contradict the virtues of honesty or candour. The argument that such behaviour is consistent with the professions' role morality is increasingly difficult to sustain. The contradictions rooted in the adversarial ethic have in the USA led to doubt that partisanship, justice and the pursuit of client's informed preferences provides a suitable framework for defining professional responsibility.[111] In the UK the adversarial ethic may be too costly to the public purse[112] and, therefore, too fragile a foundation on which to ground the legal profession's claim to special status and privilege. Some of the darker practices of adversarialism, which may appear to be in the interests of clients, are contrary to the obligation not to be involved in deception or suppression or in any other conduct which may mislead the court. While the *Guide* may countenance a lack of frankness and candour, if it is in the overriding interests of clients, this is inconsistent with other views such as those expressed in the Marre Report that a professional should not "restrict the field of his or her vision or advice so as to avoid embarrassment, but must advise clients of their obligations and observe the rules of court, even where this may appear to be against the client's interests".[113]

Principled approaches to litigation and bargaining, which depend on honesty and problem solving, offer a more coherent theoretical basis for the lawyer's role in dispute resolution, not only because they are often more effective, but because they harness the "power of legitimacy".[114] Conducted properly, problem-solving bargaining is more rigorous and resistant to exploitation than an

---

[109] Canon 28 (*ibid.*, at 1262).

[110] *Ibid.*, at 1263. Although, in the context of litigation in the 1930s, the rules could be seen to be an attempt to curtail actions between the wealthy and business classes (*ibid.*, at 1256).

[111] A. Gutmann, "Can Virtue be Taught to Lawyers?" (1993) 45 *Stanford Law Review* 1759.

[112] T. Shneyer, "Moral Philosophy's Standard Misconception of Legal Ethics" [1984] *Wisconsin Law Review* 1529.

[113] Marre Report, n. 2 above, para. 6.4.

[114] Indeed, Condlin argues that the most valuable contribution made by principled negotiation to co-operative strategy is the legitimacy added by the injunction "yield only to principle, not pressure": Condlin, n. 58 at 26.

adversarial approach based on positional strategies. This supports the idea that lawyers in civil dispute resolution should be *required* to co-operate with each other and with non-lawyer representatives of other parties.[115] Adopting this approach would reinforce the efforts of the BVC and LPC to adapt problem-solving bargaining to adversarial contexts. At present, problem solving methods of bargaining tend to be conflated with more adversarial styles. This deepens confusion regarding the lawyer's obligations and makes it more difficult for problem solving to take root in the legal culture. Revising the adversarial ethic in civil litigation, including establishing a different culture of negotiation, may be a long-term project for the profession.

---

[115] *Ibid.*, at 93. Indeed, this is the ethic contained in the *Code of Conduct for Lawyers in the European Community*. This states that "the corporate spirit of the profession requires a relationship of trust and co-operation between lawyers for the benefit of their clients and in order to avoid unnecessary litigation. It can never justify setting the interests of the profession against those of justice or of those who seek it": *Law Society Guide*, para. 5.1.1.

14

Advocacy Services

"In order to further justice, in order to ensure that the machinery of justice is not perverted, those who operate the machinery must not merely know how to operate it, they must have a deep sense of things that are done and things that are not done. They need the guiding restraint of the professional spirit to prevent misuse of that machinery, to prevent waste of public time in useless wrangling, to promote proper forensic treatment of witnesses so that witnesses will not be unwilling to come forward to testify. They need to be able to inspire confidence on the part of the courts in being able to rely on what counsel represent to them instead of having to waste time in looking up everything because unable to assume the face of things as presented by the advocates."[1]

A. INTRODUCTION

Advocacy involves the professional presentation of another's point of view, which may or may not coincide with the advocate's personal convictions.[2] All lawyers are advocates in this sense. In terms of legal services "advocacy" has a more restricted meaning, limited to trial advocacy, still largely the monopoly of barristers, at least in superior courts and tribunals.[3] The rationale for a distinct core of advocates is that the thorough, honest and skilful presentation of cases saves the time of courts and so public time and expense.[4] The right to provide advocacy services has been a recurring source of friction between the two branches of the profession. The Bar has dominated advocacy though, at times, its supremacy has been threatened.[5] Until recently solicitors were restricted to

---

[1] R. Pound, *The Lawyer from Antiquity to Modern Times: With Particular Reference to the Development of Bar Associations in the United States* (St. Paul, Minn., West Publishing, 1953), at 127.

[2] For consideration of various conceptions of advocacy, see R. Audi, "The Ethics of Advocacy" (1995) 1 *Legal Theory* 251.

[3] The Courts and Legal Services Act definition, adopted in The Law Society's *Code for Advocacy* (para. 1.2), suggests that "advocacy services" mean "any services which it would be reasonable to expect a person who is exercising, or contemplating exercising, a right of audience in relation to any proceedings, or contemplated proceedings, to provide" (s.119); "court" means: (i) any court of record (the House of Lords, the Court of Appeal, the High Court, the Crown Court, country courts, magistrates' courts, coroners' courts); (ii) any tribunal which the Council on Tribunals in under a duty to keep under review; (iii) any court-martial; and (iv) a statutory inquiry within the meaning of s.19(1) of the Tribunals and Enquiries Act 1971; "litigator" means an authorised litigator as defined in Section 119 of the Act; "member" in relation to any authorised body means a member as defined in s.119 of the Act; "rule of conduct" means rules of conduct as defined in s.27(9) of the Act.

[4] Pound, n. 1 above, at 27.

[5] When the county courts were introduced in 1834, and solicitors were given rights of audience in them, the size of the Bar declined because the county courts took work away from the circuits, on

advocacy in the county courts, magistrates' courts and in tribunals; the right to conduct advocacy in higher courts was the exclusive preserve of barristers. In 1982 the Law Society, anticipating the decline of income from conveyancing, began to lobby for rights of audience in higher courts. This coincided with the government's desire to open up the market for advocacy.[6] The ending of the Bar's monopoly of higher courts became inevitable with the passage of the Courts and Legal Services Act 1990. The statutory role given to the Lord Chancellor's Advisory Committee for Education and Conduct,[7] included recommending that the Lord Chancellor approve "authorised bodies" for the purpose of accrediting advocates and litigators.[8]

In 1993 the Law Society became a body authorised to grant of rights of audience in higher courts to solicitors in private practice. In addition ILEX has been authorised to grant rights of audience for certain proceedings. Bodies like the institute for chartered surveyors are also making progress in this. The Act provides that a professional body, or other body seeking authority to grant either the right to conduct litigation or rights of audience, must have rules of conduct, effective mechanisms for enforcing them and be likely to do so.[9] The rules themselves must be "appropriate in the interests of the proper and efficient administration of justice".[10] In the case of rights of audience only, the rules of conduct must make "satisfactory provision" to prevent members offering advocacy services withholding those services on the ground that the nature of the case, or the conduct, opinions or beliefs of the client, is objectionable or unacceptable to him or to any section of the public or any ground relating to funding of the legal services.[11] The expansion of rights of audience to new groups has been slow, partly because of the procedures established for the granting of such rights[12] and partly because of economic, structural and cultural forces operating on solicitors.[13]

---

which barristers had exclusive rights: A. Thornton, "The Professional Responsibility and Ethics of the English Bar" in R. Cranston (ed.), *Legal Ethics and Professional Responsibility* (Oxford, Clarendon Press, 1995), 53 at 57.

[6] *The Work and Organisation of the Legal Profession*, Lord Chancellor's Department, (London, HMSO, 1989).

[7] See further on this Courts and Legal Services Act 1990, s.19(1) and on ACLEC's function s.20(1): "the general duty of assisting in the maintenance and development of standards in the education; training and conduct of those offering legal services", having "regard [under s.20(3)(b)] to the desirability of equality of opportunity between persons seeking to practice any profession, pursue any career or take up any employment, in connection with the provision of legal services".

[8] See s.27 for rights of audience and s.28 for litigation.

[9] Courts and Legal Services Act 1990, s.17(3)(b)(i)–(iii).

[10] *Ibid.*, s.17(3)(d).

[11] *Ibid.*, s.17(3)(c)(i)–(iii).

[12] M. Zander, "Rights of Audience in the Higher Courts in England and Wales Since the 1990 Act: What Happened?" (1997) 4 *International Journal of the Legal Profession* 167.

[13] J. Flood, A. Boon, A. Whyte, E. Skordaki, R. Abbey and A. Ash, *Reconfiguring the Market for Advocacy Services: A Case Study of London and Four Fields of Practice* (London, Report for the Lord Chancellor's Advisory Committee on Legal Education and Conduct, 1996), hereafter *ACLEC report*. Under the Access to Justice Bill 1998 solicitors will enjoy full audience rights in the same way as barristers.

This chapter considers four aspects of the provision of advocacy services: first, the issue of competence is considered in relation to the qualification requirements of both branches of the profession; secondly, the duties owed to clients by the providers of advocacy services; thirdly, the wider public duties which impinge on those practising advocacy; finally, we consider the responsibility of the legal profession to ensure that access to justice, where advocacy is a critical component of access, is provided to those who need such services.

B. QUALIFICATION AND COMPETENCE

Qualification

Barristers who complete all stages of education and training (including pupillage), are called to the Bar and have maintained a practice for three years may offer advocacy services in all courts. The advocacy services provided by the Bar are highly specialised. Newly qualified barristers, however, undertake a wide variety of work, including advocacy of a kind which solicitors could perform. Such barristers, by offering competitive rates, develop their forensic skills in minor cases and progress to more serious cases as their skills, experience and reputations permit. The upper echelon of the ranks of barristers, Queen's Counsel, are instructed in the most important and difficult cases and are the group from which the vast majority of judges are selected. Below the rank of Queen's Counsel there are virtually no formal distinctions between barristers. Upon qualification a barrister is often referred to as a junior barrister and, informally, those of more experience are often referred to, particularly by solicitors, as senior juniors. In theory, there are no restrictions on the right of barristers to represent a client in court. Subject to the three-year rule, admission to the Bar is the sole criterion.

The regulations which enabled solicitors to gain a higher courts qualification came into force from 8 December 1993[14] following a period of consultation which had started in April 1991, during which time aspects of the Law Society's proposals were amended to take account of ACLEC's views.[15] Solicitors must apply for, and be granted, a higher courts qualification before they can appear

---

[14] These included:
- Practice Rule 16A (solicitors acting as advocates);
- The Law Society's Code for Advocacy;
- Practice Rule 16B (choice of advocates);
- guidance on choice of advocate (for inclusion in client care booklet);
- Guidance on the interpretation of para. 4.1(e) and paras. 2.4 and 2.5 of the Code for Advocacy;
- the Higher Courts Qualification Regulations 1992.

[15] For a more detailed analysis of the process see, The Lord Chancellor's Department, *Rights of Audience and Rights to Conduct Litigation in England and Wales: The Way Ahead* (London, The Lord Chancellor's Department, 1998), Annex C.

in higher courts.[16] The Higher Courts Qualification Regulations 1993[17] provides the framework whereby the Law Society[18] may grant applicants who have practised for three years[19] one of three qualifications to conduct higher court advocacy for all proceedings, criminal proceedings only or civil proceedings only.[20] A higher courts qualification may be granted under regulation 4 to solicitors with "appropriate judicial or higher court advocacy experience"[21] as defined in Schedule 1 to the Regulations.[22] For those who cannot claim such experience, higher courts qualification can be gained in two stages. The first stage requires that the solicitor must "satisfy the Society that they are suitably experienced and suitably qualified to exercise rights of audience in the proceedings relating to the qualification for which they have applied".[23]

Schedule 2 relates "suitable experience" to "the range,[24] frequency, regularity[25] and quality"[26] of advocacy experience[27] in the "recent past".[28] The

[16] The Courts and Legal Services Act 1990 approved the arrangements established by the Bar Council for the training of advocates and the conduct of advocacy on the day the Act came into force. The existing rights of audience of barristers in all courts and of solicitors in lower courts were also preserved.

[17] *Professional Standards Bulletin*, No. 10, at 10.

[18] As an authorised body under the Courts and Legal Services Act 1990 s.27 and by virtue the Solicitors' Act 1974 s.2.

[19] The Higher Courts Qualification Regulations 1992, reg. 2 (Applications).

[20] (a) The Higher Courts (All Proceedings) Qualification which permits the holder to conduct advocacy in all courts and in all proceedings; (b) The Higher Courts (Criminal Proceedings) Qualification which permits the hold to conduct advocacy in the Crown Court in all proceedings and in other courts in all criminal proceedings; (c) The Higher Courts (Civil Proceedings) Qualification which permits the holder to conduct advocacy in the High Court in all proceedings and in other courts in all civil proceedings.

[21] Reg. 4(a).

[22] Those who do not satisfy the Law Society under this regulation may be required to take "additional steps". "The steps may include the gaining of more advocacy experience, the submission of references, the passing of the appropriate Test and the passing of the appropriate Course": Sched. 1(2).

[23] Reg. 5(i).

[24] For the criminal proceedings qualification a solicitor "may be expected to have appeared in the normal range of magistrates court criminal work, and to have appeared in bail applications, adjournment applications, committals, summary trials and guilty pleas. It would also be expected that the range of charges dealt with would encompass summary offences, either way offences and indictable offences" (Sched. 2(5)). For the civil proceedings qualification the solicitor would be expected to "have conducted a full range of county court work, including interlocutory applications, pre-trial reviews and hearing involving final orders of judgement, including contested trials" (Sched. 2(6)). The all proceedings qualification requires a mix of experience but not of the combined quantity required of applicants for the other two qualifications. Experience in higher courts gained by use of either of the other qualifications will be important (Sched. 2(7)).

[25] Frequency and regularity involve making a minimum of 20–25 appearances a year or before courts and tribunals (Sched. 2(3)). However, the Law Society is prepared to take into account limited opportunities for advocacy in the particular region (Sched. 2(8)), area of practice (Sched. 2(9)) or because of "career breaks, job changes, illnesses or disabilities" (Sched. 2(10)).

[26] Large numbers of simple, routine experiences carry little weight, while experiences which have lasted for a number of hours or days will count for more (Sched. 2(4)). However, "higher court experience" as an instructing solicitor in the court for which qualification is sought, with access to case papers and discussion of case handling with the instructed advocate, is also regarded as valuable (Sched. 2(11)). [27] Sched. 2(1).

[28] Sched. 2(2). Sched. 2(1) states that the Law Society's decision will be based on the record of experience in the two years preceding the application.

application must be supported by two references "from those who have first hand experience of the solicitor's advocacy work and whose standing as members of the judiciary, the court service or the legal profession would enable them to offer informed opinions".[29] If the solicitor satisfies the Law Society in relation to the first stage the Society issues a certificate of experience and eligibility to proceed[30] to either the Test of Evidence and Procedure in the Higher Criminal Courts and/or the Test of Evidence and Procedure in the Higher Civil Courts.[31] Passing the test is normally[32] a prerequisite of attending the appropriate course(s).[33] The structure, content and assessment methods of the course are set out in Schedule 4 to the Regulations.[34] The course is intensive and difficult. Preliminary reading may be sent to participants who may be required to leave the course if they "clearly have not read it".[35] The minimum duration of the course is 34 hours, of which 17 hours "should be spent on oral and written practical exercises".[36] These exercises form the basis for assessing whether the participant is competent to conduct advocacy in the relevant courts.[37] The criteria for performance assessment are not currently published. This complex set of regulations will be swept away as a result of Lord Irvine's Access to Justice Bill 1998. Under clause 30 (2) solicitors on qualification will have advocacy rights in all courts as well as the right to conduct litigation. The relevant qualification regulations will require approval by the Lord Chancellor under the Bill[38]

---

[29] Sched. 2(1).

[30] Reg. 5(ii).

[31] Reg. 6(1).

[32] Reg. 6(5).

[33] The Higher Criminal Courts Advocacy Training Course or the Higher Civil Courts Advocacy Training Course in each case provided by authorised and monitored providers (Reg. 6(2)).

[34] The Sched. provides, *inter alia*, that the aim of the course is that participants shall perform competently as an advocate in the relevant higher courts and that the course should therefore enable a participant to: (a) prepare an action for trial . . .; (b) develop a case presentation strategy . . .; (c) identify admissible evidence to be used in the presentation of a case and . . . make submissions concerning the admissibility of evidence; (d) examine, cross-examine and re-examine witnesses effectively and in accordance with the rules of evidence; (e) demonstrate a sound understanding of the Law Society's Code for Advocacy and of courtroom formalities; (f) formulate and present a cohesive argument based upon facts, general principles and legal authority in a structured, concise and persuasive manner; (g) analyse personal and other advocates performances to assess their effectiveness and identify the action necessary to deal with identified weaknesses; (h) draft pleadings relevant to the conduct of proceedings in the relevant courts including applications for leave to appeal and notices of appeal.

[35] The course specification appearing in the Regs. suggests that preliminary reading comprises course papers and documentation on practical exercises: the *Law Society Guide* including the Law Society's Advocacy Code and The Inns of Court School of Law coursebook *Advocacy, Negotiation and Conference Skills*. Participants must bring copies of the *Supreme Court Practice* or *Archbold*, as appropriate (Sched. 4(2)).

[36] Sched. 4(3).

[37] Sched. 4(4).

[38] The Bill is based on proposals contained in the Consultation Paper *Rights of Audience and Rights to Conduct Litigation in England and Wales: The Way Ahead* (London, The Lord Chancellor's Department, 1998), and the White Paper *Modernising Justice*, Cm 4155 December 1998.

Competence

Although competence is often seen as a personal quality, it is also a product of education, training and experience. Both branches of the profession now teach advocacy, procedure and evidence at the vocational stage of education. Since 1988 the Bar vocational course has placed a "double weighting" on advocacy compared to the other skills taught on the course. The LPC includes a significant advocacy component but it is of equal weighting to the other skills.[39] Neither the Bar nor the Law Society imposes any further training requirement related to advocacy following the acquisition of the right to appear in any particular court. Solicitor-advocates are obliged by the Code of Advocacy to organise their practices appropriately, to maintain libraries and to ensure that employees are aware of obligations arising under the code.[40] When solicitors instruct barristers to conduct advocacy they retain a responsibility to provide proper instructions.[41] Barristers are also under restrictions in the way they organise their practice, and these are considered below. The most powerful quality control may, however, be fierce competition for work. The Royal Commission on Criminal Justice recognised that "the best barristers are outstanding and that many are very good" but that a small number were "incompetent, prolix and poorly prepared".[42]

Although there are few formal restrictions on the difficulty of work which can be undertaken by barristers, there are strong cultural expectations concerning the kinds of case which it may be appropriate for barristers of different experience to handle. Barristers' clerks do not wish their barristers or their chambers to fall into disrepute and there is therefore a disincentive to overstretch the capabilities of junior members of chambers. Both branches of the profession impose an obligation on practitioners to assess their own competence to conduct any advocacy which arises from their instructions and to refuse instructions which

---

[39] The introduction of the new postgraduate vocational course for intending solicitors, the Legal Practice Course (LPC) and a new compulsory course for trainees, the Professional Skills Course (PSC) coincided with the higher advocacy rights regime. The PSC has a heavy bias towards advocacy at the expense, for example, of negotiation.

[40] Part 3 of the Code provides, at para. 3.1, advocates must have or have ready access to library facilities which are adequate having regard to the nature of their practice. Para. 3.2 states that advocates must take all steps which it is reasonable in the circumstances to take to ensure that: (a) their practices are administered competently and efficiently and property staffed having regard to the nature of the practice; (b) proper records are kept; (c) all employees and staff in the practice:(i) carry out their duties in a correct and efficient manner; and (ii) are made clearly aware of such provisions of this Code as may affect or be relevant to the performance of their duties.

[41] On the requirements for giving competent instructions to counsel, see S. Payne, "Instructing Counsel" in S. Payne (ed.), *Instructing Counsel* (Croydon, Tolley Publishing, 1994), at 3. This is the substance of the requirement that solicitors attend court with counsel so that, in cases where this requirement can be dispensed with, the solicitors should ensure that the brief is sufficiently comprehensive to compensate: *ibid.*, at 4.

[42] A. Owen, "Not the Job of a Judge", *The Times*, 6 Dec. 1994 at 39.

they are not competent to handle.[43] Such rules are expressed to be in the interests of both client and the justice system and are of fundamental importance because, as we have noted previously, both solicitor advocates and barristers enjoy immunity from actions in negligence brought by clients. In *Rondel* v. *Worsley*[44] the House of Lords held that a barrister[45] was immune from an action for negligence in relation to the conduct and management of the case in court and the preliminary work such as drafting pleadings.[46] This immunity covers trial work and work so intimately connected with trial work that it constitutes a preliminary decision on the conduct of the case.[47] Therefore, no challenge can be launched by the client in relation to such matters, even where an advocate takes a decision contrary to a client's wishes.[48] This immunity is based on public policy and long usage[49] and is intended to allow a barrister to conduct a case "fearlessly and independently", to prevent the retrying of litigation and so as not to undermine the cab rank rule.[50]

[43] Under para. 601 of the *Code of Conduct of the Bar of England and Wales* (London, The General Council of the Bar of England and Wales, 1990), hereafter *Bar Code*, a practising barrister: (a) must in all his professional activities be courteous and act promptly, conscientiously, diligently and with reasonable competence and take all reasonable and practical steps to avoid unnecessary expense or waste of the Court's time and to ensure that professional engagements are fulfilled; (b) must not undertake any task which: (i) he knows or ought to know he is not competent to handle;(ii) he does not have adequate time and opportunity to prepare for or perform; or(iii) he cannot discharge within a reasonable time having regard to the pressure of other work; (c) must read all briefs and instructions delivered to him expeditiously; (d) must have regard to the relevant Written Standards for the conduct of Professional Work (which are reproduced in Annex H of the code); (e) must inform his professional client forthwith and subject to para. 506 return the instructions or the brief to the professional client or to another barrister acceptable to the professional client: (i) if it becomes apparent to him that he will not be able to do the work within a reasonable time after receipt of instructions; (ii) if there is an appreciable risk that he may not be able to undertake a brief or fulfil any other professional engagement which he has accepted.

[44] [1969] 1 AC 191.

[45] A majority held that a solicitor acting as an advocate enjoyed the same immunity, although Lord Pearson recognised the difficulties with this (see 294).

[46] Lord Upjohn thought that the immunity should commence on the sending of the letter before action.

[47] See s.62(1) Courts and Legal Services Act 1990; *Saif Ali* v. *Sydney Mitchell & Co.*[1980] AC 198; *Rees* v. *Sinclair* [1974] 1 NZLR 180, 187 (CA); *Kelly* v. *Corston* [1997] 4 All ER 466; and *Acton* v. *Pearce* [1997] 3 All ER 909.

[48] *R.* v. *Gantam* [1988] CLY 574 (allegedly incompetent cross examination). See also *R.* v. *Ensor* [1989] 1 WLR 497 (decision by counsel not to apply for separate trials where defendant was charged on two counts of rape where the defence to both was the absence of sexual intercourse and consent). See also *R.* v. *Swain* [1988] Crim. LR 109.

[49] *Rondel* v. *Worsley* [1969] 1 AC 191; *Somasundaram* v. *M Julius Melchior* [1988] 1 WLR 1394 [1988] 1 All ER 129 (action for negligence against solicitor who persuaded defendant to plead guilty to imprisonment and assault of his wife. A civil action attacking a final judgment of a court was contrary to public policy even where the advice was not protected from immunity); and *R.* v. *Roberts* [1990] Crim. LR 122—counsel's decision not to introduce medical evidence not a valid ground of appeal even if wrong unless there was flagrantly incompetent advocacy; once a court announced a decision it regards itself as *functus officio*. See also *Munster* v. *Lamb* (1883) 11 QBD 558 which held that the immunity could be claimed even where a defamatory attack by an advocate was malicious, not negligent. For a case where liability in negligence was established, see *Acton* v. *Pearce* [1997] 3 All ER 909.

[50] It was not therefore, as had sometimes been thought, connected with the rule that a barrister could not sue for fees.

C. THE INDEPENDENCE OF ADVOCATES

Independence is a strong theme in the narrative of the Anglo-American legal profession as we have already noted. It is a theme with many threads including independence from the state, independence from clients and independence in the way in which work is organised and performed. The importance of independence to the advocate is captured in the response of the Bar to the battery of changes proposed in the 1989 Green Papers. The Bar considers that its strength:

"lies in its independence, and in the "cab-rank" rule, made possible by the independence of barristers in private practice as sole practitioners, and in its being a consultant profession acting on referral from solicitors and other professionals."[51]

The Law Society's Code for Advocacy also emphasises the importance of independence. Solicitor advocates must not:

"(a) permit their absolute independence and freedom from external pressures to be compromised;
(b) do anything (for example accept a present) in such circumstances as may lead to any inference that their independence may be compromised;
(c) compromise their professional standards in order to please their clients, the court or a third party . . ."[52]

These different aspects of independence are now dealt with in greater detail.

Independence from the State

Freedman argues that the adversarial process, whatever its defects, minimises the harms and maximises the benefits that characterise most processes of dispute resolution. One of these benefits is that it offers the best guarantee of the independence of a legal system, for:

"there is only one way to keep the law "trustworthy"—only one way to keep the bureaucrats honest, and to make the law work, that is, by making sure that there is an independent Bar, prepared to challenge government action and to do so as zealously and effectively as possible."[53]

The claim of lawyers to independence is most strongly expressed in relation to advocates. As we saw in Chapter 1, the rhetoric of the profession casts the advocate as a champion, one who must be willing to advance her client's case freely without fear of public or professional disapproval.[54] The advocate is a

---

[51] General Council of the Bar, *The Quality of Justice: The Bar's Response* (London, Butterworth, 1989), at paras. 2.3–2.4.

[52] *Ibid.,* Para. 2.6.

[53] M. H. Freedman, "Are There Public Interest Limits on Lawyers' Advocacy" [1977] 2 *The Journal of the Legal Profession* 47 at 54.

[54] S. L. Jacobs, "Legal Advocacy in a Time of Plague" 21 *Journal of Law Medicine and Ethics* 382.

partisan representative whose role is to present the strongest case possible. The adversarial system requires this because it proceeds by evaluating two "versions of the truth". Advocates in common law systems are trained to present a "theory of the case", consistent with both the evidence and the desired result.[55] The implications of this professional duty are perceived differently by laymen and lawyers. While George Bernard Shaw observed that "[t]he theory of the adversary system is that if you set two liars to exposing each other, eventually the truth will come out",[56] Freedman argues that the adversary system serves public policy in a uniquely important way:

> "[It] proceeds from the assumption that the most effective way to determine truth is to pit against each other two advocates, two adversaries, each with the responsibility to marshall all the relevant facts, authorities, and policy considerations on each side of the case, and to present their conflicting views in a clash before an impartial arbiter. In the performance of that adversarial role, zealous advocacy is, of course, an essential element in producing an effective clash of opposite views."[57]

The lawyers' role in the adversary system, intelligible to lawyers, makes observers doubt their integrity. Public opinion may be outraged when lawyers achieve the acquittal of criminal defendants on a technicality. The state, however, has both power and resources at its disposal. The individual citizen is at a massive disadvantage when these resources are marshalled against him. So, Freedman argues, the interests of the state "are not absolute, or even paramount . . . the defendant is at least afforded that one advocate, that 'champion against a hostile world', whose zealous allegiance is to him or her alone".[58]

Independence from Clients

Despite his partisan role, the advocate should also be independent of the client. This is regarded as a virtue by the Bar, a guarantee that barristers will not succumb to the unjustified demands of clients and, thereby, compromise their duty to the courts. Distance from clients is maintained in formal ways and expressly underpins the Bar Council's Code of Conduct.[59] Examples include the fact that

[55] A. Boon, *Essential Legal Skills: Advocacy* (London, Cavendish Publishing, 1993), at 58–60.
[56] Quoted in M. J. Saks, "Accuracy *v.* Advocacy: Expert Testimony Before the Bench" (1987) Aug/Sept *Technology Law Review* 43.
[57] Freedman, n. 53 above at 47.
[58] *Ibid.*, at 48.
[59] The statement setting out the general purpose of the Bar Code (n. 41 above) contains several references to "independence", i.e., para. 102 states the purpose of the code is:
"to provide the standards of conduct on the part of barristers which are appropriate in the interests of justice in England and Wales (and so far as applicable elsewhere) and in particular:
  (a) in relation to barristers in independent practice to provide common and enforceable requirements and prohibitions which together preserve and enhance the strength and competitiveness of the independent Bar as a whole in the public interest by requiring such barristers:
  (i) to be completely independent in conduct and in professional standing as sole practitioners;
  (ii) to act only as consultants instructed by solicitors and other approved professional persons;

barristers can accept work only where it is referred by other approved professions[60] and the fact that a barrister's fees are the responsibility of the firm of solicitors which instructs the barrister rather than that of the client who is represented. Barristers may appear in court only if their professional client is present unless they have a specific agreement with the professional client[61] or in an emergency.[62] The "cab-rank" rule is not only a formal expression of the commitment to professional obligation of neutrality, it also ensures that barristers are not reliant on a single paymaster. Therefore, barristers must accept a case unless they have a reason, which the Bar's Code of Conduct recognises as valid, for not doing so.[63] Likewise, having accepted a brief, a practising barrister cannot withdraw from a case except in specified circumstances[64] and subject to specific requirements for the return of the brief.[65]

These rules are often put forward as the ethical principles essential to independence. Indeed, it is the inability of employed lawyers to submit themselves to

(iii) to acknowledge a public obligation based on the paramount need for access to justice to act for any client (whether legally aided or not) in cases within his field of practice".

[60] While the original arrangement was that barristers would accept instructions only from solicitors, this has been broadened to include a range of other professions (see *Bar Code*, n. 44 above, at Annex E, "The Direct Professional Access Rules" and Chap. 5, above).

[61] Para. 608 of the *Bar Code* states that, provided a barrister is satisfied that the interests of the lay client and the interests of justice will not be prejudiced he may agree with his professional client that attendance by the professional client and his representative may be dispensed with for all or part of any hearing (a) in a magistrates' court or a county court; (b) provided that he has been supplied with any necessary proofs of evidence in any other Court.

[62] Para. 609 of the *Bar Code* provides that a barrister who has been briefed in a case may: (a) if the attendance of his professional client has been dispensed with pursuant to para. 608; or (b) if he arrives at court and neither the professional client nor his representative is in attendance and there are no other grounds on which to request an adjournment and no practicable alternative conduct the case on behalf of the lay client and if necessary interview witnesses and take proofs of evidence.

[63] The "cab-rank rule" obliges a barrister (except as otherwise provided in paras. 501, 502 and 503, of the *Bar Code*) in relation to any field in which he professes to practise, in relation to work appropriate to his experience and seniority and irrespective of whether his client is paying privately or is legally aided or otherwise publicly funded to (a) accept any brief to appear before a court in which he professes to practise; (b) accept any instructions; (c) act for any person on whose behalf he is briefed or instructed; and do so irrespective of the party on whose behalf he is briefed or instructed (ii) the nature of the case and (iii) any belief or opinion which he may have formed as to the character reputation cause conduct guilt or innocence of that person.

[64] I.e. where he is satisfied that (a) his brief or instructions have been withdrawn (b) his professional conduct is being impugned, or (c) there is some other substantial reason for so doing (*Bar Code*, para. 505).

[65] Para. 506, *Bar Code* requires that the barrister must not:
(a) cease to at or return a brief or instructions without having first explained to his professional client his reasons for doing so;
(b) return a brief or instructions to another barrister without the consent of his professional client of his representative;
(c) if he is a barrister in independent practice return a brief which he has accepted and for which a fixed date has been obtained or (except with the consent of his lay client and where appropriate the court) break any other professional engagement to enable him to attend a social or non-professional engagement;
(d) except a provided in para. 504, return any brief or instructions or withdraw from a case in such a way or in such circumstances that his client may be unable to find other legal assistance in time to prevent prejudice being suffered by the client.

the cab-rank rule that was one of the arguments used to deny them higher rights of audience.[66] The ACLEC Report referred to concern about the realities of pressures on CPS lawyers in denying them the opportunity to gain higher rights of audience.[67] The role of advocate, it is argued, should be separate from, for example, the decision to prosecute, and even from the task of case preparation.[68] But despite the importance attached to the cab rank rule its observance in reality is patchy. Barristers may sometimes "discover" prior obligations in order to refuse a brief. There have even been proposals to abrogate the rule in legal aid cases where legal aid costs do not cover the barrister's full fees.[69] In general, however, it is thought that the cab-rank rule works well compared to the situation in the USA where there is no equivalent rule.[70]

Solicitor advocates do not enjoy this structural protection from the direct influence of clients and may, unlike barristers, be in formal partnerships with other solicitors. The Law Society's Code for Advocacy stresses that solicitor advocates are "individually and personally responsible for their own conduct and for professional work . . . they must exercise their own personal judgement in all their professional activities and must not delegate such responsibility to another advocate".[71] Solicitor advocates are also subject to a rule similar to the cab-rank rule. The Code for Advocacy prevents a solicitor advocate from declining instructions on grounds of the race, gender or sexual orientation of the prospective client or because "the nature of the case is objectionable to the advocate or any section of the public" or because "the conduct opinions or beliefs of the client are objectionable to the advocate or any section of the public". Nor can a case be refused because of the nature of the financial support which the client may properly receive.[72] Solicitor advocates are, however, entitled to refuse a brief on the grounds that they will not be adequately remunerated (as are barristers).[73]

Solicitor advocates should not accept a brief if they realise that to do so would cause them "professional embarrassment".[74] Similarly, solicitor advocates

---

[66] Zander, n. 12 above, at 186–8.

[67] *Ibid.*, at 187.

[68] This was raised by the Bar Council in opposition to Crown Prosecutors being granted higher rights: see Thornton, n. 5 above, at 62. CPS lawyers and other employed lawyers will obtain advocacy rights under the Access to Justice Bill 1998.

[69] See Ch 3, section C.

[70] R. Cranston, "Legal Ethics and Professional Responsibility" in Cranston (ed.), n. 5 above, at 28–9.

[71] *Law Society Code for Advocacy*, para. 2.7.

[72] *Ibid.*, para. 2.4.2. As regards financial support, solicitors must not refuse clients supported under the Legal Aid Act 1988.

[73] *Ibid.*, para. 2.5 provides that an advocate is not required to accept instructions if there are reasonable grounds for the advocate to consider that having regard to:
  (i) the circumstances of the case;
  (ii) the nature of the advocate's practice; or
  (iii) the advocate's experience and standing the advocate is not being offered a proper fee.

[74] If they lack sufficient experience or competence to handle the matter (4.1.(a)), they lack adequate time and opportunity to prepare (4.1.(b)), the brief limits the discretion of an advocate in the conduct of proceedings in court or imposes an obligation to act against the provisions of this Code (4.1.(c)), where there are likely to be witnesses connected with the advocate (or of any partner or

should return a brief if they are likely to be professionally embarrassed if they continue with a case.[75] They are allowed to withdraw from a case where they are satisfied that the brief has been withdrawn or their retainer terminated, their professional conduct is being impugned or there is some other substantial reason for doing so.[76] Solicitor advocates must not, however, (a) cease to act or return a brief without having first explained to their client their reasons for doing so; (b) return a brief to another advocate without the consent of the client; (c) return a brief which they have accepted and for which a fixed date has been obtained or (except with the consent of the client and where appropriate the court) break any other professional engagement so as to enable them to attend a social or non-professional engagement; or (d) save as provided above return any brief or withdraw from a case in such a way or in such circumstances that their client may be unable to find other legal assistance in time to prevent prejudice being suffered by the client.[77]

Structural Protection of the Ethos of Independence

The Bar's Code of Conduct contains rules which seek to ensure that, in the way the practice of a barrister is structured, his independence is secure. The formal prohibition of partnerships[78] at the Bar is based on "the traditional conception of members of the Bar as individual practitioners enjoying an independent and

---

other associate of the advocate) whereby it will be difficult for the advocate to maintain professional independence or the administration of justice might be or appear to be prejudiced (4.1.(d)), where the legality of any action taken by the advocate is in dispute in the proceedings or if they are company directors and the company is a party to the proceedings (4.1.(e)), where there is a risk of a conflict between the interests of the advocate (or any other partner or other associate of the advocate) and some other person or between the interests of any one or more of their clients (4.1.(f)), where there is a risk of a breach of confidence (4.1.(g)).

[75] Part V, para. 5.1, of the Code provides that advocates should cease to act and return any brief if continuing to act would cause them to be professionally embarrassed with the meaning of para. 4.1 unless they are only likely to be witnesses on a material question, in which case they may retire or withdraw only if they can do so without jeopardising the client's interest or, in cases of conflict of interest or breach of confidence the clients do not all consent to the advocate continuing to act. Similarly they should surrender a brief if, in civil or criminal cases, it is clear that Legal Aid has been wrongly obtained by false or inaccurate information and action to remedy the situation is not immediately taken by the client (5.1(c)), if the client refuses to authorise them to make some disclosure to the court which their duty to the court requires them to make (5(1)(e)); if having become aware of the existence of a document which should have been but has not been disclosed on discovery the client fails forthwith to disclose it (5.1(f)); or if, having accidentally obtained and read a document "belonging to another party by some means other than the normal and proper channels" they would thereby be embarrassed in the discharge of their duties by their knowledge of the contents of the document provided that they may retire or withdraw only if they can do so without jeopardising the client's interests' (5.1(g)).

[76] *Law Society Code for Advocacy*, para. 5.2.

[77] *Ibid.*, para.. 5.3.

[78] Barristers must be in sole practice and not in partnership: *Bar Code*, n. 43 above, para. 207(a).

individual status".[79] There are features of practice at the Bar which undermine this claim to independence, individualism and service. These include the fact that solicitors tend to select barristers from chambers with reputations for particular kinds of work, the persistence of "devilling"[80] and the return of briefs so late that a solicitor has no practical alternative but to instruct another member of the same chambers.[81] More recently, in corporate/commercial work, it has been said that barristers are selected because they are "good team players, willing to go along with the client's wishes".[82] Although barristers appear to be free of ties to any particular paymaster, the pressure to specialise may make the barrister reliant on a small number of solicitors' firms with regular instructions in a particular area of work. The independence of advocates may be enshrined in formal rules in the code of conduct, but it may be undermined by the reality of practice.

Solicitor advocates, even those entitled to practise in the higher courts, are not subject to restrictions on partnership. Part II of the Law Society's Code for Advocacy does, however, prohibit solicitor advocates from engaging "directly or indirectly in any occupation if their association with that occupation may adversely affect the reputation of advocates or prejudice their ability to attend properly to the interests of clients".[83] A problem may arise when a client needing advocacy services is introduced to a firm with an advocate who is not suited to the particular case. In those circumstances the case should be referred to a suitable advocate elsewhere. There may be a temptation to try and keep the work if the advocacy is potentially lucrative or when the firm fears it may lose the client if it acknowledges that it cannot handle the case. The Law Society's Code for Advocacy attempts to protect clients in a number of ways. It provides that "[a]dvocates (whether or not they are also litigators and whether they are instructed on their own or with another advocate) must in the case of each brief consider whether consistently with the proper and efficient administration of justice it is appropriate for them to accept a particular brief".[84] The criteria against which this decision must be made involve the solicitor advocate asking whether in:

(i)   the circumstances including the gravity, complexity and likely cost of the case;

---

[79] From the report of a special committee set up by the Bar Council in 1959 under the chairmanship of Geoffrey Lawrence, QC. The Committee reported in July 1962 and the report appears in the *Bar Council Annual Statement, 1961*, at 40 and is discussed, and condemned, by M. Zander, "Partnerships at the Bar" in M. Zander, *Lawyers and the Public Interest: A Study of Restrictive Practices* (London, Weidenfeld & Nicolson, 1968), at 253–69.

[80] The farming out of papers to, often more junior, colleagues without either the professional or lay client knowing that this has been done.

[81] For discussion of these practices and the issue of barrister partnerships generally see Zander, n. 12 above.

[82] *ACLEC Report*, n. 13 above.

[83] Para. 2.1(b).

[84] *Ibid.*, para. 4.3.1.

(ii) the nature of their practice;
(iii) their ability, experience and seniority;
(iv) their relationship with the client;

the best interests of the client would be served by instructing or continuing to instruct them in that matter.[85]

Solicitor advocates are under an additional obligation to consider whether or not theirs is the most suitable firm to conduct work, considering the nature of the case and the expertise available in-house, and to advise the client accordingly.[86]

The enforcement of these rules presents problems as clients cannot sue advocates in negligence (and, in the case of barristers, cannot complain of advocacy services).

C. THE DUTIES OF ADVOCATES

The Advocate's Duty to Clients

Freedman argues that, in the USA at least, the importance of the lawyer's adversarial role as a bulwark against the power of the state imposes an obligation of zealousness on advocates. It follows, he suggests, that a defence lawyer in a criminal trial must do everything she can on a client's behalf to attempt to discredit a witness who she knows to be telling the truth, to allow a witness who she knows will commit perjury to give evidence and to advise a client in such a way as to enable the client to give perjured evidence. These are, he argues, the three "hardest questions a defence advocate must face".[87] It is almost certain that the legal profession in England and Wales does not subscribe to Freedman's view but it is less clear exactly where the limits of adversarialism lie in this country. It is clear that an advocate's duty is to say on behalf of a client what a client would say for himself. The precise wording of paragraph 2 of the Law Society's Code for Advocacy is, however, instructive. It says that advocates "must promote and protect fearlessly and by all proper and lawful means the clients' best interests and do so without regard to their own interests or to any consequences to themselves or to any other person (including professional clients or fellow advocates or members of the legal profession)"[88] and "must act towards clients

[85] Solicitors' Practice Rule 16B(2) requires a solicitor providing both litigation and advocacy services to consider these issues from "time to time": *Client Care: A Guide for Solicitors* suggests that the client be guided on choice of advocate and cost and that he or she should be provided with adequate information on which to make an informed choice on these matters.

[86] Solicitors' Practice Rules 16A (solicitors acting as advocates)—any solicitor acting as advocate shall at all times comply with the Law Society's Code for Advocacy. Practice Rule 16B (choice of advocate)—a solicitor shall not make it a condition of providing litigation services that advocacy services shall also be provided by that solicitor or by the solicitor's firm or the solicitor's agent.

[87] M. Freedman, 'Professional Responsibility of the Criminal Defense Lawyer: The Three Hardest Questions' (1966) 64 *Michigan Law Review* 1469.

[88] N. 86, above para. 2.3 (a).

at all times in good faith".[89] It will be apparent that the "zeal", which is implied in paragraph 2, is limited by the phrase "proper and lawful means". Therefore, we conclude, in the UK the advocate's obligations to clients does not include the zealousness conceived by Freedman. One of the main constraints is the duty owed by an advocate to the court. This is a feature of both the British and American systems.

The Duty to the Court

Certain duties owed to the justice system transcend the duty to clients; such a duty is usually expressed as a duty owed to the court.[90] In *Rondell* v. *Worsley*, Lord Reid expressed the balance the advocate is expected to hold between these duties as follows:

> "every counsel has a duty to his client fearlessly to raise every issue, advance every argument, and ask every question, however distasteful, which he thinks will help his client's case. But, as an officer of the court concerned in the administration of justice, he has an overriding duty to the court, to the standards of his profession, and to the public, which may and often does lead to a conflict with his client's wishes or with what the client thinks are his personal wishes. Counsel must not mislead the court, he must not lend himself to casting aspersions on the other party or witnesses for which there is no sufficient basis in the information in his possession, he must not withold authorities or documents which may tell against his clients but which the law or the standards of his profession require him to produce."[91]

Therefore, although a practising barrister must place the client's best interests over those of fellow members of the legal profession, professional clients and the legal aid fund,[92] the duty to the client is subject to an overriding obligation to promote justice. This is interpreted, broadly, along the lines indicated by Lord Reid, i.e. as a duty not to mislead the court.[93] This is not an inevitable interpretation of what a duty to the court means. It can be argued, for example, that a duty to the wider system is discharged by a conscientious fulfilment of the primary obligation to the client combined with due deference and courtesy to the judge and the judicial institution.[94] In England and Wales the duty to the

---

[89] Practice Rule 16B, para. 2.3 (c).

[90] The introduction to the Law Society's Code for Advocacy states that "[f]or the purpose of maintaining the proper and efficient administration of justice this Code sets out the principles and standards to be observed by all solicitor advocates when acting as such. These obligations are in addition to and do not replace those imposed by law or required by other Law Society Rules".

[91] N. 49 above at 227.

[92] Bar Code, n. 43 above, at para. 203.

[93] The Bar Code provides that "[a] practising barrister has an overriding duty to the Court to ensure in the public interest that the proper and efficient administration of justice is achieved: he must assist the Court in the administration of justice and must not deceive or knowingly or recklessly mislead the Court": Bar Code, n. 43 above, para. 202). The *Law Societys Code for Advocacy* contains a similar formula: see para. 2.3(b).

[94] S. Ginossa, "The Lawyer's Divided Loyalties: An Introductory Note" (1981) 16 *Israel Law Review* 1.

court is more developed than a requirement of courtesy and, in other ways, goes beyond a basic formula. It requires the exercise of ethical discretion because the precise circumstances that the advocate has to deal with may be unpredictable.

Barristers are given wide discretion regarding the conduct of proceedings in court[95] but may not express a personal opinion in relation to either law or fact.[96] This avoids the possibility of unseemly arguments with the judge. But, further, paragraph 609 of the Bar Code contains detailed provisions dealing with conduct in court, for example relating to the handling of witnesses. It also states that the obligation of advocates is to "ensure that the Court is informed of all relevant decisions and legislative provisions of which he is aware whether the effect is favourable or unfavourable towards the contention for which he argues and must bring any procedural irregularity to the attention of the Court during the hearing and not reserve such matter to be raised on appeal".[97]

The overriding rule binding all advocates is that that they must not mislead the court. But what constitutes "misleading the court"? It is not possible to be clear on the limits of the obligation because it is only possible to examine the views of the judges in those cases that have come before courts. This means that it is only those cases where the behaviour of lawyers was discovered and arguably affected the outcome of the case that opportunities to seek judicial opinion present themselves. In such cases it is clear that the judges perceive that the duty to the court is broadly based but imprecise; an advocate is expected to

---

[95] *Bar Code*, n. 43 above,, para. 610(a), provides that a practising barrister when conducting proceedings at court "is personally responsible for the conduct and presentation of his case and must exercise personal judgement upon the substance and purpose of statements made and questions asked".

[96] *Ibid.*, para. 610(b): "[a barrister] must not unless invited to do so by the Court or when appearing before a tribunal where it is his duty to do so assert a personal opinion of the facts or the law".

[97] *Ibid.*, para. 610. The Law Society's Code for Advocacy provides, in para. 7.1, that advocates, when conducting proceedings at court:
  (a) are personally responsible for the conduct and presentation of their case and must exercise personal judgement upon the substance and purpose of statements made and questions asked;
  (b) must not unless invited to do so by the court or when appearing before a tribunal where it is their duty to do so assert a personal opinion on the facts or the law;
  (c) must ensure that the court is informed of all relevant decisions and legislative provisions of which they are aware whether the effect is favourable or unfavourable towards the contention for which they argue and must bring any procedural irregularity to the attention of the court during the hearing and not reserve such matter to be raised on appeal;
  (d) must not adduce evidence obtained otherwise than from or through their client or devise facts which will assist in advancing their client's case;
  (e) must not make statements or ask questions which are merely scandalous or intended or calculated only to vilify, insult or annoy either a witness or some other person;
  (f) must if possible avoid the naming in open court of third parties whose character would thereby be impugned;
  (g) must not by assertion in a speech impugn a witness whom they have had an opportunity to cross-examine unless in cross-examination they have given the witness an opportunity to answer the allegation;
  (h) must not suggest that a witness or other person is guilty of crime, fraud or misconduct or attribute to another person the crime or conduct of which their client is accused unless such allegations go to a matter in issue (including the credibility of the witness) which is material to their client's case and which appear to them to be supported by reasonable grounds.

sense when his or her behaviour might undermine justice. Obiter statements in early cases, where the courts dealt with disciplinary charges against solicitors, are indicative of the standards of behaviour required. In *In re Mayor Cooke*,[98] for example, it was said that:

> "it was a part of [a lawyer's] duty that he should not keep back from the Court any information which ought to be before it, and that he should in no way mislead the court by stating facts which were untrue . . . How far a solicitor might go on behalf of his client was a question far too difficult to be capable of abstract definition, but when concrete cases arose every one could see for himself whether what had been done was fair or not . . . if he were to know that an affidavit had been made in the cause which had been used and which, if it were before the Judge, must affect his mind, and if he knew that the judge was ignorant of the existence of that affidavit, then if he concealed that affidavit from the Judge he would fail in his duty . . . if he were to make any wilful misstatement to the judge he would be outrageously dishonourable."[99]

The application of these principles is often more difficult than their expression however. This is particularly true when the issue before the court is whether a new trial should be ordered because the court has been misled in the course of proceedings. In such cases the issue is not whether the advocate has been negligent but whether the failure to order a new trial would be an injustice. The behaviour of the advocate is a critical factor in such cases. In *Tombling* v. *Universal Bulb Company Limited*[100] counsel for the plaintiff conducted an examination in chief of a witness and established his home address, his previous employment as a prison governor and his subsequent employment without referring to the fact that the witness was at the time of the trial serving a prison sentence for a driving offence. The Court of Appeal refused to set aside the decision of the court below because it could not be shown that this fact would have affected the outcome of the trial. Somervell LJ thought that counsel was probably not under any duty to disclose the witness's convictions but that it would have been better had plaintiff's counsel not put the relevant questions to the witness. He was not attracted by the argument that the perpetration of a trick by counsel,[101] even if proven, should itself be a basis for ordering a new trial.

Denning LJ would have been disposed to order a new trial had there been any improper conduct by the successful party. But, he said, there was nothing improper in the conduct of the plaintiff's counsel. Had the questions been put to the witness with the intention of misleading the court, it would have been a different matter. His Lordship was, however, satisfied that it had not been put with that intention. Singleton LJ took a less forgiving line, saying that, regarding the conflicting duties owed by advocates, "in this case counsel thought only of his duty to his client to the exclusion of the duty which he owed to others, and, in

---

[98] *In re G. Mayor Cooke* (1889) 5 *Times Law Reports* 407.
[99] *Ibid.*, at 408.
[100] [1951] 2 *Times Law Reports* 289.
[101] Presumably, presenting the witness as more credible than he in fact was.

particular, that which he owed to the court".[102] He would have ordered a retrial on the basis that this witness's evidence was material to establishing the plaintiff's case. Further, he said, there was a need to see that courts should be above suspicion and parties should feel that they had a fair deal.

In *Meek* v. *Fleming*,[103] a case with broadly similar facts, the decision went the other way and a re-trial was ordered. This was an action in which witness credibility was central, a civil action by a journalist claiming damages for an uncorroborated assault by a senior police officer. The defendant's counsel, a QC, took full responsibility for concealing from the court the fact that his client had been demoted for a deception on a court of law in the course of his duty as a police officer. At the trial the defendant had been deliberately dressed in civilian clothes and was addressed as "Mister" throughout. Yet his status and seniority had clearly been a material factor in the trial. It was held that to uphold the decision at first instance would be a miscarriage of justice. Holroyd Pearce LJ accepted Denning LJ's argument in *Tombling* that the intention of the advocate was material. The instant case, he said, was different from *Tombling* in that the court was deceived as a "premeditated line of conduct".[104] Wilmer LJ said that counsel's decision had "involved insufficient regard being paid to the duty owed to the court and to the plaintiff and his advisers.[105] In both *Tombling* and *Meek* the ethical decisions made by advocates for the benefit of clients had direct and adverse consequences for those clients. In both cases two factors detemined the court's decision; was the court deliberately misled by the advocate and did the fact that the court was misled affect the outcome of the case? An alternative interpretation of these cases, that an advocate has no positive duty to correct an impression innocently created, has been dispelled by two recent cases.

In *Vernon* v. *Bosley*[106] the plaintiff was awarded substantial damages for nervous shock resulting from the death of his two daughters. Following the first instance judgment, the defendants' counsel received copies of a judgment in proceedings relating to unconnected family proceedings which suggested that the plaintiff had substantially recovered by the time the judgment was delivered on his claim. Stuart-Smith LJ held that the relevant papers should have been disclosed to the defendant. It was the duty of every litigant not to mislead the court or his opponent. The plaintiff might mislead the court, not only by giving evidence that he knew to be untrue, but by leading the court to believe that circumstances, which were once true, had not changed. The duty continued until the judge had given judgment. His Lordship gave examples of instances where it may be permissible to stand by while the court is misled. Where a barrister knows of his client's previous convictions he is not under an obligation to disclose them but must not assert the good character of his client. Similarly, he is

102 N. 99 above, at 296.
103 [1961] 2 QB 366.
104 *Ibid.*, at 379.
105 *Ibid.*, at 383.
106 [1997] 1 All ER 614.

not bound to call evidence which does not support his case. But where evidence has been presented of material facts which are known to be untrue, counsel has an obligation to advise his client to make disclosure. If the client refuses this advice "it was not, as a rule, for counsel to make the disclosure himself, but he could no longer continue to act". The non-appearance of the plaintiff's counsel and solicitor would alert the defendants' advisers, and the judge, that there was something amiss.

Evans LJ, dissenting, sought to blame the plaintiff's expert witnesses, who had given evidence in both sets of proceedings. The plaintiff's counsel, he said, did not mislead the court or act improperly in any way. He was particularly concerned at the implications when expert witnesses, having given their evidence, changed their minds. Thorpe LJ argued that the current reform of civil justice must include "strengthening the duty to the court". He argued that counsel would know instinctively or intuitively that a course of action felt wrong and that, in such cases, he should not follow it. His Lordship suggested that the correct course of action was for the plaintiff's counsel to make disclosure to the opposing counsel in order to avoid the likelihood that injustice would be done.[107] In Thorpe LJ's judgment we see at least some lack of sympathy for role morality. To the extent that counsel might feel that what he did was wrong, it would have been "ordinary morality" which told him so. This view is interesting because, as we have seen, lawyers are normally encouraged not to be guided by ordinary morality but by the specific morality of their adversarial role.

A similar case is *Haiselden* v. *P&O Properties*.[108] A litigant in person commenced an action for damages for personal injury in the County Court. The sum involved required that the court should enter the case for arbitration but, in error, the case was put on the path to trial. The error remained undetected and, the plaintiff not realising the error, the case was tried and the plaintiff lost. Costs were awarded against him. Had the case been arbitrated, this would not have been possible. On appeal to the Court of Appeal, Thorpe LJ said that the defendants' advocate had:

> "very creditably and candidly informed us that at all stages the defendants perceived the advantage to themselves of the error of the court service . . . They thought that they would win on liability; they did not want an arbitration determination; they wanted determination by trial so that they had the prospect of recovering the costs of their defence. Accordingly they took advantage of the judicial error and felt able to do so because they considered that it was still arguable that some administrative notice of reference to arbitration needed to be issued. They comforted themselves by saying, "if and when such a notice is issued we will then apply to the judge inter partes for a ruling rescinding the reference to arbitration."[109]

The plaintiff succeeded in having the order for costs set aside on the basis that there should never have been a trial. But there was no hint of criticism in the

---

[107] See comment by D. Pannick, "When Counsel Should Come Clean", *The Times* ,14 Jan. 1997.
[108] Court transcript, 5 May 1998. See also *Law Society Gazette*, 3 June 1998.
[109] *Ibid.*, at 7.

judgment of the advocate who, realising the court's mistake, had allowed the process of trial to continue.

The trend discernible in these judgments is that the courts are moving towards a more onerous conception of the advocate's duty to the court. What emerges is an obligation to ensure that justice is done which goes beyond a prohibition on deliberately misleading the court.[109a] To be less than scrupulously honest with the court could have adverse consequences for the client and the advocate's reputation. A similar obligation of honesty subsists in relation to the specific provisions of the Legal Aid Regulations. Advocates should not, for example, certify a case as suitable for Legal Aid, knowing that, in fact, it has very little chance of success. In this respect, the obligation to protect public funds also transcends duties to clients. This is less clearly the case in relation to the actual performance of the advocacy task. In short, there is no duty to be succinct. Any observer of court television from the United States will note that advocates in serious cases are anything but brief, and proceedings are correspondingly lengthy. Pound attributes this tradition of "untrammelled advocacy" in the United States to the frontier reliance on self-representation.[110] But in the UK, particularly in serious cases, a similar tradition persists. In *The English Bar: The Tribute of an American Lawyer*, Hollander celebrates the link between untrammelled advocacy and the English barrister thus:

> "It should be remembered that if counsel fails to appear the opposing counsel will take his place and in the best of faith adduce the facts and state the law that he must meet and overcome. Here is 'priesthood'. Patience and thoroughness is the rule of the Bar and the Court; time is never more than a passing consideration and counsel are permitted to exhaust the argument . . . no warning light and cutting short as in the U.S. Supreme Court—'Justice is seen to be done'."[111]

But, to some extent, this is a distortion. Historically, the Bar discouraged verbosity. Pound relates an example of a barrister who was presenting a speech when a boy fell asleep in the well of the court and fell and broke his neck. Instruments of murder were, at that time, forfeit to the Crown. Presumably in the spirit of "comradely humour" which characterised the Bar at that time, the barrister was indicted by the Circuit "for murder with a certain dull instrument to wit a long speech of no value".[112] In the UK there are strong suspicions that advocates whose clients are legally aided in civil cases tend to be prolix, one of the reasons underlying Lord Woolf's proposal for judicial case management.

While in general the assertion that lawyers in England and Wales owe a duty to the court seems clear enough, the way in which the duty to the client and the

---

[109a] This may include an obligation to correct a mistake of fact made by the court but, for a contrary view, see M. Stobbs 'Ethical Issues Facing the Bar' (1998) 1 *Legal Ethics* 27. It should also be noted that the Bar Code requires a barrister to continue to represent a client who claims that he did not commit an offence but wishes to plead guilty (Bar Code n. 44, para. 12.5 Annex H).

[110] Pound, n. 1 above, at 239.

[111] B. Hollander, *The English Bar: The Tribute of an American Lawyer* (London, Bowes, 1964).

[112] Pound, n. 1 above, at 127.

court should be reconciled is not always obvious. Some lawyers identify strongly with the individuals they represent and may be tempted to place loyalty to them above the duty to the court.[113] "Cause lawyers", for example, sometimes use methods frowned upon by the judiciary and the profession to delay the execution of their clients.[114] In the UK immigration field, barristers, in order to delay the deportation of a client, may certify cases as appropriate for Legal Aid when they are clearly not.[115] In pursuing these "causes" lawyers may leave the purely professional realm of technical expertise and enter the political sphere. In one notable case in the USA involving an appeal against the death penalty, the court criticised the accused's lawyers for "abusive delay, which has been compounded by last minute attempts to manipulate the legal process".[116] Others, however, have observed that although cause lawyers represent a "deviant strain" in the legal profession they do reconnect the idea of law and morality. Paradoxically, this may undermine the law's legitimacy but it may legitimise the legal profession's role in society.[117]

In contrast to the cause lawyer, some advocates acting for defendants in criminal cases may facilitate the smooth processing of their work by placing their relationship with court staff and professional opponents above their duties to clients.[118] Recent empirical work suggests that defence solicitors routinely adopt a non-adversarial approach because they share similar social and crime control values as prosecutors. They adopt a routinised, if not casual, attitude to presenting facts to courts. This is illustrated by an excerpt from a transcript of

---

[113] See J. F. Sutton, and J. S. Dzienkowski, *Cases and Materials on the Professional Responsibility of Lawyers* (St. Paul, Minn., West Publishing Co., 1989), at 2 (lawyers often are unaware of the extent to which they get caught up in the emotions and ambitions of their clients . . . Often clients come to consider the lawyer as "the best friend they have . . . with such an attitude, the client may harbour certain magical expectations, for instance, that the lawyer is able to accomplish any manipulation or transaction which the client desires"); J. P.Tomain, "False Idylls of Lawyering" (1985) 35 *Journal of Legal Education* 157 (questioning whether a lawyer should attempt to meet, as opposed to mediate, client expectations). Scheingold and Bloom suggest that there cause lawyering represents a continuum. At one end 'transgressive' cause lawyers deploy the law for political purposes, at the other end 'conventional' cause lawyers seek reform or to make the state live up to its ideals (S. Sheingold and A. Bloom, "Transgressive cause lawyering: practice sites and the politicization of the professional" (1998) 5 *International Journal of the Legal Profession* 209 at 245.

[114] See generally A. Sarat, "Bearing Witness and Writing History in the Struggle Against Capital Punishment" (1996) 8 *Yale Journal of Law and the Humanties* and A. Boon and P. Hodgkinson, "Life and Death in the Lawyer's Office: The Internship in Capital Punishment Studies" (1997) 30:3 *The Law Teacher* 253, particularly 259–60 and 266–9.

[115] *ACLEC Report*, n. 13 above.

[116] *Gomez v. US* (1992) 112 S Ct. 1652, 1653.

[117] A. Sarat and S. Scheingold (eds.), *Cause Lawyering: Professional Commitments and Professional Responsibility* (Oxford, OUP, 1998); and see A. Sarat, *Between (The Presence of) Violence and (The Possibility of) Justice: Lawyering Against Capital Punishment* (USA, Amherst College, 1974) and "Bearing Witness and Writing History in the Struggle Against Capital Punishment" (1996) 8 *Yale Journal of Law and the Humanities.*

[118] See generally A.S. Blumberg, "The Practice of Law as a Confidence Game" (1967) 2 *Law and Society Review* 15; M. McConville, J. Hodgson, L. Bridges and A. Pavlovic, *Standing Accused: The Organisation and Practices of Criminal Defence Lawyers in Britain* (Oxford: Clarendon Press, 1994), chap. 2.

an interview taken from the research of McConville *et al.*[119] In this excerpt a solicitor interviews a client, who has admitted purchasing cannabis, with a view to establishing what can be said in mitigation:

Solicitor:	Are you a cannabis user or was this your first time?
Client:	(smiling) This would have been the first time!
S	(laughing) Straight up?
C	(with mock assertiveness) Yes!
S	Is there anything else we can say? You've had it before obviously—not that we"ll tell them that . . . What was your last job?
C	I was a waiter about six months ago.
S	And before that?
C	I was on a scheme.
S	Before that?
C	A youth training scheme.
S	Any prospects of work? Can we say that you're pissed off not working and that's why you decided to do it?
C	I don't think it would be wise to say that.
S	Okay, I'm here to take instructions from you. Just a one off then?
C	Yes.
At court	
Solicitor:	This may be a young man who, unfortunately, is not able to find work and may have thought he would find release via this.[120]

There are several ethical objections to this lawyer's behaviour. As the authors of the research observe, the solicitor offered to help the client construct mitigation, misled the court and involved the client in the lie. It should also be noted that this lawyer also ignored the client's clearly expressed preference that nothing should be made of his employment situation. The solicitor therefore denied the client's right of self-determination.

D. THE BALANCE: STANDARDS OF FAIRNESS AND PROBITY IN ADVOCACY

Standards of probity in advocacy are important, not only to the administration of justice, but to the reputation of the legal profession and to the confidence which government and public place in legal professionals. Advocacy is a highly visible professional activity; one which is newsworthy and open to more official and public scrutiny than any other activity undertaken by lawyers. This is perhaps why, when the Law Society published its own Code for Advocacy it

[119] *Ibid.*
[120] *Ibid.*, at 209.

emphasised that "[a]dvocates must not: (a) engage in conduct whether in pursuit of their profession or otherwise which is: (i) dishonest or otherwise discreditable to an advocate; (ii) prejudicial to the administration of justice; or (iii) likely to diminish public confidence in the legal profession or the administration of justice or otherwise bring the legal profession into disrepute".[121] Many of these rules were already covered elsewhere in the *Guide*. Their reiteration in the context of advocacy must, therefore, have symbolic force. They underline the idea that the advocate carries special responsibilities. More specific rules also underline the public nature of the advocate's duties. So, for example, barristers should not use their immunity from action to impugn the character of witnesses or others.[122] Solicitor advocates must not treat any person, i.e. witnesses, "less favourably" than other persons on the grounds of, *inter alia*, race, gender or sexual orientation.[123]

These examples create significant doubt regarding Freedman's assertion that lawyers are obliged to place the interests of clients above the integrity of the justice system. Freedman's account of the advocate's obligations has also been challenged in the USA. Noonan argues that Freedman misrepresents the philosophy of the justice system. By conceiving of trials as "battles", in which the advocate is bound to do everything possible in a client's cause, Freedman is able to justify the acceptance of dishonesty in witnesses, including his client.[124] But, Noonan argues, the advocate's duty is to assist the judge in making an impartial, wise and informed decision; to seek to establish the truth. Therefore "the advocate plays his role well when zeal for his client's cause promotes a wise and informed decision of the case".[125] Both visions have merit and are, to some extent, reflected in the contemporary conception of the advocate's role. Freedman, for example, makes a good point when he argues that a client must reveal all of the facts to the lawyer in order to allow the best defence to be put forward. If the

---

[121] Para. 2.1.

[122] The *Bar Code* provides, at para. 6.10, that barristers, (e) must not make statements or ask questions which are merely scandalous or intended or calculated only to vilify insult or annoy either a witness or some other person; (f) must if possible avoid the naming in open court of third parties whose character would thereby be impugned; (g) must not by assertion in a speech impugn a witness whom he has had an opportunity to cross-examine unless in cross-examination he has given the witness an opportunity to answer the allegation; (h) must not suggest that a victim, witness or other person is guilty of crime, fraud or misconduct or make any defamatory aspersion on the conduct of any other person or attribute to another person the crime or conduct of which his lay client is accused unless such allegations go to a matter in issue (Including the credibility of the witness) which is material to his lay client's case and which appear to him to be supported by reasonable grounds."

[123] The Law Society's Code for Advocacy, para. 2.4.1 provides: "[a]dvocates must not in relation to any other person (including a client or another advocate) on grounds of race, ethnic origin, gender, religion, sexual orientation or political persuasion treat that person for any purpose less favourably than they would treat other such people".

[124] See further Freedman, n. 87 above and W. Simon, "The Ideology of Advocacy: Procedural Justice and Professional Ethics" (1978) 29 *Wisconsin Law Review* 30 at 34, which criticises both Freedman and Noonan as naive but concludes that the only alternative to the philosophical contradiction inherent, in advocacy is non-professional advocacy with personal advocacy the ideal (pp. 130–144).

[125] J. Noonan, "The Purposes of Advocacy and the Limits of Confidentiality" (1966) 64 *Michigan Law Review* 1485 and Simon, n. 124 above.

lawyer must refuse to act on discovering facts which compromise her belief in the honesty of the client, there arises the unappealing prospect that clients may move from lawyer to lawyer, adjusting their story until they find one who can act without being compromised. There are ways of dealing with suspicion that one's client is guilty without "knowing" that the client is guilty. Lawyers interviewing clients may seek to pre-empt the client's attempt to reveal embarrassing facts. On the other hand, having revealed a version of events which does not sound credible the client may be told "I do not think that the court will believe your story but my job is to put your case before the court. If this is what you are telling me, that is what we will tell the court".

On the other hand, Noonan's view is that the clash of committed adversaries does not always reveal the truth. Therefore, lawyers undermine the system of justice when they allow clients to subvert the truth. As Richard Nixon, himself a lawyer, observed:

> "the only way justice can truly be done in society, is for each member of that society to subject himself to the rule of law—neither to set himself in the name of justice nor to set himself outside the law in the name of justice."[126]

These issues can be usefully explored against the background of the debate between Freedman and Noonan in which Freedman's "three hardest questions" served as examples. They are not the only problems which confront the advocate[127] but, through them, it is possible to explore the tensions between expectations of "zeal" and probity. By considering the conduct rules in England and Wales and the cases set out above, we may cast some light on the issue of whether our courts and legal profession subscribe to the "battle" or the "informed decision" explanation of the adversarial system.

It must be remembered that the Freedman and Noonan were exploring the limits of "zealous advocacy" as promoted by the ABA standards. As we have noted, "zeal" is not a concept adopted by the codes in the UK. It will also be noted that Freedman's justification of procedural abuse as a part of the adversarial role of lawyers explicitly applies to criminal defence only. Criminal prosecutors, as representatives of the state, are often placed under specific constraints. Criminal defence lawyers are often cast as protectors of individual liberty. There are strong arguments, as discussed in the last chapter, for not extending "the adversarial excuse" to civil proceedings.[128] The rules of professional conduct, however, make no distinction between the responsibility of

---

[126] R. Nixon (1971) 7 *Trial* 45 (May/June) cited in Sutton and Dzienkowski, n. 113 above, at 16.

[127] How, e.g., should an advocate deal with a client who claims innocence but wishes to plead guilty to avoid the possibility of conviction and a heavier sentence? By allowing a client to admit guilt and privately claim innocence a lawyer is subverting justice particularly when it is known that the court will not accept an ambiguous "guilty" plea: *R. v. Turner* [1970] 2 QB 321, suggests that the advocate should seek to dissuade an innocent client from pleading guilty, but see M. McConville, "Plea Bargaining: Ethics and Politics", (1998) 25 *Journal of Law and Society* 562.

[128] D. Luban, "The Adversary System Excuse" in D. Luban (ed.) *The Good Lawyer: Lawyers' Roles and Lawyers' Ethics* (Totowa, NJ, Rowman and Allenheld, 1984).

advocates in civil and criminal proceedings. Freedman's "three hardest questions" are now examined in greater depth.

Should an Advocate Attempt to Discredit a Witness Known to be Telling the Truth?

It is the job of the advocate to expose *dishonesty* in opposing witnesses. Freedman states that the advocate should also attempt to discredit a witness "known" to be truthful.[129] The problem is how does the advocate know the witness to be truthful? Often this can itself be discovered only by a vigorous cross examination in order to test the witness.[130] Such a cross-examination may lead the advocate mistakenly to question the witness's reliability. Equally, even where the witness is seen to be honest, the evidence may be undermined without attacking the witness's integrity.[131] It is very difficult to draw a line in such cases, but to attack a witness who is plainly honest appears unethical to the ordinary person and also is likely to lose the sympathy of judge and jury.[132]

The hostile treatment afforded honest witnesses was recently given a high profile in England by cases in which victims of rape were subjected to gruelling cross-examination. In one case a man eventually convicted of rape opted to conduct his own defence and subjected his victim to six days of cross-examination. The barrister prosecuting the case was reported as saying that he now felt "completely schizophrenic" on the issue of whether sex offenders should be allowed to cross-examine their alleged victims personally. He added, "half of me says this should never happen again. But the other half says the defendant was exercising a centuries-old right that should not be simply swept away".[133] In another case the victim of gang rape was cross-examined over a period of 12 days by *lawyers* for multiple defendants. Boal J said, on convicting the attackers, "[f]or over thirty hours this girl had to relive the ordeal in a public court in front of total strangers. Outrageous suggestions were put to her on your instructions. You, not your counsel, added insult to injury and heaped further humiliation on her."[134]

---

[129] Freedman, n. 88 above, illustrates his argument with the example that the judge may, mistakenly, permit an honest witness to give irrelevant testimony (see also Pepper, who asserts that a challenge to a truthful witness is permissible in all circumstances: S. Pepper, "The Lawyers' Amoral Ethical Role: A Defense, A Problem and Some Possibilities" [1986] *American Bar Foundation Research Journal* 613). While Freedman argues that the opposing lawyer may then be obliged to discredit the witness, rather than the testimony, Noonan, n. 125 above, argues that the advocate must trust the judge to exclude such testimony. A lawyer, he says, must not pre-empt the role of the judge or jury in assessing the truth.

[130] R. Audi, "The Ethics of Advocacy" (1995) 1 *Legal Theory* 251 at 276.

[131] F. Loftus, " 'Eyewitness Testimony' and Impact of Expert Psychological Testimony on the Unreliability of Eyewitness Identification" (1980) 65 *Journal of Applied Psychology* 9.

[132] Boon, n. 56 above, chap. 6.

[133] See *The Lawyer*, 27 Aug. 1996 and 3 Sept. 1996.

[134] See *The Guardian*, 24 Aug. 1996 and 5, 7 Sept. 1996.

The judge's remarks absolved the lawyers in the case from blame. They, in the judge's view, were performing the duty which the adversarial system requires of advocates. This explanation of the lawyer's behaviour must, presumably, be based on the view that they had no option but to accept these instructions. Otherwise, would not the defence advocates have perceived that the suggestions that they were instructed to put to the victim crossed the line between establishing the truth and causing an honest witness to forsake her pursuit of the truth? The fact that they felt bound to put "outrageous suggestions" must be because they had adopted Freedman's, rather than Noonan's, view of their role. Ironically, the victim in the first of the cases discussed above has applied to the European Court of Human Rights on the ground that her cross-examination by her attacker breached the requirement of the European Convention of Human Rights that criminal proceedings should be organised so as to prevent "degrading treatment, discrimination and violation of the right to privacy".[135]

Should an Advocate allow a Witness who the Advocate Knows will Commit Perjury to Give Evidence?

In civil litigation it is generally regarded as legitimate for either side in a case leading to trial to reveal only the witness statements of witnesses who are known to support the case being advanced. In criminal cases the prosecution is obliged to reveal details of certain witnesses they do *not* propose calling and are obliged to produce witnesses who appeared in committal proceedings.[136] The freedom not to call witnesses also applies to expert witnesses who are often selected, not only for their expertise, but for their predisposition to support the case of those instructing them.[137] While this is not improper—it follows the rules established for the presentation of evidence—it does present problems. In particular this kind of practice is another illustration of how the adversarial system can blur the boundaries between conduct which is acceptable, i.e. witness selection, and behaviour which is not, i.e. suborning perjury. This is exemplified in the selection of expert witnesses:

> "Long before the expert and lawyer arrive in court, a bond has formed between them. The influence of the lawyer is considerable. He or she may authorise a limited budget for analysing the evidence and restrict the information provided to experts about the case. The attorney expects help and co-operation from experts, who know that the

---

[135] *The Lawyer*, 29 Oct. 1996.

[136] See re expert evidence CCR, O.20 r.27 and RSC, O.38 r.37; and A. Keane, *The Modern Law of Evidence* (London, Butterworths, 1994), chap. 5. The defence now has (limited) duties of disclosure under the Criminal Procedure Investigations Act 1996, Part I.

[137] In personal injury cases, e.g., it is common to obtain medical reports from specialist consultants who are known to be plaintiffs' consultants or defendants' consultants. There are some exceptions to the rule in relation to expert witnesses in children's cases.

lawyer could hire someone else. The question is how far they are willing to be drawn out onto the forensic limb."[138]

Lord Woolf's report seems to accept the fact that the adversarial system leads to the possibility that evidence is strained or distorted by expert witnesses. The costs wasted by testing expert evidence are one of the considerations behind his proposal to replace "partisan experts" with court-appointed experts.

Having recognised these definitional problems, there are still cases where it is known to the lawyer that a witnesses proposes to present incorrect and material facts before the court. Noonan argues that the presentation of such evidence must be unethical because it will lead to injustice. Freedman's position is that there may be circumstances where justice will ultimately be achieved by presenting such evidence.[139] The profession in the UK clearly rejects Freedman's position. The *Marre Report* emphasised the advocate's duty to the court:

> "In criminal cases there is a rule against self incrimination which protects the client. Accordingly, the lawyer's duty of disclosure to the court in these cases is more limited, but he still must not take any positive steps nor make any positive statements which mislead the court. A lawyer may not, directly or indirectly, lend himself knowingly to any false story being put before the court. If he is asked to do so, he must immediately cease to act for the client. Because of the doctrine of legal professional privilege, which shields from outside eyes what passes between a lawyer and his client, the observance by the lawyer of his duty to the court is of particular importance."[140]

Tombling clearly shows that a witness should not be allowed to create a misleading impression, let alone commit perjury.

Should an Advocate Advise a Client in such a Way as to Enable the Client to give Perjured Evidence?

In Chapter 7 we noted the difficulty surrounding a request from a client for advice which might assist him in breaking the law. The difficulties are compounded where there is a risk that an advocate's duty to the court may be compromised. Freedman envisages a situation where a client does not ask a question directly. Rather, in a question-and-answer session between lawyer and client, by

---

[138] Saks, n. 57 above, at 44 (this is potentially of huge significance . . . it is widely believed that both judges and juries attach more importance to the scientific evidence than evidence of fact: see M. J. Saks and R. Van Duizend, "The Use of Scientific Evidence in Litigation" [1983] *National Centre for State Courts: USA* 5.

[139] This is contradicted by cases decided under US state laws: *McKissick v. United States*, 379 F2d 754 (5th Cir. 1967)—admission of perjury to attorney was good cause for withdrawal from case; attorney would be subject to discipline if continued defence without reporting to the court; *Dodd v. Florida Bar*, 118 So. 2d 17 (Fla. 1960)—advising several persons including client to perjure themselves warrants disbarment: G. C. Hazard, "The Future of Legal Ethics" (1991) 100 *Yale Law Journal* 1239 at 1257.

[140] Lady Marre CBE, *A Time for Change: Report on the Committee on the Future of the Legal Profession* (London, The General Council of the Bar, The Law Society, 1988), para. 6.6, hereafter the *Marre Report*.

positive and negative answers to the client's questions, the lawyer helps the client to identify which facts may help to acquit him. Noonan suggests that the complexity of the process by which advice is given, which includes evaluation of facts outlined by the client, renders this example irrelevant in all but the most extreme circumstances.[141] As far as the codes in England and Wales are concerned, it is clear that it is improper to allow a client to construct facts based on legal advice, but neither the Bar's nor the solicitors' code of advocacy deals with Freedman's example explicitly. Paragraph 6.10(d) of the Bar's Code of Conduct provides that "a barrister must not adduce evidence obtained otherwise than from or through his professional client or devise facts which will assist in advancing his lay client's case". Paragraph 607 also states that out of court a barrister must not pressurise a witness to give "other than a truthful account" or rehearse, practise or coach witnesses. The Law Society's Code for Advocacy also prohibits solicitor advocates from devising facts "which will assist in advancing their client's case and must not draft any originating process, pleading, affidavit, witness statement or notice of appeal containing (a) any statement of fact or contention (as the case may be) which is not supported by the client or by their brief or instructions [and] (b) any contention which they do not consider to be properly arguable".[142]

Whether or not these rules cover the behaviour described by Freedman depends on the interpretation of phrases such as "devising facts" and "properly arguable". There may be a difference between "devising facts" and interviewing a witness in the manner suggested by Freedman. What is "properly arguable" may depend on whether one adopts Freedman's or Noonan's view of what is proper. Other provisions in both codes give clues to the intention of the draftsmen but are not definitive. For example, the Law Society's Code for Advocacy also provides that "[a]dvocates must not when interviewing a witness out of court (a) place witnesses who are being interviewed under any pressure to provide other than a truthful account of their evidence; (b) rehearse, practise or coach witnesses in relation to their evidence or the way in which they should give it".[143] Is Freedman's example an instance of "rehearsing, practising or coaching" the client? While Freedman's argument can be rejected using ethical arguments it is flawed in other ways. Inaccurate evidence is dangerous to the side that advances it, as the quotation from a litigation solicitor suggests:

[141] n.197 at p.488
[142] Para. 6.6, which continues:
(c) any allegation of fraud unless they have clear instructions to make such allegation and have before them reasonably credible material which as it stands establishes a *prima facie* case of fraud;
(d) in the case of an affidavit or witness statement any statement of fact other than the evidence which in substance according to their instructions the advocate reasonably believes the witness would give if the evidence contained in the affidavit or witness statement were being *viva voce*; provided that nothing in this paragraph shall prevent an advocate drafting a pleading, affidavit or witness statement containing specific facts, matters or contentions included by the advocate subject to the client's confirmation as to their accuracy.
[143] Para. 6.5.

"courts to most people are daunting, and the way they give their evidence is coloured by their fear and their conception of what they are doing . . . I have seen witnesses lie when there is absolutely no need to lie and it causes all sorts of problems."[144]

Various ways of addressing these problems in the form of rules have been proposed. It has been argued that any advocate should in presenting a case "(1) have, (2) be genuinely motivated by, and (3) offer, or at least be willing to offer good reasons" for the judgment they seek.[145] This means that an advocate should not give spurious reasons, claim disproportionate force for their reasons or give reasons which they believe have only a superficial appeal. On this view the advocate should be convinced that the reasons given are good.[146] Such a position may be difficult to maintain as a representative lawyer. Advocates sometimes offer weak reasons because there are no good ones and because the underlying rationale of the adversary system is that clients are entitled to their day in court. Where an advocate believes that a client may be guilty of a criminal charge, but that there is insufficient evidence to convict, most lawyers would argue that it is not only ethical but essential to press for an acquittal.

E. ACCESS AND CHOICE

The final issue considered in this chapter is that of access to advocacy services. This is a precondition of access to justice, since the ability to hire a specialist advocate confers an advantage in legal proceedings. Access can be restricted by formal rules, such as restrictions on who may brief advocates, or by factors such as cost. Advocates have limited options if they are obliged to accept clients. There are only two relevant decisions; whether to represent and how to represent. Once the client has been accepted it is a "betrayal of trust to provide the client with a defence which is less than the law allows".[147] As regards cost, different ways of organising legal professions may affect access to advocacy services. Access is facilitated where services are available for a fee appropriate to the level of expertise necessary. Barristers are selected by solicitors or other approved professionals and, subject to satisfying themselves that they have the experience to handle a case, barristers need not concern themselves with the degree of choice exercised by the lay client. The choice of barrister is likely to be made by a solicitor rather than by a lay client except where the client is a knowledgeable "repeat player". In the case of solicitor advocates the issue of choice is more problematic, partly because firms may offer an advocacy service or

---

[144] A. Boon, "Assessing Competence to Conduct Civil Litigation: Key Tasks and Skills" in P. Hassett and M. Fitzgerald (eds.), *Skills for Legal Functions II: Representation and Advice* (London, Institute of Advanced Legal Studies, 1992).

[145] Audi, n. 130 above, at 263.

[146] *Ibid.*, at 265.

[147] Freedman, "Professional Responsibility of the Criminal Defence Lawyer" (1996) *Michigan LR* 1469 at 000.

because the litigator is also an advocate. The lay client is less able to decide whether she would be better served by another advocate.

The decision to give full rights of audience in higher courts to solicitors has profound implications both for the profession and for access. The provision of advocacy services in higher courts is the *raison d'être* of the split profession and there is an argument that the present system is both cost-effective and efficient. In a fused profession there is a risk that the supply of high quality advocacy services would be concentrated in a small number of elite firms. This would limit access to such services. At least five studies of the attitudes of solicitors to extended rights of audience have been conducted.[148] Most suggest that there is unlikely to be a rush by solicitors into higher court advocacy. A questionnaire sent to the heads of litigation of 85 City firms established that there was a large majority in favour of a split profession[149] and against the establishment of in-house advocacy units[150] or independent solicitor advocates.[151] Views were more evenly divided on the "one-stop shop" concept, whereby solicitors within firms provide advocacy in the cases in which they are dealing.[152]

While the rationale for extending rights of audience is to increase competition and choice[153] the separation between solicitors and barristers had advantages as well disadvantages. The "double manning" required by the split profession, with both solicitors and barristers acquainting themselves with the same set of facts and both being required to attend court, costs more than it would cost for one person to prepare and present a case. But, by virtue of the way in which the Bar is organised, and in particular the low practice overheads which barristers enjoy compared to solicitors, barristers are cheaper to instruct for advocacy than are solicitors. These arguments do not convince Lord Irvine, however, whose consultation paper on higher rights of audience proposes that barristers and solicitors should have equal access to higher courts on qualification, subject to whatever requirements are imposed by professional bodies. In his introduction to the proposals Lord Irvine writes:

> "Professions and industries throughout Britain have changed to meet the challenges of greater competition and increasing consumer demands. Working practices have been modernised and have become more flexible, while old restrictive practices have been swept away. The legal profession cannot and should not be immune from this process,

---

[148] F. Belloni, *British Solicitors and Barristers: Change in the Legal Profession*, Paper presented to the Law and Society Association and the Research Committee on the Sociology of Law of the International Sociological Association Joint Meetings (Glasgow, 10–13 July 1996); *ACLEC Report*, n. 13 above; R. Annand, G. Davis, J. Hasler, R. Kerridge and T. Press, *The Impact of Solicitors' Higher Court Rights upon the Advocacy Market in Bristol* (Bristol, 1996); The City of London Solicitors' Company, Whittington Committee, *Report of the Working Party on Solicitor Advocates in City Firms* (London, 1996); and A. Coles, *Solicitors in the Higher Courts* (London, The Law Society, 1997).
[149] 67% with 25% having no view.
[150] 48% against, 14% for.
[151] 54% no, 21% yes, 12% no objection and 9% no view.
[152] 42% no, 38% yes and 20% no view.
[153] *Modernising Justice*, Cm 4155 1998 at para. 2.26.

but there remain features of the way the profession is organised which the Government believes stifle innovation and maintain rigid structures, limiting consumer choice and increasing the expense of going to law. One particular example is the restriction on the right to appear as an advocate; members of the public often complain that they are required to hire two lawyers, where one would do. Any restrictions which inhibit access to justice have no place in modern Britain."[154]

Even if solicitor advocates do not produce any tangible cost benefits to clients, there may be advantages in terms of continuity, familiarity with the client and case and, therefore, in efficiency.[155] The concentration of specialist advocacy in the barristers' branch prevents the far more numerous solicitors' branch developing the necessary skills. If, however, the Bar ceases to be viable as a result of increased solicitor advocacy, then both choice of advocate and the cost of advocacy may be adversely affected. While senior barristers will continue to be used by solicitors, competition from solicitors and the declining availability of legal aid and criminal work may deprive the junior Bar of the work on which it has traditionally "cut its teeth". In the longer term many aspiring advocates may choose the solicitor branch of the profession, where they will be cushioned from the financial difficulties of establishing themselves. The independent bar may wither as a consequence.

The arguments against extending rights of audience also include concerns that the specialisation produced by a split profession maintains standards of competence in advocacy. Standards of probity and independence amongst advocates are enhanced where they are (a) insulated from the pressure to accede to client's wishes and (b) committed to ensuring the integrity of the legal process. Another benefit of an independent Bar with a monopoly of advocacy in higher courts is the wide availability of specialist legal advice[156] based on familiarity with the processes of adjudication, including trial advocacy. The coexistence of these two functions in one branch of the profession is not necessary, but may be desirable. The decline of the Bar would diminish the availability of an independent and objective view, both in advocacy and advice giving. Small solicitors' firms which do not have solicitor advocates on staff may find it increasingly difficult to find an advocate who is not affiliated to another firm. This would lead to the concentration of litigation services in larger units and would reduce rather than increase choice for "the consumer" of legal services. On the other hand, solicitor advocates may, over time, opt to set up their own "chambers", not connected to a particular firm, or join the Bar. In that case "independent" advocates could be more widely available. If moving between the branches of the legal pro-

---

[154] See summary of the proposals in Lord Chancellor's Department, *Rights of Audience and Rights to Conduct Litigation in England and Wales: The Way Ahead* (London, Lord Chancellor's Department, 1998), Annex A, and for comments on the proposals: L. Tsang, "Lord Irvine Says the Bar's Open", *The Independent*, 26 June 1998, and H. Hallett, "No Bar to Properly Qualified Solicitors", *The Independent Friday Review*, 26 June 1998.
[155] The City of London Solicitors' Company, Whittington Committee, n. 149 above.
[156] Thornton, n. 5 above, at 53.

fession became easier, the old debates regarding fusion would become redundant.[157] The market would both decide who would continue to offer advocacy services and, in theory at least, operate to reduce the cost of advocacy.

CONCLUSION

Whilst there are concerns regarding the standards of probity of some advocates appearing before our courts, these concerns are secondary to concerns relating to the failure of lawyers both to be sufficiently adversarial and also to recognise the limits of adversarialism. Even the judges are divided on what information a lawyer is obliged to reveal to a court. Therefore, it should not be surprising that clashes between duties to the client and to the notion of justice may frequently be resolved in favour of clients. Although ambiguity and uncertainty are not an inevitable consequence of the adversarial system, the way in which lawyers are expected to resolve this fundamental conflict is far from clear. The last two chapters have identified a significant challenge for legal ethics; to more clearly delineate the boundaries of adversarialism. The difficulties inherent in doing this raises the question of whether so-called Alternative Dispute Resolution (ADR) offers an environment more hospitable to ethical conduct. The potential of ADR and the role of lawyers in realising this potential are explored in the next chapter.

---

[157] See P. Reeves, *Are Two Legal Professions Necessary?* (London, Waterlow Publishers, 1986).

15

Alternative Dispute Resolution

"Why . . . are lawyers, in essence, such obscure men? Why do their undoubted talents yield so poor a harvest of immortality? The answer, it seems to me . . . is their professional aim and function [is] not to get at the truth, but simply to carry on combats between ancient rules."[1]

A. INTRODUCTION

Most common law jurisdictions have sought ways of avoiding the cost and delay of litigation by exploring the use of Alternative Dispute Resolution (ADR), particularly mediation, to supplement or to replace it.[2] Litigation has come to be seen as a process that is too formal, that may exacerbate conflict and delay the resolution of problems that are in reality economic, social or political problems.[3] The method of dispute resolution used must therefore be appropriate to the kind of conflict dealt with.[4] It is, however, less easy to identify which methods are embraced by the label ADR or to see what ADR is an alternative to. Terminology is not yet fixed and there are definitions of conciliation in some jurisdictions which could be treated as mediation in others. Methods of dispute resolution which may be regarded as alternative including mini-trial,[5] arbitration[6] and expert determination,[7] share features of litigation.

[1] H. L. Mencken, "Editorial", *American Mercury*, Jan. 1928, at 35, 36.
[2] A. J. Pirie, "The Lawyer as a Third Party Neutral: Promise and Problems" in D. P. Emond (ed.), *Commercial Dispute Resolution: Alternatives to Litigation* (Aurora, Canada Law Books Inc, 1989), 27 at 29.
[3] D. P. Emond, "Alternative Dispute Resolution: A Conceptual Overview" in *ibid.*, 1 at 4.
[4] W. F. Felstiner, R. L. Abel and A. Sarat, "The Emergence and Transformation of Disputes: Naming, Blaming, Claiming . . ." (1980–1) 15 *Law and Society* 631 and particularly at 640–1.
[5] This is a shortened version of a full trial presentation to senior executives of the parties to the dispute, or a retired judge, who informs the parties about the relative legal and or factual merits of the case and sets the stage for realistic high level negotiations: see J. F. Davis and L. J. Omlie, "Mini Trials: The Courtroom in the Boardroom" (1985) 21 *Will. L Rev.* 531; B. C. Hart, "Alternative Dispute Resolution: Negotiation, Mediation and Minitrial" [1987] FICC. *Quarterly* 113; and C. Ervine, *Settling Consumer Disputes: A Review of Alternative Dispute Resolution* (London, National Consumer Council, 1993), at 12.
[6] Arbitration is defined as a non-judicial proceeding in which disputing parties submit their conflict to an impartial person or group of persons instead of to a judicial tribunal. Awards tend to be binding, final and enforceable in the courts: see B. H. Goldstein, "Alternatives for Resolving Business Transactions Disputes" (1983) 58 *St. John's L. Rev.* 69; M. P.Reynolds, *Arbitration* (London, Lloyd's of London Press, 1993), Part 1; and B. J. Thompson, "Commercial Dispute Resolution: A Practical Overview" in Emond, n. 2 above, at 91.
[7] For a brief description of this process "by which parties to a contract jointly instruct the third

The most notable common feature of these alternatives to public courts is that a third party, an impartial judge, adjudicates at the end of the process.[8] He or she, having adopted a passive role throughout the proceedings, must finally decide between the competing parties' contentions, on the basis of the evidence. Therefore, some methods classified as "alternative" are not alternative in terms of process. They may be alternative in the sense that they are not state sponsored.[9] However, this is not always the case either. Conciliation has long been a requirement of certain kinds of divorce proceeding, arbitration is compulsory for small claims in the county courts and mediation will soon become compulsory in family cases and possibly as part of Lord Woolf's proposed fast track or as a factor, for example, in awarding costs.[10]

In the light of these facts it is only possible to say that *some* methods of dispute resolution, notably mediation and conciliation, pursue the *consensual* resolution of the problem through the medium of a third party, as a facilitator.[11] The third party will not impose a decision or solution. Mediation and conciliation involve helping:

'the disputants co-ordinate their meanings: to assist in creating a story commensurate with each person's goals and to help each party make sense of the other party's story. For mediators, the objective is to restore a moral and ethical order apart from the disputant's experiences of their particular set of meanings."[12]

The process is therefore radically different from adjudication, which chooses between stories. Mediation and conciliation processes are more informal and flexible than court processes. Even arbitration, the most formal process, will often take place in informal surroundings. In mediation and conciliation, the third party encourages the parties to explore perspectives and may try to bring about agreement. Because of the informality of the process, mediation and conciliation afford opportunities for the participation of the lay client in the process. It is probably for this reason that some surveys show a public preference for ADR over court-based dispute resolution.[13] Even where there is ultimately an

party 'expert' to decide an issue", see J. Kendall, "Simpler Dispute Resolution", *Solicitors Journal*, 29 Nov. 1996, at 1152. It is said e.g. that the process is similar to arbitration and produces a binding decision but with less formal and with less judicial control and potentially, significantly cheaper.

[8] P. Gulliver, *Disputes and Negotiations: A Cross-Cultural Perspective* (New York and London, Academic Press, 1979).

[9] G. C. Hazard, "Court Delay: Toward New Premises" (1986) 5 *Civil Justice Quarterly* 236.

[10] Lord Woolf, *Access to Justice (Final Report)* (London, HMSO), 4–12.

[11] See generally A. Bevan, *Alternative Dispute Resolution* (London, Sweet and Maxwell, 1992); and J. M. Haynes, *Alternative Dispute Resolution: Fundamentals of Family Mediation* (Horsmonden, Old Bailey Press, 1993).

[12] L. M. Cooks and C. L. Hale, "The Construction of Ethics in Mediation" (1994) 12 *Mediation Quarterly* 77.

[13] In a recent survey published by the National Consumer Council (NCC) three quarters of respondents suggested that they would have preferred some form of ADR to the process of civil litigation they had actually experienced. Six out of 10 people involved in personal injury or divorce cases said they would have preferred mediation. Fewer than one in 10 favoured a full trial as the best means of resolving their dispute: *Seeking Civil Justice* (National Consumer Council, 1995) at 11. See

adjudication, as in arbitration, there is more party control over the process. Thus, in arbitration the parties can agree in advance what procedures will be followed. These distinctive features of ADR, and the implications of these for the ethics of lawyers, are now considered in more detail.

B. CONSENSUAL PROBLEM SOLVING

The use of ADR processes is the result of either a contractual provision, on the initiative of the parties after the dispute arises, or it may be mandated or permitted by court procedures. An example of the latter are family disputes referred to mediation under the Family Law Act 1996.[14] Despite this supposed advantage, however, it seems that alternative processes may not solve certain kinds of problems but, rather, provide a process by which the parties come to accommodate, or think of ways to deal with, the problem.[15]

Control by Parties

In mediation and conciliation the relative informality of process, venue and structure increase opportunities for disputants to play a role in settling their conflict. Informal processes encourage exploration of the causes of conflict,[16] permit a wider range of solutions which reflect the values and priorities of the parties,[17] and may encourage a high degree of compliance with the outcome.[18] In theory, these methods offer a more consensual approach to solving disputes, focusing on underlying interests rather than positions. Mediation is often compared to problem-solving negotiation using a third party intermediary[19] and, indeed the process has been characterised as a process in which the parties learn

also A. Ogus, M. Jones-Lee, W. Cole and P. McCarthy, "Evaluating Alternative Dispute Resolution: Measuring the Impact of Family Conciliation on Costs" (1990) 53 *Modern Law Review* 57.

[14] Part I, which is due to come into force in early 2000.

[15] See R. Young, "Neighbour Dispute Mediation: Theory and Practice" (1989) 2 *Civil Justice Quarterly* 319.

[16] Modern society and laws also produce more complex disputes, with multiple parties, high level of interdependency between parties and issues, polycentricity (interlinking of issues so that dealing with one impacts on others, unclear linkages and poor understanding of issues by parties): Edmonds, n. 2 above, at 14.

[17] Conflict arises in different ways and for different reasons; conflicts over scarce resources are materially different from situations where there are different percepetions of a situation. The potential for conflict may be increased when the values held by the different sides in a dispute clash, a possibility enhanced by the increasing pluralism of society: Edmonds, n. 2 above, at 13.

[18] There is some evidence that the mere act of signing a mediation agreement may secure greater compliance in some kinds of mediation compared with compliance with court orders. See further C. A. McEwen and R. J. Maiman "Small Claims Mediation in Maine: An Empirical Assessment" (1981) 33 *Maine Law Review* 237

[19] C. Menkel-Meadow, "Lawyer Negotiations: Theories and Realities: What we Learn from Mediation" (1993) *Modern Law Review* 361.

to negotiate.[20] For these reasons ADR creates the possibility of more accessible and community-orientated forms of dispute resolution and less expensive, more efficient ways of resolving disputes. The promise is of more acceptable process(es) producing more "satisfying results".[21] It has been suggested , however, that this "consensual" model of facilitative mediation is only one of a range of possibilities. This tends not to be recognised in the literature because dispute resolution theorists sometimes fail to recognise "power" mediation, in which the third party acts more like a negotiator and uses leverage to coerce a settlement.[22] This distinction may, however, be particularly relevant to the introduction of compulsory ADR as an alternative to adversarial dispute resolution.

Court-annexed ADR

The provision of ADR mechanisms by the state has been the subject of a long debate in the United States and, with the Woolf proposals, this debate will certainly take centre stage in the United Kingdom.[23] Court-annexed ADR schemes have substantially reduced court congestion in some jurisdictions.[24] They tend to be less expensive than independent schemes because the cost of accommodation and other overheads are absorbed by the court system.[25] The objections to ADR in general are not necessarily addressed by annexation to court structures.[26] Adding ADR to court-based processes may increase the net cost of settling disputes overall, particularly when the process fails and its costs are then added to the cost of litigation.[27] Moreover, processes which are not a part of the judicial process are the more likely to be effective in relation to the satisfaction

---

[20] See P. H. Gulliver, *Disputes and Negotiations: A Cross-cultural Perspective* (New York, Acadamic Press, 1979), and, for a summary, M. Roberts, "Who is in Charge? Reflections on Recent Research on the Role of the Mediator" (1992) 14 *Journal of Social Welfare and Family Law* 372 at 374–6.

[21] Emond, n. 2 above, at 3.

[22] R. Dingwall, "Empowerment or Enforcement? Some Questions about Power and Control in Divorce Mediation" in R. Dingwall and J. Eekelaar (eds.), *Divorce Mediation and the Legal Process* (Oxford, Oxford University Press, 1988); J. D. D. Smith, "Mediator Impartiality: Banishing the Chimera" (1994) 31 *Journal of Peace Research* 445.

[23] For a succinct exposition of the main issues see N. Fricker and J. Walker, "Alternative Dispute Resolution: State Responsibility or Second Best?" (1994) 13 *Civil Justice Quarterly* 29. It should be noted that Lord Woolf did not propose court-annexed ADR but favoured the position that the court should be able to take into account unreasonable refusal of ADR or unreasonable behaviour in ADR in relation to costs (*Final Report*, section 1 para. 18).

[24] D. R. Hensler, "What We Know and Don't Know About Court Administered Arbitration" (1986) 69 *Judic.* 270; W. K. Edwards, "No Frills Justice: North Carolina Experiments With Court Ordered Arbitration" (1988) 66 *NCL. Rev.* 395; and Pirie, n. 2 above, at 35.

[25] Ogus *et al.*, n. 13 above, at 66.

[26] See generally R. L. Abel, "The Contradictions of Informal Justice" in R. L. Abel (ed.), *The Politics of Informal Justice* (New York, Academic Press, 1982), and J. Auerbach, *Justice Without Law? Resolving Disputes Without Lawyers* (Oxford: Oxford University Press, 1983).

[27] It was found to add approximately £150 to the cost of settling a child dispute: Ogus *et al.*, n. 13 above, at 73.

of the parties and the durability of the agreement.[28] One of the main reasons for this is that participants in court-based schemes experience pressure from the third party neutral to reach speedy conclusions.[29] Lord Woolf's proposals envisage that mediation could be a prerequisite of the right to commence litigation or of an application for legal aid.[30] This would substantially undermine the consensual element which is a part of the rationale for ADR. On the other hand, it has been argued that widespread ignorance of the potential of alternative methods may justify coercion to participate.[31] Although it has been suggested that there is a distinction between the voluntariness within the ADR process and the freedom to choose the process in the first place, it remains a concern that, without voluntary commitment from the parties, ADR is unlikely to be successful.[32]

Formality

The formality of ADR processes often depends on the extent to which the process is public or private. This affects the scope for participation by the parties to the dispute, which is associated with informality. The degree of control parties can exercise over the resolution of the dispute can be increased provided the procedure permits and encourages this. The public or private locus also affects the accountability of representatives and the decision-making powers and levels of accountability of third-party neutrals.[33] So some kinds of negotiation, albeit taking place against a formal adversarial backdrop, allows scope for high levels of client participation.[34] Commercial arbitration is generally more formal and adjudicatory in nature[35] than, say, the small claims arbitration procedures of the county courts.[36] The role of the third party is critical. In conciliation the third party may smooth the path to agreement, provide a neutral forum to air issues and relay information between the parties. A mediator may take a more proactive role; encouraging parties to clarify values and identify possible joint gains. The third party may help to sustain dialogue when dead-

---

[28]   *Ibid.*, at 74.

[29]   n. 13 above, at 74.

[30]   Many schemes in the US provide for costs sanctions if the parties fail to improve on decisions in court-annexed arbitrations: Ervine, n. 5 above.

[31]   S. B. Goldberg, E. D. Green and F. E. A. Sanders, *Dispute Resolution* (Boston, Mass., Little Brown, 1985), at 490.

[32]   T. B. Carver, "Alternative Dispute Resolution: Why it Doesn't Work and Why it Does" (1994) 72:3 *Harvard Business Review* 120.

[33]   Emond, n. 2 above, at 20–1. Therefore, e.g. in *Road Rejuvinating and Repair Services* v. *Mitchell Water Board and Another* [1990] ADRLJ 46 it was said "[a]rbitrators are not mediators. It is not their function to deal directly with disputants where legal representatives are retained."

[34]   Edmonds, n. 2 above, at 22.

[35]   And even here there are differences between kinds of commercial arbitration: see J. Flood and A. Caiger, "Lawyers and Arbitration: The Juridification of Commercial Disputes" (1993) 56 *Modern Law Review* 412. Note also that constuction disputes are now subject to a process called adjudication.

[36]   Ervine n. 5 above, at 8.

lock threatens and will remind the parties, sometimes persuading and cajoling them, of the advantages of agreement.[37] They will also facilitate a fuller understanding by the parties of the other side's perceptions, circumstances and feelings so as to bring about rational communication and negotiation.[38]

The claim of alternative dispute resolution to offer purely neutral problem-solving through mere facilitation is, as with most such broad claims, contestable both theoretically and empirically.[39] As with adjudication processes, no particular model of mediation, for example, enjoys universal support. Used selectively, however, these processes offer considerable advantages over adjudication in resolving some types of dispute. The increasingly widespread availability of such mechanisms, and the possibility of support for them from the public purse, raises important issues about the involvement of lawyers in such processes. Two questions are critical for the legal profession; if the spread of alternative methods to adjudication is inevitable, can lawyers, as the existing experts in the field of dispute resolution, afford not to participate in this growth and, if they must participate, what are the implications for professional ethics in general, and the adversarial ethic in particular?

C. ALTERNATIVES TO COURTS?

There are signs that the great proliferation of ADR programmes in the USA during the 1980s[40] may now be replicated in the UK. At both ends of the ADR spectrum, from commercial matters to small claims, there appears to be massive growth potential. Alternatively, it is possible to see current developments as a cyclical reaction to problems created by legal formalism which will quieten if and when these are resolved,[41] or as an attempt by business lawyers to legitimise their preferred method of dispute resolution.[42] Credibility is lent to these alternative views by the recent history of arbitration. Although arbitration had declined in popularity in the UK, in part because the regulatory framework was inadequate,[43] the introduction of the Arbitration Act 1996 offered the prospect

---

[37] Emond n. 3 above, at 20.

[38] See Roberts n. 20 above, at 375 citing Gulliver, *Disputes and Negotiations: A Cross-cultural Perspective* (New York, Academic Press, 1979).

[39] Roberts, n. 20 above; R. Dingwall and D. Greatbatch, "Who is in Charge? Rhetoric and Evidence in the Study of Mediation" (1993) 15 *Journal of Social Welfare and Family Law* 367; Roberts, n. 20 above; and R. Dingwall and D. Greatbatch, "Family Mediation Researchers and Practitioners in the Shadow of the Green Paper: A Rejoinder to Marion Roberts" (1995) 17 *Journal of Social Welfare and Family Law* 199.

[40] M. Galanter, "Law Abounding: Legalisation Around the North Alantic" (1992) 55 *Modern Law Review* 1 at 11.

[41] Y. Dezalay, "The Forum Should Fit the Fuss: The Economics and Politics of Negotiated Justice" in M. Cain and C. B. Harrington (eds.), *Lawyers in a Postmodern World: Translation and Transgression* (Buckingham, Open University Press, 1994), 155.

[42] *Ibid.*

[43] "Fair Speedy and Cost Effective Resolutions of Disputes" (1996) *Solicitors Journal*, 23 Feb.

of a revival of the UK as a centre for international arbitration.[44] The Act distinguishes between mandatory and non-mandatory provisions.[45] The sections dealing with conduct of proceedings[46] are mainly non-mandatory, affording parties new opportunities to design their own method of binding dispute resolution[47] without fear of intervention by the court, except in limited circumstances. Its main rationale is to recapture international arbitration business. But the commercial sphere is not the only growth area for ADR. Since the mid-1970s, the most significant growth in alternative dispute resolution in the UK has been in employment disputes, through the medium of ACAS, and in the field of family conciliation.[48] The latter was precipitated by a six-fold increase in the rate of divorce since the 1960s and concern over bitter custody battles and the cost of this to the Legal Aid scheme. Lawyers were often blamed for fuelling the conflict inherent in these family disputes. Conciliation schemes were set up by local professionals, lawyers, social workers and probation officers, and were unofficially annexed to some divorce county courts and magistrates' domestic courts.[49] The initiatives often suffered from lack of funding and lack of formal structures, and yet were frequently used by solicitors in an attempt to avoid the emotional battles which tend to accompany divorce proceedings. Mediation has now been embodied in the law under the Family Law Act 1996, which is due to come into force in 2000.[50]

ADR does not, of course, offer the only alternative to adjudication. As we have noted, the vast majority of disputes are settled by negotiation, including those disputes in which proceedings have been instituted. The success of negotiation in resolving disputes is due to the availability, as a last resort, of the coercive powers of the court. Negotiation takes place "in the shadow of the law"[51]

---

[44] In particular it was hoped that the UK would "retain pre-eminence in the field of international arbitration, a service which brings this country very substantial amounts indeed by way of invisible earnings": Saville LJ, chair of the Departmental Advisory Committee of the Department of Trade and Industry: see M. Rutherford, "Arbitration Act Update" (1996) *Solicitors Journal*, 22 Nov. at 1125 and for a synopsis of the Act see P. R. Ellington, "The New Arbitration Act 1996" (1998) 3 *Amicus Curiae* 14.

[45] S.4.

[46] Ss.33–95.

[47] S. York, "Privatisation of Disputes in 1997" (1996) *Solicitors Journal* at 1153.

[48] Lady Marre CBE, *A Time for Change: Report on the Committee on the Future of the Legal Profession* (London, The General Council of the Bar, The Law Society, 1988), para. 11.10, hereafter the *Marre Report* (and, in relation to labour disputes, see R. Singh, "Dispute Resolution in Britain: Contemporary Trends" (1995) 16 *International Journal of Manpower* 42.

[49] See Ogus *et al.*, n. 13 above, who suggest at 59 that conciliation was tried to explore the possibility of saving marriages in magistrates courts before Second World War.

[50] The Act was based on the Law Commission Report, *The Ground for Divorce* (Law Commission No.192, London, HMSO, 1990).

[51] The word "negotiation" sometimes describes a broad process including all interactions between parties. Hence, Galanter describes the process of litigation and settlement as "litigiotiation": M. Galanter, "Worlds of Deals: Using Negotiation to Teach About Legal Process" (1984) 34 J *Legal Education* 268. Bargaining "generally describes a narrower process including attempts to reach agreement, face to face": D. A. Lax and J. K. Sibenius, *The Manager as Negotiator: Bargaining for Co-operation and Competitive Gain* (New York, Free Press, 1986). For simplicity we distinguish here between "litigation" and "bargaining".

and the high cost of litigation encourages parties to settle. Yet, many who settle before trial are less satisfied with the court system than those who did not start legal proceedings or those who went to trial.[52] Critics of ADR, and informal settlement generally, argue that the terms of settlements are more likely to reflect the resource inequalities of the parties than are the outcomes of trials.[53] The poorer party is less able to pay for expert preparation of the case, and is therefore less likely to be able to predict adequately the outcome of adjudication. It will more often be subject to financial pressure to settle prematurely.[54] The very informality of some ADR processes permits people to behave less reasonably than they might in a formal setting.[55] The success of mediation may depend on the intimacy, reciprocity and permanence of the social context[56] and may be more inclined to fail where these conditions do not exist. For these reasons ADR does not always produce higher degrees of client satisfaction, particularly if the method adopted is not seen to be fair.[57]

There are other objections to the indiscriminate use of mediation processes. Even if one accepts that the wholesale rejection of ADR is unreasonable, there are arguably whole categories of cases which may not be appropriate for the use of consensual dispute resolution; abuse in relationships may be an example.[58] Whereas the judge in adjudication "struggles against inequalities of wealth", such inequalities are accepted by bargaining or ADR. This, the negative side of ADR processes, is increased when courts are reluctant to use coercive powers to enforce consensual arrangements. Despite these points, the difficulty of arguing for adjudication and against ADR is that the English civil procedure encourages settlement by negotiation and, therefore, institutionalises many of the features of ADR which are seen as its weaknesses.[59] Moreover, courts are monopolised by complex actions brought by corporations rather than by individuals[60] and cannot, apparently, cope with contemporary society's demand for efficient processing.[61] The central problem, the incommensurability of these competing

---

[52] NCC, *Seeking Civil Justice,* n. 13 above, at 7.

[53] Auerbach, n. 26 above.

[54] O. Fiss, "Against Settlement" (1983) 93 *Yale Law Journal* 1073 at 1076.

[55] R. Delgado, C. Dunn, P. Brown, H. Lee, and D. Hubert, "Fairness and Formality: Minimizing the Risk of Prejudice in Alternative Dispute Resolution" [1985] *Wisconsin Law Review* 1359.

[56] Auerbach, n. 26 above.

[57] See, e.g., *Out of Court: A Consumer View of Three Low Cost Trade Arbitration Schemes* (London: National Consumer Council, 1991).

[58] F. E. Raitt, "Informal Justice and the Ethics of Mediating in Abusive Relationships" [1997] *Juridical Review* 76.

[59] Ogus *et al.,* n. 13 above.

[60] Increased use of courts involves companies as plaintiffs and defendants rather than individuals. It is reflected in an increase in actions for breach of contract between 1975 and 1989; a growth rate five times as large as that for writs in general: Galanter, "Law Abounding", n. 40 above, at 10; but see R. Cranston, "What do Courts do?" (1986) 5 *Civil Justice Quarterly* 123.

[61] In England and Wales the number of actions started in the High Court increased from 140,003 in 1963 to 262,761 in 1988 and, in the county courts over the same period, from 1,521,594 to 2,285,125: Galanter, n. 40 above, at 8. The problem of increasing complexity of litigation is a phenomena already common in many jurisdictions: see H. Per Lindblom and G. D. Watson, "Complex Litigation: A Comparative Perspective" (1993) 12 *Civil Justice Quarterly* 33.

conceptions of justice, presents difficulties for the profession. Moreover there is the risk that, whatever view the profession contributes to the debate, it will be seen as self serving.

D. THE LEGAL PROFESSION'S RESPONSE TO ADR

Long before Lord Woolf endorsed the use of mediation, the professional bodies had embraced ADR. A joint working party was set up by the Law Society's Family Law Committee to consider the role of family mediators and to draft Standards of Practice for lawyer mediators,[62] and a proposal for a family court with annexed conciliation services was welcomed by the Marre Committee.[63] This enthusiasm jarred with the views of lawyers who defended the link between justice and adversarial processes. In the USA, in contrast, some legal academics had argued forcefully for adversarial justice and rejected compromise and settlement. Their case was that the search for consensual processes of dispute resolution is misplaced; that settlement reached through negotiation or ADR is "a capitulation to the conditions of mass society" which deprives the common law of the cases which force large-scale structural changes in political and social institutions.[64] ADR, it was said, undercuts substantive law, permitting parties to reach solutions which might ignore public standards and the interests of third parties. These considerations, which might be taken into account by judges, produce an uncertain environment which may actually encourage disputing.[65] In the UK, in contrast, the generally warm reception from the profession for ADR was only qualified by a report prepared for the Law Society in 1991[66] which suggested a number of circumstances where ADR would be inappropriate. These included cases where issues of principle of a public nature where involved,[67] where there were power imbalances between parties or where ADR was used as a tactic, for example to delay litigation.

Despite these reservations, the involvement of lawyers as mediators was firmly endorsed by the Beldam Committee, which was set up by the Bar and included representatives of the Law Society.[68] Implying that lawyers had a natural place in ADR processes, the Committee did not address the multiple motives of those pushing for the expansion of ADR. These motives were prob-

---

[62] *Marre Report,* n. 48 above, para. 11.16.

[63] *Ibid.,* para. 11.19.

[64] Fiss, n. 54 above, at 1075; Edmonds, n. 3 above, at 24–5.

[65] Ervine n. 5 above, at 16.

[66] H. Brown, *Alternative Dispute Resolution,* prepared for the Law Society's Courts and Legal Services Committee (July 1991).

[67] For further consideration of this issue see M. A. Scodro, "Arbitrating Novel Legal Questions: A Recommendation for Reform" (1996) 105 *Yale Law Journal* 1927.

[68] *Report of the Committee on Alternative Dispute Resolution* (London, General Council of the Bar, 1991).

ably extremely diverse. The government wanted to reduce its spending on courts; the judges to relieve the weight of legal business processed by courts; professional groups wanted to secure new areas of work; consumer pressure groups were demanding more effective and less expensive ways to deal with disputes.[69] Solicitors were soon permitted to offer ADR services[70] as part of their practice[71] or as a separate business.[72] Despite the enthusiasm of the professional bodies, early experiences of lawyer participation have not been encouraging. In the well-established field of arbitration in the construction industry lawyers have been accused of "juridifying" the process, thus contributing to a pattern of delay.[73] Solicitors were found to be generally hostile to a pilot scheme of court-annexed mediation operated at the Central London County Court. They were reported to believe that mediation was suited to litigants in person and preferred to use "known litigation strategies".[74]

The implications of this expansion for the ethics of the profession are profound. Not least are the implications for lawyers of offering a "new" approach to resolving disputes as a part of their portfolio of services. While the ABA has issued Standards of Practice for lawyer mediators which distinguish between their role as mediator and traditional legal advisor,[75] the profession in the UK has only begun to accommodate this new area of work in its standards. The *Guide* provides no separate code of conduct for solicitors engaged in arbitrations, and only three paragraphs relating to the provision of ADR services generally which defines ADR so as to include arbitration.[76] It is unclear whether mediators should be subject to ethical requirements or merely held subject to ordinary civil liability for breach of contract, breach of fiduciary duty or professional negligence. Finally, the desire to incorporate these radically new areas of work has not been reflected in adjustments in the core curriculum of legal education. ADR is not a compulsory part of the syllabus in law degrees, nor the LPC, nor the BVC. In their enthusiasm to secure jurisdiction over a new area of work the professional bodies have glossed over the difficulty of colonising an area which might require a fundamental re-evaluation of an ethic which is wedded to adversarialism.

---

[69] S. Roberts, "Mediation in the Lawyers' Embrace" (1992) 55 *Modern Law Review* 258 at 259.

[70] See para. 22.01 of N. Taylor (ed.), *The Guide to the Professional Conduct of Solicitors* (London, The Law Society, 1996), hereafter the *Law Society Guide*, which defines ADR service as acting as an independent neutral, e.g. mediator, conciliator or arbitrator.

[71] When they are covered by the Solicitors' Indemnity Fund up to the current limit of indemnity: *Law Society Guide*, n. 70 above, para. 22.01.2.

[72] When they must observe the provisions of the Solicitors' Separate Business Code (Annex 3D, 102 of *ibid.*) and obtain separate indemnity insurance (para. 22.01.3).

[73] See Flood and Caiger, n. 35 above, and N. Gould and M. Cohen, "ADR: Appropriate Dispute Resolution in the UK Construction Industry" [1988] *Civil Justice Quarterly* 103.

[74] L. Tsang, "Research Finds Solicitors are Hostile to Mediation Scheme", *The Lawyer*, 4 Aug. 1998, at 2.

[75] *Marre Report*, n. 48 above, para. 11.8.

[76] Chap. 22.

E. THE NEED FOR LAWYERS IN ADR

The enthusiasm of the professional bodies for ADR is surprising given that its main advantages are that it is quick and cheap and does not necessarily use a lawyer.[77] Cynics might argue that this was because the profession was convinced that the introduction of ADR was inevitable and that, in the UK at least, it would not involve the exclusion of lawyers.[78] Although lawyers are not necessary participants in ADR there may be good reasons for using them. Lawyers have a facility with complex information, are familiar with the issues raised by disputes and may be able to draw on their legal background. The main problem for lawyers in adapting to provide ADR services lies in their relationship with clients. The value which is pushed to the fore in ADR is, arguably, autonomy; the acceptance of individuals as rational, problem-solving entities.[79]

Ethics are at least as central to the mediator's role as they are to the advocate's role.[80] The roles do, however, have substantially different ethical orientations. In order to acclimatise lawyers to the environment of ADR, it has been suggested that there is a need to modify their paternalistic, competitive and aggressive traits. In some senses these processes are already under way. Lawyers are, nowadays, more likely to be taught client-centred interviewing techniques and principled negotiation. This involves the development of a package of skills which are distinctive from those developed within the adversarial tradition. The modern approach is to regard empathy, genuineness, listening and probing as the core skills of interviewing. By adding to these creativity and foresight, analysis and advice and explanation and co-operation we have the core skills of counselling. In addition, skills of strategy, persuasion and conciliation complete the core skills of problem solving negotiation.[81] This package of skills operationalises the principles of client autonomy and co-operation. But a thorough revision of the curriculum of legal education to reflect this is no simple process. It is necessary to develop new techniques and skills at the same time as developing the traditional adversarial skills. If such skills are taught insensitively, or in isolation, the risk is that students will "think cynically of their craft, to regard it as the mastery of the arts of interpersonal manipulations".[82]

---

[77] Ervine, n. 5 above, at 35.

[78] *Ibid.*

[79] Autonomy can be understood as freedom from coercive restraint, as freedom to choose, as informed reasoned choice or as choice based on the recognition of moral value. The last of these, the highest level of autonomy, incorporates respect for the autonomy of others and may, therefore, be inconsistent with the preceding three: S. C. Grebe, "Ethics and the Professional Family Mediator" (1992) 10 *Mediation Quarterly* 155 at 160; and see also Cooks and Hale, n. 12 above, and D. P. Joyce, "The Role of the Intervenor: A Client Centred Approach" (1995) 12 *Mediation Quarterly* 301.

[80] C. Morris, "The Trusted Mediator: Ethics and Interaction in Mediation" in J. Macfarlane (ed.), *Rethinking Disputes: The Mediation Alternative* (London, Cavendish Publishing, 1997), at 301.

[81] R. M. Bastress and J. D. Harbaugh, *Interviewing, Counseling and Negotiating: Skills for Effective Representation* (Boston, Toronto and London, Little Brown and Company, 1990), at 5.

[82] P. D. Carrington, "Civil Procedure and Alternative Dispute Resolution" (1981) 34 *Journal of Legal Education* 298. See also P. Brest, "The Responsibility of Law Schools: Educating Lawyers as

It is, therefore, worth considering the ways in which lawyers might be more attuned to the ADR process. The concern is that the role that lawyers have played in litigation and adjudication has had a profound effect on the collective professional psyche of lawyers. Traditionally, students have been trained in a way which anticipates the system's need for adversarial argument. Can such a strong commitment to adversarialism, in working methods, legal education and in the professional ethic, be reconciled with a vision of lawyers as "healers of human conflict"?[83] Four requirements have been identified; appropriate training in techniques of ADR; the capacity to conduct an informal but orderly proceeding; the ability to identify issues; skills in dealing with people.[84] What are the problems to be overcome in reconciling the lawyer's predispositions with a role in ADR?

The first problem lies in the lawyer's skills and the scope of the lawyer's vision. Whereas one strength of ADR is the breadth and flexibility of the possible solutions which can be proposed, lawyers are used to working in a system which provides only two basic remedies; damages and injunctive relief. Lawyers tend to be more concerned with the process by which these goals are reached, the analysis of facts and law, rather than solutions. Lawyers are trained to be legal technicians, not creative problem-solvers. Therefore, the weakness of the adjudicatory process, its blindness to creative, innovative solutions, is reproduced by lawyers when they negotiate by anticipating the will of the court.[85] This is probably because lawyers see this as their role in negotiation. It is a moot point whether a training which is geared to dealing with problems in one way can be successfully attuned to new methods and goals.

The second problem is whether the immersion of lawyers in adversarial and formal processes has created a barrier between lawyers as a group and clients as a group. A state of dependency is engendered by the traditional professional relationship between lawyers and clients. Lawyers are accused of assuming that they are acting in their clients' best interests rather than discovering what their clients' preferences are[86] and also of mystifying the process so as to impede informed decision-making by clients.[87] By acting in this way lawyers remove an important constraint on the pursuit of justice, or at least litigation: their client's wishes. Paradoxically, by so doing and thereby promoting costly adversarial processes above other means of resolving disputes, they reduce access to justice. Denying clients a role in decision making, essential for effective use of ADR, is

---

Counsellors and Problem Solvers" (1995) 58 *Law and Contemporary Problems* 6, arguing that, as law schools teach more about methods of influence they must also consider "the morality of influence" (at 2).

[83] W. Burger, "Isn't There a Better Way?" (1982) 68 *American Bar Association Journal* 274.

[84] R. B. McKay, "Ethical Considerations in Alternative Dispute Resolution" (1990) 45 *The Arbitration Journal* 15 at 22.

[85] Emond, n. 3 above, at 9.

[86] A. Gutmann, "Can Virtue be Taught to Lawyers?" (1993) 45 *Stanford Law Review* 1759.

[87] *Ibid.*, at 1762.

both paternalistic and undemocratic.[88] Further, by adopting a technical approach to the problems presented in ADR processes, and by attempting to create formal and universal rules governing the field, lawyers may undermine the client-centred approach demanded by ADR.[89] It is open to question, therefore, whether it is appropriate for lawyers to have any role in ADR, at least while the ambiguities of their formal and adversarial role are unresolved.[90]

F. LAWYERS AS NEUTRAL THIRD PARTIES

One of the roles which lawyers can fulfil in ADR processes is as neutral third parties, i.e. as arbitrator, mediator or conciliator. Other professional groups are also used here. In the construction industry, for example, lawyers are a minority of those who appear as arbitrators.[91] In some circumstances a multi-disciplinary perspective is required. Mediators, for example, may need to work with professionals from complementary disciplines.[92] The need for co-working may be increased where there is a wish that perspective will be a critical determinant of outcome or that gender[93] or cultural background[94] may impinge on perspective. As is clear, different kinds of ADR process are subject to different degrees of judicial control. Where the parties have agreed on expert determination, it is difficult to challenge the decision of the expert and difficult also to avoid the contractual agreement to refer the matter to an expert rather than court.[95] Some ADR processes produce little in the way of case law and it is difficult to state precisely what obligations third party neutrals are under. The obligations which bind third party neutrals focus on the virtues of honesty, integrity, neutrality, impartiality, candour with the parties, conflicts and appearances of conflicts of interest, fees and fee arrangements.[96] Arbitration practice, being more heavily regulated than other ADR processes, has given rise to a developed case law regarding the obligations of the arbitrator.[97] Analysis of codes of conduct for mediators suggest that a number of themes are common; disputant self-

---

[88]   *Ibid.*, at 1769.

[89]   Joyce, n. 79 above.

[90]   Carrington, n. 82 above.

[91]   Flood and Caiger, n. 35 above, at 414, suggest appointment of lawyers in construction disputes in 1991 was less than 10%.

[92]   In family mediation solicitors and social workers sometimes co-work on all issues. See Roberts, n. 20 above, at 373.

[93]   G. Davis and M. Roberts, *Access to Agreement: A Consumer Study of Mediation in Family Disputes* (Milton Keynes, Open University Press, 1988).

[94]   S. Shah Kazemi, "Family Mediation and the Dynamics of Culture" (1996) 6:3 *Family Mediation* 5.

[95]   See *Mercury Communications Ltd.* v. *Director of Telecommunications* [1993] AC 334, and Arbitration Act 1996 s.9(2).

[96]   T. Arnold, "Reviewing Ethics Issues in Mediation" (1995) 19 *ALI-ABA Course Material Journal* 53.

[97]   The Arbitration Act 1996 may however change this by giving parties more control over the processes they choose: York, n. 47 above.

determination, informed consent, mediator impartiality and mediator neutrality.[98] In three vital areas, those which touch on the ethical nature of the role, arbitration case law provides useful insights into how third parties in mediation or conciliation should perform their roles. These areas—competence, neutrality and confidentiality—are dealt with in the next sections.

Competence

The role of the third party neutral varies according to the ADR process[99] and competence to act as third party neutral therefore depends on the nature of the process. The obligation of competence is based on the common law and will be subject to interpretation. Therefore, the requirement that an arbitrator should possess the formal qualifications provided for in the original agreement is open to interpretation.[100] Incompetence in a third party neutral may have a number of consequences. So, for example, an arbitrator inexperienced at the level may cause delay and increased cost and be more likely to be subject to appeal.[101]

In relation to mediation, incompetence in handling the matter by the third party neutral may have a more direct consequence. This is because mediation is usually voluntary and any party, or the mediator, may terminate it at any time.[102] The voluntary nature of mediation is fundamental and those involved must protect this dimension of the process.[103] Mediators have no authority to impose decisions[104]; their primary purpose is to allow the parties to explore a wider range of options for settlement than might otherwise be the case.[105] The responsibilities of a mediator can include exploring the interests of the parties, the most suitable options for satisfying those interests and the costs and benefits of these options. However, even this description of the role is not universally accepted. Some codes of conduct suggest that mediators should discuss which method of dispute resolution is most suitable and others do not.[106] Mediated agreements are "ordinarily intended to be binding on the parties only when they have been recorded in writing and signed by the parties"[107] and are enforceable

---

[98] Cooks and Hale, n. 12 above.

[99] So, e.g., in Med/Arb. a third party neutral attempts to mediate between the parties but, in default of agreement, can make an arbitral award: Thompson, n. 6 above, at 92.

[100] *Pan Atlantic Group Inc. and Others* v. *Hassrieh Insurance Co. of Israel Ltd.* [1992] *ADRLJ* 179. The primary issue is competence—where an arbitrator loses a position proscribed by the agreement he may still retain the competence which the holder of such a position was intended to possess.

[101] Thompson, n. 6 above, at 117.

[102] Specimen code of practice, para. 1.2.

[103] Bevan, n. 11 above. Note that the problem of court-annexed schemes is that the power to mandate mediation conflicts with this principle.

[104] *Law Society Guide*, n. 70 above, mediation—specimen code of conduct-practice information, at 375.

[105] Specimen code 1.4.

[106] Bevan, n. 1 above: see generally 36–60 and 34–5 citing the Centre for Dispute Resolution (Denver, Colo., *Code of Professional Conduct for Mediators*).

[107] Specimen code, para. 6.1.

as contracts.[108] They may also propose packages or mechanisms for reaching agreement, steps towards "operationalising" the agreement, evaluation and monitoring and enforcement procedures.[109] Mediators can play an active or passive role. Although they have no decision-making powers, active mediators can have a profound influence on the outcome of the process.

A solicitor mediator is insured under the Solicitors' Indemnity Fund Professional Indemnity Policy provided the fees earned go to the practice rather than the mediator personally.[110] The *Guide* recommends that "solicitors wishing to offer ADR services should undertake appropriate training and work with one of the bodies which provide training and a regulatory framework".[111] It also recommends that solicitors who offer ADR services comply with a code of practice,[112] and a specimen code is provided in the *Guide*. This is designed for use in civil and commercial matters and provides guidance on "ethical issues which can arise".[113] The specimen code of practice provides that the role of the mediator is to "help parties to work out their own principles and terms for the resolution of the issues between them". It goes on to provide that:

> "the mediator may meet the parties individually and/or together and may assist the parties for example: by identifying areas of agreement, narrowing and clarifying areas of disagreement; defining the issues; helping the parties to examine the issues and their available courses of action; establishing and examining alternative options for resolving any disagreement; considering the applicability of specialised management, legal, accounting, technical or other expertise; and generally facilitating discussion and negotiation, managing the process and helping them to try to resolve their differences."[114]

This leaves open the degree to which mediators should evaluate options and pressure the parties to accept these[115] or misrepresent circumstances to achieve what the mediator believes to be a "right" result.[116] This ambiguity is cause for concern because, as noted above, in some ADR schemes there is a tendency for authoritative neutrals to coerce and manipulate the parties.[117] Whether this is a

---

[108] Although they may be made the subject of consent orders in arbitration or court proceedings: see specimen code, para. 6.1.

[109] C. W. Moore, *The Mediation Process: Practical Strategies for Resolving Conflict* (San Francisco, Cal., Jossey Bass, 1986), at 14, cited by Pirie, n. 2 above, at 41.

[110] Bevan, n. 11 above, at 27.

[111] *Law Society* Guide, n. 70 above, para. 22.01.4.

[112] *Ibid.*, para. 22.04.

[113] Note to 22.04. The specimen, "Mediation—specimen code of practice—practice information" appears as Annex 22A at 375 of the *Law Society Guide*, n. 70 above.

[114] Specimen code of conduct, 1.5.

[115] The Beldam Committee also perceived mediation to be largely faciliative and left these questions unanswered: Roberts, n. 69 above, at 260.

[116] Bevan, n. 11 above, at 33.

[117] Abel, *The Politics of Informal Justice* n. 26 above; Auerbach, n. 26 above; D. Greatbach and R. Dingwall, "Selective Facilitation: Some Preliminary Observation on a Strategy used by Divorce Mediators" (1990) 28 *Family and Conciliation Court Review* 1; R. Dingwall, "Empowerment or Enforcement? Some Questions about Power and Control in Divorce Mediation" in Dingwall and Eekelar (eds.), n. 22 above, and discussion by Roberts, n. 20 above, at 377 ff. criticising the methodology.

legitimate part of any process is doubtful. The explicit aim of the process is that the parties make their own agreements. This means that the mediator's role should be "consciously unobtrusive and non-directive".[118] As noted above, the skills described in the specimen code, or implicit in the process, are not naturally a part of the adversarial lawyer's training. These skills include facilitation, building trust and empathy and creative problem solving.[119] It is important that third party neutrals are able to distinguish different kinds of ADR from more familiar processes such as negotiation and other legal processes.[120] If and when processes of ADR become more mainstream, legal education will need to pay more attention to these skills.[121] Finally, how far should mediators check the veracity of information passed on during the course of negotiation? The common law is capable of dealing with such cases as issues of negligence. The interpretation of exemption clauses in mediation clauses is, however, unresolved.[122]

Neutrality

Although neutrality can be distinguished from impartiality,[123] for practical purposes they are very similar.[124] In essence, those acting as arbitrators, mediators or conciliators must not be seen to be predisposed towards, or lean towards, either side. A particular problem arises for lawyers because of the perception, arising from their familiarity with an adversarial role, that they cannot resist taking sides.[125]

Arbitration

The test for the removal of an arbitrator on the grounds of bias is whether the issues could fairly be determined in the way which the arbitrator on the basis of

---

[118] *Ibid.*, at 383.

[119] Pirie, n. 2 above, at 43.

[120] Roberts, n. 69 above, at 382.

[121] Indeed, the second report of the Law Society Courts and Legal Services Committee (June 1992) proposed a syllabus for an introductory case on ADR (see Ervine, n. 5 above, at 26). See further M. Minnow, "Some Thoughts on Dispute Resolution and Civil Procedure" (1984) 34 *Journal of Legal Education* 284.

[122] See Bevan, n. 11 above, at 33.

[123] Roberts, n. 20 above, at 376.

[124] The dictionary definition of neutrality: "not supporting or assisting either side in a dispute or conflict and . . . impartiality, not favouring one more than another" (*Oxford Paperback Dictionary* (Oxford, OUP, 1979)) implies that neutrality is a pre-existing state whereas partiality may develop.

[125] A. J. Pirie, "The Lawyer as Mediator: Professional Responsibility Problems or Profession Problems?" (1985) 63 *Can. Bar Review* 378. But see A. T. Kronman, *The Lost Lawyer: Failing Ideals of the Legal Profession* (Cambridge, Mass., Belknap Press of Harvard University Press, 1993), at 113, who suggests that the "case method" encourages judgement and practical wisdom by forcing students constantly to shift perspective (from judge to advocate) in analysing a set of facts.

evidence and arguments to be adduced before him.[126] The arbitrator's conduct must be viewed from the perspective of a reasonable man.[127] In *Christopher Alan Turner v. Stevenage Borough Council*,[128] an application to remove an arbitrator for bias was rejected. Before entering upon the arbitration the arbitrator had requested an interim payment from each party. The applicant did not pay, although the other party did. It was held that this did not give rise to justifiable concern that the arbitrator would be biased against the applicant and the case was remitted to the arbitrator.[129] In the French case, *Kuwait Foreign Trading Contracting and Investment Co.*,[130] it was held that, for the bias of an arbitrator to be established, there had to be "material" or "intellectual" connections with one of the parties. The chairman of an arbitration panel was an English QC. One of the parties instructed a barrister from the same chambers, a fact of which the other party was not aware until the publication of an interim award. The court held that an English barrister's membership of chambers did not create "common interests or any economic or intellectual interdependence among its members" because the sharing of chambers was not a material connection. This must have been because barristers are often required to plead against each other. There being no other evidence that the chairman's independence had been compromised, the claimant's application for annulment failed.

An arbitrator fulfils an adjudicatory role and therefore assesses evidence but, unlike a judge in most circumstances, he usually has the power to call his own witnesses.[131] Although arbitrators must use their own knowledge and experience in interpreting evidence they must not use that experience to supply evidence which the parties have not chosen to supply themselves "for then he would be discarding the role of an impartial arbitrator and assuming the role of

---

[126]   *The Ellisar* [1984] 2 Lloyd's Rep. 84, approved in *Town Centre Securities Plc. v. Leeds City Council* [1985] ADRLJ 54.

[127]   In *Tracomin SA v. Gibbs Nathaniel (Canada) ANOR* [1985] FTCR 1.2.85, an arbitrator was observed sitting behind one party's counsel, apparently giving instructions. The reasonable man would think that the arbitrator was in the enemy's camp and that there was a real likelihood of bias.

[128]   [1997] EGCS 34.

[129]   In *Bremerhandelsgesellschaft mbH v. Ets Soules etc. cie & Anor* [1985] FTCR 4.5.85, application by commodity seller for removal of director of commodity from house from Board of Appeal refused. There was nothing in the individual's record to suggest bias towards buyers rather than sellers. See also *Fletamentos Maritimos SA v. Effjohn Internation BV* [1996] LTL 21/2/97 (unsuccessful attempt to remove an arbitrator who had provided a witness statement highly critical of applicants' solicitor and who failed to formally disclose the possible conflict). The potential problem had been drawn to the applicants' attention by their solicitor earlier in the proceedings and there had been no evidence that the arbitrator's actions reflected any bias (note that it was held here that the court only had jurisdiction to correct procedural errors in extreme cases). See also *L/S A/S. Gill Brakh v.. Hyundai Corporation* (1987) ILR 2.11.87 (an error over admissability of evidence did not by itself, amount to misconduct by an arbitrator.

[130]   Paris, Court of Appeal 1991 (1993) ADRLJ part 3.

[131]   But note that in *Top Shop Estates Ltd. v. C. Domino* (High Court 1984) 1992 ADRLJ 47, an arbitrator's award was overturned, inter alia, on the ground that he gathered evidence without the consent or knowledge of the parties and accepted unsupported evidence without affording an opportunity to challenge his interpretations. Although there was no imputation on his personal conduct or sense of fairness he had misconducted the proceedings.

an advocate for the defaulting side."[132] Arbitrators must apply the law unless the parties agree otherwise and the particular jurisdiction permits this.[133] Judicial review may be available on the grounds of the arbitrator's misconduct such as bias, or a failure to apply the principles of natural justice.[134] Appeals may be allowed on the grounds that arbitrators did not follow agreed procedures.[135] In the Australian case *Road Rejuvenating and Repair Services* v. *Mitchell Water Board and Another*,[136] it was held that an arbitrator "must present himself to the parties as an unbiased adjudicator". In this case the arbitrator, the second defendant, had accepted into evidence, without the consent of the plaintiff, material which was extremely damaging to that party containing hearsay and much irrelevant material. On other occasions he had arrived at the building site which was at the centre of the dispute, driven by an officer of the first defendant. This was an "inexcusable alignment of an arbitrator with one party" and the arbitrator was removed.[137]

Other ADR Processes

Mediators are under a duty to act fairly, although this does not extend to attempting to counteract any power imbalances between the parties.[138] The specimen code of conduct, provided for solicitors, states that

> "if a mediator believes that any party is abusing the mediation process, or that power imbalances are too substantial for the mediation to continue effectively or that the parties are proposing a result that appears so unfair that it would be a manifest miscarriage of justice, then the mediator will inform the parties accordingly and may terminate the mediation."[139]

The obligation of neutrality can, sometimes, be broader than the obligation to be even handed. In family conciliation for example, the third party neutral

---

[132] Lord Denning MR in *Fox* v. *P.G. Wellfair Ltd* [1981] 2 Lloyds' Report 514 and see *Top Shop Estates Ltd.*, *ibid.*, where the arbitrator conducted a "pedestrian court" without the knowledge of the parties.

[133] Thompson, n. 6 above.

[134] H. J. Kirsh, "Arbitrating Construction Disputes" in Emond, n. 2 above, 175 at 180.

[135] *Oakstead Garages Ltd* v. *Leach Pension Scheme (Trustees) Ltd* (1996) 24 EG 147. Appeal allowed against decision of arbitrator in a rent review who had told parties that he would inspect relevant comparable properties but failed to do so (and see Mabanafit *GBMH* v. *Consentino Shipping Company SA Times Law Reports* 15 May 1984. Arbitrators decision based on theory not raised with the applicants. It was an issue of fact and degree whether a party should have an opportunity to deal with such points).

[136] Supreme Court of Victoria, Nathan J. (1990) *Arbitration and Dispute Resolution Journal* 1992 46.

[137] Although the first defendant was ordered to pay the plaintiff the arbitrator was ordered to indemnify. The judge suggested that the Institute of Arbitrators, who had nominated the second, should bear the full costs of the parties.

[138] Bevan, n. 11 above, at 34.

[139] *Law Society Guide* (1996) Annex 22A, Mediation—specimen code of practice—practice information" para. 3.2.

may be expected to counteract attempts by a stronger party to exploit the weaker while remaining true to the neutral role.[140]

Some rules intended to guarantee impartiality are structural rules. For example, a solicitor is prevented from acting as mediator in relation to former or present clients[141] or may be permitted to do so only with the written consent of the parties. A solicitor cannot "provide an ADR service in connection with a dispute in which he or she, or a member of his or her firm, has acted as a professional adviser to any party. If a solicitor has provided an ADR service neither the solicitor , nor a member of his or her firm, can act for any participant individually in relation to the dispute.[142] Additionally, *The Guide* attempts to reinforce the neutral role of solicitors by providing that "a solicitor who provides ADR services must inform the parties to the dispute in writing, and the parties must agree, that the solicitor will be independent and impartial and will not advise either party".[143] For this reason it may be unwise to meet either party in private caucus in some kinds of mediation, e.g. family mediation. A mediator may easily discover information which, although subsequently disclosed to the other party, they may not be able to evaluate the information in the same way.[144] Making a recommendation so as to avoid breakdown of the mediation, even at the request of the parties, may be seen to compromise neutrality.[145] Mediators may, however, make recommendations to parties "as to the desirability of seeking further assistance from professional advisers such as lawyers, accountants, expert valuers or others".[146]

Confidentiality

Conciliation

Privilege attaching to communications during the course of family conciliation is well established. As a result of early cases on divorce conciliation it is clear that communications in conciliation sessions hosted by a third party neutrals who are not lawyers, are privileged unless both the parties consent to disclosure

---

[140] *The Ground for Divorce* (1990) Law Commission No. 192 para. 5.34, cited by Roberts, n. 20 above, at 373.

[141] While rules vary in the USA and Canada mediators are often prohibited from acting in matters involving former clients and/or are prohibited from acting for either party in the future (see Pirie, "The Lawyer as a Third Party Neutral: Promise and Problems", n. 2 above, at 45 discussing the rules published in British Columbia and by the ABA). The Law Society provides for this.

[142] *Law Society Guide*, para. 22.03 which applies to ADR services operated by a solicitor as a separate business. See also para. 1.6 of the Mediation—specimen code of practice which is expressed in very similar terms.

[143] Specimen code of practice 1.3. and 22.02.

[144] For example, where a wife in an access and custody dispute tells the mediator that she may take the child abroad and, at the mediator's instigation, tells the husband but says it is less of a possibility than the mediator believed it to be (Arnold, n. 000 above, at 63).

[145] Thompson, n. 6 above, at 92.

[146] Specimen code of conduct para. 5.3.

to the court.[147] The general rule is that privilege extends from the parties or their legal advisors[148] but the earlier cases suggest that the third party neutral cannot claim privilege if the parties waive it.[149] Special confidentiality provisions apply to matrimonial conciliation and proceedings under the Children Act 1989.[150] Therefore, communications from parties to a marriage, which are aimed at reconciliation, are protected if they are made to official parties, like probation officers or priests, or to private individuals appointed as conciliators.[151] Similar privilege covers proceedings under the Children Act unless it relates to evidence of a propensity or an intention on the part of one of the parties to harm a child.

Mediation

The confidentiality of information disclosed in mediation is problematic. As we have seen, for the process of mediation to be effective, full disclosure by both sides, at least to the mediator, is desirable if not essential. Mediation processes do not *require* the parties to produce specific relevant documents although this may be desirable in order to resolve misunderstandings; in general, discussion and agreement are the means by which information is verified.[152] It is not clear that the privilege exists in relation to documents or other communications that exists in conciliation covers mediation also. This is because, in relation to family conciliation, the state is said to have a vested interest in facilitating matrimonial conciliation.[153] Although it clearly has a general interest in facilitating the settlement of other kinds of dispute, there is understandable caution about extending the sphere of confidentiality. At present, the confidentiality rules governing mediation are based on the privilege offered by ordinary negotiation which, again derives from the desire to facilitate settlement of disputes.[154] The discussions or correspondence for which privilege is claimed must have the aim of settling proceedings involving the same subject matter.[155] This intention is usually signalled by including the words "without prejudice" in relation to discussions or correspondence relating to proposed mediation.[156] It is clear,

---

[147] *McTaggart v. McTaggart* [1949] P 94, [1948] 2 All ER 754 *Mole v. Mole* (1950) P 21. The privilege applies whether reconciliation was attempted by the parties or brokered by a conciliator see *Henley v. Henley* [1955] 1 All ER 590.

[148] *La Roche v. Armstrong* (1922) 1 KB 485.

[149] *McTaggart v. McTaggart*, n. 147 above.

[150] See generally A. Keane, *The Modern Law of Evidence* (London, Dublin and Edinburgh, Butterworths, 1994).

[151] *Mole v. Mole*, n. 147 above and *Theodoropoulas v. Theodoropoulas* [1964] P 311.

[152] Mediation specimen code para. 4.2.

[153] *D. v. NSPCC* [1978] AC 171.

[154] See *McTaggart v. McTaggart*, n. 147 above, where the Court of Appeal held that communications in the case of negotiation towards attempted reconciliation were, *prima facie* privileged.

[155] *Muller v. Linsley & Mortimer, The Times* 8 December 1994.

[156] Bevan, n. 11 above, at 31.

however, that the substance of the discussion and its relevance to settlement is more important in a claim for privilege than the use of this formula.[157]

While it is only settlement discussions that are covered by the cloak of privilege[158] it should be noted that there is no reason in principle why, if mediation communication is privileged, this privilege should not extend to discussions which take place with a view to avoiding litigation.[159] Doubts about the effectiveness of the "without prejudice" formula to protect communication from being used as evidence leaves some doubt as to whether information received by mediators in the course of a mediation is covered by privilege. The mediation processes meets the basic criterion of an attempt to reach settlement but, because the mediator is not a "party" making a proposal in settlement, doubt is cast over the extent to which she can refuse to give evidence of information gleaned from the mediation. Claims for privilege in relation to information learned by mediators in the process of mediation have been upheld in two Canadian decisions.[160] Continuing doubts about the risk of third party neutrals being required to give evidence in subsequent court proceedings have led to suggestions that no notes or records should be kept of confidential discussions.[161]

The Law Society's specimen code provides that the process will be confidential and that the mediator will not disclose information discovered in the course of mediation "except to the extent that such matters are already public or with the consent of the parties".[162] It goes on to provide that "all discussions and negotiations during the mediation will be regarded as evidentially privileged and conducted on a 'without prejudice' basis, unless such privilege is waived by the parties by agreement, either generally or in relation to any specific aspect"; nor is such information to be referred to in any "subsequent proceedings".[163] Under the code, no party can require the mediator to give evidence nor have access to a mediator's notes[164] although the situation in law seems more complex. The code does, therefore, present a genuine ethical dilemma for solicitor mediators. If they adopt the Law Society's code, and a court does not recognise a "mediatior's privilege" in the circumstances of the case, a solicitor mediator may have

---

[157] *South Shropshire District Council* v. *Amos* [1986] 1 WLR 1271 and see J. McEwan, "Without prejudice: Negotiating a Minefield" (1994) 13 *Civil Justice Quarterly* 133.

[158] In *Redifusion Simulation* v. *Link Miles* [1992] FSR 196 a defendant applied to have struck out, under R.S.C.O.41, r.6., passages in an affidavit by the plaintiff in support of an application to the judge. The passages were not plainly inadmissable as a result of the "without prejudice" rule because P was not seeking to use in evidence any statement made by way of offer or compromise or by way of an express or implicit admission of liability or fact (following *Rush & Tomkins* v. *Greater London Council* [1988] 1 All ER 549.

[159] *Rush & Tomkins Ltd.* v. *Greater London Council, ibid.*

[160] See Pirie, n. 2 above, at 48–49 and *Porter* v. *Porter* (1983) 40 O.R. (2d) 417, 32 R.F.L. (2d) 413 (U.F.Ct.). (Wigmore's conditions for granting privilege found to be present following family mediation) and *Sinclair* v. *Roy* (1985), 20 D.L.R. (4th) 748, 65 B.C.L.R. 219, 47 R.F.L (2d)15 (S.C.).

[161] B. E. Larson and S. B. Hansen, "Ethics in ADR" (1992) 22 *The Brief* 14.

[162] Para. 2.1 (and see para. 2.2 which maintains the confidentiality of information obtained from separate meetings with parties subject to consent).

[163] Specimen code 2.3.

[164] Para. 2.3.

to choose between contempt of court or violating the code under which the mediation was carried out.

The Law Society's mediation code deals with some other difficult ethical issues but, regrettably, not very satisfactoraly. For example, if a mediator discovers information in the course of the mediation which suggests "that the life or safety of any person is or may be at serious risk"[165] the code provides that the mediator "shall try to agree with the person furnishing such information as to how disclosure shall be made".[166] This does not make it clear whether, in the absence of agreement, disclosure shall still be made. By analogy with the position of solicitors generally, one assumes that confidentiality requires that they do not disclose information even in order to prevent harm to third parties. The mediation code, perhaps understandably, fudges the issue. Another example is where a mediator is aware that an agreement reached through mediation is based on false information or bad faith. Here it is not clear how the duty of confidentiality applies. It has been suggested that a mediator should try to persuade the parties to rectify the problem and, if this fails, to withdraw. Whether or not the mediator is obliged to bring the irregularity to the attention of those outside the process is a moot point. It has been suggested, for example, that mediators should not allow the obligation of confidentiality to override the criminal law.[167]

G. LAWYERS AS REPRESENTATIVES IN ADR PROCESSES

A lawyer advising a party on the question of whether or not to participate in an ADR process must consider the kind of dispute resolution method which is most appropriate, given the preferences of the client and the nature of the problem.[168] The general duties of competence and diligence demand that lawyers should be familiar with the alternatives before offering advice in relation to any dispute.[169] For, as one litigation solicitor has said:

---

[165] Para. 2.1.

[166] Para. 2.1.

[167] Bevan, n. 11 above, at 32.

[168] Carrington, n. 82 above, suggests the following:
- what qualifications, status, mix of participant dispute resolvers?
- how are disputes channelled to correct dispute resolver?
- what mechanisms for ensuring fidelity to any controlling law?
- must process adhere to any procedural norms?
- on what information will process be based and at what cost will it be gathered?
- how will mechanism be protected from abuse of process? (e.g., costs, criminal sanctions, tort liability or professional sanctions for lawyers)
- how will representation be provided and costs controlled?
- will the ADR mechanism be able to terminate disputes?
- can the enforcement of decisions and awards be managed solely by contract?

[169] Note that in both Texas and Colorado lawyers are under specific obligations to advise the client regarding the availability and/or advisability of ADR (Arnold, n. 96 above).

" . . . an initial overall view must be taken which allows the solicitor to know early on if there is a problem, such as it costing more than the likely reward . . . or whether evidence will be difficult to find . . . I listen to what the client is saying; everything they say. I might think initially; "Ah-ha, litigation!", and it may not be their concern—they may want something else. So I must listen overall and use my judgement/ experience to decide whether they are looking for a remedy through the courts . . ."[170]

But, unlike in many states in the USA the professional codes of lawyers in England and Wales impose no obligation to identify the objectives of the representation or to advise on the basis of this what methods of dispute resolution may be most appropriate.[171] Unless this is prescribed by rules of court it will be necessary to consider at which point in the course of litigation mediation should take place or, if negotiation has been attempted, whether it should be take place at all. The extent to which representatives should use offers to mediate for tactical reasons in litigation is open to question. It has been suggested for example, that an offer to mediate might be the subject of a *"Calderbank offer"*, a "without prejudice" proposal which can be referred to in a subsequent court case in relation to the award of costs.[172] In considering these possibilities lawyers must confront previously absent ethical problems. By having to consider the use of such adversarial tactics are they undermining the prospects of consensual dispute resolution?[173] Even if they decide to remain outside of ADR processes for this reason they must not allow their familiarity with, or personal preference for particular methods, to colour their advice to their clients.[174] Further, they should ignore their personal financial interests, i.e. the fees earned, in offering advice on the client's choice of method. They should also consider whether they will be present during the mediator's attempts to facilitate settlement.[175]

If a lawyer proposes to participate in ADR processes as a representative the lawyer should possess a level of appreciation and skill which enables them to facilitate the emergence of a solution which meets the clients interests.[176] It is in

---

[170] A. Boon, "Assessing Competence to Conduct Civil Litigation: Key Tasks and Skills" in P. Hassett and M. Fitzgerald (eds), *Skills for Legal Functions II: Representation and Advice* (London, Institute of Advanced Legal Studies, 1992).

[171] Arnold, n. 96 above.

[172] Therefore a distinction could be drawn, in terms of confidentiality, between the offer to mediate and the material discovered in the process of mediation. Bevan, n. 11 above, at 29.

[173] It has been observed that "posturing" or the desire to receive a decision rather than recommend a settlement, to an extent attributes of the advocate, are a hindrance in mediation (see Thompson, n. 6 above, at 116).

[174] ADR has not been the first choice of many litigants. A pilot out of court mediation scheme in Bristol backed by the Law Society, had only 24 cases in its first year and only two reached the mediation stage, York, n. 47 above. It has been agreed that lawyers should be under a duty to advise clients about alternative methods (see S. Widman, "ADR and Lawyers Ethics" (1994) 82:3 *Illinois Bar Journal* 150).

[175] Roberts, n. 69 above, at 260 points out that a number of possibilities are presented including no lawyers, only lawyers or lawyers permitted at option of parties. The last of these, recommended by Beldam, is arguably the option least likely to facilitate agreement (section 14 at 10).

[176] This may mean, in a business setting for example, that the lawyer must be aware of the commercial context of the dispute, the interests of the party in a continuing relationship, the potential

this context that the NCC asserts that a "mediator without legal knowledge is definitely preferable to a lawyer who is deficient in mediation skills".[177] The specimen code of conduct envisages that solicitors may take part in discussions or meetings without the parties being present[178] and that the parties may consult legal advisers to formalise draft heads of agreement or for advice before entering a binding agreement based on the mediation.[179] When lawyers participate in ADR proceedings they should seek to assist the third party neutral in finding the best way to handle the dispute and not seek legal redress if they are not satisfied with initial proposals for dealing with the matter.[180]

CONCLUSION

In Part I we saw that the adversarial role of lawyers has been fundamental to the professional ethics and professional culture. Now there is some dissatisfaction with what lawyers offer in terms of their adversarial approach to dispute resolution. Society is less tolerant of a professional culture which appears to be profligate with social and economic resources. A system of civil justice which is burdensome to the state, for which lawyers are held at least partly to blame, makes a role as facilitators of dispute resolution more attractive both in terms of negotiation and litigation strategies. It also raises the possibility that lawyers will find substantial new areas of work as neutral third parties, arbitrators, fact finders, mediators or conciliators in the processes of disputing. The incentive for lawyers to colonise new areas of work has been matched by a growing demand in certain areas, for example in the mediation of commercial disputes. Whether or not they act as mediator or conciliator, or maintain an advisory role in relation to their client, their participation in the process requires that they focus more on the interests of parties to disputes instead of, or as well as, their legal rights. This requires a resolution of some of the unresolved anomalies of the adversarial role.

The field of dispute resolution exemplifies the crisis of the legal profession both in terms of its jurisdiction and ethics. As Lord Woolf's proposals demonstrate, one of the main pressures for the deprofessionalisation of lawyers has arisen because lawyers' "trained psychic aggression" inflames disputes and render legal services more expensive. This is no longer perceived as "a good" for either individuals or to society and poses a fundamental problem in terms of the professional ethic and in terms of the education and training of lawyers.

for mutually beneficial agreement and so on (see Thompson, n. 6 above, at 90). The exceptions include those ADR processes, including mini-trial and arbitration, where the process may be adversarial.

[177] Ervine, n. 5 above, at 34.
[178] Specimen code para. 5.1.
[179] Specimen code para. 6.2 and 6.3.
[180] See *Colt International Ltd.* v. *Tarmac Construction Ltd.* (1996) *Arbitration and Dispute Resolution Law Journal* 328 (application by party to remove arbitrator for bias or incompetence).

Without a significant shift in the way that lawyers perceive their role, or are trained to fulfill that role, the question remains; "are lawyers appropriate participants in ADR, either as representatives or third party neutrals"? Are they able to complement legal acumen with a facilitative role? A case may be made for those who have based their practice on negotiation but it is less obvious what advocates can contribute to ADR processes. If these concerns are well founded they present particular problems when, as is often proposed, ADR schemes exist as adjuncts to court processes or deal with cases which could also be taken through the courts. If lawyers fail to adapt to a role of facilitators of consensual dispute resolution it may well be the legal profession, rather than ADR, which is the long term casualty.

Epilogue

A. INTRODUCTION

This chapter outlines future developments which may be a catalyst for changes in professional ethics. Some areas of work will clearly decline. Methods of organising work, such as the formal barriers between solicitors and barristers, will become less significant.[1] It seems likely that the solicitors' branch will become increasingly dominant, both economically and numerically, and will ultimately absorb groups of barristers. Changes in the social and economic power relationships between different kinds of lawyers mean that professional coherence will depend on the ability of lawyers to reinterpret their role and function and claim a common ideology and social purpose behind the way they provide and sell their services.[2] If they can to do this, change will not be detrimental but may produce a new kind of professionalism.[3] In order to achieve this, the profession must dispel the suspicion that its ethics are a mirage; merely a means of enhancing professional control and prestige.[4] What are the trends which will shape these developments?

B. PROFESSIONAL WORK AND PROFESSIONAL REPRESENTATION

Specialisation, routinisation of work and bureaucracy will continue to change the nature of lawyers' everyday work. The process by which professional knowledge is undermined is, apparently, inexorable. Richard Susskind, in *The Future of the Law*,[5] predicts that legal services will move away from the provision of legal advice on an individual lawyer/client basis and towards the provision of legal information by increasingly sophisticated IT packages. This will shift the work of lawyers away from their current major role as reactive crisis-solvers and towards helping clients to manage legal risks in advance. Much of this will be managed by IT packages provided to clients and their employees. In this way, he says, much legal work will become "routinized and proceduralized."

---

[1] Glasser predicts that the criminal bar will not survive and will become absorbed in legal aid firms as solicitors take up rights of audience in Crown Courts. Further, there is a risk that litigation generally will become a publicly funded service, C. Glasser, "The Legal Profession in the 1990s: Images of Change" (1990) 10:1 *Legal Studies* 1.

[2] Glasser, *ibid*.

[3] See also H. Perkin, *The Rise of Professional Society: England Since 1880* (London, Routledge, 1989).

[4] See chap. 2.

[5] R. Susskind, *The Future of the Law* (Oxford, Clarendon Press, 1996) and see T. Purcell, "Technology's Role in Access to Legal Services and Legal Information" in R. Smith (ed.), *Shaping the Future: New Directions for Legal Services* (London, Legal Action Group, 1995) at 66.

" . . . those who are guided become users, the lawyers who analyse and organise the material will become legal information engineers."[6] It is entirely conceivable that some legal markets may be served by a mixture of professional and self-help, thus raising new problems regarding the scope of professional responsibility.[7] This vision of the future will require a fundamental change in the current ideas of a professional service provided by a lawyer to a client.

The fragmentation of lawyers into different kinds of employment threatens to further undermine the cohesion of the profession and its commitment to common ideals. Even amongst private practitioners changes in the kind of work undertaken, and the rewards reaped for that work, raises questions about existing professional boundaries and status. We might, therefore, expect the debate about whether the Law Society should separate its regulatory and representative functions to surface periodically. Given the change in the relationships between professional bodies and the state, the Law Society is probably correct in its view that the promotion of the profession is an exercise that can only be effectively undertaken in collaboration with its membership.[8] However, the membership need to be aware that it is in its own interest that the profession retains, or restores, its image of trustworthiness and ethical conduct. This, after all, is what it is selling to the public and what distinguishes it from occupations which still do not share the privileges and prestige of professionals.

C. ADVERSARIALISM

If the adversarial ethos is substantially and successfully revised, at least in civil work, what will happen to the role morality created around it? Will the obligations owed by lawyers to parties other than their clients increase? Placing client interests above all others will not be tenable. Now even Freedman, an outspoken supporter of partisanship, argues that lawyers should be under an obligation to prevent a crime against the public, such as the marketing of a potentially lethal drug.[9] There is judicial support for the proposition that "danger to the

---

[6] *Shaping the Future: New Directions for Legal Services* (London, Legal Action Group, 1995) at at 268. This vision of the future promoted by Susskind is obviously dominated by the large corporate solicitor's firm. Whether such developments will affect the individual client (in particular the accused client) is doubtful. Susskind also notes that the use of IT brings us "to the brink of an entirely new era of mankind, very few philosophers or social commentators have explored the [ethical] ramifications in the depth that it surely merits" (n. 5 above, at 69). Neither does he explore them. Computerisation clearly raises some immediate ethical problems, e.g., of confidentiality and of the personal responsibility of IT package users for negligence etc.

[7] F. S. Mosten, "The Unbundling of Legal Services: Increasing Legal Access" in Smith, n. 6 above, at 47.

[8] Negative images of uninteresting work carried out in victorian offices, or of an inward looking, defensive profession persist in some peoples minds. Promotion of an image which is more positive and more accurate must be the responsibility of the profession as a whole (The Law Society, *The Recruitment Crisis* (London, The Law Society, 1988), para. 4).

[9] M. H. Freedman, "Are There Public Interest Limits on Lawyers' Advocacy" (1977) *The Journal of the Legal Profession* 47 at 52–53.

state or public duty may supercede the duty of the agent to his principal".[10] The Government wishes to strengthen the lawyers' duty to the interests of justice by making it a statutory duty. In clause 38 of the Access to Justice Bill 1998 every advocate has "a duty to the court to act in the interest of justice" which overrides "any obligation which the [advocate] may have (otherwise than under the criminal law) if it is inconsistent" with it. In the commentary on the Bill it is emphasised that this duty to the court reinforces the fact that a barrister or solicitor "must refuse to do anything required, either by a client or by an employer, that is not in the interests of justice (eg. suppress evidence)". It is arguable that the professional codes should go further than they do in specifying the scope of a lawyers public duty of disclosure.[11] Yet client confidentiality is central to the role of many professionals and is probably a critical part of the legal profession's commercial advantage. If lawyers were not bound to respect client confidences, even in limited circumstances, it would be bad for business. Nevertheless, it is to be anticipated that a change in the balance between duties to clients and to wider social obligations may be demanded of lawyers. What are the implications for the lawyer and client relationship? A major change may well be a further development of the idea of "informed consent" towards participative decision-making between lawyer and client.

D. DEPROFESSIONALISATION

In former times professional mystique, the "language of the law", reinforced professional identity and excluded outsiders, potential competitors. In the process it also distanced clients from the proper discussion of their legal problems. This went largely unquestioned in an age of paternalism where professional authority and judgement was itself not questioned. This process of exclusion reinforced the dependence of the client on the lawyer and encouraged a tendency among lawyers to "depersonalise clients, to treat them paternalistically or to manipulate them".[12] Public resentment of this has fed a desire to deprofessionalise the high status professions, to weaken their professional autonomy so as to eliminate "defective interpersonal relationships" between professionals and clients.[13] One way to assuage this particular pressure towards deprofessionalisation is to move to a model of participative decision making. Although such a move may, at first sight, appear further to diminish the status of lawyers, this is not necessarily the case. A critical test of lawyer's power is not

---

[10] Lord Findlay in *Weld-Blundell* v. *Stephens* [1920] AC 596 cited in Bankes L.J. in *Tournier* v. *National Provincial and Union Bank of England* (1924) 1 KB 461.
[11] See M. Brindle and G. Dehn "Confidence, Public Interest, and the Lawyer" in *Legal Ethics and Professional Responsibility* Ed. R. Cranston (Oxford: Clarendon Press) at p 115.
[12] R. Wasserstrom, "Lawyers as Professionals: Some Moral Issues" (1975) 5 *Human Rights* 1 at 17.
[13] Wasserstrom, *ibid.*, at 19.

whether they *determine* tactics or technique but whether they are successful in *modifying* their client's goals or objectives.[14]

In any case, it is sad if a profession's status is dependent on professional mystique and domination of its clients. The role of advising, informing, helping and encouraging clients to achieve appropriate and satisfactory solutions to their problems should not be regarded as a low-status activity but part of a widespread movement affecting business as a whole as well as the professions.[15] This reconception of the professional role in relation to clients would be consistent with a role in dispute resolution which is more co-operative. While this strikes at the heart of the legal profession's traditional ethic[16] there are strong arguments for lawyers seeking a new social role as "managers of conflict". Some may feel that this would be premature; that it is the duty of lawyers to uphold and defend adversarialism as the best method of dispute resolution available. Others would argue that the public and government are unlikely to be convinced of this and that it is time to recognise that diverse methods of dispute resolution is the shape of the future.

E. PUBLIC SERVICE

Until recently the profession's perception of its public service obligations have been narrow. The practice of law has become more commercialised and this may, initially at least, have exacerbated this tendency. The ability of the profession to serve the "whole public" is hampered by the fact that ordinary members of the public are, by the professions' own admission, ignorant of what services lawyers can provide. More revealing perhaps, even in today's allegedly claims-conscious society, they have been reluctant to use lawyers.[17] If nothing else, the revitalisation of professional ethics must address the nature of public service obligation, not just for the individual client, but for the community as a whole. In this respect it will be necessary to delineate what entitlements clients have as a result of these shifting obligations. It is also important that lawyers are identified with causes which bring the public's attention to their commitment to social goals. In some cases, for example in advancing unpopular causes, a reconciliation will be difficult and may even, on occasions, seem to run against the profession's desire to be seen as socially responsible. Yet, guaranteeing representation is a justification for the professional monopoly which it would be foolhardy to disregard.

On the other hand, lawyers might regain some degree of public trust if they pursue worthy causes which would not otherwise have legal support. This is

---

[14] J. P. Heinz, "The Power of Lawyers" (1983) 17 *Georgia Law Review* 891 at 897.

[15] T. J. Johnson, *Professions and Power* (London and Basingstoke, Macmillan Press, 1972) at 13.

[16] E. E. Sward, "Values Ideology and the Evolution of the Adversary System" (1989) 64 *Indiana Law Journal* 301 at 355.

[17] B. Abel-Smith, M. Zander, and R. Brooke, *Legal Problems and the Citizen: A Study of Three London Boroughs* (London, Heinemann Educational, 1973) at 233.

now beginning to happen but there is some way to go before the profession can justify the claims made for its pro bono work. There will, undoubtedly, be continuing debate about the best way that lawyers can help the poor and disadvantaged, with demands for new kinds of engagement.[18] If lawyers fail to respond to the demand for a public service orientation, then they will lose control over much of their work. Much of the legal aid debate has been about delivery; whether by voluntary schemes, salaried bureaucracy, community agency or contracted services.[19] Of these models, the most consistent with the existing practice and organisation of lawyers is contracted service and, with legal aid franchising, this has been the starting point. If this limited degree of state mediation fails, the prospect of an extensive national legal service becomes a significant possibility. The current government's proposal for a community legal service is a step in that direction. The details of the Community Legal Service, provided for in the Access to Justice Bill 1998, are as yet unknown but will clearly remove more lawyers from private practice and place them in the direct or indirect employ of government.[20] The most likely areas to be affected would be welfare and criminal defence. This raises acute ethical questions. Are such lawyers expected to be as zealous on behalf of the state as they might be expected to be on behalf of citizens *against* the state? Should they be subject to different ethical codes than the private profession?[21] Based on experience of public lawyers in the USA, new measures would then be needed to ensure the quality of service offered to non-paying clients, such as the right to dismiss the first assigned representative.[22]

State mediation as a model of occupational control has a number of implications. As the occupation becomes incorporated within the frameworks provided by government agencies, individual relationships with clients become secondary. The notion of a fiduciary relationship with clients is modified or abandoned. In defining notions of quality, different criteria are used. The current criteria of quality are the orientation of service to clients, accuracy of advice, efficiency of service (was it quick and cheap), effectiveness of service (did the

[18] See G. P. Lopez, *Rebellious Lawyering: One Chicano's View of Progressive Law Practice* (Westview Press, 1992) and A. Southworth, "Taking the Lawyer out of Progressive Lawyering" (1993) 46 *Stanford Law Review* 213

[19] T. Goriely, "Law For the Poor: The Relationship Between Advice Agencies and Solicitors in the Development of Poverty Law" (1996) 3:1/2 *International Journal of the Legal Profession* 215 at 216.

[20] See, for example, the proposals of the National Consumer Council which envisage the introduction of "multi-door" dispute resolution centres and the use of salaried lawyers, volunteer lawyers or paralegals in a network of advice, referral and representation services (M. A. Winfield, *A Community Legal Service: The First Steps* (London, National Consumer Council, 1998)).

[21] Commenting on the position in the USA Lanctot argues that the same ethical codes must apply, i.e., state agencies are entitled to the same commitment from their lawyers as are private individuals. Policy decisions regarding the interests of the public interest and the interests of the people are the province of policy makers (C. J. Lanctot, "The Duty of Zealous Advocacy and the Ethics of the Federal Government Lawyer: The Three Hardest Questions" (1991) 64 *Southern California Law Review* 951.

[22] See generally P. D. Carrington, "The Right to Zealous Counsel" (1979) 6 *Duke Law Journal* 1291 particularly 1304 *et seq.*

client win, how much did s/he get/ retain). In the future, a choice between these criteria may have to be made.[23] With state mediation of the relationship between producer and consumer it is likely that lawyers would need to be more concerned with the broad social consequences of their actions. Efficiency will become the major determinant of the preferred organisational form.[24] It is worth remembering that, while numerous studies have suggested, as one might expect, that legal advice and representation improves the prospects of claimants[25], it does not matter whether or not it is provided by lawyers, as long as it is competent and expert.[26]

F. LEGAL EDUCATION

It can be argued that the Law Society has pursued regulation at the expense of ethics[27] and that the time has come to redress the balance. Incorporating ethics as a part of the curriculum for lawyers could have considerable implications but certain preliminary problems need to be addressed. What are the different responsibilities of the undergraduate and vocational stages? In the USA the educational task has been conceived as one of inculcating "professional responsibility". The curriculum implied by such a project is potentially voluminous; it would certainly involve perspectives which went far beyond codes of conduct, although these would inevitably play a part.[28] Detailed examination of professional ethics by students would, however, reveal many ambiguities and raise some unanswerable questions. It is not clear how far the profession is prepared for thoroughgoing examination of ethics and conduct in the curriculum or how many academics, and therefore Law Schools, would be able to deliver such

[23] T. Goriely, "Debating the Quality of Legal Services: Differing Models of the Good Lawyer" (1994) 1 *International Journal of the Legal Profession* 159.

[24] Johnson, n. 15 above, at 79–83.

[25] Abel-Smith, Zander and Brooke, n. 17 above, at 221.

[26] H. Genn, and Y. Genn, "Tribunals and Informal Justice" (1993) 56 *Modern Law Review* 393.

[27] This conclusion is hinted at by the Head of Policy of the Professional Ethics Division of the Law Society who suggests that only Practice Rule 1 concerns "core legal or ethical duties" and that, in 1993 alone, her division dealt with nearly 50,000 enquiries from solicitors (A. Crawley and C. Bramall "Professional Rules, Codes, and Principles Affecting Solicitors (Or What Has Professional regulation to do With Ethics?)" in *Legal Ethics and Professional Responsibility* Ed. R. Cranston (Oxford: Clarendon Press) 100 pp.107–109.

[28] Writing on the content of such a curriculum in the USA Bundy argues that "a lawyer cannot accurately grasp the contours, significance, or potential for reform of US law without understanding the core material of legal ethics. That material includes, at a minimum, the role of lawyers in making, shaping compliance with, and enforcing the law, this country's increasingly controversial attachment to the adversary system, and the circumstances under which actors have access to legal counsel or advocacy. A legal ethics course is also the natural setting to discuss the policy preferences that underlie our nation's perennial (and presently heated) national debates about regulation, litigation, and the role of lawyers. Those include our continuing national preferences for weak, poorly funded, and highly politicised governmental and judicial authorities, for litigated, rather than consensual, solutions to problems of governance, and for political and legal processes dominated by private parties and their lawyers" (S. M. Bundy, "Ethics Education in the First Year: An Experiment" (1995) 58 *Law and Contemporary Problems* 19 at 32).

programmes. Such a project is, however, essential if any kind of general ethic underlying the diverse forms of legal practice is to be formulated.

G. GLOBALISATION

One intriguing possibility is that, far from disappearing, legal ethics will become 'globalised'. The notion of globalisation is complex and imprecise. For the present we take globalisation to be a movement towards a universal global culture precipitated by the increasing interdependence of global economies, technologies and political systems. One dimension on this is the production of international codes of professional ethics for lawyers, two of which are considered below. In Chapter 1 we referred to Giddens' notion of globalisation in which local systems of reference and understanding the self and the world gave way to global systems; i.e. time and space became less significant impediments to the presentation of information. But globalisation can be seen to have its own drivers, particularly trade, which creates a momentum for the exchange of ideas across national barriers. This process has waxed and waned for millenia but has been accelerated by electronic communication and travel. Globalisation may imply the declining significance of national systems of governance, the harmonisation of culture, political ideologies and values. The immediate relevance of globalisation to ethics is raised by the participation by lawyers in international deal making and international commercial dispute resolution. There are however, other dimensions to the issue. The field of international practice has recently been dominated by the Anglo-American legal professions and, therefore, any global legal ethic may be dominated by adversarial assumptions. Yet, the three main legal cultures of the world, common law, civil law and Islamic law, produce very different legal professions with very different traditions.[29] Differences between these legal cultures may be a considerable constraint on the evolution of a global ethic for legal professions.

The Forces Behind the Globalisation of Professional Ethics

International trade is often depicted as the driving force behind the globalising process in law. Therefore, it is international lawyers who are at the heart of the process. A senior French international lawyer recently observed that:

> "The development of law in international relations is a factor of economic progress, in particular because it ensures greater security for its participants. However, international business law is also a factor of peace and stability and is one of the essential,

---

[29] J. Flood, "The Cultures of Globalisation: Professional Restructuring for the International Market" in *Professional Competition and Professional Power: Lawyers, Accountants and the Social Construction of Markets* (eds. Y. Dezalay and D. Sugarman) (London & New York, Routledge, 1995) 139.

even if rarely perceived, elements in the development of a more harmonious and peaceful world order. The globalisation of the economy, in particular with regard to international trade and investment, has led governments more completely to define and to guarantee the rules for such trade through institutions, of which the GATT is a prime example."[30]

The same lawyer suggested, probably over optimistically, that international business lawyers carried with them the same cultural values; fundamental human rights and civil liberties, monitoring the constitutional guarantee of those rights, the independence of judges and respect for the principles of fair trial.

Yet it is in the international financial markets where the international trade is primarily conducted. These markets are confined to three main regional markets, North America, Europe and the Pacific Rim, and activity is largely confined to micro-markets. Flood, however, argues "that with the political economy of the nation state giving way to that of the super region . . . any profession that serves corporate finance and commerce will be in danger of withering unless it can at least attempt to transcend traditional boundaries. But this is not to say that organisational and institutional forms that now exist can be produced on a grander global scale".[31] In particular it must be asked whether the relational ideology, characterised by ethics, is appropriate to the transactional context of international trade. That is to say, ethics can be used as a weapon of big business. A classic example concerns transactions and disputes where only relatively few lawyers have the necessary experience to handle the matter. This provides fertile ground for alleged conflicts of interest, the litgation from which can significantly delay the resolution of the main dispute.[32]

Another point of interaction between legal professions is in relation to dispute resolution. Some countries have become established as centres of international commercial dispute resolution. In 1989 in the UK 30% of the Commercial Court's dockets were between non-British disputants[33] generating a significant volume of trade by the home legal professions.[34] Since, however, the disputants tend to be represented by lawyers from the *forum conveniens* there is little need for interaction between lawyers of different jurisdictions. The growth of international arbitration and mediation does, however, require lawyers from different jurisdictions to work together. In some cases this arises from the nature of the dispute. A classic example was the Maxwell insolvency in which a UK business held almost all of its assets in the US. As a result of the general collapse of the Maxwell financial empire, the UK business found itself under a UK administration order and in the regime known as US Chapter 11 simultaneously. These incommensurable insolvency regimes could only be reconciled by the active collaboration of American and English lawyers who

---

[30] R. Badinter, "Role of the International Lawyer" (1995) 23 *International Business Lawyer* 505.
[31] Flood, n. 29 above, at 140.
[32] *Ibid.*
[33] 'Competition, fees, partnerships, appointments' *The Times* 20 July 1989, 4.
[34] In 1988 British law firms generated £300 million in overseas earnings (*Law Society Gazette* ??? 1989).

devised a private legal system to solve these problems. This was accepted by the courts in both countries as the only approach which would avoid expensive litigation. This was clearly an exceptional case in terms of both complexity and expense but the nature of international business could see such privately negotiated legal regimes becoming more common. Clearly, these circumstances require that the lawyers of different countries develop a high degree of common understanding.

One of the manifestations of increasing cross border activity is the development of transnational practice and multi-national law firms. This dates from the 1980s.[35] Solicitors are permitted to be in partnership with registered foreign lawyers in England and Wales, provided such lawyers do not conduct litigation or advocacy.[36] There are relatively few restrictions, even of this kind, on solicitors practising wholly outside England and Wales.[37] Multi-national practice remains relatively insubstantial with only the American and English firms, the common law countries which permit large firms, maintaining a significant presence abroad and then at low levels relative to the numbers of the domestic professions.[38] Firms tend to be concentrated at the international centres of finance, London, New York and Tokyo, of arbitration, London and Paris, and of government, Brussels, Luxembourg and Strasbourg.[39] Abel argues that firms which aspire to be transnational must be transactionally based rather than advocacy based and that this creates problems in fulfilling a public service role, e.g. performing *pro bono* work.[40] Abel predicts that within a few decades the legal professions of all countries significantly integrated into the global economy will be stratified with the corporate and commercial sector, presumably, in the service of those linked most closely to international markets.

Finally, we note the political pressures toward globalisation. Halliday and Karpik argue that the world political movements towards democracy, particularly in Latin America and Eastern Europe—has moved the market theory of professions from the national to the international sphere.[41] The process of globalisation linked to economic development can be conceived of as a battle between political philosophies in which the West seeks to promote liberal democracy as the universal model of world government.[42] The irony of this

---

[35] R. L. Abel, "Transnational Legal Practice" (1993–5) 44 *Case Western Reserve Law Review* 737.

[36] *The Law Society Guide*, Principle 8.01 at 140–1. Barristers are able to accept instructions from foreign lawyers but have tended not to encourage this work (see N. Cooper, "Jeux Sans Frontières", *Counsel* December 1998 at 16).

[37] *Ibid.*, para. 8.01.5.

[38] Abel, suggests that law firms from the US, the most heavily represented overseas, have fewer than 2000 lawyers in foreign branches and many of these are local lawyers (n. 35 above, at 738).

[39] Abel, *ibid.*, at 743.

[40] Abel, *ibid.*, at 743 and 749.

[41] T. C. Halliday and L. Karpik , *Lawyers and the Rise of Western Political Liberalism: Europe and North America From the Eighteenth to Twentieth Century* (Oxford, Clarendon Press, New York, Oxford University Press, 1997) at 349.

[42] The role of financial institutions in promoting government according to the rule of law is suggestive. For example, the European Bank of Reconstruction and Development will only lend money to countries committed to promoting the rule of law.

development is that the rule of law is a defining feature of the strategy of the Western liberal democracies, and the *raison d'être* of the legal professions which their governments have attacked.[43]

The Internationalisation of Ethics

Following from these pressures for a 'globalised ethic' for lawyers we consider two attempts to internationalise ethics. The first, the CCBE (The Council of the Bars and Law Societies of the European Union) Code of Conduct for Lawyers in the European Community, applies to the cross-border activities of lawyers within the European Community.[44] The second, the International Bar Association's International Code of Ethics[45] "applies to any lawyer of one jurisdiction in relation to his contacts with a lawyer of another jurisdiction or to his activities in another jurisdiction".[46] We also consider the IBA's General Principles of Ethics which are intended as a yardstick against which members can judge their rules of conduct " . . . without prejudice to the direct application of any such Code of Ethics which Member Organisations may currently have in house".

The CCBE Code

The rationale of the CCBE Code is "The continued integration of the European community and the increasing frequency of the cross-border activities of lawyers within the community . . ." and the need to "mitigate the difficulties which result from the application of double deontology . . ."[47] The Code is to be adopted by each local bar or law society in relation to the cross-border activities of EC lawyers and "be taken into account in all revisions of national rules of deontology or professional practice with a view to their progressive harmonisation".[48] In fact it is far less comprehensive or detailed than the rules of conduct promulgated by the Law Society which, that body would surely argue, amply meet the requirements of the European rules. The exception relates to disputes between lawyers from different member states which must, first, be settled "in a friendly way", if possible or, if not, referred to the lawyers' own bars or law societies for the purpose of mediation.[49]

---

[43] Halliday and Karpik, n. 41 above, explore the ways in which lawyers have affected the rise of modern political liberalism, i.e., assisted in the creation of an order in which rights confine states and protect citizens. And conclude that bar self governance becomes an instrument to constrict the power of the state.

[44] See generally *The Guide to the Professional Conduct of Solicitors* (London, The Law Society, 1996) at 172 and para. 1.5.

[45] The *Law Society Guide, ibid.,* at 159.

[46] *Ibid.,* "Preamble".

[47] Para. 1.3.

[48] *Ibid.*

[49] Para. 5.9.

Despite the absence of divergent rules the CCBE Code is interesting, for its conception of ethical imperatives which underly the code itself. Unusually for such codes the CCBE code is prefaced by a statement delineating "the function of the lawyer in society" which begins, "in a society founded on respect for the rule of law the lawyer fulfills a special role . . . a lawyer must serve the interests of justice as well as those whose rights and liberties he is trusted to assert and defend".[50] The preamble proceeds to note the possibly conflicting legal and moral obligations imposed on lawyers. In addition to those obligations owed to clients, courts and the legal profession, the code notes an obligation to "the public for whom the existence of a free and independent profession, bound together by respect for rules made the profession itself, is an essential means of safeguarding human rights in the face of the power of the state and other interests in society".[51]

The International Bar Association's International Code of Ethics and General Principles

The IBA's Code is an even shorter document and, like the CCBE Code, it contains nothing unique in terms of the ethical principles espoused. The prohibitions of the IBA Code are often subject to national codes, for example in relation to advertising and soliciting and the delegation of work to non-qualified personnel.[52] The IBA limits the purpose of its code to being "a guide to what the IBA considers to be a desirable course of conduct by all lawyers engaged in the international practice of law" although it does state that "the IBA may bring incidents of alleged violations to attention of relevant organisations".[53]

The General Principles were drafted by the IBA's Professional Ethics Standing Committee and were endorsed by a number of IBA member organisations. They state that:

1. Lawyers shall at all times maintain the highest standards of honesty and integrity towards all those with whom they come into contact.
2. Lawyers shall treat the interests of their clients as paramount, subject always to their duties to the Court and the interests of justice, to observe the law and to maintain ethical standards.
3. Lawyers shall honour any undertaking given in the course of their practice, until the undertaking is performed, released or excused.
4. Lawyers shall not place themselves in a position in which their clients' interests conflict with those of themselves, their partners or another client.

[50] Para. 1.1.
[51] *Ibid.*
[52] Paras. 8 and 20.
[53] *International Code of Ethics of the International Bar Association* (1988 Edition) "Preamble" (*The Law Society Guide*, n. 44 above, at 159).

5. Lawyers shall at all times maintain confidentiality regarding the affairs of their present or former clients, unless otherwise required by law.

6. Lawyers shall respect the freedom of clients to be represented by the lawyer of their choice.

7. Lawyers shall account faithfully for any of their clients' money which comes into their possession, and shall keep it separate from their own money.

8. Lawyers shall maintain sufficient independence to allow them to give their clients unbiased advice.

9. Lawyers shall give their clients unbiased opinion as to the likelihood of success of their case and shall not generate unnecessary work.

10. Lawyers shall use their best efforts to carry out work in a competent and timely manner, and shall not take on work which they do not reasonably believe they will be able to carry out in that manner.

11. Lawyers are entitled to a reasonable fee for their work. A demand for fees should not be a condition of the lawyer carrying out the necessary work if made at an unreasonable time or in an unreasonable manner.

12. Lawyers shall always behave towards their colleagues with integrity, fairness and respect.[54]

The Significance of International Codes of Ethics

John Toulmin QC became a representative of the United Kingdom legal profession at the CCBE in 1983, was vice president in 1991–2 and was President of the CCBE in 1993. He asserts that, while there important differences in the ethical codes of legal professions in the United States and Western Europe, they have much in common. He argues that "they are like two trains on the same track with the US train in the lead.[55] If the will existed, he believes, it would be possible to base a worldwide code on the US model rules, the Japanese Code and the CCBE Code.[56] Some of the areas of incompatibility, including secrecy and confidentiality, advertising, conflicts of interest and contingency fees, are, he argues, "greater in theory than they are in practice".[57] But, is there a genuine need for a universal ethic for legal professions around the world? There are clearly contrary trends. As countries around the world are re-erecting barriers to free trade[58] the global free market may not be seen as inevitable or an unal-

---

[54] (1995) Summer, *International Bar News* at 23.

[55] J. Toulmin, "Ethical Rules and Professional Ideologies", Paper for the Cornell Law School Seminar in Paris, 4–5 July 1997.

[56] *Ibid.*, and see also J. Toulmin "A Worldwide Common Code of Professional Ethics?" (1992) 15 *Fordham International Law Journal* 673.

[57] N. 55 above, at p16.

[58] J. Gray, *False Dawn: The Delusions of Global Capitalism* (London: Granta, 1998), P. Kennedy, "Coming to Terms with Contemporary Capitalism: Beyond the Idealism of Globalisation and Capitalist Ascendancy Arguments" (1998) 3 *Sociological Research Online*.

terable reality.· Yet there are also indications that new international systems of dispute resolution could substantially increase the activity of lawyers in this area.[59] This would exacerbate the problem of the "double deontology"; of lawyers operating across national boundaries creating obligations of some complexity. Principle 9.03 of Guide, for example, states that solicitors engaged in overseas practice must comply with local rules of conduct if there is a specific local obligation to do so but, if there is not, that they should "observe the standards of conduct applicable to local lawyers so far as possible without breaching solicitors' conduct rules or hindering the proper exercise of his or her profession".[60]

Might the international codes also be intended to foster understanding between lawyers from different cultures? It is doubtless the case that international legal practice raises significant problems of cultural difference. Thus, US and UK law firms are larger and more entrepreneurial than their civil law counterparts, perhaps feeding the perception, for example, that US lawyers are too "pushy" in Europe.[61] But, it is precisely the niceties of cultural misunderstanding that ethics are inadequate to resolve. The CCBE code is confused regarding its purpose. Rather inconsistently, it notes that "it is neither possible nor desirable that they [the rules of each bar] should be taken out of their context nor that an attempt should be made to give general application to rules which are inherently incapable of such application. The particular rules of each bar and law society nevertheless are based on the same values and in most cases demonstrate a common foundation".[62]

Picciotto suggests an alternative explanation for the attempt to establish international codes of ethics. The period between 1915 and 1975, he argues, saw the increasing dominance of an internationalist ruling class. This domination was based on corporate liberalism and Atlantic unity.[63] One of its features was the emulation of institutions and corporate forms. The recognised inadequacy of the international state system in regulating business led to the growth, since the 1960s of what Picciotto calls "international economic soft law",[64] such as codes of conduct for international business promulgated by international bodies. These codes, he argues, are largely symbolic; "a reaction to and an attempt to contain the growing criticisms of and actions against transnational corporations from the 1960s onwards".[65] The international codes of legal professions, by emulating this aspect of the activity of their organisational counterparts in business, could be seen as a part of this development.

---

[59] P. Ruttley, "The WTO's dispute settlement mechanism" (1997) *Amicus Curiae* 4.

[60] The *Law Society Guide*, Principle 9.03.3 at 145.

[61] Flood, n. 29 above, 151.

[62] CCBE. Code para. 1.2 (*The Law Society Guide* at 17).

[63] S. Picciotto "The Control of Transnational Capital and the Democratisation of the International State" (1998) 15 *Journal of Law and Society* 58 at p64.

[64] Id at p70.

[65] Id. at p71. (See also R. Tomasic and B. Pentony, "Insider Trading and Business Ethics", (1989) 13 *Legal Studies Forum* 151).

A prime motivation for globalising ethics may, however, be political in a broader sense. Although Halliday and Karpik may be correct in identifying the role of lawyers in building the liberal state, poverty law, welfare law and discrimination were not the concerns of liberalism. There are therefore, many reasons why in the late twentieth century, powerful commercial forces are attenuating lawyers' engagement with political liberalism, whether in terms of the apolitical model characterised by the UK or the political model characterised by France.[66] One of the reasons for disengagement are recent attacks on legal professionalism. These have transformed the relationship between legal professions and their respective states. For, in the UK for example,

> "By transforming the previous balance of power, and by seeking to put under state control what previously belonged to civil society, Mrs. Thatcher created a new situation in which legal professions as collectivities needed to deploy political weapons against the state and to mobilize the public in its defence".[67]

It is consistent with this view that legal professions around the world see new dangers for civil society in the increasing power of the state.[68] Although attempts to counteract these dangers can be seen as a political act, and not the province of professions, it can be justified; the state, after all, does not always prioritise the rule of law as much in its practice as in the rhetoric of its politicians.[69] This tendency may increase as national governments around the world, driven by the need to create conditions for competitive trade, seek to control the cost of legal services by deprofessionalising legal practice. Yet, as Johnson noted, if state encroachment on professional privilege can be checked, world wide alliances of professional associations might yet provide important checks on the accumulation of state power in the service of trade and corporations. Indeed they may "provide an important channel of communications with the intellectual leaders of other countries, thereby helping to maintain world order".[70]

The Future of International Codes

The increasing fragmentation of legal professions at national level and the attempt to harmonise international ethics may seem to be contrary trends. At

---

[65a] See C. Harlow, review of Halliday and Karpik, n. 41 above in (1998) 25 *Journal of Law and Society* 657.

[66] i.e., Lawyers in these different countries have located themselves in different relationships to the state so that in England, for example, professional self government is a pillar of civil society and a bulwark of liberal political society (Halliday and Karpik, n. 41 above, at 8).

[67] Halliday and Karpik, n. 41 above, at 38.

[68] Flood, n. 29 above.

[69] The government recently replaced two moderate judicial members of the House of Lords, who had retired, with two "conservatives". *The Guardian* commented that this was a move "that will swing Britain's highest court to the right, just as it gears up to take on a politically sensitive role under the new Human Rights Act." (*The Guardian* 18 July 1998).

[70] Johnson, n. 15 above, at 14 quoting K. S. Lynn *The Professions in America* (Daedalus, 1967) at 653.

a practical level there seems to be little need for the regulation of lawyers on the international stage. Indeed, Abel argues that transnational lawyering should be deregulated on the grounds that (a) in international legal business there are fewer of the information asymmetries which are often taken to justify ethical rules designed to protect clients and (b) the market for international legal services favours the client rather than lawyers.[71] There is considerable force in this argument particularly if the protection of clients is seen as the *raison d'etre* of professional ethics. Even Toulmin, as an advocate of a univeral ethic, recognises that large firms in New York or Chicago have more in common with with similar firms in London or Brussels than with the single practitioner in these jurisdictions.[72] Moreover, he perceives that there are likely to be significant differences in the way in which the work of lawyers in different jurisdictions develops.

A classic example is the provision of access to justice. Article 3 of the Maasticht Treaty provides that member states should inform and consult one another with a view to coordinating action on providing access to justice. Toulmin argues that this issue is assuming greater signficance and that "unless the lawyers take the lead . . . procedures will be introduced for the resolution of disputes which will by-pass them. Computers will be harnessed to set out the law to be interpreted by lay people. Lawyers will be excluded from representing clients in a range of civil cases".[73] This possibility is more real in some jurisdictions than others. There may less need for the the addition of alternative methods of dispute resolution to supplement court procedures in civil law countries than in common law countries because civil law procedures are less confrontational and less expensive than in the adversarial tradition.[74] The extent to which legal professions continue to share a common conception of their role in dispute resolution may, therefore, vary considerably.

This is significant because the tendency of international codes to call in aid the defence of the rule of law links the spread of legal professionalism to the spread of capitalism and liberal democracy throughout the world. But, as MacBarnet notes, the rhetoric of the rule of law is a difficult one for business lawyers, who are in the vangaurd of this movement, to support with any degree of conviction. They often work against the spirit of law in offering corporate advice, for example on tax, which leads to avoidance of regulation; "far from being means to the implementation of rights . . . lawyers create the devices which *obviate* them and

---

[71] Abel, n. 35 above, at 762. Powerful jurisdictions, with major international business, should, he argues, negotiate the lowering of foreign barriers. He does however, propose that each jurisdiction should establish a register of foreign lawyers practising in that jurisdiction areas of reserved practice and disciplinary proceedings and facilitate the requalification of foreign lawyers—he suggests that foreign jurisdictions should not try to regulate fees of overseas lawyers and that contingency fee arrangements should be permitted and home disciplinary proceedings should apply at the instance of clients.

[72] Toulmin, n. 55, above at p2.

[73] Id. at p13.

[74] Id. at p8.

render them ineffective".[75] Therefore, in order to claim legitimacy for international codes, elite groups must remain in professional unity with groups of lawyers who actively support the rule of law at national level; lawyers working in the fields of criminal defence, civil liberties or welfare law. Yet, despite the fact that international codes depend on national enforcement, the capacity of these groups to influence their professions and their codes remains marginal. At the international level they face the additional problem that they are divided by language and geography.[76] Although, therefore, there are arguments for distinct codes dealing with the work of different groups of lawyers across national borders, the interest of elites in claiming the legitimacy of common codes makes such a development unlikely.

Whether the professional elites seeking a global order can carry their own professions with them is a moot point. It has been predicted that globalisation may precipitate "political struggles over the goals, identity and control of the profession, usually between segments of professions differentially exposed to the force of transnational developments".[77] At a time when there is great potential for the spread of the rule of law there is also increasing conflict within national professions. The ability to carry forward a liberal political agenda in the globalisation of ethics depends on the ability of the international bar to dissolve the tensions of economic and political globalisation.[78] One of the pressures on professionalism throughout the common law world, the growth of international business, draws lawyers into its wake. As political and economic contacts increase, highly evolved legal professions have been actively promoting their ideologies. Given that their vision is based on professional autonomy, status and prestige it is understandably attractive to lawyers in countries with less well developed professional frameworks. Many countries share common understandings of the role of legal professions, often as a result as a result of adopting European professional traditions.[79] It is unlikely, however, that, at least in the short term, either economic or cultural globalisation will change the way that most lawyers work or their understanding of their ethical obligations.[80]

[75] D. MacBarnet "Law, Policy and Legal Avoidance: Can Law Effectively Implement Egalitarian Policies?" (1998) 15 *Journal of Law and Society* 113 at p118–119.

[76] Picciotto, n. 63 above.

[77] Halliday and Karpik, n. 41 above, at 361.

[78] *Ibid.*, 369.

[79] The Nigerian legal profession, for example, is modelled on the English profession introduced in the second half of the 19th Century. J. O. Orojo, *Conduct and Etiquette for Legal Practitioners* (London, Sweet & Maxwell, 1979).

[80] See generally T. C. Halliday and L. Karpik, "Postscript: Lawyers, Political Liberalism, and Globalization", in Halliday and Karpik, n. 41 above, at 349.

CONCLUSION

The legal profession in England and Wales faces choices in the way that it develops its ethical commitments. It may agree with the inevitability of "deprofessionalisation", concluding that "we have become like grocers; grocers don"t have ethics".[81] This is unlikely because the elite of the profession is critically concerned with professional identity, status and standards. At the very least they must uphold exacting standards in order to justify high fees. Another possibility is that the profession will further elaborate and more rigorously enforce its codes of conduct. This is expensive and imposes greater burdens on practitioners. Poorer members of the profession are likely to object to the cost of the bureaucracy which high service standards require. They will, in any event, be increasingly subject to state regulation of their activities as it seeks to guarantee quality standards in the conduct of legal aid work. This raises the possibility that the profession will formally split into groups with more homogenous interests and abandon any claim to a single distinctive ethical foundation for legal practice. This raises the interesting prospect of collaboration by professional interest groups *across* national boundaries in relation to a number of issues, including ethics.

By increasing professional rules, and the effectiveness of regulation, lawyers will, by definition, be increasingly criticised and disciplined. This may reinforce the public impression of incompetence and lack of ethics. There is also another risk inherent in the elaboration of the professional code. Hazard notes that, over the past 25 years, the norms of the profession in the USA have become "legalised" so that professional codes are no longer seen to be the sole preserve of the profession but constitute a code of public law, enforced by normal adjudicative processes.[82] This has, to some extent, weakened "professionalism" in the sense of *self*-regulation, but can be seen as an effective way of reducing the pressure and uncertainty of ambiguous role morality.[83] An alternative therefore, is to renew the commitment to professional ethics in terms of the values which the profession espouses, which it attempts to imbue in its entrants and which it seeks to sustain in its practitioners. This would involve an ambitious attempt to relocate the role of the profession in a constitutional democracy. It is probably also an essential development if the unification of the ethics of a profession that is becoming diverse is to be acheived. A unifying ethic can be constructed only if the basic ethical concepts behind the rules governing the way lawyers work are thoroughly examined and clearly articulated. The rules may then become less detailed but more principled. Lawyers would thereby regain professional autonomy in interpreting their ethical obligations.

Such a policy could inform developments at the macro and micro levels. It

[81] A comment by an old colleague of one of the authors on being told about this book!
[82] G. C. Hazard, "The Future of Legal Ethics" (1991) 100 *Yale Law Journal* 1239 at 1241.
[83] J. Weinstein, "On the Teaching of Legal Ethics" (1972) 72 *Columbia Law Review* 452.

could involve a thorough review and reformulation of the goals of legal professionalism. The enlightened policies of the professional bodies, for example
attempts to encourage more entrants from ethnic minority communities, would
be reflected in recruitment policies, particularly among elite solicitors' firms.
The idea that the choice of a legal career is made not for financial reasons but
because of the opportunity it affords to fulfil a worthwhile role in society would
have to be supported by suitable policies and structures. Following the Lord
Chancellor's Advisory Committee for Education and Conduct's initiative,
ethics would be incorporated into legal education at every stage and the common ideal of public service reinforced intellectually and structurally.[84] The profession may need to reformulate, even invent, a notion of what such
commitment involves. This is essential not only for the guidance of practitioners, but also to inform clients of the service that they can legitimately expect
from the legal profession.

[84] C. Glasser, "The Legal Profession in the 1990s—Images of change" (1990) 10 *Legal Studies* 1.

Index